Part One: Studying Social Agreements

1. Sociology as Point of View

This introductory chapter examines the nature of agreements and the points of view they are based on. It introduces the point of view that sociology offers for the study of social agreements.

2. Theoretical Points of View

Sociology actually provides several points of view for studying human group life. Some focus on the creation of agreements, others on the organization and perpetuation of those agreements, and others on disagreement.

3. Scientific Sociology

Sociology offers a scientific approach to the study of human group life. We'll see what science is and then look at the logic and techniques that make sociology scientific.

Part Two: A Conceptual Overview

4. Culture: The Basic Agreements

The set of interrelated agreements shared by the members of a particular group constitutes their "culture." It includes symbols, beliefs, values, norms, social statuses, and the roles associated with those statuses.

5. Socialization: Learning the Agreements

For a group to persist, those born into the group must learn the agreements on which group life depends.

This process also provides the new members with personal identities and positions within the group.

6. Social Networks: Relations, Groups, Organizations

Group life is structured in a variety of ways. Some social relations are intimate, others more distant. People deal with one another in small, informal groups and in large, impersonal bureaucracies.

Part Three: The Structure of Agreements

7. Institutions and Institutionalization

Some agreements disappear once they've achieved the purpose for which they were created; others seem to last forever. Institutions are persistent sets of agreements that govern broad areas of social life so as to support the survival of group life.

8. Kinship and the Family

Agreements regarding the structure and function of family relations serve the group need for replacing members. At the same time, they serve many other group and individual needs.

9. Religious and Educational Institutions

These two institutions offer views of reality and meaning in life. Sometimes they provide a basis for agreement on a particular view; other times they conflict and create disagreements.

10. Political and Economic Institutions

These institutions contain a group's agreements regarding the distribution of power and scarce goods. They are a source of cooperation and also a source of competition and conflict.

11. Social Stratification and Mobility

In all known societies, people are arranged hierarchically. Social pecking orders have a number of different bases, often relating to a society's major social institutions.

12. Minorities

Just as individuals are arranged hierarchically in societies, so are subgroups of those societies. These minority groups—based on race, ethnicity, religion, sex, and other factors—are denied an equal share in the good things of life.

Part Four: Changing Social Agreements

13. Deviance and Social Control

People are continually breaking agreements, in many ways and for many reasons. Some agreement breaking is perceived and labeled as "deviant," however, and punishment results.

14. Collective Behavior and Social Movements

Not all group behavior is governed by the established agreements. People join together in spontaneous actions—such as fads, panics, and riots—and they often mobilize in an effort to influence the agreements per se.

15. Social Conflict and Social Change

Groups cannot exist without agreements, but group life is not always peaceful and harmonious. Society is the scene of a continuing struggle among points of view, and the prevailing points of view are continually changing.

Part Five: Mass Society

16. Population and Health

Some of the most significant changes in recent social development can be traced to the rapid growth of populations. In large part, the "population explosion" can be traced to our handling of health and illness.

17. Technology, Urbanism, and Environment

Increasingly we have acted on the point of view that human beings are the masters of the physical environment. Our advanced technology and large cities are a reflection of that view. We are now coming to recognize that our agreements in this regard can be our undoing.

18. Communication in Mass Society

Agreements are created and perpetuated through communication; in the process, we create our view of reality. In a mass society, not everyone participates equally in the creation of group reality.

19. Sociologists in Mass Society

The social problems we face are side effects of the agreements we have created to make group life possible. Solving those problems requires a full understanding of the nature of our agreements, and that's what sociology is all about.

SOCIETY BY AGREEMENT

AN INTRODUCTION TO SOCIOLOGY

Earl R. Babbie
University of Hawaii

with fiction

THE DISCOVERY OF ADAMSVILLE

by Agnes Czerwinski Riedmann
University of Nebraska, Omaha

Wadsworth Publishing Company, Inc.
Belmont, California

Sociology Editor: Stephen D. Rutter
Production Editor: Joanne Cuthbertson
Designer: Nancy Benedict
Special Projects Editor: Sheryl Fullerton
Copy Editor: Judith Chaffin
Part Opening Illustrator: Robert Bausch
Technical Illustrator: John Foster
Cartoonist: Tony Hall
Photo Researcher: Barbara Hodder
Dedication Page Photo: Steve Bartlett

Printed in the United States of America
3 4 5 6 7 8 9 10—81 80 79 78 77

Library of Congress Cataloging in Publication Data

Babbie, Earl R
    Society by agreement.

    Bibliography: p.
    Includes indexes.
    1. Sociology.   I. Title.

HM51.B16   301   76-41716
ISBN 0-534-00461-X

A *Student Study Guide*, by Robert Huitt,
to accompany

**Society by Agreement
An Introduction to Sociology**

is available from your bookstore.

Contents

    Agreements   103

        Heredity and Environment   104
        The Creation of Social Selves   104
        Status, Role, and Identity   108
        The Transmission of Culture   112
        Agents of Socialization   117
        Adult Socialization and Resocialization   119
        Socialization and Cultural Variations   121
        Socialization and Social Change   122
        Summary   122
        Suggested Readings   124

    The Discovery of Adamsville
    Episode Five   125

6. Social Networks: Relations, Groups,
    Organizations   131

        What Is a Group?   131
        Primary and Secondary Groups   136
        Voluntary Associations   139
        Bureaucracy   141
        The Trend toward Secondary Relations   147
        Summary   149
        Suggested Readings   151

    The Discovery of Adamsville
    Episode Six   152

Part Three   The Structure of
Agreements   157

7. Institutions and Institutionalization   159

        Agreements: A Balance Sheet   160
        Institutionalization   161
        Linkup in Social Space   163
        Institutions and Individuals   165
        The Dilemma   167
        A Preview—How We'll Look at
        Institutions   167
        Summary   171
        Suggested Readings   171

    The Discovery of Adamsville
    Episode Seven   173

8. Kinship and the Family   179

        Functions of the Family   179
        Dimensions of Variation   182
        Changes in the American Family   185
        The Search for Alternatives   192
        Summary   193
        Suggested Readings   194

    The Discovery of Adamsville
    Episode Eight   195

9. Religious and Educational Institutions   201

        Functions of Religious Institutions   202
        Varieties of Religious Institutions   206
        Religion in America   207
        The Structures of Religious Experience   208
        The Experience of Religious Structure   212
        Functional Alternatives to Religious
        Institutions   212
        Summary—Religious Institutions   213
        Functions of Educational Institutions   216
        Dimensions of Variation in Educational
        Institutions   219
        American Education   221
        Experiencing the Structure of Learning   227
        Functional Alternatives   228
        Summary—Educational Institutions   229
        Religion and Education in Review   229
        Suggested Readings   230

    The Discovery of Adamsville
    Episode Nine   231

10. Political and Economic Institutions   237

        Functions of Political Institutions   238
        Varieties of Political Structures   241
        Power in American Politics   242
        The Individual in American Politics   245
        Political Alternatives   248
        Summarizing Political Institutions   248
        Functions of Economic Institutions   249
        Varieties of Economic Institutions   252
        American Economic Structures   254
        The Experience of Economic Structures   256
        Some Economic Alternatives   259

Contents

Contributed Boxes

A Note to the Reader

It seems ironic that prefaces—appearing first in a book—are almost always written last. Written at the completion of a major undertaking, they provide an occasion for reflection.

As I look back across the two and a half years I've just spent writing this introductory textbook, it occurs to me that I've been considering myself a sociologist for about half my life. And yet this is the first time I've tried to bring together all the miscellaneous bits and pieces of my chosen discipline into a coherent whole. In the course of writing the book, I have found a power and an excitement in sociology that I had not experienced before. That's what I want to share with you.

Part of my excitement about sociology stems from my more practical concerns about the current and future state of the world. Like you, perhaps, I've grown increasingly concerned about the many ways in which our world simply doesn't "work." War, prejudice, poverty, and pollution are only a few of my concerns. Whereas I once felt that such problems might be amenable to technological solutions, it is now clear that technology is not enough. There is no magical "superbomb" or "doomsday machine" on the technological horizon that will solve the problem of war. Nor is there a "clean" energy source about to be discovered that will solve the problems of environmental pollution forever.

Ultimately you and I are the source of the kinds of problems I've mentioned, and we represent the only possible solution to them. Our problems stem from the social agreements we and our ancestors have made for living together in groups; if we are to solve them—and survive—we need to understand those social agreements. This is the only way we'll ever succeed in creating the kind of world we want for ourselves and others.

Sociology is going to be increasingly important in the years to come. Physicists can develop nuclear power, but the decision to use that power for peace or war is the result of a social process. Chemists and biologists can develop effective methods of contraception, but a social process determines whether the methods are used. Without a firm sociological understanding of those social processes, we will end the human interlude on earth with a warehouse full of unused or impractical technological solutions.

My intention in writing this book has been to make the broad field of sociology accessible both to students who will go on to become sociologists and those who will not. Sociology cannot fully serve all our interests in society if the field is only understood by professional sociologists. Thus, I have tried to provide a fundamental grounding in sociological points of view and findings appropriate both to further study *and* responsible participation in society.

The Agreements Theme

The power and promise of sociology stems largely from the breadth of substantive and conceptual territory it covers. Ultimately, it subsumes all other sciences. However, sociology's breadth and diversity also present a problem to beginning students who often have difficulty grasping and managing the field's many points of view, concepts, and research findings. Brute memorization often seems the only solution, since the logical scheme that holds all of sociology together is not always apparent.

The difficulty of understanding the diversity of sociology is at least matched by the difficulty of presenting it in lectures or textbooks. For teachers and authors, it has often seemed necessary to choose between (1) presenting a biased view of the field by focusing on a single point of view and/or subject area or (2) burying students under an avalanche of unconnected and often conflicting views and materials. It's never been a happy choice.

The chief contribution of this textbook—what excites me most about it—is the way it handles this problem. As a perpetual student of sociology and as a professor, I have found the notion of *agreements* an extremely effective device for organizing the field of sociology and a context for "holding" everything that comprises it.

In briefest summary, this book presents sociology and human social life in terms of the agreements that people continually make, organize, break, and change. As we'll see, agreements are necessary for the survival of group life. Those agreements are created continously through social interaction, and they are organized and perpetuated in the form of institutions. Social life, however, is as much a matter of disagreement as agreement. There is a continuing competition over *which* points of view will be established and institutionalized, and every institution becomes a source of dissatisfaction for some members of the society. Sometimes people simply break the agreements that dissatisfy them; sometimes they seek to change those agreements. Ultimately, agreements and disagreements are like two sides of the same coin. There will be conflict, deviance, and social change as long as there are institutionalized social structures.

The agreements theme provides a context for us to observe and understand all these different aspects of social life.

It is not my intention to offer a new *theory* of society. The agreements theme is not intended as a competing point of view within sociology. Its chief value, I find, is that it provides a context for existing theories and points of view. It is possible therefore to look at all that the different views have to offer without choosing which is "true." Moreover, the agreements format makes the links between different points of view easier to grasp and hold.

Special Features of the Book

In addition to providing an integrated and comprehensive introduction to the field of sociology, I wanted to explode some myths about higher education—myths that I've found troublesome. Chief among these is the myth that learning is painful, akin to the belief that powerful medicine has to taste lousy. Both as a student and as a teacher, I've found the most powerful learning experiences were also the most exciting and even fun.

A related myth suggests that Introductory Anything is by nature dull and lifeless. What ought to be a magical adventure in a field of newly discovered flowers gets dried into a dustbowl by this myth, and that seems a shame.

Finally, there is a myth that rich and complex ideas can only be presented in difficult, complicated language. I have not found this to be true in my own writing: Whenever I begin writing in clumsy and difficult prose, I have found it more a reflection of my own lack of understanding than of the complexity of the idea.

With an eye toward exploding these myths, it has been my intention to make this book both informative and enjoyable. I have wanted it to be both simple and entertaining since I feel those qualities contribute to learning rather than detracting from it. A number of special features of the book have that purpose.

Agnes Riedmann

Fiction   One of the more unusual features of the book is the science fiction story that runs throughout it. Each chapter of the book concludes with a new installment in the story of Adamsville, illustrating the main sociological concepts introduced in the chapter. The story was written by Agnes Riedmann, a nationally recognized short-story writer who also teaches introductory sociology at the University of Nebraska, Omaha. Although I'm sure you'll enjoy the story in its own right, it also provides an opportunity to see sociological concepts within a dynamic, human drama.

Boxed materials   This book is unusual among recent sociology textbooks because it has just one author. While this was essential in giving the book a

central, integrating theme, it also created a problem, since no one sociologist can hope to master the entire discipline in depth today. Throughout the book, therefore, you will find boxed inserts, written by experts in specialized areas, that present topics of special interest. These inserts give the book a breadth and currency that no one person could hope to provide. I've acknowledged the authors of the boxed materials later in these introductory comments.

Graphics   Sometimes concepts and information can be expressed more effectively in graphic form than in words. Where appropriate, we have used a variety of graphics. There are cartoons by Tony Hall, a British cartoonist whose imagination and wry sense of humor allow him to create the proverbial "picture worth a thousand words" again and again. We have used photographs to bring life to concepts and events, as well as show you sociologists past and present who might otherwise be lifeless names in footnotes. Finally, we have used a variety of graphs and diagrams to present information in an easily grasped form.

Glossary   A glossary in the back of the book defines and illustrates key sociological terms. These terms appear in boldface type in the text to signal that they are in the glossary. If you find some of the definitions in the glossary somewhat "off-the-wall," (I hesitate to say *which* wall), please realize that writing them allowed me to remain relatively sane in completing the task I enjoy least.

Other student aids   There are previews and reviews throughout the book, aimed at keeping the specifics in perspective. You may have already noticed that the inside of the front cover contains a conceptual introduction to the text called "Society at a Glance." Inside the back cover, the fictional characters and their world are introduced.

Each of the book's five parts begins with an overview, and each separate chapter begins with a topic outline. Finally, each chapter ends with a summary and suggested additional readings. All these features aim to make sociology more easily grasped and held.

Student study guide Robert Huitt has prepared an excellent student study guide that both reinforces the materials contained in the text chapters and creates opportunities to go beyond the text through a variety of projects and activities.

I want to conclude this preface by thanking you. If you are an instructor, I want to thank you for your willingness to share your experience of sociology with your students and for letting me participate in that process. It's truly an honor to take part in the education of the Meads, Parsons, and Marxes of future generations.

If you are a student, I want you to know that your willingness to take a look at sociology enables me to share something I enjoy very much. Everytime I find a way to communicate an idea to you, I understand that idea better myself. In a sense, you teach me sociology at the same time I teach you. I enjoy it immensely and hope you do too.

To Aaron Robert Babbie:

Intrepid explorer,
   he discovered a new world,
Took me to it,
   and let me play there.

Acknowledgments

It is customary to acknowledge "all those people" who had a hand in the way a book turned out. I guess you have to write a book like this one to realize how genuine such acknowledgments are. It's a humbling experience to review all the people who contributed to the creation of a book that has your name on the cover.

I want to begin with a special acknowledgment of my colleague, Dave Arnold at California State College in Sonoma. Near the beginning of the project, we had planned to coauthor the book, and Dave participated actively in the formulation and organization of topics. He did extensive library research and commented on early drafts of the manuscript, as well as pretesting chapters with his students. As it turned out, we decided not to coauthor the book, but Dave's early participation is still reflected in the final draft. I am grateful to both Dave and his students.

Students in my own introductory sociology course at the University of Hawaii tested later drafts of the manuscript. I appreciate both the contributions of the some 400 students who heard repeatedly about agreements in society and the support of my teaching assistants: Wanda Chong, Jerry Goldberg, Clyde Kawahara, Lei Tanaka, Gene Ward, and Chung Wing Yung.

During the final revisions of the book, I taught a graduate seminar dealing with the place of agreements in society. It was the most exciting course I've ever given or taken, reflecting the participation and enthusiasm of the students in the course: Jim Dannemiller, Tom Davis, Becky Gilbertson, Dave Gowe, Rick Harter, and Steve Molnar.

In one way or another, all my colleagues at the University of Hawaii have made contributions to the book. I'd like to especially acknowledge Dave Chandler, Joe Seldin, Ed Volkart, Eldon Wegner, and Mike Weinstein. Jody Yamamoto was a valuable library researcher. Many of the gaps between a good idea and a book were bridged by Jessie Ohta and Janet Tanahara.

A major draft of the book was produced during five months as a Visiting Scholar at the University of California, Berkeley, and I am grateful to the Department of Sociology for their support. John Clausen loaned me his office (and his books). Neil Smelser, Charlie Glock, and Margaret Stetson were congenial hosts. Neil, Charlie, Herb Blumer, and Don Stone were valuable critics.

Most of the book was written "on the road," and I am grateful to several organizations for making that possible. The University of Hawaii provided a sabbatical leave. Financial support in the form of research/writing grants from the Haas Community Fund, *est* of Hawaii, and The *est* Foundation made it possible for me to devote my leave exclusively to the book. Finally, the St. Lucia Archeological and Historical Society provided a place in which to begin the actual writing of the book.

I suppose it's unusual to give music credits in a sociology textbook, but these comments would be incomplete without acknowledging my friend, John Denver, for the joy and enthusiasm his music provided during the writing of the book. Office neighbors stretching from St. Lucia to Honolulu will attest to that.

Earlier, I mentioned the boxed materials that appear throughout the text, and I want to acknowledge the people who wrote them:

Joan Acker, University of Oregon
Robindra Chakravorti, California State University, Sacramento
Linda Marie Fritschner, California State University, Sacramento
Jeanne Gobalet, Stanford University
David Gold, University of California, Santa Barbara
Virginia Hiday, North Carolina State, Raleigh
Anthony LaGreca, University of Florida
Charles B. Perrow, SUNY, Stony Brook
Laurence J. Peter, The Peter Press

John Shelton Reed, University of North Carolina, Chapel Hill

Joseph Sheley, Tulane University

Stephen Steinberg, City University of New York

Donald Stone, University of California, Berkeley

Jonathan Turner, University of California, Riverside

Writing a textbook is an excellent exercise for learning to take criticism. In addition to the valuable comments of all those previously mentioned, eighteen colleagues around the country reviewed the manuscript or portions of it and suggested ways to improve it. Sister Kristen Wenzel at the College of New Rochelle gave especially detailed comments as the book neared completion, and the following people made substantial inputs:

Ruth Andes, Genesee Community College

Dennis Berg, California State University, Fullerton

Barbara Bolaños, College of the Desert

Peter Chroman, College of San Mateo

Caroline Coffey, Cabrillo College

Stephen Cutler, Oberlin College

Jeanne Gobalet, Stanford University

David Graeven, California State University, Hayward

Betty Green, Hamline University

Violet Hover, Blackburn College

Nancy Mazanec, University of Missouri, St. Louis

Nina Clark Powell, Wayne Community College

Robert Sherwin, Miami University, Ohio

Robert Stebbins, University of Texas, Arlington

Win Steglich, University of Oklahoma

Joseph Vandiver, University of Florida

Jules Wanderer, University of Colorado

Vic Gioscia, a friend and colleague in San Francisco, deserves a special acknowledgment as a constructive critic. Vic read an early draft of the manuscript and made numerous comments. Later, he came to Hawaii for a short vacation, and for four days we drew charts and diagrams, made outlines, tore it all up, and started over, eventually getting a handle on the ways social institutions operate. Chapters 7–10 have Vic's fingerprints all over them, just as the early drafts had his footprints on them.

Since our use of science fiction is something new and untried in a sociology textbook, we felt it was important to test it on some students. Robert Cherry, Sally Hayse, and Paul Kroeger undertook the task.

It should be clear by now that this book represents more than an author sitting at a typewriter writing. One person, more than any other, was responsible for that difference. Steve Rutter, sociology editor at Wadsworth, is the model of what an editor should be. I'd sum it all up by saying that Steve is a magician—with secret powers for transforming good ideas into books. The mutually supportive relationship that Steve and I have had through two books so far is the kind of joy I'd wish on any author.

Steve has been supported by many people at Wadsworth. Sheryl Fullerton was the special project editor for this book, supervising its early development through several drafts and preliminary designs. Joanne Cuthbertson was the production editor and truly a partner in the book. Nancy Benedict created its handsome and functional design. Judy Chaffin was the copy editor—sifting through the manuscript to find what I really wanted to say. Barbara Hodder dug up over two thousand photos, and I want to acknowledge the pain she experienced over all the good ones we didn't use. Finally, Betty Messersmith and Barbara Cuttle provided the assistance that allowed Steve to work his magic.

It wouldn't be possible for me to put words together that would adequately describe the nurturance and support I received from my family during the writing of the book. My mother, Marion, my wife, Sheila, and my son, Aaron, all made it their own purpose to have the book turn out just the way it did; I couldn't have asked for more.

Finally, I want to thank my friend, Werner Erhard, for all the value I've gotten from my association with him, especially as it was reflected in the writing of this book. Where I once went into sociology looking for satisfaction and excitement, Werner showed me how to bring satisfaction and excitement with me, into sociology, into writing, into everything.

Part One
Studying Social Agreements

Sociology is the study of the **agreements** that people make, organize, break, and change. It's also the study of **disagreements.** Before you've read very far in this book, it will be clear to you that *you* have been studying those agreements and disagreements all your life. The purpose of Part One is to show you what makes the sociological study of them different.

Chapter 1 introduces several concepts that set the stage for the rest of the book. I'll begin by discussing **points of view:** different views of the world around us. I want you to realize that people see the world differently depending on their points of view. After that, we'll examine the concept of agreement as it is used in this book. We'll see that people, in groups, have tendencies both to agree on certain points of view and to disagree.

Then, at the conclusion of Chapter 1, I want to look at what sociology is, especially in comparison with other academic disciplines. I want to distinguish sociology from some of the other studies you might confuse it with. Most important, however, is for you to notice that sociology is a point of view, a way of looking at the world.

The purpose of Chapter 2 is to explore the sociological point of view in depth. You are going to discover that sociology actually embraces several different points of view. Although these views of the world have enough in common to justify their being gathered under the name "sociology," there are some fundamental differences in the ways various sociologists look at and understand agreements and disagreements. You should come away from Chapter 2 with an appreciation of the special insights to be gained from looking at the world through a variety of sociological points of view.

Chapter 3 takes up a sometimes controversial topic: the *scientific* quality of sociology and the other "social sciences." The debate over whether human social life can be studied and understood scientifically comes about largely because of misunderstandings about what **science** is. I want to begin, therefore, by discussing what makes scientific inquiry different from nonscientific inquiry. After that we'll be in a position to examine some of the key problems sociologists must deal with in studying social life scientifically, and we'll look at some of the specific techniques that sociologists use in their research.

All in all, you should come away from Part One with a sense of what sociology is and how it might be useful to you. You should also have a broad, general framework within which to place the more specific materials presented in the rest of the book.

1

Sociology as Point of View

This is a book about agreements. Its purpose is to provide an introduction to sociology—to some of its research findings and, more importantly, to the conceptual framework that sociology provides for looking at the world. We'll be examining the same world you've been looking at all your life, but in a different way. This book introduces you to what sociologists "see" when they look at that world.

When I talk about the way a sociologist sees the world, I don't mean "vision" in the physiological sense. I mean that the sociologist experiences the world in terms of a particular point of view. All of us experience the world through our personal points of view, and my intention in this book is to give you an opportunity to try out and look through a new point of view, the point of view called sociology.

When sociologists look at the world, they see the stated and unstated agreements that people make and share, and they see how those agreements are organized to produce orderly social relations. Just as important, sociologists also see the *disagreements* that exist. They see people breaking the agreements that others make and share, and they see agreements change.

In this chapter, I'm going to talk about points of view and agreements and disagreements, and in the process I'll describe what sociology is and what it isn't. By the time you finish this chapter, you should have a sense of what sociology is about.

Points of View

Points of view provide the basis for agreements and disagreements, so let's begin by discussing them. Keep in mind that sociology itself is a point of view.

A point of view is a way of looking at things. What you see reflects your point of view. The accompanying cartoon illustrates how a person might look from three different points of view.

Although the three drawings in the cartoon are all of the same person, he looks different depending

on whether we view him from the front, side, or back. Now ask yourself this: Which drawing shows how the person "really" looks? Does he "really" look like the front view? The side view? The back view? Your answer has to be either "all of them" or "none of them." Each of the drawings portrays a point of view. Each presents the "real" view from a particular point, but nothing more. Points of view are only points of view.

Picasso, a founder of cubism, was once confronted by a critic who had just examined a Picasso painting entitled *Fish.* "It doesn't even look like a fish," the critic complained. "It's not a fish," Picasso retorted. "It's a *painting* of a fish." What I'm saying to you with this story is this: Fish are fish, pictures are pictures, and one shouldn't be confused with the other. Every point of view gives you only a *partial* picture of whatever you are looking at. To see what's "really" there, you'd have to be able to look at it without the distortion of a point of view.

Unhappily, however, points of view are like eyeglasses in a world where everyone needs glasses to see anything. Different glasses let you see different things, but you have to use some glasses—some point of view—to see at all. The accompanying cartoon

illustrates what I mean. By the same token, you simply cannot see the person in the first cartoon without looking *from* somewhere, and where you look from determines what you see.

You look at the world from many different points of view. So do I. Some of these points of view affect how we view physical objects, others affect how we behave, and others affect how we think and feel about things. You and I may see some things (a sunset, perhaps) from the same point of view, or we may have different points of view. We probably see a course in introductory sociology differently.

For sociologists, the "point" or "place" from which people view things is *social* rather than geographic. If you and I "see" introductory sociology differently, it is because you are looking at it from a place we call "student" and I am looking from a place called "sociology professor." Sociologists call these places **statuses**—I'll have more to say about them later in the chapter.

Human social life can be usefully examined in terms of the similarities and differences in people's points of view. Thus, for example, Karl Marx observed that workers had a particular point from which to view economic production and that capitalists had another. Marx then devoted most of his life to raising workers' awareness of their own point of view: what he called "class consciousness."

The Nature of Agreements and Disagreements

Sociology is the study of the agreements and disagreements people have regarding their points of view. It is the study of harmony and conflict, order and disorder, persistence and change. Let's take a closer look now at the nature of agreements and disagreements.

Defining Agreement/Disagreement

In this book, I'll be using the term "agreement" pretty much the way mathematicians do when they say two sides of an equation agree. They mean the sides are the same, or equal. An agreement, then, is a condition of being the same, and a disagreement is a condition of being different.

When you and I "make an agreement," we are simply creating a condition of being the same in some regard. When we agree to have lunch together, we create a shared expectation about lunch: We both expect the same thing. We would disagree if you expected that we have lunch together and I did not.

The agreements and disagreements that sociologists study, however, do not necessarily reflect the acts of people getting together and making agreements. Indeed, the greater part of sociology is devoted to agreements that have never been openly discussed and formed by the people who share them.

People can agree without knowing that they agree or even without knowing each other. This is an essential point. For example, even though we've never met each other, you and I can agree that war is bad. Or we can disagree.

There's another aspect of social agreement that may not be immediately evident: You don't have to *like* an agreement in order to make it. When you were younger, for example, your parents may have set a time for you to be home. That curfew was an agreement, and you shared it with your parents even if you didn't like it. You may have had a different point of view on the necessity or justice of the curfew, and you may have argued with your parents about it. If you still accepted the expectation that you would get home on time, you and your parents had an agreement.

Throughout this book, we're going to see that some people have the ability to impose their points of view on others, to *force* an agreement. Some social agreements, then, cannot be understood without reference to **power.** In the Marxian example, both the capitalists and the workers agreed in the sense that they had the same (capitalistic) expectations regarding economic relations. They agreed even if the workers were unhappy about it. As you examine your own life within society, you'll find that you've agreed to behave in accordance with many points of view that don't really correspond to your self-interest or desires; nor do they necessarily make you happy.

The relationship between power and agreements is a subtle one, often more than a matter of force. Sometimes it is impossible to see who is exercising power over whom, but the power of agreements themselves in shaping your behavior operates in every aspect of your life.

As a student, you share a number of agreements with fellow students, with your instructors, with college administrators, with your friends and parents, and with other kinds of people. There are agreements about studying, taking exams, taking vacations, filling out forms. There are also agreements about asking your instructor a complicated question just as class is about to end.

As you begin to think about it, you will find that agreements—and disagreements—are involved in every aspect of your life. It's always been that way, and it always will be. Some of those agreements relate to what's "true," some relate to what's "good," and others relate to what's "expected."

To get a clearer picture of how the agreements you share with others directly affect your life, let's look at the place agreements have in games.

Agreements and Games

The agreements in the games we play have four main characteristics. Knowing these will be useful to you as you try to understand how agreements operate in social life:

1. Agreements are *essential* in games.

2. Those agreements are often *arbitrary.*

3. Some agreements are more *appropriate* to the games than other possible ones would be.

4. Sometimes we begin to think that agreements represent "reality" rather than being just agreements; we *reify* them.

Agreements are essential   You can't have games without agreements. Some of the agreements are formally stated as rules, while others seem so obvious that they don't even have to be stated. You can't play craps without an agreement that rolling a 7 (on the first roll) is better than rolling a 2. Imagine a craps game in which you want rolling a 7 to win and I want it to lose.

Most games are based on an unspoken agreement that it's better to win than to lose. *That* agreement is so obvious that it doesn't even get written inside the cover of the box the game comes in. Try to imagine a game of chess in which your strategy was to win and mine was to lose. It wouldn't be much of a game.

Even though this probably seems obvious to you, children have to learn about games and why and how they're played. The accompanying box, "Learning about Games," describes what Jean Piaget discovered about the stages that children go through in learning those rules that you and I take for granted.

Agreements are often arbitrary The agreements by which we play games are "made up." They

don't have to be the way they are. In Monopoly, for example, Boardwalk isn't of itself any more valuable than Baltic Avenue. You could play Monopoly just as well if all the players agreed to make Boardwalk less valuable than Baltic Avenue. We need an agreement to have the game, and we just happened to agree that Boardwalk would be more important.

Football would not be affected much if the playing field were 110 yards long instead of 100. Players could adjust to going a little farther for a touchdown. (Canadian football, incidentally, *is* played on a 110-yard field.) Some agreement on how far you must go for a touchdown is necessary, however, and Americans happened to agree on 100 yards.

Some agreements are more appropriate than others Although the agreements involved in games are often arbitrary, some seem to work better than

Learning about Games

Swiss psychologist Jean Piaget has spent a lifetime observing children, how they develop physiologically, emotionally, and socially. His classic examination of how "moral judgment" is developed in children begins with a study of the games they play.

Piaget has concluded that a child comes to grips with the game of marbles in four stages.

1. *Motor stage.* At this first stage, children merely *handle* the marbles, guided only by desires and motor habits. There is no sense of "rules" for playing marbles.

2. *Egocentric stage.* Sometime between the ages of two and five, children learn from others the "idea" of rules. They may then make up and employ some set of rules in their solitary play with marbles, or they may begin playing marbles together—each with his or her own set of rules. As Piaget notes, "everyone can win at once."

3. *Cooperation stage.* Around ages seven or eight, children begin trying to *win*, which means there must be rules that will allow losing. The rules tend to grow out of the game in progress. " . . . While a certain agreement may be reached in the course of one game, ideas about the rules in general are still rather vague."

4. *Codification of rules.* By ages eleven or twelve, children have formalized the rules of the game. "Not only is every detail of procedure in the game fixed, but the actual code of rules to be observed is known to the whole society."

What are some other "unspoken" rules about games such as marbles that young children must learn? How do you suppose they learn those rules that you might consider too obvious to mention?

Source: Jean Piaget, The Moral Judgment of the Child, *trans. Marjorie Gabain (New York: The Free Press, 1965), pp. 26–27.*

others. So, while football can be played as easily on a 110-yard field as on a 100-yard field, and while kids manage to play football in much less space, it probably wouldn't work to play football on a field 10,000 yards long. Having to run over 5 miles for a touchdown probably wouldn't work. At the least, football would become a less exciting spectator sport than it is now.

People tend to reify the agreements   "Reification" means "to make real" or to think something is real when it isn't. One of the strangest things about the agreements in games is that people often begin thinking they are "real" instead of just being agreements. You may know someone who plays Monopoly as though people were going to move into those hotels on Boardwalk and Park Place and feels depressed for days after losing all his or her "play" money in such a game. People often forget they are only playing games.

Two Kinds of "Reality"

I've asked you to look at the place agreements have in games because these agreements have the same characteristics as those that operate in the rest of your social life. First, they are essential. You couldn't have a society like the one you live in without them. Imagine what your daily life would be like if you and others did not agree on what language to speak and which side of the road to drive on. Agreements are necessary in thousands and thousands of similar instances.

Second, the agreements that form the structure of your life in society are—like those in games—often arbitrary. Traffic flows as well with everyone driving on the left side of the road as on the right. Conversations can be conducted in French as well as in English.

Third, some of the agreements in your life are more appropriate than other possible ones. Societies operate more smoothly with an agreement that you shouldn't kill other people than they would if there were an agreement that killing was all right or an agreement that everyone *had* to kill one person a day.

Finally, in societies, as in games, people have a tendency to reify the agreements they make. Put somewhat differently, people reify the points of view that they have agreed on and begin thinking that those points of view represent ultimate reality. Because the operation of armies requires clear systems of authority, for example, militaries have the agreement that generals have authority over privates. Rather than regarding this as a logical arrangement for getting a job done, however, people tend to begin feeling that generals are "really" superior to privates. If the general and the private meet twenty years later when both are civilians, they are still likely to experience, to some degree, the earlier authority relationship that began as a logical agreement for getting a particular job done. The "private" will still defer to the "general" even though such deference would not be logically necessary in their new situation.

If you look carefully at your own life, you should be able to see that you have reified countless agreements. You and I share an agreement, for example, that telling the truth is better than lying. That agreement makes a lot of sense because it makes communication easier. But suppose that you found out I had lied to you about something in this book. Would you merely say "He shouldn't have done that because it gets in the way of communication" or would you feel that I was "really" wrong to have lied? Would you regard my lying as merely an inconvenience or also as immoral? Is "telling the truth" merely an agreement for you, or is it something more?

We have an agreement not to murder each other, and, like an agreement to tell the truth, it makes a lot of sense. Things would be pretty chaotic and disorderly without that agreement, and we probably wouldn't be able to live together in groups as we do now. But do you regard the agreement on murder as merely a convenient arrangement or as something more?

Realize that when you were a young child, you didn't feel that lying and murder were "really" bad. In your very beginning, you didn't feel they were wrong at all, and you didn't know about the agreements those around you shared. As you grew up, however, the agreements were taught to you. As you learned them, you had a tendency to think they represented something on the order of truth. Try the exercise on the nature of the relationship between

Points of view on the exposure of the human body illustrate changing agreements in a single society. (above *Library of Congress,* top right *Popperfoto,* bottom right *Elliott Erwitt, Magnum*)

"truth" and agreements in the box on page 10 "How to Find 'Truth'."

In a sense, you live in a world of two realities. Some things seem real to you because you experience them directly. Other things seem real to you because of the agreements you share with others, because you have reified the points of view you hold in common with those around you.

You may have had the direct experience of loving someone. You may not have been able to explain or justify the feeling; you just *knew* that you loved that person. You may also love your parents, but this may be because we have an agreement that everyone loves his or her parents. If you've ever had doubts about whether you love your parents, if there have been moments when you hated your parents, you have probably felt guilty. We are all *expected* to love our parents. That's the agreement we share.

I don't mean to suggest that you can't or don't have a direct experience of loving your parents quite aside from the agreement to do so. I'd simply like you to notice that some of the many things that seem

How to Find "Truth"

Look up the definitions of "true" and "truth" in a large, unabridged dictionary. Write down all the *key* words used in those definitions, words like "real," "actual," "fact," and "being."

Now look up the definitions of all those key words and write down all the key words used to define *them*. Keep repeating this process.

The first thing you'll discover is that language is circular. Something is "true" if it is "real," and it is "real" if it is "true." Most of the "meaning" of truth is lost in this circularity.

If you repeat the process long enough, however, you'll find that "truth" ends up as a matter of agreement. Essentially, something is "true" if people *agree* that it is—or not true by the same process. Something exists if a lot of people say they see it.

Can you think of something you know to be "true" quite aside from other people's agreement with you? How do you know it's "true"?

"real" to you grow out of agreements you have learned from others and have subsequently reified. It's difficult to distinguish **experiential reality** from **agreement reality,** moreover, because they both "feel" real.

Consider the following situation. Suppose you are visiting in someone's home and your host offers you a chocolate candy after dinner. You try one and find it tastes "really" good. You eat five or six of them. Then your hosts tell you that you've been eating chocolate-covered *worms.* You might very well throw up; you certainly wouldn't feel good. The feeling in your stomach would be very real, yet it should be clear that it stems from the agreement you share with others in our society that eating worms is awful. Realize also that people living in other societies around the world have agreements that eating bugs, worms, and grubs is okay, in some cases, more than okay. The creatures are a delicacy.

You live in a world of two realities. Both feel real, and they are often difficult to distinguish. Yet one is based on your own direct, personal experience of things and the other is based on the agreements you share. This situation is illustrated in the box describing the Sherif experiment, "Creating Agreements out of Nothing."

The Survival of Groups

The reality created by agreements is important in many ways. First, it makes group life possible. People cannot get along together in groups without agreements, although a wide variety of different sets of agreements is workable in this regard. The business of government, for example, gets accomplished by democracies, monarchies, and totalitarian dictatorships alike. The exchange of goods and services gets accomplished under **capitalism, socialism,** and barter systems. None of these would work, however, without an agreement on what system was operating.

Sociologists use the term **institution** to refer to the agreement system that organizes some general aspect of group life. "Government" is an example of an institution, as, more specifically, is "democracy" or "monarchy." Democracy, then, is an institution made up of the agreements that govern political relations in America. Other major institutions that interest sociologists are the **economy, religion,** the **family,** and **education,** and each of these institutions

---

Creating Agreements out of Nothing

Several decades ago, Muzafer Sherif conducted a set of experiments that should cause you to take everything you experience and believe with a grain of salt. Sherif studied the development of group norms in regard to what are called *"autokinetic effects."*

In Sherif's experiments, a group of people were placed in a totally darkened room. Mounted on a far wall was a small, stationary point of light. I've emphasized that the light was stationary because if you were to sit in a totally darkened room, with no visible walls, floor, or ceiling to serve as a frame of reference, you'd eventually get the feeling that the point of light was moving around. That's what Sherif's experimental subjects experienced.

In addition to signaling the experimenter whenever they saw the light move, the subjects were also asked to estimate the distance that it moved. Since the light was stationary throughout all the experiments, it's not surprising that estimates of how far it moved varied greatly. More surprising, however, was the discovery that whenever a group of subjects viewed the light together, they quickly reached an agreement as to the distance it moved, even though the initial estimates of different members of a given group disagreed greatly. By the end of each observation session, all members of the group were experiencing the same amount of movement. (Different groups, incidentally, arrived at quite different agreements.)

What does this experiment suggest to you about those things that "everybody knows"? What does it suggest about those things you personally "experience" as real?

Source: Muzafer Sherif, The Psychology of Social Norms *(New York: Harper and Row, 1936).*

---

is discussed at length in Part Three of this book.

To the extent that the institutions of a particular society remain unchanged, people are able to get along with each other in habitual ways. There are rules about the ways things are done, and everyone knows what to expect of everyone else. Voters in a democracy, for example, know that they will have an opportunity periodically to elect public officials, and politicians know that they must at least appear to represent the interests of their constituents. Businesspeople in a capitalistic economy know that they can purchase goods at wholesale and sell them at retail, turning a profit in the process.

In a broad sense, institutions are made up of agreements about the ways in which people will get along with each other in a particular society. As such, all institutions represent the establishment of certain points of view in favor of others. This means that in every society, there are some people who disagree with established ways of doing things, people who have different points of view. Sometimes these people simply break the agreements. Sometimes they seek to establish new ones.

Sociologists study all these different aspects of society—agreements and disagreements, established institutions, breaking and changing agreements. These concerns are what sociology is about. Now, let's get even more specific and put sociology in the context of some things it is *not* about.

What Is Sociology?

Sociology is the study of the agreements that people make, organize, teach, break, and change. It is also the study of the disagreements involved in the same processes. Some sociologists are chiefly interested in the processes through which agreements are continually being made and then remade through disagreements. Others are more interested in the extent to which certain agreements are perpetuated. We'll look at different sociological points of view in Chapter 2.

Sociology is a science, a scientific study of agreements. As a science: (1) Sociology aims at a rational, logical, systematic understanding of social agree-

Social interactions are the source of agreements. As this lovers' quarrel illustrates, interactions also highlight differences in points of view, conflict, and disagreements. (Bernard Wolff, Magnum)

ments; and (2) it continually tests such understanding against careful observations of events in the world we seek to explain. Chapter 3 considers the scientific aspect of sociology in depth and some of the specific **research methods** sociologists use.

At this point, it will be useful to look at sociology as the study of agreements and disagreements that are involved in **social interaction** and **social relationships.**

Social Interaction

"Action" means pretty much what you think it does: Action is something you *do*. Voting, talking, listening, selling, or being perfectly still are all ac-

tions. "Inter"action is what goes on between "actors." Typically each action is shaped somewhat by the actions that precede it, and each action in turn helps shape those that follow.

A tennis match is an excellent example of inter-action. So is a conversation. Suppose that you and I are meeting for the first time. I tell you my name and hold out my hand. You tell me your name, shake my hand, and tell me it's good to meet me. I suggest that we sit down, and you agree, asking me what I do for a living. I respond. This is an example of inter-action.

Of course, there's nothing to prevent you from interacting with a dog or a machine, and many people interact in that way. We use the term "social" interaction to make a distinction, to refer to interaction among human beings.

Social interaction doesn't need to be harmonious. A fistfight or a mugging is social interaction. The mugger points a gun at you, and you hold up your hands. The mugger demands your money, and you comply. If you refuse to hold your hands up or to hand over your money, your action will affect what the mugger does next.

Sociologists are interested in social interaction since agreements are formed that way. If you realize that the mugger wants you to hold your hands up, you've struck an agreement with regard to that intention. If you comply with the mugger's intention, you've made another agreement. If you refuse to raise your hands, the agreement-making process continues. In an important sense, social interaction is a matter of **communication.** (Chapter 18 examines communication more fully.)

When you have a "picture" in your mind—whether it's a piece of information, a desire, or a feeling—you may want to create that same picture in my mind. That's what communication is. You attempt to communicate through your actions—talking or gesturing, for example—and you learn whether you succeeded by observing my actions. If you've created the same picture in my head—if our pictures agree—you've communicated; if not, you haven't. (You would have communicated *something* in any event, but it might not be what you were trying to communicate.)

Many sociologists study how people communicate through interaction and how agreements are formed in the process. Some focus on what is being communicated, others on the actions involved; still others are primarily interested in the nature of the agreements and disagreements that are created. We'll look at these several points of view in Chapter 2.

Social Relationships

Agreements are formed in the course of social interaction, but this does not mean that none existed before interaction. All interactions occur within a framework of preexisting agreements and are shaped by that framework. Language, for example, is a set of agreements, and all conversations occur within that

set and are shaped by it. Even though we make new agreements about language (agreeing on a specific meaning for a key word we are using, for example), our interaction begins within a preexisting agreement framework. If the previous example of our meeting each other made sense to you, that reflects our agreement that when I say my name and hold out my hand, you are expected to say your name, shake my hand, and say you're pleased to meet me.

Sociologists are especially interested in how the agreements governing social interactions between people reflect their relationships with each other. Social relationships are based on the social locations people have with reference to each other. Let me introduce the notion of "location" with a physical illustration.

Imagine for the moment that *you* are the only thing in the entire universe. There are no other people, no stars, no planets, nothing but you. Now ask yourself, "Where am I?" Your answer has to be either "nowhere" or "everywhere." You simply can't have a location except in relation to something else. Now imagine that *I* also exist. Now *you* can be somewhere. You can be in front of me, in back of me, above or below me, near or far away. Where you are, however, only has meaning with reference to me: It is a matter of the relationship between us in space.

People have social locations in relation to each other, too. You could be my parent or my child, but notice that you can't be a parent without reference to a child, nor can you be a child without reference to a parent. That's true of all social relationships. You can't be a leader without followers; you can't be an employee without an employer; you can't be a student without teachers.

Sociologists use the term "status" to refer to the social locations people have in relation to each other. Statuses and status relationships are important to sociology because many of the agreements that govern social interaction refer to specific statuses. There are different sets of agreements pertaining to interactions between mothers and daughters, privates and generals, salesclerks and buyers, muggers and victims.

Different social statuses are also linked to different points of view. Your social location influences what you "see" just as your geographical location does. Imagine how differently a package of employee benefits (wage raise, retirement, and medical care, say) "looks" to a worker, a stockholder, and a government economist. Physicians, patients, and insurance agents "see" major surgery differently according to where they are located in the network of social relations.

Many sociologists focus their attention on the ways in which statuses are organized in a group such as a society. Every status has a set of privileges and duties associated with it that define how individuals occupying that status should interact with individuals occupying other statuses. Sociologists use the term **role** to refer to what people do and are expected to do because of the statuses they occupy.

It is useful to look at the organization of roles and statuses because many of the lasting agreements in a group are those defining interactions between specific statuses. The concept applies well beyond the interactions of two people. A complex organization such as a corporation or a factory can be seen as the structuring of statuses: established agreements about interactions between workers and supervisors, planners and production people, presidents and boards of directors, and so forth. Some sociologists are primarily interested in examining the structure of statuses per se, and others are more interested in the kinds of social interactions that actually take place within the structures.

Sociology, then, offers special points of view from which to observe and "see" the world around you. Since sociology is often confused with other points of view, I'd like to make a distinction between it and some of them. Please realize, though, that there are no rigid boundaries between them.

Sociology Is Not Psychology

Psychologists study what goes on inside your head and adjoining parts of your body. They study such things as thinking and emotions. As a very general distinction, psychology deals with individuals, and sociology deals with what goes on *between* individuals.

Sociology and psychology have important things to say to each other, of course. How a person thinks and feels will affect the way he or she interacts with other people, and those interactions will affect how he or she thinks and feels. There is a special field of *social psychology*, in fact, that addresses the links between sociology and psychology.

The main distinction between psychology and sociology, then, is one of emphasis, with psychology emphasizing the personal and sociology emphasizing the interpersonal.

Sociology Is Not Anthropology

Anthropology is a lot like sociology. Anthropologists also study social interactions and social relationships. Traditionally, however, anthropologists have studied preliterate peoples while sociologists have studied what are called—sometimes erroneously—"civilized" ones. In recent years, this distinction between anthropology and sociology has grown less clear, with anthropologists paying more attention to modern, complex societies, and sociologists occasionally examining preliterate ones.

Anthropologists sometimes study aspects of social life that sociologists tend to ignore. Anthropologists, for example, are more concerned with *artifacts:* human products such as arrowheads, pottery, weavings, and other objects that people make in certain ways because of the groups they live in. Physical anthropologists study the physical characteristics of people, such as the width of their skulls and lengths of their arms. Archaeology, the study of past societies, is generally regarded as a subfield of anthropology.

Sociology Is Not Economics

Economists study relationships and interactions among people also, but economics is more limited in scope than sociology. Basically, economists are interested in the exchange of goods and services, how people get what other people have. Economic exchange is important to sociology, too, but sociologists study *noneconomic* relationships and interactions as well. (In Chapter 2, we'll discuss "exchange theory," which is an attempt to adapt the economic exchange model to social interactions and relationships.)

Sociology Is Not Political Science

Political science is another specialized field, focusing on power relationships among people. Thus, political scientists study different kinds of governments (different ways of distributing power in a group) and the interpersonal processes, such as voting, war, and bureaucratic administration, through which power is exercised.

Power relationships are important to sociology, just as economic ones are, so political science and economics are both useful to sociology. By the same token, economics and political science have both profited from the theories and research of sociologists.

Sociology Is Not Social Work

Many people confuse sociology with social work. Basically, the difference is this: Social workers *help* people; sociologists *study* people. Sociologists aren't against helping people, and most sociologists engage in helping people in many ways. It's just that *sociology* isn't about helping; it's about understanding.

At the same time, understanding people is often the first step toward helping them. Understanding social problems is the first step toward solving them. Sociology is very *relevant* to the issue of helping, and sociological research is often specifically designed to improve social conditions. Too, the efforts of social

workers often reflect the understanding sociology provides.

Sociology Is Not Socialism

Socialism is an economic system in which the government, rather than private capitalists, owns the means of production. Some sociologists are in favor of socialism. Some are in favor of capitalism. Some favor something else altogether. Sociology is a useful point of view for studying both socialism and capitalism. Sociological findings might be useful to both socialist and capitalist countries, and sociologists are active in both.

There is one link between sociology and socialism that you should be aware of, however. Karl Marx, the founder of modern socialism, was a sociologist (among other things), and much of his work reflects a sociological point of view. Marx has also influenced the points of view of other sociologists. Moreover, he regarded his sociological analyses as intimately related to his efforts to establish socialism as an economic system in the modern world. Many contemporary "Marxist" sociologists take the same view, particularly those in socialist countries.

Is Sociology Social Reform?

Finally, I'd like to distinguish sociology from social reform, though you should realize that the issue is controversial. Sociology is not necessarily about making the world a better place to live in—any more than sociology is social work—but proficiency in sociology would probably make you a more effective social reformer.

No one disputes that some sociologists *as citizens of societies* engage in efforts at social reform—fighting poverty, prejudice, war, and other social problems—just as others do not. In recent years, both within sociology and outside it, there have been heated debates over whether sociologists support or resist social reform in their activities *as sociologists.* Some people think that sociologists are out to restructure society—through socialism, for example. Others, however, feel that the study of social order as it exists inevitably supports the maintenance of that order.

In addition to the dispute over what sociologists

do, there's a disagreement about what they *should* do. An increasing number of sociologists have urged that sociology be practiced within a context of social reform, that it have the improvement of social conditions as its ultimate goal. They urge this course even granting disagreements about what would be "better" or "worse" conditions. We'll consider the issue further in Chapter 19.

A Useful Point of View

Throughout this chapter, I have repeated that sociology is a point of view, with different, more specialized points of view within it. Points of view do not reveal the "Truth," but some are more useful than others in particular situations and for particular purposes. If you were interested in learning about cross-pollination in flowers, you would find biology a more useful point of view than poetry. A socialist point of view may convince you that your car broke down because of capitalistic greed and corruption, but taking a mechanic's point of view is more likely to get your car running again.

Sociology can be a very useful point of view. It can offer an understanding of things that other points of view do not provide. Let's look at one illustration.

For years it has been widely believed that the black American family was matriarchal, that is, dominated by the wife and/or mother. Empirical evidence has somewhat substantiated this belief. In a number of surveys, some black men and women have reported that their mothers made most of the important decisions while they were growing up and that their mothers were more powerful in family matters than their fathers. Similarly, among some black couples, husbands and wives have indicated that the wives make most of the important decisions.

For years, political conservatives have used such evidence to support their belief in the weakness and submissiveness of black American males. Such supposed character flaws were used as an explanation for why blacks have fared so badly in American society.

Those with a liberal point of view, on the other hand, have taken the evidence as an indication of the ways in which the black American family has been weakened by discrimination, inhumane welfare regulations requiring fathers to desert their families to get government assistance for them, and other influences. These conflicting points of view have been expressed repeatedly in every possible medium of communication.

Notice how differently you might "see" the survey reports of female dominance in black families, depending on whether you were looking from a conservative or liberal point of view. There is another point of view, a sociological one.

Herbert Hyman and John Reed (1969) looked at the matter according to a sociological point of view. To begin, they confirmed that the surveys did indeed suggest that black women were more powerful than black men in family life. Then they looked at something others had overlooked: the answers given by *white* men and women in the same surveys. The answers given by white respondents were the *same* as those given by blacks! Thus, Hyman and Reed concluded, if black families were dominated by women, so were white families. If this meant that black men were weak and submissive, then white men were equally weak and submissive.

In Chapter 3, we are going to look at some of the characteristics of sociology *as a science* that would lead sociologists to see things that others might overlook. In that context, you will be able to gain a clearer understanding of why sociology can be a useful point of view for looking at the world around you.

Summary

A point of view is a way of looking at things, a place to view things from. Your point of view, moreover, determines what you see, as in the illustration of looking at a person from the front, back, or side. Points of view present you with pictures, but the pictures are incomplete.

You can *only* see the world through a point of view. It's as though everyone needs glasses in order to see, and each pair of glasses shows things a little differently. Despite this seemingly chaotic state of affairs, people often act as though they see things similarly, and sociology is largely about how that happens—and how it fails to happen, too.

Sociology is the study of the agreements people make, teach, organize, break, and change. Sociology is also the study of disagreements. In this book, two points of view agree if they are the same. We might also say that two people agree if they have the same point of view, if they see the same thing. People disagree, on the other hand, if they see things differently.

People can agree even without knowing it. They don't even need to know each other. Much of sociology deals with those agreements that people don't even recognize as agreements, those agreements that are too implicit even to discuss.

We can learn a lot about the nature of social agreements by examining the way agreements work in games. They have four main characteristics. First, agreements are essential: You can't have games without rules. Second, they are often arbitrary: Different agreements would also work. Third, some agreements are more appropriate than others: Some just seem to work better. Finally, people have a tendency to reify the agreements in games: They forget that the agreements are only agreements and begin thinking that they represent an ultimate reality.

The agreements in social life have the same four characteristics. It is especially important to notice that people often reify their social agreements. People have a tendency to believe that the points of view they share represent "reality." Some people believe it's "really" better to drive on the right side of the road than on the left. Other people believe that democracy is "really" better than monarchy.

The social agreements that people reify constitute an agreement reality, and most of what we take to be a direct experience of things is an experience of those reified agreements. This is not to deny that our experiences "seem" real, but people who do not share those agreements would not have the same experiences.

People can't live together in groups without agreements, and the reification of an agreement reality provides a persistent set of agreements. Reification, then, allows groups to survive. Sociologists use the term "institution" in reference to the system of agreements that organize some general aspect of social life. The major institutions that sociologists

study are family, economy, government, religion, and education. In all societies, some people disagree with the points of view represented by the established institutions. Sometimes they break the agreements and sometimes they seek to establish new ones.

In their study of social agreements, sociologists often deal with social interaction and social relationships. In both connections, they examine the statuses people occupy—social "locations" in relation to one another—and the roles associated with those statuses.

Although sociology shares common interests with other academic disciplines, sociology is *not* psychology, anthropology, economics, political science, or social work. Neither is it the same as socialism. Finally, there is disagreement within sociology as to whether it should or does either foster or impede social reform.

When all is said and done, sociology is a point of view. It reveals things we can't touch, smell, taste, hear, or even see directly. Like all points of view, it reveals only a picture of what it addresses, yet it is a useful and enlightening one. Sociologists see a rich and fascinating invisible world that exists all around us, and the purpose of this book is to share that world with you.

Suggested Readings

Berger, Peter L.
1963 *Invitation to Sociology: A Humanistic Perspective.* Garden City, N.Y.: Doubleday.
This eminently readable little book offers an excellent introduction to the sociological point(s) of view. Berger illustrates the nature and utility of sociology within the context of day-to-day social life, showing how sociologists see a much different world than other people. Sociology, you'll see, can be practiced as a pastime as well as a profession.

Berger, Peter L. and Thomas Luckmann
1967 *The Social Construction of Reality.* Garden City, N.Y.: Doubleday.
A study in the "sociology of knowledge," this book explores what I have called "agreement reality" in

depth. The book examines individuals' subjective experiences of reality, how those experiences are communicated through interaction and language, and how agreements on the nature of reality are established in the form of institutions.

Mills, C. Wright
1959   *The Sociological Imagination.* New York: Oxford
          University Press.
Here is an introduction to the sociological perspective within a context of social criticism and social reform. Mills shows how the sociological imagination can reveal the failings of society and point the way to

greater social justice. In the process, he criticizes those sociological points of view that he feels impede social reform.

Williams, Robin M., Jr.
1959   *American Society: A Sociological Interpretation.*
          New York: Knopf.
This classic overview of American society illustrates (in readable form) some of the ways sociologists examine social life. Given the familiarity of the subject matter, you should gain a clearer and more comprehensive picture of what makes sociology different from other points of view.

The Discovery of Adamsville

Prologue

By the year 2020 the United States showed promise of recovery. What had been the longest and most painful economic depression in human history had at last begun to weaken.

The entire planet had suffered upheaval. Throughout the final quarter of the twentieth century the Middle East oil cartels had grown increasingly stronger, unmercifully demanding higher and higher prices for their black gold, the lifeblood of industrialized nations. Meanwhile the oil-rich countries, along with other formerly underdeveloped nations, had quickly urbanized. Using energy supplies as rapidly as their Western industrialized clients, these newly modernized countries had accelerated the already rapid depletion of earth's energy reserves.

By the turn of the twenty-first century, a barrel of oil cost the United States fifty times what it had in 1980. Moreover, the Alaskan pipeline had proved a dismal solution. Fraught with labor disputes and engineering difficulties, the pipeline pulsed not even half the oil that had once been anticipated. What the line could supply cost consumers far more than was originally estimated.

As a result, food production had become a serious national—and international—problem. United States farmers needed energy to operate their machinery. Many who could not afford to continue in business allowed their acres to go untilled. They planted what they could by hand, bending their own backs to cultivate their meager harvests, much as their ancestors had done 200 years before. These farmers fed their families, but little was left for those standing in the breadlines of the nation's cities. Americans were hungry and cold.

Then, in 2018, a small corporation located in the Arizona desert announced plans to manufacture solar transistors. Hope returned.

Engineers had made use of solar energy for heating a small number of homes and office buildings since the 1970s. By 1990 nearly three-fourths of those few United States factories still in operation had been converted to solar energy. Also by 1990 some experimental solar-powered vehicles existed.

But solar-powered plants and motor vehicles faced an important difficulty: They could not operate for long periods without direct sunlight. Solar energy could be stored only several hours; during long weeks of haze or overcast skies—and in winter when daylight hours were fewer—solar energy proved an inadequate solution.

Solar transistors (S.T.'s) promised to change all that. Ranging in size from that of a dime to an automobile battery, the transistors could emit stored solar energy for up to six months. An S.T. as small as a quarter could, the corporation asserted, heat a small room for several weeks.

With the further development of solar-powered engines and relatively simple conversion procedures, factories and farmers might—it was hoped—resume full capacity. By 2020 Detroit's unemployed looked forward to taking up their positions on the city's assembly lines, where they would fasten bolts in solar-powered vehicles equipped with S.T.'s. Farmers saved what cash they could for down payments on forthcoming S.T.-powered combines. Homemakers dreamed of a return to the affluence of their grand-parents: Perhaps one day power companies would use S.T.'s to produce electricity and even dishwashers would hum again.

Renewed hope caused curiosity. Journalists sought interviews with the executives of Solar Transistors, Inc. But requests for interviews were categorically denied. "It is official policy," S.T., Inc. announced in a national press release, "to deny requests for personal interviews with any S.T.I. personnel and further to deny entrance to S.T.I. property to anyone other than properly identified employees of this corporation."

The press release created a challenge. Competing for the first scoop, free-lance writers, radio and television reporters, and newspaper and magazine journalists struggled frantically for a glimpse inside the revolutionary factory.

Solar Transistors, Inc. still remained shrouded in secrecy. Those few who had by 2019 ordered S.T.'s had done so by mail, they reported. Only one company, a steel producer based in Gary, Indiana, told of personal contact with anyone representing S.T.I. Granting an interview to *Newsweek*, the steel executive described the sales representative who called upon him. "He was polite, cooperative, and well informed," the executive said. "I offered to take him to lunch, but he declined."

On March 10, 2020, Josephine Langley and Robert Parks, reporters for the *Phoenix Herald*, successfully invaded S.T.I. headquarters. Having parked the car in which they approached some distance away, they entered the premises under cover of darkness. Crawling past several armed guards and carrying portable telephones, Parks and Langley tunneled under the fence bordering S.T.I. property and once inside crept almost a mile. They came upon a single-story, glass-roofed building that they correctly supposed to be the corporation's main quarters. Jimmying doors and scurrying tiptoe through the darkened corridors, the two happened upon offices belonging to S.T.I.'s board of directors.

Langley and Parks spent several hours reading, photographing, and telephoning information from S.T.I. files. Receivers at the *Phoenix Herald* picked up the electronically transmitted data.

The corporation, the journalists reported, was owned by a large family or clan, all descendants of a man named Adam Jones III, deceased. While over 625 members owned shares in the corporation, more than half the stock was held jointly by Ruth and Michael Jones, Adam's two living children.

Adam Jones III had purchased 2500 acres along the Arizona-New Mexico border in 1965. He was forty-five years old at the time.

Jones's father, Adam, Jr., had amassed a considerable fortune in the manufacture of small electric home appliances after World War II. When he died in 1950, he left his son, an only child, a substantial inheritance. Adam III, moreover, increased his father's fortune by investing wisely in the stock market.

Adam Jones III had married young and fathered five children, who, in 1965 when he purchased the Arizona–New Mexico property, ranged in age from thirteen to twenty-six. Adam's wife had divorced him in 1964. Jones had apparently gained custody of their minor children, and during 1966—records showed—he built on the desert property a large home for himself, his children, and "any future posterity."

Ann, Jones's eldest descendant, had married at age seventeen and was herself divorced eight years later. She had borne four children and in 1966 she returned with the children to her father's home. By 1970 all five of Jones's children and at least eleven grandchildren had joined him. Parks and Langley found no record of the presence of Jones's children's spouses at the estate.

In 1971 Mary, Adam's youngest daughter, then nineteen, and her older brother, David, thirty, were brutally beaten by hoodlums as they attended a movie in nearby St. Johns, Arizona. Mary was pronounced dead on arrival at a Tucson hospital. David died within the following week, leaving three children.

Shortly after the incident Adam installed an electric fence around the whole property, positioned family members as guards near the three entrances, and began to insist that those residing on the estate remain within its boundaries whenever possible. After that, it appeared, the Jones clan became increasingly secretive. While the family's youth often left to attend colleges and universities, they were strongly encouraged to return before their twenty-sixth birthdays and thereafter to remain upon Jones's territory.

One further incident increased Adam Jones's determined attempts to shield his family from the rest of the world. In 1980 his daughter Ann, while standing guard duty, was fatally wounded by a shot from an outsider's high-powered rifle.

By 1985 Jones's grandchildren were growing up, and according to records that Parks and Langley discovered, some had intermarried rather than seeking mates outside the estate. By 2000, the year of Adam's death, the property sheltered some 250 people. That number had increased to over 575 by 2018.

Adam Jones had educated his children in the best American universities. While still in graduate school, Adam's son Michael had demonstrated promise in the field of electronics. Upon his subsequent return to his father's estate, he had begun to experiment with solar radiation. Michael's older sister Ruth, herself an engineer, had collaborated in these early experiments.

In 2005 the pair received a $500,000 federal grant from the Energy Resources Development Administration (ERDA). The money was to aid private industry in the development of new energy resources.

It appeared, Parks and Langley transmitted, that neither Ruth nor Michael had dealt personally, however, with anyone from the United States government. According to the records David Jones's grandson,

Larry, then twenty-one, had made several trips to Washington, D.C., during 2004. Apparently it was Larry who convinced ERDA of his family's potential for successfully harnessing solar energy.

The thirteen years between 2005 and 2018 were spent in secluded research. Again and again, minutes of S.T.I. board meetings revealed, members considered means for ensuring absolute secrecy. It had become important to the family that they be the first—and only—producers of solar transistors.

Moreover, Larry—board member along with Ruth and Michael—often urged stronger measures for the family's defense. In 2015, records showed, Larry was successful in persuading the corporation to set aside a substantial portion of its annual budget for the development of "a complete solar weapons system."

Two years later the family had begun testing a solar laser that would, when perfected, beam death to "any potential enemy within a 10-mile radius." Also by that time the corporation had initiated the design of solar shields, future defense weapons.

But the primary interest of S.T.I. remained in creating a device for solar energy storage. In 2018, in a mailed press release to the *New York Times,* the corporation publicly announced its success.

Faced with the need to market its solar transistors, the family permitted a handful of its young members to leave the estate in order to act as sales representatives. By 2020, the journalists transmitted, the corporation employed five such representatives, all between twenty and twenty-four years of age.

What happened shortly after 4 A.M., the morning of March 11, 2020, is not exactly clear. Langley whispered into her transmitter, "Someone's coming." After a short pause she gasped one additional sentence. That sentence was followed by what sounded at the *Phoenix Herald* like a scuffle. Minutes later a

male voice—probably that of Parks—stuttered a frightened, "We'll get back to you." An abrupt click followed, after which all transmission ceased.

At 5:30 A.M. March 11, the car in which Parks and Langley were returning to Phoenix left the road, striking a power pole. The accident proved instantly fatal to both. Subsequent investigation by the Arizona state police revealed that the driver was speeding and had lost control of the vehicle.

On March 12, 2020, the *Phoenix Herald* issued a special edition. Across its front page the paper ran the following headline:

TWO REPORTERS KILLED;
THEIR FINAL STORY:
S.T.I. DIRECTORS ARE GREEN!

"Greens" had appeared on earth. The beings resembled humans except that their skin color took on an increasingly green cast as they approached their late twenties. In 2024 biochemists, working with what data they could uncover, reported the creatures could photosynthesize. The mossy flesh tone, these scientists asserted, was due to the presence of chlorophyll within epidermal cells.

While no one could state with certainty the causes for the mutation, some evolutionary scientists theorized that it was a response to the worsening world food shortage. Others of equal stature argued differently. The mutation, these latter scientists believed, could only be retrogressive: a throwback to an earlier evolutionary period, a reversion to something resembling plant life.

"We must come to an agreement soon," the president of the United States anxiously admonished his secretary of the interior in February 2026. "The country is going crazy!"

"Sir," Secretary Steinburg began.

"It's six years now," the president interrupted, "since those two reporters turned this country upside down. What we've got is bedlam. Half the people want greens executed. 'We can't live with monsters,' they're screaming. The other half say, '*Leave them alone, let them sell us solar transistors, let them ASSIMILATE, for God's sake!*'"

"We do need the energy, sir."

The president paced. "We've spent 400 million dollars," he said quietly, "on espionage directed specifically at greens, and still we can't come up with the formula to manufacture our own S.T.'s." He paused, then slammed his fist on his desk. "Now some crazy liberal group is claiming we've violated the creatures' civil rights!"

"That is a valid issue, Mr. President."

"How do you know that, Steinburg? We can't even be sure they *have* civil rights. We haven't yet decided whether the things are *human*."

"Sir," Steinburg ventured cautiously, "Are you personally in favor of annihilation?"

"I'm not in favor of anything yet," the president snapped. "Most of these greens don't need to eat. What if they're multiplying in China? In Australia? Suppose Canada has its own green monsters, lets them alone, lets them assimilate. And we kill ours. Then what? Then you've got a country of people who hardly even need to eat living next door to a nation whose people are hungry. Hungry, Steinburg." He repeated the word for emphasis. "Then what happens? Canada could stockpile a grain surplus while we would be experiencing a shortage. That would put Canada in a position to demand exorbitant prices for their surplus food."

"So maybe we need the greens. Is that what you're saying?"

The president sat behind his desk. "Sit down," he said.

Steinburg slid into a chair and faced the president from across the desk.

The chief executive leaned forward. "The CIA report came in this morning. It's classified 'top secret.'" The president paused. "Steinburg," he said finally, "greens have working solar weapons—a solar laser and defense shields."

The secretary stared in silence. "What kind of creatures *are* these?" he whispered.

The president's voice was unusually loud. "I'm saying find out, Steinburg." "FIND OUT!"

Questions

1. The fact that members of S.T.I.'s board of directors are green shocks the world. What unconscious agreement (about the acceptable colors of people) does this point out?

2. What is the "point of view" of the president of the United States concerning greens?

3. What do you suppose a sociologist could contribute to solving the president's problems regarding the greens?

4. What sorts of questions do you suppose a sociologist, a psychologist, and a political scientist would ask if they were to study the greens?

2

Theoretical Points of View

Sociologists are not alone in wanting to understand society. All of us from our youngest childhood try to make sense out of the social world around us. But sociology offers several special ways of looking at society. This chapter presents the different theoretical points of view that sociologists use.

It will be useful for us to look at these points of view early in the book because if you are to understand society you must first know what to look for. Each of the theoretical points of view in sociology reflects a slightly different picture of what's important, and you must be aware of these differences in order to understand the materials presented in later chapters of the book.

We'll begin with a brief examination of some of the more important intellectual influences on sociological theories past and present. Then we'll turn to discussions of some of the key points of view being used and developed right now. If you're wondering what theory has to do with you, the box "Why 'Do' Theory?" on page 26 may start you on the road toward some answers.

Some Influences on Sociological Theory

In reviewing early human intellectual history, it is difficult to separate what we would now call sociology from social philosophy. For many of the early social thinkers, the question of "what is" was largely inseparable from "what ought to be." Moreover, many of the earlier points of view were deeply embedded in religious beliefs, and explanations for the social order lay within the supernatural realm.

During the past two or three hundred years, however, this situation has changed. Theories of society have more and more come to be shaped by intellectual influences that are largely devoid of moral philosophy and also devoid of the supernatural. Let's look at some of those influences.

The Problem of Order

In 1651, Thomas Hobbes (1588–1679), a British philosopher, said something about human affairs that has been near the heart of social thought ever since, and it is important to sociology today. Hobbes said that the "natural state" of humankind must have been a "war of all against all." Without governments, laws, religions, or other factors, everyone would have followed only the dictates of his or her own short-run self-interest. People would have taken what they wanted and given no thought whatever to anyone else.

Hobbes (1651:100) described early human history as "continual fear, and danger of violent death; and the life of man, solitary, poor, nasty, brutish and short." In Hobbes's view, without the influence of a strong leader (called the Leviathan), no social order could have arisen.

Social thinkers since Hobbes have differed in their feelings about the necessity of a strong leader, but each has had to deal in some fashion with what has come to be known as the "Hobbesian problem of order." Even in the worst of times, people are more civil than Hobbes described as our natural state. Why is it that we get along as well as we do?

A century after the publication of Hobbes's *Leviathan,* the French philosopher Jean Jacques Rousseau (1712–1778) offered an answer to the problem of order that did not require the participation of a totalitarian leader. In *The Social Contract,* Rousseau (1762:5) said that social order did not come from force: "The strongest—unless he transforms force into right and obedience into duty—is never strong enough to have his way all the time." He expressed this thought in another passage as well (1762:2) and said also that the social order did not rise automatically out of human nature: "In any case, social order is a right—a sacred right, which serves as the basis for all other rights; it does not, that is to say, flow

---

Why "Do" Theory?

Theory has sometimes had a "bad press" among sociology students. Some consider it dry, vague, difficult, and irrelevant. Such objections largely reflect a misunderstanding of what theory is and what it does.

What is theory? In simple terms, it is a system of abstract statements about relationships between events and units that answers the question "Why?" Why do social agreements break down? Why do bureaucracies become centralized? Why is there prejudice, crime, and war?

If sociological theory sometimes seems irrelevant to important questions like those, it is because theory is, by nature, *abstract.* An abstract statement is one that is not tied to a particular time and place. Rather than making theories less relevant, however, this fact gives them *greater* relevance to your understanding of daily life. Let's see how that works.

You are already familiar with perhaps the most famous theoretical formula of recent years: Albert Einstein's $e = mc^2$. This formula tells us the amount of energy that is released whenever matter is transformed into energy. It is an abstract statement about events and units because it applies to *every* time that *any* matter is transformed into energy. It is not limited, for example, to the explosion of an atomic bomb over Hiroshima in 1945. It also applies to the generation of electrical power in nuclear reactors.

Now, let's take a sociological illustration. Georg Simmel once said, "The greater the degree of conflict between two groups, the greater each's respective internal solidarity." While this does not always happen in practice, it provides a good illustration of the utility of abstract theories.

Notice that Simmel's statement makes no reference to particular groups, specific places, or specific times. In fact, it brings together and makes sense out of a diverse set of sociological observations. We observe that nations become nationalistic during wartime. We observe that street gangs become more tightly knit as they approach a "rumble." We observe that high school social clubs become more cliquish when they compete with one another for an award.

All of these diverse observations suddenly make sense in the light of Simmel's abstract statement: Conflict between groups increases solidarity within each. Abstract theory, then, explains things we have observed, and it also suggests new things to look for. It may allow us to predict future events.

Without theory, we can only describe, record, and react to the confusion of the world. With it, we can see events in context, find similarities and patterns, and make sense out of the confusion.

Can you think of other examples to illustrate Simmel's abstract statement? Where do you suppose theories come from? How do you suppose Simmel arrived at his statement?

Thomas Hobbes 1588–1679 (Popperfoto)   *Jean Jacques Rousseau 1712–1778 (Bulloz)*   *Auguste Comte 1798–1857 (Snark International)*   *Emile Durkheim 1858–1917 (The Bettman Archive)*

from force. Yet it does not flow from nature either. It therefore rests upon agreements."

Social order was, for Rousseau, the result of a social contract entered into by people bound by it, not the result of an agreement imposed on them by a strongman. His theory had a significant impact on social and political philosophy,* and it's also an important one for sociology.

Positivism

Auguste Comte (1798–1857) is frequently cited as the "father of sociology" for more reasons than his coining of the French term *sociologie*. Not only did he urge the development of sociology as a *science* similar to physics and biology, but he also suggested that such a development would represent a pinnacle in human intellectual achievement. Indeed, he referred to one of his own major works as "the great discovery of 1822."

Comte's primary influence arises from his "positive philosophy" or **positivism** (Lenzer 1975). Comte urged that social behavior be studied and understood logically and rationally and that rational/logical explanations be tested against empirical observations. In this, Comte suggested modeling sociology after the experimental method that had been developed in

*Thomas Jefferson and other American founders were greatly influenced by Rousseau, for example, and Rousseau's writings were even more directly influential in the French Revolution.

biology and the other natural sciences. To appreciate the significance of this point of view, you should realize that before Comte most social theories were based on speculation and, very often, religion.

Comte recognized that biology had been separated from the religious point of view. He suggested that psychology would next be separated, and that with the separation of sociology the emancipation of human reason from religion and superstition would be complete.

Comte's positivistic point of view has had a lasting influence on sociology. Sociology as a social science could not have developed without an acceptance of positivism. Today many sociologists argue that positivism has also had negative consequences for sociology, and we'll look at some of their views later in this chapter.

Functionalism

Sociology has been influenced by biology in many ways, as we've just seen in the case of positivism and the experimental model. **Functionalism** is another example of a point of view influenced by biology. From the point of view of functionalism, the elements of a society are understood in terms of the functions they perform for the society as a whole. For example, the function of schools is to teach new generations the society's agreements. The function of labor unions is to promote the collective interests of workers.

This type of "functional" analysis developed in biology during the nineteenth century as the different parts of the body were looked at in terms of their contributions to the body as a total system. The idea of "system" is an important one. Clearly, the human body as we know it is more than a mere collection of cells, tissues, bones, and organs. These different parts are *related* to each other, and they interact with one another. The lungs fill blood with oxygen, the heart pumps blood to the brain, the brain directs the lungs to fill with air again, and so forth. We say, therefore, that the body operates as a system. The term "system" refers to the interrelatedness and interaction of the parts.

The functional analysis of the body as a system represented a significant advance in biology. Organs that could be removed and examined in isolation from the rest of the body could only be understood in terms of the functions they served for the body as a total system.

Comte, Emile Durkheim (1858–1917), and others suggested that the same point of view be adopted in the study of society. In this point of view, Durkheim (1895) thought that society as a system had a "reality" quite apart from the components of that society.

The functionalist point of view became very influential in anthropology also, because it offered an explanation for many seemingly bizarre practices—e.g. worshipping trees, magic, etc.—among preliterate people. As anthropologists examined the functions such practices might serve for the social whole, they often found parallels in their own societies. Thus, for example, restrictions against killing or eating certain kinds of animals were often seen to serve a religious function for a preliterate society—a function served by churches in more modern societies.

In more recent times, Robert Merton (1957a) has drawn attention to the subtlety of some social functions, speaking of the **manifest** (overt) and **latent** (hidden) **functions** of elements in society. The manifest function of schools, for example, is education. One of their latent functions is keeping young people out of the job market for a number of years.

Overall, functionalism has had two "functions" in sociology. First, it has offered explanations for the ways in which different elements of society fit together. Second, it has prompted the study of "system needs," the functions that must be served for a system to survive. We shall return to the idea of system needs in the discussion of **social systems theory** later in the chapter.

Evolution

Another major influence that biology had on sociology came from the evolutionary point of view advanced by Charles Darwin (1809–1882) and others. The biological evolutionists suggested that mutations (new life forms) appeared by chance and that their survival potentials were tested by the environments in which they appeared. Darwin spoke of "natural selection" and "survival of the fittest" in explaining how some new life forms established themselves in nature by reproducing themselves and thereby giving persistence to their "kind." The long-term effect of the evolutionary process, moreover, was the gradual development of complex organisms—such as people—from those very simple organisms that marked the beginning of life itself.

Social evolution as a point of view has come and gone in the history of sociology ever since. The evolutionary point of view gained tremendous popularity in sociology following the publication of Darwin's works on biological evolution. Herbert Spencer

Robert Merton 1910– (Jill Krementz)

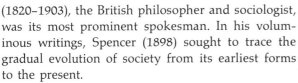
Charles Darwin 1809–1882 (Popperfoto)

Herbert Spencer 1820–1903 (Historical Pictures Service, Chicago)

Karl Marx 1818–1883 (Popperfoto)

(1820–1903), the British philosopher and sociologist, was its most prominent spokesman. In his voluminous writings, Spencer (1898) sought to trace the gradual evolution of society from its earliest forms to the present.

We'll return to the evolutionary point of view from time to time throughout this book and especially in Chapter 15 where I'll discuss social change. It's useful to note at this point, however, two of the more serious criticisms raised against it.

First, an unsophisticated view of social evolution suggests that evolutionary "progress" is all for the good, that modern, complex societies must be "better" or "fitter" than simple ones. This view has been roundly criticized, in much the same manner that many people today criticize the view that industrial "progress" is necessarily good.

Second, some sociologists have questioned whether societies actually evolve in a single direction —from simple to complex, for example—in all cases. Some, such as Pitirim Sorokin (1889–1968), have suggested *cyclical* theories of social change, and we'll look at those in Chapter 15.

Marxism

Karl Marx (1818–1883) had a profound influence on sociology although he is, of course, more commonly associated with economics and politics. Two issues raised by Marx had the greatest impact on subsequent sociological theory: **economic determinism** and **class conflict.**

First, Marx suggested that all human social existence could be understood in terms of economics. All social agreements could be traced back to economic determinants. Where Max Weber (1905) was to point to the influence of religion (ascetic Protestantism) on economic systems (capitalism), Marx insisted, in contrast, that even religion flowed from economic factors. In characterizing religion as "the opiate of the masses," he suggested that the capitalists used religion as a device to keep the mass of workers in check.

Marx is often compared with Georg Hegel (1770–1831), the German philosopher, and Marx acknowledged being influenced by Hegel's thinking. Hegel saw human progress as a "dialectical" process: An idea (thesis) would be followed by its opposite (antithesis), and both would be followed by their synthesis. Marx accepted the Hegelian view of human progress, but with an important difference. Marx argued that the dialectical process involved not ideas but economic conditions and relations. Thus, Marx's point of view on history is often referred to as **dialectical materialism.**

Marx's second major influence on sociology reflected his dialectical materialism. He argued that all history was the history of class struggle: the conflict between economic classes. In contrast to the functionalist point of view, which focuses on the harmonious interrelations among the elements of society, Marx suggested that societies were structured so as to produce conflict rather than harmony.

As long as societies were organized around dominant and subordinate classes of individuals, Marx argued, conflict would result. More to the point, Marx saw societies organized around a class of people who owned the means of economic production, on the one hand, and the exploited class of workers, on the other. It was inevitable, Marx felt, that the workers would struggle to attain equality, and it seemed to him that it was the obligation of scholars to educate and organize the masses for an effective struggle.

As we shall see later in this chapter, a part of Marx's legacy to sociology is what we now call **conflict theory.** It represents a radically different point of view from that of functionalism and social systems theory.

Idealism

The final theoretical influence I want to discuss is quite different from the others. It came to sociology from the German idealist tradition in philosophy and had its main impact by way of the writings of Max Weber (1864–1920), particularly from his discussion of **ideal types** (Weber 1925a).

Essentially, an ideal type is a model against which to compare the world we observe. The ideal type is intended to capture the essential qualities of a class of things we observe around us, even though it does not correspond exactly with any specific observation.

Weber (1925a), for example, provided a detailed description and explanation of bureaucracy as a form of social organization. Although his development of this ideal type reflected his observations of real-life bureaucracies, his purpose was not to incorporate all the details of each. Rather, he sought to describe a "perfect" bureaucracy, thereby offering a model against which to compare and understand those bureaucracies we observe.

Realize that when I refer to a "perfect" bureaucracy, I do not mean to imply that you would *like* one that completely reflected the model. The terms "idealism" and "ideal type" in this context are based on the notion of "idea" and do not imply any kind

of evaluation. You could, for example, construct an ideal type for dictators, murderers, or rapists without being in favor of them.

Think for a minute about the different kinds of professors you've come across during your studies. Perhaps there were some who were warm and friendly, treating you more like a friend than like a student, and others who were more formal, maintaining the traditional distance between students and professors. You could construct an ideal type for each kind of professor, describing all the most significant characteristics of each. Those ideal types would be useful tools for you in summarizing your observations about professors in general.

Ultimately, ideal types describe what a society's agreements would be like if they were totally logical and rational, if society were totally understandable. Actual societies and social relations, then, can be understood as approximations of the ideal types.

Let's turn now to some of the contemporary, theoretical points of view in sociology. In Chapter 1 I mentioned that some sociologists are particularly interested in the structure and perpetuation of agreements, while others are more interested in the disagreements that result in a struggle over the change of agreements. I'm going to discuss these two points of view as social systems theory and conflict theory. I'll also describe a sociological point of view called symbolic interactionism. This view deals with the creation of agreements. You will see that these points of view offer very different perspectives on society and social relations. These different views also complement each other. I'd like you to notice how, for a well-rounded picture of the world around you, you have to entertain each.

Symbolic Interactionism

Since we're going to be talking about agreements throughout this book, we should find out where they come from. Social agreements are created through communication in interaction. When people interact, they communicate with words, actions, postures, symbols, gestures, and other signs, and they form agreements with each other in the process.

The sociological point of view called **symbolic interactionism** deals primarily with the communication of symbols through interaction. This orientation within sociology is most directly associated with the so-called Chicago school that was centered around the University of Chicago during the first part of this century. The key figure in that school was George Herbert Mead, a philosopher and sociologist.

I'll begin with a review of the ideas Mead and others put forward to explain how our systems of social agreements were established. Then I'll turn to some of the contemporary symbolic interactionists in American sociology.

In the Beginning . . .

Georg Simmel (1858–1918) was one of the first sociologists to draw attention to the simplest of social phenomena: small-group interaction. For Simmel, the organizations of large-scale religions, governments, economic systems, or whole societies were merely extensions of the process of interaction that could be observed between two people (a **dyad**) or among people in slightly larger groups.

Simmel made many important contributions to sociology, and we shall return to some of them later in the book. Someone else, however, traced the full implications of the creation of agreements through social interaction. This was George Herbert Mead (1863–1931) at Chicago.

Like Simmel, Mead felt that all the large-scale social phenomena we observe were the products of the interaction process, but Mead went even further. For Mead, our *minds* and our conceptions of our *selves* were also the products of interaction.* Neither mind, self, nor society existed before interaction (Morris 1934).

To begin, Mead regarded interaction as inevitable among human beings. More generally, it is inevitable among species that reproduce through sexual union

*As I'll use the term in this discussion, "mind" is a process rather than a thing. Your mind is what goes on in your brain, most familiar to you, perhaps, as the little voice in the back of your head. Your "self," on the other hand, is your individual identity: who you are. It is clear to you that you are not your father, your mother, your best friend, or your sociology instructor. *Who* you are is your "self." Your name is the label we've agreed to use in talking about your self.

Georg Simmel 1858–1918 (Bibliotèque Nationale) *George Herbert Mead 1863–1931 (Historical Pictures Service, Chicago)*

and whose offspring require parental care through infancy. Moreover, it seems clear that the human race could not have survived had it not learned to cooperate. Our ancestors, like ourselves, were neither the fastest, the strongest, nor the best-protected animals in the primeval neighborhood.

Looking about him, Mead saw three characteristics of the human mind that made human beings unique among animals. First, they were able to assign symbols to represent the objects around them, giving those objects names and using those names in communication. Humans developed and used far more complex languages than other animals. Second, humans could imagine what would happen if they pursued different lines of action in relation to the objects around them. They could imagine what would happen if they punched a tiger in the nose or crashed a Green Bay Packer team party. They could imagine what would happen without actually taking the actions. Finally, humans seemed able to choose appropriate actions from among those they had rehearsed in their minds.

Mead did not believe that our earliest ancestors had these abilities at first; instead, the abilities developed over hundreds of thousands of years. Without being able to explain exactly how they developed, Mead described what probably happened in the course of developing minds, selves, and societies.

Mead pointed to communication as being essential to the development process. People, like other animals, first communicated through gestures, a form

This prehistoric painting in the Lascaux caves is an attempt to communicate symbolically the experience of the hunt. George Herbert Mead said such communication was a keystone in the development of mind, self, and society. (Popperfoto)

of communication that predated language. You are already familiar with hundreds and thousands of different gestures: a dog's bared teeth, a cat's purr, a baby's smile. Gestures such as these seem to communicate to us directly, without having to be transformed into words or concepts. Other gestures can communicate directly, too. Our earliest ancestors would not have had to possess very large brains to understand what someone shaking a fist and throwing rocks was communicating.

Communication through nonverbal gestures laid the foundation for the development of language. We don't know exactly how the first verbal symbols, the first words, were developed or what they were.* Nobody could write an account of the creation of language any more than the person in the cartoon in Chapter 1 could tell how he'd look without glasses. Probably the first words were a lot like grunts and screams.

Over a very long time, a body of agreements on verbal symbols accumulated. There were words to represent physical objects, words to represent emotions, and words to represent actions. A person could

*There have been three major theories regarding the first words uttered by humans: (1) "Where is the bathroom, please?"; (2) "You're standing on my foot"; and (3) "This is a stickup. Gimme your pelts." None of these has been proven, however, and the debate continues.

not only recognize an angry gesture but also could communicate about it verbally, using a word for "anger." Different collections of people in different places developed words and languages distinct from one another.

People were able to communicate verbally using a shared language. An individual could also communicate effectively with himself or herself, using words and the concepts that words gave substance to. In this fashion, people gained the ability to imaginatively rehearse possible courses of events. Through language, they could not only imagine possible actions but also could imagine how they and others might feel about those events. People were able to reflect on their day-to-day existences. Thusly, people developed *minds*.

The combination of interaction and language, for Mead, was also necessary for the development of the *self*. With language, which allowed a person to mentally represent such emotions as anger, fear, and love, it was possible to include other people's mental states in the imaginative rehearsals of possible future events, anticipating how people would feel in various circumstances. In this sense, Mead spoke of a developing human ability to "take the role of the other," to take on someone else's point of view. It became possible to look at the world the way others saw it.

Think what might have taken place had you been one of our earliest ancestors, just beginning to look at the world through someone else's point of view. One of the first things you probably would have seen would have been yourself. That probably would have been the most profound thing to happen to you since you first looked into a pool of water and saw your face reflected in it. By looking at yourself through other people's points of view, you would have discovered that they regarded you as one of the objects in their environment, just as you regarded them as objects in yours. The more you looked at yourself through other's eyes, the more you would have developed a consciousness of yourself, a self-image, or what Mead simply called your "self."

The full development of mind and self came, Mead said, when individuals were able to take the role of the **generalized other,** to recognize and look through the points of view that the members of the group generally shared. In addition to learning that a

particular neighbor was likely to hit you over the head with a club whenever possible, you could also learn that most members of your group felt such behavior was improper. In addition to learning that one person thought you were ugly and another thought you were pretty, you could also learn that most members of the group thought you were so-so.

Once an individual learns the point of view of the generalized other, that individual begins to govern his or her behavior by it. Having learned it is the general consensus of the group that stealing food from others warrants a punishment by death, most individuals would be hesitant to steal. Having learned that it is the general consensus of the group that the best hunter should get the most food to eat, most would try to excel in the hunt.

This body of group agreements was, for Mead, **society,** or "institutions," a term he seems to have preferred. Society developed out of interaction, and, once developed, it controlled the interactions that followed. Once you agree to something, you are bound by that agreement.

To summarize, George Herbert Mead attributed the development of our minds, our selves, and our societies all to the process of social interaction. Non-verbal communications through gestures led to the development of language. The combination of language with continued interaction made thinking possible. This, in turn, allowed us to "take the role of the other" and look at the world through other

people's points of view. Finally, each individual learned the points of view that were generally shared by members of his or her group, and those shared points of view had the effect of at least partly controlling subsequent interaction.

Mead could only speculate about the historical events that produced human minds, selves, and societies, but you can observe something similar to what must have taken place by watching young children develop. Watching them learn language and the other social agreements can offer insights into how it all began, and we'll return to that process in Chapter 5 on socialization.

Other founders of symbolic interactionism include Charles Horton Cooley (1864–1929) and W. I. Thomas (1863–1947), and we'll look at their contributions to sociology later in the book. At this point, let's turn to the current status of this point of view and to some of the sociologists most closely associated with it.

Contemporary Symbolic Interactionism

Herbert Blumer (1900–), a student of Mead's at the University of Chicago, is generally regarded as the key figure in symbolic interactionism today. Early in his career, he undertook empirical studies of such phenomena as collective behavior to demonstrate the interactionist point of view in practice. In more recent years, he has become involved in elaborating interactionism as theory (Blumer 1969).

In direct contrast to the social systems point of view to be discussed shortly, Blumer regards society as an ongoing *process* of mutual adjustment among individuals. He acknowledges that people develop habitual patterns of behavior, but his primary attention is on the continual creation of agreements as individuals define the meaning of situations, communicate, and interact.

The work of Erving Goffman also fits within this perspective. In particular, Goffman is interested in the ways we present ourselves to each other in our everyday interactions. The titles of Goffman's books indicate this interest, for example: *Presentation of Self in Everyday Life* (Goffman 1964). In addition, he has found insights into the nature of interaction by studying behavior in mental hospitals (Goffman 1961) and

Talcott Parsons 1902– (The American Sociological Association)

in studying how people with physical defects manage their "spoiled identities" (Goffman 1963).

The best statement of the symbolic interactionist point of view in social psychology is in the work of Tamotsu Shibutani (1961). More than Blumer, Shibutani is interested in how the agreed-on meanings that grow out of interaction become perpetuated. He notes that "meanings, once they have been formed, tend to be self-sustaining" (Shibutani 1961:108).

The self-sustaining quality of agreements is the chief concern of another important point of view in sociology: social systems theory.

Social Systems Theory

Sometimes called "structural-functionalism," the social systems point of view is an important and influential one in sociology today. I've already mentioned the roles played by Comte and Durkheim in

regard to functionalism, but the elaboration on the idea of a social "system" didn't take place until later.

Early in this century, a Harvard biochemist, L. J. Henderson (1878–1942), crossed departmental boundaries to lecture in sociology and to write a "physiologist's view" of the works of Italian sociologist/economist Vilfredo Pareto (1848–1923) (Henderson 1935). Pareto's great contribution, Henderson urged, was to suggest that society functioned as a system, a system analogous to economic and biological systems. This, Henderson insisted, was the most fruitful point of view for sociologists to take.

While Henderson and his works are little known in contemporary sociology, one of his students at Harvard took his insistence on a systems approach seriously. Talcott Parsons (1902–), with previous university training in both biology and economics, went on to devote his professional career to an elaboration of the social system.* Parsons' *The Social System* (1951) remains the chief representation of this point of view, and Parsons' name is regarded as synonymous with that view.†

Let's look now at the key features of the social system as laid out by Henderson, Parsons, and others.

System

First and foremost, there is the concept of "system." As I've already indicated, this concept comes to sociology primarily from biology and economics. Important advances in each of those fields were associated with a systemic point of view, and similar advances have been sought in sociology.

The primary characteristic of a system is the interrelationships and interdependence of the component parts making up the system. Throughout the body, for example, the heart pumps blood, providing nourishment for the other tissues and organs. It permits the lungs to survive, enabling them to take

---

*Another student in the class, George Homans, will be discussed later in this chapter.

†Parsons acknowledges the role of Henderson in the preface, saying: "The title, *The Social System*, goes back, more than to any other source, to the insistence of the late Professor L. J. Henderson on the extreme importance of the concept of system in scientific theory, and his clear realization that the attempt to delineate the social system as a system was the most important contribution of Pareto's great work" (p. vii).

in air from the environment, with that air becoming part of the blood's nourishing quality.

The "free market" model of supply, demand, and prices offers an example of a system in economics. Changes in one part of the system affect other parts. In a situation in which the supply of a commodity increases a great deal and the demand remains constant, for example, prices are likely to be depressed. Or, if supply remains constant and demand increases, prices are likely to rise.

The same interrelationships and interdependence of component parts may be seen in a social system. Organized cooperation of individuals in a group makes achievements possible that would lie beyond the ability of an individual or even a collection of unorganized, uncooperating individuals. The industrial factory provides an excellent illustration, with different specialized workers supporting each other's efforts in the accomplishment of the group goal—the finished product.

Equilibrium

An essential characteristic of systems is equilibrium. The interrelationships among the component parts of a system must be such that the system will survive as changes in one component are "balanced" or "compensated for" by other parts. This simplest form of equilibrium, called static equilibrium, has the effect of maintaining the status quo.

A familiar, physical illustration can be used to demonstrate the concept. In a house with central heating, governed by a thermostat, we have a system that functions to keep the temperature of the house constant. If the temperature begins to drop, the thermostat is designed to turn on the furnace and raise the heat to the desired level. Once the temperature has reached the specified level, the thermostat is designed to turn the furnace off.

In many ways, your body operates to maintain equilibrium. If you get too hot, you sweat (or perspire, depending on your upbringing), and that has the effect of cooling the surface of your skin. Economists have observed that economic systems have the same equilibrium-maintaining characteristic as in the example, regarding the relationships among supply, demand, and prices.

The social systems point of view is an attempt to understand the elements in society in terms of the functions they serve within the whole. (John Hodder)

Social systems also have the characteristic of equilibrium. The fact that an increase in the crime rate is likely to result in more intensive crime-prevention efforts—increasing the size of the police force, for example—is an illustration of equilibrium maintenance. Or if the lathe operators in a factory are unable to keep up with the other production units, it is likely that more lathe operators will be hired and trained. Social systems, like biological and economic ones, are continually involved in the balancing and rebalancing necessary to survive as systems.

Social systems theorists don't insist that systems always maintain the status quo, however. In place of static equilibrium, they suggest, some systems are characterized by *moving* equilibrium. In this view, a system may change continually in a certain direction, but it does so in an *orderly* fashion, maintaining a dynamic balance among its parts. Let's look at an example of moving equilibrium.

It has been observed that as the educational level of a population increases there is a tendency for job requirements to be upgraded. Positions that once required a high school diploma now require a college education. Upgrading job requirements, however, encourages people to get even more education, which, in turn, results in a further upgrading of job requirements. Although the level of education in the population and the educational levels required for employment are continually changing, they are continually balanced against one another. Despite the continual changes, the educational/employment system survives.

System Imperatives

The observation that systems operate in such a way as to survive as systems has resulted in a persistent controversy in sociology and elsewhere. In the case of sociology, it has been centered on the concept of **system imperatives,** sometimes called "functional imperatives." This concept combines the functionalist point of view with that of maintaining equilibrium in a system so as to provide for its survival *as a system.*

Let's examine the concept itself first, and then we'll see why it has been controversial. Parsons, who has written most on this subject, has suggested that any system must accomplish four basic tasks or functions if it is to survive as a system. The letters A, G, I, and L have come to symbolize this point of view.

A   Adaptation: The system must have the ability to get resources from the environment and distribute them through the system. The *economy* is an example of adaptation in a society.

G   Goal attainment: The system must have the ability to establish goals, set priorities, and move its parts toward achieving them. *Government* is an example of goal attainment in a society.

I   Integration: The system must have the ability to achieve coordination and effective working relationships among its parts. The *laws* of a society are an example of the integration function in a society.

L   Latency:* The system must have the ability to maintain patterns of "proper" behavior by its components and to handle any strains or tensions that arise. *Religion* is an example of the latency function in society.

Unless a social system provides for the satisfaction of each of these functions, Parsons suggested, it cannot survive. Since the social systems that sociologists study have survived, he continued, it makes sense to examine the ways in which different societies have performed the several functions.

Social Structure

The persistent agreements of societies are organized so as to promote system survival. Even if the system itself cannot "act" in ways appropriate to its survival, the agreements that make up the system lead individuals to act that way. By and large, people obey the laws and customs of their societies, and generation after generation teaches those agreements to its children. In every society, some individuals assume a special responsibility for enforcing the agreements, and, in the process, they often resist the pressure to change.

A novelty item that you may be familiar with illustrates what I am saying about people resisting the pressure to change. It's a small black box with an on/off switch on top of it. If you flip the switch to the "on" position, a door opens on top of the box and a small, mechanical hand reaches up to push the switch back to "off." Every time you flip the switch

*Parsons originally called this "latent pattern maintenance and tension management."

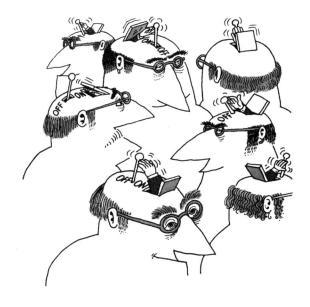

to "on," the little hand pushes it back to "off." This mechanical system is constructed in such a way as to keep the switch in an "off" position.

Social systems theorists observe that the agreements of societies are "constructed" and organized in such a way as to enhance their chances of survival, and we'll look further into that matter in the discussion of culture (Chapter 4) and in the examination of institutions (Part Three).

From a social systems point of view, disagreement and change are problems. This is not to say that systems theorists personally oppose disagreement and change, but these threaten the survival of systems *as* systems. From the social systems point of view, sociologists focus their attention on how the system "deals with" such problems in the pursuit of system survival. Not all sociologists think that disagreement and change threaten systems as systems, however, as we'll see now.

Conflict Theory

So far, we've noted that interactionists look at the world in terms of interpersonal communication and formation of agreements. Structural-functionalists, on the other hand, focus on the orderliness of

social relations in terms of organized and perpetuated agreements. Yet a third camp is made up of sociologists who see the world primarily in terms of conflict and power.

In this section, you are going to meet four sociologists associated with **conflict theory** in sociology. In comparison with the discussion of social systems theory, you'll get a clear picture of how differently sociologists see the world, depending on their sociological points of view.

Karl Marx

The conflict point of view is an old one in modern sociology. Emile Durkheim, one of the early functionalists, was born in 1858. That same year, Karl Marx wrote Friedrich Engels to say how much he had just profited from his reading of Hegel's *Logik* and to indicate that "If ever the leisure for such work returns, I should very much like to make intelligible to common human understanding (in a short work) the rational aspect of the method which Hegel discovered but at the same time mystified" (Bottomore and Rubel 1956:1).

The Hegelian method that Marx referred to was the dialectic mentioned earlier in this chapter. Although Marx was never to write the short work he spoke of, his reinterpretation of Hegel did appear in 1867 in the monumental *Das Kapital*. The conflict view was firmly established in sociology.

Although Marx recognized the systematic and organized quality of social relations, he found conflict a more important aspect. Not only did he observe a great deal of conflict in day-to-day affairs, but he also saw the ways in which the very structuring of agreements *created* conflict.

Marx observed, for example, that all societies had agreements regarding the unequal distribution of scarce resources such as wealth and power. All societies were organized in such a way that some people had more of these than others. Such agreements, Marx indicated, made conflict inevitable, as the "have nots" struggled to gain a larger share of the things enjoyed by the "haves."

Taking the class struggle as inevitable, Marx was especially interested in the dynamics of it. In particular, he examined the process of communication

Lewis Coser 1913– (The American Sociological Association)

Ralf Dahrendorf 1929– (The London School of Economics)

the class struggle would run its course with or without Marx—and he regarded it a just price for eradicating inequality and injustice.

Marx's point of view focused on the historical struggle between societywide classes of people. Georg Simmel, another German sociologist, focused on smaller-scale conflicts.

Georg Simmel

As I noted in the earlier discussion of symbolic interactionism, Georg Simmel (1858–1918) regarded the dynamics of small-group interaction as the foundation on which larger social phenomena were based. His observations of human interaction suggested two fundamental and persistent tendencies in human affairs: agreement and disagreement. He called these tendencies "monistic" and "antagonistic," bringing to mind Hegel's notions of thesis and antithesis (Simmel 1908a).

One of the facets of the disagreements that people have with one another that particularly interested Simmel was their varying levels of intensity. He found conflicts more intense when the people having the disagreements were emotionally involved and intimate with one another. Disagreements among members of a tightly knit group were especially intense and even more so when the people having the disagreement felt it threatened the *group's* survival as opposed to affecting individual goals and interests only (Turner 1974).

Simmel had a greater interest than Marx did in the functioning of social systems, more akin to the point of view of social systems theorists. Marx and Simmel shared the view that social structures produce conflicts and that conflict threatens the survival of social systems, but Simmel had an additional interest in the ways in which conflicts could *support* the survival of social systems. A contemporary conflict theorist, Lewis Coser, has elaborated on this latter view.

Lewis Coser

The work of Lewis Coser (1913–), sometimes called "conflict functionalism," might be regarded

whereby the members of an oppressed class became aware of the implications of their shared status. Marx had a special interest in the beliefs that composed what he called "false consciousness" and constituted a barrier to the working class's struggle for equality. The religious view that each individual's place in society is ordained by God is an example of beliefs that Marx felt the dominant groups in a society encouraged among oppressed groups as a device for "keeping them in their place." Religion, for Marx, was an instrument of power in the hands of rulers.

Out of his desire for social equality, Marx directed much of his attention to the process of communication by which members of oppressed groups saw the lie of false beliefs, recognized the true state of affairs, and developed a unified "class consciousness" with a plan of social action. For Marx, the class struggle was largely a struggle for agreement on divergent points of view. The dominant class attempted to promote and enforce—through socialization and other means—the point of view that maintained its favored position in society. For the oppressed class to gain equality, it needed to establish and gain agreement for a different point of view—first among its own members, then throughout the society.

Marx recognized that as workers increasingly agreed among themselves about their true class interests and attempted to gain societywide agreement for their point of view, the struggle would become more violent. The battle over ideas would be bloody and people would die. Marx saw this as inevitable—

as an integration of the systems and conflict points of view. In part, Coser (1956) regards conflict as a "signal" that the system needs readjustment and rebalancing, just as the cooling of air in a house signals the thermostat that it "needs" to turn the furnace on. In all, Coser has sought to elaborate the process of conflict in a system and has examined the causes of conflict, the varying levels of intensity, and variations in duration. He is best known, however, for his descriptions of the ways in which some kinds of conflict can support the survival and functioning of social systems. Here are some of his major conclusions.

1. Conflict between groups increases cohesion and solidarity *within* each of the groups. This effect is particularly felt when the conflict is intense and group members perceive the conflict as impinging on them.

2. Conflict draws attention to structural problems in a system and can stimulate innovative attempts to resolve them.

3. Frequent, unintense conflicts allow people to blow off steam and thereby avoid the buildup of tensions.

4. Conflicts between groups can clarify the perception of the agreements that the members of a particular group share.

5. Conflicts between groups can lead each to seek and form coalitions with other groups.

Ralf Dahrendorf

The contemporary German sociologist Ralf Dahrendorf (1929–) is one of those who has drawn renewed sociological attention to the Marxian view of social conflict as the struggle between parties seeking domination over each other. He has criticized the view that sees conflict as a functioning mechanism within basically orderly societies.

In Dahrendorf's (1959) reformulation of Marx's dialectical process, the organization and perpetuation of agreements involve what he calls **imperatively coordinated associations** (ICAs). In any social setting, Dahrendorf suggests, some participants have the power to impose their points of view on others. An

ICA, then, is an association of individuals that functions harmoniously because some have the power to dominate others. The mutual cooperation of master and slave in an orderly fashion, for example, occurs only because of the power of the master over the slave.

Social conflict, in Dahrendorf's view, is the continuing competition for power to dominate, to impose one's own point of view. It will persist as long as people occupy different positions and have different points of view. In short, according to Dahrendorf, conflict is inevitable. Moreover, social conflict operates dialectically in that once a dominated class has gained the power to impose its point of view on others, the "others" begin the struggle for power.

Other Theoretical Points of View

We have now discussed the three major theoretical points of view in sociology today. Interactionism addresses the process of agreement formation. Social systems theory, or structural-functionalism, focuses on the organization and perpetuation of agreement structures. And, finally, conflict theory takes primary note of the disagreements that are always present in social relations. The box, "Looking at the World from Different Perspectives," on page 40 presents a final look at these points of view.

Before concluding this chapter, I want to describe briefly some additional points of view that supplement, integrate, or elaborate on the major ones already discussed. These are **exchange theory, role theory,** and **ethnomethodology.**

Exchange Theory

In economic relations, people exchange goods and services with one another, each hoping to profit or at least break even on the exchange. Over the years, a number of anthropologists and sociologists have suggested that a similar model might be used to explain social behavior in general. Exchange theory represents the adaptation of an elementary economic model to social relations. When people interact, it has been suggested, they do so with expectations that

Looking at the World from Different Perspectives

The same events appear different according to different theoretical perspectives. Different theoretical perspectives make us see different things. Development of theory in a relatively young discipline such as sociology is always characterized by such competing orientations. Each seeks to find the "real" truth and the "real reality" of events. Let us illustrate the different realities that you would see if you looked at your college or university using the three main theoretical perspectives in sociology: functionalism, symbolic interactionism, and conflict theory.

With functionalism you would view your college as a system of interrelated roles: student, administrator, instructor, service roles, and the like. These roles would probably be seen as subsystems of the overall college system, and each of these subsystems would then be analyzed according to how it functions to meet the survival needs of the college. Instructors might be seen as meeting goal-attainment needs, administrators, integrative needs, students, adaptive needs, and so on. The college as a whole might then be viewed as a subsystem of the overall system of higher education in American society, and, in turn, the functions of higher education for meeting the functional requisites of the society in general might be assessed. Through functional analysis, one views the world as a series of systems and subsystems, each with survival requisites.

You would see your college much differently with symbolic interactionism. Interactionists are interested in how various people playing roles—students, teachers, administrators—define, interact in, and adjust to various situations. For example, a symbolic interactionist might examine your class in sociology by initially trying to understand the definitions of the classroom situation held by students and the teacher. Then, over the course of the term, the interactionist would examine the interaction between you and the instructor, noting your gestures, your assessments and reassessments of the situation, and your changed behavior. From observations of concrete patterns of symbolic interaction among actual people, the interactionist would attempt to develop laws of the basic processes of interaction that make human organization possible.

If you were a conflict theorist you would see your college (or any social unit) as a system of conflicting interests—usually, though not always, conflicting economic interests. You would analyze the different interests of different groups of participants: for example, students would be viewed as having one set of interests (getting diplomas and jobs), instructors another (broad liberal arts instruction in their areas of expertise so that they can keep and justify their jobs), and administrators still another (maintaining order and control). These diverse interests would then be viewed as periodically coming into conflict. Students might be more interested, for example, in getting degrees and jobs quickly than in doing so in an orderly fashion. Such pressures might conflict with instructors' interest in maintaining a broad curriculum that would legitimate their areas of expertise. Thus, the conflict theorist asks these questions: How are the diverse interests of participants likely to come into conflict? What is the power of each conflict group? And how will conflict and its reconciliation create new arrangements, or social agreements? For the conflict theorist, then, the operation of your school involves the perpetual working out through conflict of diverse interests.

Each of these theoretical views reveals a different picture of your college or university. Each gives only a partial picture, yet each draws attention to aspects of the situation that might be overlooked if you used one of the others. The best policy is to look at the situation through several points of view.

How would the three theoretical points of view present different descriptions of and explanations for a student demonstration in opposition to grading policies? Which of the three points of view would be the most *useful* in explaining how students form opinions of specific faculty members?

they will get out of the interaction at least as much as they put into it. To take a simple example, if I invite you to my home for dinner, I hope that my investment—in time and money—will be repaid to me in terms of pleasure in your company, future friendly relations between us, and, perhaps, an invitation to dinner at your house.

The sociologist most closely associated with exchange theory is another of L. J. Henderson's former students at Harvard: George Homans (1910–). In his development of exchange theory, Homans (1961) has devoted most of his energies to two fundamental issues. First, he has set about specifying the various units involved in social exchange, such concepts as costs, investments, rewards, values, and profits. In this context, Homans has introduced the concept of "distributive justice": a "fair" profit for all parties to the exchange.

Homans has also sought to develop the fundamental axioms of social exchange in order to permit the derivation of a formal theory. An example of an axiom is Homan's assertion that a person is likely to engage in an activity if that same activity has been rewarded in the past. In developing the axioms of exchange theory, Homans has insisted that the axioms of any social theory must, themselves, be psychological in nature, thereby laying himself open to the charge of psychological reductionism,* the view that all social behavior may one day be explained in terms of psychological processes.

Role Theory

Some sociologists work with a theoretical point of view that focuses directly on the concepts of role and status that were introduced in Chapter 1. I'll have more to say about these two concepts in Chapter 4, but I want to say a little here about the special view of society that this theory can provide.

For role theorists, social life is analogous to a play in the theater, a view anticipated by William

*"Reductionism" is an important, logical concept in science. Some people hold the view, for example, that one day all psychological behavior may be explained in terms of biology. Such a view is an example of "biological reductionism."

Shakespeare in *As You Like It* nearly four centuries ago:

All the world's a stage
And all the men and women merely players:
They have their exits and their entrances;
And one man in his time plays many parts.
(act 2, scene 7)

From the role theory point of view, people are seen as occupying statuses in society, just as actors fill parts (roles) on the stage. A society's agreements are analogous to the script in a play. And just as different actors play a particular role a little differently, so do people in society—though occupying the same status—behave somewhat differently, partly in response to differences in those with whom they interact. In role theory, a good deal of attention has been paid to the interactions and mutual expectations that shape the way roles are played (Biddle and Thomas 1966).

Erving Goffman's analyses of everyday interpersonal behavior, mentioned earlier in connection with symbolic interactionism, provide illustrations of this point of view in use. Goffman has applied it successfully to the study of mental hospitals, to understanding how people cope socially with physical handicaps, and in other contexts.

Ethnomethodology

The final theoretical point of view that I'll discuss is relatively new in sociology, although, like all those discussed earlier, traces of its main ideas can be found throughout the history of social thought. As a sociological view, ethnomethodology is most closely associated with the work of Harold Garfinkel (1917–) (1967).

In understanding this point of view, it will be useful for you to recall the way we have discussed "agreement" in this book. Two things agree if they are the same; thus, we may say that two people agree about something if their points of view on it are the same. In this sense, we have been looking in this book at some of the ways people agree and some of the ways they disagree.

In an important sense, however, people *never* agree totally. They only *disagree.* If you think for a moment of all the subtle nuances in your view of, say, the desirability of world peace—considering all the different international situations that can arise—you'll see how unlikely it is that *my* view of the matter is exactly the same as yours. Even though you and I may both say we prefer peace, it seems certain that each of us means something different when we say it. We probably wouldn't even be able to agree on what world peace *is* or what it might look like if it existed.

The task of sociology, as seen from the ethnomethodological point of view, is to discover the processes through which people *pretend* to agree. How do you and I go about convincing ourselves that we feel the same way about world peace?

Ethnomethodology addresses the way people construct "agreement reality," their reified and shared view of the way things are, as discussed in Chapter 1. One way ethnomethodologists have sought to clarify the nature of agreement reality is through the violation of heavily reified agreements and the observation of people's reaction to such violations. Garfinkel's students have on occasion treated their parents like total strangers, openly cheated at games, and broken other unspoken agreements in an effort to learn more about those things people take for granted.

Summary

Sociology, as we've seen in this chapter, is not a single point of view but several. Different sociologists see the world around them quite differently. None of the sociological points of view I've discussed gives a total picture of the way things are—they are *only* points of view—yet each reveals things the others do not. Taken together, they offer you a kaleidoscopic peek at the invisible world sociologists see.

Contemporary sociological theories have been influenced by a number of notions over the course of history. Hobbes's 1651 discourse on the "problem of order" has laid in the background of social thought ever since. How is it that people get along together

as well as they do? Hobbes said that it all began with a strong man, the Leviathan, who imposed a set of agreements on those around him. Rousseau, a century later, suggested the reason lay in a social contract.

Comte's positivism pulled sociology away from speculation and supernatural explanations toward science, in the hope that the modern study of social relations would be as rational and precise as biology and physics. Another influence of biology on sociology is to be found in the functionalist view: The elements of a society are to be understood in terms of the functions they serve for the whole.

Evolution provided still another influence of biology on sociology. Many sociologists have regarded the development of social forms—from simple to complex societies, for example—as analogous to the biological evolution of higher forms of life.

Marxism has provided a different kind of influence. Where other sociologists sought to solve the "problem of order" by analyzing the structure of social cooperation and coordination, Marx drew attention to the persistence and significance of conflict in social affairs. In doing so, he emphasized the importance of economic class struggle, employing a modification of Hegel's dialectical process.

German philosophy provided another influence on sociological theory, in the form of ideal types as elaborated by Max Weber. In this view, the concrete events of daily life could be understood as approximations of abstract and logically consistent models.

Three major points of view in sociology today are symbolic interactionism, social systems theory (or structural-functionalism), and conflict theory. These three major views address, respectively, the primary concerns of sociology: (1) how agreements are formed, (2) how they are structured and perpetuated, and (3) how people, as individuals and in groups, resist established agreements, seek to change them, and compete for power in the process.

Symbolic interactionism is traced primarily to the work of George Herbert Mead. Mead suggested that humans had three important abilities that other animals lack: (1) They could assign symbols to represent objects and communicate with those symbols; (2) they could imaginatively rehearse different courses of action; and (3) they could choose the most appropriate course of action from among those rehearsed in their minds. Mead did not believe that human beings had those abilities in the beginning of our species, however. Rather, he felt they were developed in the course of interaction. In particular, by "taking the role of the other," individuals developed minds and self-identities. In the same process, a body of shared agreements—in the form of the "generalized other"—laid the basis for society.

Social systems theory addresses the organization and perpetuation of agreements that are formed through interaction. Although people still create new agreements in the course of their interactions, they do so against the backdrop of previously established —and often reified—agreements. Social systems theorists seek to understand the persistence of agreements by understanding the ways in which they are interrelated and self-supporting. They have a special concern for the functional needs a system has in maintaining equilibrium: either static equilibrium or orderly change over time. The sociologist most associated with this point of view is Talcott Parsons.

Conflict theory is chiefly concerned with disagreement: how individuals and groups compete for power to change established agreements. As I've indicated, Karl Marx was responsible for establishing this point of view in sociology, and Ralf Dahrendorf has sought to reformulate the Marxian position through an analysis of the continuing struggle for power in society. Georg Simmel examined microconflict through the study of small groups. In addition, he introduced the notion that conflict often has positive functions for the stability of social systems. This latter view has been elaborated by Lewis Coser.

The chapter has concluded with a brief overview of three other points of view in sociology. Exchange theory applies the economic model of exchange to social relations. Role theory focuses on the organization and interrelations among roles and statuses, building on the analogy of actors in a stage play. Finally, ethnomethodology asks how people persuade themselves that they agree when, in fact, they never do.

Suggested Readings

Nisbet, Robert A.
1966 *The Sociological Tradition.* New York: Basic Books.
Nisbet's purpose is to trace the history of theoretical concern in sociology regarding several fundamental issues: community, authority, status, the sacred, and alienation. He shows how different sociological theorists living in different historical settings have dealt with the separate issues and their interrelationships.

Parsons, Talcott et al., Eds.
1961 *Theories of Society.* New York: Free Press.
This large, two-volume collection presents the major theoretical writings of social thinkers ranging from Machiavelli to the present. Editorial introductions by Parsons and the other editors place the selections in a contemporary, sociological context. Although you might not be inclined to read the entire collection from beginning to end (not a bad idea, though), it's an excellent place to explore further some of the theoretical ideas discussed in this chapter.

Turner, Jonathan H.
1974 *The Structure of Sociological Theory.* Homewood, Ill.: Dorsey.
This is an excellent presentation of the major theoretical points of view that were introduced in this chapter. Turner discusses the historical development of each point of view. Then he extracts the major theoretical propositions of each writer, making it possible for you to compare the implications of the different theoretical points of view in sociology.

Wallace, Walter L., Ed.
1969 *Sociological Theory.* Chicago: Aldine.
Wallace begins with a discussion of what theory is and where it fits within sociology as a whole. Then, he summarizes eleven (count 'em, eleven) major points of view. The remainder of the book is devoted to selections by representatives of each of the theoretical perspectives discussed.

Episode Two

"They photosynthesize, ladies and gentlemen. Our problem, simply put, is to define them."

The date was May 15, 2026. In Washington, D.C., United States Secretary of the Interior Allen Steinburg was opening the first National Conference on Human Mutations.

Dr. Louise Roanoke, forty, single, internationally known sociologist, listened, intent. She had flown from Chicago in order to address the conference later that afternoon.

"We must know," the secretary pursued dramatically, "what these creatures are. Are they human mutants? It would appear so. Are they then ultimately beneficial to humankind—or harmful throwbacks bent on taking over civilization? Esteemed scientists, are they humans or monsters?"

Steinburg wiped his forehead and took his seat. It had been done, just as the president had ordered: Two hundred of the world's top behavioral, natural, and physical scientists were marshaled to solve what appeared to be one of the most pressing national—and human—problems since the beginning of the species.

Now Dr. Roanoke exchanged glances with a fellow sociologist, Dr. Constance Batterson.

"Nervous?" the latter mouthed from across the room. Roanoke nodded.

Speaking was an American historian who had been researching greens since the turn of the twenty-first century.

"The first green mutant, Adams Jones III," he read from his notes, "had been living in Phoenix as a recluse from the time he was twenty-six because he could no longer pass as normal. His normal wife, it appears, thought Jones to be suffering from some previously unheard-of disease and remained with him as nurse and companion until 1964, when she divorced him. We do not know the reasons for the divorce. We can hypothesize that Mrs. Jones refused to follow her husband to his newly acquired desert estate.

"Adam Jones's descendants multiplied rapidly. Perhaps to lessen confusion, they had, by the third generation, begun to adopt last names other than 'Jones.'

"By the year 2025," the historian continued, "mutants in Green Colony numbered close to 800."

Steinburg shifted in his chair. What *were* these things? How was his government to deal with them? What national policies were to be formulated?

The historian had finished. Dr. Charles Turquet, a French psychologist, stood at the podium now. He told the audience that greens were probably just as aggressive as normal humans—but not more so.

Dr. Batterson listened with interest. As a conflict sociologist, she wondered whether aggression levels could be explained successfully from only the psychological point of view. It seemed to her, rather, that people became aggressive when they as a group began to feel that they had been imposed upon by society's more privileged.

Still, argued the psychologists, some members of an underprivileged class react more aggressively than others. That, they emphasized, can be explained by either psychology or social psychology.

Nervously Steinburg lit a cigarette. Soon it was Roanoke's turn to speak. She was a small-boned woman. Her dark hair had begun to gray. She wore it in tight curls close to her face, a style which accented her nicely formed features. Adjusting her glasses, she approached the podium.

"Allow me first," she began, "to introduce two American University sociologists who are equally involved with me in the scientific study of greens. It is by two flips of the proverbial coin that I stand before you now, rather than one of them.

"One of my colleagues is Dr. Constance Batterson. Will you stand please, Connie?"

Batterson stood. Tall, thin, thirty-seven, the woman wore a large-brimmed leather hat over her waist-length hair. She smiled, raising a slender hand in a slight wave toward the audience. Before entering the academic world, Batterson had worked five years as a political cartoonist for the *Washington Post*. Her husband was a free-lance photographer.

Roanoke resumed speaking. "My second colleague—and I would like to ask Brad to stand also—is Dr. Bradley Duncan."

Duncan stood: A man of fifty-six, his hair cropped close according to the fashion of the day, he was married to a computer programmer. A symbolic interactionist, Brad was interested in studying how Green Colony's values, beliefs, and norms had emerged—and continued to emerge. He smiled now, bowing almost imperceptibly. He was a person who felt more at ease having a beer with students after an evening class than attending a symposium such as this. Momentarily, Roanoke caught Duncan's eyes. The latter winked his support.

"Now let me tell you," Dr. Roanoke continued, "what we have learned so far—and what we are aiming to learn—about the sociology of greens.

"I must first admit that what we have learned so far is minimal. We have many questions and few answers."

Steinburg winced. How long could the government wait?

"A green mutant, ladies and gentlemen, looks exactly like an average olive-skinned Caucasian from birth until approximately age twenty-five. Greens' respiratory, circulatory, reproductive, and nervous systems appear virtually equivalent to those of normal humans. Their digestive and excretory systems, while capable of reducing food, are probably somewhat atrophied.

"Some greens, we think, remain normal in appearance until they reach thirty. Gradually, however, as mutants age, the chlorophyll within their skin becomes more pronounced in hue. Why the skin is not green at birth is not within the realm of sociology; biochemists are presently at work on that question.

"What is important to the sociological perspective is that greens appear normal for a significant number of years after their birth. We have hypothesized that many during the latter part of this normal period choose to pass; that is, they attend schools, become employed, and perhaps even vote in mass society."

Roanoke paused.

"At the same time we have not one recent reported incidence of any green mutant living among normal humans once he or she has begun to bear evidence of the mutation. This raises a myriad of sociological questions. How and precisely why is it that chlorophyllics are forced from normal society? Or are they? Where do they go once they have 'turned', so to speak?

"Our hypothesis is that they return to Green Colony—or some such other community that we do not know of yet.

"We are, if our hypotheses are correct, presented therefore with a society whose young people move out at some early age, then return as young adults. When and whom do these greens marry? *Do* they marry? What of their children? Do they marry normals? If so, what happens to these marriages?

"What functions do greens perform once they return to the colony? How does the colony prepare for their return? How do they support themselves? In what manner are they socialized before they first remove themselves from the colony?

"What rules for personal and social conduct have chlorophyllics established? Do they have religion? If so, of what nature is it? How does it function to serve their psychological and social needs?

"What types of political and economic institutions exist in Green Colony? Is there evidence of social stratification within the community itself? Where would greens find themselves within the social stratification system in our present national society?"

Louise paused.

"As a functionalist," she resumed, "I see Green Colony as a social system. I am interested in the community's interrelated parts—how they work together, how they influence and support one another. In what ways does the social institution of family in Green Colony, for example, support the community's social institution of religion or government?"

Dr. Roanoke adjusted her glasses.

"As you can readily see, fellow scientists, we have many, many questions, a few hypotheses, a tremendous need for data—but virtually no answers."

Roanoke paused. "Now I would like to make," she said, "what my colleagues and I feel to be a startling and exciting announcement. Just yesterday, the three of us were granted official permission from Green Colony leaders to visit their community."

The crowd buzzed at this revelation.

"The visit will take place during the week of June 26 of this year. Particular arrangements are yet to be made. As I said, we have many questions. I can only predict that when the answers do come, many of them will surprise us."

On June 25, 2026, in Chicago, Illinois, Gabriel Knapp, thirty-two, carefully locked the door to his private office and reread a physician's report. It had been an excruciating physical. He should never have agreed to it, he reprimanded himself, in spite of a new company policy that required executives to undergo thorough medical examinations every five years.

Gabriel's eyes snagged at salient terms and phrases: abnormal metabolic rate, chemical imbalance, chlorophyll.

He buzzed his secretary. "Mr. Jacobs," he said, "I'm going to be out of the office this afternoon. Something's come up. If anyone calls, take care of it, will you?"

Fifteen minutes later Gabriel Knapp exited the Chicago National Insurance building on Michigan Avenue, the medical report tucked safely under his arm. He would go home to think.

He walked the several blocks to Shore Towers, a high-rise apartment complex on Lake Shore Drive. It was a plush structure, and, as he approached the familiar uniformed doorman, Gabe felt pleased that he could live so well in times like these. The Great Depression had made Americans more security-conscious than they had been. As a result, the insurance business remained relatively stable.

When he had entered his apartment, Gabe made himself a cup of coffee and removed his suit coat and shirt. He walked out onto the terrace. There he could stand in the late afternoon sunlight.

"Now you have to think," he told himself. "Think." He placed his fingers near the top of his forehead, then moved them back across his skull, absently parting his thick black hair. He could burn the report, inform the board of directors that it had been lost. There was a chance they would not pursue the matter.

Perhaps he should hire Monica to represent him. An attorney, she could argue in court that the company had no right to demand such personal information of its employees. But, he considered, whether he won or not, his favorable position at Chicago National would surely be jeopardized. A lawyer was not the answer.

He might make an appointment with Hopkins, president of the company, and tell her the truth. Explain to her that it was probably no problem, that he was thirty-two years old now and had not experienced any changes whatsoever, that he expected the mutation might never become glaringly noticeable. He was in a position now, he would argue, where his experience in and knowledge of the insurance industry were valuable. It would be foolish of the company to let him go. And anyway, this was only a medical report, only something different going on in his metabolism—something no one could see.

Gabe lit a cigarette—a habit he had formed recently—and made himself another cup of coffee. He placed the report in a secret compartment of his briefcase. Burning it, he realized, would do no good. There would be questions—another physical perhaps. It would all come out eventually anyway. He had known—and tried not to know—that for several years now.

The phone rang.

"Gabe? Larry Jones here. I called your office and they said you were out for the afternoon, so I thought I'd try you at home."

"I can't talk now, Larry."

"Well, you'd better; it's important. This won't take long. I'm on long distance."

"Larry, please. Not now."

"Listen. There's a boy baby, Leonard Decker's son, in Lake Hospital there. Born this morning. We can trace his lineage back to Adam."

"Larry, I can't. Not now."

"You're the only one who can do this assignment, Gabe. There are no other posers available in the lake area. Everything's in order."

Gabe's tone became anxious. "I've got problems here myself," he said.

"That's tough, Gabe. You're overdue anyway and you know it. They're getting angry here. Now listen: You get the baby and this Wednesday, June 28, you fly with him to Phoenix. U.S.–Russian Airlines non-stop out of Chicago, 2:40 P.M., flight 742. Someone will be there to meet you."

Gabe replaced the receiver, then picked it up again and dialed. Once Chicago National executives read the medical report, the thought came to him,

they would get suspicious. Begin investigating. Find out the rest.

"I'd like to speak with Monica Roanoke," he was saying.

"Ms. Roanoke is with a client. May I ask who's calling, please?"

"Gabe Knapp. Tell her it's important."

"I'm sorry, Gabe," came the receptionist's response. "I didn't recognize your voice. I'll ring her."

Gabe waited. "Monica," he said finally, "I have to see you. Would you come over here after work? It's really important."

Questions

1. How would you describe Secretary Steinburg's "point of view" concerning greens?

2. Roanoke, Duncan, and Batterson will approach the study of greens from their different theoretical perspectives. Can you guess some of the ways that these three social scientists might differ in this respect?

3. Roanoke (a functionalist) has already described how a social systems point of view might be used to examine life in Green Colony. How do you suppose Roanoke might look at Green Colony as a component of the United States as a social system? How would Batterson, the conflict theorist, see Green Colony as part of the United States?

4. How would Roanoke and Batterson view Gabe Knapp's situation within the insurance company now that he's been discovered to be a green?

3

Scientific Sociology

All science is a matter of observing and making sense out of what is observed. Both theory and research are involved. Theory provides the basic points of view from which to make sense of things; research requires observation. Research also includes techniques for making sense out of things.

In this chapter, we're going to examine some of the research methods used in sociology and see how they fit within the larger context of science in general. We'll begin with an overview of the nature of inquiry: human, scientific, and social scientific. We're going to see that people observe in order to understand and that sometimes they make mistakes. We'll see how scientists try to avoid the errors common to nonscientific inquiry, and we'll see what makes science science.

Following the overview of inquiry, we'll look at two of the more basic considerations involved in designing and undertaking—and even reading and understanding—sociological research. The first consideration deals with **conceptualization** and the second with **sampling.**

Once we have covered the two basic considerations, we're going to look at several popular methods of research in sociology: **field research, experimentation, content analysis,** and **survey research.** In each case, I'd like you to gain a general familiarity with the method so that you'll recognize it whenever you read a report of a sociological study that used it. Beyond that, however, I want to impart a sense of the relative strengths and weaknesses of the different

methods so that you'll be able to evaluate the studies you read about. It is not my intention to train you to *use* the different methods, although you should be well prepared to begin learning how to do research after you have finished this chapter.

The materials I've mentioned so far are primarily concerned with preparations for observation and actual observing. The chapter concludes with a look at sociological analysis: how sociologists make sense out of what they've observed. Once again, my intention is primarily to prepare you to read, understand, and evaluate the reports of research other people have done rather than to train you in analysis per se.

The Nature of Inquiry

Inquiry seems to be a native human activity. From the time we are very young, we snoop around our environment, observing things and trying to understand them. At least in part this reflects a desire to predict what's going to happen. In particular, we want to be able to predict the consequences of our own acts. What will happen if we stick our finger in the shiny electric socket? What will happen if we pull the cat's tail?

We learn to predict even when our inquiring doesn't reflect a desire to do so. When you were a young child, you probably learned to predict what would happen if you wet your diapers while you were sitting in someone's lap or what would happen if you tried to crawl out into a busy street.

All of us learn the regular patterns of objects and events in our environment, and out of the specific patterns we observe we develop a more general understanding of how our universe operates. This understanding, in turn, allows us to predict future conditions—which helps us to survive.

Sometimes we observe and reason more effectively than at other times. Let's look briefly at some of the errors we can make.

Errors in Inquiry

Inaccurate observation Sometimes we are simply sloppy in our observations, mistaking what we observe for something else or simply failing to observe what's there. Eyewitnesses at the scene of a crime, for example, often disagree in their descriptions of the criminal.

Overgeneralization The desire to *understand* what you observe can lead you to assume that specific events represent general patterns. If this is your first course in sociology, you might be tempted to assume that all sociology is like this.

Selective observation A danger of overgeneralization is that your satisfaction with the understanding you've developed may lead you, subsequently, to observe only phenomena that confirm your pictures of how the world operates. If you've concluded, for example, that all politicians are liars, you may have a tendency to overlook the ones who don't lie.

Deduced information When you do observe something that contradicts your ideas, you may be tempted to find reasons to explain the discrepancy so that you can protect your understanding of the way things are. If you've concluded that all shopkeepers are crooked, for example, and one walks 4 miles to return your purse or wallet, your general picture of shopkeepers is threatened. One solution is to assume that the shopkeeper is attempting to gain your confidence so as to cheat you in a grand manner later on.

Illogical reasoning Sometimes we try to make sense of things in ways that make *no* sense. A common example of this is reliance on the idea that "the exception proves the rule." This idea is often used to protect pictures that are threatened by disconfirming observations. There is simply no way in heaven or earth that observing a friendly sociologist can "prove" that all the rest are unfriendly. What it "proves" is that *not all* sociologists are unfriendly; it might even suggest that there are several friendly ones.

Premature closure of inquiry Many of the errors I've mentioned characterize premature closure of inquiry: deciding that you understand the way things are before all the facts are in. One way of expressing this is by saying, "I already understand that. Don't try to confuse me with facts."

These, then, are some of the pitfalls along the road to human understanding of what's going on. What makes science special is that it offers safe routes around such pitfalls. Scientists share a number of agreements about how to observe and understand, and those agreements appear to offer protection against faulty observation and understanding. Let's look at what makes science different.

Science Is Different—Sometimes

The first agreement that scientists share is that observation ought to be a careful and conscious activity. Most of the time people observe things casually, sometimes nearly unconsciously. Try to remember, for example, what your sociology instructor was wearing during your last class meeting. Scientists—when they do research—carefully plan what kinds of observations they are going to make, and they make those observations carefully and consciously.

Second, scientists are equally careful and conscious in drawing conclusions from what they observe. I suspect that when you read the word "alcoholic," what comes to mind is a picture that represents your general understanding of alcoholics. Now ask yourself how you formed that picture. What were the specific observations that led you to your conclusions

Even when specific behaviors are not formally prescribed, people create patterns of social regularity. Sociologists try to discover and understand such patterns through careful observation and measurement. (Louis Goldman, Photo Researchers, Inc.)

about alcoholics? If you're having trouble remembering exactly how and why you formed the picture you have, you're no different from most of us. Scientists, however, have agreements that make the forming of conclusions a more careful and conscious activity.

Finally, the public nature of scientific inquiry offers protection against the common errors of human inquiry. Notice that you are under no obligation to tell anyone what you think about alcoholics, and if you keep quiet about it, nobody can challenge the quality of your observations or the wisdom of your conclusions. The results of scientific inquiry are useless, however, unless they are communicated. Making the results public opens them up to scrutiny by other scientists.

I don't want you to think that scientists never commit the errors that other people do. In the non-scientific portions of their daily lives, scientists can be as casual and unconscious about observing and understanding as nonscientists. Even when they do research, scientists make mistakes. Sometimes, moreover, those mistakes go unnoticed for years, decades, or centuries. The point is that science offers protections against the common errors of human inquiry—even if the protections aren't always effective.

The Nature of Scientific Inquiry

The preceding section concluded with some general comments on how science differs from ordinary, human inquiry. In this section, I want to be more specific in describing some of the agreements that scientists share regarding inquiry.

Two Kinds of Logic

People often err in inquiry by illogical reasoning. While scientists are also guilty of faulty reasoning at times, they are generally more careful and more conscious in that regard than nonscientists. Scientists use two distinct logical systems: **deductive** logic and **inductive** logic.

Deductive logic may be defined as reasoning that proceeds from general principles to particular cases. The classical illustration of deductive logic is the syllogism: "All men are mortals. Socrates is a man; therefore, Socrates is mortal."

Inductive logic works in just the opposite direction: The reasoning is from particular cases to general principles. Thus, you might observe that Socrates, a man, was mortal, observe a number of other men to be mortal, and conclude that "all men are mortal."

Let's see how these two different logical systems might be used in a research project. I'd like you to imagine that you are interested in learning about the relationship between how much students study for a final examination and the grades they get on the exam.

First, you might begin by analyzing the matter logically. You might decide that the reason students study is to familiarize themselves with the course

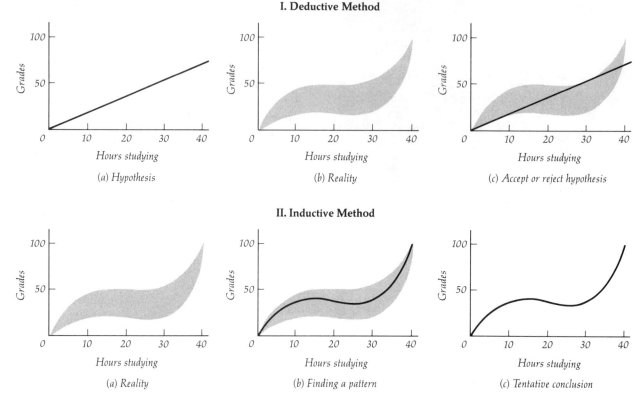

Figure 3·1 Deductive and inductive methods.

materials and that examinations measure familiarity with the course materials. You'd probably conclude that the more students study, the better their examination grades will be.

What I've just described is deductive logic; the conclusion you reached corresponds to a "general principle." In a research context, this general principle would serve as the basis for a **hypothesis,** an expectation about the way things are. You might hypothesize, therefore, that on a forthcoming examination students who study most will receive the highest grades and that the grades received will consistently reflect the amount of study.

Look now at Figure 3·1. Part (a) of section I, ("Deductive Method") illustrates your hypothesis: The more students study for the exam, the better their grades on it. If you were conducting a research project on this topic, you would next collect data to test your hypothesis, an activity known, appropriately, as **hypothesis testing.** Part I(b) in Figure 3·1 represents the data that might be collected in such a project. Each point within the shaded area represents a single student. Where a given point is in relation to the horizontal scale tells you how many hours the student spent studying for the exam. The relationship of a point to the vertical scale tells you the grade that student received on the exam.

Notice that the "reality" in this example and your hypothesis do not exactly correspond. The two are shown together in part I(c) of Figure 3·1. Some students received higher grades, given the hours spent studying, than you would have predicted, and others received lower grades. The "reality" roughly approximates what you hypothesized, however. The decision you must make is whether the observations are "close enough" to the hypothesis for you to conclude that

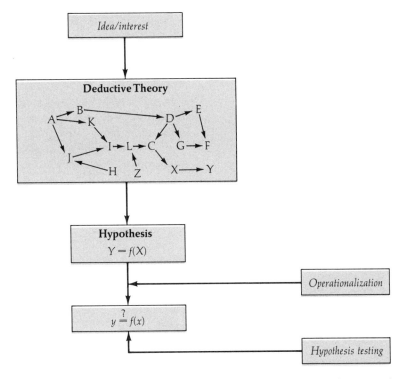

Figure 3•2 The traditional image of science. Operationalization, *to be discussed shortly, is the process through which the researcher specifies operations and observations that will provide concrete measures of theoretical concepts.*

the general principle is an accurate summary of how things are.

The second approach you might take is illustrated in section II("Inductive Method") of Figure 3•1. You might begin by observing the hours studied and the grades of the students in the course, doing this without any hypothesis linking the two (*a*). Using your observations as a base, you might look for a general pattern that will provide a reasonable summary of all those specific observations. The curved line shown in (*b*) is an example of the pattern you might find.

Notice what this pattern suggests about the relationship between studying and grades. Grades appear to improve with study among those who study between 0 and 20 hours. At that point, however, grades begin to decline somewhat with additional study—up to the point of studying 30 hours. Grades generally improve, however, for each additional hour

spent in study above 30 hours. (Realize that this example is only *hypothetical*, not something you can use to govern your own study habits.)

Using the inductive method, you might frame a *tentative conclusion* (*c*) based on the pattern best summarizing the observations you made. This, then, is an example of working from particular cases to a general principle.

The Traditional Image of Science

Science courses and textbooks tend to link "the scientific method" and the deductive system. They suggest that scientific research begins with contemplation and logical reasoning, is followed by the framing of hypotheses derived from that theoretical reasoning, and concludes with empirical tests of the hypotheses. Figure 3•2 illustrates that traditional image of science.

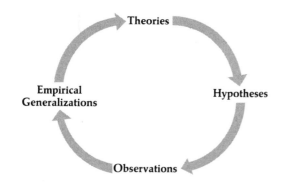

Figure 3·3   A more realistic image of science. Adapted from Walter Wallace, The Logic of Science in Sociology *(Chicago: Aldine-Atherton, 1971).*

Although Figure 3·2 is a useful model of how science operates, science doesn't always operate that way. Nor is science less "scientific" when it follows an inductive rather than deductive pattern. Both approaches to scientific inquiry are legitimate and valuable.

A More Realistic Image of Science

Walter Wallace (1971) has provided another picture of how science operates. His seems to be more realistic than what we have portrayed so far. He sees science as a circle made up of theories, hypotheses, observations, and empirical generalizations. His image of science is presented in Figure 3·3.

The significant feature of this model is that scientific research can *start* anywhere. Further, researchers may move around the circle many times. Observations are generalized, theories are framed that suggest hypotheses which form the basis for new observations, revised generalizations produce revised theories, and so forth.

Some Characteristics of Science

Whether proceeding through the use of deductive or inductive logic or both, scientists agree on certain general approaches to inquiry. It will be useful for you to bear these in mind when we turn, shortly, to an examination of specific techniques and methods

in sociological research. Research techniques are an essential part of what makes sociology scientific.

The first characteristic that distinguishes science from nonscience is that scientists seek a general understanding of the world around them. Thus, although a sociologist of religion might do research to discover why some Episcopalians are more religious than others, the major goal of the research would be to develop a general understanding of religiosity that would apply to Methodists, Catholics, Jews, Hindus, Buddhists, and all other religious groups. Ideally, such research would also explain why some people have *no* religion.

Another characteristic of science is that while it is aimed at generality, it is specific. Scientists agree that research methods should be reported explicitly. The value of any conclusion depends largely on the manner in which it was reached, and scientists plan their methods carefully, follow them diligently, and report those methods in detail. A sociologist would not report that politically conservative people are generally more religious than politically liberal people without telling exactly how political orientations and religiosity were measured and among whom.

Another function of explicitness in science is that it permits **replication,** or repeating, of studies. Scientists agree that replication is valuable. When research methods are described in detail, it becomes possible for another researcher to repeat the study, with all the same methods, to see if the same results are produced the second time. If two studies produce the same results, confidence in those results is increased.

In developing an understanding of the way the world operates, scientists seek parsimony: a combination of powerful explanation and simplicity. Let me give a practical illustration. If I could learn 1,328 specific things about you, I could guess with almost utter certainty who you favored in the last presidential election. Moreover, if I could learn the same 1,328 specific things about anyone else, I could be equally certain who that person favored. It would be more parsimonious, however, if I could achieve the same degree of certainty by only knowing two or three things instead of 1,328. When you shop around before making a purchase, you are trying to get the most value for the least amount of money. Scientists seek the same kind of "bargain" in terms of understanding.

Empirical verification is the keystone in the agreements that distinguish science from nonscience. Whenever a scientist develops an understanding of how something operates, the next essential step is to *test* that understanding with additional observations. If you were to conclude that women are, on the average, more religious than men, your next step would be to undertake an empirical study—make observations—to test the accuracy of your conclusion.

These, then, are some of the agreements that scientists share—agreements that distinguish science from nonscience. Everything I've written is true, but only *to a degree.* You should realize that scientists do not always behave the way I've described, just as nonscientists sometimes *do* behave those ways. There is no magical dividing line between science and nonscience. Even so, the kinds of characteristics we've been looking at do distinguish scientific inquiry from other forms of human inquiry. They are what make "science" special.

Science and Determinism

Another characteristic of science is different enough from those I've discussed to require special treatment. This characteristic is **determinism.** All science is based on a deterministic view of things, but this can present problems for people as they approach *social* science. Determinism conflicts with our implicit, personal feelings about **free will.**

The deterministic view assumes that some things are determined or caused by others. If you ask an astronomer why the moon doesn't fly off into space, he or she will tell you that the moon's orbit is caused by the gravitational pull of the earth. The astronomer wouldn't say anything about the moon's "desires" in the matter, and you probably wouldn't think to ask. The moon isn't a human being after all. How can it have any say in the matter?

But what about the scientific study of *human* behavior? In sociology and the other social sciences, it proceeds from a deterministic view the same as that of astronomy, physics, and biology. Later in this

book, for example, we'll ask why some people are more prejudiced than others. We'll look at some of the "causes" of prejudice that sociologists have discovered involving educational, religious, economic, and other factors. Nowhere in that discussion will we consider whether people "choose" to be prejudiced or not. Instead, we'll look at the factors that "make" people prejudiced, factors over which they have little or no control.

The deterministic view of human behavior implies that *you* have no personal say in how tolerant you are, how religious, how liberal or conservative, how hard-working or lazy. You have no control over any of the things that make up your image of who you are. Scientists assume that people are totally determined in what they say or do when they study human behavior. You don't have to *believe* this assumption, but you should be aware of it in advance. Otherwise, as we look at various sociological attempts to explain and understand social life, it might become an unrecognized source of discomfort.

Let's turn now to some of the ways sociologists do scientific research. I want to begin with the general issue of **conceptualization** and **operationalization,** and then we'll examine some specific research techniques.

Conceptualization and Operationalization

"Concepts" are pictures in your head, vague mental images that summarize the observations you make. Concepts categorize observations. I cannot know with certainty what your concepts look like, and you cannot know with certainty what mine look like. Yet concepts are an essential part of communication and interaction. To facilitate matters in this difficult situation, you and I agree to associate certain terms with our concepts, with our mental images.

"Conceptualization" is the process of refining and specifying exactly what is meant by the terms we associate with concepts. If I told you that young people don't know enough to vote intelligently, you'd probably be offended. If I were to specify that by "young" I mean people under one year old, I would have communicated my meaning more clearly, and you'd probably agree with my assertion (and not be offended).

Sociologists frequently use terms that people already associate vague mental images with, so careful conceptualization is all the more important. You probably have some mental picture that you associate with the term "liberalism," for example, and it is very likely different from mine. If I were to undertake a study of liberalism, ultimately reporting my findings on why some people are more liberal than others, it is unlikely that the observations I based my study on would correspond exactly to your conception of what "liberalism" means. For my study to have meaning for you, then, I need to specify what I mean by the terms I use. Even if you disagree, you'll at least know what I mean by my research conclusions and what my observations mean to you.

It is essential for you to realize that none of the terms we associate with our mental pictures has a "real" meaning. My concept of "liberalism" is no more "correct" or "incorrect" than yours. The closest we can come to the "real" meanings for terms are the *agreements* we make for the purpose of communication. "Liberal" is only a word, after all, a word that we agree to use in summarizing certain observations. Our agreement is a concession we make in the interest of communication. The process of conceptualization is a further concession, in that we specify an even narrower range of observations in the interest of even greater communication.

Conceptualization has a function aside from communication. Very often, the "reconceptualization" (*revision* of our mental images) of what we observe can offer new insights into the way the world operates. You and I agree, for example, that automobiles can reasonably be summarized in the concept "modes of transportation." An economist, however, would also include automobiles in the concept "consumer purchases," and a psychologist might include them in the concept "parent figures." Sociologists might include automobiles in the concept "status symbols." Sometimes reconceptualization enables us to make sense of things that make no sense otherwise.

Attributes and Variables

Sociologists typically deal with two kinds of concepts: **attributes** and **variables.** Attributes are characteristics of people or things. Attributes can be described, for example, by such terms as "tall," "heavy," "blue," "upper-class," "four-year-old," and "male."

Variables are logical sets of attributes. "Male" and "female" are attributes, for example; "sex" and "gender" are variables composed of those two attributes. "Color" is a variable composed of such attributes as "red," "blue," and "green." "Social class" is a variable composed of such attributes as "upper-class," "middle-class," and "lower-class."

The relationships among attributes and variables are at the core of the two goals of scientific research: description and explanation. Scientists *describe* the way things are by reporting the distribution of attributes on a particular variable. We describe the "sex composition" of a population, for example, by telling how many men and women there are in that population. Scientists *explain* why things are the way they are by noting **correlations**—"co-relations"—among variables, by noting that certain attributes of one variable typically appear in the presence of certain attributes of other variables. Thus, for example, we note that the attribute "liberal" appears more often with the attribute "young" than it does with the attribute "old." We say that "liberalism" and "age," as variables, are related to each other. Making sense out of the observation that some people are more liberal than others, then, involves, in part, the matter of age. We'll look at the processes of description and explanation in more detail near the end of the chapter.

Operationalization

Operationalization is an extension of the process of conceptualization, specifying the meanings to be associated with certain attributes and variables. The most explicit way I can tell you what I will mean, in my research project, by my use of the terms "liberal" and "conservative" is to detail the operations I will undertake in classifying people as liberal or conservative. "Operationalization" is the process of determining the operations I'll use.

I might decide, for example, to base my **operational definition** of political orientations on such specifics as the political party people identify with, whom they have voted for or whom they prefer, or on their attitudes on specific political issues. Although the definition I choose will inevitably lack the "richness of meaning" that you (and I) associate with the terms "liberal" and "conservative," my definitions will at least be clear to us both. The use of operational definitions in sociology, then, is one aspect of the characteristic of explicitness that I discussed earlier.

In general, conceptualization and operationalization are processes by which sociologists prepare to measure what they observe. Let's discuss now *what* they observe.

Sampling Observations

Sociologists and other social scientists have a problem. Much of what we do is based on observations—we observe and make sense out of what we observe—yet it is impossible to observe everything relevant to a particular investigation. Suppose, for example, that you want to discover how people decide how to vote on election day. It would be simply impossible for you to observe every voter in the process of reaching a decision. And the decision-making processes of the few voters you observe might be different from those you didn't observe.*

Typically, we want to draw conclusions—descriptive and explanatory—about a "population," a large group or class of people, such as "all Americans," "Nebraska teenagers," or "naval officers." Since we are unable to observe all members of the population in question, we select a sample for actual observation and analysis. We select some members of the population and try to make our selection in such a manner as to ensure that those we *do* observe closely resemble

---

*Notice that this is less of a problem for physical scientists. The chemist who wants to study the properties of carbon, for example, doesn't need to worry about "which" carbon is observed: All carbon is the same. Because of the heterogeneity of people, however, the social scientist cannot study whatever person is convenient and assume that all other people will be like the one studied.

those we do not. The term **representative sample** is used to refer to a sample that has the same essential characteristics as the population from which it was selected. The technique of the representative sample is used by political pollsters like Gallup and Harris. It accounts for their ability to interview 1,500–2,000 voters across the nation and predict with uncanny accuracy how some 80 million voters will vote on election day.

Scientific sampling is based ultimately on the process of **random selection,** a process most commonly illustrated by flipping a coin. Random selection gives all members of a population an equal chance of being selected into the sample. This, in turn, ensures that those who *are* selected will closely reflect the characteristics of the total population from which they were drawn. While actual sampling methods can be complex and almost never involve flipping coins, the fundamental logic is the same as what I've described. Sampling methods have not always been as effective as they are now, as the box "For Pollsters, 'More' Doesn't Always Mean 'Better'" on page 59 illustrates.

We've now seen how sociologists decide who to observe. Now let's look at some of the ways sociologists actually observe people in society.

Modes of Observation

Just as sociologists have a variety of different theoretical points of view, they also have several methods for observing people and other aspects of society. In this section, I am going to describe three major research methods often used in sociology, and I'll mention some additional ones more briefly.

Field Research

Perhaps the most obvious way to observe social life is to go where it's happening and watch. If you want to study how people behave during a riot, you could pick the riot of your choice and watch it unfold. If you're interested in student-faculty interaction in the classroom, you can go to a class and watch students and faculty interact. It's as simple as that—almost.

This research method is sometimes referred to as **participant-observation,** and that name points to one of the key decisions a field researcher needs to make.* Will you *participate* in what you study or will you only observe? Either decision has strengths and weaknesses. Participating directly in what you study (getting a job as a coal miner, for example, to study coal mining) can give you insights that might escape you otherwise. On the other hand, personal participation can interfere with the scientific "detachment" that seems essential to analytical observation.

If you decide to participate directly in what you study, you face another decision. Do you identify yourself as a researcher to those you will study? Again, there are reasons to support either conclusion. Concealing your identity—saying you are just another coal miner, for example—encourages those you are studying to act "naturally." They might change their behavior if they knew they were being studied. There are some kinds of behavior, moreover, that probably can't be studied if you identify yourself as a researcher. When Laud Humphreys (1970) set out to study homosexual behavior in public rest rooms, he told participants that he would serve as a lookout,

*Raymond Gold (1969) has examined these issues in detail and has suggested there are four roles the researcher might play: "complete participant," "participant-as-observer," "observer-as-participant," and "complete observer."

having concluded that identifying himself as an on-the-job sociologist would have an effect on his subjects.

If you act as and become accepted as a full participant in whatever you are studying, there is a good chance that you'll shape the events under study. When Leon Festinger and his colleagues (1956) pretended to be full members in a small Midwestern group that believed flying saucers were about to make contact with a few chosen earth people, they were frequently asked what they felt the group should do next. Should the group try to recruit more members or just lie low until the saucers came? This was a problem for the researchers, since they were largely interested in the conditions under which the group attempted to recruit new members.

The steps involved in *doing* field research are largely a matter of refined and sharpened common sense. If you were to undertake field research on a topic—understanding the popularity of a new religious sect, for example—you'd want to begin by finding out all you could about it. You'd want to study books and articles written about the group and about any similar groups. If there were people familiar with the group, you'd probably want to talk to them, learning as much as you could before beginning your own direct observations.

Field research is fundamentally a matter of going where the action is, and you begin your observations by planning where and when you can be in the presence of what you want to study. If you are studying a new religious group, you should find out when and where they are having meetings. Go there. See what happens.

Often field research involves interviewing participants. If you've identified yourself as a researcher, you can conduct the interviews in that context. If you've pretended to be a participant yourself, you can still conduct interviews in a conversational form.

Note taking is the backbone of field research. Observing is not enough. You need to record what you observe. Styles of note taking vary from individual to individual. Shorthand is useful if you have that ability. If conditions permit, you may be able to tape-record at least the audio portion of what you're observing, devoting your note taking to the visual. As you review and reinterpret what you've observed, your research is likely to gain focus: As you begin to discern what appear to be important patterns, you will focus your attention on those things in later observations. This aspect of your research is not that different from the procedures a good detective or newspaper reporter follows, except that you'll bring a sociological point of view to bear on the subject.

For Pollsters, "More" Doesn't Always Mean "Better"

Just before the election of 1936, *The Literary Digest*, a widely read and influential magazine, announced the results of its presidential preference poll. The New Deal was going to be repudiated; FDR would be swept out of office. Alf Landon would be the next president, taking nearly 60 percent of the two-party popular vote. The announcement was made with a great deal of hoopla. The *Digest* modestly quoted a reference to itself as an "oracle, which, since 1920, has foretold with almost uncanny accuracy the choice of the nation's voters. . . ." And, after all, hadn't they mailed out over 10 million "secret ballots" to voters all over the nation, after ransacking tax rolls, telephone directories, automobile registration and magazine subscription lists for names? And hadn't they heard from more than 20 percent of the nation's voters in return?

At the same time, a young man named George Gallup was predicting a Roosevelt landslide. His employees, he said, had interviewed a "scientifically selected sample" of voters, and a solid majority of them were planning to vote for Roosevelt and the New Deal. How large was his sample? Less than one-thousandth the size of the *Digest*'s. Obviously, nobody paid much attention to the "Gallup Poll."

Today, of course, few remember *The Literary Digest* (and many don't even remember Alf Landon). Within a week of the *Digest*'s announcement, Landon had been soundly defeated: He got less than 40 percent of the vote and carried only two states. A little more than a year later, the *Digest* went out of business. Its credibility was destroyed (as we would put it now). On the other hand, the forecasts of the Gallup Poll and its competitors are front-page news today, and politicians generally regard the polls as accurate assessments of public opinion.

With such a large sample, how could *The Literary Digest* have been so wrong? The answer is hidden in the first paragraph. How did the *Digest* decide which 10 million voters to send ballots to? In 1936, what kinds of people had telephones? What kinds had automobiles? Who subscribed to magazines? Clearly, the *Digest*'s sample of voters—although extremely large—was not *representative*. It was not an accurate cross section of *all* voters: It included too few of the kinds of people who were benefiting from the New Deal's economic programs, and too many of the kinds of people who were likely to oppose those programs. (Obviously, the *Digest* could have done worse: Suppose it had drawn its sample from lists of contributors to the Republican party.)

How could Gallup be so accurate with a sample of only a few hundred? Workers in his organization worried less about *how many* people they heard from than about *what kinds* of people. Statistical sampling theory told them that, beyond a point, sampling more voters didn't increase their accuracy very much and that they could concentrate on making sure that they sampled the right proportions of well-off and poor, employed and unemployed, rural and urban, and so forth. With a few modifications (some of them introduced after Gallup went wrong in 1948 and predicted a Dewey victory), the methods Gallup used in 1936 are the basis not only of modern public opinion polling, but of market research and government and academic survey research as well.

The *Literary Digest*'s fiasco in 1936 resulted from a lack of representativeness. To have been accurate, *whom* should it have represented: (1) all those eligible to vote, (2) all those registered to vote, (3) all those who voted? Granting that national samples of around a thousand respondents provide adequate accuracy in political polling, larger samples would be more accurate. Why do you suppose pollsters don't use larger samples?

Among the methods available to sociologists, field research has some special advantages. More than any other of the methods I'm going to discuss, this one allows you to study social life in its natural habitat. In that sense, it offers you a more comprehensive picture of what you want to study. By being there you can *sense* things that would be totally lost in an experiment or a survey.

Field research also has disadvantages. It is generally less rigorous and less precise than other methods. A survey, for example, can determine, say, voter intentions with considerable accuracy and precision, something that cannot be accomplished in field research. Also, as you begin to focus your attention as a field-research project unfolds, you run the risk of reaching a premature conclusion and failing to observe other things of equal or greater importance.

Undoubtedly, the quality of field research improves with practice, and practicing it is relatively inexpensive and easy. As you read this discussion, it may have occurred to you that you've been doing field research all your life. You may not have been as consciously rigorous as sociologists are, but you were doing field research all the same. You have also been engaging in the next mode of observation we shall discuss.

Experiments

All of us experiment copiously in our attempt to understand the world around us. All adult skills are learned through experimentation: eating, walking, talking, riding a bicycle, swimming, and so forth. Students learn how much studying is required for academic success through experimentation, and that's how professors learn how much preparation is needed for successful lectures.

Basically, experiments involve (1) taking action and (2) observing the consequences of the action. In preparing a stew, for example, we add salt, taste, add more salt, and taste again. In defusing a bomb, we clip a wire, see if the bomb explodes, and clip another. Scientific experiments need to be carefully planned, however.

A classical scientific experiment has three major components: (1) an **independent** and **dependent variable,** (2) **experimental** and **control groups,** and

(3) **pretesting** and **posttesting.** Let's look at each of these components in turn.

Experiments typically test the effects of one variable on another: the effects of an independent variable on a dependent one. If you want to find out, for example, whether a movie dealing with black American history reduces prejudice among those viewing it, prejudice is the dependent variable. The movie is an experimental stimulus (in this case), and whether or not people see the movie is the independent variable. The question to be answered by an experiment is whether the independent variable (seeing the movie or not seeing it) has an effect on the dependent variable (prejudice).

The "experimental group" is a group of people (called "subjects" in experiments) who are exposed to the experimental stimulus. In the present example, the black history movie is shown to the experimental group. The "control group" is made up of subjects who are similar to the experimental group in all respects except one: They are *not* exposed to the experimental stimulus.

A typical method for testing the effects of an experimental stimulus is the use of pretesting and posttesting. Measurements of the dependent variable are made before and after the administration of the experimental stimulus. In the present example, you might give a questionnaire to all subjects in both the experimental and control groups to determine their levels of antiblack prejudice. If the members of the two groups are similar to one another, the average level of prejudice in the two groups should be about the same. Then you show the movie to members of the experimental group only. Afterward, you measure prejudice among all members of both groups. If the movie reduces prejudice, you expect to find a reduction in the level of prejudice in the experimental group but not in the control group.

Control groups are especially important in experiments because they pinpoint the effects of the experimental stimulus. Suppose, for example, that you had been conducting an experiment on the black history movie in April 1968, working *without* a control group. You had measured your subjects' prejudice, shown them the film, and made arrangements to remeasure their prejudice a week later, on April 10, say. In the posttest, you might have discovered a dramatic reduction in antiblack prejudice, but you'd be unable to tell how much of that was due to the movie and how much was due to the assassination of Martin Luther King, Jr., on the day before the retesting. Had you been using a control group, however, the amount of reduction in prejudice among them would have allowed you to determine the independent effects of the movie.

Control groups also guard against the effects of the experiment itself. Very often people modify their behavior and attitudes just by virtue of their participation in an experiment.

"Evaluation research" is the name associated with an increasingly important type of social research in connection with natural experiments. Whenever new social programs are put into effect, social researchers may be asked to evaluate their impact and success. Such situations are essentially large-scale experiments within natural social settings (Moursund 1973).

Suppose, for example, that a prison warden wants to experiment with "home visits" as a way of improving inmates' morale and hastening their rehabilitation. A sociologist might be invited to study the innovation and evaluate its effectiveness. Prisoners might be divided into experimental and control groups, with the former permitted home visits. In a comparison of the morale and rehabilitative progress of the two groups, the sociologist could assess whether or not the program achieved its objectives.

Not all experimental research in sociology involves the testing of a particular experimental stimulus. A good deal of research on small-group behavior is conducted in laboratories (Bales 1950). Groups are assembled and given tasks to perform. Sociologists, frequently concealed behind one-way glass mirrors, observe the manner in which group members interact in dealing with the task. The nature of the task, the structuring of rewards and punishments, and other elements in the situation may be modified to further clarify the nature of human group behavior.

Experiments have both advantages and disadvantages. The primary advantage lies in the researcher's ability to control the variables under study. If you are interested in the effects of a black history

Sometimes it is possible to bring social behavior into the laboratory for observation. The sociologist in the foreground is concealed behind a pane of one-way glass. (Hugh Rogers, Monkmeyer Press Photo Service)

movie on prejudice, the experimental method allows you reliably to rule out the effects of other variables.

The chief disadvantage of the experiment is its artificiality. (Natural experiments are an exception, of course, but they cannot be greatly controlled.) Human behavior is studied under "unnatural" conditions for the purpose of learning about human behavior in general. The persistent danger is that what is learned in the laboratory will not apply in the world outside it.

Let's turn now to what is probably the most popular research method in sociology. If you browse through the research reports in a sociological journal, you'll find that they are based on, more than anything else, survey research.

Survey Research

Surveys have a long history if you take into account their similarity to **censuses.** For thousands of years, people have sought to describe and understand populations by asking standardized questions of individual members. A census involves all members of the population. The term "survey," in contrast, typically implies a "sample survey." Using methods we have already discussed in this chapter, a usually large (hundreds or thousands) sample is selected from a population, those selected in the sample are questioned, and their responses are analyzed for the purpose of describing and understanding the larger population.

The questioning in a survey can take one of two forms. Interviewers may contact the respondents (either face-to-face or by telephone), read the questions, and record the answers. Respondents may also be asked to read and complete "self-administered" questionnaires either handed to them or sent through the mail.

A variety of information can be collected in surveys. Respondents may be asked to provide routine descriptive information about themselves—such as age, sex, race, education, and income—that can be brought together in a composite description of the population. Many surveys tap people's attitudes, opinions, and beliefs. Quite aside from sociological studies, this aspect of survey research is used in political polling, consumer-product marketing, and other similar endeavors. Surveys can also ask people to report previous behavior and can ask them to speculate about how they may behave in the future.

Writing good questions for a survey is more complicated than it might seem. First, you need to decide what you want to know and in what form. Then, bearing in mind who will be questioned, you must frame your questions so that they are likely to be understood.*

Sometimes questions are constructed in an open-ended format. A question is posed and the respondent gives an answer in his or her own words. You might

*Survey research is an undertaking in which the "customer" is always right. If a respondent misunderstands a question and gives a useless answer, you lose regardless of how stupid you may feel the respondent is.

ask, for example, "What do you consider to be the most important problem facing the United States today?" The respondent writes an answer or gives it orally to an interviewer who writes it down.

More frequently, perhaps, "closed-ended" questions are asked, questions accompanied by a set of possible answers. The respondent then picks the answer that suits him or her. Figure 3•4 presents a portion of a questionnaire used in a self-administered survey of medical school faculty members.

The chief advantage of survey research is uniformity. Hundreds or thousands of people carefully sampled from a population answer the same question. Often the respondents even answer using a uniform set of responses. This uniformity makes it possible to draw general conclusions about the whole population.

Surveys have the advantage of being relatively efficient ways for collecting large masses of information, another benefit of standardizing the inquiry. By standardizing the inquiry, however, surveys overlook the subtle varieties of attitudes and conditions that exist for people. The respondent who protests that none of the standardized answers is a satisfactory one presents a problem for survey research.

Survey research, like field research and experiments, represents a compromise. Each of the methods I've discussed has its special strengths and weaknesses. I've tried to give you an overview in Figure 3•5. Figure 3•5 is not based on precise mathematical calculations, but it should give you a useful sense of the different methods. It also makes the point that with research methods, as with theoretical points of view, a combination of approaches is more effective than reliance on only one.

Other Modes of Observation

Survey research, field research, and experiments are commonly used methods in sociology. They are not the only ones, however, and I want to conclude this section by mentioning briefly some other sociological research methods.

Content analysis Sometimes sociologists study human communications as a way of learning about people (Holsti 1969). They analyze the content of

The Teaching Physician

Instructions

Either pen or pencil may be used to complete the questionnaire. Please disregard the small numbers and letters next to each question; these are for the use of IBM tabulating machine operators.

In the first section, we would like to learn something about your interests and opinions regarding a number of issues which concern the medical profession in general and medical schools in particular.

Part I. Professional Interests and Opinions

1. While some medical students find it more natural to view each patient as an individual person, others are more likely to perceive him as an example of a disease entity. Do you feel the overall medical school experience at the school where you teach has any effect on the way students ultimately view patients in this regard?

01 ^{8}/A ☐ Yes, it creates a shift toward viewing the patient as an individual person.

B ☐ Yes, it creates a shift toward viewing the patient as an example of a disease entity.

C ☐ No, there seems to be no effect.

2. Do you feel medical school training *should* encourage either or both of these views, or do you feel the issue is irrelevant to medical training?

^{9}/A ☐ It should encourage a view of the patient as an individual person.

B ☐ It should encourage a view of the patient as an example of a disease entity.

C ☐ It should encourage both views equally.

D ☐ The issue is irrelevant to medical training.

3. When students have their first prolonged contacts with particular patients, do you feel there is generally a greater tendency for them to become overly involved with their patients, or a greater tendency to remain overly detached?

^{10}/A ☐ There is a greater tendency to become overly involved.

B ☐ There is a greater tendency to remain overly detached.

C ☐ Both seem to occur about equally.

Figure 3·4   Example of a self-administered questionnaire. Source: Earl Babbie, Science and Morality in Medicine *(Berkeley, Calif.: University of California Press, 1970). Copyright © 1970 by the Regents of the University of California; reprinted by permission of the University of California Press.*

such productions as books, newspapers, poems, songs, paintings, and radio broadcasts. To determine the key news issues of the 1960's, for example, G. Ray Funkhouser (1973) pursued two lines of inquiry. In one, he examined the public-opinion polls (a form of survey research) to see what people said were the most important issues for them. In the other, he undertook a content analysis of three major newsmagazines. He selected a sample of issues of each; then he measured the amount of space devoted to different news issues.

Historical research   When sociologists look at history, they often have a different point of view from historians. The historian may seek to learn all the specific details of a particular event or era; the sociologist, in contrast, is more likely to seek general patterns. Thus, for example, Max Weber (1905) turned to history in an attempt to understand the religious foundations of capitalism. In large part, he looked at the religious and economic histories of many nations—including those that had and had not developed a capitalist economy. Years later, Robert

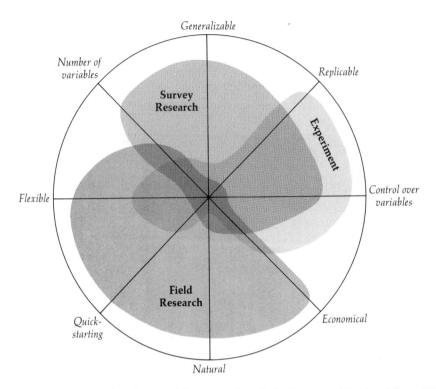

Figure 3•5   An overview of the strengths and weaknesses of three research methods. Terms are defined as follows: "Generalizable"—extent to which the results of a specific study can be assumed to apply to social behavior in general; "replicable"—extent to which a specific study can be repeated exactly by another researcher; "control over variables"—degree to which a researcher can determine which specific variables have which effects; "economical"—how inexpensive the method is to use in general; "natural"—extent to which the method offers an observation of social behavior in its natural setting; "quick-starting"—speed with which a study can be designed and launched using the method; "flexible"— extent to which the researcher could modify a research design if appropriate in mid-study; and "number of variables"—the number of variables that can be measured and analyzed effectively in a given study.

Bellah (1959) turned to Japanese history in an effort to determine whether Weber's conclusions also explained the development of capitalism in Japan.

Analyzing existing statistics   So far in this section I've been talking about the "collection" of data for study. Sometimes sociologists analyze data that have already been collected by someone else, perhaps for some other purpose. Official government statistics are often used in this fashion. The best-known example of this research method occurs in Emile Durkheim's (1897) classic study of suicide. From a painstaking analysis of suicide rates in different countries and different regions of particular countries,

Durkheim was able to draw conclusions about the motivations of individuals.

Secondary analysis   In addition to analyzing published statistics, sociologists have, increasingly in recent years, reanalyzed the data collected by others in sample surveys. Suppose that I have conducted a large-scale survey for a particular purpose. I analyze my data and report my results. Quite possibly I will have collected data that would be useful to you in examining some other topic. Rather than conducting a survey of your own—costing both money and time—you can obtain a copy of the data collected in my survey and reanalyze them for your own research purpose (Hyman 1972).

As secondary analysis has become more popular in sociology and other social sciences, "data libraries" have been established around the nation. Sets of IBM cards or magnetic tapes containing the data collected in surveys are filed and stored the same way that books are handled in a conventional library (Nasatir 1967).

Analyzing total societies   Most early sociologists took a very broad view of society and social development. Over the years, however, they have tended to limit their inquiries to smaller subgroups or to specific issues. More recently, there has been a renewed interest in the broader view. Gerhard Lenski's (1974) epic study of human societies is a good example of this renewed interest. It brings together masses of data describing hundreds of preliterate and modern societies around the world.

These, then, are some of the many facets of sociological observation. I'll conclude the chapter with a discussion of some ways sociologists *analyze* what they observe in their search for understanding.

Quantitative Data Analysis

With the exception of field research and historical studies, most sociological research involves the collection and analysis of quantitative data, information transformed into numbers. In this concluding section, I want to cover some of the logic and techniques involved in quantitative data analysis.

Descriptive Analyses

Description is a fundamental purpose of much social research. Recalling my earlier discussion of variables and attributes, description involves the distribution of attributes making up a variable. For example, "male" and "female" are attributes making up the variable "sex." We might describe a population in terms of the numbers of men and women.

Percentages often replace numbers in sociological descriptions. Pursuing the above example, then, we might simply report that, say, 53 percent of a given population are females.

Averages are also used in description. Rather than reporting the numbers or even percentages of a population who are of particular ages, we might report that the mean age is 24.7 years. To arrive at the mean, we add all the individual ages and divide that total by the number of people.

Descriptive analyses are sometimes deceptively simple in appearance. The interpretation of "the simple facts" can make a great difference in conclusions, as the box "Half Empty or Half Full? Making Sense of Statistics" on page 66 illustrates.

Explanatory Analyses

Most sociological analyses of data go beyond description, seeking to explain. While it might be interesting to know what percentage of a population consider themselves very happy, a sociologist would be more interested in learning what causes happiness and unhappiness. Why are some people happy while others are not?

Subgroup comparisons are an intermediate step between description and explanation. The observation that young people appear happier than old people suggests that there is something about age that is relevant to happiness. From a sociological point of view, we would say that the two variables "age" and "happiness" are related to each other. Particular attributes of one variable are associated with particular attributes of another variable.

Notice that while sociologists may observe people, those people are seen primarily as the "carriers" of attributes, and it is the relationship between the attributes of different variables that we seek to discover in the **explanatory analysis** of data. Thus, we might look for the relationship between age and happiness, religion and prejudice, education and income, and so forth. People in such studies are the units of analysis: They are units that can be described in terms of the variables under study.

How to Read a Table

Explanatory analyses are often presented in the form of percentage tables,* and I want to say some-

*These are also called "contingency tables" or "cross-tabulations."

thing about how to read such tables. In order to read an explanatory percentage table, you must recall the distinction between independent and dependent variables as discussed in the section on experiments. In terms of a simple "cause-effect" model, the "cause" is the independent variable and the "effect" is the dependent variable.

Suppose, for example, that you are interested in learning whether age is related to attitudes regarding the legalization of marijuana. Which of these would be the independent variable? Which variable would "cause" the other? Often you can determine which

of two variables is the independent one by noting the time order in which they occur. In this case, a person's age (the date of birth) occurs long before an attitude toward marijuana is formed. Thus, while there could be something about being young or old that would have an effect on attitudes toward marijuana, there is no way that an attitude could affect a person's age. In this case, age is the independent variable.

Table 3·1 is an illustration (using hypothetical data) of a percentage table. It is constructed from the results of the examination of people's attitudes toward the legalization of marijuana. Notice that 75

Half Empty or Half Full? Making Sense of Statistics

In 1965, Daniel Patrick Moynihan, then an official in the Department of Labor, wrote a memorandum called "The Negro Family: The Case for National Action." Among other symptoms of strain on black family life, Moynihan pointed to what he saw as a pattern of "matriarchy" by saying, "A fundamental fact of Negro American family life is the often reversed roles of husband and wife." (In the ensuing conflict, many lost sight of the fact that Moynihan was merely echoing the conclusions of two generations of social scientists and other observers—black and white.)

Suppose we look at the answers black respondents gave to a Gallup-poll question in 1951, "When you were growing up, who was the most important influence on you—your father or your mother?" Of those who answered 73 percent said that their *mother* was the more important influence.[1] Surely this supports Moynihan's assertions about the matrifocality of the black family. Or does it? That figure—73 percent—takes on a rather different meaning when we discover that virtually the same proportion of whites (69 percent) gave the same response. This situation illustrates a general difficulty: It is hard to know *what*

to make of many statistics unless you have something to compare them with.

One way to "lie with statistics" is to imply a comparison where none exists. Suppose we discover that a quarter of the students at some college say they have cheated at one time or another. We know that figure probably understates the proportion who have actually cheated, and it would be easy to write about "the cheating epidemic," saying wise things about the effects of increased pressure to get into graduate and professional schools. We would be misleading, however: A national survey of college students in the middle 1960s, subject to the same sort of underreporting bias, reported a figure of 50 percent.

In another example, from 1960 to 1973, United States yearly defense expenditures increased by 66 percent, "a substantial increase by any standard." By any standard? Compare it with the increase in the wholesale price index (43 percent), in national income (154 percent), or in government social welfare expenditures (311 percent).

When used with statistics, the words "fully" and "only" should provoke skepticism. Compared with what? Is the figure higher or lower than that for similar phenomena? Is it higher or lower than that for other populations? Is it higher or lower than it used to be?

[1]Herbert H. Hyman and John Shelton Reed, "'Black Matriarchy' Reconsidered: Evidence from Secondary Analysis of Sample Surveys." *Public Opinion Quarterly* 33 (Fall 1969): 346–54.

Table 3·1 A Hypothetical Percentage Table		
Attitudes toward legalizing marijuana	Age	
	Young	Old
In favor	75%	33%
Not in favor	25	67
N[a] =	(1,292)	(1,567)

[a]The numbers in parentheses represent the number of people, or "cases," upon which the percentages are based. In these hypothetical data, there were 1,292 young people, 75 percent of whom (969) were in favor of legalization. There were 1,567 old people, 33 percent of whom (527) were in favor.

Table 3·2 A Hypothetical Three-Variable Table				
Attitudes toward legalizing marijuana	Residence			
	Urban		Rural	
	Young	Old	Young	Old
In favor	82%	43%	59%	13%
Not in favor	18	57	41	87
N =	(890)	(1,079)	(402)	(488)

percent of the "young" people favor legalization and 25 percent do not. Also notice that 33 percent of the "old" people are in favor, while 67 percent are not. In analyzing the relationship between age and attitudes toward legalizing marijuana, we would note that young people are more in favor of legalization than are old people: 75 percent versus 33 percent. We conclude, therefore, that something about age affects attitudes toward legalizing marijuana. We conclude there is a relationship between the two variables.

Very often, more than two variables are used in the presentation of a percentage table. Suppose, for example, that we think that attitudes toward marijuana might *also* be related to whether people live in urban or rural areas. We will then see a table that will reveal the simultaneous effects of the two independent variables (age and residence) on the same dependent variable (attitude toward legalizing marijuana). Table 3·2 is a hypothetical example of such a table.

The new hypothetical table tells us that the young are more likely to favor legalizing marijuana both in the city and in the country. It tells us something else as well. Urban people support legalization more than rural people regardless of age. The urban young are more in favor of legalization than the rural young, and the same pattern appears among the older people under study.

Finally, Table 3·2 tells us that age and residence have a cumulative effect on attitudes toward legalization of marijuana. If you know a person's age and

residence, you can make a pretty good guess at his or her feelings about legalizing marijuana.

These hypothetical examples illustrate the basic method of explanatory analysis in sociology. Very often, the researcher begins with a dependent variable (such as prejudice or voting behavior) and then sets about finding the independent variables that determine it. As an alternative, the researcher sometimes begins with an independent variable and tries to find all the dependent variables it causes. You might want to ask, for example, what the various consequences of prejudice are.

Sociological explanatory analyses are by no means limited to percentage tables. Sometimes graphs are an appropriate format for examining the relationship between variables. More complex tables or figures include correlations, regressions, factor analysis, path analysis, smallest-space analysis, and countless others. The fundamental logic of these more advanced explanations may be found in the percentage tables that have been discussed above.

Sociologists and Detectives

I want to conclude this chapter with some comments on the place of luck and intuition in scientific inquiry. There is a misconception about science that suggests these factors have no place in science. If you are to understand what sociological research is about, it is essential that you realize that the scientist's task, like that of the investigative detective, is to find the answers to questions: Who killed Cock Robin? What causes prejudice? Finding the answer is what makes a good scientist, just as it makes a good detective. Merely going through the steps generally associated with scientific research or criminal investigation does not make you a scientist or a detective.

Intuition is perfectly acceptable in science as in detective work. An answer to a question is no less valid because it came to the investigator through intuition. A detective may "get a feeling" that "the butler did it," and a sociologist may "get a feeling" that education is the main key to reducing prejudice.

Luck is perfectly all right in science and in detective work too. The detective who just happens to be at the scene of the crime when the murderer sneaks back to erase a clue is simply lucky. A sociological researcher may "just happen" to collect data about a variable that turns out to be the critical one. Such lucky events do not diminish the validity of the answers they provide.

If intuition and luck are acceptable in the solution of scientific and detective problems, then why worry about specialized methods of inquiry? The specialized methods and the logic underlying them serve two important functions in careful inquiry. First, the methods typically followed by professional scientists and detectives increase the likelihood that intuition, insight, or good luck will occur. The detective's standard methods of criminal investigation place him at the scene of the crime; sociologists routinely pay attention to certain variables that have proved generally important in previous studies. The standard methods of science and detecting tend to put you where the luck happens.

Second, although intuition is legitimate in obtaining the answer to a problem, it is not sufficient demonstration that you really have the answer. The detective may have a feeling that the butler is guilty, but such a feeling is not enough—nor should it be—to convict the butler. A "gut feeling" that education is the key to reducing prejudice does not prove the case. The standard methods of inquiry, and especially the logic that underlies them, provide rules of proof. My purpose in this chapter has been to show you some of the logic and techniques that reflect the agreements sociologists have in this latter regard.

Summary

Science is a matter of observing and making sense out of what is observed. Research involves observation and includes techniques for making sense out of things.

Inquiry seems to be a native human activity, based in part on the desire to predict. We learn the regular patterns of events around us and develop general understandings of how the world operates.

Natural human inquiry is beset by perils. Sometimes we simply observe things inaccurately. The desire to understand can lead to overgeneralization, which, in turn, fosters selective perception. To protect our "understandings" further, we sometimes make up "facts" that explain away inconsistencies. Sometimes we reason badly or conclude our inquiry prematurely.

Scientific inquiry differs from other kinds of inquiry by providing some established safeguards against such errors. First, scientists have an agreement to make observation a careful and conscious activity rather than just a casual one. Second, scientists are equally careful and conscious in drawing conclusions. Finally, the public nature of science makes it possible for the errors of one scientist to be pointed out by others. Science and scientists are not perfect in these regards, of course.

Science operates within two different systems of logic: inductive and deductive. Inductive logic involves the development of general principles from specific observations, and deductive logic involves the development of specific expectations, hypotheses, from general principles. Science in practice is a never-ending cycle of induction and deduction.

The traditional image of science suggests that it is a relatively straightforward and routine process largely flowing from the deductive system of logic. This view is inaccurate and oversimplified. The actual practice of science is more like detective work.

Some of the general characteristics of science are as follows. First, it is based on a deterministic view of the world, including human beings. It aims at ever-more-general understandings of things, an aim that it achieves by being explicit in methods, definitions, and conclusions. Replication is essential to science;

repeating studies and arriving at the same conclusions as the first ones guards against possible biases and chance. Scientists seek parsimony, a combination of powerful explanation and simplicity. Finally, empirical verification is the keystone of science. Theoretical conclusions must correspond with actual observations.

Concepts are pictures in your head, and conceptualization is the process of refining and specifying those pictures, those mental images. Some concepts refer to attributes, or characteristics of people and things. Other concepts refer to variables: logical groupings of attributes. For example, "male" is an attribute contained in the variable "sex." Operationalization, specifying the methods (operations) by which attributes and variables are to be observed and measured, is a step beyond conceptualization.

While science involves observation, it is typically impossible to observe everything of relevance to an inquiry. Methods of probability sampling make it possible to observe only some things and draw conclusions that extend far beyond what has been observed. For example, a sample of voters may be interviewed whose voting intentions can reflect the voting intentions of the entire electorate.

Sociologists use a variety of different modes of observation. Field research is directly observing whatever is under study. To study riots, find one and watch it. Experiments typically involve the administration of a stimulus and observations of its effects. Sometimes, however, it is possible to study "natural experiments," and evaluation research is still another use of the experimental method. Survey research involves the use of questionnaires, either administered by interviewers or completed by the respondents themselves. There are other modes of observation in sociology, and all have special strengths and weaknesses. The soundest inquiry is one that uses several different modes.

Descriptive and explanatory analyses of the data produced by observations constitute the "making sense" part of research. People are often the units of analysis in sociology, but the goal of explanatory sociological inquiry is to discover relationships among the variables that characterize and distinguish different people.

Suggested Readings

Babbie, Earl
1975   *The Practice of Social Research.* Belmont, Calif.: Wadsworth.
This lucid, up-to-date, charming, witty, and generally wonderful (you thought maybe I'd say it was lousy?) introduction to the logic and methods of social science research pursues in more depth the materials covered in this chapter. My intention was to present the basic logic and ideal techniques of sociological inquiry in a context of research realities, showing the compromises that have to be made.

Madge, John
1962   *The Origins of Scientific Sociology.* New York: Free Press.
Madge describes several classic examples of sociological research, representing a variety of methods. In addition to gaining familiarity with the specific studies, you should gain a more comprehensive view of the potential for sociological inquiry. The biographical quality of Madge's presentation makes this a fascinating and engaging book.

Stouffer, Samuel A.
1962   *Social Research to Test Ideas.* New York: Free Press.
I've suggested this collection of articles by a giant of sociological research for inspirational as well as educational purposes. No one exemplifies the sociologist as detective better than Stouffer. Addressing a variety of research topics, this book illustrates the manner in which a sociologist transforms an interesting idea or puzzling question into a strategy of observation and interpretation.

Wallace, Walter L.
1971   *The Logic of Science in Sociology.* Chicago: Aldine-Atherton.
This is an excellent presentation of scientific inquiry as a cyclical process involving theories, hypotheses, observations, empirical generalizations, and back to theories. As Wallace demonstrates, scientific inquiry can begin at any point on the circle and goes round and round thereafter. Here's an excellent antidote to the view of science as a routine, lock-step undertaking.

Episode Three

Gabriel Knapp flipped a switch. The custom-installed fluorescent tubes above his bed receded and were subsequently hidden by a false ceiling. Monica would arrive soon.

He dressed, examining himself as he had done methodically for the past eight years. The evidence had been located, he thought, through medical technology. It was only a matter of time now.

More than three years ago Gabe had conceived the private hope that he was somehow to escape his future, that perhaps—in spite of all he knew to be true—he was not one of Adam's people.

He couldn't help feeling bitter now. Seven years ago, he mused, he had been ready. Prepared to return. Anxious for maturity. Anxious even in spite of the fact that his skin showed little promise of becoming true green and that, as a result, his status at home would never equal that of greens like Larry Jones or Rebecca Lockwood.

But today? Today there was the private executive office at Chicago National. Today there was the Lake Shore apartment. Today there was Monica. He was thirty-two years old now, he mused, and had lived more than one-third of his life on the outside. He had made friends here, made a home here. He had told no one of his mutation.

"What's wrong?" Monica was saying as she arrived.

"Nothing."

"Well, it must be *something*. You sounded awful on the phone this afternoon."

Gabe fixed two drinks.

"What *is* it?" Monica whispered finally. "You're staring."

"I just needed to talk to you." Silently he sipped his drink. Whatever he had wanted to talk about, Monica realized, he was having difficulty approaching it now.

"Say," she changed her tone. "The firm's planning a big deal for July Fourth—picnic, fireworks—they're even splurging for real beefsteaks. Want to go?"

"I might have to be out of town."

"Where's the insurance industry sending you this time?"

"Phoenix." He shifted. "But maybe I'll be back by the Fourth. When do you have to know?"

"At least half an hour before I pick you up."

He was lucky, he thought. She gave him room, didn't pressure.

They had discussed marriage once. It had been he who initiated the conversation. How foolish, he grimaced now, even to dream that his mutation might remain secret.

Anyway, the discussion had not gone well. Monica had surprised him. "I think I'd like to have children right away," she had blithely announced.

"Right away?" He was incredulous.

"Why not?"

"We've got our careers now," he explained calmly. "We'll concentrate on our careers for the next few years, and then we'll raise children."

"Well," Monica was playing now, "what if I get pregnant on our wedding night?"

"We'd give it away," Gabe had responded automatically without reflection.

Monica's chin dropped. "Gabriel," she breathed, "that's a horrid joke."

The conversation had occurred several months before. Now Gabe gazed at Monica. Slowly he was beginning to realize that someday he would have to tell her exactly who he was.

"Monica," Gabriel asked, "how about another drink?"

Batterson, Duncan, and Roanoke departed American University in Chicago and landed in Phoenix early the next morning, June 28, 2026. There they rented a car and drove toward Green Colony.

Located in a sparsely populated area of the Arizona–New Mexico desert, the community proved difficult to find. The trio had driven within what they knew to be the general vicinity of Green Colony for some hours before they were stopped by an armed guard. A wrought-iron gate bearing the sign "Adamsville" curved across a narrow, unpaved road.

"May I help you?" asked the female attendant. She was young, Duncan noted, and scantily attired for such an "official" position. Her hair was long, bleached from overexposure to a blistering sun. Her skin was like that of a nonmutant. She carried a rifle.

"We are looking for Green Colony," Duncan offered from his position in the driver's seat.

"There is no Green Colony here," came the terse reply.

Roanoke leaned across Duncan. "We are looking for a colony of mutants that we know to be located somewhere near here."

"This is private property," the woman said. "No one is admitted without official documents."

"We have with us a letter from a Michael Jones-the-Elder," Duncan responded quickly, pulling the briefcase which contained the letter into his lap. He passed it to the guard. The letter granted permission for a two-hour interview. The team was expected to depart the community by 2 P.M. that day, the communication read.

"I will have to phone ahead," she said. She walked toward a small, glass-roofed booth near the edge of the road. When the guard returned, she announced with noticeable surprise, "You have received clearance to the next gate."

At a second gate, the team was greeted by a woman in her fifties, her skin a dark emerald.

"I am Rebecca Lockwood," she introduced herself. "I will take you to the home of my forebears." Without invitation she opened the rear door of the sociologists' rented auto and slid into the seat behind the three visitors. "If you will just drive slowly ahead," she began, "we will soon be in town. From there I will direct you to Elderhome."

"Elderhome?" Roanoke repeated.

"The home of Adamsville's two remaining elders."

"Has Green Colony always been your home?" Constance asked, turning slightly from her position in the front seat.

"There is no Green Colony," Rebecca Lockwood answered firmly. "The name of the community is Adamsville. Outsiders have written about 'Green Colony' for several years now. But there is no such place."

"What you're implying," Duncan suggested, "is that while outsiders—scientists, politicians, journalists—have chosen to call your community 'Green Colony', the folks here do not accept that name."

"There is no such thing as 'Green Colony'," the woman repeated. "There is only Adamsville, named by my grandfather shortly after he established the community."

The vehicle approached the center of the colony.

The town was small. A spacious park occupied what appeared to be the hub of the miniature city. Adjacent to the park stood a modern, single-story building of adobe and glass. This was Elderhome.

"Turn left and stop just ahead," Lockwood directed.

After Duncan parked the car, the four stepped out into the glaring desert sun.

"My uncle and aunt will have finished noon light-break shortly," Lockwood advised. "Then they will see you. Meanwhile, I shall show you into the Elderhome parlor."

As the party entered the adobe structure, Duncan noted the clean, uncluttered lines of the architecture.

"Won't you be seated?" Lockwood suggested. "Allow me to offer you some refreshment," she added politely, pushing a button on a wall panel behind her. The roof receded, and the three felt pierced by the sharp sunlight.

"Make yourself comfortable," Lockwood said. "The elders will be here shortly."

Connie Batterson yearned for her sunglasses. Duncan wiped his brow. Finally two persons, advanced in age, entered the room. Their green skin dazzled.

"I presume you are the sociologists from American University," the female began. "I am Ruth Jones, the eldest living of Adam's children. This is my brother, Michael. Together we govern Adamsville."

As the party walked to the glass-enclosed "ruling center," the sociologists introduced themselves. Once in the official administrative office, Michael and Ruth took their places behind a long table. They faced their guests who sat in comfortable chairs along the other side of the table.

"Now," Ruth began, "I want to be brief and to the point. This is an important day in the history of Adamsville. It is the first time that we have responded favorably to a request from outsiders to enter our community. We have done so for two reasons: First, we know that information on the colony is leaking to the outside. That leaked information is not always correct. Often it is gathered haphazardly. Someone sneaks in, talks to one or two of us maybe, and goes off. The resulting information is often biased. By the time the story gets into the newspapers, it may be grossly inaccurate.

"We figure it is time, since information is leaking out anyway, to allow people here who will gather the facts systematically and report what they see without bias.

"The second reason we have allowed you here," Ruth continued, "is that we believe what you discover may help us. We are beginning to experience a serious problem. Some of our young people are not fulfilling their obligations to the community. They lack loyalty. We want to know why."

The five talked at length.

"How can you be sure that what you find will be accurate?" Michael challenged the sociologists.

"We can't," Duncan said. "We can only be reasonably certain. And we can promise that we will strive to be systematic, logical, and open-minded. We will not jump to conclusions."

"We do not pretend to have come here without personal values," Constance said. "But as scientists we can try to recognize these values. Then, aware of them, we will not unconsciously let them influence either our observation or analysis."

"I must explain," Michael said, "that some factions within the community are not in favor of your being here. They resent being studied. They feel their privacy is a sacred thing, not to be infringed upon. You cannot expect cooperation from every member of this community."

"Some fear your being here," Ruth added. "They feel that it is best for us to remain living in complete secrecy. They trace the beginnings of many of our community's troubles to the invasion by those two reporters six years ago. They feel that the more the world knows about us, the more endangered we become. Sometimes outsiders picket our gates. They carry signs that say horrible things, like 'KILL THE GREEN MONSTERS'. We never experienced that before ungreens came poking around."

"How do you answer your dissenters?" Louise asked.

"We believe," Michael said, "that the outside must be told who we are. We are the saviors of the world, a new people, the fathers and mothers of a new humanity. The world cannot survive without us. Once people realize this, we will be accepted."

"Indeed," Ruth said, "we will be more than accepted. The earth will be ours."

Batterson and Roanoke exchanged glances.

"But we must know," Ruth shifted the focus of the conversation, "how you plan to gather your information."

Duncan responded. "I would like to be allowed to return," he said, somewhat hesitantly, "to live here for a time with your people, to participate as well as I can in the lives of your people."

"Why?" Ruth demanded.

"It is one of the best ways I know," he said, "to practice social science."

"We can arrange that," Michael replied. "Some will think it an unwise decision, but Ruth and I are convinced otherwise. We are moral people and we want outsiders to understand that. Nothing ill can come of the truth."

Ruth sat quiet a moment, apparently engaged in heavy thought. "This afternoon," she said suddenly, "the community will have a welcoming ceremony. According to our previous plans, you were to have left Adamsville before the ceremony began. But we would like you all to stay for the welcoming. You will enjoy it. It is a wonderful celebration."

Michael Jones-the-Elder pushed a button on the table in front of him. A gentleman of forty, his complexion the color of fresh limes, entered the room.

"Mr. Alexander," Jones announced, "these people are guests of Ruth and myself. They have been invited to attend the ceremony this afternoon. Please escort them. You will be their host."

The man nodded. "Come with me," he said.

Questions

1. The Elders feel that information about their community has, until now, tended to be inaccurate. What "errors of inquiry" might people who have investigated the colony before have been inclined to make?

2. How might the forthcoming sociological inquiry avoid the errors of inquiry that you mentioned above?

3. Is the result of sociological research a "matter of agreement" or does it approach "absolute truth?"

4. The Elders want the world to know that greens are "a moral people." Can this conclusion be drawn from scientific sociological research?

Part Two
A Conceptual Overview

In Part Two of this book, we are going to look at some of the fundamental concepts that sociologists use in their study of social life.

Chapter 4 will examine the variety of agreements that people make in structuring their societies. Sociologists and others use the term **culture** in reference to the collections of shared agreements that shape the way members of a society think, feel, and act. You'll see that there are certain kinds of agreements that sociologists are particularly interested in: **symbols, beliefs, values,** and **norms.**

In addition, we're going to look more closely at the concepts of "status" and "role" that were touched on in Chapter 1. I noted in Chapter 2 that the "role theory" point of view is based fundamentally in these concepts, and you'll see that they have a special importance for sociologists in general.

Chapter 5 addresses the process by which a society's agreements are passed from one generation to the next, the manner in which they are taught and learned. This process is called **socialization.**

Socialization, as you'll see, has two essential functions: (1) A society's agreements are perpetuated to the extent that new generations of members enter into those agreements, and societies are able to survive; and (2) socialization provides for the formation of individuals' social identities. I touched on this in Chapter 2 in the discussion of symbolic interactionism, and we'll look more deeply into the matter in Chapter 5.

In Chapter 6, we're going to look at some of the ways individuals are linked to one another. We'll begin with an examination of **primary** and **secondary** relations, noting the kinds of groups that are formed in connection with each. Then we'll broaden our view to include an examination of additional types of social groups. The chapter concludes with a discussion of formal organizations, giving special attention to **bureaucracy.**

By the time you finish Part Two, you should understand sociological concepts well enough to be able to look at and understand the substance of sociological inquiry. That's what we'll do in the remainder of the book.

4

Culture:
The Basic Agreements

Throughout Part One, I pointed to a number of ways in which the agreements people make influence how they live together and interact with one another. In this chapter, I want to take a broader view, looking at how the many agreements people share are organized and interrelated so as to provide a comprehensive framework within which social life occurs.

"Culture" is a general term sociologists, anthropologists, and others use to refer to the whole collection of agreements that the members of a particular society share. It includes all the shared points of view that define what's true and what's good and what kinds of behavior people can expect of one another. In large part, culture includes those ways of thinking, feeling, and acting that the members of one society simply take for granted, but which might seem very strange to an outsider.

To get a sense of all I'm including when I speak of culture, I'd like you to do a short exercise. In this exercise, I want you to close your eyes for a minute or so and imagine some things. Read the instructions first, then do the exercise, and then come back to the book.

After you've finished reading these instructions, close your eyes and imagine a hundred or so prehistoric cavemen and cavewomen, a collection of small, unrelated families. Imagine that none of the families has ever seen other human beings before. They've just been wandering through the forest and the plains looking out for their own survival needs. In the pic-

ture you create, have all the families suddenly converge on the same water hole and discover each other. Notice what happens when they meet.

Those are the instructions for the exercise. Close your eyes for a couple of minutes, do the exercise, notice what goes on when the people meet, and then come back here.

Welcome back. I'm glad you escaped safely. They can be a pretty rough bunch, those human beings. I can't guess exactly what you saw, of course, but there was probably quite a bit of confusion, fear, and possibly some violence. Don't worry, however, if what you imagined wasn't anything like that.

I've suggested that you try the exercise so that you will have a point of comparison for the discussions of culture in this chapter. Now I'd like you to look at the people around you or remember the last time you were with a large group of people.

You will probably notice that all the people around you are speaking the same language. They're not just using the same utterances to stand for the same physical objects, but they're also expressing some pretty complex ideas. Notice the ways they are dressed. Given all the possible states of dress and undress, the similarities you see will probably be greater than the differences. Notice how people meet each other, say hello, and perhaps shake hands. Think about the things the people around you eat and drink. How do they move around? What do they do for entertainment?

Compared to the picture you had of that sudden meeting at the water hole, the people around you must seem pretty orderly. Given the range of possibilities of ways people *could* behave, the people around you are remarkably similar to one another. The similarities in the ways people around you think and act reflect the fact that they share a common culture. A culture is the collection of agreements that a people share.

You are living in a veritable sea of agreements. The fact that you can read this book is a matter of agreements as to the meanings of the words I've used and an agreement that a book is something to keep words in. The fact that you wear clothes when you go out of the house (as well as the kinds of clothes you wear), the fact that you don't punch everybody you see on the street, the fact that you say "hello" to people and ask them how they are even if you don't really care how they are—all these things make up the culture you share with those around you. Many of those agreements seem so natural, so "right," that you probably don't even think about them.

If you reflect, you'll see that there's no obvious reason for the existence of many of the agreements that make up your culture. Why do men wear ties when they dress up, for example? It doesn't make any sense at all if you think about it. To find out how real that agreement is, though, try getting into a fancy restaurant without a tie, *if you're a man, that is.* If you're a woman, you don't need a tie, of course. Of course? Why? What sense does *that* make?

Young children frequently regale the adults around them and add to the store of "family stories" by asking "why" about things that adults find obvious and don't question. Why can't the family dog eat dinner at the table with the rest of the family? Why can't you tell someone he or she has a funny-looking nose? Why can't you take all your clothes off when it's hot?

Every generation of children in a society draws attention to the discrepancies between the world of direct experience and the agreement reality that has become reified in the society. We laugh at children, however, and they soon learn they can't "belong" until they participate in the agreement reality shared by everyone else. Generation after generation, children give in and take for granted what "everybody knows."

Sociologists are more persistent. We've learned, for example, that what "everybody knows" in one society is very often different from—even directly contradictory to—what "everybody knows" in another society. Sociologists are unwilling to accept agreement realities as true and obvious.

The sociological view of culture also draws attention to and clarifies the existence of disagreement in any society. Although a society's culture represents the generally agreed-on patterns of living together, some people in any society disagree with some aspects of that culture. They have different points of view. Rather than viewing such differences as weird or antisocial, the sociological view reveals the ways in which such sets of disagreements actually constitute a separate culture—or **subculture**—within the society.

This chapter discusses all the different aspects of culture that I've mentioned. We'll begin by looking at some of the separate components of culture. Then we'll take a look at how cultural agreements are structured, how they're organized and related to one another. We'll see that cultures are more than mere "collections" of agreements: They are systematically interwoven so that the "whole" hangs together and even makes sense.

Some Components of Culture

In this section, we are going to look at some of the different kinds of agreements that have historically made up cultures around the world. As we shall see, these agreements have general effects on interaction. In the section that follows this one, we'll look at some agreements that have an even more direct effect.

Symbols

A "symbol" is a representation of something else. A symbol communicates information in shorthand form, and it can evoke feelings associated with what it represents. The dove, for example, is a symbol of peace; the cross is a symbol of Christianity. Two

Much symbolism is limited to a single culture. This French advertisement for Levi's *is a re-creation of the well-known (among the French)* La Marseillaise *sculpture at the Arc de Triomphe de l'Etoile. (left* Bulloz, *right* Levi Strauss & Co., Europe)

people can agree to let the cross symbolize Christianity even though they have different feelings about Christianity itself.

We discussed symbols in Chapter 2 in the discussion of language. A "language" is a symbol system, with words representing objects, actions, feelings, and other aspects of our experience. Because we have agreed on a symbol system called the English language, it is possible for me to communicate with you through this book.

Symbols that represent emotion-charged things can, themselves, evoke high emotions. National flags, the swastika, the star of David, and the hammer and sickle can evoke strong positive feelings in some people and strong negative ones in others. There are

"dirty words" that titillate some people and horrify others. There are "dirty names" that have the same effect. There are racial epithets that can spark a riot.

I chose not to give examples of "dirty words" because I knew that you or other readers might be offended. I am less reluctant to say *"merde"* in this book, however, because I know that most English speakers don't have *any* meaning associated with that collection of letters, let alone feelings of offense. Some French speakers, however, would be horrified. The point is that symbols don't mean anything in and of themselves: They symbolize things only by agreement.

The language you speak is more a part of your experience of things than you may realize. As Edward

Sapir (1960) has suggested, languages both reflect and shape the ways people think, feel, and act. You've probably heard that Eskimos have a large number of words for "snow" or that members of certain tropical societies distinguish among a number of parrots. The impact of language goes deeper than the number of distinctions made among objects in the environment, however.

A particularly fascinating view of the impact of language comes from studies of bilingual people. In one such study, S. Ervin-Tripp (1964) interviewed Japanese-American women in both languages. The interviews, separated by a period of time, were identical in content, but the answers from given women were interestingly different. Asked to complete the sentence "I will probably become . . .," one respondent replied "housewife" when the interview was conducted in Japanese and "teacher" when it was conducted in English. Similarly, when asked to complete the sentence "When my wishes conflict with my family . . .," she replied "It is a time of great unhappiness" in the Japanese-language study and "I do what I want" in the English-language study. What can we conclude about the way this woman "really" felt about career and family matters? About all we can conclude is that her feelings depended on

the language she was speaking at the time and the culture it represented for her.

Our languages are deeply woven into our experiences of the world. Consider such mainstays of "reality" as time and space. When I mention "time," you probably think of calendars and clocks, years, days, hours, minutes, and seconds. Most Westerners tend to view time as something linear that can be broken up into chunks—chunks that can be assigned, scheduled, invested, spent wisely, or wasted. This view of time is not universal, however, as different languages indicate.

Edward Hall (1959) reports that the Sioux Indians have no words for "time," "late," or "waiting." The Sioux, like other American Indians and other peoples around the world, live in the present, doing what they feel is appropriate to the moment. Things happen when they happen and take as long as they take. This orientation to time has contributed to countless conflicts between the Indians and the white American majority.

Notions of space, especially what it symbolizes in interpersonal relations, differ from society to society. In his discussion of the "silent language" (1959), Hall notes the difference in the ideas of North Americans and Latin Americans about how much distance should separate two participants in a conversation. "In Latin America the interaction distance is much less than it is in the United States. Indeed, people cannot talk comfortably with one another unless they are very close to the distance that evokes either sexual or hostile feelings in the North American" (p. 164).

Hall recounts episodes in which Latin Americans move close to North Americans in conversation, only to have the North Americans back away. The moving close is misinterpreted as aggression, and the backing away is misinterpreted as cold and unfriendly. The implicit symbolism of interpersonal distance, although deeply ingrained in each, is different in the two cultures. Even the facial expressions that you and I take for granted reflect cultural agreements in part, as the box "Are Facial Expressions Universal?" shows.

Symbols, then, are a part of culture. They represent agreements that are shared by members of one society, but which vary across societies. Let's turn to some other components of culture.

Beliefs

"Beliefs" are points of view about what's true in the world. By definition, beliefs are views that have been reified. Every culture contains many broadly shared statements about what is true. Some beliefs are held across cultures.

The belief that God exists is a widely shared agreement. The belief that God does not exist is also widely shared. The belief that thousands of gods exist is an agreement shared by hundreds of millions of Hindus and others. The belief that "godness" or the godhead pervades all creatures and objects of the universe is an agreement among millions of people around the world.

All this illustrates a fact about beliefs. Some people have agreed to beliefs that directly contradict the beliefs other people have agreed to. As you look around you, you'll find both agreements and disagreements about what is true.

Some beliefs seem strange to us. During World War II, the American military built airstrips on tiny islands throughout the Pacific. The purpose of these airstrips was to facilitate the shipment of men and supplies in support of the war effort. The natives living on these islands observed the construction of the airstrips and, subsequently, observed the landing of airplanes, carrying tons and tons of cargo.

Once the war was over and the troops had left, anthropologists discovered that the natives on many of the tiny islands were building airstrips! Not only that, they expected airplanes to begin arriving with supplies for them. These "cargo cultists," as they came to be known, shared an agreement that building airstrips caused great birds to come out of the sky bearing gifts. You may think their belief strange. That's another thing about beliefs: The ones you don't share can seem pretty silly. When the anthropologists told them that the airplanes weren't going to land, the cargo cultists thought the anthropologists were stupid.

Some people believe that the number 7 is lucky and that 13 is unlucky. Some people believe it's bad luck to have a black cat cross your path or to walk under a ladder. Some people believe that Libras and Cancers always spell trouble for each other. Some people believe that peace is better than war. Some

people believe that the different races are equal in human value. Another thing about beliefs is that they don't seem at all silly if you happen to share them.

Between 1939 and 1945, approximately 6 million Jews were murdered because of an agreement among

---

Are Facial Expressions Universal?

Language and symbolic gestures, such as nodding one's head to indicate approval, have agreed-on meanings within cultural groups. However, these agreements do not always extend from one culture to another, and a symbolic gesture or word may have very different meanings for different groups. For example, a Tibetan sticks out his tongue to greet a friend, but an American sees this as a disrespectful gesture. Research indicates that unlike the situation with symbolic gestures and language, some facial expressions that indicate basic emotions may be universal, signifying the same things to all humans.

According to researcher Paul Ekman,[1] through biological evolution all humans may have come to share a number of facial expressions and interpretations for them, such as happiness, sadness, anger, and disgust. Ekman found that people from South America, Europe, Asia, North America, and New Guinea, regardless of whether they are literate or have had contact with people from other cultures, have learned, recognize, and interpret arbitrary facial expressions in the same way. To Ekman, this suggests that humans inherit the tendency to link certain facial expressions with particular emotions, although cultures vary in when and how people use the expressions.

In what other ways might one explain the similarity Ekman found in facial expressions and their interpretation across cultures?

[1]"Face Muscles Talk Every Language," *Psychology Today*, September 1975, pp. 35–39.

members of the Third Reich that Jews were inferior human beings and that they constituted a threat to the purity of the Nazi superrace. Some beliefs seem absolutely dangerous. *That's* a belief also, of course.

Beliefs, to review, are views about what's true, typically in the form of agreements that people share. People also disagree about what's true. If you agree with a belief, it seems very *real* to you. Beliefs are, by definition, reified agreements.

Usually beliefs don't appear as isolated items but as parts of belief systems. For example, physicists believe that all matter is composed of molecules. They believe that molecules are composed of atoms, and they believe that atoms are composed of electrons, protons, and other subatomic particles. These beliefs exist within a context of beliefs about electromagnetic attraction, centrifugal and centripetal forces, and countless other related beliefs.

Social beliefs also occur as systems. Communists believe that the excesses of capitalism will generate revolutions among the disgruntled masses. They also believe that revolutions by the masses result in socialist governments. Communists also believe that socialist governments will eventually experience a withering away of the state, leaving a classless, communist society.

All of us share agreed-on belief systems. One belief supports another, just as one hand washes the other. As we shall see shortly, moreover, beliefs are linked to other components of culture.

Values

Values are points of view about what's good. People have many agreements about values. Some people feel it is better to permit people to achieve the full extent of their potential even though inequalities are inevitably created in the process. Other people prefer that everyone have all the necessities of life rather than allowing some people to accumulate more than they need. Capitalism and socialism, respectively, hold these two different values. Capitalists pretty much agree that achievement is more important than equality, and socialists pretty much agree that it should be the other way around. Notice that the values of achievement and equality are inevitably

in tension with one another, since achievement implies the opportunity to be unequal.*

Democracy is based on the value of self-government. Monarchy is based on the value of hereditary leadership. Peace is based on an agreement that it's bad for people to kill each other. War is based on an agreement that it's all right to kill to get what you want. (Notice that you can't have a war unless *both* sides agree to this, even if one side only feels that it's all right to kill to get peace.)

Like beliefs, values are usually no casual matter. Values, by definition, are statements that some things are *better* than others. People are killed in disagreements over whether democracy is better than monarchy or vice versa. People get killed in disagreements over whether peace is better than war.

Values are often reified, just as other kinds of agreements are. We tend to believe that the things we think are good are "really" good. If you feel peace is better than war, you probably don't regard this as a simple matter of personal preference. You feel peace is "really" better, and you probably have hundreds of reasons to back up your point of view. That's because values also appear as components in larger systems of values. If you share (with me, incidentally) the values of human life, dignity, and freedom, these values support your view on the value of peace over war.

Values are related to beliefs. As a general rule, values are justified by beliefs. For example, our American value of democracy is often justified by the belief that all people are the equal children of God. For some people, then, the preference for democracy is based on a belief about what's true, and the value follows logically from the belief. Notice that monarchy is sometimes justified by the belief that God has specially chosen the monarch to rule.

Looking at the relationship between beliefs and values from the other direction, we see that values *specify* beliefs. The belief that all people are the equal children of God doesn't, by itself, say anything about what's good or bad. A value specifies what ought to be good if what's true is true. The value of equal representation in government, then, specifies the

*Seymour Martin Lipset has suggested that much of American history can be read as the conflict between these two values. See *The First New Nation* (New York: Basic Books, 1963).

"best" kind of political structure if the belief that all are the equal children of God is true.

Norms

Norms are agreements about what's expected. Norms typically describe the kinds of behavior we have agreed to expect of one another. In the United States, for example, there is a norm that automobiles will be driven on the right side of the road. In England, by contrast, the norm is that automobiles will be driven on the left side of the highway. As this example illustrates, laws are norms, but there are other kinds of norms as well.

In poker, the norm is that the person on the left side of the dealer bets first, and the betting proceeds in a clockwise direction from there. Recall that in Chapter 1 I said you couldn't have games without agreements, without rules. The rules I talked about were norms.

Norms are related to values the same way that values are related to beliefs. Values legitimate norms just as beliefs legitimate values. For example, the norm that says no one shall drive over 25 miles per hour is legitimated by the value of traffic safety, the value of preserving human life. If you were to protest the inappropriateness of the norm to an arresting officer, he or she would probably respond with this justification. From the arresting officer's point of view, by violating the norm, you are violating the value.

Looking at the relationship from the other direction, norms specify values. Neither beliefs nor values say anything directly about how we should behave. Norms specify what we should expect in behavior if what's good is good and what's true is true.

Beliefs legitimate values which then legitimate norms, and norms specify values which then specify beliefs. Why are you going to the library tonight instead of going to a movie? Because going to the library is one of the things you are expected to do if you feel education is good. Why do you feel education is good? Because you believe that education will set you free, perhaps, or make you happy or rich, or whatever you believe education will do for you.

Beliefs, values, and norms are all interwoven, then, and norms can be reified just as beliefs and values can. We begin to think that the ways we've

agreed people should behave are the ways they "really" should behave. If you feel there is "really" something wrong with walking naked down the street, you've reified a norm shared in American culture. Realize, however, that many people around you have reified that norm, so you'd better keep the agreement. What happens when you don't keep your agreements is the topic we'll turn to next.

Norms and Sanctions

I've talked about the fact that agreements are created through interaction and that those agreements subsequently govern interaction. Now it's time to consider how the agreements govern interactions. After all, the existence of a norm specifying how you should behave is not, in and of itself, enough to ensure that you will behave that way.

"Sanctions" are the elements in a culture that ensure the keeping of agreements. There are both positive and negative sanctions: rewards and punishments. Some norms have stronger sanctions than others, and sociologists often try to figure out why.

Sanctions play a critical role in your learning of norms. Positive sanctions reinforce and encourage behavior that keeps the agreements, and negative sanctions discourage behavior that violates the agreements. Praise, displays of affection, and good things to eat are a few of the positive sanctions sometimes used in training children in normative behavior. Spanking, scolding, and the withdrawal of love are some negative sanctions. Sanctions function to teach you the agreements and to ensure that you keep them once you've learned them.

Lest the earlier discussion of norms, values, and beliefs seem too neat and orderly, beware. It's not that way. In any given culture, you will find norms in conflict with one another, norms in conflict with values and beliefs, and so forth. The box on page 84 on the Ik of East Africa, "Norms and Social Disorganization," illustrates how such conflicts and social change can be created by external forces. Conflicting beliefs, values, and norms can also exist side by side for years.

Alongside the American value of equality, countless norms of inequality have persisted throughout our national history. Both formal and informal norms have denied equal treatment to women and to racial and religious minorities. The norms of free speech

and free assembly—embodied in the Bill of Rights—have existed side by side with laws making it a crime to "conspire to advocate" certain ideas.

Americans value peace, yet we have fought nine major wars during our first two centuries of nationhood. Even during peacetime, we spend billions of dollars on preparations for war. We value truth, and yet we spend billions of dollars lying about soap, medicine, deodorants, cosmetics, and politicians. The person who unfailingly told the truth would be regarded as cruel, insensitive, and antisocial.

Sociologists use the term "integration" to refer to the extent to which norms, values, beliefs, and other elements of culture agree with one another, and we haven't found a totally integrated culture yet. The extent to which a culture *is* integrated, however, explains why social life is as orderly as it is.

Artifacts

The physical productions of a society represent another aspect of culture. The artifacts of a society reflect the agreements that people share. Examples of artifacts include such diverse things as handwoven blankets, pottery, abstract art, music of all sorts, high rises, religious objects, and beer cans. Artifacts represent an interaction between people and their environment.

People transform their physical environment in countless ways, leaving behind traces of their having been there. The ways we transform the environment and the nature of the artifacts we produce reflect the agreements we share. Socialist realism in art reflects politico-economic agreements. American factories dramatize our value of efficiency. Feathered headdresses speak plainly of the Indian's belief in harmony with nature.

All animals transform their environment, and some of the artifacts they produce might be regarded as works of "art": the spider's web, the bird's nest, the beaver's dam. Yet for such animals as these, the production of artifacts is a matter of instinct. Human beings appear to be the only animals who shape their artifacts, their physical creations, by agreements that lie outside the realm of instinct.

Symbols, beliefs, values, norms, and artifacts are all parts of what sociologists refer to as "culture."

Norms and Social Disorganization

Anthropologist Colin Turnbull lived with and studied the Ik in East Africa. The creation of a national game reserve had forced these people to abandon nomadic hunting, the traditional basis for their culture, and had caused gradual social disintegration. Though the Ik were encouraged to become settled farmers, the land they were given was drought-ridden and generally unsuitable for agriculture. As a result, food was extremely scarce, and under this pressure norms and institutions such as the family virtually disappeared, leaving only the desperate quest for individual survival. Only food and its acquisition remained important, and the Ik became unfriendly, uncharitable, inhospitable, and selfish. Parents allowed children to die; the aged and weak were allowed to starve; people were reduced to eating bark, pebbles, earth, and uncooked grass seeds. Children's games were based on competing for food. The Ik came to define "goodness" as the individual possession of food and a good man as one who has a full stomach. Even when food became more plentiful, cultural changes endured: People continued to eat alone because they no longer wished to share with others. They stole from each others' fields and did not store surpluses to meet future needs, continuing to behave as they had in times of scarcity. Turnbull believes the Ik were once a generous, charitable, hopeful, loving, cooperating people, but under pressure of individual survival needs they abandoned society itself.

Do you suppose that a severe ecological crisis such as a famine could have this kind of effect on other societies?

Source: Colin M. Turnbull, The Mountain People *(New York: Simon & Schuster, 1972).*

People do many of the same things in all societies, but their styles differ. Differing styles are a source of ethnocentrism. (left Lawrence Ploetz, Black Star; right Lennart Nilsson, Black Star)

More than mere collections, the components of a given culture are systematically related to one another. They "fit together," though never perfectly.

Ethnocentrism and Cultural Relativity

Throughout this section, I have noted that people often reify the agreements that make up their culture. We often lose sight of the fact that agreements are only agreements and start thinking they represent some kind of ultimate reality. What we agree is true seems "really" true; what we agree is good seems "really" good; and what we agree is proper behavior is "really" proper. We tend to see those people who disagree with us as more than just different: They seem *wrong.* Sociologists have a name for this tendency: **ethnocentrism.**

Ethnocentrism is the reification of one's culture. Extreme ethnocentrism can even blind us to the fact that other people have different agreements; we assume that everyone everywhere must be pretty much like us. When confronted with indisputable evidence that someone disagrees with us, the ethnocentric person can experience amusement, concern, or even a violent rage.

Cultural relativity is the opposite of ethnocentrism. It is based on the recognition that different peoples have different sets of agreements and that agreements are neither right nor wrong. They are only agreements. You can drive on the right side of the road in America while recognizing that it is no more correct ultimately than driving on the left side. You can value equality over achievement while recognizing that it is no more valuable ultimately than achievement. Sometimes you can step back from your beliefs and see them as merely different from the beliefs other people have agreed to.

Without a heavy dose of cultural relativism, you might never comprehend the seemingly bizarre practices reported by Horace Miner (1956), for example, in his classic analysis of body ritual among the Nacirema. This contemporary tribe, he reports (p. 505), has "an almost pathological horror of and fascination with the mouth, the condition of which is believed to have a supernatural influence on all social relationships."

> Were it not for the rituals of the mouth, they believe that their teeth would fall out, their gums bleed, their jaws shrink, their friends desert them, and their lovers reject them. . . .
> The daily body ritual performed by everyone includes a mouth-rite [which] consists of inserting a small bundle of hog hairs into the mouth, along with certain magical powders, and then moving the bundle in a highly formalized series of gestures.

Strange as the mouth rite of the Nacirema might seem to you, it makes perfectly good sense to the members of that tribe. Indeed, the high priests associated with the mouth rite—among the wealthiest members of Nacirema society—could probably persuade you of the wisdom of the rite, but only if you could rise above your ethnocentrism and Miner's backward spelling habits. (Look again at the word "Nacirema" if this doesn't make sense.)

If I've presented ethnocentrism as a "bad" thing, there's another side to the matter. As we'll see more clearly in Part Three, reification and ethnocentrism can be functional for society. In general, societies survive best when people keep the agreements making up their cultures, and they're more likely to do that if they believe that their points of view are really true, really the best. But as a sociological orientation cultural relativism works better than ethnocentrism.

Sociology fosters a culturally relative point of view in at least two ways. First, sociology will bring you into contact with so many sets of agreements that contradict your own that you may begin to question the special "truth" of your own beliefs, values, and norms. Second, you will find it difficult to under-

stand how other cultures work if you have the point of view that only your own culture is correct. You will find cultures seemingly based on error after error that function very nicely.

Sociology offers an opportunity for you to look at the world through a variety of cultural points of view. Taking advantage of this opportunity will allow you to understand your own culture even better, allowing you to function more effectively within it. This is equally true if you want to change that culture or just get along smoothly within it.

Social Structure and Agreements

Thus far in this book, we've seen how social interaction results in a collection of agreements that make up a people's shared culture. We've seen, further, how those agreements subsequently affect how people act, think, and feel. But the collections of agreements are more than simple collections. Agreements are directly related to each other in logical and systematic ways.

An agreement that a primitive tribe's survival depends on hunting is likely to produce a view that the best hunter is the most important person in the tribe. An agreement that the gods intervene in every aspect of the tribe's daily activities suggests that the priest is the most important member of the tribe. Either of these agreements, moreover, would probably produce further agreements on how people should act toward the hunter, the priest, and other members of the tribe.

Many of the agreements making up a culture govern behavior by specifying social relationships. Social relationships refer to one person's social "locations" in terms of others. Mother-daughter is an example of a social relationship, and every culture contains some agreements about the ways in which mothers and daughters should interact with one another.

The agreements governing interactions in different social relationships, however, are also more than mere collections. Those agreements are also interrelated. The agreements governing mother-daughter interactions are related to the agreements governing father-daughter interactions, for example.

Social structure is a term sociologists use to refer to persistent patterns of social relationships and the interactions expected in those relationships. The term "structure" reflects the organized character of those relationships and interactions.

In this section, we'll look at the sociological point of view, which allows an examination of social structure. The discussion is organized around the concepts that sociologists use and the links among those concepts.

Status and Role

Everything I've said so far seems to indicate that the agreements making up a culture govern the interactions of *people,* but that's not totally accurate. They specify the relationships among social *locations.* People get involved only because they occupy those locations. In a sense, there are no agreements in your culture specifying how *you* should behave, only how a student should behave, how an American should behave, how a young woman, young man, friend, enemy, son, or daughter should behave. Your behavior is governed by agreements only as you occupy social locations.

Sociologists use the term "status" to represent a social location and the term "role" to represent the behavior that cultural agreements prescribe for a status. Ralph Linton, an anthropologist, defined and distinguished status and role this way (1936:114):

> A status, as distinct from the individual who may occupy it, is simply a collection of rights and duties. . . . A *role* represents the dynamic aspect of a status. The individual is socially assigned to a status and occupies it with relation to other statuses. When he puts the rights and duties which constitute the status into effect, he is performing a role.

A status, then, is a position or a location that a person may occupy. Here are some statuses that are very familiar to you: student, professor, woman, man, old person, tall person, minister, judge, police officer, criminal, Buddhist, employer, Democrat. Any term you might use to describe or identify yourself or someone else is probably the basis for a status.

Ralph Linton 1893–1952 (Field Museum of Natural History, Chicago)

Everybody occupies a very large number of statuses. You might glance through the short list in the preceding paragraph and see which ones you occupy. You might think up some others you occupy. In a sense, your identity—who you are—is the collection of statuses you occupy. I'll have more to say about that in Chapter 5, which is about how you become who you are.

Some of the statuses you and other people occupy are called **ascribed statuses.** You don't have to "earn" them. "Female" is one example of an ascribed status. Your race and your age are ascribed statuses. Probably your nationality is an ascribed status for you, if you were born into it.

Other statuses you occupy are **achieved statuses,** meaning that you have to do something to occupy them. "College student" is an achieved status. So is "professor," and so is "parent."

Whether a status is ascribed or achieved is, many times, a matter of agreement. And those agreements vary from place to place and from time to time. "President of the United States" is an achieved status while "queen of England" is an ascribed one. ("Prime minister" of England is an achieved status.) Not long ago, the following statuses were primarily ascribed by sex in America: police officer, nurse, barber, secretary, engineer, airline cabin attendant. Now these statuses are becoming more a matter of achievement only. The agreements are changing.

Both in Linton's definition of status and in my discussion of it in Chapter 1, it was pointed out that individuals occupy statuses "in relation to other statuses." Most statuses directly imply one or more other statuses. "Wife" implies "husband." "Teacher" implies "students." "Pitcher" implies "catcher" and "batter." The fact of relationship makes possible the dynamic aspect of status, which is role.

If your status is a description of who you *are*, the role associated with that status describes what you

do because of who you are. "Student" is a status. The role of a student is all the things students are expected to do: going to class and to the library, reading, learning, taking examinations, writing papers. Roles are sets of agreed-on expectations we have about the behavior of people who occupy the statuses associated with those roles. The box "Who Is Normal?" illustrates how expectations are associated with statuses.

The statuses we occupy also create points of view. Corporation executives, for example, are expected to earn large profits for their stockholders, while union leaders are expected to get large raises and fringe benefits for their members. It is hardly surprising that they bring different points of view to contract talks.

Who Is Normal?

Psychologist David L. Rosenhan and seven other sane people voluntarily became pseudopatients in mental hospitals. Their experiences led them to conclude that psychiatric hospital personnel cannot distinguish between the sane and the insane and that mental patients are labeled and depersonalized.

To gain admission to the hospitals, the researchers reported hearing voices, but ceased simulating any symptoms of abnormality after entering the psychiatric ward. Despite this, none of the pseudopatients was detected or even questioned, and all were released after an average of 19 days with the diagnosis of schizophrenia "in remission." Pseudopatients' extensive note taking was never questioned and was seen as evidence of their illness. Apparently staff members judged the pseudopatients' roles in terms of their surroundings: Since they were in psychiatric wards, they must be insane. Interestingly, though, it was quite common for patients to recognize the pseudopatients' sanity, some guessing they were, in fact, researchers.

Rosenhan suggests that once a person has been diagnosed as insane, it is expected that he or she will continue to be insane. Mental health professionals may convince family, friends, and the persons themselves to accept the diagnosis. The result may be changes in an individual's self-concept, particularly if reinforced by socialization to the bizarre setting of a psychiatric hospital. The diagnosis may be a self-fulfilling prophecy whereby the individual internalizes and enacts the role of "insane."

Rosenhan suggests that the trends toward community mental health facilities, crisis intervention centers, behavior therapies, and the human potential movement may encourage focus on specific problems and behaviors and may help the distressed avoid being sent to insane places. These people would be labeled as generally crazy rather than as having a specific problem. Rosenhan recommends working to increase the sensitivity of mental health workers and researchers and to improve the quality and quantity of their interaction with patients.

How are ideas of normal, abnormal, sane, and insane relative to cultural norms? What are the advantages of participant-observer studies? The disadvantages? Risks to the researcher?

Source: David L. Rosenhan, "On Being Sane in Insane Places," Science, *19 January 1973, pp. 250–58.*

Some of the roles associated with statuses have developed gradually over the course of many centuries of interaction. Other roles are the results of specific agreements by specific people at specific times. For example, if the president of the United States dies in office or resigns, the vice president is expected to assume the duties of president. That's one of the things we expect him or her to do because of *being* vice president. This expectation was agreed upon by the founding fathers in their drafting of the United States Constitution.

Interestingly, however, the founding fathers did not specify whether the vice president would occupy the status of president or *acting* president. This issue was still unresolved, moreover, when, in 1841, President William Harrison gave his inaugural speech in the rain, caught pneumonia, and died a month later—becoming the first president to die in office. Harrison's vice president, John Tyler, to the unhappiness of many, simply declared himself to be the president, not the acting president. His decision was not successfully challenged, and a new agreement was born.

After discussing beliefs, values, and norms earlier, I cautioned that things were not as orderly as the presentation might make them seem. The same caution should be added to the discussion of statuses and roles.

Since people play many roles, they very often experience what sociologists call **role conflict.** The different statuses you occupy frequently demand conflicting behavior of you. Your role as "friend," for example, may involve going to the movies tonight, while your role as "student" may involve studying, and you experience role conflict in deciding what to do. You also experience role conflict when your parents expect you to come home for their wedding anniversary the week before finals.

Even when your different roles don't conflict, you may experience what sociologists call **role strain.** A single status that you occupy can carry more role expectations than you seem able to handle. The status "leader" very often produces the experience of role strain. So does the status "college student." By the same token, a single status may have conflicting roles. Wives, for example, may have difficulty doing piles of dirty laundry *and* being beautiful, charming, and witty.

Sometimes role conflict can be resolved through compromise: You fly home for the *day* of your parents' anniversary, for example. Often, however, you must choose between one role and another, choosing to keep one set of agreements while violating another. In extreme cases of role conflict or role strain, you may resolve the situation by choosing to leave the status you occupy. If you find you simply cannot keep all the agreements expected of a college student, you may drop out.

Violating the role associated with a status while still occupying the status can have a variety of consequences. You may find yourself removed from the status against your will. Or, you may find yourself participating in changing the roles associated with statuses. This happened in 1955, for example, when a black woman in Alabama chose to violate the agreement that persons occupying the status "black" should give up their seats on the bus to persons occupying the status "white."

Social Organization

From a sociological point of view, the statuses you occupy and the roles associated with those statuses describe who you are, and they have an important effect on what you do. Status and role have another function for sociologists. They make it possible to understand how social interactions are organized.

Social organizations—a factory, for example—are composed of statuses, and they operate through roles associated with those statuses. "Lathe operator" is a status you might find in a factory, and the role associated with that status describes the ways a lathe operator is expected to behave. The role describes agreements regarding interactions with other lathe operators, with foremen, and other statuses in the factory.

Or consider the structuring of families—more specifically, for example, the relationships between husbands and wives. All societies have agreements about how husbands and wives relate to one another, yet they differ from one society to another. In traditional Japanese and Chinese cultures, for example, wives were extremely submissive in their relations to their husbands. The husband in those societies was

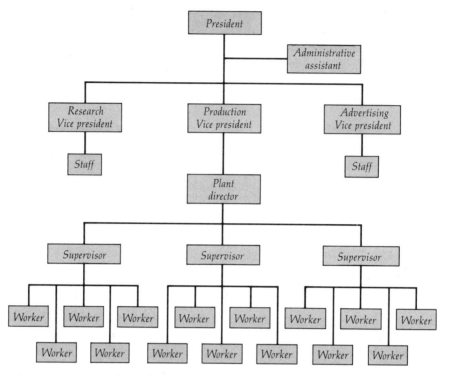

Figure 4•1 A chart of organization. The titles in the chart represent statuses. The lines connecting statuses represent roles, the behaviors expected of workers in their interactions with supervisors or the behaviors expected of supervisors in their interactions with workers, the plant director, or others.

clearly the lord and master of his family. Among the Hopi Indians of the American Southwest, just the opposite was true. Wives totally dominated their husbands. Finally, in contemporary, white, middle-class American families, husband-wife relations are more egalitarian. Despite cultural differences such as these, however, you should note that status relations are structured and organized in all societies.

"Tables of organization" are diagrams of the statuses that make up a formal organization. Figure 4•1 is an example of a table of organization. Job descriptions are examples of the specification of the roles associated with statuses, even though the entire set of expectations making up a role is never fully spelled out.

Institutions

We've seen how some social-interaction patterns are woven together into concrete social organizations

such as a family or a factory. Some aspects of social life may be seen in terms of more general structures called institutions. An "institution" is a relatively stable and integrated set of symbols, beliefs, values, norms, roles, and statuses relating to some aspect of social life. "Religion" in general is an example of an institution. A particular church is a social organization composed of statuses and roles, but religion in general is an institution.

A given family can be regarded as a social organization, but "the family" in general is an institution. A given factory can be regarded as a social organization, but "the economy" in general is an institution. Other institutions of interest to sociologists include education, government, medicine, the military, and science. Chapters 8 through 10 examine some specific institutions in detail.

Institutions are important to sociological analysis since they contain systems of beliefs, values, and norms that govern the activities of specific social organizations. Thus, for example, although no two individual families are exactly the same, the institution of the family in American culture represents broadly shared agreements about what families should be and do. That individual families are expected to provide for the welfare of their young members is a part of family as an institution, even though different individual families do this differently and to different degrees.

The preceding discussion of social structure—including roles, statuses, organizations, and institutions—should have expanded your understanding of the *social-systems* view that we discussed in Chapter 2. Sociologists using that point of view are particularly interested in the functional interrelationships among the different elements of social structure and culture.

Concepts like culture and social structure are relevant to other sociological points of view as well. In the next section, I want to return to a point made earlier in the chapter: No society is totally integrated in the sense that all of its members happily consent to all the many agreements making up their culture.

Cultural Disagreement

Generally speaking, a "society" is a group of people who share a common culture. One of the basic characteristics of a society is that its members share an extensive body of agreements: symbols, beliefs, values, norms, and so forth. From the systems point of view, a society is a large social system with people living in it.

As the term is usually used, a "society" is also a political unit associated with a territory. The nations of the world would be considered societies. A small, preliterate tribe might also be considered a society. An isolated community within a larger society, the Amish in America, for example, might be considered as a separate society for sociological purposes. When sociologists look at a particular society, they are often interested in learning about that society's *generally* shared agreements. In this regard they often speak of the society's "dominant" culture. Thus, for example, when Robin Williams (1959:388–440) examined con-

temporary American society, he pointed to the following dominant values:

1. "Achievement" and "success"
2. "Activity" and "work"
3. "Moral orientation"
4. "Humanitarian mores"
5. Efficiency and practicality
6. "Progress"
7. Material comfort
8. Equality
9. Freedom
10. External conformity
11. Science and secular rationality
12. Nationalism-patriotism
13. Democracy
14. Individual personality
15. Racism and related group-superiority themes

Williams was careful to point out that not all Americans shared the values he enumerated; certainly the values were not shared equally by all members of the society. His criteria for identifying the "dominant" values included: extensiveness (the proportion of people sharing the value), duration (how long the value had persisted), intensity (seen in the severity of sanctions, for example), and the prestige accorded the "persons, objects, or organizations considered to be bearers of the value" (1959:382–83).

Williams's approach to "dominant" values must also be taken with regard to other aspects of a society's culture. We may speak of the beliefs or norms, for example, that are generally shared by members of a society but must realize that there is probably no belief or norm that is shared by *all* members of any society. We can speak of a dominant culture, but we must do so with caution.

Subcultures

In any large, complex society, it is possible to find, in addition to a dominant culture, several "subcultures," sets of agreements shared by specific subgroups in the society.

"Black culture," including black jargon, afro haircuts, black heroes, African dress, and so forth, constitutes a subculture in America today. The hippie

Conformity is not limited to any subculture; agreement within a group is what gives it a special identity, distinct from other groups. (Jeffrey Blankfort, BBM)

movement in America offers another example of a subculture, a special set of symbols, beliefs, values, and norms. There is a small jet-set subculture in America and a poverty subculture.

Subcultures develop whenever people occupying certain statuses in a society have shared experiences quite different from those of others in the society. In the case of immigrant groups, subcultures may merely represent a continuation of their earlier cultures. The subculture of Jewish immigrants to America contained the languages, occupational preferences, religious beliefs and practices, food preferences, and family values that had characterized them in Europe before immigration.

Sometimes the experiences members of a subgroup share make the dominant culture of their

society seem irrelevant or dysfunctional. For people deeply mired in poverty, for example, the values of education, hard work, and thrift seem grossly inappropriate if they have any meaning at all. What hand one's fork should be held in while cutting one's chateaubriand has little relevance for one who has no meat to eat. The box on page 94 discusses one researcher's idea of the "culture of poverty."

Subcultures are composed of agreements that are relevant to the particular conditions experienced by a group of people. Whatever their situation, people create agreements—through interaction—as to what is true, good, and expected.

Sometimes subcultures generally agree with a society's dominant culture; sometimes they disagree. The norms and values of the American Jewish sub-

culture, for example, were in general agreement with the dominant American norms and values. If anything, Jews were harder working and thriftier than others in a nation that generally valued hard work and thrift. On the other hand, in contrast to the general American value on honesty, we may find among some subcultures the value that "breaking the law is all right if you don't get caught." These subcultures range from urban ghettos to the high circles of government and industry.

Whenever elements of a subculture disagree with the dominant culture, we can expect conflict. This may take the form of intergroup prejudice and hostility, negative sanctions levied against members of a subgroup, or, in the extreme, insurrection and civil war.

Cultural Domination

Even though the dominant culture of a complex society often contains elements from its several subcultures, you should not imagine that this is a simple matter of egalitarian democracy. More often, the dominant culture of a society reflects the subculture of a dominant group in it. It often reflects the domination of one subgroup over others, as we discussed in Chapter 2 when we examined conflict theory. Consider, for example, the "elite subculture" described in the box on page 95.

The English language is perhaps one of the most widely shared elements of American culture. Government is conducted exclusively in English, and your participation in government as a citizen depends on

Oscar Lewis and the Culture of Poverty

Anthropologist Oscar Lewis developed the idea that some Western societies have a distinctive subculture, which he called the "culture of poverty." He believed people in this subculture feel disengaged from and do not participate in the larger society, are not organized beyond the family level, have short childhoods in matriarchal families, and feel fatalistic, helpless, dependent, and inferior. He thought the culture of poverty should be eliminated but felt it would be easier to cure poverty itself than to undo the subculture because children are socialized into it early in life. Subculture members are usually unemployed or underemployed, receive low wages, and have little property, so they cannot acquire the resources to break out of poverty's vicious circle.

Lewis emphasized that there are many poor people around the world who do *not* belong to the culture of poverty, who are relatively integrated into the larger society, are socially well organized, and have feelings of satisfaction and self-sufficiency. He believed that the culture of poverty is most likely to develop in free-enterprise, pre-welfare-state, capitalist societies and studied examples of the subculture in Latin America and the United States.

Lewis's research methods centered on observing and interviewing carefully selected rural and urban families (rather than individuals or whole communities). His methods are included in what social scientists call "ethnography," the description of specific cultures. He published accounts of his field research and developed his culture-of-poverty idea in numerous works.[1]

His death at age 55 in 1970 cut short his career and has left others to elaborate on and criticize his concepts. Although his work is widely known and respected, critics[2] have questioned his research methods, suggested that the culture of poverty may be an ethnocentric middle-class stereotype, and pointed out the need for understanding the social characteristics that create class differences and limit choices open to the poor.

Can you identify any people in the United States who might belong to the "culture of poverty"? How might the subculture's "vicious circle" be broken?

[1]Among them: *Five Families: Mexican Case Studies in the Culture of Poverty* (New York: Basic Books, 1959); *Tepoztlan: Village in Mexico* (New York: Holt, 1960); *The Children of Sanchez* (New York: Random House, 1961); *Pedro Martinez* (New York: Vintage Books, 1964); *La Vida: A Puerto Rican Family in the Culture of Poverty, San Juan and New York* (New York: Random House, 1966); and *Anthropological Essays* (New York: Random House, 1970).

[2]Eleanor Burke Leacock, Ed., *The Culture of Poverty: A Critique* (New York: Simon and Schuster, 1971); Charles A. Valentine, *Culture and Poverty: Critique and Counter-Proposals* (Chicago: University of Chicago Press, 1968).

your ability to use English. Education, commerce, and other aspects of American life are conducted almost exclusively in English.

The dominance of English in America was hardly achieved democratically, however. The native Indians, Hawaiians, and Eskimos whose descendants are now Americans didn't speak English. Neither did the Scottish, Welsh, African, German, Irish, Italian, French, Mexican, Polish, Russian, Chinese, Japanese, or other immigrants who came to America. If we were to trace the ultimate national ancestries of all of today's Americans, we'd find that only around 20 percent of us come originally from English-speaking

An Elite Subculture

G. William Domhoff investigated and described a subculture based on status. He suggested that the upper-class elites of America are united by family connections, school cliques, and membership on corporate boards, policy-making organizations, and social clubs. In his research, Domhoff found considerable overlap in membership among six social clubs and three policy-making groups, and he asserted that this overlap is good evidence of the unity of America's ruling class.

According to Domhoff, ruling-class members develop cohesiveness and agreement on issues during interaction in exclusive men's clubs such as the Bohemian Club (especially during the members' annual two-week encampment in the redwoods north of San Francisco) and organizations such as the Business Council, the Council on Foreign Relations, and the Committee for Economic Development. Leaders in business, government, academia, the media, and the arts develop consensus on economic, social, and political policy and try out new ideas on each other before presenting them to the public. Formal and informal in-group communication and interaction have, in Domhoff's view, led to the development of a distinctive status subculture.

Why might "playing together," relaxing and interacting informally as well as formally, help a group to develop common ideas and agreements?

Source: The Bohemian Grove and Other Retreats: A Study in Ruling-Class Cohesiveness *(New York: Harper & Row 1974); see also "How Fat Cats Keep in Touch," Psychology Today, August 1975, pp. 44–48.*

people. English as an element in the dominant culture, then, represents the domination of one subculture over others in America.

The dominance and domination of the English language in America is no mere "academic" matter. Children raised in non-English-speaking subcultures today do poorly in school, just as their parents do poorly in the job market.

Capitalism is the dominant economic form in American culture. Its persistence through our national history has sometimes involved the suppression, imprisonment, and execution of those Americans who preferred something else. Monogamy (one husband or wife at a time) is the legally required form of marriage in America, and its persistence has involved the suppression (historically) of Mormons and others. And when antiblack discrimination had legal support in America, the persistence of that cultural element required the suppression of those who felt it was wrong.

When sociologists speak of the "dominant" culture in a society, then, you should remember two things. First, the elements of that culture are probably not shared equally by all members of the society. Second, the dominant culture probably represents the domination of one subgroup over others.

Summary

"Culture" is a general term used by sociologists and others in reference to the basic agreements generally shared by members of a society. Culture is what makes societies different from one another. The main elements of culture include symbols, beliefs, values, norms, and artifacts.

As discussed in Chapter 1, people have a tendency to reify their group's agreements, and this may be seen in the case of culture. "Ethnocentrism" is the term used in reference to the view that your culture is "right" and "true" rather than simply different from other cultures. Cultural relativity is the opposite of ethnocentrism.

Cultures are more than mere "collections" of agreements and artifacts. They are "structured," or organized. The various elements of culture are linked to one another in a mutually supportive fashion. Symbols, beliefs, values, and norms specify and justify one another, for example.

The structuring of cultures can also be seen in terms of roles and statuses. A status is a position you may occupy in a society, and a role describes how the occupant of one status interacts with the occupant of another status. The linking of statuses in this fashion can be seen most clearly in the case of formal organizations.

Cultures are structured in another fashion as well. "Institutions" are those relatively stable and integrated sets of symbols, beliefs, values, norms, roles, and statuses that govern general areas of social life. Institutions include the family, religion, education, the economy, and government. While the form of a given institution may differ from one society to another, the major ones are present in some form in every society. Every society has some set of agreements regarding family relations, even though the agreements may differ.

The terms "society" and "culture" are often used in defining each other. A society is a large group of people who share a common culture, while a culture is the system of agreements shared by the members of a given society.

References to a society's culture usually imply a "dominant" culture, since virtually no agreement is shared equally by all members of a given society. The dominant culture is typically the one shared by most members of the society.

All large, complex societies contain "subcultures," the agreements shared by members of subgroups within the larger society. Subcultures sometimes reflect the cultural origins of immigrant groups; sometimes they reflect a shared experience or condition in the larger society.

Subcultures may agree or disagree with the dominant culture of a society. When they disagree, however, conflict is likely, ranging in expression from prejudice to war.

The dominant culture of a society usually reflects the domination of one subgroup over others. Thus, the dominant culture of the whole society is often the subculture of a dominant subgroup. Powerful subgroups impose their agreements on less powerful subgroups.

Suggested Readings

Liebow, Elliot
1967   *Tally's Corner: A Study of Negro Streetcorner Men.* Boston: Little, Brown.
This very readable account of aspect of black subculture in America shows patterns of day-to-day interactions against the backdrop of interrelated subcultural agreements. Liebow's humanistic portrayal of life in the blighted inner city (Washington, D.C.) illustrates one of the ways people create a set of social agreements appropriate to the situation they find themselves in.

Parsons, Talcott
1951   *The Social System.* New York: Free Press.
In spite of its being difficult reading, this book is the classic statement of the social systems view of the interrelationships among sociocultural agreements. Parsons examines the many components of social structure and their connections with one another in forming an integrated whole.

Roszak, Theodore
1969   *The Making of a Counter Culture.* New York: Doubleday.
Growing out of the protest movement of the 1960s, Roszak's examination draws attention to those aspects of contemporary American culture that were the targets of opposition and reform. It highlights a number of fundamental issues regarding human social existence that lie, often hidden, behind particular cultural forms.

Sapir, Edward
1924   "Culture, Genuine and Spurious." *American Journal of Sociology* 29:401–29.
The sociological view of culture derives largely from the research and writings of anthropologists, since the study of very foreign forms of social life draws attention to the most implicit agreements in our own culture. This classic discussion of culture by a great anthropologist remains insightful and useful for those just approaching sociology today.

Episode Four

The weather was dismal in Chicago Wednesday, June 28. It had rained for several days, and the morning forecast offered no hope for early change.

Gabe stood on Lake Shore Drive, the wind beating beads of water into his neck and face. Tugging at his jacket collar, he tried to hail one of the city's fewer and fewer cabs. In his left hand he carried a small brown suitcase. He kept his head lowered, in defense against the stinging rain and also to lessen his chances of being recognized.

He had called in sick to Chicago National, complaining of a summer cold. He had told Monica he must leave town on business. He would not risk being recognized.

A taxi stopped. "Lake Hospital," Gabe announced abruptly, sliding into the back seat, his head lowered. Hidden beneath his jacket was a sling used to carry very young babies.

Once in the hospital lobby, Gabe located a rest room. He entered, locked himself inside a toilet stall, and opened the suitcase. He pulled a mustache from the case, positioned it above his lip. He smoothed a light-brown wig over his own dark hair. He removed the blue jacket he had been wearing and replaced it with a tan one. Having stuffed the blue jacket into a waste bin, he closed the suitcase and left the rest room.

At a flower stand in the lobby he purchased a bouquet. Near the elevator door he scanned the directory posted on the wall. "Maternity," he read, "2." Gabe entered the elevator and pushed the button for the second floor.

"Suppose you get caught," he asked himself repeatedly as he had done since the night Larry called.

The elevator door opened; Gabe was on the second floor.

A nurse approached. "You look lost," he smiled. "May I help you?"

"My wife just had a baby," Gabe said. "I haven't seen him yet. Which way is the nursery?"

"Congratulations," came the response. "Just down the hall to your left."

Gabe walked along the hall that the nurse had designated. When he approached the windowed nursery, he observed a nurse attending the infants. He noted the closed door into the room and positioned himself so that he could peer through the glass window and also stand as near as possible to the door.

He scanned the identification tags at the foot of each bassinet. In the row nearest him he spotted what he was looking for: "Decker," the tag read, "male; 7 pounds, 5 ounces."

"And he's near the door," Gabe thought. "This was meant to be."

Gabe turned, searching for a stairwell. He knew there had to be one; it was mandatory due to fire regulations. At the end of the hallway he spotted a metal door, marked "EXIT." Casually he walked toward it, opened it, saw that it led to a stairway and that the stairway exited onto an outside street two flights below. He returned to his previous position at the nursery window.

The attendant had begun systematically to change diapers. She began at the far side of the room and, as Gabe watched for several minutes, he noted that often, for as many as ninety seconds, the attendant's back was turned toward him. It would be possible, he considered, to open the door, grab the Decker child, and escape down the back stairway without being seen. If the attendant continued to work systematically around the room, she would not look directly into the Decker crib for almost fifteen minutes.

Gabe waited. Again he counted the seconds during which the nurse kept her back to him.

The attendant finished changing a baby, patted it on the bottom, and moved to the next. "It's time now," Gabe told himself. "Do it."

Slowly he opened the door. Tiptoeing into the room, he scooped up the Decker infant, placed his hand over its tiny mouth so as to muffle a possible wail, and moved quickly from the room.

Once in the hall he dropped the freshly cut flowers into a drinking fountain and dashed toward the stairway. In the sling over his left shoulder Gabe smuggled the baby, partially hidden under his jacket. In his right hand he clutched the suitcase.

Gabe entered the enclosed fire stairway and hurried down the steps. He was unconcerned now with the infant's crying; he would be on the street in seconds.

He shoved through a heavy, metal door to the outside. It was still raining. Unseen, Gabe darted across the street into the rear rest room of a deteriorating service station, locking the door behind him. There he removed the mustache and flushed it down the toilet. He jerked the wig from his head, opened the suitcase, and carefully set the baby down on a brown sweater which he had earlier crumpled inside it. His arms free now, he lifted the cover from the toilet tank and removed the tan jacket he was wearing. He stuffed the jacket and wig into the toilet tank, stepping aside so that the dispersed water, spilling onto the grimy floor, would not soak his shoes. With one foot he gently shoved the suitcase aside so that it would not be wet by the overflow from the tank.

Gabe reached into his pocket and found a comb. Squatting to peer into the small, cloudy mirror which hung precariously on the wall, he combed his hair.

The baby had begun to cry. He picked it up and soothed it. From the suitcase he pulled a baby bottle filled with milk and offered it to the child. Still holding the infant, Gabe later pulled the sweater from the suitcase and put it on.

He knelt beside the open suitcase, balancing the quieted infant upon his knees. From the suitcase he pulled a flannel blanket and a heavier one of waterproof material. He wrapped the baby in the flannel comforter, then folded the bundle into the waterproof shield. He took a pacifier from the suitcase and placed it in the baby's mouth.

Gabe reclosed the case and stood, replacing the child in the sling against his shoulder. With his right hand he pulled several paper towels from a dispenser and wiped his fingerprints from the handle of the emptied case. Then with his foot he wedged it between the toilet stool and the rest-room wall. Gabe shoved open the door and with the infant walked outside.

Again on the street, Gabe boarded a bus to Shore Towers, using the parking garage elevator to get to his apartment. There he changed into a gray business suit. He diapered the infant, then laid it on his bed under the glare of the fluorescent tubes. "You'll feel better shortly," he soothed, "I promise."

He poured himself a cup of coffee. "Damn rain," he said to himself, lighting a cigarette and then immediately extinguishing it.

He returned to the bedroom. The baby had fallen asleep. "We've got to go," he said quietly, working his arms into the sleeves of a full-length raincoat. Gently he scooped up the sleeping seven pounds.

Outside Gabe quickly walked several blocks toward a Loop hotel. The rain was coming down harder now, and Gabe shielded the infant beneath his raincoat. In front of the hotel the two boarded a bus for the airport.

Seated toward the rear, Gabe looked closely into the infant's vulnerable face, then leaned to kiss its forehead. "Soon," he said, "everything will be okay. In just a few hours you'll be home."

The three sociologists followed their guide through a glass-enclosed walkway to a waiting solarmobile. "We do not encourage visitors from the outside." Alexander's tone was cold. He opened the rear door of the readied vehicle. "Consequently," he said, "we have not developed official methods for hospitality. I'm sure you understand."

"Of course," Batterson smiled.

Roanoke settled herself in the solar auto and checked her watch. It was 2:30 P.M. Already, she thought, her colleagues and she had had a long day.

Duncan wiped his forehead. He was hot and hungry. "Excuse me," he leaned forward to address Alexander. "Is there any place near where we might get something to eat? I'm afraid," he added with a forced chuckle, "it's past our lunchtime."

"There are no restaurants in Adamsville," Alexander responded.

"No restaurants?" Batterson asked.

"Eating is a weakness," Alexander said. "To go to restaurants after maturity is against the law."

The vehicle swerved through the small community. Glass sun decks protruded from the west and south sides of each residence. "I'll take you to a liquidhouse."

Sunlight Liquidhouse resembled a tavern. A bartender stood behind a counter. A man of about forty, his skin was moderately green. A large jar of mineral tablets rested on the bar behind him.

"Jake," Alexander said as the four entered, "these ungreens are invited guests of Ruth and Michael. We thought maybe we could get a drink before you close up for the welcoming."

Jake stared. It was apparent he had known nothing of the outsiders' expected visit. He filled four glasses, garnished the drinks with sprigs of parsley, then set the refreshments on the bar. "You're not taking them to the ceremony?" he asked Alexander, incredulous.

Alexander nodded. "On order from Elderhome," he said.

"What are you serving today?" Batterson asked the bartender in an appreciative voice.

"Water. That's mostly all the people want.

Liquidhouse down the way a block or so serves coffee now. Young folks got the notion they like coffee."

"Well, it's got to be the best water I've tasted," Batterson said. "That sun is vicious."

Jake stared at the three ungreens. Alexander shuffled. He seemed embarrassed, anxious. It was as if Batterson had committed blasphemy.

"Well, Jake, see you at the ceremony." Alexander set his glass on the counter and turned to exit. Three somewhat confused sociologists followed.

The ceremony was to take place in the park. A crowd had gathered. Alexander escorted the three toward an elevated platform near the edge of the park.

Sparked by scientific curiosity, Batterson decided that she must ask as many questions of her host as he would allow.

"What kind of ceremony will we see today?" she began.

"A welcoming ceremony."

She could see his answers were going to be brief. "Does Adamsville have welcoming ceremonies often?" she pursued.

"We hold the welcoming ceremony whenever it is appropriate," Alexander replied.

"What is a welcoming ceremony?" inquired Roanoke.

"We are welcoming a green infant," Alexander answered.

"Do you have this ceremony whenever a green is born?" asked Duncan, expecting an affirmative answer.

"No," said their host. "Only when the infant has been rescued from the outside."

"Who bore the infant?" asked Batterson.

"It is not important who bore the infant." Alexander turned his back to the triad.

Batterson was unwilling to curtail her inquiry. "We've noticed," she said after a brief silence, "that Adamsville residents are many shades of green. Why is that?"

"Our children do not look green. The mature citizens of Adamsville look green," Alexander answered.

"But even among the adults," Duncan interjected, "some are very green while others show almost no evidence of chlorophyll in their skin."

"A green is a green, Mr. Duncan. I have difficulty answering your question."

The four stayed away from the center of the crowd. Nearer the platform about thirty mutants lay on the ground, as if sunbathing.

"The ceremony will begin when our rescuer arrives," stated Alexander. "We will wait here quietly."

Alexander removed his shoes, socks, and shirt. He positioned himself on the ground, his face projected toward the sun.

The sociologists searched one another's faces. Batterson shivered, in spite of the heat. "What is he doing?" she demanded of her companions. The others shrugged.

"They *are* different shades of green," Roanoke whispered. "Yet Alexander refused to discuss it."

"Perhaps they themselves don't see it," offered Duncan. "It isn't important to them."

"Or they do see it, even more vividly than we do," Batterson offered, "and Alexander simply refuses to share any information with us."

A limousine came to a halt near the expectant crowd. The mutants began to cheer. "Welcome, welcome, welcome," they shouted in unison. "Welcome to your family. Welcome to Adamsville. Welcome to your home."

The shouting, much like a football cheer, went on for several minutes. "Welcome/welcome/welcome," sang the throng. "Welcome to your family/welcome to Adamsville/welcome to your home."

The door of the car opened. Meanwhile Ruth and Michael Jones-the-Elder had appeared in the doorway of their home. Gallantly they proceeded toward the solarmobile. The crowd continued its chant. Ruth ushered from the vehicle a man who was from all appearances not a mutant. He carried in his arms an infant. The three proceeded to the platform.

"From where was this child rescued?" Roanoke asked Alexander.

"From the outside," came the answer.

"Who bore the child?"

"An outsider."

Roanoke cleared her throat. She had forgotten her hunger. "Then the infant is not a green?"

"The infant is a green, the son of a green father."

"Then the infant is half green?" Roanoke pursued hesitantly.

"The infant is green," insisted Alexander. "A green's chromosomes are always dominant. It is right that the infant be raised in Adamsville because he is green."

"Who is the rescuer then?"

Alexander did not reply. The crowd had ceased its chant. All eyes focused on the platform. There the normal-appearing man, evidently the rescuer, stood with the infant still in his arms. He was flanked now by Ruth and Michael Jones.

The rescuer approached the microphone. "I have saved the life of this infant boy," he began the ritualistic litany.

"You have saved the life of this infant boy," returned the crowd.

"Born of green, he is green," the rescuer called. The crowd repeated the decree.

"Greens, raised outside, die," led the rescuer.

"Greens, raised outside, die," the mass replied.

A stillness ensued. The rescuer placed the infant into the arms of Ruth Jones-the-Elder. A band began to play. Michael Jones approached the microphone.

"Ladies and gentlemen," he said, "we welcome today not only an infant, but a hero. Gabriel Knapp, gone from us for so long, has today demonstrated his loyalty."

The crowd responded with the now-familiar cheer: "Welcome/welcome/welcome . . ."

Roanoke searched her mind. Gabriel Knapp. The name sounded unnervingly familiar.

Questions

1. A culture is the collection of agreements that a people share. What are some of the agreements shared in Adamsville?

2. What are some of the beliefs, values, and norms composing green culture? How are they related to one another?

3. How does the belief that a green's chromosomes are always dominant dictate a value? What value?

4. What are some examples of ethnocentrism in the greens' view of outsiders?

5. What are some examples of *your* ethnocentrism that are becoming apparent as you learn more about the greens?

5

Socialization:
Learning the Agreements

William James once described the world of the newborn baby as "a blooming, buzzing confusion." Jean Piaget's extensive observations of newborns seem to support that view, leading him to conclude that "in the first weeks of life the universe is [not] really cut up into objects, that is, into things conceived as permanent, substantial, external to the self and firm in existence . . ." (1954:5).

It would appear that you and I came into this world making no distinctions between ourselves, our bodies, and the rest of our environment. We apparently experienced an undifferentiated reality in which our own arms, legs, and cries were no less a part of the whole than walls, cribs, parents, and the sound of a truck passing by. We certainly did not share the symbols, beliefs, values, and norms of those around us—but we learn.

"Socialization" is the process by which people learn the agreements of the group. It has two key functions. First, through socialization individuals gain social identities, their sense of self as discussed by Mead and as reported in Chapter 2 of this book. Second, socialization is the process through which a society's agreements are transmitted from one generation to the next. We're going to examine both of these functions in this chapter.

Since socialization involves your discovery of who you *are*, I want to begin the chapter with a discussion of the persistent debate over the effects of heredity and environment in personal development. As we'll see, what you are today is a product of both your genetic inheritance and your experiences. The remainder of the chapter will be devoted to an examination of the latter of these two influences.

Socialization and personal development is a topic of special interest to psychologists. Their theories have been influential in framing sociological points of view, and I want to say something about a few of the more prominent ones.

For sociologists, socialization is largely a matter of status and role, two concepts that we have already discussed. We'll return to these once more to see how they shape the sociologist's view of socialization. Then we'll look at some of the mechanisms of socialization and its "agents"—the people and groups who socialize others.

For the most part in this chapter, we'll be focusing on the socialization of children. Socialization is *not* limited to children, however, and later in the chapter we'll look specifically at adult socialization and "resocialization."

The chapter concludes with an examination of the implications of socialization for society. How does it create continuity, harmony, and order, on the one hand, and how does it foster disruption and change, on the other?

Heredity and Environment

One of the oldest debates in the study of human beings has revolved around the relative contributions of hereditary and environmental factors. Is a person primarily the reflection of his or her genetic heritage —what he or she was born with—or primarily the reflection of what happens after birth, during the growing-up process? This is sometimes referred to as the "nature-nurture" controversy.

There is truth in both positions, of course. We are inescapably the products of our genetic heritages. Born humans, we cannot simply flap our arms and fly. Many of our characteristics—such as sex, race, eye color—are determined at the moment we are conceived. And if we are born male, we simply cannot conceive and bear children of our own. Some aspects of who we are, then, are clearly a function of genetics, and some of those—race, for example— depend on who our parents were.

We also possess characteristics that are unquestionably a matter of upbringing rather than biology. You were not born speaking the language you now speak, for example. You were not born feeling the way you do now about politics, religion, and sex. Nor did your biological makeup determine how you would turn out in these regards. All these characteristics developed over the course of your growing up and were influenced by your environment. They are a matter of agreements: agreements that were a part of your culture before you were born and agreements that you had a hand in making during your lifetime.

Other aspects of who you are seem to reflect both genetics and environment. Intelligence is a good example of such an aspect. It is illustrative of the interplay of heredity and environment in the development of personal characteristics. Both are important. I suspect that you regard your intelligence as an important aspect of who you are. Take a moment to imagine yourself having an IQ twice as high as you now have. You'd probably be a very different kind of person. Or imagine yourself having an IQ only half as high as your present one. Again, you'd be a very different kind of person.

The interplay of heredity and environment has been demonstrated by studies of IQ-similarity among different pairs of children. A greater IQ-similarity is found, for example, between identical twins (born of the same egg) than between fraternal twins (born at the same time but of different eggs). Even those identical twins who were raised apart in different families had greater IQ-similarities than fraternal twins who were raised together. This would point to the influence of genetic factors and heredity (Erlenmeyer-Kimling and Jarvik 1963).

Studies of foster children, however, point to the importance of environmental factors. These studies (for example, Erlenmeyer-Kimling and Jarvik 1963, Jones 1946) show IQ-similarities between children and parents who are biologically unrelated to one another. Genetics aside, then, children raised by high-IQ parents tend to have higher IQs than those raised by low-IQ parents. Intelligence can only be a product of *both* heredity and environment.

The question of which personal characteristics are more a matter of genetics and which more a matter of environment is subjected to continuing research, and new discoveries are being made continuously. Most researchers at this point would agree with the statement "We are born with certain genetic limitations and potentials, and environmental factors determine the extent to which we realize our potentials."

As we turn now to the first function of socialization, the creation of social selves, we are going to focus only on environmental factors. The sociological point of view sees who you are as a function of your culture and your experiences within it. Sociologists do not deny the influence of biological factors; they simply deal with the environmental side of the coin.

The Creation of Social Selves

How do you become the person you feel you are? The sociological answer to this involves your culture and the social experiences you have within that culture. Psychologists have taken a similar view, and many psychologists have been influential in the development of sociological points of view. Let's begin, then, by looking at how some influential psychologists have seen the matter.

Sigmund Freud

Sigmund Freud (1856–1939) was an Austrian neurologist and physician who is best known as the founder of psychoanalysis (Freud 1909). Early in his professional career Freud became particularly interested in the study of hysteria.* Hysteria was a fairly common mental disturbance in Europe during Freud's time, one that frequently had no discoverable, physiological cause.

The further Freud probed into patients' minds, the more aware he became of a bizarre mental life previously unknown. He found that patients had countless thoughts and memories that were hidden below the surface of their conscious awareness. In particular, Freud became interested in those childhood experiences that had been hidden in the dark recesses of what he began calling the "unconscious." Increasingly, he found "repressed" sexual desires and fantasies to lie at the base of adult emotional disorders. Making patients aware of those repressed thoughts and memories, moreover, often alleviated their disturbances. But why, Freud asked, had such thoughts been hidden and repressed in the first place?

Freud eventually came to regard personal development as a struggle between two powerful forces. One of these forces was made up of the pleasure-seeking drives and instincts that all humans share, including the pleasure of being nursed at the mother's breast and other bodily pleasures. Freud referred to this aspect of the individual, representing all the inborn tendencies to seek pleasure, by the term "id." Set against this inherent tendency to seek pleasure were the demands of society.

Freud recognized that societies could not survive if all individuals followed their pleasure-seeking instincts without restraint. Thus, Freud suggested, each individual also had a "superego." The superego was an internalization of all the beliefs, values, and norms that ensure group survival.

What Freud (1927, 1930) saw as a continuing combat between the individual and society, he also saw internalized within each person as the id and the superego. Mediating between these powerful

Sigmund Freud 1856–1939 (Snark International)

forces and influenced by them was the "ego," Freud's term for what George Herbert Mead (whom we discussed in Chapter 2) called the "self": your sense of who you are.

Freud's psychoanalytic theory, then, offers one view of the influence of society in the development of individuals. We'll return to the combat between the individual and society in Parts Three and Four.

Erik Erikson

A somewhat happier picture of ego development has been presented by one of Freud's most prominent students: Erik Erikson (1902–). In Erikson's view (1963), development occurs over the course of several stages. In each of the stages the ego faces a crisis.

In the first stage of development—in earliest infancy—the child must develop a sense of hope that

*Hysteria is a psychiatric condition characterized by emotional excitement, excessive anxiety, or such physical disorders as blindness or deafness.

Jean Piaget 1896– (Swiss National Tourist Office)

forms a foundation for all later development. This sense of hope grows out of the basic trust that the infant may develop in regard to its parents. Parental responses to the child can either foster trust or hinder it, promoting a sense of basic mistrust.

In succeeding stages of development, the child may develop a sense of autonomy (versus shame and doubt), initiative (versus guilt), industry (versus inferiority), and, in the fifth stage of development, identity (versus role confusion). Erikson says of the fifth stage (1963:261): "The sense of ego identity, then, is the accrued confidence that the inner sameness and continuity prepared in the past are matched by the sameness and continuity of one's meaning for others."

With the onset of adolescence, we pull together the lessons and discoveries of childhood to form a picture of who we are, a picture that we compare with the pictures other people seem to have of us. The fifth stage is a difficult time, however, since it is also a period of significant physiological and social changes. In this stage we may be thrown into confusion.

The crisis faced during young adulthood, the sixth stage, in Erikson's view, is one of intimacy versus isolation. Having established our*selves* as individuals, we enter into intimate relationships with others or remain apart. Largely, this stage centers on the formation of love relationships, and young adults must balance the risk of being hurt in making a commitment to a relationship against the lonely protection of refusing to make such commitments.

In the next stage, spanning young adulthood and middle age, Erikson speaks of the crisis between generativity versus stagnation. Generativity includes the ideas of productivity and creativity, including the production of new generations of children. At the final stage of old age, Erikson sees a crisis involving ego integrity versus despair. This is a time when a person reviews his or her life and prepares for death. Such a review may produce a sense of value, worth, and kinship with past generations, or it may result in "the feeling that the time is now short, too short for the attempt to start another life and to try out alternative roads to integrity" (1963:269).

Let's turn now to a rather different psychological view of how selves develop. In contrast to the psychoanalytic views of Freud and Erikson, the next one to be examined centers on cognitive development: how children learn the nature of the physical and social reality into which they are born.

Jean Piaget

As I mentioned at the outset of this chapter, Jean Piaget (1896–) is an internationally renowned child psychologist who has spent his career in direct observations of child development. In large part, Piaget is concerned with how children learn to understand the physical and social world.

According to Piaget's research on newborn babies, we begin life with absolutely no sense of our selves. We begin as observers of a multidimensional motion picture, having no sense of the distinction between the observer and the observed. As Piaget suggests (1954:xii), newborns are ironically self-centered for ones with no sense of self: "It is precisely when the subject is most self-centered that he knows himself the least, and it is to the extent that he discovers himself that he places himself in the universe and constructs it by virtue of that fact."

To find out who you are, then, you must separate yourself from your environment, and Piaget has examined the process through which this occurs in detail. Much of his research centers on the manner in which children learn the nature of physical reality: learning, for example, that objects don't really disappear when they are out of sight. Similarly, children must learn the relationships between objects and the environments in which those objects exist.

During the first stage of development, children have difficulty learning the concept of individual people separated from their contexts. Children do not automatically equate "Mother in the kitchen" with "Mother in the bedroom." Piaget notes in this regard the trick adults sometimes play on young children, saying, "Go up to my room and see if I'm there." Young children often fall for this, not recognizing that the person talking to them is the same one they are being sent to look for.

During the intuitive stage (from two to seven years), children expand their understanding of the physical and social worlds, influenced by their growing ability to communicate with others through language. Increasingly, they experiment with the points of view of others, although they often do so clumsily.

As Foss reports (1973:19):

> One of Piaget's earliest and most useful concepts is that of egocentrism in thinking—an inability to see the world from anyone else's point of view. Egocentrism of most kinds extends well beyond the fifth year. A child is asked how many brothers he has. "Two, Paul and Henry." And how many brothers has Paul? "One, Henry."

Eventually, children develop a greater ability to take on the point of view of others, making it possible for them to see themselves the way others would see them. Ironically, as Piaget suggests, young children are too egocentric to discover their egos. Initially, they see the world so totally through their own point of view that there is no way for them to recognize the existence of the person standing behind that point of view.

Notice how closely Piaget's studies of children mirror George Herbert Mead's theory of self-development as discussed in Chapter 2. We discover ourselves by taking the role of the other, eventually developing a sense of the "generalized other"—how we are seen by other people in general.

Charles Horton Cooley

The notion of the "generalized other" in reference to the development of self was elaborated by one of Mead's colleagues at Chicago: Charles Horton Cooley (1864–1929). Cooley suggested that those around us act as mirrors, providing us with a reflection of ourselves. He called what an individual sees in such a mirror **the looking-glass self.**

> A social self of this sort might be called the reflected or looking-glass self:
> "Each to each a looking-glass
> Reflects the other that doth pass."
> As we see our face, figure, and dress in the glass, and are interested in them because they are ours, and pleased or otherwise with them according as they do or do not answer to what we should like them to be; so in imagination we perceive in another's mind some thought of our appearance, manners, aims, deeds, character, friends, and so on, and are variously affected by it.
> A self-idea of this sort seems to have three principal elements: the imagination of our appearance to the other person; the imagination of his judgment of that appearance; and some sort of self-feeling, such as pride or mortification (Cooley 1902:184).

If others regard you as beautiful, you come to have that same regard for yourself. If others see you as a thief and a scoundrel, you take on that self-image. In this view, then, who you think you are is a matter of who you think other people think you are.

To empirically test this view Miyamoto and Dornbusch (1956) undertook a study of the self-conceptions of several groups of college students. Each student in each group was asked to evaluate

himself or herself in terms of (1) intelligence, (2) self-confidence, (3) physical attractiveness, and (4) likableness.

Since all the members of a given group (sororities and fraternities) knew each other, every person was also asked to evaluate all the other members of his or her group in terms of the same four characteristics. Then they were asked to guess how their group would evaluate *them.*

The researchers compared individuals' self-images with their perceptions of group evaluations and with the group's actual evaluations. In the majority of cases, students correctly perceived how their group saw them. Their self-conceptions corresponded closely with the group evaluations as well, thereby supporting the notion of the looking-glass self as a source of self-identity.

In his autobiography (1965), Malcolm X told how, since he got better grades than any of the white students in his class, he had come to regard himself as a bright student. He began thinking he would become a lawyer. To his great disappointment, he found that even a trusted white counselor saw him primarily as a "nigger" and encouraged him to pursue a trade as a carpenter. Malcolm X found his looking-glass self directly contrary to his growing sense of

self. Individuals can also rise above their looking-glass selves to break and finally change the agreements they find around them.

The ideas of "generalized other" and "looking-glass self" point to the critical role other people play in your development of a self-image, a sense of who you *are*. At the same time, they can make matters seem too simple. Actually, none of us has *one* self-image that sums up all that we think we are. As William James (1842–1910) observed, a person has "as many social selves . . . as there are distinct groups of persons about whose opinions he cares" (1890:294). Let's turn now to this more complex state of affairs and the ways in which sociologists view it.

Status, Role, and Identity

Introductory sociology students are often asked to complete an exercise that requires them to give ten or twenty answers to the question: "Who am I?" (Kuhn and McPartland 1954). They give a variety of answers, as you might imagine, and many of their answers are like the following: a student, a woman, a Japanese-American, a Jew, an athlete. When strangers meet at a party, they often begin their conversations with the question "What do you do?"

From a sociological point of view, then, you might see yourself—your social self, that is—as the collection of statuses you occupy. Recall from Chapter 4, however, that the statuses you occupy only have meaning in terms of other, complementary, statuses. You can't be a parent without children, for example, or a teacher without students.

Your social self, in terms of your statuses, is a function of your interactions with people occupying complementary statuses. The people occupying those statuses constitute countless looking-glass selves for you. Robert Merton (1957) has used the term "role set" in reference to those complementary statuses. Figure 5•1 is a graphic illustration of a person's social self as defined by the statuses that person occupies and the role sets that give those statuses meaning. The circles represent statuses, while the lines connecting statuses represent the actual and expected

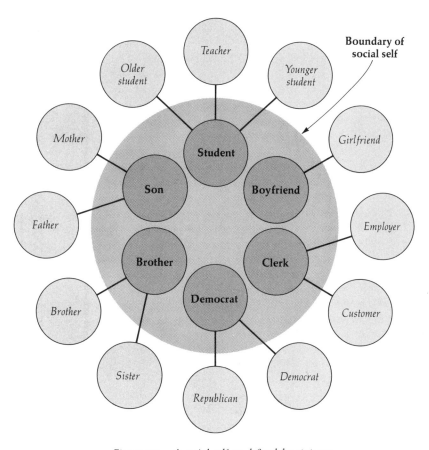

Figure 5·1 *A social self as defined by statuses.*

behaviors between specific pairs of statuses. The large circle encloses the set of statuses that constitute the person's social self.

The lines connecting statuses represent the roles that define and condition the interactions between those statuses. If you are a student, there is a set of agreements relating to the interactions between students and teachers. The ways you are expected to behave in interactions with your teacher are a part of who you are, also. "You" are a person who is respectful to teachers and obeys their instructions, for example. The link between status and interaction is further illustrated in the box on page 111 "Who Talks in Committee Meetings?"

Your social self, then, is largely a matter of the social web spun out of the statuses you occupy and the roles you play. Cooley made the case for this point of view in 1902 when he wrote that "individuals" as well as the groups they belong to were "an abstraction unknown to experience." He elaborated on the point as follows:

> "Society" and "individuals" do not denote separate phenomena but are simply collective and distributive aspects of the same thing.
> . . . Through both the hereditary and the social factors in his life a man is bound into the whole of which he is a member, and to consider him apart from it is quite as artificial as to consider society apart from individuals (pp. 1–3).

Figure 5·2 presents this sociological view graphically. Despite its apparent complexity, the illustra-

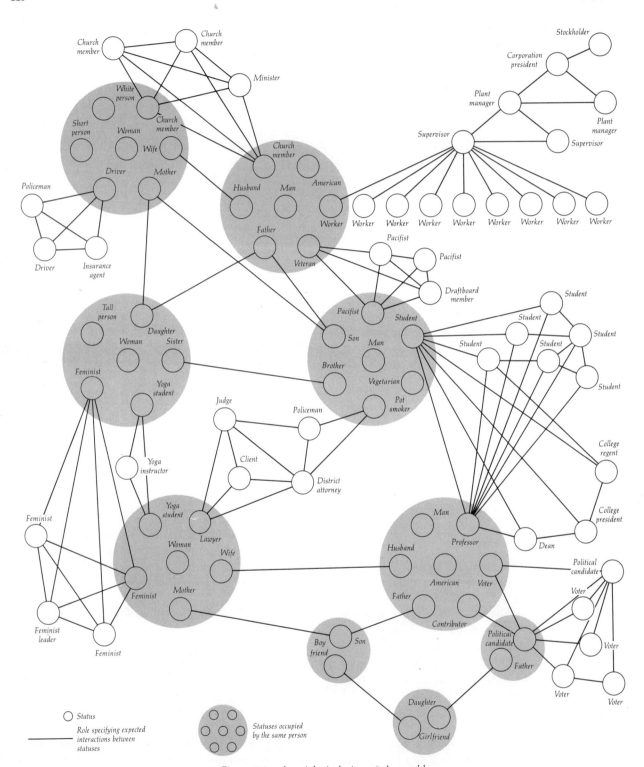

Figure 5·2 A sociological view of the world.

tion is a gross oversimplification of the way things are. Its purpose is to give you a picture of how statuses and roles can be seen to constitute both individual selves and social organizations.

Each of the small circles in the figure represents a social status, and the lines connecting statuses are roles defining the interactions between statuses. Larger shaded circles denote collections of statuses we would normally think of as individual persons.

The illustration is grossly oversimplified because it presents only a tiny fraction of the statuses and roles that make up the social selves of real individuals. And for any given status, only a tiny frac-

tion of the complementary statuses forming its role set have been shown.

Another oversimplification characterizes this discussion. The agreements describing relations between a pair of statuses are never as explicit and precise as I may have implied. To pursue an example already introduced, you may disagree about students' respecting and obeying teachers. Regardless of how you feel about it, it's clear that not all students and not all teachers share your view. The mere fact that you occupy the status of student, then, doesn't totally determine how you behave in relation to others. Other factors complicate matters still further.

Who Talks in Committee Meetings?

Sociologists have long been interested in the relationship between a person's social status and how he or she interacts with others. Research into this issue has been conducted for at least the last forty years. In theoretical research programs sociologists have focused on developing theory and conducting experiments that analyze how people in small problem-solving groups, such as juries and committees, develop opinions of each others' abilities and how these opinions affect the interaction.

According to researchers, people who come together for the first time in informal task-oriented groups develop a hierarchy according to their statuses or, if they have about the same age, sex, occupational, and educational statuses, according to their relative abilities to perform the group's task. Committee members try to identify each others' competencies and rank each other accordingly. The highest-ranked group members are given more opportunities to talk, and others tend to defer to their opinions. If all members care about the goals or tasks of the committee, they want to find who is best equipped to provide information and solutions. Role differentiation, including choice of group leaders, may be based on group members' abilities, or if no information about abilities is available, on group members' social statuses.

Strodtbeck, James, and Hawkins[1] conducted an experiment using mock juries. They found that both sex and occupational status were associated with being chosen as jury foreman and with relative rates of participation in the deliberations. Men were chosen as foreman more often than women, and males participated more in the discussions than females. Proprietors were chosen most frequently as foremen, followed by clerks, skilled workers, and unskilled laborers. The same order applied to rates of participation in the deliberations. Many other studies reinforce the idea that "status organizes interaction."

The next time you work in a small problem-solving group such as a class discussion group, a committee, or even a sports team, you might observe whether you organize yourselves and participate according to each others' statuses and abilities.

Can you think of group tasks that would result in women being chosen as group leaders more often than men? What do you suppose would happen if the women in the mock juries had actively sought the position of foreman? What would the other members have thought of them?

[1]Fred L. Strodtbeck, Rita M. James, and Charles Hawkins, "Social Status in Jury Deliberations," *American Sociological Review* 22 (1957): 713–19.

In your real-life interactions with other people, it is unlikely that you actually limit your behavior or your expectations of the behavior of others to that appropriate to single, specific pairs of statuses. You are likely to respond to several of the statuses another person occupies, and your actual behavior is likely to reflect many of your own different statuses. When you are sitting in class, you may define your relationship with your instructor as primarily one of professor and student. If you are a political liberal, however, something your instructor says or does may strike you as politically conservative, and a part of your definition of the situation takes on a political coloring. Something else your instructor says or does may start you thinking: "What does a woman (man) know about that?" When you finally rise to ask a question, your feelings and actions may reflect several different status relationships.

Very often, the multiplicity of status possibilities creates role conflicts. Suppose you and your best friend are taking an examination together. Your friend quietly asks you for the answer to one of the questions on the exam. One expectation associated with the status of student is that you will refuse to cheat on an exam. One of the expectations of a friend is assistance, however, and you are caught in a bind. In fact, Gregory Bateson, an anthropologist, has called this sort of situation a "double bind." You lose—whatever you do.

Different people occupying the same status have different styles in how they perform the role associated with that status. Whether you are basically relaxed or tense or whether you are basically quiet or aggressive will affect the "kind" of student you are, how you behave as a student. Ultimately, all the statuses you occupy will affect the way you perform the roles associated with individual statuses.

A final complicating factor in the discussion of roles and statuses is that there are disagreements on the roles that ought to be associated with a given status. Even when there is a very broadly shared set of agreements about the behavior expected of those occupying a given status, someone who does not share those agreements may choose to violate them. You may disagree with your instructor on the appropriateness of holding all questions until the end of class and choose to violate the agreement by asking one in the middle. Doing this may subject you to negative sanctions, you may end up changing the agreements, or both.

In summary, then, your social statuses and roles govern your behavior, but not totally. Moreover, the set of statuses you occupy is unique. While you may share each of your statuses with other people—there are other students, for example—and may have several statuses in common with some people, there is no one else in the world who occupies exactly the same set of statuses that you do. Your statuses make your social identity unique at the same time that they weave you into the cultural whole.

Ensuring that you are part of the cultural whole of your society leads to another important function of socialization. I've already mentioned it earlier. Now let's look at it in detail.

The Transmission of Culture

The second major function of socialization is the transmission of culture across generations within a society. In learning those agreements that lie at the base of who you are, you also learn the agreements that make your society what it is.

Some culture learning takes place through formalized instruction, but a great deal occurs in an informal, almost unconscious manner. We are going to look at both kinds of socialization in this section. To do that, I want to organize the discussion around the different kinds of agreements that constitute culture.

Symbols

All symbols are a social creation, and they must be learned. Language is a good example. No child is born speaking his or her "native" tongue. Children are born *hearing* it, however, and they eventually come to understand and use it.

Christian children learn the symbolism of the cross, just as children among the Australian aborigines learn to revere their clan's totemic emblem, the witchity grub. American children learn the national symbolism of the stars and stripes, just as Russian children learn of the hammer and sickle.

Some symbols are learned by observation and imitation, others through formal instruction. Most are probably learned through both modes.

Beliefs

Recall that I've defined "beliefs" as views about what's real and true. A society's agreed-on beliefs are also learned through socialization. As Alfred Schutz (1962:13–14) noted:

> Only a very small part of my knowledge of the world originates with my personal experience. The greater part is socially derived, handed down to me by my friends, my parents, my teachers and the teachers of my teachers. I am taught . . . the system of relevances accepted from the anonymous unified point of view of the in-group.

Sometimes children can learn the beliefs of those around them by merely observing what they say and how they act. Many beliefs are specifically taught—by parents, peers, teachers, and others. That's how children learn about Santa Claus, the Easter Bunny, and the tooth fairy.

Some shared beliefs appear to grow directly out of experience. Young children learn about gravity long before they can be told about it. Every time they get off balance, they get a direct experience of gravity, and they learn a set of behaviors appropriate to it. Only later do they learn about the *concept* of gravity.

It's possible that you are uncomfortable thinking about "real" things like gravity as beliefs that people share. Regardless of whether gravity is real, experience is not a sure test of what is real and what is not real, especially when agreements are involved—and they are always involved.

Centuries ago, people observed that the earth appeared to end at the horizon. Not surprisingly, they concluded that if they reached the end of the earth they would drop off into space. Generation after generation of children were taught the dangers of venturing out to sea, and they believed what they were taught. If history teaches us anything, it is that

beliefs about what's true are continually being overturned and replaced. It can be difficult to regard your own beliefs as simply agreements, however, and each new generation learns the beliefs of its society as hard, cold facts of life.

Values

In Chapter 4, we noted how agreements about what's good or preferred vary from society to society and how the values of a given society constitute an important part of its special character. Sociologists and anthropologists have found some societies to be basically warlike and others more peaceful. Some, like traditional China, have a special reverence for the past, while others, like the United States, are more oriented to the future. Some societies place religious values above economic ones, and others do just the opposite.

Whatever the values of a given society, it is essential to the society's survival that those values be passed from one generation to the next.

Jean Piaget has written (1965), "All morality consists in a system of rules, and the essence of all morality is to be sought for in the respect which the individual acquires for these rules" (p. 13). In his observations of moral learning among children, Piaget concludes there are "two moralities." The first consists of the child's unilateral responsibility to obey adults. Later, however, children adopt a view of morality based more in a sense of cooperation, reflecting a greater degree of individual intention and choice.

Much of Piaget's research focuses on the idea of "responsibility," and probably all societies have some type of value defining the responsibilities and duties of individuals to other members of their groups.

One researcher interested in the moral development of children is Lawrence Kohlberg (Kohlberg and Gilligan 1971). Kohlberg traces six stages. In the early "preconventional" stages, children conform to expected behavior, first out of fear of punishment, then out of a recognition that "proper" behavior can be traded for favors. Not until the third stage (around age thirteen among American children) do they begin associating "proper" behavior with general notions of right and wrong, seeing the values that lie behind norms. By stage four, children are learning specific moral rules, completing what Kohlberg calls the "conventional" level of moral development. In the final, "postconventional," two stages, children (becoming young adults) gain insights into some of the moral disagreements around them, and, finally, develop some notions of universal values such as justice, human dignity, and human rights.

Kohlberg's empirical research on moral development takes the form of moral dilemmas posed to children. Suppose a man needs money to buy lifesaving drugs for his wife and can only get the money by stealing. What should he do? Using typical answers given by children of different ages in different cultures, Kohlberg has been able to describe the development patterns characterizing different countries. All the children studied appear to progress through all the sequential stages, however.

Norms

From the beginning of your life, you began learning about the patterns of expected behavior agreed on by those around you. You did this by acting and by observing the consequences of your actions. During the first months of your life, you began observing events around you and learning from them. You

learned, for example, that crying usually caused someone to come and pick you up. You learned that smiling and cooing when people were around attracted their attention and often resulted in displays of warmth and affection.

As you learned what actions would get you the things you wanted and what actions would get you things you didn't want, you were learning about the role of a baby. You learned, and probably accepted to an extent, the agreements that governed the interactions of babies with other people. You learned how to *play* the role of baby, even though you didn't realize it at the time, and the process of role playing has continued and will continue all through your life.

As a baby you also observed the ways in which other people behaved, not only in relation to you, but in relating to each other as well. You noticed how your parents behaved, for example. Some psychologists (Bandura 1969) feel that much of socialization takes place through observational learning.

Once you gained sufficient skills in moving around, talking, and manipulating things, you began a process of imitation, reflecting what you observed in the behavior of others around you. You began acting out the same behaviors you witnessed in others, most notably your parents. No one is certain *why* children imitate. Piaget, for example, suggests that imitation is a drive in *all* children, simply a given. Other psychologists disagree.

Whatever the reasons for imitation, it is extremely common in children. A father picks up a hammer and pounds a nail, then sees his young child attempt the same act with no understanding of the purpose of pounding nails. A mother may take her child for a drive in the car only to find the child later sitting on the floor making engine noises and steering an imaginary car.

"Role taking" refers to the imitation that reflects a child's acting out of the role behavior of someone else. The term derives from Mead's "taking the role of the other," as discussed in Chapter 2.

Much role taking involves social interaction, as is the case when children play house or cops-and-robbers. On the basis of their observations of how adults occupying their various statuses behave, the children interact in ways they feel reflect the "significant" aspects of adult role behavior. Probably every

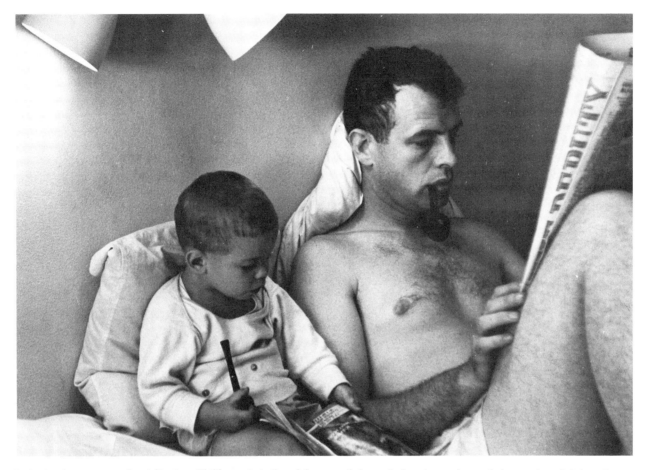

Imitation is one aspect of socialization. Children mimic the adults around them whether they understand the meaning of their actions or not. (Erika Stone, Photo Researchers, Inc.)

parent has been embarrassed on learning what aspects of his or her behavior children consider significant.

Role taking often serves as preparation for role playing. As children we imitate the behavior of the adults we observe, and what we observe and imitate very often carries over into our behavior once we become adults. This phenomenon has many obvious functions. It permits us to grow into statuses gradually by practicing role behavior long before it is expected of us. Observational learning through role taking can also be dysfunctional in that we may not understand the reasons behind what we observe and imitate.

Much socialization involves "selective reinforcement." This term simply refers to the use of positive and negative sanctions, rewards for behaving the ways your parents want you to behave and punishments for behaving contrarily.

Sanctions can take many forms. Positive sanctions, or rewards, include kind words, displays of affection, special treats, money, special privileges, and a variety of other good things. Negative sanctions, or punishments, also vary: angry words, the withdrawal of affection, the withdrawal of privileges and treats, and a whole host of unpleasant things.

B. F. Skinner, a psychologist, has put forth (1953) a theory of all learning that he calls "operant con-

116 Socialization: Learning the Agreements

ditioning." He suggests that all our behavior (as well as that of animals) is conditioned through sanctions.

Sex Typing

Every culture known to science makes some distinctions regarding the roles expected of men and women. Traditionally in America, boys have been socialized to take on occupational statuses, while girls have been primarily socialized for the household statuses "wife" and "mother." And, generally speaking, boys have been encouraged in aggressiveness, while girls have been encouraged to be more submissive. While there have been radical changes in these patterns of socialization in recent years, the old patterns remain strong.

Interestingly, while all cultures make some distinctions between the expected behaviors of men and women, different cultures differ greatly in the distinctions they make. Among the Tchambuli tribe of New Guinea, the kinds of behavior expected of men

and women are just about the opposite of what we expect of men and women in America. Women are dominant, impersonal, and aggressive, whereas men are more submissive and emotionally dependent. Margaret Mead, who studied (1935) the Tchambuli, also studied the Mundugumor tribe and found both men and women to be dominant, impersonal, and aggressive. Among the Arapesh, the third tribe studied by Mead, both men and women were submissive and dependent. The complexity of this issue is further illustrated in the accompanying box on sex-role socialization.

While differences exist across cultures in sex-typed socialization, a few patterns appear to be common, as an examination (Barry, Bacon, and Child 1955) of child-rearing practices in 110 preliterate cultures shows. In those cultures where data were available on training for "nurturance," the quality of being helpful toward younger brothers and sisters and other dependent people, 82 percent taught nurturance primarily to girls. The remainder taught it

---

Sex-Role Socialization

Feminists and others have recently begun to urge that we adopt new styles of sex-role socialization, free of stereotyped notions of femininity and masculinity, and allow people to acquire the traits that best suit them. Some people feel that this androgynous pattern (having both male and female characteristics) might allow people more flexibility in their lives and more potential for self-expression.

Sandra Lipsitz Bem, psychologist at Stanford University, investigated whether sex-typed people are indeed more limited and androgynous people more adaptable.[1] She developed a questionnaire to measure how masculine, feminine, or androgynous a person is and found that of the 1,500 Stanford undergraduates she studied about half adhered to the sex role appropriate to their gender, about 15 percent followed the role of the opposite sex, and

[1]"Androgyny vs. the Tight Little Lives of Fluffy Women and Chesty Men," *Psychology Today,* September 1975, pp. 58–62.

about 35 percent were androgynous. She and others conducted further studies and found that those who followed traditional sex types were more restricted than androgynous people in their behavior. Masculine men did "masculine" things well, such as being assertive and independent, but did not do "feminine" things at all, such as expressing warmth, playfulness, and concern. Feminine women did "feminine" things, but not "masculine" things. Androgynous men and women did nearly everything equally well, regardless of sex-role stereotypes. Bem concluded that traditional sex roles do limit people, although both "masculine" and "feminine" traits are useful to people in our society. She felt androgyny allows people more of the flexibility needed to cope with everyday life.

How could patterns of sex-role socialization be changed to allow people more freedom from sex-role stereotypes? What kinds of people might object to androgyny?

equally to boys and girls. None taught nurturance primarily to boys. In 85 percent of the cultures, as another example, the value of "self-reliance" was taught primarily to boys, 15 percent taught the value equally to both boys and girls, and none taught it primarily to girls.

The Internalization of Culture

Socialization, as the transmission of culture, involves a process called **internalization.** The survival of society and the perpetuation of its agreements is most assured when the new generation of members take those agreements within themselves. Typically, this requires the reification of agreements. Children come to feel that the beliefs shared by those around them are really true, the values are really good, and the behavior specified by norms really proper.

Socialization is most successful when people "feel" the agreements of their society. Suppose you stole something from a store and nobody ever found out about it. Would you feel guilty nonetheless? If you would, that indicates your internalization of the norm against stealing and the value of honesty that lies behind it.

I want to return to the topic of internalization through the reification of agreements at the end of this chapter where we'll look at its implications for social change. At this point, however, it will be useful to consider who is responsible for the socialization that takes place. Who are the socializers?

Agents of Socialization

We have been examining the manner in which a young child is shaped according to the dictates of other people. The child's beliefs, values, behavior, and even self-identity are largely a function of what *others* believe, value, expect in the way of behavior, and see as the child's identity. The impact of socialization you experience as a child stays with you for your entire life.

Who are those "other people" who wield such an influence over you from the time you are born? Who tells you what to believe and value, how to behave, and who you are? The accurate, though perhaps un-

satisfactory, answer is "everybody." Literally everybody around you had a hand in your socialization.

Some kinds of people seem to have more influence than others, however. Let's look briefly at three important agents for socializing children: family, peers, and schools.

Family as Socializers

The members of your family surely had the earliest influence on your socialization. That's not surprising since you spent most of your time with them and were dependent on them for your survival.

When I speak of your "family," I mean the people who brought you up, even if they weren't your biological mother and father. In Chapter 8 we'll look at the variety of family structures that have been agreed on in different cultures. For now, it is enough to know that in some cultures the agreed-on family structure is the *"nuclear* family," a family consisting of a mother, father, and their children. In other cultures, the "extended family" is the norm, with grandparents and perhaps other relatives living with the mother, father, and children. Still other cultures have even different agreements as to the structure of the family.

Whatever your family's religious beliefs, they became yours when you were young. Whatever their language or dialect, it became yours. You learned and shared in their racial prejudices or their lack of prejudices. You learned their version of what love is and how to express it.

You might find it interesting to take just a moment to think about the things you learned from your family that are still "real" for you. You will never totally escape what you learned at home as a child.

Peers as Socializers

Your **peers** are people you know who are like you. They are people who occupy the same status(es) you do. If you are a college student, for example, your classmates are your peers. If you are a professor, your peers are your fellow professors. Since you have many statuses, you have many peer groups, and since you change statuses over time, your peers keep changing also.

The primary peer group for young children is based on age. When you were a child, the other children you knew and played with were your peers, and they had an important influence in your socialization.

Psychologists Mussen, Conger, and Kagan (1974: 515) describe the socializing role of peer groups this way:

> The peer group provides an opportunity to learn how to interact with age-mates, how to deal with hostility and dominance, how to relate to a leader, and how to lead others. It also performs a psychotherapeutic function for the child in helping him deal with social problems. Through discussions with peers the child may learn that others share his problems, conflicts, and complex feelings, and this may be reassuring. . . . Finally, the peer group helps the child develop a concept of himself. The ways in which peers react to the child and the bases upon which he is accepted or rejected give him a clearer, and perhaps more realistic, picture of his assets and liabilities.

After a review of the research that has been done on the influence of peer groups, Boyd McCandless (1969) concluded that peers are more powerful socializers than either teachers or siblings. Only parents are more powerful.

Your childhood peers may be even more important than adults in creating your picture of who you are. Before they learn the agreements as to what may or may not properly be said, children are often more candid reporters of a culture. If you grew up with any kind of defect or peculiarity, for example, it is unlikely that adults told you directly that it was something to be ashamed of, even though they may have felt that way. Your childhood peers would have told you directly that your nose was too big, you were too skinny, or that you were the shortest kid on the block.

Schools as Socializers

Schools are charged with the formal task of passing on many of a culture's symbols, beliefs, values, and norms. Instruction in language and in mathematics is one way two symbol systems are passed from one generation to the next.

Schools also play an important role in the transmission of beliefs. Thus, American schools today teach children that the earth revolves around the sun just as earlier schools taught that the sun revolved around the earth. As we've seen a number of times in this book, agreements about what is true change over time, and the schools have the function of teaching children the current agreements of their society.

In addition, schools transmit cultural agreements regarding values and norms. As is the case with symbols and beliefs, the agreements to be transmitted change. The function of the schools, however, is to assist students in learning whatever agreements exist at a given time.

Schools sometimes reinforce or extend the socialization received in the family. Children begin learning language in the family, for example, and the schools carry language instruction even further. Sometimes, however, schools modify or undo the socialization received in the family. This is likely to occur whenever the family's agreements are different from those of the main culture.

I'll have more to say about schools in Chapter 9, "Religious and Educational Institutions."

Socializing the Socializers

You may recall that I began this section by saying that everybody around you had a hand in your socialization. I'd like to close the section by examining the implications of that statement. It appears that through social interaction everybody is socializing everybody else.

While a mother is teaching her baby what it means to be a baby, the baby is teaching its mother what being a mother means. At the same time your professor is showing you what it means to be a student, you are showing him or her what it means to be a professor. There's a story about a man visiting a dude ranch and asking, "Do you have a horse I can try? I've never ridden before." The answer was, "Sure, try this one. He's never been ridden before, so you can learn together." Socialization is like that in one sense. We are all learning together, from each other. Moreover, socialization goes on forever; it never stops, no matter how old you get.

Peer groups are a powerful socializing agent. They tell us what the agreements are, and they exact a price for disagreement. (Abigail Heyman, Magnum)

Adult Socialization and Resocialization

Socialization happens to adults as well as to children. Every time you interact with someone, you are being further socialized by that person, and you are socializing him or her. When you buy something in a store, you learn just a little more about being a customer, and the salesperson learns a little more about being a salesperson. You may not have noticed it, but your understanding of the role of customer probably changed just a little in the process.

Some societies, like ours, have formal schools for adults. College is a good example of a formal school. A "liberal education" is explicitly designed to put

students in touch with their cultural heritage. Vocational and professional schools are examples of training for specific (occupational) roles. On-the-job training programs sponsored by many large corporations also illustrate socialization into occupational roles.

Military boot camp is a perfect example (if you're not going through it) of adult socialization and **resocialization.** Socialization of trainees involves their being taught the beliefs, values, and norms of the military. Trainees are drilled in the specific behaviors expected of military personnel in various roles. Military training also is an example of "resocialization," the *un*learning of agreements previously learned. Trainees must unlearn many aspects of their civilian socialization. The American civilian value of equality, for example, does not fit well with the military rank structure and the special privileges and duties associated with senior and junior ranks. Interestingly, during the Vietnam war, the military established special programs to resocialize returning veterans:

Adult Resocialization: Becoming a "Surplus Person"

What happens to a person's self-concept and attitudes about society when he or she loses a job and has difficulty finding new employment? According to Dorothea Braginsky and Benjamin Braginsky, they are "surplus people," expendable in society's eyes. Classification as surplus may result in lowered self-esteem and increased alienation, changes in goals, life-style, and expectations, and feelings of depression, insignificance, and cynicism that affect them even after they become reemployed. The Braginskys interviewed forty-six jobless and fifty-three employed men of similar backgrounds and found the unemployed men felt unwanted by a callous society that judges people by their productivity. They found that the effects were most pronounced upon high-status men who lost their jobs suddenly. Although men who were reemployed felt somewhat more useful and regained some of their self-esteem, they remained cynical about society. The Braginskys concluded that the impact of unexpected unemployment can include lasting changes in individuals' concepts of self, society, family, and friends.

Why does society define certain individuals and groups as expendable ("surplus")? What other groups are socially defined as "surplus"? What are the effects of being unwanted on them?

Source: "Surplus People: Their Lost Faith in Self and System," Psychology Today, *August 1975, pp. 69–72.*

The purpose was to reorient them to the agreements of civilian life in America.

None of this is to say that adult socialization and resocialization is always a smooth and harmonious process. Countless soldiers and sailors have refused to accept the agreements of military life. Some have refused to obey orders; others have deserted. From time to time, sailors have mutinied. In some instances, the only result has been the punishment of the "offenders." In other instances, things have been changed. American enlisted men today, for example, enjoy many privileges unheard of a decade or two ago. None of these changes would have occurred without disagreement.

When adults change statuses, their resocialization often includes subtle changes in their points of view. Seymour Lieberman (1963) found this to be the case, for example, in a study of industrial workers. Comparing the attitudes of workers recently promoted to the position of foreman with those of a control group of similar workers, Lieberman found the new foremen to be more pro-management and anti-union.

The effects of promotion on attitudes were even more telling when Lieberman examined long-term occupational patterns. Studying workers' attitudes in three different years, he was able to detect the changing points of view of particular workers. Those promoted to foremen were more critical of the union than they had been before they were promoted. Some of those promoted, however, were subsequently demoted. These became less critical of the union after demotion. The accompanying box on becoming a surplus person describes the consequences of an even more disturbing occupational change.

Socialization and resocialization will follow you to the edge of your grave. Senior citizens learn that many of the behaviors expected of them earlier are no longer appropriate. The elderly couple who get drunk at a party and start dancing wildly are likely to be regarded as a pitiful sight rather than as a happy spectacle of people enjoying themselves. Aging parents may learn that their children no longer expect them to offer guidance on child rearing and would even prefer that they didn't.

I DON'T KNOW WHO OR WHAT THEY ARE—BUT THEY'VE **ALWAYS** HOVERED AROUND ME......!

A person bedridden and near death learns there are behavior expectations for that status that are different from those previously learned. Other aspects of the dying role are strikingly similar to those a young, totally dependent child learns.

Socialization and Cultural Variations

Both as children and as adults, then, individuals are socialized into the acceptance and perhaps internalization of the agreements shared by the groups to which they belong. In the process, the groups' agreements are perpetuated and the individual members develop their own social identities by learning the roles they play in the groups. Since different groups have different sets of agreements, people are being socialized every day into very different points of view, different cultures, and subcultures.

China and the United States have different cultures, so Chinese and Americans are taught different points of view. Upper-class and lower-class Americans have different subcultures, so people socialized into those different subcultures are taught different

points of view. Chicanos and Japanese-Americans have somewhat different points of view in America. Urban and rural people have different points of view, as do people living in the North and those in the South. All these differences and many, many more are reflected in the socialization of different individuals.

The statuses we occupy and the roles we play affect our points of view. So do the specific interactions we engage in. No two people in the world have exactly the same collection of points of view any more than two people have exactly the same fingerprints.

Sociologists are especially interested in studying the points of view that a particular group of people—a nation, an ethnic group, a subculture, a primitive tribe—agree on. Sociologists are also interested in studying the points of view that different groups *disagree* on.

Monogamy, for example, is a widely shared agreement in American society. We tend to feel that every husband should have only one wife at a time and that every wife should have only one husband at a time. This agreement is not universally shared, however, as we shall see in Chapter 8, which deals with the family.

Moslems, for example, feel it is permissible—even preferable—for a man to have several wives, an arrangement called "polygyny." The Mormons during the nineteenth century in America also thought polygyny was desirable, and they put their point of view into practice. As you may already know, the Mormons were severely sanctioned for their disagreement with the agreement on monogamy that was a part of the general American culture.

Here's something you might not know. Only a minority of the world's societies share our American agreement on monogamy. In an examination of 915 societies throughout the world, Gerhard Lenski (1974) discovered, "industrial societies are the only major type in which [polygyny] has never been socially approved. Among preliterate societies, only 13 percent insist on monogamy . . ." (p. 421). This does not mean that a majority of families in the world are polygynous. It does mean, however, that most societies disagree with ours on the value of monogamy.*

In Chapter 4, I spoke of ethnocentrism as the reification of agreements, the tendency to regard our agreements as being *true* rather than merely agreements. It would be ethnocentric to feel that monogamy is "really" the proper basis for a family. From the sociological point of view, monogamy is only one possible agreement that is shared in some cultures and not in others.

Socialization and Social Change

If the preceding discussions have made socialization seem like a force for stability and the perpetuation of the status quo, that's only a part of the picture. In a variety of ways, socialization also produces social change, disrupting and destroying the status quo.

Before World War II, for example, black Americans had been socialized to a set of agreements that placed them in an inferior, second-class status in American society. The need for fighting men, however, was color-blind, and the same demands were made of blacks as of whites. In the military, moreover, blacks were socialized to a greater equality with whites than they had experienced in civilian life. Once the war was over, the socialization to equality couldn't be undone, and the experiences of returning black soldiers were undoubtedly influential in shaping the militancy of the civil rights movement and black power movement that followed.†

Socialization can also result in social change whenever a group's "official" culture is different from what actually goes on in the group. Sociologists often speak of a society's having an "ideal culture" (the *stated* beliefs, values, and norms) and a "real

culture" (the *actual* state of affairs in day-to-day life). For example, many Americans have been personally troubled by the discrepancy between their childhood socialization involving internalizing the stated American value of peace and their later resocialization in terms of the frequent wars we engage in. The peace movement that paralleled the Vietnam war is an example of what can happen when an attempt is made to socialize people into contradictory points of view.

These latest examples notwithstanding, socialization is basically a conservative process. It aims at the perpetuation of agreements, the maintenance of the status quo. Maintenance of the status quo is accomplished, moreover, by building many of those agreements into our very conceptions of ourselves.

We have constructed our societies in such a fashion as to perpetuate what we have constructed. Notice that we are not saying anything about the appropriateness of the perpetuated agreements to the needs, desires, or aspirations of individual members of those societies. As Piaget (1965:13–14) has said,

> Now, most of the moral rules which the child learns to respect he receives from adults, which means that he receives them after they have been fully elaborated, and often elaborated, not in relation to him and as they are needed, but once and for all and through an uninterrupted succession of earlier adult generations.

Summary

Socialization is the process through which people learn the agreements of their group. It has two main purposes. First, it enables individuals to gain their social identities. Second, it permits the perpetuation of the group's agreements across generations.

The socialization process must be seen against the controversy over the relative effects of heredity and environment as determinants of individual development. While the question of these relative effects has not been resolved, it is clear from a great

---

*Since the industrial societies are generally the most populous, it seems likely that the majority of *people* in the world live in societies that demand monogamy. The point, however, is that among all the cultures people have devised in the world, only a minority involve the demand for monogamy.

†The resocialization inherent in wars usually results in social change. During World War I, for example, a popular song was entitled "How You Gonna Keep 'Em Down on the Farm (after they've seen Paris)?"

volume of research that each is important. Sociologists are mostly interested in social environmental factors.

Sigmund Freud, the founder of psychoanalysis, saw individual development as a battle between two forces: the innate drives and instincts of the id and the social agreements internalized in the individual as superego. The result of this combat was the "ego," a term corresponding generally to Mead's concept of self (as discussed in Chapter 2).

Erik Erikson, one of Freud's students, sees ego development as a matter of crises that the individual must face over the course of a lifetime. Erikson has spoken of eight stages of development, in each of which the individual has a critical choice to make. The first stage is characterized by a trust versus mistrust crisis, the last, late in life, by an ego integrity versus despair crisis.

Jean Piaget is another prominent psychologist who, while studying child development, has analyzed individual development at length. Piaget has been interested in learning how children develop their most fundamental understandings of the physical reality around them, how they separate themselves from it—discovering their identities in the process—and how they develop moral senses.

Charles Horton Cooley, a contemporary of George Herbert Mead, extended Mead's concept of the "generalized other" in his discussions of the "looking-glass self," the mirror composed of the views of those around us. The mirror tells us who we are. Subsequent research has confirmed his view that our self-images very much match the images others have of us.

To a very large degree, we learn who we are in the process of learning to occupy statuses and perform roles. We identify and describe ourselves to other people in terms of our agreed-on positions in society. The status of "student" is probably an important part of your image of who you *are*.

The second major function of socialization is the transmission of culture from one generation to the next. As a newborn baby you did not share any of the agreed-on symbols, beliefs, values, and norms that made up the culture of those around you. You learned them, and in the process, your society stayed

the same even though its membership was changing.

Children learn the agreements that make up their culture in a number of ways. In part, they are taught the agreements as a conscious and even formal process. Much learning takes place through simple observation and imitation. Role taking is a way in which children learn the agreements relevant to the statuses of others around them, and they often prepare themselves to occupy those statuses later.

Socialization, in serving the second function, represents an internalization of culture. Individuals take the society's agreements inside themselves, making those agreements a part of their personal makeup. Individuals often keep agreements because it "feels right," quite aside from any fear of punishment for breaking them.

Socialization is carried on by everyone in a society. Everyone socializes everyone else. At the same time, certain people and agencies seem especially important. In the socialization of children, the three most important are family, peers, and schools.

Socialization is not limited to children. All of us continue being socialized (and socializing others) throughout our lives. Adults are resocialized whenever they change statuses, such as in the case of a person who leaves an assembly-line job to become a supervisor. Changes in status and the attendant resocialization is often a painful process for the individuals involved.

Since socialization is a matter of cultural transmission, it stands to reason that different societies pass on different sets of agreements. Even within a complex society, different subcultures may teach different agreements to their new generations.

While the culture-transmission aspect of socialization is basically a conservative process—one of maintaining the status quo—socialization can also be a source of social change. The resocialization of black Americans to greater equality with whites in the World War II military is a case in point. Blacks were unwilling to return to the civilian status quo once the war was over.

Socialization is one of the most important of social processes. Through it, individuals gain social identities, and established social agreements are perpetuated over time.

Suggested Readings*

Erikson, Erik H.
1963 *Childhood and Society.* New York: Norton.
Erikson's classic statement of the eight stages of ego development is cast in a broader context of socialization and its consequences for the individual and society. A number of cross-cultural and individual case studies are presented to illustrate Erikson's view. This is an easily readable, insightful, and important book.

Mead, Margaret
[1928] *Coming of Age in Samoa.* New York: New
1949   American Library.
Often the socialization process is seen most clearly in the case of agreements that are unfamiliar to you. Margaret Mead's classic examination of adolescence and the learning of sexual norms in Samoan society provides an excellent illustration of this assertion. While the problems of adolescence and of socialization are fundamentally the same in early Samoan society and in the modern United States, the manner in which those problems are handled is very different in many respects.

Piaget, Jean
1954 *The Construction of Reality in the Child.* Trans. Margaret Cook. New York: Basic Books.
Piaget is without peer in the careful and detailed observation of childhood learning. In this book, Piaget chronicles the painstaking process through which young children make sense of the physical world in which they live, learning the permanence of objects, causation, movement, and other concepts that adults take for granted.

Skinner, B. F.
1953 *Science and Human Behavior.* New York: Macmillan.
Skinner's view of operant conditioning is one of the most controversial in the current literature on socialization. This report of his research on the power of positive sanctions in shaping behavior among animals lays the theoretical foundation for his more recent and even more controversial book, *Beyond Freedom and Dignity* (New York: Knopf, 1971).

*Brackets indicate original publication date.

Episode Five

Gabriel Knapp was born March 1, 1994, in Nogales, a village along the southern Arizona border. His physical mother was a posing green. Her husband, Gabe's physical father, was Mexican. Gabe remained primarily of his father's complexion and facial characteristics. Yet the chlorophyllic chromosomes of his physical mother had lent an olive cast to his skin.

When Gabe was three months old, his birther noticed that her skin was beginning to turn green. With the aid of two posing rescuers, she fled with the infant to Adamsville. There she contracted the infant to the home of a fellow chlorophyllic, Jonathan Knapp. Gabriel knew nothing of his physical parents. He had never thought to ask. Birthers were, in Adamsville, irrelevant.

Gabriel knew that as a baby he had been rescued from death on the outside. Since a chlorophyllic's chromosomes were always dominant, he was taught only that he had been born a green. Therefore, he had been told from the time he could understand the language of his green parents, it was necessary that he be nurtured as a green.

Furthermore, Gabriel learned early, he owed much to the community that had saved him. The very best thing he might do in appreciation was one day to perform a rescue mission of his own.

And so Gabriel Knapp, from the time he was two years old, had been groomed as a rescuer.

He sat now, July 4, 2026, gazing into Lake Michigan. He had accepted Monica's invitation to her firm's holiday picnic. It had turned into an extravagant yet comfortably casual affair at the lakeside home of one of the firm's senior partners.

Behind Gabe as he stared across the water—but much within his memory—was Lake Hospital. The ungreens around him buzzed over the recent kidnapping, their angry tones pendulum-swinging between disbelief and fear.

Monica Roanoke, sitting beside Gabe, was twenty-eight years old. A year ago she had graduated fifth in her class from the University of Detroit Law School. Today she sought in vain to gain the attention of her preoccupied escort. "Gabe," she asked, "would you like to join the egg toss?"

"Not now," he mumbled apologetically. His thoughts wound back to a game *he* had played all through childhood.

Rescue was the equivalent of cops-and-robbers or cowboys-and-Indians in Adamsville. Children ducked in and out of alleys, galloped up staircases, banged screen doors, and upset trash cans. "I have a baby," one would call. "I have a green baby!"

"Come back, come back," another would chant. "It's mine, it's mine."

"No, no, no, no. It isn't yours," the retort might ring. "It's Adam's. Adam wants his green baby!"

Gabriel had played all the parts. When very young, he had been cast in the role of rescued infant. "You were *really* rescued, Gabriel," the little girl down the street had reminded him. "You be the baby."

And Gabriel would pretend to cry. "I want Adamsville," he would wail. "I want to go home."

As Gabe grew older, he played rescuer. Sometimes he carried a toy pistol, sometimes a rope, occasionally a handkerchief to quiet a wailing birther. Sometimes he carried no weapon at all. But essentially his role was the same: to snatch the wailing infant to freedom, to dignity, to health, to life, to Adamsville.

Gabriel had occasionally played the birther. Sometimes when he played the birther he chased his playmates, the rescuers. Other times he handed the child over with acquiescence. "This baby is sick," he would say. "You can make him well."

"Gabe," Monica interrupted his reverie, "remember what I promised? Real beef!"

Eating, Gabriel considered, was for these people a social occasion. It appeared they put things into their mouths while in the presence of one another as a way of saying "I like you." He would never get used to that.

Gabe looked around him. One of Monica's fellow attorneys was slicing a watermelon. Several from her secretarial pool sat on a blanket devouring fried chicken. Someone had fired a large open grill. The steaks awaited on a nearby picnic table. Sporadically the crack of fireworks startled him. But in spite of all this, it occurred to Gabriel with glaring realism, the Fourth of July was not, to his way of thinking, a *real* holiday.

"Now Adam's Birthday, that was *something*," he said to himself, surprised at the pangs of homesickness he was feeling. He would have liked to talk to Monica about Adam's Birthday. He would have liked to tell her about the green velvet costume he was allowed to wear for the first time when he was twelve—and wore on every holiday thereafter until five years ago when he stopped going back. He would have liked to tell her of his tremendous anticipation—when he was in his teens—for the time when he would no longer need the green costume because his own skin would dazzle with more brilliance than any velvet cloak.

Gabriel jerked. This nostalgia was ridiculous. In the years he had not been to Adamsville, Gabe had nearly forgotten Adam's Birthday, nearly forgotten

his unquenchable teenage thirst for entrance into Adamsville Hall. He had in recent years chosen *not* to participate in the maturing ceremony. They had invited him. "You are green," they had said. "Your skin is olive now. Come home. Mature."

Gabe had witnessed more than a dozen maturing ceremonies while growing up in Adamsville. The rite marked the passage of a green to chlorophyllic adulthood. Under ordinary circumstances the ceremony took place after the greening of a young mutant's flesh. Usually this occurred following his or her return to the colony after a period of posing. Adamsville residents held that every green should mature both physically and ritualistically. They believed that all chlorophyllics should one day wear skin which dazzled in its greenness.

Often, however, a mutant's flesh became—and remained—only dull green. Occasionally a chlorophyllic's skin evidenced virtually no sign of the mutation. Failure of a green's skin to change color was interpreted as evidence of some inner intellectual or emotional disloyalty to the colony. Hence, those whose skin did not attain its potential brilliance—while they were expected to participate in the maturation rite before their thirtieth birthday—often found themselves the victims of considerable discrimination. Upon their return to Adamsville after a period of posing, these "dull" or "less" greens were denied access to prestigious positions and enjoyed little voice in decision making. They were made constantly aware that, because of their evidenced lack of commitment to Adamsville, they were to be trusted and respected only with reservation.

Consequently Gabe viewed an eventual return to the colony with mixed emotions. While once he had joyfully anticipated becoming a true, brilliant green, he knew now that his flesh would never change. Meanwhile he had become accustomed to and even grown to enjoy many elements of life on the outside.

"Cheer up, Gabe," Monica's secretary was saying, "its the Fourth of July!"

"Are you all right, Gabe?" Monica questioned. "You haven't seemed the same since your business trip to Phoenix last week."

"I'm fine," he muttered, becoming aware that

he was rudely ignoring Monica. "I'm just a little tired. I'm sorry."

What she had said was true, of course. The trip had taken him back to a past he evidently could not shed as readily as he had thought. Since the rescue, he had been haunted by memories from his Adamsville childhood.

"Want to claim a steak?" Monica suggested.

"Sure." Gabe had learned to accept eating much as the commuter accepts fighting rush-hour traffic. If he was to live on the outside, if he was to keep the executive office at Chicago National Insurance, if he was to continue with Monica, then occasional social eating was a fact of life.

Gabriel had, of course, from the time of his rescue, taken "supplements." All green babies received supplement, usually milk. But as the children grew older, they drank milk only within the privacy of their homes—and always with the expectation that one day, probably shortly before their maturity, the practice would no longer be necessary. Supplements were, Gabriel learned early, at worst a sign of weakness or disloyalty, at best a sign of immaturity. "Take your supplement now," his soft parent would say, handing him a glass of goat's milk, "before we go out." "Supplement is a private matter," his stern parent would admonish. "You musn't speak of it to anyone."

Now as Gabe placed a piece of meat upon the grill, he remembered an incident which occurred when he was nine. He had gone to school one day as usual. But when the class broke at noon for light-break, Gabe and four classmates became adventurous.

"Let's not go to light-break," Joey, a ten-year-old, had teased. "Let's go for a walk."

The children had walked quite a way before they approached the Adamsville gate.

"We'll get in trouble if we go through," Gabriel had hesitated.

"Oh, come on," coaxed a small girl. "The guard's not even looking."

"What's out there anyway?" someone asked.

"Let's go see," Joey urged, slipping around the gate.

The children skipped along a single-lane road, intoxicated by their mischief. Eventually they approached a combination roadside grocery store and gas station.

"Well, what might I do for you?" asked a rotund clerk, girdled in a white butcher apron.

None of the wayward youngsters responded.

"Aren't you in school today?" asked the grocer.

No one answered.

"How about a piece of chocolate?" he offered.

Gabriel reached to meet the grocer's extended hand. He fingered the strange, foil-wrapped rectangle. He had never seen anything like it before.

"Go ahead," encouraged the man, opening one for himself and thrusting it into his mouth.

Each of the children took a piece of candy. Gabriel could still recall, some twenty-three years later, the sensation as the chocolate touched his tongue.

"Good, isn't it?" the grocer had encouraged.

Gabriel wasn't sure.

"Haven't met a kid yet that doesn't like chocolate. Here, want some more? . . . Go ahead, it's okay. . . . Here, honey, have another piece. Isn't it good?"

The children had departed the strange establishment licking their palms.

"Where were you?" asked their teacher, Mary Colvin, when they returned. Colvin was a mature green of thirty-one who had received her master's degree in elementary education while still posing. "You were not at light-break."

The children were silent.

"Where were you?" she repeated.

"We went for a walk," offered Joey.

"What is that, Gabriel?" the woman asked then, noticing candy smeared on his shirt.

"Chocolate," he said. "A nice man gave it to us. He said it was good."

"And was it good?" questioned the teacher.

"I don't know," Gabriel answered slowly.

"Greens who often disobey," the teacher warned then, "sometimes do not fully mature. Their skin stays dull and lifeless."

Gabe was getting a stomachache. "My stomach hurts," he complained.

"Your stomach aches," explained Ms. Colvin, "because you have eaten. You did not enjoy the taste of the chocolate and now it has given you a stomach-ache. Eating is never enjoyable."

"Eating is never enjoyable," Gabe thought now, as

he positioned a sharp knife over his 6-ounce steak.

"Want some more potato salad?" someone asked. "You didn't take much."

Louise Roanoke dug into her half of a barbecued chicken.

"More corn on the cob?" Bradley Duncan passed a platter of buttered corn along his backyard picnic table. It would be the last party he would host for these friends and colleagues for a long time. He was scheduled to leave the next morning to begin a period of field experience in Adamsville.

"This sure beats work," laughed Duncan's wife, Alice. "We ought to have July Fourth more often."

"Every couple weeks, at least," Brad nodded.

"What would you say," Louise Roanoke asked slowly, "is the manifest function of the Adamsville welcoming ceremony?"

"Hey," Connie Batterson interjected, winking toward her spouse, "I promised my husband we wouldn't talk business today."

"Five minutes," Louise promised.

"The manifest function of the welcoming ceremony?" Brad repeated. "To welcome the stolen baby, change his status."

"Change his status how?" asked Alice, a computer programmer by profession.

"From a stolen baby to a green, from an outsider to an insider."

"How about latent functions? What are some possible latent functions of the welcoming ceremony?" Louise pursued.

"Legitimation of the rescue mission," Constance offered. "Positive sanctioning of the rescuer. Socialization."

"Socialization of whom?" Duncan urged.

"Everyone who was there," Connie answered. "Children, adults—everyone. Did you hear them respond to that litany? I mean they *believed* what they were saying."

"Socialization of the rescuer, too, of course," added Brad.

"I surely would like to know where that baby came from," remarked Roanoke.

"Well, I'd say from the headlines you've got a pretty good estimate," offered Batterson's husband, Paul.

"You think the child was kidnapped from Lake Hospital?"

"Makes sense to me," Paul said. "They catch that guy, they'll hang him."

"Aha," laughed Connie, "now doesn't he talk like he's married to a conflict theorist?"

Louise Roanoke had become too serious for humor. "Gabriel Knapp," she mused. "Somehow I feel I've heard that name before."

"Your niece mentioned a Knapp," Brad recalled casually, "last time she was in the office."

Questions

1. How does Gabe Knapp's heredity contribute to his social identity? What aspects of his social identity seem to reflect both genetics and environment?

2. Discuss several socialization functions served by the rescue game that green children play. How do you suppose the game ever began?

3. How did Gabe's family, peers, and school act as socializers?

4. The baby that Gabe rescued was taken from the outside to Adamsville. When he becomes a young man, he may move outside again for school and work; as he matures, he'll return to Adamsville. Discuss the resocialization required by each of these moves.

5. The general process of adult socialization and resocialization can lead to role conflicts. How does this statement apply to Gabe Knapp?

6

Social Networks:
Relations, Groups, Organizations

In the preceding chapters, I've used the terms "group" and "relationship" rather casually, knowing that you'd have a general understanding of them. In this chapter, however, we're going to examine those terms more carefully. In particular, we're going to examine some of the different kinds of groups that sociologists study, and we'll be especially concerned with the kinds of relationships that characterize different kinds of groups.

I want to begin the chapter with a discussion of what sociologists mean by the term "group." In our everyday language, we use the term to mean a variety of things, and sociologists have something more specific in mind.

Next we'll examine two ideal types that have reappeared from time to time throughout the history of sociology: **primary groups** and **secondary groups.** I'll discuss the ways different sociologists have seen these two types of groups, and we'll look at the implications of primary and secondary groups in social life.

Following the discussion of primary and secondary groups, we'll look at some of the special types of groups that have interested sociologists. Separate sections will address **reference groups, voluntary associations,** and bureaucracy.

The chapter concludes with further words on primary and secondary groups. First we'll look at the matter of primary relations within secondary groups; then we'll examine the general trend toward sec-

ondary relations in contemporary societies. We'll also look at some countertrends.

The purpose of this chapter is to give you a sense of the different social networks that people create in their relations with one another. It should also give you some insights into your own relationships with other people.

What Is a Group?

The term "group" is used in everyday language in a variety of ways, reflecting many meanings. We speak of a "group" gathered at a bus stop, and the "group" that used brand X toothpaste. We also speak of "groupies," people who follow rock music stars around. In this section, I want to spell out the meaning sociologists usually associate with the term, and in doing so I'll mention some related terms. For example, sociologists usually distinguish groups from **categories** and **aggregations.**

A "category" is a set of people who share a characteristic. Examples include black Americans, blue-eyed people, all those who use brand X toothpaste, and so forth. Members of a category don't necessarily know each other or interact with each other. They belong to the same category merely because they share a characteristic.

An "aggregation" is a gathering of people in the same physical location. Those people gathered at the bus stop are an example, as is a theater audience. Members of an aggregation need not know one another or interact with one another, and there is no expectation that they'll ever gather together again.

Imagine a noonday street scene in a busy city. People are hurrying anonymously past each other on the sidewalk. Then they notice someone about to jump off the top of a tall building, and they stop to watch. A crowd forms. That crowd is an aggregation. The person they are watching atop the building has a change of heart and disappears inside the building. Eventually the crowd drifts away, never to assemble again.

Characteristics of Groups

Although sociologists do not totally agree in their use of the term "group," it is possible to detail some of the qualities most commonly agreed on:

1. *Shared interests.* Members of a group agree in some degree on values, norms, goals, and so forth. For example, the members of a PTA share an agreement on the desirability of "quality" education, and they may agree on the means for achieving it.

2. *Interaction.* When sociologists speak of a group, they usually assume some degree of interaction or communication among the members, based on the fact of their membership in the group. Thus, members of a family interact because of their membership in the family.

3. *Identity.* The members of a group must have a sense of membership in or of belonging to that group. At some level, the group constitutes an element in the individual's definition of who he or she is. A group is, in some degree, a *union* of individuals, and it is useful to consider the notion of "*reunion*" in this context. Class reunions, for example, reflect the group identity characterizing the graduating class. It is unlikely that you'd contemplate or wish for a reunion of the crowd that gathered to watch a suicide attempt.

4. *Structure.* Unlike categories or aggregations, groups have structure—agreed-on relationships among statuses. The structure present in a group may be either formal or informal or explicit or implicit.

The sociological use of the term "group" covers a broad variety of things. Examples of groups include a family, a bureaucratic office, a high school graduating class, a John Denver fan club, a Communist party cell, a sociology department faculty, and a political party caucus within a legislature.

Groups are important in sociology for two major reasons. First, they provide an important part of an individual's social identity. Your sense of who you *are* is largely a function of the groups you belong to. Second, they are a key to understanding much social behavior. Many sociologists have studied the dynamics of interaction within groups—particularly small groups—thereby gaining insights into social interaction more generally. Further, the behavior of individuals within society is largely a function of their membership in particular groups. I'll be elaborating on each of these points through the rest of this chapter.

Dyads and Triads

Georg Simmel, whom I've mentioned earlier in connection with social conflict, is also noted for his investigations of the smallest of groups. He (1908b) introduced the German term *zweierverbindung,* literally translated as a "union of two," and more commonly translated into English as **dyad,** a two-member group.

For Simmel, the dyad was the most elementary social unit, what he called a "superindividual unit." The dyad had an existence and reality that transcended the existence and reality of individuals. Still, Simmel recognized that the existence of a dyad was dependent on the membership of each individual, either one of whom could terminate the group by withdrawing. The group as a reality apart from individuals became more apparent and persistent when a third member was added: "The dyad, therefore, does not attain that super-personal life which the individual feels to be independent of himself. As soon, however, as there is a sociation of three, a group continues to exist even in case one of the members drops out" (1950:123).

Sociologists have used the term **triad** in reference to groups of three or more, and as Simmel suggested, the triad differs from the dyad in two important ways. First, each member of a dyad recognizes that the "groupness" depends directly on his or her continued membership. The members of a triad, on the other hand, recognize that the group has a reality that extends beyond their individual membership in it. When two people make agreements with each other, each recognizes his or her part in making the agreements. The agreements shared by members of a larger group appear to have more substance, more "reality," as opposed to being merely agreements.

The second important distinction between dyads and triads is similar to the first, representing only a different point of view. Triads have a greater survival potential than dyads, making them more significant in the overall structuring of societies. Simmel was particularly interested in the "immortality" of larger social groups, how although the membership of groups changed the groups themselves continued forever.

The survival of social units is one of the critical elements in society. The U.S. Senate as a social group has survived for 200 years, even though its membership has changed totally. Despite the continuous changing of membership, the Senate is, in many important senses, still the Senate.

The "superpersonal" life of groups—the group survival that transcends the survival of individual members of it—is a central issue in sociology, and I'm going to discuss it at length in Chapter 7. We'll see how agreements individuals make become **institutionalized** and persist as the basis for group organization and interaction long after the individuals who originally made those agreements are dead and forgotten. But for now, let's keep our attention on the nature of groups.

Coalitions

Another aspect of "microgroup" life that has interested sociologists is the formation of temporary or permanent partnerships called "coalitions." Very often individuals enter into coalitions for the purpose of gaining advantages that they could not enjoy as individuals. Such coalitions, moreover, are formed in opposition to someone else.

Theodore Caplow (1920–) has done the most extensive theoretical work (1959, 1969) on this subject in recent years. Caplow has been especially interested in the formation of coalitions in connection with creating power, asking which two members of a triad would most likely form a coalition against the third member.

The trade union movement offers a clear illustration of this. Individual workers in a particular factory were powerless in challenging the owner, in demanding better pay and improved working conditions, but a united coalition of those same workers generated a power equal to or greater than that of the owner. The union composed of workers in a given factory is an example of a "group" as sociologists use the term.

In-groups and Out-groups

Earlier I said that a sense of "belonging" is an element in defining groups. The sense of belonging is also important to another distinction that sociologists make, that between **in-groups** and **out-groups.**

Most simply put, an "in-group" is a group you belong to. Since membership in a group is a status and statuses define your social identity, your membership in an in-group contributes to the social definition of who you are. Whether you belong to an exclusive country club or are a member of an impoverished urban ghetto, such membership is a part of your social identity, who you are in society.

In-group membership has no meaning, however, unless there are *non*members, people who do not belong to your in-group. In-group membership takes on social significance to the extent that the nonmembers belong to distinct groups of their own, groups that are in some degree of competition with yours.

An in-group is composed of people you refer to as "we"; an out-group is made up of people you call "they." The "we feeling" that characterizes in-groups has implications for both the individual and the society. I have already mentioned that your own social identity is partly based on the groups you belong to. "We" includes "I," as illustrated by Kipling in the box "We and They."

In-group membership affects your personal feelings as well as your identity. Many of your in-groups provide you with feelings of support, loyalty, and even affection. Because an in-group is typically based on shared points of view, you may feel more comfortable interacting with members of your in-groups than with other people. This is all the more the case to the extent that you have reified the points of view that your in-groups share.

From a societal point of view, in-groups and out-groups provide important bases for both stability and conflict. Within-group cohesion and solidarity keep knots of people bound together in persistent groups, whereas between-group tensions and conflict provide a continuing source of stress, strain, and change.

Often, in-groups and out-groups are the basis for social divisiveness and inhumane actions, as was the case in the relocation of West Coast Japanese-Americans during World War II. During the same war, the Nazis excluded Jews from the human species, and the Japanese took essentially the same approach to the Chinese. Earlier in our own history, white Americans essentially excluded American Indians from the human species. Once a group of people has been defined as outside the in-group of human beings, even the most basic, shared agreements regarding the relations of humans to humans are suspended, and atrocities often follow.

You now should have a better idea of what sociologists mean when they use the term "group." We've seen that sociologists distinguish groups from aggregations and social categories. We've also seen that members of a social category can be transformed into a group. Now I want to conclude this section with an examination of another type of group that has interested sociologists, the reference group.

Reference Groups

In Chapter 5 we discussed Cooley's concept of the looking-glass self, suggesting that we learn who we are by seeing ourselves reflected in the eyes of others. Certain groups and categories around us also provide us with the standard against which we evaluate ourselves. These are called "reference groups."

Reference groups operate in two ways. First, they can provide a measure of how well or poorly we are doing. For example, would you regard a grade of B as a "good" or "bad" grade in this course? Your answer is likely to reflect the grades your friends are receiving in their courses or the grades other students in this course receive or both. If you received the

---

We and They

Father, Mother, and Me
Sister and Auntie say
All the people like us are We
And every one else is They.

All good people agree,
And all good people say,
All nice people, like Us, are We
And every one else is They.

Source: From Rudyard Kipling's Verse, Definitive Edition. *Copyright 1940 by Doubleday & Co., Inc. Reprinted by permission.*

only B in the course and everyone else did worse, you'd think that B was a good grade. If everyone else got an A, you'd take a much different view of your B. We tend to judge ourselves in comparison with other members of our groups.

Comparing ourselves in relation to others lays the foundation for what sociologists call **relative deprivation.** We experience deprivation whenever our situation seems worse than that of those around us—regardless of the objective circumstances.

During World War II, Samuel Stouffer and several colleagues formed a research branch in the U.S. Army for the purpose of conducting social scientific research relevant to the war effort. Many of the studies (Stouffer et al. 1949) examined the conditions under which high and low morale occurred. One specific aspect of army morale centered on the promotion system, with the researchers reasoning that rapid promotions would be associated with higher morale than slow promotions. The studies conducted in relation to this topic turned up some surprises, however.

The army air corps (the forerunner of the air force) enjoyed the fastest promotions in the army, while in the military police the situation was just the opposite: Promotions were slow and few. Yet when the researchers asked soldiers if they felt the promotion system was "fair," those in the army air corps were far more likely to complain that it was not.

The explanation of this surprising finding, Stouffer suggested, lay in the concept of relative deprivation. Soldiers in the army air corps, more likely to have been promoted themselves, compared themselves with others in their unit. No matter how far and how fast a man had been promoted, he probably knew others who had been promoted further and faster. In the military police, on the other hand, the soldier who had not been promoted at all was likely to find his lot the same as those around him, and not feel deprived relative to them. Soldiers in the army air corps and the military police, then, had different reference groups.

Reference groups also can be composed of those people whose opinions we respect, providing a some-, what different standard for us. Suppose you want to become a ballet dancer. Let's assume further that you are the best dancer in your college. Your dance

Samuel A. Stouffer 1900–1960 (The American Sociological Association)

teacher and those around you might, reasonably, regard your stature as a dancer very highly. If your reference group is the Bolshoi ballet company, however, you are likely to have a very low regard for your abilities.

Reference groups have an important socializing effect in providing goals for us to work toward in our personal development. Very often this takes the form of an attempt to gain membership in the reference group, whether it is an exclusive "jet set," a university faculty, or a street-corner gang.

Robert Merton (1910–) has written extensively on the subject of reference-group theory (Merton 1957a). One of his important contributions to this topic involves the distinction he has made between "cosmopolitans" and "locals." In his study of personal influence within a small Eastern seacoast town, Merton found some residents to confine their interests largely to the small town in which they lived, giving little thought to national and world issues. These people were the "locals." Other residents, the "cosmopolitans," took a much broader view.

Clearly, the "locals" and the "cosmopolitans" had different reference groups. A similar observation

Primary groups are marked by close, intimate relationships and create a "we feeling." Though membership and activities change, many of your lifetime experiences will occur in primary groups. (above Burk Uzzle, Magnum, right Michael D. Sullivan)

has been made with regard to university faculty members. Some tend to identify primarily with their own campus, while others identify primarily with their national profession. A "local" professor would value being appointed to an important campus committee, but a "cosmopolitan" professor would take greater pride in being asked to address a national convention.

The reference group, then, is another way in which the sociological point of view can organize and clarify familiar aspects of social life. Now I want to turn to an issue concerning the quality of groups and interpersonal relationships that has interested sociologists for a long time. Basically, this interest grows out of the observation that some relationships

and groups are characterized by warmth and intimacy while others are more detached and casual. Our discussion of voluntary associations and bureaucracy later in the chapter is based on the following discussion of primary and secondary groups.

Primary and Secondary Groups

In this section, we'll look at some of the writings of three sociologists: Charles Horton Cooley, Emile Durkheim, and Ferdinand Toennies. Each of these men has addressed the subject of the quality of group relations in society.

Cooley: The Primary Group

In 1909, Charles Horton Cooley drew attention to a special type of social group, and his characterization has remained near the heart of sociology ever since. He called this kind of group the "primary group," saying: "By primary groups I mean those characterized by intimate face-to-face association and cooperation. They are primary in several senses, but chiefly in that they are fundamental in forming the social nature and ideals of the individual" (1909:23).

Cooley went on to say that primary groups were characterized by a "we feeling" and that individual members of primary groups personally identified with the group and group goals. He said that the intimate association in a primary group creates a feeling of "wholeness" with the group that "involves the sort of sympathy and mutual identification for which 'we' is the natural expression."

The family is an example of a primary group. Although you may grow away from your parents, sisters, and brothers as you get older, there is a sense of identification and belonging that you can probably never escape fully. When you were young, probably no group of people represented more of a primary group than your family.

Families are not the only primary groups, however. If you belong to a clique of close friends, that is also a primary group, characterized by intimacy and identification. You share many of your innermost feelings and most personal experiences with them and they with you. Each of you is important to the others, and the joy and sadness that one of you experiences affects the others to some extent.

Cooley was careful to caution that primary-group relations are not always friendly and harmonious. You may fight with members of your primary groups, verbally and even physically. When you do, though, you are likely to feel the unhappiness more deeply than you would after a fight with other people.

Primary groups are usually based on shared points of view. You and the members of your primary groups are likely to agree on many aspects of life. Even when you do not actually discuss those agreements, you have a "sense" of agreement that runs deeper than words. Herein lies the basis for the feeling of "wholeness" with the group.

While Cooley never spoke of "secondary groups" as such, the contrast between them and primary groups was implicit in his writings on the primary group, and subsequent sociologists have added this term to the discussion of social groups. Secondary groups are characterized by more superficial and more casual relations. They lack the intimacy and feeling of belonging that characterize primary groups.

Your sociology class would probably be a good example of a secondary group. Although your class meets periodically, you interact with one another, and the class is somewhat structured by statuses and roles, it is unlikely that you experience the kind of intimacy and belongingness that characterizes your experience of your family.

Two European sociologists, Emile Durkheim and Ferdinand Toennies, had also noted and written about the distinction made by Cooley, although the time lag between initial publication and translation into English delayed the impact of their ideas on American sociology. Each man lived through the Industrial Revolution, and each saw the growing influence of technological change on social life.

Durkheim:
Mechanical and Organic Solidarity

Emile Durkheim, the prominent French sociologist, was particularly interested in the issue of social

order. As I noted in Chapter 2, he is regarded as one of the founders of the structural-functional view in sociology. In studies of both preliterate and modern societies reported in *The Division of Labor in Society* (1893) he found different bases for orderliness.

Social order in preliterate societies, Durkheim suggested, was based on implicit agreements that were taught and enforced through face-to-face relations, among people composing what Cooley would have called primary groups. This was possible because of the direct contacts among people in such societies and also because of the great similarity among the members in those societies. Durkheim called this form of social order "mechanical solidarity" and spoke, in this regard, of a "collective conscience," or "common conscience" (p. 79).

Modern societies differed from preliterate ones in a number of ways. Because of the division of labor and other forms of social specialization, members of society differed from one another far more than in preliterate societies. Also, the greater size of modern societies reduced the dominance of face-to-face, primary-group relations; modern societies were more characterized by secondary-group relationships. In such societies, Durkheim noted the greater importance of formal rules, needed to create order among diverse people, and he introduced the term "organic solidarity" to characterize that situation.

Durkheim, like Cooley, saw the trend toward secondary-group relations that was part of modernization and urbanization. So did the German sociologist Ferdinand Toennies (1855–1936).

Toennies:
Gemeinschaft and Gesellschaft

Although Toennies's major work in social organization *Community and Society* was originally published in 1887, it was not translated into English until 1957. Nonetheless, it has become a sociological classic, and two German terms used by Toennies have become standard concepts in American sociology.

Toennies distinguished between two distinct types of large-scale social organization: **gemeinschaft,** translated as "community," and **gesellschaft,** translated as "society." In the context of terms we are

Ferdinand Toennies 1855–1936 (Franziska Toennies Heberle)

already familiar with, gemeinschaft would be characterized by primary-group relations and mechanical solidarity, while gesellschaft would be more characterized by secondary-group relations and organic solidarity.*

In introducing these terms, Toennies was responding to the social change he was witnessing as small rural communities of the preindustrial era were transformed into large urban societies. Toennies was struck by the impersonal, contractual nature of relationships in the gesellschaft, and he saw a general trend toward such relationships everywhere. Clearly, he did not welcome this trend, and he spoke of the gesellschaft as cold and anonymous.

Two types of social organizations common in modern society illustrate the secondary relationships

*Toennies, like Durkheim, used the terms "mechanical" and "organic," but he used them with exactly the *opposite* meanings. Toennies wrote: "Accordingly, Gemeinschaft (community) should be understood as a living organism, Gesellschaft (society) as a mechanical aggregate and artifact." While Toennies's use of the terms has more agreement with common sense, Durkheim's meanings have become the accepted ones in sociology.

that both Durkheim and Toennies foresaw: voluntary associations and bureaucracy. Let's examine each of these. Then I want to return to these questions: Is there a trend from primary to secondary relations? Is it continuing? Is there a countertrend?

Voluntary Associations

"Voluntary associations" are secondary groups formed around a set of shared interests. A PTA is an example of a voluntary association. So is a sociology club. Students for a Democratic Society and the Daughters of the American Revolution are other examples.

Some associations have a charitable or altruistic purpose. Examples include the American Cancer Society, the American Heart Association, the American National Red Cross, the Cooperative for American Relief Everywhere (CARE), and Big Brothers of America. There are occupation-based associations such as the American Sociological Association and the American Anthropological Association, and there are politically based associations such as the Democratic and Republican national parties.

Some associations, such as the American Civil Liberties Union (ACLU), have as their purpose the enforcement of the formal agreements of the larger society. Some associations, such as Zero Population Growth, have as their purpose the changing of society's informal agreements.

So far, I have mentioned only a few of the thousands of national voluntary associations. Every state, community, and neighborhood has more of its own. Community associations organize to protest the building of a highway, and others organize to demand its construction. Associations form to support voluntary abortions, and others form to oppose them. Wherever and whenever people share a common interest, they are likely to form a voluntary association in support of that interest.

Voluntary associations serve two functions. First, and most obvious, they provide a vehicle for sharing common interests. The American Contract Bridge League, for example, is a vehicle for getting people together to play bridge. Your local chamber music society is a vehicle for people's listening to it together.

Second, voluntary associations in America are also potent political forces. Often the interests that association members share are affected by governmental actions, and the association is a vehicle for affecting those governmental actions. The National Association of Manufacturers, for example, seeks legislation favorable to industry. The American Legion seeks legislation favorable to veterans. The National Rifle Association opposes legislation to require the registration of firearms.

Within a democracy, voluntary associations achieve political power because of the effect they can have on the election or reelection of officials. Typically, effect is measured as money or votes or both. Thus, an elected official may see there is "public good" to be gained from granting a rezoning request for the construction of a steel mill in a residential community if his or her reelection campaign fund might increase in the process. The mill could seem like a bad idea, too, if a community association in the area of the proposed mill submitted an irate petition signed by 80 percent of the voters in the district.

Americans have a special penchant for voluntary associations. Membership generally also seems more common among men than among women. Table 6·1 shows voluntary-association membership rates for five nations in the early 1960s with men and women shown separately.

Alexis de Tocqueville 1805–1859 (Bulloz)

Alexis de Tocqueville, early in the last century, saw Americans' tendency to form voluntary associations as a critical guard against despotism.* In *Democracy in America* (1835, 1840), he wrote that as long as citizens can organize freely to advocate their special interests, no despot could assume totalitarian control over the nation.

More recently, William Kornhauser (1959) has spoken of large-scale associations as an important part of a democratic infrastructure† in mass society. Such associations are more accessible to citizens than

Table 6·1 Voluntary Association Membership, by Nation and Sex

	Total	Men	Women
		Percent who belong	
United States	57	68	47
Great Britain	47	66	30
Germany	44	66	24
Italy	30	41	19
Mexico	24	43	15

Source: From The Civic Culture: Political Attitudes and Democracy in Five Nations, *by Gabriel A. Almond and Sidney Verba, copyright © 1963 by Princeton University Press, published for the Center of International Studies, Princeton University. Reprinted by permission of Princeton University Press.*

*"Despotism" is a form of government in which the power of the ruler in charge is unlimited.

†"Infrastructure" means the underlying foundation on which the survival of a society depends. Some elements other than voluntary associations that are a part of America's democratic infrastructure are the commitments to free speech and religious tolerance.

Max Weber 1846–1920 (Historical Pictures Service, Chicago)

government itself, yet they are large enough to exercise political power. The impact of associations formed by racial minorities, women, environmentalists, and others in recent years support the conclusions reached by Tocqueville and Kornhauser.

Secondary-group relationships epitomized, however, are to be found in still another type of social organization, the bureaucracy.

Bureaucracy

"Bureaucracy" is a word that people use frequently, and we commonly distinguish among several types of bureaucracy: "stupid bureaucracy," "petty bureaucracy," "bungling bureaucracy," "damned bureaucracy," and worse. Bureaucracy has a "bad press" in America and elsewhere. For most people, bureaucracy means long lines, red tape, impersonality, forms, and frustration. It doesn't *have* to be that way, as the box on pages 142–143, "Why Nothing Works," shows.

What Is Bureaucracy?

From a sociological point of view, "bureaucracy" is simply one way in which social statuses and social relationships are organized. Max Weber (1846–1920) did the earliest comprehensive analysis (1925a) of this form of organization, and his observations are still generally applicable to today's bureaucracies.

Weber saw the following as the key characteristics of bureaucratic organization.

1. Jurisdictional areas were officially fixed and generally governed by rules. The required regular activities of the organization were specified as official duties. The structure of authority in the organization was clearly spelled out, as were the means by which each member of the organization would fulfill his or her official duties.

2. The organization was structured hierarchically, with specified levels of authority. Like a pyramid, the organization had fewer people at each higher level of authority, ending with a single person at its head.

3. The organization was managed largely through the preparation, maintenance, and use of written files.

4. Those holding positions in a bureaucracy were especially trained for their jobs.

5. The fully developed bureaucracy required the full working capacities of those holding positions in it. Administration was a full-time job. In this regard, Weber was contrasting modern bureaucracies with earlier enterprises in which management was treated as a secondary activity.

6. All of the organization's official activities were governed by formalized rules, and knowledge of the rules itself constituted a special skill.

In summary, bureaucracies engage in the business of "administration," and they do so through officially specified agreements regarding status relationships and role expectations. The bureaucracies of Weber's day were very different from the governmental and business organizations that preceded bureaucratization.

Advantages of Bureaucracy

Weber felt that bureaucracy was technically superior to other forms of organization in the same fashion that machine production was technically superior to handwork. Bureaucracies were faster, more precise, clearer, more certain, more effective,

Why Nothing Works

Public-service agencies—police, firefighters, school systems, welfare agencies, motor-vehicle bureaus, and so forth—are the fastest growing organizations in the United States, the most likely to help or rub raw the average citizen, and the most criticized. Too often they appear to be "organizational insanities," hamstrung with red tape, inefficient, filled with time-serving civil servants who can't be fired or political appointees. They seem, at times, to have been devised primarily to provide the jobs that our rationalized and automated industry can't provide.

The explanations for the inefficiency and non-responsiveness of public bureaucracies are many: They lack clear-cut goals and measurable outputs (How do you evaluate services to welfare clients or schoolchildren? What should we be doing to them anyway?); they are staffed by political appointees who don't work hard and are mostly concerned with preventing embarrassing scandals; they are entangled in red tape, much of it the result of fruitless efforts to protect the public's money through all sorts of fiscal controls; people in secure jobs won't work hard; and there is no chance for customers to switch to brand X if they don't like the municipal brand.

Perhaps. But public agencies need not be this way. A recent study[1] of government-owned liquor stores in two states shows that none of these factors is conclusive. These stores had a monopoly on the

sale of liquor. The efficiency of the service can be precisely measured; it is like private business in this respect with data on sales per employee, costs of sales, growth of sales, rates of profit, growth of profit, and so on.

The monopoly in state A conforms perfectly to the stereotype of an inefficient, overstaffed, non-innovative bureaucracy with underworked and secure public servants. Its growth was slow; it barely moved into efficient self-service stores, preferring traditional counter-service stores; its profit per employee or per bottle sold was small; the manual of operation for the store manager was 250 pages, covering every eventuality (but using more pages, for example, on how to take care of the store safe than on inventory management); the financial controls were multitudinous and time-consuming; inspections were frequent; the work was not hard; pay was good; and morale was high. The top officers were political appointees, of course.

The monopoly in state B, however, had a profit rate double that of the one in state A, a rapid growth rate, many self-service stores, acted like private industry in innovations in inventory control, merchandising mechanism, automated stock handling. Further, its manual was only 50 pages; it committed only one-twentieth of the resources to fiscal audit and control that state A did; it was rarely visited by top management; the employees worked harder, longer, and for less pay; and their morale was lower. Top management people were also political appointees, but were turned out if they did not produce high profits.

What accounted for the difference? Why did the bureaucracy in state B operate so efficiently, almost

[1]William E. Turcotte, "Control Systems, Performance, and Satisfaction in Two State Agencies," *Administrative Science Quarterly* 19(1974):60–73.

and more efficient than nonbureaucratic organizations.

In addition, Weber saw an advantage in the continuity of bureaucracies and their files. Individual members of a bureaucracy could come and go, but the structure of statuses and the written records of past activities gave the organization a life of its own that outlived the service of individual bureaucrats. The continued functioning of the United States civil service in spite of the frequent changing of politically appointed officials is a contemporary illustration of this feature of bureaucracies. Bureaucrats tend to continue performing their specified duties regardless of personnel changes above, below, and around them.

---

as if it were not a public bureaucracy? The usual explanations won't work. Both had clear-cut goals and means to measure them; both had political appointees, and job security for the men. Neither had competition. It couldn't be morale, either, because the state with high morale had low productivity and vice versa. The source of the differences between the monopolies appears to be the demands made by the governors and the legislature and the uses to which they wanted to put the organization. In state A, even though the revenue from the agency was huge—over 40 million dollars a year—it was only 2 percent of the state budget and a drop in the bucket considering the state's debt. There was no incentive to make the operation more profitable, so no one compared its profitability with that of other states. There was an overriding concern, however, that there not be any scandals associated with it that might embarrass the ruling political party, so there was considerable incentive to flood it with sophisticated fiscal controls that consumed the time of the store managers. Each year it proposed a modest increase in sales and was given a comparable increase in personnel and expenses, so profits stayed the same!

For state B, the profit of the monopoly constituted 20 percent of the state revenues (the state had no sales or income tax), so there was an enormous incentive to increase sales and profits. Top management people were actively involved in the business, not limiting their participation to ceremonial affairs. The governor's office regularly increased targets in the light of past performance, but the store managers were not given explicit targets, as in state A. Instead, they were constantly exhorted to do better. Questionnaire data "suggest a stronger willingness of state B managers to accept more responsibility and effort. The data became more significant considering that state B managers were already about twice as productive as state A managers, were working longer hours, and had no pay or promotion linked to increased volume."

The lesson seems to be not that you should drive your employees, but that top management should establish different expectations for their organizations. The essential differences between the two monopolies were the goals set by the governor, legislature, and top management (the commissioners). Left to its own devices, an organization will not raise its targets, push its people, innovate, or emphasize service. Why should it? State A did very well with what its leaders demanded of it—error-free operation, no scandals, and an easy sinecure for those at the top. But it did not do much else. In state B, it was a tool for generating increasing revenues, and everything was bent to this. The result was lower taxes for the population and probably better service in the stores. Both were "political" goals in one sense; political parties run states and their agencies. But only one state used its resources and the skills and effort of its employees to the best advantage. Organizations are tools; they can be used for different ends and well used or poorly used. Whether they are public bureaucracies or private businesses may not be the important thing.

What does this analysis have to say about other public bureaucracies, such as the military and state universities? This analysis has employed a structural-functional point of view. How would a symbolic interactionist examine the two kinds of liquor stores?

AS YOU NO LONGER HAVE ANY USEFUL FUNCTION DUE TO THE RECENT RE-STRUCTURE, WE'VE FOUND YOU A NEW JOB......

Weber cited the technical expertise of members of a bureaucracy as another advantage of that form of organization. Only in a bureaucracy was it possible for people to develop extreme competence in extremely narrow specialties and for all those special skills to be coordinated into a meaningful organizational effort.

Disadvantages of Bureaucracy

Weber's description of bureaucracy, although accurate, differs greatly from the common agreement about bureaucracy among Americans today, which is more likely to be reflected by such comments as those that began this section. Despite its undeniable functions, bureaucracy can be dysfunctional.

Two popular books in recent years have pointed to some of the problems that arise in bureaucratic organization, and their popularity is an indication of the extent to which they have touched on some of the agreements people share about bureaucracy. The first is C. Northcote Parkinson's discourse (1957) on what he modestly referred to as "Parkinson's law." Parkinson stated his law as follows: "Work expands so as to fill the time available for its completion." No matter how little work is to be done or how much time is

available, the work will be stretched out enough to fit perfectly within the time at hand.

Bureaucracies are characterized by regular work hours and specified activities to take place during those hours. If too much work is expected, this discrepancy will be made known and either the work will be reduced or the staff will be increased to handle it. If, on the other hand, there is not enough work to be done by the staff assigned to it, that work somehow keeps everyone "busy" throughout working hours.

Parkinson's law would appear to extend to the case where there is no work to be accomplished. Sometimes a change in the structure of an organization or a change in the flow of business through it will leave individuals with no useful function in the organization. Typically, it is possible to stretch "nothing" enough to fill the day. Indeed, whole organizations may find themselves with no useful function. Bureaucratic organizations seldom die, however. Every year the government creates many new agencies, usually with mandates to solve specific problems. Rarely, if ever, does such an agency solve its problem and ask to be dissolved.

The Peter Principle, a more recent (1969) popular book, also points to problems in bureaucratic organization. Laurence Peter states his "principle" as follows: "In a hierarchy every employee tends to rise to his level of incompetence." Weber noted, you will recall, that technical expertise was one of the chief advantages of bureaucracy. He also noted that members of the bureaucracy could rise to ever higher positions in it. If promotions in the bureaucracy are based on demonstrated merit, a person who proves capable of doing a particular job with excellence will be removed from that job and elevated to one in which he or she has not demonstrated excellence. Often, of course, the person quickly learns the skills required in the new position and again performs with excellence—and is promoted once more. Peter suggests that members of a bureaucracy will continue to be promoted until they reach positions in which they perform terribly, and they will be left in those positions since further promotions are clearly not warranted. Many bureaucrats will occupy positions that outstrip their competence, since demotions are

UPWARD MOVEMENT ONLY!

BUREAUCRATIC MACHINE **DANGER!** BACKWARD MOTION CAUSES CHAOS.

rare in bureaucracies. There are exceptions, however, as Peter describes in the box on page 146 "Illegal Invocation of the Peter Principle."

When bureaucrats are too incompetent, and the functions of the organization are severely threatened by that incompetence, the situation is often resolved by the incompetent's being "kicked upstairs." This involves an apparent promotion, usually indicated by an impressive title and a pay raise, to an essentially unimportant position. Many corporation vice-presidents have gained their positions in this way. (Your instructor may irreverently tell you that's where deans come from—unless your instructor is a dean.)

Bureaucracies have many other problems (Bennis 1971:143–47). Those of us who are constantly in touch with them are sure of it. One of the problems is people's ability or inability to accommodate themselves to such formal structuring of social relations. Many sociologists have paid special attention to this problem.

People in Organizations

Amitai Etzioni (1964) has summarized the extent of formal organization in modern societies as follows:

Our society is an organized society. We are born in organizations, educated by organizations, and most of us spend much of our lives working for organizations. We spend much of our leisure time praying, playing, and paying in organizations. Most of us will die in an organization, and when the time comes for burial, the largest organization of all—the state—must grant official permission (p. 1).

How well do individual human beings fare in such a superorganized existence? Etzioni gives a mixed assessment. The situation is neither all good nor all bad. Since organizations operate more smoothly with happy employees, efficiency and happiness can go hand in hand. This does not always happen, however. The desires of employees must often be sacrificed in favor of organizational goals and needs.

Many people have written of the negative effects of bureaucratic organizations on the lives of individuals within them. Perhaps the most popular book on this topic was William Whyte's *The Organization Man* (1956). One of the classic sociological examinations of this issue was Robert Merton's (1957a) essay "Bureaucratic Structure and Personality."

Noting that bureaucracies are primarily characterized by formal, written regulations, Merton further noted that bureaucratic officials were largely evaluated (for promotion, for example) in terms of their "strict devotion to regulations" (p. 200). The safest course for any bureaucrat is unswerving enforcement of the formal rules. If deviation from the rules results in disaster, the bureaucrat will be blamed; if irrational obedience to the rules results in disaster, however, the rules are to blame. The sure way to avoid making bad decisions is to make no decisions at all.

Blind obedience to regulations, Merton observed, produces "timidity, conservatism, and technicism" in officials and makes bureaucracies incapable of adapting readily to new or special conditions. "Thus, the very elements which conduce toward efficiency in general produce inefficiency in specific instances" (p. 200).

Merton and others have noted that despite the appearance of robotlike obedience to regulations, detached objectivity, and bureaucratic impersonality,

Illegal Invocation of the Peter Principle

It has been my custom, when writing about the Peter Principle, to use fictitious names to protect the guilty. But in the case of Doris Judd it was unnecessary. The courts found that she had been an innocent victim.

After a two-and-one-half-year battle Doris Judd is back on the job in the campus cafeteria at the University of California at Davis. On February 4, 1973, she was fired from her food-services job as head sandwich maker for failing to spread the mayonnaise all the way to the edges of the bread.

Two courts found that the Mayonnaise Lady, so named by the California State Employees Association, had been unjustly fired. A Yolo County Superior Court decision reinstated her to the job with back pay. The Third District Court of Appeals in Sacramento unanimously upheld the reinstatement. The decision read, "Mrs. Judd's promotion to head of the sandwich department seems to have been a deliberate invocation of the Peter Principle done with the hope that she would provide her superiors with ample reasons to discharge her."

During the lengthy court battle someone else got the mayonnaise job so Mrs. Judd was rehired to do hamburgers. She now works the grill and recently demonstrated her competence, during a noon rush, by satisfactorily preparing twelve dozen hamburgers, two dozen grilled-cheese sandwiches, and some patty melts.

Although this story has a happy ending, the legal precedent has been established. It is managerial malpractice to use the Peter Principle as the means for dumping an employee.

Will Mrs. Judd spread ketchup all the way to the edge of the hamburgers? What implicit agreement was involved in management's use of the Peter Principle?

Source: Prepared by Laurence Peter for Society by Agreement.

formal organizations have a human underbelly. Every bureaucracy and other secondary group is the scene of informal primary-group relations. Even when they function within groups formally structured around secondary-group relations, people still establish patterns of primary relations and form primary groups.

Let's take an example that should be familiar to you. Your sociology class is a secondary group, most typically characterized by secondary relations. The main agreements governing behavior in the class reflect the specific purpose of providing instruction in sociology. In most classes, however, small groups of friends are formed. You get to know some of the other students in your class and develop the "intimate, face-to-face relations" that characterize a primary group.

Primary groups often form within other formal organizations as well. If you were a clerk working behind one of the hundreds of identical desks in a large insurance company, it is likely that you would join in a small group of friends. If you were in the military, you would probably be part of a similar primary group. Most soldiers have groups of "buddies."

The primary groups that form within formal organizations usually seem totally irrelevant to the formal agreements of the organization and its functions. In practice, however, they often support the official activities. In a classic study of the German army during World War II, for example, Edward Shils and Morris Janowitz (1948) found the strong primary relations among German soldiers to have been a critical factor in their morale and effectiveness. Ideological commitments to Nazism seemed largely irrelevant; rather, the German soldier was committed to supporting the fellow soldiers in his unit, his friends.

At the same time, primary relations are often dysfunctional for the secondary group, and sociologists have been especially interested in studying this. Such primary groups represent sets of agreements separate from those of the secondary group, and the two sets of agreements often conflict.

During the late 1920s and early 1930s, F. J. Roethlisberger and W. J. Dickson undertook studies of industrial behavior in the telephone "bank wiring room" of the Western Electric Hawthorne Works in

Chicago. Out of these studies (reported in the book *Management and the Worker,* 1939) came an appreciation of the significance of primary relations in secondary groups. In particular, Roethlisberger and Dickson discovered an informal agreement as to the "rate" of work that a worker was expected—by the members of his primary group—to accomplish during a given period of time. "Rate setting" was totally a function of primary-group agreements; it was not an official policy of the organization. This does not mean that it was not enforced, however. "Rate busters" were severely sanctioned by their fellow workers. The consequence of the informal agreement was to keep production lower than it might have been otherwise. Rapid workers were unwilling to outproduce the members of their primary group, thereby casting them in a bad light.

Primary groups within organizations often represent alternative lines of communication and authority. Recall that Weber characterized bureaucracies as having specified command structures, spelling out who could give what kinds of orders to whom. Primary relations often conflict with that. Suppose, for example, that you are an office supervisor in a large company, and one of your office workers asks to have a day off on Friday to go to the beach with her boyfriend. You deny the request, basing your decision on the proper functioning of the office. Later, you receive instructions from the head office to grant the requested day off because the president's son is the boyfriend in question. You have witnessed an example of how primary relations within a secondary organization can conflict with formal command structures.

Sometimes, however, the alternative lines of communication and authority can serve the organization's ultimate interests. I've already commented on the disadvantages of bureaucratic rigidity. Primary relations are often a remedy. They permit people to work around incompetent supervisors, for example, and they can make needed information and other resources available when the formal agreements get in the way of getting the job done. Every military unit of ten or more has at least one person who knows how to "get things." If the unit has orders to paint its building, for example, and other orders prohibit their being issued paint, such a person will know someone in the supply office, and the paint will appear. The box on pages 148–149, "Democratic Bureaucracies?", further suggests the functions that individual discretion can serve in formal organizations.

Formal organizations such as bureaucracies present problems for the people who inhabit them. Formal regulations can work against the achievement of organizational goals, and people can be unhappy and inefficient. One thing that people do is make their own modifications to the organizations. Sometimes these modifications serve the goals of the organizations; sometimes they do not.

Bureaucracy, then, like the internal-combustion engine, has been a mixed blessing. And, also like the internal-combustion engine, bureaucracy and other forms of secondary-group relations are steadily increasing. Let's conclude the chapter with a brief look at the trend toward secondary relations and some countertrends.

The Trend toward Secondary Relations

As is evident in the preceding sections, you spend your life in a variety of both primary and secondary groups, and it will always be that way. At the same time, the "development" of societies in general has been marked by an overall trend in the direction of larger numbers of secondary relations. Many social interactions that typically were "intimate, face-to-face relations" a century ago in America are now more typically secondary relations. Where most Americans used to buy groceries from neighborhood grocers who were personal friends as well as shop owners, today's shopping patterns more likely involve large supermarkets where the shopper may have never met the checkout clerk before. Family physicians have been increasingly replaced by medical clinics in which patients may see a different physician each time. In higher education, mass lectures have increasingly replaced small classes.

In large part, the trend we are witnessing in the direction of larger numbers of secondary relations is a function of population growth and urbanization.

The growth in the bureaucratization of social relationships reflects the fact that bureaucracies are still the most effective and efficient form of organization for carrying out large-scale activities. A supermarket can sell groceries cheaper and faster than can a small, family-owned grocery store. Mass-produced education is cheaper than that tailored to individuals.

There is substantial evidence of a countertrend toward primary relations, however. A number of experiments in education have sought to replace lectures with small discussion seminars. The Saab motor company in Sweden has started to replace its assembly-line procedures with small groups of workers assigned to assemble entire automobiles.

In the past decade or so, we have witnessed a remarkable growth in organizations and programs designed to improve the quality of human relationships by making them more personal and loving. Encounter groups and sensitivity training programs and the rapidly growing "human potential move-

Democratic Bureaucracies?

One of the problems of bureaucracy has been its tendency to pile layer upon layer of offices so that the people at the bottom and the people at the top may as well be on different planets. Everything has to go up the hierarchy for approval and then back down again (generally coming back so stretched, distorted, reinterpreted, shaved, or bloated that the originator of the matter does not recognize it).

Because things are so centralized, the people at the lower level soon lose any initiative they have. To make matters worse, they are watched closely by their supervisor, who is watched closely by his or her supervisor, and so on up the line.

The "height" of a bureaucracy—measured in levels—is related to its "width." In bureaucracies where each supervisor has a "narrow span of control" (relatively few subordinates), a greater number of levels are required to accommodate the entire enterprise. On the other hand, few levels are required if each supervisor is responsible for a large number of subordinates. There are "tall, slim" bureaucracies and "short, fat" ones, and there is reason to believe that such structural differences have implications for people's experiences within them.

We might well expect, for example, that supervisors would be more authoritarian and autocratic in those bureaucracies where they had fewer subordinates, since it would be relatively easy to watch and control the people under them. Sensibly, that's what Peter Blau assumed when he began his study of finance agencies and personnel agencies. To his surprise, he discovered the opposite to be true.[1]

Blau found that the more levels in an organization, the more decentralization there was in decision making. Those agencies with many levels were more likely to delegate decision making to lower levels of the organization. How could this be? Did a narrow span of control mean a more democratic organization and a wide one, a more centralized, autocratic one?

He also noted that "tall, slim" organizations used computers more and required college degrees of more of their personnel. There is some evidence, also, that they had more complex and sophisticated outputs. Apparently, it is quite possible that each boss and his small number of well-trained subordinates were working closely together on a fairly egalitarian basis solving complex problems while the routine work was done by machines. In the squat, traditional bureaucracies one boss was watching over many subordinates who were doing routine work, and his surveillance could have been quite authoritarian. It may even be that he wanted to keep all control to himself, so he wouldn't appoint a couple of lieutenants and delegate some authority to them.

This interpretation of Blau's finding was bol-

[1] Peter Blau, "The Structure of Small Bureaucracies," *American Sociological Review* 31(1966):179–91; "The Hierarchy of Authority in Organizations," *American Journal of Sociology* 73(1968):453–67.

ment" are aimed at getting people in touch with each other as human beings as an antidote to what is regarded as superficiality in most secondary relations. The popularity of such activities points to a rather broad-based feeling of dissatisfaction with social relations as they exist in modern society.

Part Three, which follows, addresses the organized character of social life in greater detail. Chapter 7 opens that discussion with an analysis of the conflict between individuals and their societies.

Summary

The term "group" is used in many ways in day-to-day conversation. While sociologists have something more specific in mind, the sociological usage is not totally unambiguous. As distinct from groups, sociologists use the term "category" to refer to people who merely share a characteristic, such as blue-eyed people. Similarly, "group" is distinguished from "aggregation," a mere gathering of people in the

stered by some other studies. One researcher in a large hospital found the span of control was narrow where the work was complex, nonroutine, and required many skills (such as in open-heart surgery), but the span was broad where the work was simpler and more routine (for example, "on the assembly line" in obstetrics). More striking, because they were not dealing only with span of control, but with all the other aspects of bureaucracy, such as standardization, specialization, and formalization, were two studies in England. Derek Pugh,[2] John Child,[3] and two research teams studied a large number of industrial firms and found that the more bureaucratized the organization, the greater the decentralization of decision making. Ponder that a minute. The more bureaucratic the firm, the more discretion it gives to lower-level personnel! They did not anticipate this finding any more than Blau did. Perhaps bureaucracy was not such a bad thing after all. Perhaps the squat, fat organization with few levels of authority, little specialization of functions, few rules, and little standardization of materials and tasks was not so "democratic" after all. However, the basic issue of democracy within formal organizations is a more complex one than this suggests.

Notice some of the other characteristics of those

organizations that granted lower-level authority—measured by the authority to hire, fire, and spend money without higher-level approval. The organizational goals and priorities were already quite clearly spelled out. There were standardized procedures for handling many situations, and the degree of organizational structure controlled the information available to people. In situations like that, efficiency is increased by giving people considerable latitude in using their skills, experience, and training. Given the prior set of structural controls, it is likely that people will use their talents in the interests of the organization.

Efficient, modern bureaucracies, then, *are* more "democratic" in some senses. People are not closely watched and directed in their every action. They enjoy relatively great freedom—within a narrow range of possibilities. We should not assume from this, however, that the workers in such organizations would be allowed to vote on whether the organization should be producing nerve gas, mislabeling its goods, or destroying the environment. Only at the top of the modern bureaucracy is there room for that kind of discretion.

How would a conflict theorist address the issue of how an organization's basic goals and priorities are determined? Which kind of bureaucracy do you suppose would be the more likely site of a revolt by workers? Where would you expect workers to go on strike or attempt to take over control of the organization?

[2]D. S. Pugh, et al., "Dimensions of Organization Structure," *Administrative Science Quarterly* 13(1968):65–105.
[3]John Child, "Organization Structure and Strategies of Control: A Replication of the Aston Study," *Administrative Science Quarterly* 17(1972):163–77.

same physical location. The crowd that gathers at the scene of an accident is an example of an aggregation.

When sociologists speak of groups, they usually imply (1) a sharing of interests, (2) a degree of interaction, (3) a shared identity, and (4) a degree of structure, either formal or informal. A family or a John Denver fan club are examples of "groups," as sociologists use that term.

Groups are important in two ways. First, they serve as a focus of an individual's social identity. Your social identity is partly a matter of the groups you belong to. Second, groups represent a basic building block for larger social structures. They can also offer insights into the process of social interaction at a societal level.

Georg Simmel was one of the earliest sociologists to study very small groups seriously. He was especially interested in the dyaḍ (union of two) and the triad (small groups of three or more). The triad interested Simmel since it was a "superindividual unit," something that had an existence independent of the continued participation of any single member. Such groups, because they can survive the disappearance of individual members, appear to have lives of their own.

Some sociologists, Theodore Caplow for one, have been interested in the study of coalitions. They want to learn the dynamic processes by which individuals and groups join forces against other individuals and groups.

Another way sociologists look at groups centers on the distinction between in-groups and out-groups. The groups you belong to and identify with are your in-groups. People who do not belong to your group but belong to groups of their own (that you don't belong to) are out-groups from your point of view. Your groups are out-groups to them. In-group–out-group distinctions provide bases for both stability and conflict in society. In-group cohesion and loyalty are a source of persistence and stability for the organization of society. At the same time, however, such groups conflict with each other, sometimes to the point of violent outbursts.

Reference groups are especially important to sociological analysis. One kind of reference group provides the standard against which we measure our lot in life. In his army studies in World War II, for example, Stouffer found that soldiers judged how fair their experiences of army life were on the basis of the experiences their buddies had. Stouffer spoke of "relative deprivation" in this regard. We don't feel we are deprived if everyone around us is no better off. Only when we are relatively less well off do we feel deprived.

Other kinds of reference groups provide another kind of standard. These are the groups made up of people whom we take as models for our own attitudes and behaviors—those people we aspire to be like, the people we'd like to be identified with and compared favorably with.

Robert Merton, in his studies of reference groups, drew attention to the distinction between "locals" and "cosmopolitans" in small to medium-sized communities. The former are people who tend to be interested and involved only in local issues, while the latter see themselves as part of a larger—perhaps national—community. Some university professors ("locals") would take greater pride in campus-based recognition, while others ("cosmopolitans") would take greater pride in profession-based recognition.

A great many sociologists over the years have drawn attention to a common and seemingly important difference in the quality of certain relationships and groups. Charles Horton Cooley pointed to this distinction in his classic writings on the primary group, characterized by "intimate face-to-face association" and a special "we feeling." The family is a chief example of the primary group, and sociologists have added the term "secondary group" to sharpen the distinction.

Emile Durkheim, in comparing preliterate and modern societies, spoke of two different types of social solidarity: mechanical and organic. The first of these, more typical of preliterate societies, corresponds roughly to the notion of primary-group relations, while the second, very typical in complex, modern societies, corresponds to secondary-group relations.

Ferdinand Toennies drew a similar distinction when he wrote of gemeinschaft (community) and gesellschaft (society). Toennies was particularly interested in the social change being brought about by the Industrial Revolution as small rural communities developed into large urban centers.

I illustrated the notion of secondary groups by discussions of two major forms in modern society. First, we looked at "voluntary associations," those groups formed around a shared interest, such as a PTA, a political party, or a professional association.

Voluntary associations are a source of power in society and thus have significant political implications. William Kornhauser has pointed to their importance in maintaining democracy in mass society, and Tocqueville anticipated that function when he toured the new nation more than a century ago.

The second example of secondary groups is bureaucracy. Countless sociologists have studied this form of social organization. The most noted study is Max Weber's, and Weber's ideal type describing the most salient features of bureaucracy is still useful today. Bureaucracies engage in the business of administration, and they do so through formally specified agreements pertaining to status relationships and procedures. Because of their standardized regulations and specialization of personnel, bureaucracies can be very efficient. The same characteristics, ironically, can make them not only inefficient but also frustrating and infuriating.

A common sociological observation concerns the formation of primary-group relations within secondary groups such as bureaucracies. The people who inhabit formal social structures have a tendency to create their own informal structures and relationships. Sometimes the informal structures actually support the goals of the organization; sometimes they do not.

As suggested in the work of Cooley, Durkheim, Toennies, and many others, there has been a steady trend toward secondary-group relations as societies have "developed" from preliterate to rural to urban. Increasingly, the intimate face-to-face associations of an earlier era have been replaced by more casual and impersonal secondary relations. This trend has not been without exception, however, as indicated by the popularity of such modern movements as encounter and sensitivity training.

The varied discussions of Part Two should have drawn your attention to a fundamental human dilemma. The agreements we form and keep as well as the groups we organize and live in are a mixed blessing. We profit from them in numerous ways, and we seem to lose something in the process.

Suggested Readings

Caplow, Theodore
1969 *Two Against One: Coalitions in Triads.* Englewood Cliffs, N.J.: Prentice-Hall.
I touched on this briefly in the chapter, and you might like to pursue it further. Caplow's analysis demonstrates the dynamic process of group formation. Though he focuses on a specific type of group (the coalition), the logic of creating purposeful partnerships can provide more general insights into the foundations of group life.

Hyman, Herbert and Eleanor Singer, Eds.
1968 *Readings in Reference Group Theory.* New York: Free Press.
The reference-group concept has received far more detailed attention in sociology than could be presented in an introductory chapter such as this. The Hyman-Singer collection of articles on the topic illustrates the many directions that sociologists have taken in the elaboration and application of this fertile idea.

Weber, Max
[1925] "Bureaucracy." In *From Max Weber: Essays in*
1946   *Sociology,* ed., trans. H. H. Gerth, C. Wright Mills, pp. 196–244. New York: Oxford University Press.
This work is a classic in two regards. First, it is a classic statement on the nature of bureaucracy. Second, it is a perfect illustration of the "ideal type" method of analysis discussed in Chapter 2, thus making it a wise investment of time and energy for the serious beginning sociologist (or for anyone else who wants to know why bureaucracies turned out the way they did).

Episode Six

Louise Roanoke leaned back in her office chair and sorted through a stack of mail. It was September; American University students buzzed through the halls again.

The school, situated on an artificial island anchored in Lake Michigan, had been constructed during the 1980s—just before the Great Depression. An expansive deck that encircled the floating campus was itself surrounded by the lake. To the west the Chicago skyline erupted, radiant now as the autumn sun began its slow descent.

There was so much to do, Louise worried: lectures to prepare, schedules to juggle, term projects to assign—the letter from the Department of the Interior to answer.

Roanoke straightened in her chair. At least, she decided, she would write next week's lectures before this afternoon. That way she could relax and enjoy herself tonight when she went to Monica's for dinner.

Louise removed several books from the shelf behind her. On a piece of notepaper she began to sketch an outline. But her mind strayed from the emerging lecture. She opened and reread the letter from the Department of the Interior.

The message was dated September 2, 2026. "Dear Dr. Roanoke," Louise read. "As you know, the position of United States secretary of the interior, since Allen Steinburg's untimely heart attack, is being filled by Edmund Slavik.

"Mr. Slavik has asked that I, as chairman for the acquisition of information on greens in the United States, write you.

"According to our files, you are engaged in sociological research on Green Colony. I understand, moreover, that you and two other sociologists were granted entrance to and actually visited Green Colony last June 28.

"As I'm sure you are aware, the level of anxiety in this nation is rising with regard to greens. The Society for the Protection of the Human Race (SPHR)—along with similar groups—is insisting on green extermination. Rumors are spreading nationally that greens, while passing as normals in larger society, are responsible for the rash of infant kidnappings that we have witnessed over the past forty years.

"The recently formed Association for the Prevention of Infant Kidnappings (APIK) threatens to become the modern counterpart of the Ku Klux Klan. Already this group has threatened vigilante 'law enforcement' against any green caught trespassing on private property in Arizona and New Mexico.

"I am sure you are aware of our problem: Whether greens are to be protected or prosecuted is a decision that must be reached rationally rather than emotionally. The decision must be based on fact.

"It is Secretary Slavik's sincere hope that some decisions regarding this possibly socially and economically dangerous group can be reached before or during the second National Conference on Human Mutations scheduled for May, 2027.

"It is his more immediate desire that in the meanwhile you relay to him any scientific data you may gather—or have gathered. Sincerely, Robert Grady, Assistant Secretary, United States Department of the Interior."

What Grady had not written in his letter to

Roanoke was that the FBI had been gathering information on kidnappings throughout the United States since long before the first conference the previous May.

While there was nothing official to link any kidnappings with Green Colony, some facts suggested a possible relationship. Kidnappings for ransom were understandable, but the infant thefts that had occurred increasingly over the past forty years were different. Never, in some 300 cases, had anyone demanded ransom. In all these cases, whoever had taken the infant apparently had not so much as attempted to contact the parents.

Of the 300 similar cases, 98 percent had been infant thefts from hospital maternity wings. The others were of babies still in their first year, stolen from playpens in their front yards, or from car seats while they awaited the return of their parents from stores. Three babies had been stolen by baby-sitters who had previously solicited their victimized clients.

Eleven parents of kidnapped infants had committed suicide as a result of their loss.

Roanoke reread Grady's letter. How would she respond? One thing she knew: She would like to consult first with Connie and Brad. She missed them. Connie had left three days before for the American Sociological Association annual meeting in New Orleans. She was to present a paper there on her preliminary work in developing a questionnaire to measure animosity toward greens within American society.

Brad had returned to Adamsville and was still there. He had written Louise early in August concerning an article he was preparing for the *American Journal of Sociology,* entitled "Cultural Agreements and Vocabulary."*

Brad's letter to Louise had discussed more than just his forthcoming publication. Some members of Adamsville—Duncan called them "radical militarists"—had begun to stockpile arms and ammunition.

Posers were buying the weapons on the outside and carrying them into the colony. This stockpile, along with small-scale solar weapons already existing in Adamsville, constituted a considerable arsenal.

The Elders exercised official control over the solar weaponry developed by the Adamsville corporation, Solar Transistors, Inc. But they remained unaware of the recent smuggling of arms from the outside. Duncan was unclear as to whether the stockpile was intended for use against outsiders or against Elderhome. He supposed both were possibilities: The radical militarists spoke increasingly of their distrust for the Elders and at the same time seemed concerned about threats of physical attack from hostile outside groups.

The Elders, and those who supported them, Brad termed "cooperationists." The essential difference between this group and the radical militarists, Brad wrote, was that the former stressed cooperation with outsiders while the latter insisted upon complete separation and isolation of Adamsville. Radical militarists maintained that total secrecy was necessary to the well-being of the colony and supported establishing an autonomous Green State separate from the United States.

Ironically the cooperationists appeared unaware of the radical militarists' growing strength. They seemed more concerned with a different problem —one they often referred to as a lack of loyalty on the part of some of their youth. Some greens, the Elders complained, were not assuming their full genetic potential. This malady could only be caused by their secret lack of commitment to Adamsville. One green poser, moreover, had delayed returning for the maturation rite until well after his thirtieth birthday. The cooperationists hoped Duncan could tell them why.

Duncan hoped so too, he wrote, but he could not be sure how long the compromisers would exercise authority over the colony. "If and when the radical militarists gain control of Adamsville," Brad concluded, "you can expect I'll be evicted immediately if not sooner."

Louise put Grady's official communication under a glass paperweight that her niece, Monica, had given her for her thirty-fifth birthday. She would consider her reply again tomorrow.

*In that scientific essay Brad had argued that a group's word choice in certain instances can be evidence of broader beliefs, values, and norms. Duncan had contrasted the implicit connotations of several pairs of words: "posing" and "passing," "rescue" and "kidnap," "birther" and "mother," "Adamsville" and "Green Colony."

Meanwhile, Gabriel Knapp had gulped a carton of milk—his mid-morning supplement. An interoffice memo stared up at him from his desk. He was to see the director of health services for Chicago National Insurance Company employees at 10:30. It was almost that now.

Gabe left his desk and took the elevator down to the health services department.

"Sit down, Mr. Knapp," the director suggested after they had shaken hands. "We keep files on each of our employees, as you know," he said, reaching for a legal-sized folder beside him.

"There was a time as recent as twenty-five years ago," the man smiled, "when this department operated primarily as a clinic. We dispensed aspirin, bandaged cuts, and took blood pressure. Now that most Americans monitor their own blood pressure we find we can turn our attention to related things."

"Yes," said Gabriel.

"We're missing the report of your recent physical, Mr. Knapp." Gabriel uncrossed, and then recrossed his legs.

"We have made a vigorous search of our files."

"I see," said Gabriel.

"Could it be, Mr. Knapp, that you inadvertently forgot to forward the report to this office?"

"I can check with my secretary," said Gabriel.

"This department," the director explained, "must send quarterly reports on all executives to the board of directors. That report is due at the end of this month. We must have your file complete by then, Mr. Knapp."

Gabriel rose, "I understand," he said.

He climbed the three flights to his office; elevators were difficult to think in. There was no medical report now. He had destroyed it before the rescue mission.

"He's been released," a co-worker offered as the two passed on the stairs.

"Who?" Gabriel called behind him, still ascending.

"That guy they arrested for the Lakeside kidnapping," called the other, descending from view.

"He came up with an alibi so they let him go."

Gabriel stopped his climb. How long could he continue to pose, he asked himself. There had been three ungreens in the crowd that afternoon. Who were they? Could they identify him?

And letters were coming again—friendly messages telling of his Adamsville family and friends. His stern parent had written suggesting Gabe spend the next few months as a kind of a rescue expert. The Chicago mission had gone so well, she wrote, Gabriel might consider several more missions. There was word of a birther pregnant in South Bend and due to deliver sometime in February.

How long could this go on? Gabriel resumed his climb. More immediately, he thought finally, he must get through the evening. He had consented to meet Monica's aunt for dinner at Monica's apartment.

"You'll love her," she had predicted. Later she added, laughing, "She's a sociologist, but you'll like her anyway."

When Gabe entered Monica's apartment that evening, the pungent aroma of soybean teriyaki greeted him. Monica offered him a glass of wine.

"No, thanks," he apologized, "just water for now. When's your aunt coming?"

"Pretty soon."

Gabe paced.

"Sit down," Monica suggested. "Don't be nervous."

Gabe positioned himself on the sofa. "Who said I'm nervous?" he protested, smiling.

The doorbell rang. Gabe remained on the sofa; he was not in direct view of the doorway. "Aunt Louise," he heard the pleasure in her voice, "come in! I have a friend here, someone I want you to meet. Here, let me take your coat."

"Monica, Monica," Gabe heard the older woman say, "it's good to be here."

"Come on, I want you to meet someone," her voice came closer.

"Aunt Louise, this is Gabe Knapp. Gabe, this is the aunt I've told you about."

Questions

1. How does Robert Grady's letter to Louise Roanoke illustrate one of the advantages of bureaucracy discussed by Weber?

2. How does the conversation between Gabe and the director of the company health services illustrate Parkinson's law?

3. Gabe attempts to conceal his inclusion in the category "green." How might inclusion in certain social categories affect a person's individual life?

4. Brad Duncan has discovered two factions in Adamsville: the radical militarists and the cooperationists. What factors do you suppose might lead a person to align with one faction in preference to the other? Would Roanoke, Batterson, and Duncan come up with different explanations because of their different theoretical points of view?

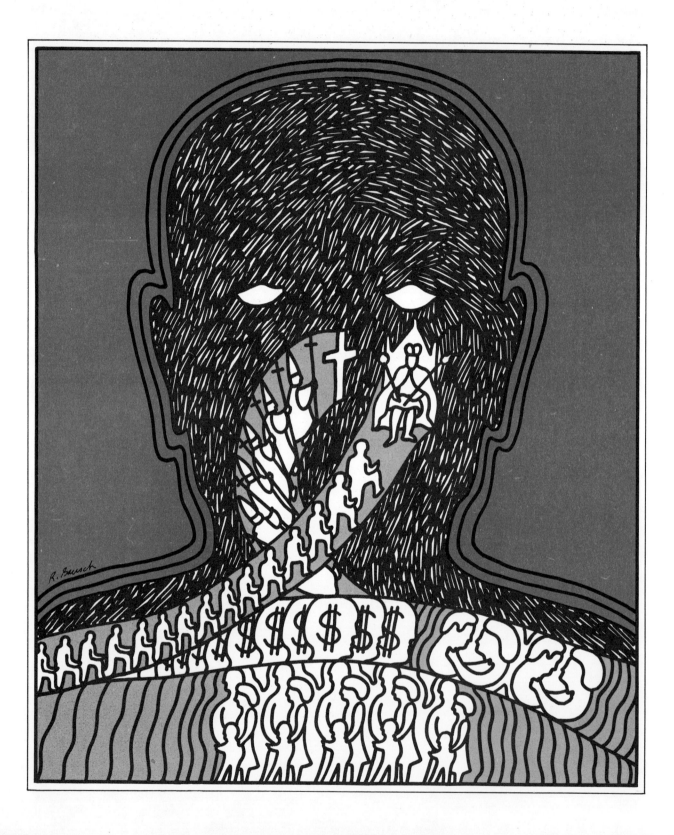

Part Three
The Structure of Agreements

Whether society has the same degree of "reality" as individuals is a matter that has concerned philosophers, sociologists, and others for a long time. You can't touch, kiss, or hit a society, and yet you know it's there. As we saw in Chapter 5, society is not only all around you, but it's also *inside you.*

The social reality that you observe and that lies within you is what I called an "agreement reality" in Chapter 1. It is composed of those agreements people have made, organized, and perpetuated. To the extent that we believe these agreements to be "real," they affect our attitudes and behavior. The six chapters in Part Three of this book address the ways in which we define our situations as real, and we are going to look at some of the consequences of those definitions.

As you'll recall from Chapter 4, "institutions" are sets of agreements relating to general aspects of social life. Examples include the family, religion, and government. Chapter 7 examines the process of institutionalization—how institutions are created—and we'll look at the links connecting the institutions of a given society. I also want to examine the implications of institutions for the personal experiences of individual human beings.

Chapters 8 through 10 discuss specific institutions. Chapter 8 addresses the family, an institution that exists in every known society but takes radically different forms. Chapter 9 deals with religious and educational institutions. Chapter 10 covers political and economic institutions. In each of these discussions, we'll see both the varieties of institutional forms in different societies and the dynamic processes that operate within those different forms.

Chapter 11 is a discussion of social stratification and mobility. We'll see that people are hierarchically ranked in all societies but that the dimensions along which they are arranged differ from society to society. These dimensions of stratification correspond to the major institutions of a given society. In some cases, the major ranking is in terms of wealth; in others, it revolves more around kinship, religion, power, or something else altogether. We'll look at the consequences of these rankings for individuals, and we'll also examine ways people move "up" and "down".

Groups as well as individuals are subject to the stratification process: Some are ranked higher than others. Chapter 12 concludes Part Three with an examination of minority groups. We'll see how minority groups are defined in societies and what difference it makes in the lives of their members. I'd also like to look at the role minority groups play in connection with the overall organization of society.

All in all, then, Part Three deals with the *persistent* "substance" of social agreement reality. Once you've finished these six chapters, you should understand more clearly how the agreements you make and the ones that were made before you got here affect your daily life and how they make life in social groups possible.

7

Institutions and Institutionalization

When people go into the country for a picnic, they often leave litter behind them on the landscape. The empty soft-drink bottles and cans, the paper and cellophane wrappers, cigarette butts, and garbage provide a record of their picnic—and constitute a part of the environment that later visitors experience.

When people interact with one another, they create agreements that remain long after the interaction is over. Like picnic litter, the agreements constitute a part of the environment that later "interactors" experience.

Different kinds of picnic litter, however, have differing degrees of persistence. Apple cores and orange peels are rather quickly biodegraded; aluminum and plastic stay around much longer. The same is true of the agreements created through interaction. Some disappear immediately: You and I agree to have lunch together, we have lunch, and the agreement disappears. Others—like the one against incest—seem to last forever. Sociologists have a name for the sets of persistent agreements about general aspects of social life: They call them "institutions." This chapter is about institutions and how they are created.

Before leaving the picnic-litter analogy, we might reconsider what we said about the rapidly biodegradable apple cores and orange peels. When they biodegrade, they decay, break down, and become an integral part of the soil upon which they were thrown. We tend to think they've disappeared, but, in fact, they have become a part of the foundation of life

itself. Rather than disappearing, the apple cores and orange peels have been transformed in such a way that they can never be picked up and carted away.

Something similar happens to many agreements and institutions. They become so totally ingrained in society that we can lose sight of their existence as agreements. They are no longer recognizable as "litter," having become an indistinguishable part of the social landscape itself. They become a part of the social reality—given, unquestioned, and immutable—that defines the limits of human social interactions and relationships.

Just as the physical reality of gravity prevents us from flapping our arms and flying around like eagles, the social agreements we internalize keep us from doing things we might otherwise do. The constraints that institutions place on us increase in direct proportion to the extent to which we regard them as part of "reality."

This chapter presents an overview of the ways institutions are created and how they operate in society. We'll see how they come to form a part of our social "reality," and we'll see the consequences of that process.

I want to begin the discussion with a review of the benefits and costs that agreements represent for us as individuals. Then we'll look at the ways in which agreements become institutionalized and perpetuated. We'll see how different institutions in a society are linked to and support one another, and we'll also see that they can and do conflict.

Next, I'll raise an issue that recurs throughout the other chapters of Part Three: the relationship between individuals and institutions. Institutions provide an important insight into the structure of social systems, but they also have a direct impact on the personal experiences of individual human beings.

The chapter concludes with an overview of those aspects of institutions that particularly interest sociologists. That overview will provide an organizational preview of the chapters to follow.

Agreements: A Balance Sheet

Every time you make an agreement with someone else, you both win and lose. Every benefit comes at a cost, and every cost has some benefit attached to it. This is true even in cases that appear at first glance to be one-sided.

If I offer to send you to Europe for the summer with $10,000 in pocket money and you agree to go, you will have to forfeit all those things you could do at home. If that seems a small loss to you, suppose that the alternative at home includes marrying the white knight or fairy princess and embarking on a life of eternal bliss. The bright lights of the Champs-Elysées will seem a little dimmer under those conditions, and you might not agree to accept my offer.

Or suppose I've just stuck a gun in your stomach and demanded "your money or your life." After appropriate consideration, you agree to hand over your money. As one-sided as this exchange may seem, the benefit accruing to you is evident in my initial demand. You get to live. Even if it costs you the $10,000 you were going to spend during the summer in Europe, you'll probably feel it is worth the price.

Every gain comes at a loss, then, and every cost brings a benefit. The balance is unequal, however. You don't make agreements unless the gain at least equals the loss and preferably exceeds it. No one makes agreements in which they know they will lose more than they gain. To understand this, you need to realize the variety of "gains" people get from agreements.

The gains we realize in agreements extend well beyond such obvious commodities as money, food, physical pleasures, and the like. Prestige, love, respect, obligations due to us, the inner glow of charity and altruism, thoughts of divine reward, the cessation of pain or of its threat, and countless other immeasurable rewards and anticipated rewards tip the balance in favor of this agreement or that.

All this applies to the agreements that you and I make with each other. But what about all those agreements that other people made before you and I got here? Nobody ever asked my opinion about wearing clothes during the hottest day of the summer. I don't recall agreeing to that, and I don't imagine you do either.

In an important sense, both you and I agree to the beliefs, values, and norms that were pretty much worked out before we were born. More accurately, we agree to them every day we are alive. We agree to them by *keeping* them. Every time you wear clothes in the heat of summer, you are maintaining an agreement with those around you that people should wear clothes no matter how hot it gets. You maintain agreements like that through your actions, and so do I—even when we don't think in terms of agreements.

Moreover, we "make" the agreements that were here before we were because we gain more than we lose. You make an agreement to wear clothes in the heat of summer at the cost of sweaty discomfort but with the benefit of staying out of jail. If you feel that staying cool is worth the risk of jail, you won't agree to wearing clothes.

Probably you don't regret or even question most of the agreements that were made before you got here, since the benefits to you are clearly greater than the losses. You probably don't begrudge the agreement that we won't murder each other, even though that diminishes your freedom to do as you choose. I'd guess that you willingly relinquish the freedom to drive on the left side of the freeway in exchange for the degree of safety you have when you drive on the right side.

We simply can't have a society—we can't live together in groups—without agreements. All of us benefit individually from the presence of agreements that make it possible for us to live together with a degree of protection against the intentional or inadvertent evils we might work on one another. This does not mean, however, that all the specific agreements in force at a particular time are beneficial to all or even most individuals.

Institutionalized agreements persist outside of any conscious, rational process in which we seek to create the greatest benefit for ourselves as individuals. Some persistent agreements provide benefits to a few individuals while being disadvantageous to the many. In other cases, it isn't clear if any individuals derive particular value from agreements, yet they persist anyway.

As we look at the process through which agreements are perpetuated, it will become clear that we've set up society in such a way that our agreements persist whether you and I get any personal value out of them or not.

Institutionalization

Sociologists use the term "institutionalization" to refer to the process through which the agreements people make are subsequently established, organized, and perpetuated. Large sets of established, organized, and perpetuated agreements pertaining to a general facet of social life are called "institutions."

It will be useful to begin this discussion with an example of institutionalization that reflects a conscious and deliberate act. When the American found-

ing fathers forged an alliance among the several colonies, they created an electoral college through which representatives of the new states could meet and select a president. It was a reasonable agreement, reflecting the nature of the initial alliance.

The electoral college became firmly institutionalized. It was written into the Constitution, and—at least equally important—subsequent generations of Americans ratified the agreement by electing their presidents through the electoral college system.

Many Americans argue today that the electoral college is outdated, that it is no longer appropriate or functional. We are no longer an alliance of semiautonomous states, they point out. We are a nation and should elect the president directly. It is further noted that the present system could result in one person's being elected president over an opponent who had actually received more votes. Yet the electoral college system persists.

Once established, institutionalized agreements often persist long after the conditions that made them reasonable and functional have disappeared. In part, this is a function of habit and custom.*

*William James, the American psychologist and pragmatist, suggested, "Habit is thus the enormous fly-wheel of society, its most precious conservative agent" (1890:121). I don't want to detour into an examination of the psychological functions of habit for individuals. Much day-to-day evidence supports the effect that James described.

GOOD GRIEF!! — THEY'RE STARTING TO WALK, AND DEVELOP THEIR OWN PERSONALITIES !!!

Once agreements become institutionalized, they are difficult to change. Many societies have agreements that give women the responsibility for raising children, including those tasks that men could perform. (Abigail Heyman, Magnum)

Many agreements become institutionalized by habit and custom even when they have no apparent reason or function at the outset. When Handel's great *Messiah* was first performed in the mid-eighteenth century in London, the king of England was in attendance. As the rousing "Hallelujah Chorus" began, the king rose to his feet and remained standing throughout the chorus. Nobody has ever figured out why. Evidently, no one thought to ask him, but in eighteenth-century England you didn't remain seated when the king stood up. Everyone in the audience rose and remained standing throughout the "Hallelujah Chorus," and two centuries later people who've never heard that story jump to their feet as soon as the chorus begins.

Institutionalized agreements offer a degree of predictability and security in the face of what might otherwise be chaotic and uncertain group existence. Group participation in such agreements, moreover, enhances the warm feelings of belonging and identity.

You may have experienced this if you were ever in an audience standing for the "Hallelujah Chorus," and you've probably had other experiences of it, too.

Comfort and security of habit are not the only reasons why institutionalized agreements persist, however. Vested interests exert pressure also. Examples of vested interests in the persistence of institutionalized agreements are plentiful. Those who profit most from a particular economic system—whether capitalist, socialist, or other—are the most active supporters of its continuation. People who hold political power in a society support the maintenance of the political system that gives them power.

In large degree, then, institutions persist because they are supported by the people who benefit most from them. Very often, moreover, because certain individuals are benefiting most from the current state of affairs—especially in economics and politics—they have a greater say than other people in whether the institutions persist or change. Legislatures, for example, seldom if ever vote to reduce the numbers of their legislators.

Habit and vested interests are important in maintaining institutions, but their persistence arises from an even more basic cause. Social institutions have been constructed in such a way as to support their own survival.

Institutions such as the family, education, and religion are composed of agreements governing broad areas of social life. For an institution to function, people must know and keep its agreements. Each institution is thus structured to serve the function of socialization, which is the teaching and learning of agreements.

As we saw in Chapter 5, socialization is most effective when agreements are internalized, that is, when people take agreements inside themselves and make them a part of their personal feelings and sentiments. Internalization, in turn, is most effective when the agreements are reified, when people lose sight of them as merely agreements and regard them as representing reality and truth.

Once the agreements making up an institution have become reified, the die is cast. Who would consider changing truth or reality? Those who have reified and internalized the agreements during their own socialization within an institution become the socializers of the next generation, and the institution persists.

Our social institutions, then, promote their own survival. They are aided in this function by force of habit and by the vested interests of those who benefit most from them. To understand the persistence of institutions more fully, though, you need to realize that institutions are also constructed so that they support one another.

Linkup in Social Space

In Chapters 4 and 5, we discussed role conflict, noting that the different statuses that a person occupies may require contradictory behaviors. Very often, role conflicts occur in connection with the statuses you occupy in different institutions. Think of a conflict that might arise in connection with familial and educational statuses: Suppose your parents want you to come home for their wedding anniversary on the day before your final exams begin. Role conflicts are plentiful in any society.

In a broader view, however, societies cannot survive if role conflicts are the rule rather than the exception. If everyone's role expectations disagree more than they agree, organized group life will not last very long. In societies that survive, the overall pattern is for different institutions to support one another by reinforcing the behavioral expectations of people occupying statuses in each. This process is called "integration." The institutions of a society must be integrated to some extent for the society to survive.

Religion is largely a family affair in many societies, for example, including both the United States and preliterate tribes. Early religious socialization occurs in the home. In Japan and elsewhere, family altars bring religious practices into the home. Many religions, in return, stress the value and sanctity of family life. Much of the disapproval of practices such as extramarital and premarital sexual relations that threaten the survival of the family is religious in nature and form. There is considerable accuracy in the motto "The family that prays together stays together."

Family and education are also entwined. The earliest education occurs within the family as children are given the fundamental skills and attitudes that prepare them for participation in formal educational institutions. In large degree, the motivation to do well in school reflects the desire to please parents and, in some cases, to bring honor to the family. Schools, for their part, educate children in the skills and attitudes necessary for forming and supporting their own families when they become adults.

Political values and norms are also learned first in the home. In America, the general commitment to democracy and the importance of obedience to authority are both taught first by families. The government in many societies—often in cooperation with religious institutions—controls the formation of families by determining who may marry whom and under what conditions. Some laws, like those against bigamy, support the persistence of a particular type of family. Other laws specify and formalize the legal obligations of family members to each other.

Family and economic institutions have interacted throughout the history of human social development. In many preindustrial societies, for example, the family *was* the chief economic unit. It produced, distributed, and consumed economic goods and services. In modern societies, families teach children the fundamental skills and attitudes necessary for partici-

pation in the economy, and the family is still the chief unit of consumption.

Religious and educational institutions support each other in many ways. As only one example, many of the early schools and universities were organized by religious bodies for the purpose of perpetuating their religious agreements. Many still have that purpose.

Religious institutions often support political institutions by providing divine backing for a particular form of government. The once-popular idea that kings had a "divine right" to rule is a good example. Governments, in turn, have provided special favors to religion. Tax-free status comes to mind.

The most famous sociological analysis of the links between religion and economics is Weber's *The Protestant Ethic and the Spirit of Capitalism* (1905), which describes how the Calvinist emphasis on frugality and worldly success created the economic base for the development of capitalism. Marx was concerned about the links between these same two institutions. He referred to religion as "the opiate of the masses": It distracted workers from resisting economic oppression by promising rewards in the hereafter.

Education is linked to both government and the economy, links that are clear in a society such as the United States. Schools provide education in "citizenship" and give people the fundamental skills needed for political participation. Government, in turn, owns most of the schools in America and provides financial support to others. Schools also train people for occupations within the economy. Economic institutions support education in many ways. One of those ways is by providing funds for scientific research, which benefits the economy through new technology. And students who do well in school are given better jobs in the economy.

The links between political and economic institutions, and their mutual support of one another, are especially evident. Laws can make potentially competing economic systems illegal, while economic production provides the basis in wealth that makes governments powerful. On an interpersonal level, political leaders may give favored governmental treatment to the industries and companies that have contributed most heavily to their campaign funds. C. Wright Mills's well-known analysis of the "military-industrial complex" described the width and depth of mutual support between these two institutions in contemporary America (1958,1959).

These are only a few of the ways in which the different institutions of a society support one another's survival. The interlinking of institutions is a powerful force for maintaining the overall status quo. Changes in one institution would necessitate countless changes in others. As perhaps the clearest illustration of this, consider American resistance to communism—an economic system—especially at the height of the cold war. Communism was seen as a threat to religion because of the atheism associated with it, a threat to the family largely because of reports that Russian children informed on their parents, a threat to government by being too democratic on the one hand and too totalitarian on the other ("the dictatorship of the proletariat"), and a threat to education in the form of political indoctrination. Every American—whether "for" or "against" communism—felt that a switch from capitalism to communism would do more than modify the economy.

Thus far, I have painted a picture of institutional collusion that might make social change seem impossible. Without undercutting the power of mutual support among institutions, I want to point out that the institutions of a given society are never perfectly integrated and supportive of one another.

In Part Four of this book, we're going to look at some of the ways in which society's agreements change, but it will be useful to raise that issue here since it illustrates a source of conflict and poor integration among institutions.

American women have demanded the same opportunities as men to participate in the economy. This situation has required changes in education. Women cannot have the opportunity to work as physicians, for example, without the opportunity to attend medical school. Similar changes are occurring in engineering and business education. There are also important ramifications for the institution of the family. Many women have been unable and unwilling to continue fulfilling the traditional role of full-time homemaker while attending school and working at a profession.

I could cite countless other examples of institutions getting out of phase with one another, produc-

ing conflicts. As scientists have developed ever more effective contraceptive techniques, for example, religious institutions (particularly the Roman Catholic church) have had to review their positions on birth control. Religion and science, more generally, have clashed frequently throughout history. Religious institutions have provided views about the nature of physical reality, and scientific research has produced a stream of contradictory points of view.

Institutions also conflict with one another on the basis of their vested interests. Shall businesses be taxed at a higher rate so as to provide additional funds to support education? Should more of our tax money be put into education, health care, or military defense? These are the sorts of questions that have always produced a degree of institutional conflict. The representatives of different institutions have very different points of view, just as individuals do when they have different personal vested interests.

Institutions also have "jurisdictional" conflicts with one another. Families, churches, and schools all perform the socialization function in a society, as we've seen, yet each of these institutions approaches the matter from a somewhat different point of view. Very often, a child will be taught one thing at home, another thing in church, and something else altogether in school. In instances of this sort, the several institutions subvert rather than support one another.

Throughout the remainder of Part Three, we are going to see some more of the ways in which institutions support one another's survival and the ways in which they conflict. The general conclusion to be taken away from both of these situations is that the institutions of a society are intricately interwoven. It is impossible to understand one institution without taking the others into account.

At this point, however, let's return to an issue we raised earlier in the chapter. Let's bring individual people back into the picture.

Institutions and Individuals

The institutions of a society represent *agreement* reality. Recall that I juxtaposed agreement reality and the experiential reality that flows from the direct personal experiences you and I have outside the

Institutions are organized sets of agreements that specify the kinds of experiences that individuals may have. Institutions have the primary function of supporting group survival. (Burk Uzzle, Magnum)

realm of agreements. One of the examples used earlier contrasted your experience of loving someone just because you love that person with loving someone because you are expected to.

I want to conclude this discussion by noting that within institutionally organized society, experiential reality can pose a *threat* to agreement reality. Experiences individuals have very often contradict and threaten the persistence of institutionalized agreements. The logic and dynamic by which institutions function for their own survival often produce an organized reaction against personal experiences that do not correspond with those agreements.

Imagine a society governed by a monarch whose rule has been justified by the religious institutions of that society and supported by other institutions as well. Now imagine an individual in that same society having a direct personal experience of human equality. Suppose the direct personal experience led the person to feel that ultimate truth had been revealed to him or her by God. The threat posed by that experience would extend far beyond the monarch's job security. People like that get killed.

In an important sense, religious institutions guard against the danger of individuals' having direct religious experiences that might threaten society. In the same sense, marriage and the family can be seen to guard against the danger that individuals will have direct experiences of loving one another in ways that do not support group life. As long as such experiences are channeled through established agreements, societies can continue to function with stability and harmony, but direct personal experiences are a constant threat to the survival of society. The treatment of heretics and "radicals" throughout history points to the seriousness of that threat.

I realize that it's fairly easy to find examples of "evil" people who control the institutions of a society and use those institutions against other people. This situation often occurs when powerful people attempt to protect their own vested interests. There is more to it, however.

The Dilemma

We cannot live together in groups without established and reasonably well-integrated institutions. Beyond mere survival, you and I personally benefit from our institutionalized agreements, despite the fact that we lose freedom in the process. By agreeing to speak a particular language, for example, we give up the freedom to talk gibberish but we gain the ability to communicate with each other.

Agreements don't work unless we keep them, and we are more likely to keep them if they are reified and internalized during socialization. In the process, however, we can lose sight of the fact that they are only agreements; we can begin thinking they have a truth and reality of their own.

Through the processes of reification and internalization we become the *effect* of our agreements instead of their *cause*. It's as though you and I built a house and locked ourselves inside. Later, when we became uncomfortable with the house, we had forgotten that we had the keys to unlock the door, and the house became a jail. If we could remember that we built the house and that we had the keys to it, we could go outside and build another house, more to our liking.

Two centuries ago, Jean Jacques Rousseau wrote: "No man has any natural authority over his fellow-man, and might makes no right. We have nothing left save agreements, then, as a basis for all legitimate authority among men" (1762:6).

We can't live together without agreements. If we are to take charge of our agreements, creating and perpetuating only those that have value for us, we must first recognize that agreements are only agreements, and we must understand how they function. In an important way, that's what sociology seeks to do.

A Preview—
How We'll Look at Institutions

Chapters 8 through 10 examine the five institutions that sociologists have studied most. These institutions are extremely complex, so we have to limit our discussions somewhat. In this section, I want to outline some of the specific topics that are of special interest to sociologists. In the chapters that follow, we will use these topics to guide our examination of each institution.

Experiential Reality

I'll begin the consideration of each institution with a reference to some of the common, human experiences that predate the institution and form bases for it. We'll see that such experiences are common though varying, and we'll also see that they potentially threaten the survival of organized society.

Not surprisingly, we'll find that people have made agreements regarding the kinds of experiences in question. In the form of established institutions, those agreements describe the structure of experience that supports the survival of the society as a whole.

Functions Served

The primary function of any institution is the survival of society, the survival of continuing social-group life. Inseparable from that is the function of the institution in perpetuating itself.

Each of the institutions we discuss serves a number of more specific functions for society. We'll see that some of the specific functions flow directly from the experiences giving rise to the institution. Other functions are only indirectly linked to the primary experiences.

In the discussions of the functions of institutions, we'll consider both "manifest" and "latent" functions. The former refers to the formal, stated function of the institution. The latter refers to the less obvious, indirect functions served by institutions. As an example, the primary manifest function of the American school system is to educate young people. A latent function of the same institution, however, is to keep young people out of the job market. A knowledge of both manifest and latent functions is essential to the understanding of institutions, and we'll look at both.

Structural Varieties

Having examined the key functions of a given institution, we'll look at some of the different forms it takes in different societies. It will become apparent that a wide variety of social structures can accomplish the functions required for system survival.

The examination of structural varieties will cover both historical variations—looking at the evolution of the institution, for example—and cross-cultural variations.

American Analysis

Once we have seen the broad range of variations in an institution historically and cross-culturally, we'll focus on American society. Although we narrow our focus, we'll see that there are many varieties of a given institution within the United States. We'll also see that the United States has developed some unique institutional forms.

Structure of Experience

As I've already indicated, institutions arise around certain experiences that people have. Institutions serve the survival of society by structuring such experiences, ensuring that individual experiences do not threaten society. I want to look at the ways in which human experiences are structured in each of the major institutions. In part, this will involve an examination of the roles, statuses, and social identities that are created in connection with those institutions.

Experience of Structure

The institutions of a society make up a good portion of agreement reality. You'll recall that the agreements that make up our points of view regarding what's true, preferable, and expected "seem real." If you've reified the view that eating worms is disgusting, you will *experience* disgust if you see someone eating a worm. You will experience something worse if you find you have eaten a worm yourself.

We do experience our agreements; we experience the institutional structures that have been created. Nonetheless, everyone has personal experiences that lie outside the institutionalized agreements of his or her society, and that experiential reality often conflicts with the agreement reality of institutions. Institutionalized agreements are very often a source of dissatisfaction for individuals, which in part is a reflection of the fundamental fact that institutionalizing one particular pattern of experience dampens others. Also, as we have already seen, institutions often survive the conditions that made them functional and satisfying, and once they are outdated they can become a hindrance to individual satisfaction.

Functional Alternatives

Given the frequent conflict between experiential and agreement reality, it should come as no surprise that people often attempt to modify the institutions that are dissatisfying to them. We'll see, for example, that some Americans are dissatisfied with the structure of the family, and new forms are being suggested and tried. We'll conclude our analysis of each major institution with an examination of some of the functional alternatives that have appeared.

At this point in human social evolution, it appears as though every institutionalized social pattern had its beginning as a functional alternative to some other pattern. Each of the "problems" that people face in this connection seems to have begun as the solution to an earlier problem. There's a reason for this.

For an institution to persist and thereby survive, it must become somewhat rigid. The process of socialization—involving reification and internalization—impedes the adjustment of social forms to changing conditions. I referred to this earlier as a "dilemma," and that's what it is.

In our examinations of the functional alternatives to established institutional forms, we are going to see that some social experiments survive and others do not. Those that survive do so through institutionalization, thereby creating the same conditions for dissatisfaction that produced them in the first place. Those new forms that "successfully" avoid institutionalization don't survive.

New alternatives to the family and to institutionalized religion, for example, aim at recapturing the

Institutionalized agreements are often a source of individual dissatisfaction and conflict. (Paul S. Conklin)

"freshness" of experience that some people feel has been lost through institutionalization. Some of the experiments appear to succeed in recapturing that freshness of experience, but they either lose it through institutionalization and the attendant rigidity, or they lose it for lack of institutionalization. Figure 7•1 provides a graphic illustration of the continuing, cyclical nature of institutionalization.

The key to unlocking the persistent dilemma of institutionalization appears to lie in recognizing and understanding the nature of social agreements. If it were possible to create sets of agreements without reifying them, it might be possible to review and modify all our agreements from time to time as conditions change. Without the recognition of agreements for what they are, it seems likely that the institutions we create tomorrow will be no more satisfying and fulfilling than those of today or yesterday.

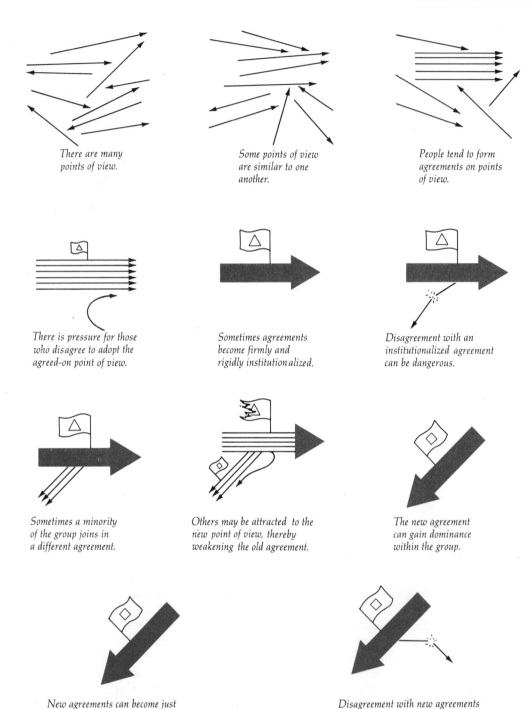

There are many
points of view.

Some points of view
are similar to one
another.

People tend to form
agreements on points
of view.

There is pressure for those
who disagree to adopt the
agreed-on point of view.

Sometimes agreements
become firmly and
rigidly institutionalized.

Disagreement with an
institutionalized agreement
can be dangerous.

Sometimes a minority
of the group joins in
a different agreement.

Others may be attracted to the
new point of view, thereby
weakening the old agreement.

The new agreement
can gain dominance
within the group.

New agreements can become just
as firmly and rigidly institu-
tionalized as old ones.

Disagreement with new agreements
can be just as dangerous as
disagreement with old ones.

Figure 7·1   Institutionalization is forever.

Summary

People are constantly making agreements in all aspects of daily life. Every agreement involves both costs and benefits, though we make agreements on the assumption that the benefits will outweigh the costs. Sometimes we are conscious of making agreements, and other times we "make" them just by the act of keeping agreements previously made by others.

The persistence of agreements "previously made by others" is one of the central topics of sociology. "Institutionalization" refers to the process whereby agreements are established, organized, and perpetuated. "Institutions" are the large sets of institutionalized agreements that pertain to a general facet of life, such as the family, religion, education, politics, and economics.

Sometimes agreements become institutionalized through custom or habit. Some are formally established, as by law. All institutionalized agreements, however, generate vested interests—people and groups who profit from them and seek to have them perpetuated.

The primary purpose of an institution is to support the survival of group life. Many powerful, individual drives, desires, and experiences could threaten the survival of the group, and institutions prescribe structures of individual behavior, thoughts, and experiences that support the continuation of the group. Many different forms seem to serve the functions of the several institutions, and great variations are found around the world.

The several institutions of a society often support one another. Thus, the religious agreements of a society may support the agreements making up the family as an institution, and the family may support religion in a similar fashion. The mutual support among institutions is a source of resistance to social change. Where institutions conflict, however, they may be a source of social change itself.

Sometimes institutions are a source of satisfaction for individuals, though this is not their primary purpose. Where institutionalized agreements conflict with individuals' experiences, however, institutions become a source of dissatisfaction. In such situations, individuals sometimes break the agreements, and

sometimes they seek to change them—substituting new institutional forms for old ones.

There is a dilemma in all this. We need institutions in order to live together in groups. Yet we have tended to create institutions as self-perpetuating "truths" rather than as convenient agreements. Through reification and internalization, we make it difficult to change agreements that no longer are satisfying to us. Whenever we create alternative institutional forms—reifying and internalizing the new agreements—we simply create a new prison to replace the old one. We lay the groundwork for later dissatisfaction.

Only through a full, sociological understanding of what agreements are and how they operate can we create social structures that will nurture individuals while making group life possible.

Suggested Readings

Durkheim, Emile
[1893] *The Division of Labor in Society.* Trans. George
1964   Simpson, pp. 233–55. New York: Free Press.
In his chapter entitled "The Progress of the Division of Labor and of Happiness," Durkheim begins his analysis of the causes of complex social organization. He examines the often-conflicting demands of individuals for happiness and the survival needs of the group, noting among other things that suicides occur only in "civilized" societies.

Freud, Sigmund
1930   *Civilization and Its Discontents.* Trans. Joan
        Riviere. Garden City, New York: Doubleday.
Here's another oldie-but-goodie. Within the context of psychoanalytic theory, Freud portrays social life as an endlessly unsatisfying struggle between the aggressive and self-destructive drives of individuals and the need for order if society is to exist. The creation and maintenance of order, moreover, frustrates individuals, requires countless renunciations of desires, and produces guilt. Freud did not have a particularly optimistic view of individuals and society.

Mead, George Herbert

1934 *Mind, Self, and Society.* Ed. Charles Morris, pp. 227–336. Chicago: University of Chicago Press.

Mead's discussion of society is the classic interactionist statement of institutionalization. Beginning with the social organization of insects, Mead examines the part played by communication, interaction, and self-discovery in the creation and recognition of social institutions. In addition, Mead examines the issue of social conflict and looks at the obstacles to the "ideal society."

Weber, Max

[1925] *The Theory of Social and Economic Organization.*
1964 Trans. A. M. Henderson, Talcott Parsons, pp. 363–86. New York: Free Press.

In his discussion of "The Routinization of Charisma," Weber expands on a point only touched on in this chapter. Some of society's institutionalized agreements have their beginnings in the ideas and actions of special, charismatic leaders. How is it that those agreements are perpetuated long after the death of their originators? This is the question addressed by Weber.

Episode Seven

Louise Roanoke and Gabriel Knapp stood facing one another, frozen. Louise Roanoke knew now—with too sudden a force —why the name had sounded familiar. Fragmented thoughts flashed through her brain. Monica dating a green! This man, from the welcoming ceremony at Adamsville, involved with her own niece?

The "rescuer" as a subject of sociological inquiry she had partially grown to understand. Indeed, the emotional and rational need to protect him, a subject, had caused much of her previous consternation over how to answer the Department of the Interior's letter. But that her niece knew and loved the mutant seemed impossible.

Gabriel was suffering himself. He had begun to perspire.

Monica watched the two, confused.

"I'm very glad to make your acquaintance," Dr. Roanoke managed, extending her hand toward Knapp.

Gabriel remembered her face. He had seen the three ungreens at the edge of the crowd that day, watching, taking everything in, soaking it up like sponges. He extended his hand to meet Roanoke's. "I've heard much about you," he stammered. "You're here in Chicago at American University?"

"Yes, right," Louise managed, taking a chair. "Yes. Right."

"Well," attempted Monica, aware of the tension between her guests, "how have your separate paths crossed before now?"

Gabriel eased himself onto the sofa, deliberately not responding to Monica's question. Louise Roanoke held the cards now, he reasoned. He would let her make the first play.

Louise searched Monica's countenance, wondering how much her niece knew about Knapp. "Get us all some wine, why don't you, Monica," she said finally.

Confused and uncomfortable, Monica poured three glasses of wine. Meanwhile Gabe had gone to the kitchen where he refilled his glass of water.

"Still only water, Gabe?" Monica asked.

"Yes, please," he mumbled.

"That's all right, Monica," the aunt's voice seemed to grow increasingly nervous. "Leave the third glass. One of us can drink it later."

"Aunt Louise," Monica insisted, "what's going on here?"

Dr. Roanoke looked first at her niece and then at Gabriel. She remained silent for a long time. "Gabe," she said at last, "how much have you told my niece about yourself?"

Quickly Monica turned toward Gabriel. "What's going on?" she demanded again.

"I haven't told her everything," Gabe murmured.

Louise helped herself to one of the wine glasses

Monica had filled. "Monica," she said, "do you remember when Brad and Connie and I went to Adamsville?"

"Yes, of course," replied the niece.

"Gabe and I saw one another in Adamsville," Roanoke said simply.

"I don't understand," Monica shrugged. Then, to Gabe: "Is that true? Were you in Green Colony?"

"Yes," responded Gabriel. "I was in Adamsville."

"Why?"

"I was there on business. I had to go."

"I didn't know Chicago National did business with Green Colony."

"It wasn't that kind of business exactly," Gabe admitted. Then after a pause he added, "Monica, I'm a green."

Monica stared, incredulous.

Gabe had begun to pace. "Could we turn up the lights?" He ran his hand through his hair. "It's awfully dark in here."

Louise flicked a switch on the wall beside her; light flooded the room.

"What kind of business were you doing in Adamsville?" Monica asked slowly. She appeared strangely calm in the immediate shock of Gabe's revelation.

"I had rescued an infant from death," came the simple, direct reply.

"What infant?" Monica asked, her voice rising.

"A baby boy, born where he should never have been born. A green who must be raised in Adamsville by his own people in order to survive. I rescued him, took him home. That's all."

"What are you talking about?" Monica insisted.

"Monica," Louise explained, "when Connie, Brad, and I were in Adamsville, we had occasion to witness a ceremony. It was called a welcoming ceremony. The colony was welcoming an infant into its midst. A member of the community had rescued the infant from death, we were told. The rescued baby had been born outside Adamsville. It was Gabe who rescued the infant."

"I'm sorry," Monica shook her head, "I still don't understand. Where did you get this baby, Gabe?"

Again Gabriel sat down. "Here in Chicago," he said.

"*Where* here in Chicago?" demanded the younger woman.

"Lake Hospital," he said.

"*You* kidnapped that baby?" whispered Monica in disbelief.

"I rescued one of our children," Gabe corrected her.

"You *kidnapped* that baby" Monica's voice was shrill. "How could you do such a thing?"

"I had to, that's all," Gabriel insisted. "The baby would have died here on the outside. He had to be raised in Adamsville by parents who know how to care for him. I *rescued* him."

"You stole him," Monica breathed. "What about his parents? Did you ever think of his parents?"

"He will have good parents," Gabe replied.

"I'm talking about his *real* parents, Gabriel! What about his mother? Have you read about his mother in the newspapers? She's so grief-stricken she had a nervous breakdown."

"Birthers do not love their children," Gabe replied calmly.

"I don't understand you," Monica shook her head.

"Birthers—people who bear babies—they don't love their infants right away. Parents must grow to love their children."

"That's crazy," Monica turned toward her aunt. "What's going on?"

Louise looked at Gabriel. "Gabe," she said, "why do your people believe that the baby you rescued is a green?"

"He had a green chromosomal father," Gabe answered.

"And his mother was an outsider?"

"Yes."

"Then the baby was only half mutant," Louise said.

"There is no such thing," Gabe flatly replied.

"I don't understand," confessed Dr. Roanoke.

Gabe took a long drink from his water. "There is no such thing as a half-green," he repeated.

"If a baby is born," Dr. Roanoke challenged, "of a green chromosomal father and a nonmutant chromosomal mother, then the baby is a partial mutant."

"A green is a green," Gabe said. "That's all there

is to it. There is no such thing as a partial green. A green mutant's genes are always dominant."

"How do you know that?" Roanoke insisted.

"I know it, that's all. It's simply the truth." Gabe was growing angry.

Monica stared into the red wine as it shimmered in her glass. Taking a long, deep breath, she shook her head almost imperceptibly. "I still cannot believe," she said slowly, "that you could do such a thing with no regard whatsoever for the feelings of that infant's real mother."

"The baby's mother," Gabriel reaffirmed wearily, "has no feelings for the child. Birthers do not love their infants."

"You really believe that what you did was right, don't you?" Monica asked, suddenly realizing that what she said was true.

"I'm a moral man. I wouldn't do anything which I considered immoral. Of course the rescue was right." Gabe lowered his voice. "You know, I risked my life to save that baby."

Knapp then explained that he was himself rescued as an infant. "If it had not been for the courage of my own rescuers," he proclaimed, "I would have perished on the outside. I had to do the same for another of my people."

"Is it an Adamsville law that green infants born on the outside must be rescued?" inquired Louise.

"Of course," Gabriel responded.

"Does the law demand that you perform a rescue?" Louise asked.

"No," Gabe said. "Conscience demands that I rescue. The religion I learned from my parents demands that I rescue."

The smell of teriyaki had penetrated Monica's apartment. "Monica," Louise said, aware that the food would soon burn, "are you still interested in serving dinner?"

Monica exchanged her emptied wine glass for the extra one she had poured previously. "I'm not hungry," she whispered.

Louise stood. "Well," she said, straightening her clothes, "you two have plenty to talk about. I think it's best if I go on now."

Monica followed her aunt from the room and, near the front door, helped the older woman with her coat. Louise kissed her niece, then suddenly hugged her. "I'm truly sorry the evening turned out this way," she said.

"I still can't comprehend it," Monica murmured.

It was 10 P.M. when Louise Roanoke left her niece's apartment, and she was tired. But rather than going home, she caught a late ferry to American University Island. For reasons of which she herself was uncertain it had become important to her that she answer Grady's letter immediately. There was no time to confer with her colleagues.

In her office Louise pushed off her shoes, slumped into her comfortably familiar desk chair, and sighed deeply. It all seemed some preposterous nightmare. Monica, her own dear Monica, dating a mutant kidnapper!

Again Dr. Roanoke read the letter she had received from the office of the secretary of the interior.

How would she respond now, she wondered. As a sociologist? As a United States citizen who believed in strict law enforcement at least for major crimes of violence? As a fond aunt, concerned and tormented over the involvement of her niece?

Just how much allegiance did she owe the government, Louise asked herself. American University had received substantial federal grants to finance the sociological research of greens. In that sense the government was her employer, was it not? Did she therefore owe the Department of the Interior the whole truth?

What consideration did she owe her subjects, the citizens of Adamsville? The sociologists had gained access to the colony on the premise that what they learned there might help the mutants—not further their chances of annihilation.

What responsibility did Louise have to future nonmutant parents who might unwittingly produce green offspring? Should she not do all within her power to stop any pain these potential victims might suffer?

Finally, how much loyalty did she owe her own niece? Louise had grown close to Monica. Like her aunt, Monica enjoyed batting ideas back and forth. As an attorney she thought deeply about legal and social issues. She believed strongly, for example, that the civil rights of individuals must be vigorously protected. She spoke often of the moral obligation resting upon lawyers, sociologists, and others to protect Americans' unalienable rights. But the women spent only a part of their time together discussing ideas. Even more often they spoke of routine activities, friends and acquaintances. Last week Monica had invited her aunt to meet a "special friend."

Monica had met him, she explained, at a lunch counter one day almost two years ago. Monica had initiated the conversation. "Aren't you eating today?" she had asked the man, noting that in front of him was only a glass of ice water and a cup of coffee.

"Not hungry," he had responded.

"Do you work here in the Loop?" Monica had asked.

"Yes," he said. "You?"

They had talked awhile, Monica told Louise, and then he asked if she would like to go for a walk. Monica agreed and the relationship had begun.

Louise realized that Monica had met many friends since coming to Chicago. Consequently she had suspected the importance of her niece's desire that her aunt become acquainted with this particular man.

"How serious are you about him?" Louise had asked in the straightforward manner their relationship demanded.

"I love him," Monica had replied.

Now Louise Roanoke sat pondering alone in her office. As Monica's aunt she found herself angry that her niece loved a mutant. As a sociologist she chided herself for that anger. Louise reflected: Would she relay to the government Gabriel Knapp's identity, surrendering a person Monica loved to an unsure but dangerous fate?

Dr. Roanoke filled a small pot with cold water and scooped ground coffee into an accompanying metal basket. Soon the aroma of coffee would fill her office.

Then she rolled a sheet of paper into her typewriter. She would rough out her response tonight.

"Two colleagues and I," she wrote, "entered Adamsville, June 28. At that time we witnessed a 'welcoming ceremony,' which marked the acceptance of an infant into the community. It is possible," Louise wrote, "that this infant was 'rescued' without the knowledge of those outsiders caring for the baby at the time.

"As a sociologist I have reason to believe that the 'rescuing' of infants may be behavior that is well institutionalized in Adamsville. It is difficult, however," Roanoke concluded, "to say more without further study."

Louise poured herself a cup of coffee. She wondered what Monica and Gabe were saying to one another.

Questions

1. Institutions can become so totally reified that we can lose sight of the fact that they are made up of agreements only. How does the episode demonstrate this?

2. Does Gabe now have a vested interest in the perpetuation of "rescue" as an institutionalized agreement? Why? What vested interests does Louise have?

3. How does Monica's reaction to Gabe in this episode illustrate some of her own reified agreements?

4. How does this episode illustrate what Simmel called the "tragic potential" of institutions?

8

Kinship and the Family

Many changes have taken place in the American family during this century, all well publicized. Divorce rates have increased greatly. Increasing numbers of young couples openly live together as husband and wife without actually getting married. Unmarried women openly become mothers and raise their children in one-parent families. Young married couples report plans and desires to remain childless. Groups of young people form communes based on the concept of "group marriage" in which sexual partners shift continuously.

Reports of these changes have been a source of horror for some and a cause for celebration for others as the box on page 180, "Is the American Family in Trouble?", reports. Many people from both camps have asked the question that titles the box, wondering whether the family will survive in America; and just as many have suggested that it won't.

The conclusion that the American family will not survive reflects a conceptual confusion, a confusion between "the family" as a social institution and one of its particular forms. The sociological point of view on social institutions (outlined in Chapter 7) can help us to understand this confusion. It can also give us a different understanding of the ongoing changes in family life.

The family, like other social institutions, is a set of agreements that structure certain human experiences in such a way as to support the survival of group life. A wide variety of family forms satisfy the needs of the group, as we can see by looking at different societies around the world.

In this chapter, we're going to study the functions the family serves as an institution. We'll look, too, at some of the different family forms that satisfy those functions. Then, using this general, theoretical understanding as a background, we'll probe more deeply into the nature of American family forms. Finally, as a way of understanding the changes that have been taking place, we'll discuss individuals' experiences of the American family.

Functions of the Family

Every institution is a reconciliation of certain group needs with certain individual experiences. The group need most relevant to the family as an institution is the need for new group members. You simply cannot have a group without people, and as long as individuals die, new ones will have to come from somewhere to take their place. The group need for new members extends beyond mere biological reproduction, however. It includes everything that lies between a newborn baby and productive participation in society. Individuals must be fed, nurtured, protected, and socialized. These functions are in large part performed by the family.

The human experience of sexuality is, of course,

Is the American Family in Trouble?

FAMILY UNIT IN TROUBLE BUT IT WILL PREVAIL SAY EXPERTS[1]

HAPPY FAMILY LIFE RATED NO. 1 VALUE[2]

FAMILY DISORGANIZATION SPREADING RAPIDLY[3]

Many American families do not fit the pattern of the ideal family of the past: father at work, mother at home, two or three children happily growing up to become like Mom and Dad. A number of trends can be noted. Mothers of young children are now going to work in large numbers. In fact, by 1973, 36 percent of married women with children under six were working full- or part-time. In addition, more and more families have only one parent. According to Isabel Sawhill of the Urban Institute, by 1975 there had been "a phenomenal growth in female headed families; from one out of ten only ten years ago to one out of seven today."[4] Also, more couples are living together while they are either postponing or deciding against marriage and children. Others are living in communes or "open marriages."

Will these trends continue, resulting in a basic change in the American family? Are they evidence of an alarming family disorganization that is undermining our way of life? Or are they evidence that Americans are working out new and more diverse ways of living satisfactory family lives? Most experts predict that although we will continue to live in families of some kind we will never go back to the old ways. The experts cannot agree, however, about whether this is a calamity or a blessing. Whatever the experts say, three out of four people questioned in a recent nationwide poll agreed that "the traditional family is important to Americans and should be preserved." Some of these people may be severely disappointed should they find themselves among the increasing numbers of Americans who are not living in traditional families.

What do you think?

[1]*Eugene* (Oreg.) *Register Guard*, headline, August 8, 1973.
[2]Ibid., May 16, 1974.
[3]Ibid., September 25, 1975.
[4]*Portland Oregonian*, September 29, 1975.

---

directly relevant to the group need for new members. Our natural, biological sex drives are sufficient for reproduction, but as I've mentioned, reproduction is not enough. Reproduction without child rearing does not ensure the survival of the group. Consider the following aspects of the problem:

1. Babies and young children require nurturance —food, warmth, and protection.

2. From the beginning, children must be socialized into meeting their own needs, into becoming more self-sufficient.

3. Children must also be socialized into patterns of interaction within the group.

4. Children need emotional support and guidance in the formation of self-image and self-confidence.

The box on page 183, "Social Identity and Extreme Isolation," describes the case of Anna, a child who was "reared" in almost total isolation. We can see the importance of the "emotional" elements of replacing society's members. Imagine a society in which all children received the treatment Anna suffered.

These needs for individual and group survival are one of the reasons why the family is often called the fundamental unit of social organization. The first human social "group" was probably some kind of family, made up of at least a mother and child and perhaps a father. Recall the discussion in Chapter 2 of George Herbert Mead and his theory of the need for cooperation. This discussion points to the importance of enlarging the family group beyond just the mother and child. If human beings were fundamentally ill equipped to survive in the presence of stronger and faster enemies, consider the predicament of a mother saddled with a dependent baby. This prehistoric problem has modern parallels that we'll see later.

No one can say how or why families developed beyond the simple mother-child dyad. If an answer to this question is ever found, it will probably involve some of the functions that families serve for their adult members. For one thing, couples living together on a regular basis can satisfy each other sexually. Families, then, can offer a way for individuals to accommodate their sexuality. Families are also a source of emotional support for adults, potentially able to provide love, comfort, security, and other forms of emotional support. Adult family members, moreover, can protect each other in the face of illness and injury. Family groups have, from the beginning, served functions for children and adults—and for society.

Although the growth of social organization involved the joining together—voluntarily or by force—of families in cooperative mutual support, the earliest human families were undoubtedly self-sufficient. We can see self-sufficiency in families in preliterate societies in the world today and in families from earlier, more developed societies. Indeed, many types of families have served *all* the functions required for the survival of group life, including political and economic ones (which we'll discuss in Chapters 9 and 10). Winch (1971:31) has described the traditional peasant family of China, for example, as "a family of great functionality," saying: "For perhaps twenty centuries there existed among the peasants of China a familial form that was just about as completely functional as is theoretically possible." In addition to the functions I've mentioned, the Chinese family carried responsibility in religious, educational, political, and economic matters.

The modern family is very different from the Chinese peasant one. Its development is often seen

The key function of the family is the replacement of society's members. (Hap Stewart, Jeroboam, Inc.)

as a process in which functions have been transferred from the family to other institutions. A great many of the family's original functions—religious, educational, political, and economic—have been shifted to separate institutions bearing the names we associate with those functions.

The family has survived as a social institution despite this shifting of functions. In a variety of forms, it continues to serve the needs of society *and* individuals with regard to reproduction, sexuality, and physical and emotional nurturance. I want to discuss this variety now. Once we see the variety of workable agreements that can satisfy the needs for group survival, we'll have a better perspective for assessing the American case.

Dimensions of Variation

In this section, we'll look briefly at two general areas of variation in family forms. We'll begin with some organizational and structural variations. Then we'll look at variations in sex roles defining interactions within families.

Organizational Differences

Family composition   For most Americans, the word "family" refers to a wife, a husband, and their children, a type of family called (technically) the **nuclear family.** Although the nuclear family is the norm in American society, it is only one type of family among many. An **extended family**—like the traditional Chinese peasant family mentioned earlier —is one that includes more than two generations. It is composed, for example, of a husband-wife couple, their children, and their children's children.

Although I've spoken of a husband-wife couple, the couple is not the only type of sexual union that exists in families. **Monogamy,** the couple, involves only one husband and one wife. **Polygamy** is an agreement permitting more than one spouse. A man can have more than one wife or a woman more than one husband.

The agreement on monogamy has been reified in America, so the idea of polygamy may seem strange to you. As children and young adults we are brought up believing and feeling that one husband and one wife is the "proper" basis for a family. It is worth noting in this connection that most societies in the world have at least permitted polygamy although none seems to have required it. Insistence on monogamy has been most typical of modern, developed countries.

Lineage   The notion of lineage or "descent" is also somewhat foreign to Americans. If I asked you to sketch out your "family tree," you'd probably begin with your mother and father, add their mothers and fathers, and the tree would branch out across successive generations. Our society has a general agreement on **bilineal descent:** We trace our ancestry back through both males and females. Other societies —the Dobu Islanders, for example—have a **matrilineal** agreement. They trace ancestry only through females. Still others—such as the ancient Jews and traditional Japanese—are **patrilineal.** They trace their descent through males.

Some patrilineal elements exist in American agreements. The clearest example has to do with our use of family names. Traditionally, women have taken their husbands' family names upon marriage. Children take their fathers' family names also. Recently, however, many American women, seeing this patrilineal agreement as evidence of sexual inequality, have objected to it and have retained their maiden names after marriage.

Location   The question of where a newly formed family should live is also a matter of differing agreements. In America, the predominant agreement reflects a **neolocal** pattern for the residence of nuclear families: They are expected to set up housekeeping on their own at a location of their own choosing.

The **patrilocal** Baganda of central Africa, however, have a different agreement. Their idea is that the new family should establish its residence with

the husband's family. The traditional Japanese (and others) share a similar agreement.

The **matrilocal** Hopi Indians see things just the opposite, as indicated in the following description of the events following a Hopi wedding.

> The bride dresses in her new clothes and returns home, where she is received by her mother and her female relatives. She is accompanied on the journey by her husband's relatives, who make a final exchange of gifts with her mother's household. During the evening the groom appears at his mother-in-law's home and spends the night. The next day he fetches wood for her and from then on is a permanent resident in her house—unless a divorce sends him packing (Queen et al. 1961:54).

The remark (in the quotation) about divorce introduces the next dimension of variation I want to consider. Sex roles within families are structured differently in different societies, particularly with respect to power and responsibilities.

Sex Roles in Families

Who was the "boss" in your family when you were growing up, your mother or your father? The sex of the person who holds the power in the family is another way in which families differ, and different societies have different general agreements on this.

Had you grown up in a traditional Japanese family, you would have had no trouble in answering the question, for the traditional Japanese are **patriarchal.** They have an agreement on the dominance of males. Your mother would have had little or no say in whether your father should establish a business or in whether you should go to college. Your

---

Social Identity and Extreme Isolation

The importance of informal social interactions with family and peers in the development of social identity and the learning of social agreements is nowhere clearer than in those rare, tragic cases of children raised in near-total isolation from others.

Anna was born in 1932, the second illegitimate child of a woman living with her own father, a stern and widowed farmer. Upset by his daughter's sexual indiscretions, Anna's grandfather refused to have the child in his house. For the first 5½ months of her life, Anna was moved around through a number of children's homes and families who considered adopting her. All attempts at adoption were unsuccessful.

At 5½ months, Anna was brought into her grandfather's house at last. Anna spent the next 5½ years lying on a bed in a dark and scarcely furnished room upstairs. Anna's mother worked all day on the farm and was away from home most evenings, so Anna saw almost nothing of her—or of anyone else. Anna was seldom fed, seldom cleaned, seldom moved, and apparently never spoken to or loved.

When Anna was discovered at age 6, she was malnourished, sick, and filthy. And she was totally lacking in any of the social skills that primary relations normally provide. She could neither walk nor talk. She gave no evidence of intelligence or communication.

After about two years of professional care, Anna demonstrated a mental development approximately that of a 1-year-old. She could walk and feed herself, but she still could not talk. By the time of her death at 10 years of age, she was talking at about the level of a normal 2-year-old and had made further progress in caring for herself and dealing with others. A clinical psychologist who examined Anna a year before her death concluded that as an adult, she might achieve the mental level of a 6- or 7-year-old.

Given her near-total lack of socialization, who or what do you suppose Anna "thought" she was? If you were to devise an alternative to the traditional American family, what child-rearing functions would you have to accommodate in that alternative?

Source: Kingsley Davis, "Final Notes on a Case of Extreme Isolation," American Journal of Sociology *52(March 1947):432–37.*

father would have made those decisions, and he would have been strongly influenced in making them by his father.

Other societies and subcultures share a **matriarchal** agreement. In this agreement women are dominant. E. Franklin Frazier (1939:125), among others, said that the matriarchal pattern characterized the black American family immediately following Emancipation.

> These women had doubtless been schooled in self-reliance and self-sufficiency during slavery. As a rule, the Negro woman as wife or mother was the mistress of her cabin, and, save for the interference of master or overseer, her wishes in regard to mating and family matters were paramount. Neither economic necessity nor tradition had instilled in her the spirit of subordination to masculine authority. Emancipation only tended to confirm in many cases the spirit of self-sufficiency which slavery had taught.

There has been considerable popular controversy in recent years as to whether the *contemporary* black American family is matriarchal. The debate on this topic has taken place against the backdrop of a belief that the typical American family is egalitarian, that is, that husbands and wives share power equally.

An increasing body of sociological research has resulted in questions, however, about both the accuracy of the egalitarian view and the generality of the pattern. Mirra Komarovsky (1962), for example, concluded that the lower-status–blue-collar families in America are relatively patriarchal, while families of higher status are more egalitarian. A study of families in Detroit (Blood and Wolfe 1960), on the other hand, suggested that neither race nor social class is as important as urban-suburban differences, finding that urban families are the more egalitarian. Finally, you'll recall from Chapter 1 that Herbert Hyman and John Reed (1969) found that blacks and whites appeared to be equally matriarchal in how they perceived power within their families.

The question of who has power within the family should be placed in the context of what men and women *do* in families: what their roles are. It has long been recognized that a given society has general agreements about the tasks men and women in

Traditionally in America, women are responsible for the internal affairs of the family. An important part of the traditional socialization of girls has been preparation for that role. (Bill Owens, Magnum)

families are to perform. It has also been recognized that those specific tasks vary somewhat depending on the society's level of development. As a very broad generalization, men hunt and fish in preliterate societies, and women gather fruit, nuts, and berries and raise the children. In industrial societies, on the other hand, a general pattern is that men work in the economy to earn support for the family while the women run the internal affairs of the family.

Talcott Parsons and Robert Bales (1955:151) have suggested a general pattern in the roles assigned to men and women in families, a pattern that crosscuts cultures and time. Using terms taken from Parsons' theoretical discussions of the social system, they concluded that men generally serve **instrumental functions** for the family (relating the family to the outside world) while women generally serve **expressive functions** (concerned with affection and emotional support within the family).

This view corresponds generally to the experiences of people brought up in developed, Western societies, but recent investigations of preliterate societies suggest that the generalization may not be as general as it appeared. A study of over 800 societies characterized by subsistence economies (Aronoff and Crano 1975) found that women played appreciable roles in satisfying the instrumental functions that Parsons and Bales assigned to men. Overall, Aronoff and Crano estimated that women produced 44 percent of the food consumed in the societies studied.

I want to return to sex roles in the family later in this chapter. We're going to see that agreed-on family roles in a society importantly affect roles of men and women outside the family. This is an issue of considerable interest in America, and we'll examine some of the research conducted relating to it.

We have seen that a variety of family structures have been created to fulfill the functions the family serves for the survival of group life. None is necessarily more effective than another, and very different forms appear to accomplish the social task. Now I want to take a closer look at the changing structure of the family in America.

Changes in the American Family

To discuss changes in the American family, we need a standard against which to measure the changes. What is the family changing from? We have already partly answered the question. The dominant agreements during this century have created a monogamous, bilineal, egalitarian (sometimes), neolocal nuclear family. The family has been grounded in marriage, typically reflecting religious as well as legal sanctions. Sexual expression has largely been limited to married couples, and divorce has been discouraged and difficult to obtain. The prime task of the husband/father in the family we describe has been the economic support of wife and children through participation in the economy. The wife/mother, on the other hand, has borne primary responsibility for running the household and raising the children.

The husband/father's participation in the economy has been a significant feature of the American family. In contrast to the farming family of years past, the contemporary nuclear family has played little part in economic production. It has, however, continued as the important unit of economic consumption. Houses, cars, food, and other consumer items are typically distributed and consumed through families. Not surprisingly, antipoverty measures have often been directed at families, as the box on page 186 on family assistance plans illustrates.

So far, I've been describing the family of the generally shared agreements of American society. Not everyone agreed that this family was best, of course, and not every family looked like the picture those agreements described. As we discuss some changes in the American family, we'll see that actual practices have gotten further and further away from what the agreements prescribed.

Sexuality and Marriage

Earlier in the chapter we noted that families provide adults with sexual security. This benefit comes at a cost. The family permitted sexual expression to married couples, but it also limited their sexuality. Couples could have each other, but they couldn't have anyone else. Marriage has thus involved a gamble that husband and wife would always find each other sexually satisfying. When the gamble has not paid off, the family agreements have been a source of dissatisfaction. (Those agreements have often been a source of dissatisfaction for the unmarried.)

As we shall see more and more in this book, people often respond to dissatisfying agreements by breaking them. The so-called sexual revolution provides an excellent illustration of this response. It

extends to all sexual behavior, not just to sexual behavior of married couples. Witness the difference
between the American agreements concerning premarital sex and the actual situation.

Despite the American institutional agreement
against premarital sex, sociologists now estimate that
between 85 and 90 percent of American men and
around 70 percent of American women have sexual
intercourse before marriage. The situation is not new,
but it is more extreme than it was before. Studies of
women born between 1900 and 1910 show a 50 percent nonvirginity rate at the time of marriage (Scanzoni and Scanzoni 1976).

Estimates of extramarital sexual relations are
harder to come by. In the 1940s, the Kinsey studies
showed that half the married men and about a fourth
of the married women had committed adultery by

The Pros and Cons of a Family Assistance Plan

Should the United States government guarantee a
minimum income to all families in the United States?
This issue was debated in Congress in the early
1970s after President Nixon proposed a family
assistance plan to replace the present welfare system. Nixon's plan would have provided for a basic
family-income floor with payments available to
working poor people as well as to those now on
welfare. Nixon's plan was not accepted, but the issue
will be raised again. The problems of poverty and
welfare have not been solved.

Supporters of a guaranteed minimum income
point out that many United States families are poor
even though one or both parents are working full
time. For example, in 1973 the official poverty line
was $4,275 per year for an urban family of four;
approximately 4.8 million families had incomes
below that level. Almost one-fourth of these families
were headed by a full-time, year-round worker. The
children in these families suffer a great deal from
the fact that their parents' jobs pay so little. The
guarantee of a minimum income would give them a
better chance in life. These are the working poor.

There are also families in which no one is able to
work either because of disability or because of
child-care responsibilities. They, too, would benefit
from a federal guaranteed minimum income plan
characterized by uniform benefits throughout the
United States. Further, such a plan might not be as
demeaning as the welfare system.

Opposition to a guaranteed minimum income
includes both conservatives and liberals. Conservatives argue that such a plan would be too expensive
and that it would destroy work incentives unless
measures to compel work were included. Liberal
critics contend that present proposals, such as the
Nixon plan, set benefits too low to take anyone out
of poverty, that the work-encouraging provisions
are coercive, and that such a guarantee would sub-
sidize employers who pay very low wages. Wages
should be raised instead, say the liberals, and jobs
provided for those who are unemployed.

The United States is the only industrial nation
in the world that does not have a program for sup-
plementing income for low-wage families. Do you
think that Congress should approve such a plan?

the time they were forty. It is generally presumed that these rates have increased since then (see Scanzoni and Scanzoni 1976:449).

Another indication of changing sex norms can be found in the increased openness with which sexuality is discussed. The accompanying box, "Research and the Sexual Revolution," describes public responses to sexuality research as an example of such openness.

In terms of the family itself, the sexual revolution

Research and the Sexual Revolution

One of the twentieth century's most sensational pieces of research on human subjects was published in 1966 in a book called *Human Sexual Response*.[1] Reporting twelve years of research on human sexual functioning, William H. Masters and Virginia E. Johnson were immediate publishing successes as well as targets for sometimes bitter criticism from other professionals. Both acclaim and notoriety derived from the same source: in addition to asking 694 women and men about their sex lives, they actually observed and photographed, under laboratory conditions, more than 10,000 male and female orgasms. In these observations, the response of the human body to sexual stimulation was, for the first time, meticulously measured and recorded during both masturbation and intercourse. In the book these data are presented in exhaustive detail. Their primary finding was that the cycle of human sexual response always proceeds through a series of phases—from arousal through orgasm to recovery—with characteristic physiological changes at each stage. The research discredited some widely held beliefs about sex: that the size of the penis affects a man's sexual performance; that there are two types of female orgasm, one clitoral and one vaginal; and that women, like men, are limited to only one orgasm during a sexual cycle.

Human Sexual Response was a best-seller, highly unusual for a technical medical treatise. At the same time, the research was attacked on the grounds that it was immoral, that the motives of the researchers and the volunteer subjects were suspect, and that it represented a dehumanization of an essentially private and intimate experience. Masters and Johnson, as well as their supporters, replied that it was no more immoral than studying the functioning of the gastrointestinal tract and that accurate scientific knowledge about sexual processes is a necessary basis for moral choice and greater personal fulfillment.

Masters and Johnson published a second book, *Human Sexual Inadequacy*,[2] in 1970. In this book they discuss the causes of sexual inadequacy and describe the treatment processes they invented to help women and men overcome difficulties in sexual functioning such as frigidity and impotence. Since the publication of *Human Sexual Inadequacy* the Masters and Johnson techniques have been adopted by many therapists—psychologists and counselors as well as medical doctors—throughout the United States. Among these, there are undoubtedly some unscrupulous imitators who have no training in the methods of treatment and whose main goal is to make a profit for themselves.

The flock of imitators is only one indicator that the work of Masters and Johnson is now accepted as a very significant scientific achievement. The knowledge developed by Masters and Johnson has helped to dissipate the ignorance, fear, and shame that surrounded sex for so many and that still often prevents satisfying sexual experiences. The critical cries of ten years ago are no longer heard.

Do you think the popularity of sex research will result in long-term changes in people's attitudes or does it just represent a passing fad? What other topics do you think might generate this amount of popular attention in contemporary American society?

[1]William H. Masters and Virginia E. Johnson, *Human Sexual Response* (Boston: Little, Brown, 1966).

[2]Masters and Johnson, *Human Sexual Inadequacy* (Boston: Little, Brown, 1970).

Source: Ruth Brecher and Edward Brecher, eds., An Analysis of Human Sexual Response *(New York: Signet Books, 1966).*

is probably likely to have its greatest impact in the growing separation of family from marriage. There are no reliable data on the numbers involved, but a

---

How Children Affect Their Parents' Marriage

Most young couples get married expecting to have a home and family. Marriage counselors advise young couples who are having problems with each other to be cautious about having children. "Don't expect to save a bad marriage by having a baby," they say. The fatigue and changes in routine following the baby's birth only add to previous tensions. But what will a baby do to a good marriage? Will the sound of little feet make a happy home happier? Since 1929 sociologists have looked at this question in numerous studies of satisfaction with marriage. The research has repeatedly shown that both men and women become less and less content with their marriages during the early years. There is a particularly sharp drop in satisfaction after the birth of the first child. After that things get worse. The low point in marital happiness, especially for women, seems to come when the children are in elementary school.

In general, childless couples are more satisfied with their marriages than couples who have children, but these findings only tell us what happens to most couples, not to every couple. Some people are happier with life after their families start to grow than they were before. Social science can never predict exactly what will happen to specific individuals from the conclusions of large studies. It can only tell us that there is a high probability that the birth of a baby will make parents less content with their relationship with each other than they were before the baby came.

What do the data suggest for the future of the family? Why do couples continue to have children?

---

great many unmarried couples now live together, maintain households, have sex, and sometimes bear children. The ritual act of marriage is the only difference between many such families and the traditional model.

Many people living together in nonmarriage families regard the arrangement as a possible prelude to marriage itself. The purpose of such "trial marriages" is to give the couple an opportunity to learn whether they are compatible enough to enter into a more binding relationship. The pattern parallels a suggestion made by Margaret Mead in 1966 when she proposed a two-stage marriage. In stage 1, a couple lives together as husband and wife but avoids having children. If they find living together satisfactory, they can move on to stage 2 and childbearing. Mead's proposal is clearly being tested although it never received serious legislative consideration.

In part, the proposal and practice of trial marriage reflects a growing recognition of the difficulties of parenthood. The accompanying box, "How Children Affect Their Parents' Marriage," discusses some of those problems. Notice as you read the box that these sociological observations contradict long-accepted views about the joys of parenthood.

Changing sex norms, then, are producing many changes in the agreements relating to family structure in America. The women's movement is having an impact, too.

Sexual Equality in the Family

Earlier in this chapter I discussed the different roles men and women in the American family play. Although we noted considerable variation, we saw that the predominant American agreement regarding roles gives the husband primary responsibility for supporting the family financially and the wife primary responsibility for managing the internal affairs of the family.

Criticisms of this agreement are not hard to find. The accompanying box on technology and the housewife, for example, describes one source of complaint. In a radical critique, David Cooper has called the American nuclear family a "fur-lined bear trap," a seductive and subtle mainstay of the capitalist society:

"The power of the family resides in its social mediating function. It reinforces the effective power of the ruling class in any exploitative society by providing a highly controllable paradigmatic form for every other social institution" (1974:360).

Other, less radical observers have noted that the American woman has generally gotten a bad deal from her particular status in connection with the family. For generations, young American girls have been taught that they could best realize their human worth as wives and mothers. Those who have sought careers outside the family have had to fight agree-

ments to the contrary. (I examine this in some detail in Chapter 12).

Both men and women have internalized the view of women as wed to the family and domestic chores, and it is hard to exaggerate the extent to which we have done this. None of us is exempt, as Sandra Bem and Daryl Bem (1971:259) report.

Consider, for example, the 1968 student rebellion at Columbia University. Students from the radical left took over some administration buildings in the name of equalitarian principles which they accused

Technology and the Functions of the Housewife

Has modern technology with all its labor-saving devices made the housewife into a lady of leisure? "Negative" is the conclusion drawn from an analysis of at least twenty studies, extending over fifty years, of how women spend their time. Most of these studies were done using guidelines prepared by the U.S. Bureau of Home Economics with the practical purpose of helping the American homemaker. They give us an unusual opportunity to compare the daily routines of several generations of housewives who kept detailed diaries of their activities at 5-minute or 15-minute intervals for a day or a week at a time.

The full-time housewife, the one who did not work outside the home, spent 55 hours per week on household tasks in the middle 1960s. This was slightly more than the 52 hours per week spent by similar housewives in 1924. Why should this be so? The data on changes in what housewives actually do suggest that higher levels of consumption have created new chores to replace those eliminated or lightened by new technology. Housewives today spend more time on laundry in spite of automatic washers and driers, probably because we own more clothes and change them more often. Increased consumption also leads to more time spent shopping and traveling on household errands. As standards change

and consumption rises, child care also takes more time.

The explanation may not be completely satisfactory, however; the studies also show one type of housewife who has lowered the hours she spends on housework. In the 1960s, the married woman employed outside the home spent only about 26 hours per week on housework. If employed women can spend so few hours at housework, why do non-employed women work so long and so hard at home? The research forces us to dismiss some plausible explanations. Full-time homemakers do not seem to have a greater burden of household tasks than working women, nor do they hire domestic help less frequently than their working sisters. Neither group of women gets much help from husbands, so the willingness of the man to take over does not explain the fewer hours spent by working wives. Available research gives us no satisfactory answer. It may be that, as Vanek suggests, the stay-at-home wife works so long to show that she is making a valuable contribution to the family. It may be that the working wife simply can't do two jobs thoroughly. Whatever the reasons for the differences, neither the full-time housewife nor the working woman/housewife are ladies of leisure.

What do you think might explain these findings?

Source: Joann Vanek, "Time Spent in Housework," Scientific American, November 1974, pp. 116–20.

the university of flouting. Here were the most militant spokesmen one could hope to find in the cause of equalitarian ideas. But no sooner had they occupied the buildings than the male militants blandly turned to their sisters-in-arms and assigned them the task of preparing the food, while they—the menfolk—would presumably plan further strategy.

Even in those presumably equalitarian "dual-profession" families in which both husband and wife pursue careers, Margaret Poloma and T. Neal Garland (1972) found a fundamental belief that the husband was ultimately responsible for the family's financial support while the wife was ultimately responsible for the internal affairs of the family. In case of conflict or crisis, the families Poloma and Garland studied would resort to the traditional sex roles. This, the researchers suggest, is the basis for women's disadvantage in the professional world.

> We wish to argue that underlying the discriminatory evidence uncovered by researchers is an institution of our society that most are very reluctant to attack—the institution of our family system. It is the family that stands in the way of a woman's career advancement and is perhaps a major reason for employers discriminating against women (1972:201–2).

I do not wish to suggest that there is anything wrong with women's occupying the family roles traditionally associated with their sex. Indeed, as is often reported, many women—perhaps a majority—prefer the traditional family role to occupational roles in society. The point is that institutional agreements become reified and internalized in such a way as to interfere with the desires and aspirations of individuals. The established agreements that make social life possible can also make it dissatisfying.

There is special irony in the reified view that in America families are for women. Against the backdrop of considerable folklore about marriage being a trap laid by women for unsuspecting men, Jessie Bernard (1972) has compiled a body of rather curious data. In terms of health, happiness, and a host of other variables, married men fare better than single men, while married women fare *worse* than single ones. If anyone profits from marriage, it is men. Table

Table 8·1   Men Profit More from Marriage than Women

Mental health problem	Men Single	Men Married	Women Single	Women Married
	Percent scoring "high"			
Depression	50	37	35	54
Severe neurotic symptoms	30	17	4	11
Phobic tendency	40	30	44	55
Passivity	66	50	57	74

Source: Adapted from Genevieve Knupfer, Walter Clark, and Robin Room, "The Mental Health of the Unmarried," American Journal of Psychiatry 122(February 1966):842. Copyright 1966, The American Psychiatric Association. Reprinted by permission.

8·1 presents some comparisons regarding mental health.

The growing concern over rights and responsibilities in marriage has produced another innovation. In all societies, marriages are by contractual arrangement, either formal or informal. They represent a set of agreements binding on the marital partners and perhaps on others as well. In the United States, the nature of the agreements has typically been specified by law and by religious traditions.

Many couples getting married today are changing this situation. They are tailoring the agreements of marriage to their own liking. In place of the traditional vows to "love, honor, and obey," many modern marriage contracts specify the details of rights and responsibilities of both the husband and wife. An excerpt from one such contract is illustrative of this practice.

> THE PARTIES AGREE to share equally in the performance of all household tasks, taking into consideration individual schedules and preferences. Periodic allocations of household tasks will be made, in which the time involved in the performance of each party's task is equal. (Reprinted in Ritzer 1974:302.)

The idea of writing such a marriage contract seems bizarre to many Americans. But is it so strange? Are there no reasons? As Susan Edmiston writes,

WE PROMISE TO LOVE HONOR AND OBEY OUR PERSONALIZED MARRIAGE CONTRACT............

Marriage Contract for Tony and Sue

"Sitting down and writing out a contract may seem a cold and formal way of working out an intimate relationship, but often it is the only way of coping with the ghosts of 2,000 years of tradition lurking in our definitions of marriage" (1973:133).

Marriage is a contractual structuring of certain human experiences so as to support the survival of society. Traditional marriage contracts represent *tested* ways in which such experiences can be structured in the interests of group survival. The innovation of couples writing their own marriage contracts, however, is further evidence that the established institution has not always been satisfying to the individuals involved.

Divorce

The clearest evidence of dissatisfaction in marriage is divorce. In the United States, divorce is a legal and—especially for Roman Catholics—a religious matter. The legal aspect is a function of state laws, so the agreements on divorce have differed greatly around the country. In recent years, however, divorce laws have been generally liberalized. Many states have instituted a "no-fault" form of divorce in which

married couples—especially if they are childless—can dissolve their marriages on the basis of mutual consent.

Our national divorce rate is evidence of one of the most radical changes in the American family during this century. In 1974, there were 2,223,000 marriages in the United States and 970,000 divorces or 1 divorce for every 2.3 marriages. Contrast these figures with 1 divorce for every 11.4 marriages in 1910 (U.S. Bureau of the Census 1975a).

Sociologists (for example, Goode 1961) have often studied the causes of divorce, including marriage at a young age, impulsive marriage, economic problems, religious differences, parental unhappiness, and differences in social class.

From the point of view of this chapter, the *consequences* of divorce are at least as interesting as the causes. We've seen that the family serves important social functions. When families fail, we should expect to see secondary effects in relation to those functions.

Recall that one aspect of the family's socialization function is to provide social identities to the children raised in the families. When families are disrupted by divorce, we should expect to see disturbances in the development of social identity among the families' children. Figure 8·1 presents the results of a study of this.

Morris Rosenberg (1965), in a study of self-image among adolescents, found that self-esteem was lower among those whose families were disrupted by divorce. Self-esteem was lowest in those cases where the mother (and the children) was relatively young at the time of divorce (indicated in the first part of Figure 8·1). The function of the family in relation to children's social identities, however, is even more evident in the second part of Figure 8·1. Children whose mothers remarried exhibited higher self-esteem than those whose mothers did not remarry.

Divorce also disrupts the family's economic support function. This is particularly evident in the case of the divorced mothers of dependent children. Besides the fact that women earn less money than men (see Chapter 12), the presence of a dependent child limits the kind of work a woman can do or adds the financial burden of baby-sitters and day-care centers or both.

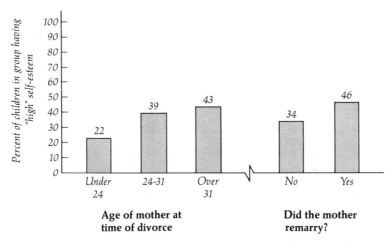

Figure 8•1   The effect of divorce on the self-esteem of children. Data taken from Morris Rosenberg, Society and the Adolescent Self-Image *(Princeton, N.J.: Princeton, 1965).*

Divorce, then, is another example of what happens when people become dissatisfied with the institutionalized agreements relating to the family. That behavior has strayed from the established norms is no surprise. Nor is it a surprise that some people have sought alternatives to the family.

The Search for Alternatives

We've already looked at some functional alternatives to the family. Premarital and extramarital sexual affairs offer alternatives to the established family as a vehicle for sexuality. Mate swapping and group sex have also been tried.

Communes are a more encompassing alternative to the family, although the new communes in America are so diverse it is dangerous to make general statements about them. Herbert Otto (1974) has named sixteen different types of communes from his own observations:

The Agricultural subsistence commune
The Nature commune
The Craft commune
The Spiritual/mystical commune

The Denominational commune
The Church-sponsored commune
The Political commune
The Political action commune
The Service commune
The Art commune
The Teaching commune
The Group marriage commune
The Homosexual commune
The Growth-centered commune
The Mobile, or gypsy, commune
The Street, or neighborhood, commune

The studies done by Otto and others suggest that the future of communes as an alternative to the family in America is not certain. Letha Scanzoni and John Scanzoni (1976:172) point to the basic dilemma:

In communes that stress individualism and personal freedom, questions of preserving group solidarity and unity must be faced; but in communes which give primary emphasis to group unity, there arise questions of where individual freedom fits in. In other words, monists must deal with the issue of pluralism; and pluralists must come to grips with the monists' concern about a central, shared core around which the group unites and through which it derives a sense of oneness.

Emotional support is an important function of families. In the search for alternatives to a particular form of the family, the provision of such functions must be considered. (Nacio Jan Brown, BBM)

As the authors suggest, some communes reflect a basic unwillingness to make and keep the agreements that will allow them to survive as a group. These wither away. Others are willing to make and keep agreements, but in doing so, they run the risk of creating the same dissatisfactions they were designed to remedy.

The Scanzonis' observations about communes apply to institutionalized social agreements more generally. Institutions like the family support the survival of society by reconciling individual experiences with the needs of the group. A variety of agreements serve that function, but each agreement carries both benefits and costs for individuals. Dissatisfaction with the costs involved in a particular agreement often results in the search for new forms for the institution. Each new form, however, carries its own benefits and costs—and the potential for further dissatisfaction and change.

Summary

This chapter began with an examination of the basic functions served by the family as an institution. Its primary contribution to the survival of group life is in replacing group members. As we saw, this is more than a matter of sexual reproduction; it involves physical and emotional nurturance as well. Families also serve the sexual and nurturant needs of adult members. Various families in history have served many additional functions, but in modern societies most of those have been transferred to other institutions.

A variety of institutional forms appear to satisfy the functions of the family. There have been varied agreements pertaining to family composition, descent, residence, and sex roles. Different agreements work, too, as we saw in looking at the changing character of the American family.

In the past sexuality has largely been limited to married couples. This agreement has changed radically in American society. Both premarital and extramarital sexual activity have increased. More directly relevant to the family itself, however, is the increased popularity of trial marriages. It is possible to form and operate a family without the marriage ritual.

No less significant is the trend toward greater sexual equality within marriage. At the same time that women have demanded equality with men in the economy and other institutions, women have increasingly rejected their traditional role within the family. One result is the framing of egalitarian marriage contracts.

The rapidly increasing divorce rate in America points to another significant change in agreements pertaining to the family. Divorce has implications both for individuals and for the functions of the family.

Dissatisfaction with the family as an institution has produced many attempts to find alternative forms for handling its functions. One recent alternative to the family in America is the commune. There are many different kinds of communes, but all are encountering the same fundamental problems inherent in institutions that have produced dissatisfaction with the family.

The family offers a prototype for the analysis of social institutions. As a means for structuring individuals' drives and experiences so as to support the survival of the group, the family exemplifies the purpose and process of all institutions. It also exemplifies the general tendency for institutions to produce dissatisfaction.

Suggested Readings

Bernard, Jessie
1972　*The Future of Marriage.* New York: Bantam.
At a time when many people are speculating about the future of the conventional norms of marriage and the family, Bernard has brought together a mass of empirical research data to provide a factual basis for such discussions. She then proceeds to draw out the implications of those data in a way that serves both those who may be contemplating marriage as well as those who are interested in studying it from a sociological point of view.

Queen, Stuart, Robert Habenstein, and John Adams
1961　*The Family in Various Cultures.* Chicago: Lippincott.

As the title suggests, this book presents an excellent cross-cultural picture of the variety of family agreements that people have created around the world and over time. This is a valuable book for sociology students, since the family is a commonly reified institution, and a healthy dose of cross-cultural disagreements enhances the kind of personal detachment that is needed in understanding the nature and functioning of social agreements.

Scanzoni, Letha and John Scanzoni
1976　*Men, Women, and Change.* New York: McGraw-Hill.
Here's an up-to-date look at the nature of sex roles in the family and other institutions. With an emphasis on *human* relationships, the authors examine the life history of a family: premarital relationships, the decision to marry, the process of being married, having children, and long-term marital relations. Like the Bernard book mentioned above, this one is useful from both personal and professional points of view.

Winch, Robert
1971　*The Modern Family.* New York: Holt.
This is one of the most respected textbooks on the sociology of the family by one of its most respected students. Winch provides an omnibus examination of all the different ways sociologists approach this institution, including its history, functions, and structures—illustrated with a good deal of cross-cultural data.

Episode Eight

Monica closed her apartment door behind Louise, then turned to face Gabe. "Listen," she said, taking a long breath, "I made the teriyaki. Do you want some?"

"I'm not hungry," Gabe said. He seated himself on the floor, then reclined so as to place his face directly within the rays of a floor lamp.

"You're a green," Monica said. "Somehow I can't believe this is really happening."

She seated herself on the floor beside him. "Tell me all about yourself," she said.

"Well, I had three parents," Gabriel began, "two men and a woman."

"You mean you had two fathers?"

"I had a chromosomal father," he said slowly, determined, "but he was not my parent."

"You were adopted."

"Monica," he said, "just let me tell you. I was raised in a large home by three parents: two men and one woman. We didn't call them 'mother' or 'father'. We called them 'stern parents' or 'soft parents', according to their personalities."

Monica opened her mouth as if to speak.

"Don't talk," Gabriel urged. "Just listen. My soft parent's name was Jonathan. Jonathan Knapp. He was the oldest of the three nurturing partners, so I received his name.

"My stern parents were Gabriel Jones and Loretta Larson. Gabriel died when I was eleven years old.

"My uncle lived with us for a while. He was Loretta's brother, and he helped with the chores, but he was not part of the contract."

"Who was your real father?"

"Real?" he repeated.

"Who was your chromosomal father?"

"I don't know."

"Don't you care?"

"He was not a chromosomal son of Adam. That much I know. My birther rescued me from him."

"Wouldn't you like to know something about him?"

Gabriel had grown impatient. "Just listen," he said. "I was the only Knapp child. When I was eighteen Loretta and Jonathan severed their nurturing contract."

"You mean they got divorced," Monica began to feel she understood.

"No. They had contracted to nurture together until I became eighteen. After that there was no contract, that's all.

"Loyal descendants of Adam contract to nurture with someone of either sex or with two or three people for at least eighteen years. If they accept more children after the first baby, then they remain contracted until the youngest becomes eighteen."

"Do the 'soft parents' and the 'stern parents' have the babies?"

"Perhaps—if they are male and female. In fact, all pure greens are encouraged to increase the race. But sometimes," Gabriel continued, "only males or only females will nurture another couple's baby." He paused. "A woman could birth an infant and then decide not to go into a nurturing contract with anyone. So she would give her baby to a nurturing family."

"Then couples who are not involved in a nurturing contract may conceive children?"

"Yes," Gabe said. "Whatever helps our people to grow in number is morally acceptable."

"What about homosexuality?" Monica asked. "You said just males or just females could enter a nurturing contract. Does that mean they're homosexuals?"

"Not necessarily," Gabe said. "But if they are it doesn't matter so long as they are doing their part either by nurturing or by working at S.T.I.—or in some other way—to help further the cause of greens."

The whole thing had become so implausible to Monica that it had taken on a fictional quality.

"What if nurturing parents want to get divorced before their child is eighteen?" Monica questioned.

"They can't," Gabe explained. "It's against the law."

"Well," she ventured, "if no one gets divorced, then there must be lots of rotten marriages—people no longer in love, just staying together because they have to."

"Parents aren't expected to love one another" —Gabriel was patient—"only to raise green children according to Adam's laws."

"But, Gabe," Monica refilled her glass, "if you and I had a baby and then decided to become nurturing parents to our own baby, wouldn't we love one another?"

Gabriel looked into Monica's eyes. His mind flashed back to a conversation he had had in Adamsville the evening after the rescue. He had gone to a liquidhouse with a fellow mutant named Jacob Lockwood.

Jacob had married on the outside, left his ungreen spouse when the first evidences of his mutation appeared, and only recently returned to Adamsville.

"Do you miss her?" Gabe had asked his friend, thinking of his own relationship with Monica.

"Not anymore," Jacob had replied, toying with the plastic straw in his drink.

"Did you love her?"

"They talk about love all the time on the outside," Jacob said, "but they can't tell you exactly what it is. We don't talk about love here, you know that."

"Why did you marry her, Jacob?" Gabe had persisted.

"I thought I loved her." Jacob motioned the bartender for another drink. "But all greens know that love between adults doesn't last."

"I know they taught that in school, and my parents always said that. And religion teaches it too. But . . ." Gabe's voice had trailed off.

"You've been outside too long," Jacob had observed. "Come home where you belong before they ruin you."

Now Gabriel pressed his palm against the crown of his head. "If you and I," he said, studying Monica's face, "were to enter a nurturing contract, we would love one another." He paused. "Monica," he said resolutely, "I do love you."

The woman shifted, "Before, when we talked about marriage," she said, "you didn't mention your being a mutant."

Gabriel sat quietly, not answering.

"Gabe," Monica continued, "last June, when you told me you had to leave the city on business for Chicago National, you lied to me."

"I'm sorry," he said. "You wouldn't have understood."

"Well, I have to agree with you there," she spurted, rising from her place on the floor and entering the kitchen where she turned off the heating surface under the teriyaki.

Returning to the living room, she asked, growing angry, "How many babies have you rescued, Gabriel?"

"Only one."

"Only the one from Lake Hospital in June? You never kidnapped any children before this?"

"No." He placed his hands upon Monica's shoulders and peered into her eyes. "You probably won't believe me, but I didn't want to do this one. I was pressured into it."

"But you thought it was right!"

Knapp shrugged, raising his arms in the air. "Yes, I think it was the right thing to do: saving an infant's life. I didn't do it before now because I'm a coward, I guess. I began to like it here in Chicago. For a while I forgot who I was. Besides," he added, "I was afraid I'd get caught."

The two remained silent for a while.

"What would your people do," Monica questioned finally, "if you were caught?"

"If they considered me a loyal Adamsville citizen they would help me however they could. But I have been disloyal, and so I don't know."

"How have you been disloyal?"

"I've disappointed my parents," Gabe said. "Jonathan Knapp, my soft parent, is ill now. I visited him after the rescue. He had expected me to return to Adamsville for good before my thirtieth birthday."

"Why?"

"It's one of Adam's laws."

"Wasn't Jonathan pleased that you had performed a rescue?"

"Yes, of course," Gabriel admitted. "But now he misses me."

"And what about your other living parent, Loretta?"

"She wants me to perform more rescues. She feels that I must redeem myself for my previous lack of commitment to the community—and for my lack of appreciation."

"Lack of appreciation for what exactly?"

"First of all for my own rescue. And then, of course, for the family life I enjoyed with her and Jonathan and Gabriel."

"Do you feel bad that Jonathan misses you?" Monica asked, unsure whether she would ever understand this man.

"Well, of course I do." Gabriel's voice sounded hurt.

"Then why didn't you stay in Adamsville with him last June?"

Gabe Knapp inhaled a long, deep breath. He rubbed his fingers over his forehead, then exhaled. "I wanted to come back," he said quietly, "to my job and to you."

Monica left her chair, resuming her former place on the floor near Gabriel. "Gabe," she said after a long pause, "did you really think we could be married?"

"I don't know," he answered then. "I think so. Some of our people have married ungreens."

"Then it's permissible in Adamsville to marry someone from outside the colony?" Monica was surprised.

"It is discouraged now," Gabe replied, "especially by some members who feel we should separate our-

selves completely from ungreens. But before there were so many of us, posing greens married outsiders often."

"And what happened once these posers turned green?"

"They went home."

Monica's features hardened. "They simply left their mates and returned to the colony, is that right?"

"Yes," Gabriel admitted. "No outsider has ever lived in Green Colony."

Monica stood. "And what, Gabriel, if these mixed couples had borne children? Did your green people kidnap their own mates' children?"

Gabe didn't answer. Against his skull the word "rescue," like a hammer, pounded over and over. "Rescue, Monica," he wanted to scream at the top of his lungs. Not "kidnap" or "steal," but "rescue." He studied the angry pain upon the woman's face. "Maybe," he said at last, "you would have wanted to come with me to Adamsville." He knew even as he heard himself say it that this had always been a frivolous, irresponsible dream. Monica could never have been comfortable in Adamsville. Gabe was not even sure she would have been allowed entry. He lit a cigarette.

"Anyway," he said, drawing the smoke deep into his lungs, "I had begun to think that maybe I wasn't really a mutant, that maybe my skin would never turn green, that perhaps I was rescued by mistake. In that case I would never have had to return to Adamsville. We could have been married and lived normally, here on the outside."

This new information confused Monica still further, momentarily diminishing her anger. "Why did you think you might not be a green?"

"When I was twenty-five or so, my skin didn't begin to turn. With every succeeding year that I didn't mature physically, I nursed the thought more and more that I was not really a mutant. Then I was thirty and still my skin hadn't greened. My parents had taught me that virtually all greens mature before their thirtieth birthday."

"But you're convinced now that you definitely are a green, that you were not rescued by mistake?"

"Yes," he said, extinguishing the cigarette, "I know now for certain that I'm green. That's largely why I decided to perform the rescue."

"Why are you certain now that you are a green?" Monica asked.

"I had a physical," he said. "The mutation showed up. I almost told you several times." He lowered his voice. "I'm really very sorry."

They sat quietly for some time. Gabe smoked a second cigarette.

It was Monica who broke the long silence. "This is why you seldom drink anything but water, why you eat so little," she said more to herself than to Gabe. Relentlessly the reality of the evening enveloped her.

"Monica," Gabe said apologetically, "perhaps we both need time to think all this over."

She nodded, sighing deeply. "I don't think we should see one another—at least for a while," she said.

Questions

1. In what ways do Adamsville agreements concerning kinship differ from those of your culture?

2. In what ways are the green agreements concerning family structure functional to Adamsville as a society? How are they dysfunctional?

3. We often hear about adopted children who, when they grow up, conduct searches to find their "real" parents. Gabe seems to have no such interest. How do you explain that difference?

4. In what ways do Gabe and Monica agree in their views on love? How do they disagree? What is love, anyway?

9

Religious and Educational Institutions

You've probably had the experience of looking up into the heavens on a quiet night, looking at all the distant stars and planets, wondering how it all began and what it means. Probably you didn't plan it; it just happened. Most people have experiences like that now and then.

I'm sure you've also had the experiences of intuition, insight, and discovery. You may have "known" that something was going to happen without being able to explain why or to justify your expectation. Or perhaps you've had the experience of grappling with a problem—trying to figure out how something worked or trying to understand a subject you were studying in school—and had what some people call an "aha!": the sudden feeling of clarity in which you broke through to an *understanding* of something. The history of science is filled with such experiences, and they are common outside science as well.

Early in the fifteenth century, a young French peasant girl of thirteen began hearing "voices." By 1428, her voices told her that she must take up arms and deliver her native France from the English. Putting on men's armor, she led the French army into battle and became a popular folk hero. Her popularity was her undoing, however, because the rulers of France came to regard her as a threat to their religious and political power. Through intrigue and treachery, they managed to have her delivered over to the English, who tried her for "heresy." The charges lodged against her involved her voices and

visions; in addition, her wearing of men's clothes figured importantly in the trial. In 1431, the trial was concluded, and the young girl was burned at the stake.

The story of Joan of Arc illustrates the danger of direct, personal experiences when seen in light of organized group life. The story of Darwin has parallels, although Darwin certainly did not burn at the stake. His insights regarding natural selection and biological evolution threatened societies that shared a belief in the Divine Creation of Man (and Woman after that).

Here's the problem. Each of us has direct, personal experiences of knowing and understanding the way things are. Yet we can't live together in societies without some agreements on the nature of reality. Religious and educational institutions embody our general agreements about the way things are as well as the values and norms that follow from that shared view. Such agreements, however, like those relating to the family, structure and limit our personal experiences, and they are a potential source of dissatisfaction.

In this chapter, we're going to look more closely at the functions served by religious and educational institutions, and we'll see some of the different agreements that appear to work. Then we'll examine the ways in which institutional structures affect our experiences of social life and how we respond to those experiences. Let's look at religion first.

Functions of Religious Institutions

The great theologian Paul Tillich (1952) said that religion was addressed to our ultimate concerns, to the fundamental problems of meaning. Religion grows out of the feelings of awe we sometimes have when we survey the enormity of the universe, the power of natural forces, or the persistent mystery of life itself. It is similarly a response to the problems of suffering and death that humans, more than other animals, can recognize, anticipate, and think about. Individual religious experiences offer personal answers to such "why" questions, and organized religious institutions provide agreed-on answers for members of a group to share.

The function of religious institutions, like other institutions, is to support the survival of group life. Clearly, we cannot continue living and interacting together without some fundamental agreements on the nature of reality and our place within it. If I felt that life would go on forever and you felt the world would end next week, think how unlikely our cooperation on a long-range project would be. Religion is an important source of our agreements on such things.

At the same time that religious institutions provide a shared view of reality, they also give people a sense of belonging. Religions define who we are and what we are doing here. They offer people another view on their identities, and those who share the same religious point of view typically have a shared identity as believers. The ancient Hebrew idea of "the chosen people" is an excellent example of people sharing an identity as believers. Religious institutions can bind people together, thereby supporting the continuation of the group.

Let's look now at some of the ways in which religious institutions serve their functions. I want to begin with a consideration of religious beliefs, values, and norms.

Beliefs

Much of what we "know" about the nature of reality can be seen as a result of direct experiences that people have. You "knew" about the force of gravity long before people could tell you about it. People also "know," in the same fashion, the changing of the seasons, the regularity of the sun's rising, and countless other things. The reasons *why* such things are the way they are, are more elusive.

In the Western world, we tend to look for explanations of the way things are in science, and I'm going to discuss that in the second half of this chapter. Science, as you'll recall from Chapter 3, is based on empirical observations and measurements of the "natural" world around us and the logical-rational understanding of what we observe. Throughout human history, however, people have also sought explanations of the natural world in a supernatural realm. What can be observed easily and directly has often been explained in terms of what cannot be so easily and directly observed. This takes us directly into the realm of gods and cosmic consciousness.

The supernatural realm is what individuals say they experience directly. Joan of Arc said that her instructions to deliver France from the English came from that realm. It is what religious institutions organize and structure. Religious institutions explain our earthly existence in terms of its being part of a much larger reality. Through them, we agree on the nature of that larger reality and its implications for our more immediate reality. How does it happen?

Many of the world's religions are so old that we can only speculate about the origins of the beliefs associated with them. Historical records of other religions, however, suggest the following pattern. An individual—such as Gautama Buddha, Jesus, or Joseph Smith (of Mormonism)—had a personal experience that created a point of view which provided solutions to the problems of meaning we have been discussing.

Just imagine for a moment that you have had such an experience. Imagine a sudden experience of total clarity on *everything*. Imagine suddenly seeing the world around you without the constraint of any particular point of view, knowing with utter certainty all the hows and whats and whys. The reports of such experiences frequently incorporate the idea of "waking up" as in the following account of the Buddha's early preaching.

"Are you a god?" they asked. "No." "An angel?" "No." "A saint?" "No." "Then what are you?"

Buddha answered, "I am awake." His answer became his title, for this is what Buddha means. In the Sanskrit root *budh* denotes both to wake up and to know. Buddha, then, means the "Enlightened One" or the "Awakened One." While the rest of the world was wrapped in the womb of sleep, dreaming a dream known as the waking life of mortal men, one man roused himself. Buddhism begins with a man who shook off the daze, the doze, the dream-like inchoateness of ordinary awareness. It begins with the man who woke up (Smith 1965:90).

Central to Buddha's "awakening" was the experience of himself as an inseparable part of the entire universe. He experienced the feeling of clearly seeing and understanding that universe in all its aspects.

Imagine having an experience like that. What would you do? Probably you'd do what people like Buddha and Jesus did—you'd want to share your experience with others. But how could you adequately tell other people about an experience that occurred far outside the established agreements about logical concepts, language, and "reality" itself? You'd probably "talk about" the experience, translating it into words, concepts, and more common experiences that other people could comprehend. What you said to your friends, however, would not be what you had experienced.

Most formal religions appear to have begun with individuals' having experiences as dramatic and powerful as Buddha's. As they have attempted to share their experience with others, however, the experience became transformed into concepts and points of view. Once that happens, people then agree on the points of view. They create beliefs about the way things are in lieu of personally having the kinds of experiences that the beliefs grew out of. In this fashion are religious points of view institutionalized.

Most contemporary Christians believe in a god who created the universe and, some believe, guides the events that occur in our day-to-day existence. For the most part, however, this belief is a matter of agreement, based on religious socialization stemming ultimately from the personal experience that

Jesus had and to his preaching "about" that experience.

The experiences that people such as Buddha and Jesus had may not have been exactly the same, although of course we cannot know that. It is clear, however, that the transformation of those experiences has produced quite different beliefs. Beliefs about the supernatural, for example, vary widely: including the monotheistic Jehovah of the Jews, the Christian Trinity, the many gods of the ancient Greeks and of Hindus, and the all-pervasive "godness" of Buddhism, animism, and other religious forms.

Max Weber (1922) has pointed out that persons having such profound experiences have communicated their experiences differently. He distinguished between "ethical" and "exemplary" prophets. The former type of prophet has felt obliged to instruct others in how to behave in this life; the latter has merely demonstrated "proper" behavior in his or her own life. Mohammed was an "ethical" prophet, Buddha an "exemplary" one. Both types of religious leaders illustrate the transformation of experiences into beliefs.

Religious beliefs, then, are agreements on answers to the basic problems of meaning that people confront in life. Such beliefs may explain such mundane matters as why it rains, why crops fail, or why commuter traffic is so heavy. And they may describe a life after death, cycles of reincarnation, or great legions of heavenly deities.

Values

Religious beliefs have a societal value in their own right because they create agreements on the nature of reality. This is only a part of the story, however. Religions also prescribe the way things "ought to be." Religious "values" are agreements about what's good and preferred, based on the agreements about the way things are.

For Christians, the belief that all are the children of God leads logically to the valuation of peace over war. For Buddhists and Taoists, the belief in the "oneness" of all things leads to the value of "flowing" with the course of events rather than resisting them.

Religious agreements sometimes provide for highly formalized rituals. The Roman Catholic Mass is one example. (William Rosenthal, Jeroboam, Inc.)

In the words of Lao Tzu (1965:206), the founder of Taoism*:

> Those who flow as life flows know
> They need no other force:
> They feel no wear, they feel no tear,
> They need no mending, no repair.

Religious values seldom prescribe specific behavior. Norms serve that function.

Norms

The survival of society depends, ultimately, on how people behave toward one another. "Norms,"

---

*From *The Way and Its Power* tr. by Arthur Waley. Reprinted by permission of George Allen & Unwin Ltd. and Barnes & Noble.

you will recall, are agreements about what behavior is expected, and religious institutions provide a wide variety of such expectations.

To begin, most religions prescribe many strictly *religious* norms: rituals and other practices that are expected of those sharing the beliefs and values of the religion. Thus, Christians are expected to attend church and partake of Communion. Jews are expected to attend synagogue and to carry out a variety of religious rituals within the family. Shintoists make pilgrimages to sacred temples and maintain family altars. Moslems bow toward Mecca five times daily. Buddhists meditate; others pray.

Of greater interest to sociologists, however, are the norms within religious institutions that prescribe expectations regarding *secular* behavior. No sociologist has shown more interest in this than Max Weber.

Twenty-one years before Weber's birth, another German sociologist, Karl Marx, had written, "Religion is the sigh of the oppressed creature, the sentiment of a heartless world, and the soul of soulless conditions. It is the opium of the people" (Bottomore and Rubel 1956:27). In that famous phrase, Marx brought religion within the umbrella of economic determinism. It was, for Marx, a tool of the powerful in maintaining their dominance over the powerless.

In much of his research in the sociology of religion, Weber examined the extent to which religious institutions were themselves the source of social behavior rather than mere reflections of economic conditions. His most noted statement of this side of the issue is found in *The Protestant Ethic and the Spirit of Capitalism* (1905).

John Calvin (1509–1564) was an important figure, along with Martin Luther (1483–1546), in the Protestant reformation of Christianity. Calvin's predestinarian point of view said that the ultimate salvation or damnation of every individual had already been decided by God. Calvin also suggested that God communicated his decisions to people by making them either successful or unsuccessful during their earthly existences.

Ironically, this point of view led Calvin's followers to *seek* proof of their coming salvation by working hard, saving their money, and generally striving for economic success. In Weber's analysis, Calvinism provided an important stimulus for the development of capitalism. Rather than "wasting" their money on worldly comforts, the Calvinists reinvested it in their economic enterprises, thus providing the *capital* necessary for the development of capital*ism*.

The examples of religiously prescribed norms that have direct implications for the survival of society are countless. Among them are prohibitions against murder, stealing, and adultery.

Group Solidarity

Religious institutions also support the survival of society by binding believers together with a sense of unity, belonging, and identity. Cooley's "we feeling," described in Chapter 6, can be generated by membership in a common religious body.

Mohammed was the founder of Islam. Aside from this, Mohammed is remembered for uniting the Arabs, no simple task. Huston Smith (1958:202) describes it*:

> Life under the conditions of the desert had never been serene. The Bedouin felt almost no obligation to anyone outside his tribe. Scarcity of material goods and a fighting mood chronically inflamed by the blazing sun had made brigandage a regional institution and the proof of virility. In the sixth century A.D. political deadlock and the collapse of the magistrate in the leading city of Mecca made this generally chaotic situation even worse. Drunken orgies often ending in brawls and bloodshed were commonplace.

During his final pilgrimage to Mecca, Mohammed essentially summarized the remarkable change he had brought about when he enjoined his followers: "Know ye that every Muslim is a brother to every other Muslim, and that ye are now one brotherhood" (p. 223). Mohammed's military and administrative prowess were essential in the creation of unity, but the perpetuation of that unity rests in a shared religious identity.

Religion and Other Institutions

The chief function of religious institutions, then, is to provide agreed-on answers to the problems of meaning and to spell out the implications of those answers for human social behavior. Religious institutions also serve another important function. They support the persistence of other institutions. Because the problems they address are so basic, religious points of view are relevant to almost all aspects of life. As I mentioned in Chapter 7, economic and political systems are frequently given religious justification. Religious support for the family in America is evident. Slavery, in the early history of America, enjoyed religious support, and many believed blacks to be a lost tribe of Israel that God had made servants for all time.

Institutions often enhance social integration through mutual support and reinforcement, but they

*Reprinted by permission.

are often a source of conflict as well. Religious differences within a society can turn citizen against citizen and interfere with orderly affairs in the schools, the economy, and government. Religious intermarriage can be a source of family conflict. Moreover, religious points of view can conflict directly with those of other institutions as we'll see later in the chapter.

Varieties of Religious Institutions

In the preceding discussions, I have mentioned several different religious institutions. In this section, I want to deal more directly with religious variations. We'll look at some of the world's different religions, noting their characteristics and the extent to which they share agreements.

Preliterate Religious Forms

Anthropologists have shown a special interest in preliterate religions, but sociologists have also studied them. *The Elementary Forms of Religious Life* by Emile Durkheim was a classic sociological study of the religious life of the Australian aborigines. In it, Durkheim searched for the roots of religion's role in modern society.

The religion that Durkheim (1915) found most elementary among the aborigines was **totemism.** In totemism, it is agreed that some animal, plant, or inanimate object possesses special powers. The members of the group sharing such an agreement see themselves as having a kinship relationship to that "totem." The totem has special symbolic meaning for the group. They take its name as their own.

Durkheim saw religion—among the aborigines and in modern society—as the basis for a "moral community." Members of the community were held together by shared beliefs, values, and norms pertaining to whatever was defined as "sacred."

Countless other religious forms are found in preliterate societies. Each, in its own way, provides a shared point of view on the nature of reality, and each binds together, in some degree, the community of believers.

The "Great Religions"

Although sociologists have sometimes examined preliterate religions, they have more typically directed their attention to the larger, more formally established religions of the world. Religious statistics are difficult to compile, but it can be estimated that nearly three-fourths of the world's population embrace one of eight religions. Indeed, over half of the world's population is either Christian, Hindu, or Moslem (*Encyclopaedia Britannica* 1976).

Table 9·1 presents the estimated religious population of the world as of 1976. Notice that Christianity as a whole is the largest religion with nearly a billion adherents. Roman Catholicism by itself is larger than any other religious body, with over half a billion members. Islam and Hinduism are the next largest.

Table 9·1 Estimated Populations of the "Great Religions," 1976 (Representing about 70 percent of the World's Population)

Religion	Number of adherents
Christianity	954,866,700
Roman Catholic	540,704,000
Eastern Orthodox	86,653,600
Protestant	327,509,100
Judaism	14,353,790
Islam	538,213,900
Shintoism	60,156,000
Taoism	30,403,700
Confucianism	186,104,300
Buddhism	249,877,300
Hinduism	524,273,050

Source: Reprinted with permission from the 1976 Britannica Book of the Year, *copyright 1976 by Encyclopaedia Britannica, Inc., Chicago, Ill.*

Some religions—like Christianity, Islam, and Buddhism—have spread from society to society; others have primarily remained near their birthplaces: Shintoism in Japan, Hinduism in India, and Confucianism in China. Reasons for this difference are many, including the extent to which the points of view embodied in the religion reflect the specific agreements of the particular culture in which the religion first appeared. In addition, while some religious leaders have openly stressed the importance of spreading the faith, others have not (Babbie 1966).

The world's major religions are of special interest to sociologists. Since religious institutions deal with fundamental issues of human existence, they have important influences on other aspects of life.

Max Weber's interest in Calvinism and its relation to the rise of capitalism, for example, must be understood in the context of his broader interest in the world's major religions as a whole. Weber was particularly interested in the point of view that religions took with regard to the temporal world. Some, such as Hinduism and Buddhism, led their believers to reject the importance of this world in favor of seeking their proper place within the larger cosmos. Others, like Islam, were very much of *this* world. As Weber described:

> There was nothing in ancient Islam like an individual quest for salvation, nor was there any mysticism. The religious promises in the earliest period of Islam pertained to this world. Wealth, power, and glory were all martial promises, and even the world beyond is pictured in Islam as a soldier's sensual paradise (Gerth and Mills 1946:264).

Different religions have different points of view on meaning. No one is necessarily "better" than another. Each is effective in its own way. What that way is can make a difference, however. The ways in which different religions serve their social functions have serious implications for the rest of society. Weber was particularly interested in the economic and political implications.

Institutional integration and general harmony in a society are enhanced by religious agreement, yet few societies are marked by total religious agreement.

The United States is a good example of religious diversity.

Religion in America

The colonization of America had important religious roots. As all American schoolchildren are taught, many of the early colonists came to the New World from Europe to escape religious persecution. Different religious groups soon concentrated in different regions of the country: the Congregationalists in New England, the Quakers in Pennsylvania, and so forth.

Robin Williams (1959) has suggested that the religious tolerance that developed in America arose more from the fact of diversity than from an ideological commitment to tolerance for its own sake. He gives the following reasons for the great degree of religious freedom and toleration in America:

1. There was a fragmented diversity of groups.
2. None was powerful enough to seize political dominance.
3. There had been no established church in America prior to settlement.
4. Most of the colonists were indifferent to organized religion.
5. Tolerance was encouraged by the generally shared Protestant view that each person had direct access to God.
6. The economic need for new immigrants reduced the significance of their religious affiliations (p. 320).

Whatever the reasons for religious tolerance in America, and despite a series of outbursts of religious intolerance, the United States has proved fertile ground for religious institutions of all sorts. All the major European religions have found homes in America. More recently, Eastern religions have become popular. And a number of new religions have been created here, including Mormonism, Christian Science, the Black Muslims, and many others.

Table 9·2   Religious Identification in America, 1964

Religion/denomination	Percent
Total Protestant	68
Baptist	19
Methodist	11
Lutheran	10
Presbyterian	6
United Church of Christ	4
Episcopal	3
Disciples of Christ	2
Other Protestant	13
Roman Catholics	26
Jews	3
None or Other	3

Source: Gertrude Jaeger Selznick and Stephen Steinberg, The Tenacity of Prejudice *(New York: Harper and Row, 1969), p. 108; and Charles Glock and Rodney Stark,* Christian Beliefs and Anti-Semitism *(New York: Harper and Row, 1966), p. 190.*

Table 9·2 presents one view of religion in America. It shows people's religious affiliation or identification based on a 1964 national survey of American adults that asked "What is your religion?"

Aside from showing the relative popularity of different religious denominations in America, Table 9·2 points to another important aspect of this institution: Virtually all Americans identify themselves with *some* religious body. Robin Williams and others have commented on the pervasiveness of religion in America, the "moral orientation" that is reflected in most of our national actions in particular. Even when we engage in wars and gross discrimination, we feel obliged to give moral justifications for our actions. It is probably not possible for the United States as a nation to enter a war openly for the admitted purpose of acquiring additional territory or resources to further our national interests (Williams 1959).

The American religious orientation, however, does not necessarily reflect a commitment to the specific doctrines of particular religions. Robert Bellah (1967) has written of a "civil religion" in America, noting the contrast between our formal separation of church and state and the persistent presence of religious sentiments and symbols in government and other aspects of "secular" life. Political leaders frequently make use of religious themes, for example, and our money says we trust in God, even though the "god" of this civil religion is not precisely identified. Other aspects of the civil religion are discussed in more detail in the accompanying box, "Civil Religion for Breakfast."

Religious institutions in America, even the civil religion Bellah spoke of, serve to structure human experiences—those experiences relating to the fundamental problems of meaning. Let's take a closer look at some of the different forms these structures take.

The Structures of Religious Experience

Sociologists have looked at the structuring of religious experience from a number of different points of view. I want to consider three of those in this section. First, we'll look at the variety of organizational structures that people have created around their religions. Next we'll examine the different kinds of religious experiences that are possible within religious institutions. Then I want to say something about the structuring of religious deviance.

Religious Organizations

Sociologists have been particularly interested in the different forms that religious bodies take, particularly those in contemporary Western societies. There are several different types of organization.

Cults   In the sociological point of view, a **cult** is a small religious group typically organized around a single **charismatic** leader or particular religious practice. Most of the world's great religions began as cults, centering around such figures as Jesus, Buddha, and Mohammed. At the present time, there are a number of tiny cults in the United States, some of which have gained national attention for practices such as "speaking in tongues," handling poisonous snakes, faith healing, and communication with the dead.

Sects   A **sect** is similar to a cult, but it is typically larger, more firmly established, and more persistent. Most sects begin when members break away from an even larger, more established religious body. Sects are characterized by personal religious fervor and religious experiences such as talking with God and seeing religious visions. Within American Christianity, sects tend to be fundamentalist and orthodox. They interpret the Bible literally, and they reify the traditional Christian beliefs.

Churches   Sociologists distinguish churches from sects. A **church,** such as the Episcopal or Methodist, is even more firmly established and persistent than a sect. It is also usually larger. The primary differences between churches and sects, however, are similar to those between secondary and primary relations and between gesellschaft and gemeinschaft (see Chapter 6 if you want to review this discussion).

Membership in a church is a more casual matter generally than membership in a sect. Church membership is typically inherited, but sect membership is often a matter of personal conversion. Sect members participate in their religion more regularly and more fervently than members of churches, on the average. Religion tends to be a more central part of the lives of sect members than of church members. Church members are less orthodox in their accep-

---

Civil Religion for Breakfast

Central to the American civil religion is the belief held by the first Puritan settlers that they were God's people chosen to bring civilization to the wilderness, to erect a new Jerusalem in the new land for all the world to see. George Washington echoed this charge in his inaugural address:

> The preservation of the sacred fire of liberty and the destiny of the republican model of government are . . . entrusted to the hands of the American people.

This theme is reiterated on our coinage as "In God We Trust," in the Pledge of Allegiance to a nation "under God," and above the pyramid on the great seal of the United States where it says in Latin "God has favored our undertaking."

Throughout our history the God of American civil religion has been called upon both to legitimize the actions taken by government and to provide some moral and humanitarian direction for them. These two possible functions of civil religion—to lend divine legitimacy to the nation or call its actions into question by appeal to a higher authority—were in abundant evidence during an annual presidential prayer breakfast. Three thousand government officials, religious leaders, and celebrities (including the Russian ambassador) gathered to ask for God's guidance and to hear testimonies by then-President Nixon, Billy Graham, and eight other leaders. In response to the prayers thanking God for the blessings of living in America, for free enterprise, and for the American way of life, Mark Hatfield, Republican senator for Oregon and an active Baptist layman, arose and criticized prayer based on such spiritual exclusivity. "Events such as this prayer breakfast contain the real danger of misplaced allegiance, if not downright idolatry." He went on to say that the Vietnam war was "a sin that scarred the national soul" and that they should seek individual and collective forgiveness for the country's role, in the hostilities there. No one in the audience was heard to say "Amen."

Can you think of any actions taken by the government in the name of God that have been considered a national disgrace? Ones that have been inspired humanitarian endeavors? What might an international or world civil religion be like?

Sources: Robert Bellah, "Civil Religion in America," Daedalus *96(1967):1–2;* New York Times, *February 2, 1973, p. 12;* Newsweek, *February 19, 1973, p. 90.*

tance of religious beliefs. On the whole, the beliefs, values, and norms of churches are more likely to be in agreement with those of the larger society than are those of sects. Finally, churches tend to be more bureaucratically organized and operated than sects.

From sect to church   A topic that has long fascinated sociologists has been the evolution of sects into churches (e.g., Glock 1964, Niebuhr 1960, Wilson 1959, Yinger 1963). Very often a sect begins with the disaffection of some group—typically the poor—within an established church. The members of the sect establish a separate religious life. As the sect becomes more established, as its members become economically more prosperous, and as the children of members inherit membership instead of being converted, the sect begins to take on many of the characteristics of a church. It becomes less fundamentalist, and its beliefs, values, and norms gradually approach those of the larger society. Eventually it becomes, in the sociological point of view, a "church," which may then be the source of subsequent sects. (I'll have more to say about this shortly.)

Ecclesia   Some established churches enjoy the status of being "state religions," having a virtual monopoly on the religious life of a society's members. The Anglican church in England and the Roman Catholic church in Spain are examples of this. While other religious bodies may be tolerated in theory or in fact, or both, the **ecclesia** is officially recognized for its central place in national life.

Dimensions of Religiosity

I've said repeatedly that religious institutions structure human experience. Now I'd like to look at some of the different religious experiences arising out of those structures. Sociologists usually look at the issue in terms of **religiosity,** or "religiousness," referring essentially to the ways people participate in religious institutions.

Religiosity can be measured along a number of different dimensions. Charles Glock (Glock and Stark 1965), for example, has suggested five major dimensions:

1. *Ritual:* Participating in the religious events and practices prescribed by one's religion, for example, attending church, praying, taking Communion.

2. *Belief:* Accepting one's religion's agreements about how things are, for example, believing in the existence of God(s), believing in reincarnation, believing in the divinity of Jesus.

3. *Cognitive:* Simply knowing about one's religion, its history, beliefs, and practices.

4. *Experiential:* Having religious experiences, such as communication with supernatural beings, and having visions and seizures.

5. *Consequential:* Living one's secular life in accord with the teachings of one's religion.

Rodney Stark and his collaborator Glock (1968) have undertaken extensive studies of the levels of these different dimensions of religiosity among the various religious groups in America. Some of their findings regarding religious experience are of particular interest in the context of this chapter.

Religious experience has received relatively little attention from contemporary sociologists. Quite likely, it has been assumed (though wrongly) that few members of a modern, scientifically oriented society would have such experiences.

In 1962, the Gallup poll asked a national sample of American adults: "Would you say that you have ever had a religious or mystic experience—that is, a moment of sudden religious insight or awakening?" One person in five reported having had such an experience (1972:1762).

A 1963 Glock-Stark study (published in 1968) limited to church members produced even more frequent reports of religious experiences. Table 9·3 summarizes some of these findings.

In earlier discussions in this chapter I mentioned that direct, personal experiences can threaten the survival of group life. Religious institutions are, therefore, a structuring of such experiences so as to alleviate that threat. What then do the Glock-Stark data suggest? Does the high frequency of personal re-

Table 9·3 Religious Experience in America, 1963

Types of religious experiences of church members	Percent	
	Protestants	Catholics
"A feeling that you were somehow in the presence of God"		
Yes, I'm sure I have	45	43
Yes, I think that I have	28	23
"A sense of being saved in Christ"		
Yes, I'm sure I have	37	26
Yes, I think that I have	23	22
"A feeling of being punished by God for something you had done"		
Yes, I'm sure I have	16	23
Yes, I think that I have	25	30
"A feeling of being tempted by the Devil"		
Yes, I'm sure I have	32	36
Yes, I think I have	20	26

Source: Rodney Stark and Charles Glock, American Piety: The Nature of Religious Commitment *(Berkeley, Calif.: University of California Press, 1968), pp. 131, 133, 137.*

ligious experience in America represent a threat to the survival of the religious agreements that support the persistence of society? The answer to this question can be found by looking at which members in American churches are likely to have such experiences.

According to Glock and Stark, religious experiences of the sorts described are most typical among people within denominations marked by a high level of orthodox religious *belief* and among those most likely to think that their particular religion is the "only true faith" (p. 214). In other words, people who have most thoroughly reified and internalized the agreements of their religious institutions are the most likely to have religious experiences. Their experiences, moreover, are in accord with the established agreements, such that the personal experiences *support* rather than threaten the group.

The fact is that the institutions of society—including religion—are structured for survival. If they weren't, they wouldn't survive. A part of that survival structuring involves socialization; another part involves social control in the face of deviance. Let's look briefly at what happens when people break the agreements of religious institutions.

The Structuring of Deviance

I began this chapter with a brief account of Joan of Arc's violation of the fifteenth-century religious agreements in France. What happened to her is not unique in the history of religious deviance. The Spanish Inquisition of the Middle Ages provides equally brutal examples. Countless religious wars throughout history also point to one solution to the problem of religious deviance. Those who disagree are killed or tortured into agreement.

There are milder solutions as well. In societies in which a particular church holds absolute religious power, persons deviating from its agreements can be denied the benefits of the secular society, employment and marriage, for example. Religious social control can operate even more subtly than that. In

his discussion of the civil religion, Bellah noted how careful all presidents are to cast their vote for God. It is unlikely that an avowed atheist will be elected president of the United States anytime soon.

Sometimes religious institutions have disagreements within their inner circles, among the clergy, for example. Phillip Hammond and Robert Mitchell (1965) have looked at some of the ways churches have dealt with the problem of radicalism. They note that during the Renaissance and Reformation, monasteries were used as a device for segregating radical priests from the rest of society. They suggest that the campus ministry serves a similar function in American Protestantism today. Their conclusion was derived from their 1963 survey of some 5,000 ministers in parishes and assigned to college campuses.

The Experience of Religious Structure

Religious critics of the modern church often complain that the church gets in the way of the individual's relationship with his or her God. Protestantism arose in response to precisely that concern, and it is ironic that contemporary Protestant churches are as subject to this criticism as the Catholic church is.

In our analysis, churches are situated between individuals and the religious experiences they might have, in the same sense that the family as an institution is situated between individuals and their experiences of love, nurturance, and sexuality. That's one of the ways in which institutions function.

We've seen that institutions do not prevent personal experiences. They merely structure and channel those experiences. Institutions represent agreement reality, and we've seen many examples of how we *experience* our agreements. People experience loving their parents and their children. And there's no denying the profound experience you can have sitting in a majestic cathedral, listening to Bach or to an inspirational sermon.

The dilemma is that religious institutions take away, just as they give. The agreements of an estab-

lished religion effectively separate people from the experiential reality they might be in touch with otherwise. People often recognize and feel that separation and experience dissatisfaction.

Functional Alternatives to Religious Institutions

As with the family, there have been many diverse attempts to develop substitutes for unsatisfying religious institutions. Christianity grew out of dissatisfaction with Judaism, and Islam grew out of dissatisfaction with Christianity. Protestantism grew out of dissatisfaction with Catholicism, and the subsequent fragmenting of Protestantism points to the continuing process of disaffection.

Recent American interest in the religions of the East marks a further continuation of the search for more satisfying religious forms. Many have characterized the drug subculture of the 1960s as another example of the same thing, best typified, perhaps, by Timothy Leary's "League of Spiritual Discovery" (LSD).

The counterculture movement of the 1960s and 1970s, represented in part by "encounter," "self-actualization," Transcendental Meditation, yoga, and the martial arts, seems to address the ultimate concerns that Tillich said formed the prime focus of religion. The box on pages 214–215, "New Religious Consciousness among Youth," discusses attempts to create alternatives to religious institutions in America.

It is too early to say what will become of these attempts, but we can recall some lessons from the past and from other institutions. To the extent that personal experience becomes replaced by belief through reification and internalization, it seems likely that the new forms will prove as unsatisfying as those they replaced.

Religious sects, you'll recall, are characterized by a greater fervor of personal experience. People do and feel things in newly formed sects that would shock and embarrass the average Episcopalian. When it comes time to socialize a new generation into the

When the established religious agreements do not satisfy individual religious experiences, people sometimes turn to new forms. The Hare Krishna movement in the United States is one such form. (David Powers, Jeroboam, Inc.)

sect, however, the fervor of personal experience is reduced. Those born into the sect usually come to believe what their converted parents experienced. The sect thus becomes institutionalized as a church. Within a few generations, it is likely to produce sects of its own, and the process continues.

Summary— Religious Institutions

We've seen thus far in the chapter that religious institutions center around the ultimate concerns that people have regarding the nature of reality and its meaning. While people sometimes have direct, personal experiences of reality and its meaning, the purpose of religious institutions is to structure those experiences so as to support the survival of group life.

Religions serve their function through systems of beliefs, values, and norms. Religions appear to rise out of the personal experiences of a founder, and they become institutionalized through the creation of beliefs reflecting the founders' experiences and agreed to by others. Religious beliefs are statements about the nature and meaning of reality, and they provide a basis for values (statements of what "ought to be") and norms (expectations about behavior).

Religious institutions also provide a source of group solidarity, based on feelings of belonging and

New Religious Consciousness among Youth

Theologians have proclaimed the death of God, and established churches have rued declining attendance, but the rise of many new religious and quasi-religious groups attests to an undeniable (though modest) religious ferment among American youth today. The Jesus People movement and the proliferation of Eastern-inspired groups and gurus have been prominently featured in the press and in TV specials. The numbers attracted vary from the more than half a million who have learned a Transcendental Meditation mantra or have received the Baptism of the Holy Spirit in the Catholic Pentecostal movement to smaller followings such as the orange-robed Hare Krishna chanters or the Jews for Jesus.

Many of the so-called Jesus freaks emphasize salvation through a personal relationship with Jesus. Charismatic gifts such as speaking in tongues or prophecy are signs of divine grace. The support provided by a communal life-style is important to participants in these recent groups, many of which arose in the 1960s and early 1970s as both an extension of and a reaction to the hippie counterculture.

Gurus who teach Indian philosophy, yogic disciplines, and altered states of consciousness have attracted sizable followings: Swami Satchidananda of the Integral Yoga Institute; young Guru Maharaj Ji whose Divine Light Mission held a "Millennium '73" gathering in the Houston Astrodome; Yogi Bhajan of the Happy-Healthy-Holy Organization. The popularization of Zen Buddhist and Taoist ideas by D. T. Suzuki and Alan Watts has provided a religious interpretation to the psychedelic experiences of the counterculture. The ecology movement with its strong sense of reverence for life has appropriated elements from native American religion. Human potential trainings such as Arica, Silva Mind Control, or *est* often involve the participants in transcendent experiences and feelings of self-realization.

In 1972 a research team of graduate students trained in sociology and theology undertook a three-year project studying these new forms of religious consciousness. The study was conducted in the Berkeley–San Francisco Bay Area where many of these groups emerged from the counterculture of the 1960s. The study had two main methods: participant-observation in specific groups and a survey of a random sample of Bay Area residents. The survey interviews indicate how many in the general population were acquainted with the new groups and disciplines and who had taken part. Additional information was obtained on beliefs, religious experiences, life-style, and family background.[1]

One element that characterizes most of the participants in these groups is the search for intense experiences of themselves and of the sacred. Central to this is direct religious experience, a sense of being in the presence of God, realizing one's true self, or fusing with a cosmic force. The content and specific revelations vary, but all share the same sense of depth, directness, and immediacy.

Many of the new groups reflect shifts from religious belief (or nonbelief) to direct experience of the sacred; from faith (or doubt) to certainty of grace. Individuals surrender to the experience of the moment, to living fully in the present. This involves a moment of consciousness outside of the ordinary judgments and evaluations of everyday life, or what Abraham Maslow has termed "peak experiences." The trigger for these experiences may be meditation as in repeating a mantra, assuming yoga postures, reading scripture, or a prayer meeting.

In some groups a dramatic encounter with God or one's True Self is normative for initiation to full membership. In others peak aspects of religious experiences are devalued in favor of tuning into the presence of God in everyday life—more of a pious "hmm" than an ecstatic "aha!"

The theology of many of these groups is wholistic, meaning that the dualistic division between

---

[1]A fuller account of the research is in *The New Religious Consciousness* edited by the project directors C. Y. Glock and R. N. Bellah (Berkeley: University of California Press, 1976) and in *The Consciousness Reformation* edited by the survey director Robert Wuthnow (Berkeley: University of California Press, 1976).

God and His people is bridged in the religious experience of unity and oneness. A Kundalini yoga student puts it this way: "Man is the finite of God and God is the infinite of man." Particularly in the Eastern and human-potential groups images of God point to something less anthropomorphic and more immediate. Cosmic energy is a favorite image.

Sources of the Quest for Religious Experience

While the backgrounds of participants in the new religious groups and the social context of their pilgrimages are as varied as their beliefs, some generalizations can be tentatively made. Most are between eighteen and twenty-eight, with equal proportions of men and women. They tend to be more highly educated and liberal than others their own age, coming from middle-class homes with affluent, well-educated, and liberal parents. These background characteristics contrast with the lower-class origins of most religious movements that emphasize direct religious experience, often characterized as "religions of the oppressed." The generation growing up after World War II came to expect a lot from life. It also had the resources and the leisure to get bored, be revolted with materialism, discover a lack of meaning in life, and call into question the moral authority of almost every social institution: government, business, industry, church, and family.

Their questioning was reinforced by an era of protest by racial minorities, the growth of the women's movement, the experimentation of middle-class youth in hippie culture, and the opposition to the Vietnam war. The interpretations of reality that had provided meaning and loyalty up until the 1960s, namely, technological progress, established religion, and utilitarian individualism, came under attack.

The lack of integration into broader society is reflected in the socially marginal situation of youth involved in these groups. They tend to be unmarried, unemployed, young, politically deviant, residentially transient. Youth in these new religious groups are twice as likely as other youth to be single, three times as likely to have finished college, and twice as likely to label themselves as "radical."

Partly through rejecting what they considered to be the hypocrisy of their elders, many youth lacked clear and acceptable images of what it is to be an adult. Coming from prosperous backgrounds, they found that the vocational opportunities open to them rarely met what they were brought up to expect. The meaningful experiences that society once provided in initiation into vocation and family life are sought through other intense experiences and alternative forms of social support.

Psychedelic drugs are one means to intense experience and a high proportion of participants have used them. Drugs can precipitate joining a religious group in at least two ways. An addict may welcome Jesus into his or her heart or seize upon meditation out of disgust with a drug habit. Alternatively, a peak experience on a "good" drug trip may open the experimenter up to another reality and encourage the search for a way to stay high all the time. As one Hare Krishna devotee said, "LSD opened the door, but Krishna allowed me to step through." Besides providing peak experiences, religious groups provide a more stable and supportive community than was generally available in the drug culture or in the nuclear families they were raised in.

In a time of crisis of authority in society generally, the sense of certainty that accompanies the direct authority of personal experience is enormously attractive. And for those reluctant to trust intuitive knowledge, contemporary religious groups provide support and validation for this experiential reality of personal experience.

Given the analysis of who participates in the new religious movements and why, would you expect them to continue growing or to die out in the near future? Can these new religious forms avoid the problems of institutionalization that have been discussed in the chapter? How?

identity. This especially supports the survival of a society in which a single, established religion is shared by all.

As we saw in the case of the family, a variety of religious forms can serve these functions. Religions with one god, three, or many—all seem to provide support for the unity and persistence of societies. Ritually devouring a totem seems to work as well for the Australian aborigines as the Eucharist does for Christians. Both rituals create a sense of moral community.

In all societies, religious institutions are relevant to other institutions and aspects of social life. Weber pointed to the implications of religious beliefs for the economy, for example.

The relatively high degree of religious tolerance in America has resulted in a great variation in religions. Religions include those transplanted from Europe and elsewhere and the many new ones born here. In addition, Bellah suggested that Americans of all faiths share in a "civil religion" that supports the generally moral concerns that characterize our national posture on issues.

Cults, sects, churches, and ecclesia are some of the different structural forms that religions take in America and elsewhere. In general, cults and sects are characterized by a greater experiential fervor, and their members are typically converts from other religions. The behavior of church members is more conservative. The membership of churches, as opposed to sects, tends to come through inheritance rather than conversion. Successful sects have a general tendency to become established as churches as the children of members become socialized into membership.

The structuring of religious experience can also be seen in terms of the dimensions of religiosity. Glock has suggested five key dimensions: ritual, belief, cognitive, experiential, and consequential. We saw that a rather large percentage of Americans —particularly church members—report having had religious experiences: feeling they were in the presence of God, being saved in Christ, being punished, or being tempted by the Devil. Such personal experiences, while they might represent a threat to the established institution, occur most typically among those who have most thoroughly reified and inter-

nalized the agreements of the institution itself. Thus, their experiences support rather than threaten the institution.

Religions deal with religious deviance in a number of ways. Historically and, less frequently, now, one solution has been death or torture to force agreement. When a religion is powerful enough, it can also punish religious deviance through secular sanctions. Churches have handled radical clergy through devices such as monastaries and the campus ministry.

Dissatisfaction with established religious institutions is evident in the continuing attempts to find functional alternatives. Today's established religions began as alternatives to unsatisfying predecessors. There is no evidence that the process is ending, and many of today's alternatives will be tomorrow's reasons for further change.

The dilemma of the church, as of the family, is a fundamental one. Institutions are structured so as to survive, and their survival typically involves the reification and internalization of agreements in place of direct, personal experience. While the experience of agreements can provide feelings of satisfaction, it does not seem to provide enough satisfaction for individuals in the long run.

Religious institutions offer one structuring of the experience of reality. Educational institutions provide another.

Functions of Educational Institutions

Certain of the experiences I've been talking about in connection with religious institutions lie outside reason and rationality. When Joan of Arc heard voices telling her to take up arms and deliver France from the English, that experience occurred on a plane aside from rational calculation and understanding. Much of our dealing with reality, however, takes place within the realm of rational analysis. We figure things out and understand them in ways akin to the methods of science. And, as I suggested at the beginning of this chapter, people have *experiences* within the realm of reasonable understanding.

When you were a small child, you may have

All of us have had the direct, personal experience of wondering, figuring out, and saying "Aha!" (Robert Foothorap, Jeroboam, Inc.)

gone through a period of trying to figure out how things "worked." Clocks are a common focus for that activity, and countless clocks have been disassembled by curious children. Maybe you accounted for one or two yourself.

I know that you've had the experiences of insight, discovery, and sudden understanding of things more than once in your life, if not with clocks, then with something else. If that weren't the case, you wouldn't be reading this book right now. I know that you've found yourself grappling with some concept or problem, that it kept eluding and confusing you, and then, in a sudden "aha!", you understood it. As is true of religious experiences, these personal flashes of insight, discovery, and understanding can present a problem for society.

Without agreements on the way things are, we can't live together. Educational institutions transmit the group's agreements about reality. Schools are in this sense inherently conservative: They perpetuate the status quo and guard against "dangerous" ideas —the flash of insight, the "disassembly of the clock"— arising from direct cognitive experiences. As we shall see, however, educational institutions contain *within* them a direct threat to their conservative orientation. Science and scholarship are a source of disagreement.

In the remainder of this section, I want to delineate the different functions educational institutions serve. Then we'll look at some of the different forms that serve those functions. We'll conclude with more specific issues regarding the experiences of individuals within educational institutions.

General Socialization

The primary function of education is, as already noted, the transmission of agreed-on symbols, beliefs, values, and norms to new generations of a society. This function has two facets. First, the society itself is perpetuated through a continuity in its agreements, and interpersonal harmony is enhanced. Second, individuals, as they learn to operate within society, gain a sense of who they *are* as seen through the point of view of the generalized other (see Chapter 2).

Special Skills

Particularly in modern societies, educational institutions have the function of training individuals in the special skills required for the operation of complex and specialized social structure. Not everyone needs to learn the skills of an auto mechanic or of a brain surgeon, but some people need to, and schools teach them.

Vocational schools have the teaching of specialized skills as their primary manifest function. American high school students, for example, may take courses of study in carpentry, farming, home economics, automobile repair, and similar occupation-related fields. Business colleges and professional schools—such as medical, law, and engineering schools—are other forms of vocational training.

Notice that this particular function of educational institutions is integrated with the needs of economic institutions. In large part, schools produce skilled people to keep the economy operating.

Mobility

In many societies, education serves the function of mobility for individuals and subgroups within society. "Getting a good education" is a way of improving your position in society. Many ethnic subgroups such as (in America) the Jews and the Japanese have achieved rapid social and economic mobility by stressing education among their young.

Mobility is relevant for the group as well as for individuals. Educational institutions can sort out those people most qualified to serve in particular statuses—regardless of their social-class origins—so as

to support the effective functioning of the social system. This is, of course, the great American dream, and it sometimes comes true.

Custody of the Young

Educational institutions often serve a function that is easily overlooked, a custodial function. Schools can serve as an alternative to the family in caring for and supervising children. This is directly represented by the term *in loco parentis*, "in the place of a parent." Schools are often granted legal and quasi-legal rights to act as parents in dealing with students.

The custodial function of schools is also relevant from the point of view of the economy. Especially in the case of mandatory schooling, education keeps young people out of the job market. The young person who might compete for jobs is required to stay in school instead. This function is further substantiated by educational requirements, a high school diploma or a college degree, for certain jobs.

Creation of Knowledge

As I've indicated, educational institutions are fundamentally conservative. Their chief function is the transmission of agreed-on knowledge and skills within the context of other institutions. Schools perpetuate agreements.

Another side to education contradicts the first. Educational institutions are also a chief source of *new* knowledge. By its nature, new knowledge often contradicts old knowledge and thereby threatens established agreements. This situation is most clearly seen in the case of modern science, but it occurs in philosophy, the arts, and elsewhere.

Medieval Europe was comfortably organized around the view that the earth was the center of the universe. Theologians were comfortable with the notion that their God had arranged the stars and planets around the human race on earth, and a carefully elaborated system of Ptolemaic astronomy made it possible to predict heavenly movement. Then Copernicus upset that comfortable knowledge of how things were by suggesting that the earth moved around the sun, which, in turn, moved around in the universe.

More recently, the physicist Albert Einstein upset our most fundamental, comfortable views on space, time, energy, and matter. Everyone "knew" that an hour was the same period of time under all conditions, yet Einstein offered a new scientific view that time ran more "slowly" at very high velocities. Everyone "knew" that matter and energy were inseparable, yet Einstein offered theoretical proof that one could be converted to the other—and then offered a dramatic demonstration in the atomic bomb. Modern-day physicists (Tobin 1975) now discuss such seemingly bizarre notions as negative time, antimatter, and black holes and white holes in the physical universe. Some are now even reconsidering the ancient Eastern notion that matter is created by cosmic consciousness.

Physics is not the only threat to what we "know" about reality. Biologists continue making inroads into understanding what was once the "sweet mystery of life," taking away both the sweetness and the mystery. Philosophers, for their part, continue their abstract inquiry into the nature of reality (ontology) and into the nature of knowing (epistemology).

Educational institutions often challenge agreements about the organization of social life. American colleges and universities were generally aligned with the views and goals of government and economics in the 1950s, but the following decade was quite different. The most radical critiques of our foreign and domestic policies came from college campuses. They were the source of major opposition to the war in Vietnam, just as they have figured importantly in the reorientation of attitudes toward race relations, women's rights, poverty, and the environment. Even in matters of "taste," educational institutions have assaulted accepted standards of what is "good" in music, painting, and literature.

Dimensions of Variation in Educational Institutions

While education is, on the one hand, a conservative institution—charged with preserving and transmitting social agreements—it is also a potentially subversive one. We'll return to this latter aspect of education later in the chapter. At this point, let's look at some of the major dimensions along which variations in educational institutions occur. The different forms that educational institutions themselves take are far too varied to cover here.

Content

Educational content includes both ideas and skills, and each of these varies in various institutions. Some schools have as their purpose the transmission of religious ideas; others focus on science, literature, philosophy, and countless other types of ideas. Skills taught have equal variety.

In addition to these cognitive orientations, education can involve more affective, or "feeling," matters. Recently in American education, for example, we have seen a growing emphasis on self-actualization, interpersonal relations, and similar concerns.

Control

Since education is so largely a matter of socialization to established agreements—whether scientific knowledge, political values, or the skills of a craft—it is important to recognize the variations in who decides which agreements are to be taught and learned.

In the United States, educational institutions have largely been run by government. Modern socialist states provide an even clearer illustration of this pattern. The linkage of educational and political institutions is particularly important from the standpoint of social control.

Sometimes religious institutions have run educational institutions. Many of the earliest universities were organized by churches, and American parochial schools are a modern illustration of this practice. Church-related schools vary greatly in the degree to which they focus on religious education and secular education.

In the United States, and elsewhere, some education is conducted by private, strictly educational, organizations. Private secondary schools such as Exeter and private colleges and universities such as Harvard represent a clearer separation of education from other institutions. Although such schools are not under the direct control of either government or religion, you should bear in mind that even private

Educational institutions structure the experience of learning and knowing. (Inger McCabe, Photo Researchers, Inc.)

schools are integrated into the rest of society and relate in many ways to other institutions.

Physical Forms

I would guess that when you see the word "school," you automatically bring up a picture of students sitting in rows of chairs in a room, being confronted by a teacher. That's only natural, since that's probably the main form your own education has taken. As I'm sure you realize, that's only one form among many.

An exciting modern innovation in the physical form of education involves the use of mass media. Children and adults alike are learning many subjects by means of newspapers, radio, and television. Prob-

ably the best-known illustration of this innovation in America is "Sesame Street." Taking much of their format from the advertising, soap operas, game shows, and dramas of commercial television, the producers of "Sesame Street" have sought to "market" education among young children. A two-year examination by the Educational Testing Service, moreover, suggests they have been successful (Ball and Bogatz 1970, 1971).

Teaching versus Learning

I want to mention a final way in which educational institutions vary, one that I'll return to later in the chapter. Increasingly, American educators have distinguished between "teaching" students and "letting them learn." This dimension runs from rote memorization at the one extreme to some form of Socratic dialogue* at the other.

The difference is important in the interplay between personal experience and institutionalization. The rote learning of the 3 Rs that characterized the one-room school in colonial America is an extreme illustration of institutionalized education. "Knowledge," in that instance, is firmly agreed-on, and the function of schools is merely to transmit the agreements from one generation to the next. By contrast, many innovations in modern education involve *leading* students to *learn* and *discover* things for themselves. The purpose of Socratic questioning is to open the way for the personal discovery and understanding of ideas and of the nature of physical reality. The fundamental dilemma of this latter orientation, as we'll see shortly, is that it does not necessarily support the agreements that, in turn, support the continuation of group life. The accompanying box, "A Pedagogy of the Oppressed," clearly illustrates this.

Now that we have considered a few of the ways in which educational institutions vary, let's look a little more thoroughly at a particular society. Let's see how the institution of American education functions in a broader social context.

> ## A Pedagogy of the Oppressed
>
> "The Brazilian teacher Paulo Freire discovered that any illiterate adult can begin to read in a matter of forty hours if the first words he deciphers are charged with political meaning. Freire trains his teachers to move into a village and to discover the words which designate the current important issues, such as the access to a well or the compound interest on the debts owed to the *patron*. In the evening the villagers meet for the discussion of these key words. They begin to realize that each word stays on the blackboard even after its sound has faded. The letters continue to unlock reality and make it manageable as a problem."
>
> What does this passage tell us about the structure of effective learning environments? If learning comes so rapidly for the Latin American peasant, how come more than 10 percent of U.S. citizens over 26 are functionally nonliterate?
>
> Source: Ivan Illich, Deschooling Society (New York: Harper & Row, 1970), p. 27.

American Education

In this section, I want to discuss two major aspects of education in America: mass education and science.

Mass Education

In many, and perhaps most, societies, formal education has been reserved for a few. In ancient Athens it was limited to young, free *men* (not available to women and slaves). A number of societies have limited education to the children of the wealthy or to the nobility.

*A method of teaching used by Socrates in ancient Greece. The method involves the teacher's asking a series of easily answered questions which inevitably lead students to a logical conclusion that the teacher foresees.

Although education in the American colonies largely reflected the European heritage, the birth of independence and the commitment to political democracy had an impact on education that is still felt today. The early national leaders, believing that an effective democracy required an educated populace, laid the groundwork for broad, public access to education. Beginning shortly after independence, public land was granted and taxes appropriated for the purpose of establishing free, public schools.

The step after education was made available to the public in America was to make it mandatory. Massachusetts was the first state to require school attendance, in 1852, and by 1918 all the states required it. Today, most states require children to attend school between the ages of eight and sixteen, and individual states have broader age ranges.

Because of compulsory attendance laws, almost all Americans complete at least eight years of elementary school. Many receive much more, as Table 9·4 indicates.

Increasing participation in education has extended well beyond the traditional four years of college. Graduate programs have expanded greatly. In 1972 alone, 46,445 persons received doctorate degrees from American universities. The largest single field was medicine with 9,253 degrees granted; next was education, with 7,037. Over 600 people received Ph.D.'s in sociology (U.S. Bureau of the Census 1975a:141–42).

Participation in education in America is undeniable. But what does this participation signify? Is education used to create the educated public the founding fathers envisioned? Has equality for all been achieved through mass education? The accompanying box, "The Uses of Education," addresses the first of these questions, and the next section addresses the second.

College in America remains available predominantly to the rich, whites, and men. As Christopher Jencks (1973) reported, 20 percent of high school

The Uses of Education

A number of studies show that educational requirements for entry into most occupations are continually increasing. Fifty years ago many engineers lacked a high school diploma. In 1950 40 percent did not have a college degree. Now a college education is essential, and perhaps by 1984 only Ph.D.'s will be hired as engineers. Why are educational requirements for employment being increasingly upgraded? When I asked this question to my students in an introductory sociology class, their response was something like this:

In an increasingly technological society, an individual's productivity depends partly on the level of skills he or she has attained. Increased education increases these skill levels and is accordingly required from those seeking employment. The value of these skills is shown by the greater prestige and income that comes with more education.

This reasoning, based on seeing the function of education as teaching technical skills, is in agreement with that of many sociologists (e.g., Clark)[1]. In recent years a number of conflict theorists have taken issue with this functional analysis. They see the purpose of education as certifying qualities unrelated to production and as legitimizing existing social arrangements rather than as teaching skills necessary

[1]Burton R. Clark, *Educating the Expert Society* (San Francisco: Chandler, 1962).

for performance on the job.[2] Relevant skills are often learned on the job as in apprenticeship programs. Many jobs now require higher levels of education for work that was done adequately by less-educated persons in the past. Once the more highly educated are hired, their performance and productivity is about the same as the less educated, and in some instances may be inferior.[3] Bowles has shown that for persons at a given level of education evidence of increased skill as measured by achievement tests does not contribute to increased income in jobs secured.[4] Much of what doctors and lawyers learn in school is undoubtedly relevant to their success in helping people get well or in winning cases for their clients, but most jobs in society with increasing educational requirements do not require this level of expertise.

If productive skills are not learned in school, what is? One thing that students learn is to accept their place in society and to feel they deserve what they get. In school, students come to believe that rewards, including access to higher education and entry into more prestigious and lucrative occupa-

[2]Randall Collins, "Functional and Conflict Theories of Educational Stratification," *American Sociological Review* 36(6)(December 1971):1002–18; Samuel Bowles, Herbert Gintis, and Peter Meyer, "Education, IQ and the Legitimization of the Social Division of Labor," *Berkeley Journal of Sociology* 20(1975–76):233–64.

[3]Ivar Berg, *Education and Jobs* (New York: Praeger, 1970).

[4]Bowles et al., "Education, IQ and Legitimization," p. 261.

graduates whose parents earned under $3,000 went to college; among those whose parents earned more than $15,000, 87 percent did so. Regardless of academic ability, high school graduates from wealthy families (Rogoff 1961) are far more likely to plan college than those from poorer families, and they are also more likely to actually attend and graduate (Havighurst and Neugarten 1968). The "elite" aspect of education is discussed in the box on page 225.

Sex is still a factor in regard to college attendance in America. Although girls have outnumbered boys

in high school graduating classes since at least the Civil War, men continue to outnumber women in college. In 1974, for example, 26 percent more men than women were enrolled in the nation's colleges and universities (U.S. Bureau of the Census 1975a).

Race continues to be a factor also. In 1974, 14.0 percent of whites aged twenty-five or older were college graduates, as contrasted with 5.5 percent of blacks in the same age category (U.S. Bureau of the Census 1975a). The role of race in American education has been the focus of a persistent debate, both within

---

tions, are based on performance on objectively measured cognitive tests. The more meritocratic the educational system appears, the better it serves to legitimize inequality of eventual incomes.[5]

Sometimes students notice that their schoolmates with the same test scores but with greater poise and more family pull seem to go further and obtain better jobs. But for the most part students internalize failure, feeling they are either too dumb or lazy to do any better than they have done.

Quasi-professions such as beauticians and morticians use educational requirements to limit entry of new practitioners and to erect hurdles in the way of future competitors. Greater educational requirements also upgrade their occupation's prestige by implying that the work involves a high level of professional expertise obtainable only through formal schooling.

Some sociologists have argued that schools *do* teach relevant skills and values, but not necessarily technical ones. By enduring sixteen years of schooling graduates have in effect been screened for passivity, deference to hierarchical authority, achievement orientation, ability to delay gratification, and ability to inhibit self-expression in the work role.[6]

Schools teach status cultures including vocabulary, inflection, styles of dress, aesthetic tastes, values, and manners. Employers use education to

select persons who have been socialized into particular cultures. For entry into managerial ranks employers look for persons socialized into elite culture, that is, the most highly educated. In recruiting rank-and-file employees they look for less educated ones who have been socialized into respect for the dominant culture and the elite that carries it. As different status cultures are obtaining more and more education, the educational requirements for jobs are raised as well.[7]

To the extent that level of educational attainment is related to family background (through influence on educational aspirations) higher education is a means for upper-class families to pass on their status. Furthermore, upper-class control of the educational institutions where sorting and certifying are done means that upper-class values will be more highly rewarded.

Educational institutions relieve employers of the burden of devising tests of relevant ability. Employers need criteria to legitimize the way they hire, and they use the school's certification function in this way. Regardless of the relevance to the skills required by the job, grade-point average and number of years in school become the criteria for justifying the selection of some individuals for employment and the exclusion of others.

How does the above discussion square with your own experience of college?

[5]Ibid., p. 239.
[6]Collins, "Functional and Conflict Theories," p. 1012.

[7]Ibid., p. 1016.

Table 9·4 Percent High School and College Graduates among Americans Twenty-Five Years and Older, 1940–1974

Year	Percent high school graduates	Percent college graduates
1940	24.5	4.6
1950	34.3	6.2
1960	41.1	7.7
1970	55.2	11.0
1971	56.4	11.4
1972	58.2	12.0
1973	59.8	12.6
1974	61.2	13.3

Source: *U.S. Bureau of the Census,* Statistical Abstract of the United States, *1975, p. 118.*

and outside the institution. Without any doubt, blacks and other minority groups have been overtly discriminated against over the years. Recently, a variety of legislation and special programs have aimed at rectifying past injustices. The formal segregation of schools on the basis of race has been illegal for years, yet **de facto** segregation of blacks and whites persists. More recent and controversial attempts to bus children from one school district to another have provoked heated and sometimes violent protests from students and parents.

The concern over racial segregation in the schools has arisen in large part from past patterns of "separate but unequal" school systems in which the educational facilities made available to blacks were grossly inferior to those for whites. Massive research efforts in recent years have made the matter more complex.

James Coleman, a sociologist, published one of the best-known recent reports on this subject in 1966. In a survey of more than half a million students in four thousand schools, Coleman found little difference in the quality of facilities in predominantly black versus predominantly white schools. More important perhaps, Coleman found that factors associated with high-quality educational facilities—libraries, laboratories, high expenditures per student, for example —had little or no effect on the scholastic achievement of students as measured by standard tests. Moreover,

Coleman found little difference in the performance of black students attending integrated schools as compared with those attending segregated schools. The most important predictors of academic achievement that Coleman (1966) could find in his data related to characteristics of the students' family and neighborhood characteristics.

The Coleman report was in extreme contradiction to much of the common knowledge Americans had about their schools, and it is still being debated. If the data and interpretations represented by the study present a valid picture of race and education in America, clearly the achievement of educational equality will be far more difficult than previously imagined.

Mass education has been an American ideal and goal throughout most of our history. In terms of sheer participation, we have been enormously successful. The ideal of equal access to education, however, has been far more difficult to achieve. There's a parallel here to the American experience in other institutions. In the economy, for example, we have achieved an unequaled standard of living *on the average.* As we'll see in Chapter 10, however, we have not achieved equal access to that high standard.

Let's turn now to another special aspect of education in America that illustrates the complex nature of institutions. From the standpoint of maintaining society's agreements, education is a "subversive" element.

Science

Early in the discussion of education, I noted that educational institutions function to *create* knowledge in addition to simply passing along established agreements about it. Nowhere is this clearer than in the case of science, pursued largely, though not exclusively, within educational institutions.

Science in education Ever since the medical universities of the Middle Ages, science has been intimately linked to educational institutions. The ever more complex and cumulative nature of scientific knowledge has required formal instruction and increasingly better trained instructors. Moreover, the growing dependence of science on sophisticated

The Education of American Elites

In most societies there are educational institutions that prepare the sons of the upper classes to rule. In these institutions they are taught confidence, leadership, teamwork, and *noblesse oblige*—elite responsibility for the welfare of the masses. In England 40 percent of the members of Parliament went to Oxford or Cambridge and a sizable proportion of these prepared at exclusive secondary schools such as Eton and Harrow. Through the "old schoolboy" network of contacts, older school alumni already well placed, they often secure high positions. Fre-

quently they marry sisters or cousins of their schoolmates, thus solidifying class and family ties.

In the United States men at the top are highly educated, with a high proportion attending the twelve most prestigious universities and the most exclusive prep schools. The table gives educational levels for corporate, governmental, and public interest leaders.

In what ways do elite schools solidify upper-class cohesion? In what ways could they help challenge the status quo?

Educational Background of Corporate, Governmental, and Public Interest Elites

	Corporate (N = 3,572)	*Public Interest* (N = 1,345)	*Governmental* (N = 286)	*All persons aged 58–64 in 1970[c]*
Average age	61	64	58	
Female percentage	0	7	1	
Schools attended				
Public	82%	73%	91%	94%
Prestigious[a]	11	18	6	0
Other private	7	9	3	6
Colleges attended				
Public	32	13	44	48
Prestigious[b]	55	79	44	5
Other private	13	8	12	47
Education				
College educated	90	96	100	17
Advanced degree	49	76	77	2

Corporate: presidents and directors of largest corporations. Public interest: trustees for universities in [b] below; trustees of largest foundations and cultural organizations; senior partners of top law firms. Governmental: executive officers of assistant-secretary rank or higher; congressional leaders, Supreme Court; presidential advisors; admirals and four-star generals.

[a]Andover, Buckley, Cate, Catlin, Choate, Cranbrook, Country Day, Deerfield, Exeter, Episcopal, Gilman, Groton, Hill, Hotchkiss, Kingswood, Kent, Lakeside, Lawrenceville, Lincoln, Loomis, Middlesex, Milton, St. Andrew's, St. Christoper's, St. George's, St. Mark's, St. Paul's, Shattluck, Taft, Thatcher, Webb, Westminster, Woodberry Forest.
[b]Harvard, Yale, Chicago, Stanford, Columbia, M.I.T., Cornell, Northwestern, Princeton, Johns Hopkins, Pennsylvania, Dartmouth.
[c]Estimated from: U.S. Office of Education Bulletin, 1933; American Council on Education, 1932; Porter Sargent, *Private Schools, 1931;* U.S. Bureau of the Census.

Source: Thomas Dye and L. Harmon Zeigler, The Irony of Democracy *(North Scituate, Mass.: Duxbury, 1975). The study was conducted in 1970 and based on* Who's Who *listings.*

equipment has similarly linked it to large organizations such as colleges and universities.

Although more than two-thirds of America's natural scientists and engineers are employed by private industry, one in seven is employed by the nation's colleges and universities (U.S. Bureau of the Census 1975a:552). In 1973, colleges and universities spent over 2.76 billion dollars for scientific purposes; more than half of that came from the federal government (1975a:548).

Science—threat to society?   As the data indicate, Americans have placed a good portion of their financial and human resources in science. Moreover, there is a broadly shared agreement that such an investment is worthwhile. As we'll see in Chapter 11, Americans have very high esteem for the occupation of scientist.

Everyone can point to benefits we have gotten from our investments in science: medical cures, advances in communication and transportation, and "bigger and better" creature comforts. Most Americans look forward to more advances, especially with regard to the cure of diseases such as cancer and heart disease. At a time of serious environmental problems, many Americans believe that science will save us all.

For all their high regard for scientists, however, Americans have reservations. Scientists are popularly portrayed as single-mindedly scientific, impractical in the nonscientific aspects of life, and generally hard to understand. A mystique surrounds science that often makes nonscientists uncomfortable and sometimes troubled.

Periodically in recent years objections have been raised to science in America, often centering on the financial investment made in it. As this chapter is being written, increased congressional concern is being expressed in regard to the research funding of the National Science Foundation, as indicated in the following report from the *Christian Science Monitor*:

"Why study the perspiration of Australian Aborigines?" was a typical complaint that pounced on seemingly trivial research and ignored the fact that the Department of Defense wanted to find out why American soldiers dehydrate in the desert while Aborigines don't. Many a congressman's constituents, hearing the criticism, have demanded that such "waste" be curbed (1975:21).

Representative Joseph Gaydos of Pennsylvania probably voiced the troubled feelings of many public officials and voters when he said "I hope we can bring this elite egghead empire under control" (*Christian Science Monitor* 1975:21).

Many Americans regard science, and education more generally, as not only wasteful but also dangerous. Education *is* a threat to society as a set of shared agreements, for education has the task of evaluating as well as perpetuating agreements. Educational institutions, and science in particular, pose a threat to the beliefs, values, and norms that the members of a society share.

Although science does not declare itself on the matter of values, its activities often reflect on our values. This happens, of course, whenever science challenges a society's beliefs, since beliefs specify values. More to the point, however, scientists often *study* those things that societies value, often examining whether they "work" or not. Thus, a scientist, although not able to say *scientifically* whether capitalism is "better" or "worse" than socialism, can examine the strengths and weaknesses of each, showing whether

they support or work against other social values.

Finally, education generally and science in particular can pose a threat to society's norms. This can happen when scientists question the beliefs and values the norms are based on. Sometimes science is troublesome for people when scientists—such as sociologists—merely point to the existence of unstated norms, showing the de facto discrimination against women in pay rates, for example.

Education and science, then, look two ways. Schools, the primary agents for passing on established agreements from generation to generation, are also charged with the questioning, evaluation, and modification of those same agreements.

Educational institutions present other problems, too. If the structuring of educational experience presents an inherent problem for society, it does the same for the individuals who inhabit that society.

Experiencing the Structure of Learning

You'll recall that our discussion of education began with our taking note of the exciting personal experiences of insight, discovery, and understanding. In the succeeding pages, we've looked at some of the ways in which those experiences become structured in educational institutions. In this section I want to examine some of the ways in which individuals experience those structures.

Creating Identities

One of the functions of educational institutions that we discussed earlier is the creation of social identities. In a society such as the United States, you cannot escape the fact that your social identity is a function of the educational system. You are required to attend school for a number of years, and you must emerge from that as a bright, average, or poor student. There's no escaping one of those identifications. In this society, moreover, you must have educational certification to get a job. In fact, the amount of education required for most jobs has been increasing steadily.

The bestowal of educationally based social identities, however, has been considerably criticized in recent years. Consider the matter of school "tracking systems." As individual schools have become larger and more complex, grouping students according to similar levels of ability has seemed a good idea. Poorer students are presumably dealt with at their own level and not forced to compete with better students. More qualified students, on the other hand, should be able to realize their full potentials, not being held back by slower classmates. That is the theory.

In practice, however, the tracking system appears to have worked against the interests of students identified as slow. Contrary to expectations, the Coleman report found that slow students performed better in mixed classes than in remedial ones. But the problem is greater even than that.

Once identified as a poor student, you are virtually trapped. It is unlikely that your teacher will ever see improvement in your performance and suggest reclassifying you. Perhaps the most frightening evidence of this pattern has been provided by an experiment conducted by Robert Rosenthal and Lenore Jacobsen (1969).

Rosenthal and Jacobsen administered what they called a "Harvard Test of Inflected Acquisition" to students in a West Coast school. The researchers then met with the school's teachers to discuss the results of the test. They identified certain students as very likely to exhibit a sudden spurt in academic abilities during the coming year, based on the results of the innovative predictive test. As measured by subsequent IQ tests, the identified students far exceeded their classmates the following year, just as the researchers had predicted to the teachers. The significant thing about this experiment? The Harvard test was a hoax! The researchers had identified the potential "spurters" *arbitrarily* from among both good and poor students.

Recall that social identities are a matter of agreement. Once an agreement has been established as to your academic abilities, it is difficult to change. The structure of educational institutions seems to support the persistence of those agreements, and the individuals involved tend to incorporate those agreements in their self-images and in their behavior.

Bureaucratized Learning

Schools are social organizations, and they have the same survival needs as other organizations. When schools are very large, they tend to be bureaucratically structured. A bureaucracy is the most efficient structure for processing students through the educational experience. Many students and others have objected, however, that "processing" is not education, and they particularly object when bureaucratic efficiency seems to take precedence over what might be the thrill of learning.

I would imagine that you have had times when the organizational requirements and procedures of your school have seemed to interfere directly with the kind of educational experience you thought school was all about. You may have been prevented from enrolling in a class that perfectly suited your intellectual curiosity. Or perhaps you succeeded in enrolling, only to discover that a thousand classmates had done the same. Instead of the excitement of personal inquiry, you found yourself listening to lectures that permitted no participation on your part. Even if you maintained your enthusiasm for the topic, your hardy enthusiasm for expressing yourself may have suffered a head-on collision with a multiple-choice examination that had no questions relating to the thrill of personal insight, discovery, and understanding.

It's a simple matter to see the problem inherent in such situations, but it is more difficult to find solutions. The organization of mass education seems inherently incompatible with the personal quest for educational experience.

Functional Alternatives

For a variety of reasons, individuals are often dissatisfied with the way the experience of learning is structured in educational institutions. As in the case of other institutions, there have been many attempts to remedy that dissatisfaction by substituting new forms and functional alternatives. Let's look at some of those.

Student Rights and Powers

The 1960s were a turbulent time for American colleges and universities. With the beginning of the Berkeley Free Speech Movement (FSM) in the fall of 1964, campuses across the nation were rocked with protest, violence, and death. In large part, the protest movement was organized around particular issues: civil rights, the war in Vietnam, and drugs. Running through these specific issues, however, were two broader questions: What rights do students have while attending school? What role should they play in the governance of educational institutions?

The conflicts over the first question highlighted the second question. Could and should students be full participants in the governing of the college—in the establishment of agreements on its operation and purpose—or were they merely clients? Should students have a say in what courses were taught, what faculty were hired, tenured, and promoted? Was "student discipline" a matter to be handled by administrators or by fellow students?

Questions such as these often were focused on extremely specific points. Ethnic and racial minorities called for courses dealing with the history of their ethnic and racial groups—plus qualified faculty to teach those courses. Marxist students called for better courses in Marxist philosophy. Women called for courses dealing with the role of women in American society. Some asked for modified admissions policies that would allow the entry of more disadvantaged students.

The implicit assumption of all such demands was that changes in the form of the institution would alleviate dissatisfactions. Overall, colleges and universities responded to the demands in part but never in full. The subsequent quieting of the nation's campuses, moreover, seems less a consequence of satisfaction with the new arrangements than a renewed interest in other matters, such as training for jobs in a tightened economy.

Free Schools

The free-school movement is another alternative to established educational forms. Allen Graubard

(1973) has described the fundamental premises on which such schools are founded:

> The basic theoretical concept is, naturally, freedom. The literature of radical school reform associated with the free schools vehemently opposes the compulsory and authoritarian aspects of traditional public and private schools. This literature attacks the emotional and intellectual effects of conventional pedagogy and projects a radical theory . . . that children are naturally curious and motivated to learn by their own interests and desires. The most important condition for nurturing this natural interest is freedom supported by adults who enrich the environment and offer help (pp. 153–54).

Graubard notes that the number of free schools in the country grew from 25 to around 600 in the space of five years, with 200 being added in a single year. Clearly, such schools are an attempt to recapture the *experience* of education that many feel is lost in the structuring of conventional schools. Whether they will be able to satisfy organizational needs such as financing and acceptance within the larger society without losing the experience they are intended to foster remains to be seen.

The dilemma of educational institutions is the same as that of religious and familial ones. They have the function of structuring personal experiences in such a way as to permit group survival, yet that function can work against the human satisfaction that might be derived from the experiences themselves.

Summary—Educational Institutions

The major functions of educational institutions include general socialization, teaching special skills, providing means for social mobility for individuals and groups, and serving as custodians. Educational institutions also serve the function of *creating* new knowledge and agreements about reality—especially through science.

A wide variety of institutional forms seem to serve these functions. Some of the dimensions of variations include the content of instruction, who controls the institution and the agreements transmitted, and the physical forms and facilities within which education takes place. There is also variation in the relative emphasis placed on "teaching" versus "learning."

The goal of equal, mass education in America reflects a political value and has resulted in a large degree of participation in educational institutions by the members of society. The goal of *equal* access has not been achieved. This is currently most notable in relation to college attendance: Women, blacks, and the poor are underrepresented.

Science, importantly, has a central place in American education. Science is, of course, directly linked to our economic and technological development, and Americans have generally esteemed scientists. At the same time, however, science (and education more broadly) is regarded as a threat to established beliefs, values, and norms.

The structuring of educational experiences within our schools, colleges, and universities has been a source of dissatisfaction for those within the institution as well. There have been many complaints that organizational needs and other aspects of institutionalization have taken the natural thrill out of learning. Innovations and functional alternatives to conventional forms have appeared as a result.

Religion and Education in Review

In this chapter, we have been looking at two different social institutions. I had a reason for treating them in the same chapter, reflecting what they have in common: the structuring of our experiences regarding the nature of reality. Both religion and education offer views of what is true and why. Both institutions—as institutions—grow out of a societal need for agreements about reality. (It doesn't matter so much what the members of a society believe as long as they all believe the same thing.)

These two institutions support each other in many ways, but I want to close our discussion by highlighting the ways they conflict. Religious views of reality originate in a realm outside rational logic. However, educational views—especially scientific ones—thrive within the realm of rational logic. Many sociologists and other observers have noted the long-term trend toward "rationalism" in social evolution and the advantage this trend has given educational institutions over religious ones. A century and a half ago, Comte was confident that science would replace religion in a short time; and contemporary writers have spoken of "the death of God."

In the American case at least, religion, like the family, has experienced a general specialization of function. Yet, like the family, religion persists. No one can tell if religious institutions will one day vanish altogether, but we can be quite certain that they will not vanish soon. The prospect, rather, is that the two separate institutions will persist as now—sometimes in harmony, sometimes in conflict—providing agreements as to the nature of reality and structuring individual experiences of it.

Suggested Readings

Glock, Charles Y., Ed.
1973 *Religion in Sociological Perspective.* Belmont, Calif.: Wadsworth.
Much of the contemporary, empirical research in the sociology of religion has been generated within the Research Program in Religion and Society at the Survey Research Center at the University of California (Berkeley) under the direction of Charles Glock. In this book, Glock has brought together a representa-tive selection of the studies conducted in that pro-gram, providing an excellent introduction to current sociological research on religion.

Jencks, Christopher et al.
1973 *Inequality: A Reassessment of the Effect of Family and Schooling in America.* New York: Harper & Row, Colophon Books.
This controversial book calls into question the im-plicit, American faith in the power of education. Much of what we expect schools to accomplish, the authors suggest, needs to be addressed in the family instead. Special attention is given to economic con-cerns such as employment and poverty.

Smith, Huston
1958 *The Religion of Man.* New York: Harper & Row.
This is an excellent introduction to the world's great religions: Hinduism, Buddhism, Confucianism, Taoism, Islam, Judaism, and Christianity. Smith describes the founders, history, and main teachings of each. Excellent bibliographies guide you toward deeper study.

Weber, Max
[1922] *The Sociology of Religion.* Trans. Ephraim
 1963   Fischoff. Boston: Beacon Press.
This is the classic work by one of the most important sociologists of religion. While this book is replete with historical and cross-cultural examples, Weber's main concern is the analytical understanding of dif-ferent religious structures and orientations. A par-ticular interest in this book, as in Weber's other studies, is the relationship of religions to other social institutions, especially economic ones.

Episode Nine

It was mid-March, 2027. Gabe sat alone on the terrace of his apartment. His sleeves rolled up and his shirt unbuttoned, he leaned back in his lounge and closed his eyes. It was early evening. The sun shone reasonably warm for the first time in months. "Relax," he thought as energy penetrated his being. "Nourish yourself."

He was troubled. A news leak from the United States district attorney's office had recently disclosed that mutants were indeed suspected of the many unsolved kidnappings which had occurred over the preceding years. Still, Gabe realized, only Monica, Batterson, Duncan, and Roanoke knew either of his mutation or of his personal involvement in the Lake Hospital mission. While he had not spoken with Monica—except briefly when their paths crossed accidentally —they had remained politely friendly. He was reasonably certain that she would not go to the authorities with information condemning him.

Constance Batterson had visited Gabriel in January, explaining that she and her colleagues considered responsibility to their subjects a matter of vital importance. The sociologists would not disclose Knapp's name. Moreover, they would refuse to testify in court should Gabe ultimately be arrested and tried.

No other outsider, Gabe repeatedly reminded himself, suspected him. He had left no evidence, no fingerprints, nothing anyone would be able to trace.

Yet he was tormented. Since the news leak had appeared on front pages throughout the nation, violence had erupted along Adamsville borders. Gangs armed with guns, knives, clubs, and rocks harassed Adamsville guards. APIK grew daily in strength,

demanding extermination of what the group now openly called "green monsters." Several other groups, each for different reasons, condemned the chlorophyllics.

The day before, a young man in Seattle had been torn from his automobile as he drove home from work and fatally beaten. A group of hostile nonmutants had thought him a poser. Gabriel knew that he was not. The growing violence disturbed him. "You're alone out here," he told himself. "Soon you'll have to go home."

But he persisted in his refusal to return. He was thirty-three now. While it had been nearly a year since the compulsory physical examination had convinced him that any doubts about his being a mutant were unfounded, his skin continued in its refusal to change.

Gabriel knew there was only one cause for the failure of a green's flesh to mature: disloyalty. And a disloyal green would forever be distrusted. He would go home to disgrace.

Resolved to "take one day at a time," Gabriel Knapp had managed so far to keep his position at Chicago National. The medical file in the department of health services had never been completed. The report had gone—several times now—to the board of directors lacking information on Knapp. Every three months Gabe received the same memo: "Please respond re your medical examination. We have no record of such in this office." Every three months, Gabriel folded the memo, took it home, and burned it.

Knapp watched the March evening sun descend. He rose and entered his apartment, pulling the sliding door shut behind him. Not sufficiently refreshed, he poured himself a glass of milk, the supplement he continued to require. Never, he chided himself as he swallowed, had he been able to do without it.

The door bell rang. When he opened a tiny aperture through which he might view his unexpected visitor, he stepped back in amazement.

The bell rang again. Gabe opened the door. "What are you doing here?" he blurted. And then, giving his guest no time to answer, "Were you followed?"

"Of course not," replied a young man in his early twenties. "Hurry and let me in, will you? I'm nervous as hell on the outside now."

The visitor shoved past Gabriel into the apartment. "It wasn't my idea to come," he said, removing his jacket. "I'm doing this for Jacob Lockwood. You and he used to be pretty good friends, he said, back in school. You snuck off and ran into some chocolate candy trouble together or something. Anyway, he's still fond of you. He persuaded me to come."

Bewildered, Gabriel ushered his guest into the living room. "Is it bright enough in here for you, Daniel? We can go into the bedroom if you like. I had some fluorescent tubes installed—"

"It's fine here, Gabriel," the younger, not-yet-matured green interrupted.

Gabe eased himself into a chair, sliding a partially full cigarette package into a drawer in the table beside him. Green religion prohibited smoking. To burn tobacco leaves was considered a symbolic infraction against "the photosynthetic universe."

"How's Jonathan?" Gabriel asked, unclear about the cause of this unprecedented visit.

"Dead," came Daniel Adamson's cold, succinct response.

Gabriel's jaw dropped. "That's impossible," he murmured.

"Greens die just like nonmutants, you know," Dan said sarcastically.

"Is that why you came here—to tell me?"

"No, Gabriel. Jonathan died several months ago. He lay in the sun on his burial bed without you."

During the religious funeral rite, Adamsville relatives place the stripped body of the deceased upon a sacred burial bed. The burial bed consists of a rock slab, 6 feet by 3 feet, over which a thick layer of green leaves has been carefully placed. Mourners keep vigil while the body lies in the sun. Once the blanket of leaves become parched, the deceased is buried, naked, with no casket of any kind.

The news of Jonathan's death had made Gabe feel weak. "Listen," he said, embarrassed, "I was just pouring a glass of supplement. Excuse me while I get it." Dizzy, he rose and went into the kitchen.

When he returned, Daniel asked, "Still taking supplement? You're too old for that, aren't you?"

"I can't help it," Gabe confessed. Shock and grief had undermined Gabriel's usual resolve to hide the weakness.

"Adam's law teaches that no green use supplement unless it is absolutely necessary," Dan preached.

"I know that," Gabe replied with impatience. "I went to school too. I learned religion just as you did. I get weak, that's all. Forget it."

"Jacob thought," Daniel ventured, realizing that he had offended his host, "that maybe by the Lake Hospital rescue you had proven yourself. He hopes you will soon begin to turn. He wanted me to encourage you to come home for the ceremony. The vernal equinox isn't far off, you know."

Adam Jones III had been a religious prophet. It was his law that all greens must mature.

Maturation rites occurred twice yearly on the occasions of the vernal and autumnal equinoxes. "Henceforth," Adam Jones III had written, "my progeny shall gather at the time when the sun crosses the equator making night and day all over the earth of equal length: that is, at the time of the vernal and autumnal equinoxes, occurring approximately March 21 and September 22. During the equinoxes, symbols of God's love and guidance, my people shall, by celebrating the onset of full greenness among their young, reaffirm their faith in God's plan."

God's plan, Gabriel and his peers had learned in school, at home, and during religious rituals, depended upon Adamsville for execution. Adam, prophet sent from God, had helped to father a new people.

The semiannual maturing ceremony had, since Adam Jones originated it, developed into an extravagant affair. During predawn hours on the morning of the equinox, the colony gathered in the park adjacent to Elderhome. It was sacred ground: To set foot in the park was to pray. As the sun rose, greens chanted thanks for the eternal source of energy, God's ultimate gift.

At noon when the sun reached the center of the sky, those who were to mature advanced to the sacred platform upon which Gabe Knapp had presented the rescued baby. The platform, draped in green velvet and flanked with cactus and desert flowers, had been decorated by Adamsville children.

Green velvet cloaks draped the candidates for maturity as they walked in procession toward the platform. A band played while they, one by one, removed their garments, letting them fall from their shoulders until they stood naked before their fellows. As those maturing gleamed green in the sunshine, Ruth and Michael Jones led the crowd in a religious chant.

"We are the future people of earth," Ruth called.

"We are the culmination of God's evolutionary plan," Michael chanted.

Later matured mutants advanced into the Great Hall, some for the first time.

All greens, Adam had written, must mature. It was later ruled, however, that if their skin did not become bright green by the time of their twenty-eighth birthday, greens must—after public repentance for their apparent sins of disloyalty—participate in the maturing ceremony.

"Outsiders have attacked our guards," Gabriel's guest had been explaining. "Gangs converge upon our gates, shouting insults, threatening murder. They may thwart God's plan.

"Now," Daniel continued, "our people are becoming separated from one another, joining factions. Larry Jones claims that the Elders are no longer capable of ruling, that they sin in their lack of commitment."

"Why?"

"They allowed three outsiders into the colony," Dan said flatly. "Larry feels that our troubles stem from that time."

"I agree," Gabriel said. "How do you think I felt, standing there chanting before our people, when I looked out into the throng and saw three ungreens? I am the one who could suffer most from this."

"The Elders," Daniel said, "thought you intended to remain in Adamsville. You were thirty-two years old, Gabriel! When you consented to perform the rescue, the Elders assumed you had chosen to repent and were returning for good."

Gabriel said nothing. The thought of a public confession sickened him.

"When you left again," Daniel continued, "it was apparent the Elders had misjudged you. Larry claims they sin by occasionally ignoring light-break. Hence, even their secular judgments are no longer valid."

Light-break, while of much lesser religious importance than either the maturing or the welcoming ceremonies, was a mandatory worship service. As greens lay on the park grounds or in their glass-roofed homes, absorbing solar energy, they became not only physically but spiritually stronger.

Daniel continued speaking. "And Larry says Duncan must go."

"Duncan is still there then?" Gabe was surprised.

"Yes. He's been there eight months now."

Gabriel rubbed his chin. "Why did Jacob send you here?" he asked after a pause.

"He wants you to come home. He believes that you have sinned. Your transgression must be confessed and forgiven before we will again be blessed with peace."

"So," Gabriel said, "*my* sin has helped cause this turmoil? What about the sins of the Elders?"

"Larry is not strong enough yet to defrock the Elders. But he wants *all* sin rooted from the community. And your sin is grievous."

Gabriel Knapp stood. "Tell them all," he said, "to tackle their most crucial problem. It is the Elders who have sinned! I admit that I have doubted. But my transgression is nothing compared to theirs!" Gabriel paused. "When Larry has accomplished the eviction of the outsider, Duncan, I will begin to consider coming home."

The visitor changed his expression. "Gabe," he said hesitantly, "don't you feel guilty for your transgressions against God and Adam?"

Gabriel thought a long time. "Daniel," he said,

"when I left Adamsville for college, I took some courses in genetics."

Daniel listened, uncertain of the relevance of this.

"I learned that some genes are either dominant or recessive, like the ones which determine eye color, for instance. If a person with blue eyes and a person with brown eyes conceive a child, the child's eyes will be blue—not bluish brown."

"I know that," Dan responded impatiently.

Gabe persisted. "But sometimes genes don't work that way. If a white outsider and a black outsider conceive a child, that child will be neither white nor black but a mixture of the two."

Dan gazed at Gabriel.

"Our religion teaches," Gabe spoke slowly, "that a green's genes are always dominant."

"Of course."

"But that religious tenet has not been subjected to scientific verification."

Dan grinned sarcastically. "And do you propose testing religious doctrines in a scientific laboratory?" he smirked.

Gabriel Knapp stared at the younger mutant intensely. "Our religion teaches," he continued, "that I drink supplements and that my skin does not mature because I have somehow been disloyal."

"Do you deny that?"

"I don't deny that I have had doubts. But there is a second possibility, Daniel."

"And what is that?"

"That mutant genes are not always dominant. That I was born of a chromosomal father who had dark skin, and I have inherited that complexion. The inherited darkness of my flesh may conceal the chlorophyll in it. And it is possible that, because I had only one green chromosomal parent, I do not photosynthesize to the extent that you do and that is why I continue to rely on supplement."

Dan stared in surprise. "You are a heretic," he whispered. "You have demonstrated here—right now—a degree of disloyalty that I have never witnessed before! It's no wonder that your skin remains dull."

"I rescued," Gabriel reminded his visitor firmly.

"And I find it difficult to understand why," Dan replied with sarcasm.

"Because my religion—while I often doubt it—is still very much part of me. When criticized by outsiders"—Gabe recalled his final evening with Monica —"I find myself defending our religious beliefs and practices vehemently."

"Larry is right," Dan said. "He wants Adamsville to establish its own university. He believes we must stop sending our young people away to schools where they can be taught heresy and untruth by outsiders."

Later Daniel explained that he had to leave. He was to catch a plane back to Phoenix that night.

When he departed, a woman of sixty, parked on the street outside, reached across the front seat of her dark-colored vehicle to a portable telephone. Drawing it to her lips, she said: "FBI Agent Garcia reporting. Green suspect presently departing Shore Towers apartments. Proceeding north on foot . . ."

Since his departure from Adamsville Daniel had been followed.

Questions

1. What are some of the values expressed within the institution of religion in Adamsville? How do these values specify norms?

2. What are some symbols within the institution of religion in Adamsville?

3. How are the institutions of religion and family interrelated in Adamsville? How does the religious funeral ceremony in Adamsville support the family as an institution?

4. Sometimes the institution of education can be at odds with that of religion. How is this illustrated in the episode? In what way would Larry Jones's proposal help to integrate these two institutions? Would this integration be functional to the colony or dysfunctional? Would it be functional or dysfunctional for another young poser like Gabe, do you think?

Functions of Political Institutions

    Power and Authority
    Codification of Norms
    Social Control
    Group Identity and Solidarity

Varieties of Political Structures

    Traditional Autocratic
    Totalitarianism

Power in American Politics

    Political Parties
    The Power Elite
    Community Elites

The Individual in American Politics

    Voting Behavior
    Political Alienation and Apathy

Political Alternatives

Summarizing Political Institutions

Functions of Economic Institutions

    Production
    Distribution
    Consumption
    Transformation

Varieties of Economic Institutions

    Capitalist Industrialization
    Socialism

American Economic Structures

    Big Business
    Big Labor
    Big Government

The Experience of Economic Structures

    Occupation as Identity:
      Satisfaction and Alienation
    The "Morality" of Work
    The Experience of Consuming

Some Economic Alternatives

Summarizing Economic Institutions

Suggested Readings

10

Political and Economic Institutions

The notion of "power" has been implicit throughout the discussions of family, religion, and education. We've seen how institutionalized agreements control our thinking, feeling, and behaving, and we've seen how those agreements put some people in positions to control others. In this chapter, as we consider political and economic institutions, we will deal with power directly—the question of whose agreements are dominant in society.

Bertrand Russell (1872–1970), the noted English mathematician and philosopher, likened power to energy, saying that power was the primary concept of the social sciences just as energy was the primary concept of physics. He also said (Russell 1938:11):

> Like energy, power has many forms, such as wealth, armaments, civil authority, influence on opinion. No one of these can be regarded as subordinate to any other, and there is no one form from which the others are derivatives. . . . The laws of social dynamics are laws which can only be stated in terms of power, not in terms of this or that form of power.

I'm sure you've had the experience of making people do what you wanted, and you've undoubtedly had the experience of doing what others wanted. You may have resented or regretted "going along" with another's wishes, but doing so is part of social life.

All of us have also had the experiences of "wanting" and of "having." In part, the desire to possess

things is related to the comfort and pleasure they offer. You enjoy having the money for a movie because the movie is enjoyable. At the same time, as Russell noted, possessions often relate to power, as a way of getting others to do what we want of them.

It is probably safe to say that all people have a "natural" desire for power and possessions, although the degree of desire varies. Normally, however, the unfettered, individual pursuit of these desires doesn't work. It would result in what Hobbes called a "war of all against all." For society to survive, it is necessary to have established agreements to regulate individual desires for power and possessions.

I am going to discuss political and economic institutions separately in this chapter, referring back and forth from one to the other as appropriate. We'll look at the functions of each institution and the structural variations that serve those functions. Then we'll look at some special issues regarding American political and economic institutions. We'll close with an examination of people's experiences of these institutions and their attempts to find functional alternatives.

Throughout, we are going to see the extent to which we experience power and possessions through institutions. This was the point of departure C. Wright Mills took in his classic analysis, *The Power Elite* (1959:10–11)*:

*Reprinted by permission.

C. Wright Mills 1916–1962 (Yaroslava Mills)

If we took the one hundred most powerful men in America, the one hundred wealthiest, and the one hundred most celebrated away from the institutional positions they now occupy, away from their resources of men and women and money, away from the media of mass communication that are now focused upon them—they would be powerless and poor and uncelebrated. For power is not of a man. Wealth does not center in the person of the wealthy. Celebrity is not inherent in any personality. To be celebrated, to be wealthy, to have power requires access to major institutions, for the institutional positions men occupy determine in large part their chances to have and to hold these valued experiences.

What are the institutions that provide, and deny, wealth, power, and fame? How do they operate? Let's

begin with an examination of the functions served by political institutions.

Functions of Political Institutions

Sometimes, the kind of power you see exercised around you seems "right," and other kinds of power seem "wrong." It might seem right and proper for your professor to "force" you to write a term paper for a course. It would seem altogether wrong and improper for one of your classmates to force you to write a term paper for him or her (under the threat of a beating, for example).

The primary function of political institutions has to do with the creation and perpetuation of agreements regarding the "proper" exercise of power. Sociologists call this the **legitimation** of power as **authority.** We'll begin with that key function, and then we'll look at some others.

Power and Authority

In Chapter 7, I quoted Rousseau as saying that nothing but agreements served as the "basis for all legitimate authority among men." Authority reflects an agreement as to who may "legitimately" exercise power over whom. For example, most societies have an agreement that parents can legitimately exercise certain powers over their children.

Max Weber was especially interested in the different bases for authority in societies. In his classic analysis, *The Theory of Social and Economic Organization* (1925b), Weber delineated three major types of authority, which represented a pattern of evolution in leadership. They were **charismatic, traditional,** and **rational-bureaucratic.**

Charismatic   "Charisma" is a personal quality that sets some people apart. A Greek word, it literally means "divine gift," and charismatic people—especially in the past—have been regarded as somehow divine.

The earliest form of authority, in Weber's view, was that which grew out of special personal qualities. Some individuals in a group simply stood out because of extraordinary strength, beauty, agility, wit, intelligence, communication skills, or the like. Such persons were granted the right to lead purely on the basis of their special qualities. I suspect that if you think back to your high school peer group, you'll be able to identify certain individuals who always seemed to take the lead in deciding what the group should do. People just seemed to agree with what those individuals suggested. That's because they had some degree of charisma.

Traditional   In the course of time, Weber said, charismatic authority gave way to "traditional" authority. Rather than depending on special personal qualities in individuals, authority became associated with certain statuses based, for example, on age or kinship. In some societies, the elders were the seat of authority, and the right to lead was passed from one group of elders to their successors. In others, authority was passed down through the generations of a particular family.

Weber spoke of the **routinization** of authority. Whereas charismatic authority appeared in an unpredictable way, the transmission of traditional authority was a regular and routine thing. The justification for traditional authority was similar to the justification for customs and traditions more generally. Things were done in a particular way because they had *always* been done that way. Thus, for example, the elders had authority because of an agreement that the elders had always had authority.

Rational-bureaucratic   Weber was particularly interested in bureaucratic authority, as we saw in Chapter 6. Bureaucracy provided for the rationalization of authority. Authority flowed not from the personal qualities of the leader, not from tradition, but from logical, rational, and explicit agreements relevant to achieving the goals of an organization. Authority was vested in officials for the purpose of supporting them in serving the interests of the group.

Whether political authority is studied in terms of the struggle to get it or in terms of how it operates at any one time, it is important to note that its legitimation—the acknowledgment of its existence—often links political institutions to other ones. For example, religious institutions may legitimate the political authority of a king through the notion of the "divine right of kings." Educational institutions also get involved sometimes. When the Congress was considering the impeachment of President Richard Nixon, for example, constitutional scholars at prestigious law schools were asked to comment on the constitutional provisions for impeachment.

In summary, the primary function of political institutions is the legitimation of power, transforming it into authority. Political institutions are sets of established agreements that specify who may exercise control over whom in what ways and under what conditions. Sometimes authority is linked to the personal, charismatic qualities of the leader, sometimes it flows from tradition, and sometimes it takes a rational-bureaucratic form. And, as we've just seen, other institutions of a society are often involved in the legitimation of political power.

Codification of Norms

Political institutions are also the focus for the creation of laws. Congresses and parliaments pass laws. Courts often clarify or legitimate those laws or do both. Monarchs pass edicts, and presidents issue executive orders.

The creation of laws represents a codification and specification of norms. We've already seen that norms are necessary for the survival of group life, and laws are a specification of the norms that apply in a given society at a given time. Sometimes laws specify the implications of the agreed-on values of a society. Some laws merely formalize agreed-on customs, and others impose norms not previously agreed on. The historic court decision in *Brown* v. *the Board of Education* in 1954, for example, clarified the implications of the American value of equality while contradicting local agreements on the norm of racial segregation in schools.

The survival of society depends on people's generally keeping the agreements of the group, and the codification of norms as laws makes that more likely. Laws also specify the sanctions associated with breaking them, which adds incentive to keeping them.

The codification of norms as laws presents a danger that we'll look at later in this chapter. Formally stating norms as laws can lead to their reification and internalization. Charles Andrain suggests that's what happened in regard to American legal documents early in our national history.

> Soon after the Constitution was accepted by each state, it began to assume sacred qualities. In some people's minds, the Constitution formed the equivalent of the ancient Hebrew covenant or even the whole Bible itself. Veneration of the impersonal law replaced reverence for the personal monarch. Thus legal norms took on sacred value (1974:79).

You can probably observe the internalization of laws in your own experience. There's an agreement in cities that you must put money in parking meters if you are going to park your car on the street. Fines are specified for breaking that agreement. It's a pretty straightforward, contractual matter. If you've received a parking ticket for breaking the agreement, though, you may have felt just a little bit "bad," as if you'd been slightly immoral or evil. If you don't feel that way about parking tickets, how about tax evasion or treason? If you feel that selling military secrets to a foreign power violates something more than a businesslike agreement individuals have with the group, then you've internalized the norms involved.

Social Control

Political institutions have the function of creating laws. They also enforce them. Police, military, courts, and bureaucracies have the job of seeing that codified agreements are kept. This function is often summarized in the phrase "maintaining law and order."

The value of social control for the survival of the society is obvious. The potential it has for the internalization of agreements should also be obvious. When political leaders speak of creating "respect for the law," what they have in mind is usually more than a recognition of the need for agreements in a society. Rather, what they have in mind is that laws should be imbued with a sanctity of their own and become "the Law."

We're going to look at the matter of social control more in Chapter 13, in the context of deviance. Let's turn now to the final major function of political institutions.

Group Identity and Solidarity

Political institutions, especially among modern societies, are the focus of group identity and solidarity. What does it mean to be an American, for example? It is virtually impossible to separate that identity from the idea of the United States as a political unit. This by no means implies that you must agree with the policies of a particular administration. It does not even mean that you support our present form of government. It's just that "being an American" refers to membership in a particular political unit, one that is distinguished from France, China, and Chile.

Andrain (1974:53) cites the "creation of a common identity" as the first basic problem of political institutions, and he mentions four possible sources: primordial, sacred, personal, and civil. As an example of the first of these, he notes that the members of some preliterate societies trace their descents back to a common ancestor. They share a common, group identity because they are relatives. Shared religious values are an example of a sacred source, and Andrain says that the personal feelings people have about a charismatic leader can also create a group identity. Finally, the source of group identity that Andrain labels as "civil" is similar to Weber's rational-bureaucratic structure of authority.

Seymour Martin Lipset has discussed the issue of group identity in America in *The First New Nation* (1963). In spite of the early conflicts and disagreements as to the form the new government in America should take, Lipset observes that a national identity was created. The difficulty of that accomplishment was not unique: "For countries, like people, are not handed identities at birth, but acquire them through the arduous process of 'growing up', a process which is a notoriously painful affair" (Lipset 1963:16).

The major functions of political institutions, then, are: (1) the legitimation of power in the form of authority; (2) the codification of norms as laws;

(3) social control; and (4) the creation of group identity and solidarity. As you will have anticipated, many different social structures can satisfy these functions. Let's look at some of them.

Varieties of Political Structures

Andrain has suggested three major types of political institutions that people have created to serve the functions we have been discussing: **traditional autocratic, totalitarian,** and **democratic.** His typology is useful for organizing our examination of this subject.

Traditional Autocratic

Strictly speaking, "autocracy" is a form of government in which all power is vested in one person, the autocrat. Monarchs and dictators are examples of autocrats, and many governments over the course of history have been autocratic. The pharaohs of ancient Egypt are one illustration; the recently ended reigns of Francisco Franco in Spain and Haile Selassie in Ethiopia are more contemporary examples.

The traditional autocrat's political authority is legitimated by tradition (leadership may be inherited, for example), by the autocrat's charismatic qualities, or by coercion. Typically, all of these are involved.

The autocrat is never the only powerful person in an autocratic society. The nobility (often landowners), the military, and the clergy possess a degree of power, and the autocrat is partly a mediator among these small elite groups. They, in turn, generally support and further legitimate the autocrat's authority.

The autocrat is the chief source of laws and the chief agent of social control. The power to make and enforce laws, however, is typically exercised to maintain the status quo rather than to develop new social and economic programs. Group identity and solidarity are primarily a matter of tradition.

Traditional autocracies have successfully served the functions of political institutions for millennia.

Organized group life has survived. It has survived through other political forms also.

Totalitarianism

The "total" in "totalitarian" has two meanings, both of which apply in the form of government called totalitarianism. On the one hand, "total" means that all members of the society are to be brought under a single set of agreements; totalitarian political institutions have no place in them for dissent. And on the other hand, the word means that all aspects of social life are to be covered by the agreements shared by all members. In this sense, every thought and action in a totalitarian society is "political."

The sets of agreements that apply to all members of society in all aspects of life in a totalitarian society are thoroughly reified in the form of a **political ideology.** The shared beliefs, values, and norms are seen as ultimately true and proper, sometimes even mystically so.

In contrast to traditional autocracies, which function to maintain the status quo, totalitarian regimes more typically represent a "rebirth" of national identity and purpose. Hitler's "superrace" and what was to be a "1,000-year Reich" were prototypes of this aspect of totalitarianism. Often a charismatic leader will come to symbolize both the group and the ideology. The society is united under a single banner, and the union is further substantiated by the identification of out-groups perceived as a threat to survival. German Jews, for example, were portrayed as particularly dangerous people, not "really" Germans.

The legitimacy of the totalitarian regime can rest on several bases. Frenzied popular support of an ideology that takes on sacred, quasi-religious qualities is one base. The personal appeal of a charismatic leader is another, and, as we've just said, the perceived threat of out-groups further supports the regime. The long-term survival of totalitarianism, however, also requires political organization.

Political parties are unusual in traditional autocracies, but they are essential to totalitarianism. Totalitarian regimes rest ultimately on tightly organized parties that enjoy a political monopoly. Totalitarian societies are single-party states. Usually only a small percentage of the population actually belongs to the party, and the party itself is usually run by a small elite. It is the party, however, that strengthens the regime's coercive ability and permits the control of other institutions in the society. In the "model" totalitarian society, the party is the vehicle for embedding the political ideology in the family, the schools, the churches, and the economy. This has the dual effect of adding immediate legitimacy to the totalitarian regime and of socializing people into agreement with the ideology.

Eric Hoffer added the term "true believer" to our popular language as a result of his examination of the great similarities among totalitarian regimes based on very different ideologies (1958). The pattern of social organization and of individual commitment to ideology and to party was the same under Stalinist Communism and Nazi anti-Communism. Hitler is reputed to have instructed party organizers to seek converts among the young Communists, realizing that Communist zealots could be Fascist zealots with little modification.

Like traditional autocracies, then, totalitarian regimes serve the major functions of political institutions. They create legitimate authority; they create laws and enforce them; and, in contrast to traditional autocracies, which enjoy a preestablished group identity, they create a renewed sense of group identity and solidarity.

The third form of political structure I want to discuss is democracy. Since democracy is closer to your own personal experience than other forms of government, we'll look into it in more detail.

Power in American Politics

In a democracy, political power is *created* by citizens' joining together in common agreements. The power of the corporate group comes from the pooling of support of many individuals. This view, although accurate, is an oversimplification of how large and complex democracies operate. Political power is actually created in many different places in America, and sociologists examine where and how. In this section of the chapter, I want to look at some of the sources of political power that have captured the attention of sociologists.

Political Parties

The Constitution makes no mention of political parties, yet the Democratic and Republican parties exercise more political power in America than any other groups outside of the government itself. The two major parties first competed with one another in 1856, and since then, no other party has elected a president of the United States, though a variety of "third parties" have tried. Individuals who run for political office as "independents" are at a serious disadvantage in comparison with candidates who enjoy major-party backing. Why is this so?

Political parties in America are a form of voluntary association, as discussed in Chapter 6. Like other associations, they derive their power from organization and knowledge, which, in turn, can create money and produce people at the polls. Suppose for a moment that you decided to run for an office such as mayor. How would you do that? You'd probably want to tell the public about the way you stood on the issues and what you'd do as mayor. One way would be to mail a statement to all the voters. For that you'd need a list of the voters' names and addresses; you'd need money to print the statement and to buy envelopes and stamps; and somebody would have to stuff the envelopes and type the names and addresses on them. But, then, would it be more effective if people went door-to-door, discussing your candidacy with voters? If you decided today to run for mayor, between now and election day you would face an unending string of unexpected problems, decisions to be made, and lessons to be learned. The special strength of established political parties is that they have faced those decisions and problems before and have learned many of those lessons. They have already organized to deal with electoral politics. Political "machines" at the local level tend to be extremely well organized.

Americans do not necessarily align themselves with political parties. More Americans do identify themselves as Democrats than as Republicans, but several times in recent years political polls have shown there to be fewer Republicans than people claiming "no party preference." See the accompanying box, "The Birth of a 'Third Party'?", for details.

Formal membership in our major political parties, moreover, has always accounted for only a small fraction of the number of votes cast for party candidates. Yet, in those states that do not have primary elections, the members of the parties are the ones who choose the candidates for office. More generally, the role of parties in a democracy can be stated this way: The people get to choose, but the parties decide what the choices are.

The Power Elite

In Dwight Eisenhower's "Farewell to the Nation" speech, given as he retired from the presidency in 1961, he surprised many by warning against the danger of too great cooperation between the military and industry.

In the councils of government, we must guard against the acquisition of unwarranted influence, whether sought or unsought, by the military industrial complex. The potential for the disastrous rise of misplaced power exists and will persist.

The military leader who led the United States and its allies through World War II had, ironically, coined a phrase that has become symbolic of the concern of some sociologists and others about the power of war-related industries in America. Three years before, C. Wright Mills had warned against the establishment of a "permanent war economy" in his ominously titled work *The Causes of World War Three* (Mills 1958). Mills contended that American industry had become so dependent on the production of war materials that the nation's economy required the continued threat of war to survive. Within this context, Mills was particularly bothered by the extent to which retired military officers entered executive positions in industry and the extent to which indus-

The Birth of a "Third Party"?

Much has been written about the rise and fall of third parties in American politics. Though they have added colorful names to American political history— Free-Soil party (1848), Greenback party (1876, 1880), Bull-Moose party (1912)—they have never attracted much support at the polls.

National electoral politics in America is a struggle between the two major parties: the Democrats and the Republicans. The Democratic party, moreover, has consistently been the stronger of the two in terms of voters' political identification.

Beginning in the mid-1960s, however, more American voters identified themselves as "independents" than as Republicans, leading some observers to suggest that the GOP had become America's first significant "third party."

Can you think of some reasons for the trends shown in the table?

Voters' Political-Party Identification

Year	Democrats	Independents	Republicans	Nothing, other, don't know
1960	46%	23%	27%	4%
1962	47	23	27	3
1964	51	22	24	2
1966	45	28	25	2
1968	45	29	24	2
1970	43	31	24	1

Source: Adapted from Robert Erickson and Norman Lutbeg, American Political Opinion: Its Origins, Content, and Impact. © 1973 by John Wiley & Sons, Inc. Reprinted by permission.

trial leaders held reserve commissions in the military.

Analysts have debated the issue of the military-industrial complex. Some, such as economist John Galbraith (1969), suggest it is more coincidental than conspiratorial. Others, such as political scientists Dye and Zeigler (1975), argue that the notion of a "war economy" has been exaggerated. No one suggests that the military-industrial complex is altogether insignificant as a source of power in American politics.

Mills's warning against the dangers of a permanent war economy is in line with his more general analysis of power in America. In 1959, he published the better-known book, *The Power Elite,* in which he argued that the nation was run by the "higher circles" of business, government, and the military.

> They rule the big corporations. They run the machinery of the state and claim its prerogatives. They direct the military establishment. They occupy the strategic command posts of the social structure, in which are now centered the effective means of the power and the wealth and the celebrity which they enjoy. . . .
>
> The people of the higher circles may also be conceived as members of a top social stratum, as a set of groups whose members know one another, see one another socially and at business, and so, in making decisions, take one another into account (Mills 1959:4,11)*.

In particular, Mills was concerned over the political power that money could buy. He spoke of "the very rich" and "the corporate rich." The recent scandals surrounding illegal corporate gifts to the Nixon reelection campaign of 1972 illustrate the danger Mills saw. As we'll discuss in the second half of this chapter, the social-structural link between political and economic institutions is even more fundamental than such political hanky-panky would suggest.

Several sociologists have questioned the validity of Mills's assertions regarding the power elite. Talcott Parsons (1957), for example, argued that wealth and power had become largely separated through the development of modern corporations. Those who owned the corporations no longer controlled them. Additionally, Parsons criticized Mills for failing to

acknowledge the power of the professions in America. He spoke specifically of lawyers, though he may have also had in mind such groups as the American Medical Association.

Parsons also raised a more fundamental question. He criticized Mills for assuming a "zero-sum" notion of power, for assuming that there was a fixed amount of power to be distributed. Instead, Parsons argued that power is continually *created* in society. Through the organization of associations is one example.

Another view on the nature of power in America is found in David Riesman's *The Lonely Crowd* (1953). Riesman and his colleagues thought national "power" was a function of veto groups that had the capacity to prevent the exercise of power by others. Whereas Mills saw a danger that a small elite could enforce its agreements on others and therefore direct the nation's destiny, Riesman and his colleagues saw the inability of any group to lead as the problem: "Where the issue involves the country as a whole, no individual or group leadership is likely to be very effective, because the entrenched veto groups cannot be budged" (Riesman 1953:257). William Kornhauser (1966) has provided an excellent, detailed comparison of the Mills and Riesman points of view.

Debate over the notion of a national **power elite** is likely to continue within the social sciences and outside them. The study of elites has had a local as well as national focus in sociology.

Community Elites

For about two decades beginning in the 1920s, an important part of American sociology involved the study of middle-American towns such as Muncie, Indiana (Lynd and Lynd 1929, 1937), and Morris, Illinois (Warner 1949, Hollingshead 1949). In their attempts to understand the dynamics of community life, researchers repeatedly discovered the presence and significance of **community elites.** In each town, either one family or a few families seemed to run everything. They owned the most important local industries. They either held political office locally or controlled those who did. Directly or indirectly, they had an influence on the day-to-day lives of everyone else.

*Reprinted by permission.

C. Wright Mills said that American society was run by a "power elite." The power elite shown here, cruising on Biscayne Bay, is composed of President Nixon (right) and industrialist friends Robert Abplanalp (left) and Bebe Rebozo (center). (Bob Sherman, Camera 5)

More recent studies of other American towns and cities suggest that the monolithic power structures of a few decades ago are less typical. Robert Dahl's study of New Haven, Connecticut (1961), Aaron Wildavsky's study of Oberlin, Ohio (1964), and Edward Banfield's examination of decision making in Chicago (1961) have pointed to **pluralistic power** structures. Each of the communities studied had several *pockets* of power that competed and cooperated in the struggle for community control.

Sociologists and other social scientists have looked at power in American democracy in a variety of ways. But since democracy is based on the agreements made by the public in the voting booth, we will now turn our attention to the average citizen, the individual voter.

The Individual in American Politics

American sociologists and political scientists have devoted a great deal of research to voting behavior. Let's see what they've learned.

Voting Behavior

In 1940, Paul Lazarsfeld and two colleagues undertook a study of voting in Erie County, Ohio. *The People's Choice* (1944), which reports their research, has become a classic account of why people vote the way they do. Foremost, the study pointed to the

Paul Lazarsfeld 1901–1976 (The American Sociological Association)

influence of "background factors" on voting choices: religion, social class, place of residence (rural or urban), and so forth. These factors related to party voting as follows:

Republican	Democratic
Protestant	Catholic
Upper class	Working class
Rural	Urban

Their effect was cumulative as well. Voters whose personal characteristics all suggested a Republican vote, for example, voted Republican, overwhelmingly. How about voters with "mixed" characteristics? They were likely to switch their preferences back and forth during the campaign and, on election day, were the most likely not to vote at all.

Subsequent studies (Berelson 1954, Campbell 1954, and others) have generally confirmed the original Lazarsfeld findings, pointing to the conclusion that there are two major types of voters in America. One type is made up of people whose social statuses indicate a particular party affiliation. These people are concerned about politics and active in political affairs, and they consistently vote according to their social statuses and their party. The other type of voter holds the power to swing elections one way or the other. These people do not always vote for the same party's candidates. They are the least interested in politics and the least likely to vote at all. More recent research on voting and political attitudes suggests that the second type of voter is becoming more common.

Political Alienation and Apathy

The 1960s have been widely regarded as a period of political alienation and disenchantment in America. While attention in this regard has been primarily focused on young people, Table 10·1 suggests that young people weren't the only ones affected. Comparing national surveys of voters in 1960 and 1968, we see increases in the numbers of people who feel that: public officials don't care what the people think; people don't have much say in governmental affairs;

Table 10·1 Growing Political Alienation in America

	Percent who agree 1960	1968
"I don't think public officials care much what people like me think."	25	44
"People like me don't have any say about what the government does."	27	41
"Sometimes politics and government seem so complicated that a person like me can't really understand what's going on."	59	71

Source: James House and William Mason, "Political Alienation in America, 1952–1968," American Sociological Review, April 1975, p. 125.

Some people have more power than others, and sometimes it may seem to you as if you have no say at all. Ultimately, political institutions are composed of the agreements people make. You can make agreements by doing nothing. (Roger Lubin, Jeroboam, Inc.)

and politics has gotten too complicated for the average citizen.

Jennings and Niemi (1975) report growing political alienation among both young people and people of their parents' generation between 1965 and 1973. Both groups were more likely to feel that: government wasted money; government officials were both crooked and inept; and government was controlled by a few big interests. In 1965, for example, 12 percent of the young people studied said that government was run by a few big interests; in 1973, 57 percent felt that way. Among the parental generation, the percentage increased from 23 to 53 percent.

The symbolic peak of political disenchantment was reached with the Watergate break-in of 1972, followed by the unfolding tale of political wrongdoing by members of the Nixon administration, and culminating with the president's resignation from office. How did the American electorate respond? From mid-May to early August, 1973, the national television networks broadcast live 235 hours of the hearings held by the Senate committee on Watergate. The hearings drew smaller audiences than the daytime soap operas they replaced, and there was a hue and cry around the country for the return of regular programming (Dye and Zeigler 1975). Subsequent revelations of antidemocratic actions by the FBI, the CIA, and other governmental agencies have not (as of this writing) outraged the public generally.

A rather large discrepancy exists between democ-

racy in theory and democracy in practice in America. Every year or so a high school or college class draws national attention by conducting a survey in which members of the general public are asked to support or oppose political positions taken directly from the Bill of Rights. Almost invariably, the Bill of Rights loses. In 1963, researcher Fred Greenstein reported that fewer than one-fourth of the adults studied could correctly cite *any* of the bill's provisions, and Herbert McClosky (1960) has shown that the nation's political leaders are far more supportive of our basic civil liberties than is the public at large.

Political alienation and apathy in America are evidenced in action as well as in attitudes. Of the nation's eligible voters 65 percent actually voted in the 1960 presidential election. In 1964, the turnout was 60 percent, and in 1972 it was 56 percent. Off-year elections traditionally draw fewer voters to the polls, and only 38 percent of the eligible voters turned out in 1974 (Dye and Zeigler 1975).

The Jeffersonian vision of self-governing citizens meeting together, discussing differing points of view, and forging a united, national agreement has proved more visionary than real. While it is an easy matter to blame the current state of affairs on an ignorant and irresponsible public on the one hand, or on an unscrupulous and conniving elite on the other, what is needed is to view the current state of American political life in terms of basic institutional processes.

Political Alternatives

The disenchantment with political institutions bears a striking resemblance to what we saw earlier in connection with the family, religion, and education. Political experiences need to be structured through agreements if society is to survive, yet the structuring of those experiences makes them less satisfying to individuals. Moreover, the continual changing of *political* forms throughout history has not remedied the basic problem. The political form alienating many Americans today began as an alternative to the unsatisfying colonial government that preceded national independence. The colonial government, however, arose as an alternative to the European politics that the colonists fled in coming to the New World.

The 1960s and early 1970s have been popularly characterized by the phrase "politics of protest." These years have been represented in part by an attempt to find political satisfaction outside of the institutionalized structure of electoral politics. Direct protest and mass demonstrations—sometimes civil, sometimes violent—were fairly common, and many observers felt American political institutions were about to be permanently altered. I am going to discuss the protest movement in more detail in Chapters 12 and 14, but I can report the basic conclusion here: Things didn't change as much as observers expected at the time. Despite specific legislation and modifications in national policies coming about in connection

with protests by minorities and antiwar demonstrators, the primary result may have been to make the reification of existing agreements among the elites and general public alike even more granitic than it had been before (see Dye and Zeigler 1975).

Many have argued that revolution is the only solution to dissatisfying political systems, but it is precisely in the case of revolution that the general problems of institutionalization are most clearly seen. The revolutionary, having successfully overturned the established political agreements, must immediately—and often autocratically—establish new political agreements. The cycle begins all over again. Without some structuring of individual political experiences, a nation cannot survive. The Maoist attempt to maintain a "continuing revolution" in China appears to be a recognition of this problem, but it does not yet appear a solution to it. Regardless of ideology or philosophy, whether democratic or dictatorial, institutionalized political agreements become reified and dissatisfying. The solution needs to be found in an understanding of the nature of social agreements themselves.

Summarizing Political Institutions

Political institutions are organized around the exercise of power in society. More specifically, they define the legitimate use of power, which is authority. Weber discussed three major types of authority: charismatic, traditional, and rational-bureaucratic. Despite a trend toward the last of these, even the most modern societies have elements of all three types of authority.

Other functions of political institutions include the codification of norms as laws, the enforcement of norms through social control, and the creation and maintenance of group identity and solidarity. In all these regards, political institutions function to support the survival of group life in societies.

Varied political forms appear to serve the necessary functions. In traditional-autocratic systems, all power and authority are theoretically vested in a single leader, although in practice the control may be less direct. Totalitarian systems operate by exercising control over all aspects of life for all members of society. Where traditional-autocratic systems tend to support a continuation of the status quo, totalitarian governments are more likely to work toward the "rebirth" of the nation, organized around an ideology. In contrast to totalitarian and traditional-autocratic systems, democracy grows out of the participation of a broad base of society's members in politics and government. In a mass democracy, people participate directly in government; in representative democracy they elect officials.

In a democracy, political power is clearly created by the joining together of people in a common agreement. In America, there are several focuses of such power. Among them, and unique, are political parties. In general, voters choose their leaders, but the parties decide who the voters will choose from. C. Wright Mills and others have written about the importance of a power elite—leaders of government, business, and the military—in running the nation. He has been criticized for taking a "zero-sum" view of power and for underestimating the power of professional interest groups. David Riesman suggests that American politics are controlled more by veto groups that have the power to prevent certain actions than by groups that direct the actions to be taken.

A number of sociological studies have examined the place of community elites in American political life. Some studies have suggested that towns are essentially run by a single family or a few families, while other, more recent, studies suggest a greater pluralism of community power.

The main way that individuals participate in American democracy is through voting, and sociologists and political scientists have studied voting behavior. The research suggests that there are two types of voters in America. One type consists of people who vote consistently in terms of their social statuses. For example, the poor would vote Democratic and the rich, Republican. Nothing is likely to sway these people from their voting pattern if several of their social statuses suggest it. These people are also likely to be interested and active in politics. The other type of voter consists of those whose statuses do not suggest a clear voting pattern. Such people are less interested in politics; they vacillate in their voting

behavior; and they are the most apathetic and the least likely to vote at all. Often, the apathetic voters hold the balance of power in American elections.

There is evidence that American voters—both young and old—have become more and more alienated and apathetic about our political institutions. They are less and less likely to think that public officials care what they think and more likely to think they have no say in government. The percentage of voters turning out for elections has been decreasing. Disenchantment with current political forms has led some people to seek functional alternatives such as mass protest. Although it is too early to tell for sure, it appears that these new political forms will be no more satisfying than the ones they oppose. Some writers have suggested that the political protest of the 1960s and early 1970s may even have furthered the reification of established political agreements among the general public.

In most societies, political and economic institutions are closely intertwined. Let's conclude our extended discussion of social institutions, then, with an examination of economics.

Functions of Economic Institutions

The stuff of political institutions is control over people. Economic institutions deal with control over the scarce things that people want. Very often the two go hand in hand. If you had control of all the world's crude oil reserves, for example, you'd be in a good position to get people to do what you wanted them to. When you were young, you may have had a sense of how powerful you'd be if you owned all the candy in the world. The situations are basically the same.

The desire for *things* is a powerful motivation in human affairs. It makes some people work hard, and it sometimes makes people lie, cheat, and kill. Clearly, the unfettered seeking after desired things would make social life chaotic and unstable. Economic institutions act to control potential chaos. They are made up of agreements that lend social order to individual acquisition. The principal functions of economic institutions revolve around the production, distribution, and consumption of scarce goods and services. I'm going to discuss each of these functions, but you should see them in two broader contexts also. First, a society's economy brings about a transformation of the environment to satisfy individual and social needs; and we'll be looking at that transformation throughout the remainder of this chapter. Second, the structure and operation of the economy is, in most societies, a keystone of social stratification. This we'll see in Chapter 11, on stratification and mobility. Now, however, let's turn to a discussion of the economic function of production.

Production

Economic production, most generally viewed, is a matter of transformation. Things people do not need or cannot use are transformed into those things they *do* need, in a form they can use. As we noted in Chapter 2, Talcott Parsons has used the term "adaptation" in connection with the functions of economic institutions. They adapt a society's environment to its needs.

Economic institutions transform many "things." Economists have generally focused their attention on three: land, capital, and labor. These are the three great resources that are transformed by economic institutions into the goods and services that people need and want.

Land   Different societies have had different agreements about land. Some have revered it, feeling obliged to bring themselves into harmony with it. Others have seen it as something to be exploited. Different agreements have also arisen regarding the ownership of land. In many preliterate societies, the notion of private ownership of land has been unthinkable; it was simply there for all to use. When these societies—such as the American Indians and the native Hawaiians—have been visited by societies favoring private ownership, the result has been disastrous for them. "Titles" to land have been given freely or sold cheaply, because the "privacy" of private ownership has been an agreement too foreign to be comprehended.

Capital   Capital might be regarded as the tool by which land is transformed in economic production. Although we tend to think of capital as "money," this is too narrow a view in the economic context. The farmer's plow is an example of capital, as is the hunter's spear. The factory capable of turning cotton into clothing is another example of capital. In modern societies, we have come to regard capital as primarily financial. It is a commodity with which to buy the plows, spears, and factories that can transform the land.

Labor   Labor, as you may have guessed, is the people who operate the tools that transform the land. Plows are useless without people to direct them, spears are useless without people to aim and throw them, and factories are useless without people to operate them. Economic institutions transform people into labor. They organize people for the production of goods and services. We'll examine this aspect of economic institutions in some detail when we discuss the organization of occupations.

Distribution

Economic institutions are systems through which the fruits of production are distributed within a soci-

Table 10·2 American Consumer Expenditures in 1929 and 1973

Item	1929 $ Millions	1929 Percent	1973 $ Millions	1973 Percent
Food and tobacco	21,239	27.5	178,676	22.2
Clothing, accessories, and jewelry	11,193	14.5	81,274	10.1
Personal care	1,116	1.4	12,315	1.5
Housing	11,530	14.9	116,367	14.5
Household operation	10,735	13.9	117,509	14.6
Medical care	2,937	3.8	62,726	7.8
Personal business	4,158	5.4	45,183	5.6
Transportation	7,612	9.9	109,228	13.6
Recreation	4,331	5.6	52,280	6.5
Private education and research	664	0.9	13,225	1.6
Religious and welfare activities	1,196	1.5	10,843	1.3
Foreign travel and other—net	511	0.7	5,595	0.7
Total	77,222	100.0	805,221	100.0

Source: U.S. Department of Commerce; as reported in Ann Golenpaul (ed.), Information Please Almanac *(New York: Golenpaul, 1975), p. 63.*

ety. Stores are an obvious example of organizations serving this function, but so are trucking companies, airlines, and shipping companies. Payroll offices, banks, and loan companies are involved in the distribution of money, which facilitates the distribution of goods and services.

In preliterate societies, distribution has been taken care of through a system of barter. Goods and services have been exchanged directly, without the intermediary role money plays in more modern societies. Notice that barter is not limited to preliterate societies. Children exchange baseball cards from packs of bubble gum. American farmers exchange many things among themselves. A bushel of fresh corn may be exchanged for the use of a tractor or a bull. People exchange favors.

Consumption

Consumption is the final stage in the operation of economic institutions; it gives production and distribution their purpose. Consumption patterns and preferences can explain much about the character of production and distribution in a society. They are a matter of agreements, and these differ from society to society. Symbols, beliefs, values, and norms shape the ways in which people consume as well as *what* they consume.

Sometimes sociologists examine consumption patterns in terms of the stated values of a society. One would assume, for example, that a widely shared agreement on the importance of, say, education would result in a significant consumption of educational services. An agreement on the value of material possessions would lead one to expect a significant consumption of such objects.

Sociologists sometimes infer a society's agreements from its actual pattern of consumption, rather than vice versa. Table 10·2 is an example of this procedure. It presents the pattern of personal expenditures by Americans in 1929 and 1973.

Personal-expenditure patterns are only one view of consumption in American society. In addition to our consumption as individuals, we consume *as a society.* In 1975, for example, Americans paid almost 100 billion dollars in individual income taxes to the federal government. When this is added to other sources of federal revenues and loans, we spent over a *quarter of a trillion dollars* as a nation, not counting state, county, and local government expenditures (U.S. Bureau of the Census 1975a:225). Table 10·3 describes our consumption pattern as a society in 1975. We can make inferences about values and priorities from this pattern, too.

We'll return to the issue of consumption later on in the chapter and examine the experience of being a consumer in a modern society. I want to close the discussion of economic functions with a brief consideration of the **transformation function** of economies.

Transformation

I've already commented on economic production as a matter of transforming the physical environment into things that people want and can use. Crude oil deposits are transformed into gasoline to run automobiles, for example.* Economic institutions effect another transformation: They transform people by structuring them into social statuses. People become consumers, workers, supervisors, and so forth. The transformation of people into statuses has an organizational function. It coordinates individual activities in the cooperative production, distribution, and consumption of goods and service. The transformation is also relevant from the individual's point of view. In many societies, "what you do" is the most important element in "who you are."

The transformation of people into economic statuses has, of course, been influenced by the division of labor in modern societies. The occupational statuses that constitute a significant part of many people's personal identities have grown increasingly specialized. It comes as no surprise when people complain that they are often regarded as tiny cogs in large machines, not as whole persons.

That transformation of individuals (like the transformation of the physical environment) is a mixed blessing we'll see in more detail later in the

Table 10·3   American Federal Government Expenditures, 1975

Item	$ Billions	Percent
National defense	85.3	27.2
International affairs	4.9	1.6
General science, space, and technology	4.2	1.3
Agriculture	1.8	0.6
Natural resources, environment, and energy	9.4	3.0
Commerce and transportation	11.8	3.8
Community and regional development	4.9	1.6
Education, manpower, and social services	14.7	4.7
Health	26.5	8.5
Income security	106.7	34.0
Veterans' benefits and services	15.5	4.9
Law enforcement and justice	3.0	1.0
Interest	31.3	10.0
General government	2.6	0.8
Revenue sharing and general purpose fiscal assistance	7.0	2.2
Undistributed offsetting receipts	−16.8	−5.2
Total	313.4	100.0

Source: U.S. Bureau of the Census, Statistical Abstract of the United States, 1975, pp. 225, 226.

chapter. At this point, however, let's look at some of the different forms economic agreements have taken in support of the social functions we've just examined.

Varieties of Economic Institutions

Throughout most of human history, our ancestors handled economic functions through hunting and gathering. Then, about 9,000 years ago, a major economic development occurred: People began planting and harvesting crops rather than simply gathering what they found in their wanderings. The development of agriculture meant that societies could form

---

*This aspect of economic institutions has important implications that will be discussed later on in the chapter. As you may have anticipated, we're going to be looking at some of the environmental problems that economic production has created in the form of pollution and the depletion of natural resources. We'll return to these problems in Chapter 17 also.

and settle down in particular areas and that more people could live together.

Our economic institutions have gone through a long history of development since the establishment of agriculture. For the purposes of this discussion, however, I want to pick up the story with the set of developments we have come to call the Industrial Revolution.

Capitalist Industrialization

Detailed occupational specialization had its beginnings in the mechanized, mass production of the first factories late in the eighteenth century. The Industrial Revolution grew out of a number of technological innovations within the British textile industry. The first of these, spinning and weaving machines, simply increased the productivity of individual workers; later innovations harnessed steam power and outstripped the productivity of individuals altogether.

The rise of mechanized factories radically restructured the economic agreements. First, economic production became far more specialized than had existed in the craft guilds. Where an individual once did everything from the spinning of yarn to the weaving and dyeing of cloth, a factory worker might have a single task of loading spools of yarn on a machine.

Second, and equally important, the worker no longer owned the result of his or her labors. The factories required large amounts of capital for buildings, machinery, and raw materials. Individual weavers lacked such funds, and a new class of capitalists invested in the factories and employed workers for wages.

With the rise of industrial **capitalism,** economic power shifted from feudal lords to capitalistic entrepreneurs and merchants. The greater profits provided by factories generated new capital for investment in expansion and even greater economic power.

Socialism

Capitalism is based on an agreement regarding private property. In practice, that agreement relates especially to big property: factories, machines, mines, and large sums of money. It is agreed that individuals may properly exercise control over such property.

In the mid-nineteenth century, Karl Marx spoke and wrote against what he regarded as the excesses of capitalism. In part, he objected to the dismal working conditions existing in factories and the low pay workers received. In part, he criticized the disassociation of specialized workers from the creative act. Primarily, however, he rejected the agreement regarding private ownership of the means of production.

The socialist set of agreements put forward by Marx and others placed ownership of the means of production with the society at large. Factories, raw materials, and industrial products, he said, should belong to the state. In this scheme, political institutions would be wedded to economic ones in the production, distribution, and consumption of scarce goods and services.

In the socialist economic institutions that have appeared in the world since Marx's time, workers are typically employees of the state. They receive wages in return for their work, and they use those wages to purchase the things they need from the state. In socialist agreements, economic institutions are centrally planned and operated since ownership of all enterprises rests with the same entity, the government. **Socialism** does not abolish private property altogether, however.

Marx looked beyond socialism in his writings to a system of **communism** that would totally abolish private ownership. All would share in the production of the society's goods, and all would enjoy them afterward. Marx summarized these sentiments in his famous dictum: "From each according to his abilities, to each according to his needs."

No major society today operates under this particular set of communist agreements. Many operate under either capitalist or socialist agreements, however, a situation that has resulted in one of the more volatile disagreements in the world today.

The economic institutions of all the world's major societies contain elements of both sets of agreements: capitalist and socialist. The United States economy is no exception. Although it is based on a fundamental agreement on capitalism, we have in practice what is often called a "mixed economy." Let's turn now to some of the structural aspects of that economy.

American Economic Structures

The most striking characteristic of the American economy is its size. Our GNP (gross national product) —the total value of the goods and services we produce as a nation—now exceeds a trillion dollars a year. This is approximately ten times what it was in 1940. In 1974, our GNP was a third more than the combined total for Asia, Africa, Latin America, the Near East, and Oceania (U.S. Bureau of the Census 1975a). With about 6 percent of the world's population it is estimated that we account for around 40 percent of the resources consumed in the world annually, a phenomenon we'll return to in Chapter 16.

In this section, we're going to look at three aspects of the "bigness" of the American economy: "big business," "big labor," and "big government."

Big Business

How big is American business? In 1972, 115 manufacturing corporations in America had assets greater than 1 billion dollars. Taken together, these corporations were worth about a third of a trillion dollars.

The immensity of American business is something that Karl Marx might have predicted as an extension of what he observed a century ago in Europe. Some twists in our capitalist agreements, however, Marx could not have foreseen. Most notably, the advent of the large corporation has deeded ownership of the means of production to the hands of the many rather than the few. In 1974, for example, American Telephone and Telegraph, the nation's largest company, was owned by nearly 3 million stockholders. General Motors had over a million "owners" (Golenpaul 1975). This does not mean, however, that all those owners participated significantly in the running of their companies.

Public ownership of business has represented a transfer of power within the economy, as A. A. Berle (1958) and others have pointed out. Today, it is the managers of business—the highest employees in the companies—who wield the power: corporate presidents and boards of directors. Corporate power is concentrated, moreover, through the phenomenon of "interlocking directorates." Certain individuals seem to turn up on the boards of directors of corporation after corporation.

The interlocking of American corporations has taken a new turn in recent years with the development of what is popularly called the "conglomerate": the giant corporation that diversifies its activities by participating in several different sectors of the economy. Conglomerates are based on the principle that diversification provides greater economic stability as the fortunes of specific industries rise and fall. They have provoked considerable controversy. David Horowitz and Reese Erlich (1972) voice the concerns this way:

> Led by such aerospace giants as Litton Industries, Ling-Temco-Vought (L-T-V) and Textron, the conglomerates are already regarded by many as the heirs apparent to American corporate power. With their feet solidly planted in the military-industrial complex, each has managed to absorb close to a hundred other corporations and to create a composite giant whose scope of industrial enterprise is truly awesome.

The transnational corporation is the latest development in the evolution of economic organization. While we've been looking at economic organizations in terms of the functions they serve within a society, the transnationals, as the name suggests, reach across societies. They may have raw materials acquired from one nation processed in other nations (where labor costs are low) and sell the finished products in still other nations (where consumer demand and wealth are high). You've probably done business with a transnational corporation yourself, perhaps buying a souvenir ashtray proclaiming the wonders of New York City and bearing the inscription "Made in Taiwan." You can look forward to doing business with more in the future.

The names of large, transnational corporations have become household words around the world. (Barbara Klutinis, BBM)

Big Labor

If big business in America is *big,* so is big labor. It would be impossible to understand the American economy or that of many other industrialized nations without an examination of the part played by unions, which were originally formed to look after and advance the interests of workers in particular occupations and industries.

The primary function of unions is to put the force of numbers behind the point of view of workers in framing the agreements that define industrial relations. For example, if one worker in a factory is unwilling to accept the agreements about working conditions, duties, pay, and fringe benefits there, he or she can be replaced with little or no disruption of the functioning of the factory. If *all* the workers in the factory unite in their disagreement, however, the matter is quite different. For this reason, "solidarity" has been the rallying cry of the union movement throughout its history.

The earliest American unions were formed of skilled craft workers, such as carpenters, electricians, and teamsters. Beginning in the 1930s, however, increasing numbers of assembly-line workers began organizing. The threat their organized power represented to management produced extreme and often violent resistance. Union organizers were fired and sometimes jailed. Union meetings were broken up and workers locked out of their jobs. Strikes were broken by the army, and people were killed in the process.

From the time of the Roosevelt administration onward, unionization has become increasingly legitimized within the American economic agreements. Federal laws now prescribe the manner in which employees of an organization can elect a union to represent them and the manner in which employers must deal with unions in collective bargaining.

The present political strength of labor unions in America is more than a matter of individual workers joining unions; unions have themselves organized into larger bodies. The American Federation of Labor (AFL) was organized in the late nineteenth century as a vehicle for coordinating existing craft unions. In 1935, following a dispute over the inclusion of unions being organized in the mass-production industries such as steel and automobile manufacture, a number of unions bolted the AFL to form the Congress of Industrial Organizations (CIO). Both organizations continued to grow until they merged into the AFL-CIO in 1954. As of 1972, the AFL-CIO was composed of 111 unions representing a total of more than 16 million members. This figure accounts for about 75 percent of the union members in America (U.S. Bureau of Labor Statistics 1975c) and nearly 20 percent of the total civilian labor force (U.S. Bureau of Labor Statistics 1976). In recent years, the organization of farm workers and government workers has represented important new directions in the union movement.

Big Government

To round out our overview of the American economic system, we turn to big government. The various levels of American government are involved in the economy in a number of ways. In 1975, over 15 million Americans—about one worker in six—were employed by federal, state, or local governments (U.S. Bureau of the Census 1975a). The federal government alone owned one-third of the nation's land and nearly half a million buildings (General Services Administration 1974). With some justification, the

federal government is sometimes called the largest "business" in the world.

A variety of government regulatory agencies exercise considerable control over the operation of private businesses. Radio and television stations, for example, are licensed, reviewed, and relicensed by the Federal Communications Commission, and that agency specifies certain agreements as to the nature of broadcasting. Other government agencies tell savings and loan institutions how much interest to pay on deposits, specify the quality of materials to be used in building construction, test and license professionals, and so forth.

The "big news" of the American economy, then, is its own bigness, reflecting big business, big labor, and big government. (That's only natural, of course, since social institutions represent the structuring of life in a big way.) But where are the individual people in the economy? And what experiences do individuals have within such economic structures?

The Experience of Economic Structures

In this section, we're going to look at some of the ways in which people experience complex, modern economic structures. We'll begin with an examination of occupation as a source of social identity and an examination of some of the interactions that occupations provide. Then we'll turn to the question of the "morality" of work for work's sake and see that attitudes and activities are both changing in that area. Finally, I want to examine the experience of individuals at the consumption end of the economic process, how they act as "consumers," narrowly and broadly defined.

Occupation as Identity: Satisfaction and Alienation

When you meet a stranger at a party, one of the first questions you'll be asked—particularly if you're a man—is "What do you do?" As you may have personally discovered, saying you're a student is not an entirely satisfactory answer. Being a student means that you don't "do" anything yet, and you may be asked a slightly sophisticated version of "What do you want to be when you grow up?" Occupation is a central source of identity in modern, industrial societies, much as kinship was in more traditional societies.

The link between occupation and social identity did not begin with modern industrialism, however. The cabinetmaker, cobbler, or other artisan of an earlier day derived his or her identity from work. Much has been written about the extent to which such people identified with the *products* of their crafts, enjoying the satisfaction of personal creativity. While such satisfactions have sometimes been overromanticized, Marx was surely correct in noting that division of labor in industry was significant in this respect. As a member of an assembly-line team, the worker could no longer regard the product of industry as a personal creation, and Marx spoke of "alienated labor."

In a modern factory hundreds or thousands of assembly-line workers repeat the same specific operation countlessly. The output of one worker becomes the input for another's specific operation. Their specific tasks typically involve the use of equally specialized equipment, and the objects of production may flow endlessly from one worker to another on conveyor belts.

The differentiated functions of the assembly line can be reasonably easily coordinated, but the further differentiation of staff positions is often the source of conflict within organizations. The corporation treasurer, with his or her point of view, may object to the equipment purchases the line personnel, with their point of view, want, and the sales staff, with their point of view, may urge modifications to the product that will be difficult to accomplish on the assembly line.

Different roles in a modern factory are interdependent. Every specific role is based on numerous agreements as to the roles others in the organization are to play. If assemblers were to stop assembling, if salespersons were to stop selling, if shipping clerks were to stop shipping, all the efforts of the rest of the organization would be useless.

Many sociologists have concerned themselves with the relationships that occur among the various occupations within industrial organizations. Some have paid special attention to work conditions and informal social relations as these affect work. They have been especially interested in such things as motivation and job satisfaction.

Numerous studies have shown that job satisfaction increases with socioeconomic status. In a study of some 400 employed men in 1955, for example, Morse and Weiss found great differences in the percentages at different occupational levels who said they would choose the same occupation if they could start over. Over two-thirds (68 percent) of the professionals said they would, compared with 59 percent of those in sales, 55 percent of those in management, 40 percent of those in skilled, manual occupations, 32 percent of the semiskilled, and 16 percent of the unskilled workers (Morse and Weiss 1955).

Part of the reason for such differences in attitude is clearly the different levels of pay. Other things being equal, people are happier making a lot of money than when they make very little. There's more to it than that, however.

Some jobs carry greater prestige and power than others, and they foster a higher level of self-esteem. In addition, high-status jobs, especially in the professions and management, call for more individual creativity and imagination, and they provide for more individual freedom and initiative than do the routinized assembly-line jobs.

High-status occupations typically also provide for a greater personal identification with the final output of an economic organization, providing the satisfaction with productivity in general that Marx said factories robbed workers of. In recent years, many corporations have instituted "profit sharing programs" and other measures to enhance workers' identification with the goals and activities of the organization. Large corporations take great pride in announcing the number of their employees who own stock in the company.

It is an oversimplification to say that people with high-level occupations get satisfaction from their work while those lower down do not, however. Much has been written about executive dissatisfaction. Probably the most popular account of this problem was William Whyte's *The Organization Man* (1956). Maintaining a high-ranking occupation in a large organization may restrict you in hundreds of ways, including who you can marry, what you must wear, and what church you must attend.

The "Morality" of Work

In part, the significance of occupation as a source of social identity in the West is linked to the "morality" of work embodied in the "Protestant ethic" we discussed in Chapter 9. In Calvinism, for example, one's economic vocation was seen as a stewardship under God. If you worked hard and well at whatever job you had, your actions glorified God. Sloth and sloppiness were a shame and a sin. The strictly religious roots of this point of view have withered, but there is still a strong agreement in America and elsewhere that working at a job—especially for men—is a moral and proper thing to do. Playboys, jet-setters, and the idle rich are targets of scorn, even when they are envied.

The view of work as moral has been considerably modified, at least in its specifics. When the average workday was reduced from twelve to eight hours, some saw the hand of the devil at work. More recent talk of a thirty-hour or twenty-hour workweek raises the same specter for some.

Unemployment is a similar, though less happy, problem. In 1975, at an 8.6 percent unemployment rate, over 7 million members of the American labor force were out of work (U.S. Bureau of Labor Statistics 1976). Added to the financial difficulties that unemployment obviously causes is the social stigma of being worthless, even "immoral." Nor is this problem evenly distributed throughout the population. Young urban blacks, aged sixteen to nineteen, had an unemployment rate of 31.4 percent in 1975 (U.S. Bureau of Labor Statistics 1976). Calvin Coolidge is reputed to have said, during his administration: "The reason we have such high unemployment rates is because there aren't enough jobs." Despite the logic of this view, a widespread suspicion remains that those without jobs are simply lazy. Even in the Great Depression, in which as many as one-fourth of the labor force were unemployed, Americans were unhappy about supporting people who didn't work. In a 1935

Gallup poll, 60 percent of those interviewed felt too much money was being spent on relief programs; 9 percent felt it was too little. In a 1938 Gallup poll, one person in five favored a proposal to deny the vote to people on relief, and the next year 78 percent said they would favor a law prohibiting "reliefers" from making political contributions (Gallup 1972). For a look at the effects of unemployment on the unemployed, see the accompanying box, "Unemployment and the Family."

The current, continuing controversy over welfare programs reflects the persistent American agreement that work is moral and not working is immoral. Popular myths, unsupported by the data, picture "welfare mothers" getting rich from an unending string of illegitimate children, the typical recipient driving to the welfare office in a Cadillac, and similar horrors.

The traditional view of work as moral is complicated by the practice of retiring employees early. The continued growth of automation further aggravates the problem. Some observers urge that we begin planning a society in which some people will never work and will be supported by government throughout their lives, but the traditional view so far appears firmly entrenched.

The Experience of Consuming

Individuals experience economic institutions both as producers and as consumers of what is produced. The more complex the economic structures, the more interdependent people are on one another in both those regards. The mere fact that you are reading this book—which I wrote, Wadsworth published, your instructor assigned, and you bought—illustrates the web of interdependencies in which you operate as a consumer. None of us is self-sufficient; we all depend on each other.

An industrial economy based on mass production has special implications for your experience as a consumer. Most apparent, your choices of what you will consume depend very largely on what manufacturers believe—on the advice of their marketing consultants—the greatest number of people will desire. Unless your tastes agree with those of the majority, you may be out of luck. At the same time, you have an opportunity to consume things that would be unavailable without mass production.

In a capitalist economy such as ours, decisions on what will be produced for consumption flow from the profit motive. Goods and services will be made available only if the producers of them can turn a profit in the process. The question of what you "really want" or how satisfied you are with what you get is irrelevant except as those considerations are translated into profits. This is not necessarily "bad"; it's just the agreement our economic institutions are based on. And like the other types of economic institutions we've examined in this chapter, it serves the function of supporting the survival of group life.

There's another way in which you are a consumer in the economy. Earlier in this discussion, I said that the function of economic institutions was the transformation of the environment. When you purchase a new car or a new stereo, you are experiencing some of the results of that transformation. The depletion of natural resources and various forms of pollution are other results of the transformation that you experience. Until recently people were not particularly conscious of or concerned about this latter aspect of the transformation. Today, however, all of us are being forced to confront it.

The experience of economic institutions—as in the case of the family, religion, education, and politics—has both satisfying and unsatisfying aspects for individuals. And, as we would expect, people's dissatisfactions have produced attempts to create alternative agreements and forms. Let's look at some of those.

Some Economic Alternatives

Dissatisfaction with the environmental damage done by modern industrialism has produced an active social movement in recent years. Recycling industries

---

Unemployment and the Family

United States unemployment exceeded 9 percent in the fall of 1975. In many localities and among blacks and young people it was much higher. Many economists believe the economic crisis will continue. How will this affect families? Although we can't be sure that history will repeat itself, we can find some clues about future possibilities from the record of the Depression of the 1930s. During those years economic troubles kept some people single and childless. And both the marriage rates and birth rates went down, particularly when unemployment was highest in the early 1930s. The divorce rate also dipped at that time, indicating perhaps that some battling couples stayed together for financial survival and that some separated couples did not have the money for a legal divorce.

Unemployment and deprivation had different effects on different families, depending upon how they had gotten along before the crisis. Happy, cooperative families pulled together to cope with disaster; families that had problems before the Depression did not do as well. Many families had to move in with relatives when they could not pay the rent. The crowded living conditions that resulted many times increased tension. The long-term unemployment of the husband/father often resulted in a shift in the family power structure. The relative power of the woman increased when the man could no longer claim to be the primary breadwinner, the head of the household. This may be one reason why unemployment led to psychological depression and physical illness for many men.

If Americans react to economic depression as did their parents and grandparents, many will postpone marriage and decide not to have children. The falling birth rate of the 1960s and 1970s will continue its downward course. There should also be a continuing increase in the proportion of young adults who are staying single. What do you think will happen to the divorce rate? Have there been any changes in recent years that might cause the divorce rate to continue its long-run rise?

have slowly begun developing as a means to stopping the depletion of natural resources. The search for new energy sources has drawn considerably more attention, yet many of the new energy sources being proposed present problems of their own. Nuclear power, for example, although it produces none of the smoke associated with oil and coal, produces problems in waste disposal. We are frequently reminded that the automobile was initially welcomed as an environmental advance, and it fulfilled the promise of clearing city streets of the ever-thicker layers of horse manure. It also filled the air with smoke and poisons.

Many environmentalists argue that the necessary solutions to current problems must be more radical than recycling and new energy sources. Economic growth, they say, simply cannot continue regardless of the technology it employs. Instead, it will be necessary to restructure societies around stabilized economies and populations. More pessimistic observers say flatly that American economic standards will, in fact, have to be lowered.

Consumer dissatisfaction with the current production and distribution of goods has taken a number of forms. Outrage over price increases has frequently resulted in consumer boycotts. Consumer cooperatives are another response, with individuals joining together in associations to purchase food wholesale, often sharing in both the financial savings and the work of distribution. In 1973, 667 such co-ops did 70 million dollars worth of business. As a partial alternative to commercial banks, 27.6 million people belonged to credit unions that handled 21.8 billion dollars in transactions (U.S. Bureau of the Census 1975a). Yet another alternative to the mass-production economy has been the renewed production of hand-crafted articles.

Dissatisfaction with the capitalist aspect of the American economy has produced many movements advocating the establishment of a socialist agreement. Some advocates have favored the evolution of socialism in America; others have urged revolution. Both groups have clearly felt that a socialist structure would remedy the problems presented by capitalism. Lurking behind the suggested change in economic form, however, is the question of what problems the new agreements would present for individuals.

Summarizing Economic Institutions

The primary function of economic institutions is the transformation of the environment in support of the production, distribution, and consumption of goods and services. A variety of economic systems and organizations have arisen to accomplish that function. Every kind of system—from hunting and gathering to capitalist, transnational conglomerates—seems to work in its own fashion.

The different economic agreements that we've examined all have the effect of structuring individual experiences. Capitalism structures economic experiences one way, socialism another. Overall, economic institutions affect individuals in two ways. Through occupations, they structure participation in the production of goods and services. The role of consumer represents another set of experiences.

Throughout the examination of economic institutions, we have seen the interweaving of institutional structures in a society. Each in its own way, and working in concert, the several institutions found in all societies have the function of structuring individuals' experiences in such a manner as to support the survival of group life. If societies are to survive, some sets of agreements must be established to control such direct personal experiences and drives as love, the search for meaning and understanding, domination over others, and acquisitiveness. We've seen there is an almost endless variation in the types of agreements that will suffice, and we've also seen that all such agreements tend to detract from the individual's experience of personal satisfaction. There is, therefore, a never-ending search for new forms and new agreements to remedy current dissatisfactions. Each new set of agreements, however, seems to produce dissatisfactions of its own, a problem inherent in institutionalization itself.

Suggested Readings

Lipset, Seymour Martin
1963 *The First New Nation.* New York: Basic Books. In an era of national liberation and nation-building around the globe, Lipset suggests that the prototypical "new nation" was the United States. In this historical

analysis, he examines the creation of national identity and political legitimacy, focusing on American values, economic matters, and the role of political parties.

Mills, C. Wright
1959   *The Power Elite.* New York: Oxford University Press.
A controversial, modern classic, Mills's thesis that American society is ruled by a small, powerful elite formed of business, military, and governmental leaders offers a graphic picture of the interrelationships among social institutions. Mills's portrayal of power in America offers a useful framework for understanding more recent events such as the Nixon administration scandals and the bribery of foreign officials by transnational corporations.

Smelser, Neil
1963   *The Sociology of Economic Life.* Englewood Cliffs, N.J.: Prentice-Hall.
In this small book, Smelser has provided the most

thoroughgoing sociological view of economics since Weber's *Theory of Social and Economic Organization.* Smelser examines the economy as an institutional social system in its own right and as a subsystem within the larger society. Special attention is given to the interrelationship between the economy and other social institutions.

Stouffer, Samuel
1966   *Communism, Conformity, and Civil Liberties.* New York: Wiley.
I want to give you a chance to see how sociologists go about studying political attitudes, and I can think of no more worthy introduction than the work of Sam Stouffer, patron saint of empirical researchers. In this classic study, Stouffer examines political tolerance and intolerance during the (Joe) McCarthy era of the early 1950s. Basing his analyses on massive surveys of political leaders and the general public, Stouffer provides still valuable insights into the fate of democracy in America.

Episode Ten

Restless and disorderly demonstrations plagued the second National Conference on Human Mutations when it opened May 10, 2027, in Washington, D.C. Divergent groups pressed unsuccessfully for admission into the auditorium where scientists who had assembled the previous year would again discuss—and attempt to define—greens.

SPHR (Society for the Protection of the Human Race) had rented three floors in a hotel adjacent to the symposium headquarters. Espousing the necessity for "human purity," SPHR vigorously opposed assimilation of "evolutionary throwbacks."

Representatives of APIK (Association for the Prevention of Infant Kidnappings) emerged to promote what they called "preventive justice." Eagerly they urged arrest and prosecution of "all green posers discovered in normal society."

Members of Concerned Citizens for National Defense (CCND) milled about, cornering scientists and distributing literature. The United States must attack Green Colony immediately, they convincingly insisted, in order to thwart an internal military threat to the government.

Still other groups demonstrated in opposition to these factions. Civil Liberty for All (CLA), an organization committed to the legal defense and protection of mutants, was recognizable by green armbands worn by its members. Representatives of the National Farmers Organization were in Washington urging gradual and "orderly" integration of greens. The food growers had grown dependent upon solar transistors. To destroy Green Colony and S.T.I., they argued, would be to destroy the world's hope for survival.

SVP (Stop Violence to Posers), a coalition of influential American businessmen, joined in the plea for harmony. It had become impossible, they noted, to contact S.T.I. sales representatives. Decreasing access to solar transistors would throw United States industry deeper into economic depression.

As Bradley Duncan labored past the noisy commotion into the conference hall where he would be principal speaker, he remarked to himself on the excess of uniformed policemen. The situation on the outside, he realized with full force, had grown critical during the period of his participant observation in Adamsville.

Upon entering the hall Brad spotted his colleagues. They stood casually near a large coffee maker at the rear of the auditorium.

"Morning," he said, approaching. He helped himself to a complimentary donut from a tray near the coffee. "Sure is nice," he chuckled, "to see food displayed like this out in public again. I was beginning to feel like some kind of pervert, sneaking quick meals, always eating in solitude."

Adamsville's Elders had granted Duncan use of an unoccupied glass residence near Sunlight Liquidhouse. Twice monthly Brad had driven into Phoenix for food and supplies.

"We hear you downed a lot of protein capsules," Constance Batterson smiled.

"And how did you survive without your beer?" Louise Roanoke laughed.

Duncan had left Adamsville just three days before. He had not yet had a long visit with his friends.

Several other conference members gathered, introducing themselves and shaking Brad's hand. "You've become something of a celebrity," Batterson teased, whispering into Brad's ear. "I hope your speech is good!"

A gavel sounded from the front of the room. Fifteen minutes later Duncan approached the podium.

"Fellow scientists," he began. "I am speaking to you today because, as a sociologist, I spent almost ten months as an Adamsville resident. When I left there just the other day," Brad announced with regret, "several Adamsville residents and I decided that it would be in their best interest if I did not return."

Duncan shifted. A ripple ran through the audience.

"During my stay there, however, I gained some understanding of green culture. It is my hope that I can share a bit of that understanding with you."

Roanoke and Batterson sat near the front of the lecture hall. Louise smiled encouragingly toward Brad. Her mind went back to her own address the previous year. So much had changed. Louise had spent months of painful soul-searching since she first met and recognized Gabriel Knapp. Her decision to relay to the secretary of interior information regarding greens' belief in rescuing, and the subsequent leak of the information to the news media, had promoted national turmoil. Louise would always feel partially responsible for the violence that followed.

While Constance Batterson had expressed sympathy throughout Louise's personal misery, the younger sociologist remained convinced that her colleague should not have sent the letter. Sociological truth, Connie maintained, could only be ascertained through vigorous refusal to cooperate with the established and powerful forces in society. In an inevitable conflict between humanity's powerful and powerless, a sociologist, Batterson believed, was morally bound not to strengthen the might of the powerful. Louise had erred, Connie had suggested, realizing even while she did that many sociologists—after considering the

moral issue seriously—would have proceeded exactly as had her friend and colleague.

But Louise had suffered over something else too. She knew that Gabe's involvement in a kidnapping had shocked and hurt her niece. "He should have told Monica about the mutation early in their relationship," Louise had complained to Connie during a discussion they'd had the previous November.

"Agreed," Connie had said. "And then what?"

"And then Monica could have broken it off long before the two became so involved," Louise had responded.

"What's this?" Connie had smirked, attempting in vain to cheer her friend. "An Ode to Homogamy?"

"Monica couldn't survive in Adamsville," Louise had said then. "She'd die of malnutrition! And Gabe wouldn't be comfortable out here." She paused. "That kidnapping was an awful thing," she murmured.

It had been several seconds before Connie spoke. "What about the concept of cultural relativity?" she ventured.

"Cultural relativity is necessary as a methodological attitude," Roanoke had replied. "It need not be a general moral conviction."

"And I thought sociologists tended to be liberal thinkers," Connie had chuckled.

"And do middle-aged aunts?" Louise had retorted.

Roanoke's attention returned to Duncan.

"Elders Ruth and Michael Jones," Duncan was saying, "have, since Adam's death, made virtually all the community's decisions. They assign community-owned land and housing to residents and exercise final authority over citizens' occupations. Adamsville's Elders are both political and religious rulers. The children of a prophet, it is reasoned, are inclined to neither sacred nor secular error. Until recently it had been assumed that Ruth and Michael would rule until their deaths.

"Changes are occurring now, however. Primarily they are the result of the charismatic personality and organizational ability of a younger mutant named Larry Jones.

"Larry Jones is a fully matured green of forty-four whose epidermis dazzles. This physical trait, I have observed, contributes to his leadership ability. Adamsville residents trust their greenest members most.

"Larry Jones is a great grandson of Adam Jones III. Larry's grandfather, David, had—before he was murdered—married a nonmutant and fathered three children. One of these offspring, a female, eventually married her first cousin, the son of Adam Jones's daughter Ann. Larry Jones was born of this union." Duncan swallowed from a glass of water which had been placed near the podium. "I burden you with this genealogical information," he continued, wiping his lips with the back of his hand, "to demonstrate that Larry Jones is—as are all mutants—the descendant of both greens and ungreens. The fact that his skin —and that of others like him—is extremely bright supports a religious doctrine in Adamsville, namely, that the color of a chlorophyllic's skin is not dependent upon chromosomal genealogy, but upon religious conviction. The more secular tenet corresponding to that religious dogma has become something of a maxim in Adamsville. 'A green is a green', the saying goes. 'A green's chromosomes are always dominant'."

Duncan paused. "Larry's luminance, then, attests to his religious loyalty. Since secular allegiance cannot be separated from religious devotion, it has long been assumed that Larry would advance to leadership upon the deaths of Ruth and Michael.

"To understand the reasons for this widespread social agreement, it is helpful first to know something about economics in Adamsville.

"Solar Transistors, Inc., began with a federal grant issued by ERDA in 2004. It was Larry Jones, then an inexperienced youth of twenty-one, who successfully convinced the federal government of his family's scientific potential.

"This fact remains much appreciated among Adamsvillers. Members of the community are aware that, as a result of their unique physiological circumstances, they face what could be a serious economic difficulty. That is, the older and more experienced members of the community have matured; the greenness of their skin forces them to remain upon family territory. As public relations ambassadors or S.T.I. sales personnel they are useless.

"The two dozen sales representatives who had until recently called upon businesses throughout the United States were all posers under twenty-five years old. It falls upon the immature and less experienced members of the colony, then, to contact prospective consumers. Often immatured greens find themselves unequal to the challenge. Larry Jones did not.

"His reward was a position as the third member of the board of directors of S.T.I. He controls 40 percent of the corporation's stock. Ruth and Michael own over 50 percent of the S.T.I. shares. That S.T.I. now manufactures solar weapons for the military defense of Adamsville attests to the influence and power of board member Larry Jones.

"The physical facilities of Solar Transistors, Inc., include several expansive, single-story buildings on the outskirts of the small city at the center of the family's property. The single most important resource to their product—solar energy—appears limitless and is considered by Adamsvillers a gift from God.

"A second necessary resource, labor, is supplied by the mutants themselves. While highly automated, the plant employs several hundred workers, all matured greens who must remain upon the property.

"Adamsville does need to purchase some materials to produce transistors. S.T.I. has obtained these from Japan. Larry, after acquiring the ERDA money, spent several months in Japan. While sources there have continued to supply Adamsville by mail, greens believe strongly that Larry's initial contact with Japanese industrialists was vitally necessary."

Dr. Duncan took another long drink of water, then continued. "I mentioned earlier," he said, "that things had begun to change in Adamsville. The once harmonious community is rocked with political rumblings. Larry Jones, charismatic and luminous, leads a faction of greens that I have come to call 'radical militarists'. They are dedicated to complete separation of greens from the outside. Larry often reminds fellow mutants that his grandfather was murdered by ungreens. But perhaps more important are the economic bases for dissension.

"Larry's goal, it appears now, is to diversify Adamsville's industrial base. He feels that the colony must manufacture goods and services that might be consumed by greens themselves—and on a large scale. As a result the colony's economy should ultimately become independent of outsiders. Then, Larry and his followers reason, Adamsville would be in the position to refuse solar transistors to outside customers at will. And with that economic hammer, radical militarists foresee the advent of national and international political power."

Duncan stopped momentarily, allowing his message to sink in. He proceeded: "The Elders, on the other hand, are convinced that Adamsville should work with ungreens. Their followers remind their fellows of the community's need to continue economic relations with ungreens in Japan, for example. Cooperationists argue that political power rests in the potential to manufacture as many solar transistors as possible. This potential must not be lessened by diversification within S.T.I. Adamsville does not yet have sufficient labor power, they contend, to diversify.

"Cooperationists argue further that only when Adamsville promotes communication with the outside will ungreens begin to understand mutants. And subsequent to that understanding matured greens might one day leave Adamsville, taking influential positions with outside-owned corporations, gaining access to policy-making positions within local and federal government, and consequently advancing the green cause."

Duncan shuffled his papers. He had talked a long time. It was almost noon when he finished. The majority of attending scientists were surprised, therefore, when the chair announced that it would consider one further motion before adjournment.

From the rear of the hall a middle-aged conference member advanced to the podium. She placed a single sheet of paper before her and read. "Be it resolved," she began in a clear, strong voice, "that this body of scientists, representing the accumulated knowledge of humanity, has determined green mu-tants to be harmful evolutionary throwbacks, pre-human beings, whose continued existence threatens humanity as we know it." Someone seconded the motion.

Batterson, Roanoke, and Duncan—along with others—were stunned. Louise Roanoke stood.

"This is impossible!" she exclaimed. "We don't have all the facts. How can we as scientists make a judgment without sufficient data? If we vote yes on this resolution we are of no more academic credibility than the groups outside struggling for the victory of their own economic, political, and social interests. If we concur with this resolution, fellow conference members, we do not deserve to be called scientists."

A long and heated debate carried into the afternoon. Several hours later the exhausted and hungry scholars tabled the resolution for one year. They did so by the small margin of five votes.

Questions

1. How does Duncan's speech illustrate what may be the beginnings of political parties in Adamsville?

2. How are the political, economic, and religious institutions related in Adamsville? Can you think of instances in which they are not integrated?

3. How does the episode illustrate charismatic, traditional, and rational-bureaucratic authority in Adamsville?

4. How does Larry Jones illustrate the concept of "self-fulfilling prophecy?"

5. Are greens human beings?

11

Social Stratification and Mobility

Sometime or other you've probably had a direct personal experience of what we might call "human worth." That experience probably cropped up unexpectedly in the context of seeing a person treated as if he or she were not worth much. Maybe once when your classmates were making fun of a kid for having torn and dirty clothes, you had the feeling that they were being cruel and unfair. Maybe you read about someone dying, someone poor, unknown, and unimportant, and you felt that it was treated too casually. You may have felt that at some level every human being is worth the same as any other.

I know you've also had an experience of feeling that some people were worth more than others. There've been times when sides were being chosen for a game and you desperately wanted to be picked by the "right" side. You've either experienced the pride of being friends with the most popular child in school or the sadness of being passed by and ignored. Even now, I know that you have a sense of which people around you are more important than others. And I know that from time to time you wonder where *you* fit into the ranking of who's who and who isn't. Other people wonder, too, as we'll see.

This chapter will examine the many faces of social inequality. Regardless of whether people were created equal, they typically live in a state of inequality. In every society, some people are more powerful than others, some have more of the good things than

others, some can do things others cannot, some can be what they want to be while others cannot. I'm going to limit the discussion of inequalities to those within one society, but the box on page 268, "Global Stratification—The Rich Get Richer and the Poor Get Poorer," indicates how we might look at inequalities *between* societies as well.

Sociologists use the term **social stratification** to refer to the organization of inequality in society. From the geological point of view, "stratification" means the appearance of layers of different kinds of

....I LIKE TO THINK I'M ACCEPTED IN **ANY** SOCIAL STRATA....

rock, one on top of another. To sociologists the word means the same thing, except that it is different kinds of people who are layered one on top of another instead of rocks. The layers, in sociology as in geology, are called "strata."

Our discussion of social stratification will begin with an examination of several sociological points of view. As we'll soon see, sociologists do not agree on the best way to regard stratification. In particular, we'll examine the differences between conflict and functionalist views of stratification and the difference between **strata** and **social classes.**

Next we'll look in some detail at the many different dimensions of stratification, the different bases for stratifying people and groups of people. We are going to see that different societies have different agreements regarding proper ways to rank people. Then

we'll examine some of the ways in which sociologists measure social status.

Different social classes are sometimes regarded as subcultures within a society, each with its own sets of agreements as to what is true, good, and proper. We'll look at how those different sets of agreements conflict within a society.

A major section of the chapter is occupied with the consequences of social stratification. What does it matter if you live out your existence in one stratum or class rather than another? The answer is that it matters greatly. We'll examine why.

The chapter concludes with a discussion of social mobility, movement from one stratum to another. Your membership in a particular stratum or class is a matter of agreement. Agreements can be changed, and in the concluding section, we'll see how.

Global Stratification—
The Rich Get Richer and the Poor Get Poorer

The most glaring inequalities may be those that exist between societies. Our world is a collection of separate nations, but they are all connected in one complex socioeconomic structure. The existence of multinational corporations, which span the boundaries of many countries, is only one piece of evidence (among many) that our globe is one world. Stratification exists on a worldwide basis, produced fundamentally by the political and economic factors that produce stratification within nations. The upper class of the world are the wealthy, industrialized countries, with the list headed by the United States. At the other end of the scale are the economically distressed countries filling much of Latin America, Africa, and Asia. Compare, for example, Canada with Burma. These two countries have about the same population, but one represents the top stratum in world stratification and the other, the bottom. Canada's per capita GNP (gross national product) was $5,400 in 1973; Burma's per capita GNP was only $80 in the same year. The rates of economic growth in the two countries permitted little hope that Burma would ever catch up with Canada: Dur-

ing the years between 1965 and 1973, Canada's economy grew by a rate of 3.5 percent per year; during the same period, Burma's growth rate was only .7 percent per year.[1]

The double trouble of recession and depression has hit the poor countries harder than the rich countries. As an example, contrast the United States with Chile. In 1975, 40 percent of the Chilean labor force was unemployed as contrasted with from 11 percent to 12 percent in the United States.[2] In the two-year period 1974–75, the inflation that agitated the people of the United States was only 15.2 percent; the inhabitants of Chile survived an inflation explosion of 999.7 percent.[3]

Inequality on a global level seems to be increasing. Is it possible that our affluent life in the United States is bought with the misery and starvation of the people of countries like Chile?

[1]*New York Times,* January 25, 1976, Section 3, p. 1.
[2]Ibid., p. 16.
[3]Ibid., p. 48.

Points of View on Stratification

In this section, we are going to look briefly at some of the points of view that sociologists and other social thinkers have taken regarding stratification. This discussion should give you an idea of how the notion of stratification has developed over time and an idea of what its standing is now.

Early Social Theorists

Stratification has probably existed among human beings ever since the first time one cave dweller beat another into submission. It seems very likely that the first, prehistoric, agreement that one person was superior to another was created with a club or rock. We have been using clubs, rocks, and subtler devices ever since.

Beginning with the earliest attempts to reflect on and organize human social existence, stratification probably seemed both inevitable and "natural." When Plato and Aristotle set about designing ideal societies, they devoted the greater part of their attention to the unequal distribution of power and privilege: the proper arrangement of affairs among rulers, common people, and slaves. Throughout most of human history, it has been assumed that inequalities among people were the result of natural or divine ordination. They were the way things were supposed to be.

Jean Jacques Rousseau

Even before the American and French revolutions, Jean Jacques Rousseau (1712–1778) and other social thinkers began suggesting that social stratification was more arbitrary than had previously been assumed. Rousseau, for example, concluded that there were two kinds of inequality: one natural and the other the result of agreements:

> I conceive that there are two kinds of inequality among the human species; one which I call natural or physical, because it is established by nature and consists in a difference of age, health, bodily strength, and qualities of the mind or of the soul; and another, which may be called moral or political inequality,

because it depends on a kind of convention, and is established, or at least authorized, by the consent of men (Rousseau 1750:101).

The same century in which Rousseau wrote those words witnessed the reigns of Kings George III of England and Louis XVI of France, neither of whom demonstrated a "natural" ability to rule over the affairs of others. Each enjoyed his high social rank by virtue of agreements that God had ordained them through family descent. Each was said to rule by "divine right." The belief in the divine rights of kings represented an agreement created and accepted on earth.

Rousseau, along with Voltaire, Montesquieu, and others, drew attention to the fact that the agreements placing one person in a position superior to others were only agreements, not ultimate truths. These men were, in contemporary terms, "consciousness raisers." They made people conscious that such agreements were only agreements and could be changed. Bloody revolutions in America, France, Russia, and elsewhere have flowed from that realization, and many basic agreements have been irrevocably altered. Still, stratification among people persists.

Karl Marx

Karl Marx was, in large part, a sociologist of revolutions, including those sparked by Rousseau and his contemporaries. Marx lived through most of the nineteenth century, and he was in an excellent position to examine the American, French, German, and—most important—Industrial revolutions.

From a personal, political point of view, Marx sought greater equality among people. In the Industrial Revolution in Europe, however, he saw increasing inequality. The system of economic capitalism, he thought, established two distinct classes of people: those who owned the means of production (the bourgeoisie) and those who did the work (the proletariat). In his view, capitalism was based on the exploitation of one class by another. Members of the proletariat were forced to sell their labor to the owners of industry as the box on page 270 "Karl Marx and the Impoverishment of the Working Class" describes.

Marx saw human history as the history of "class

struggle" in which the exploited classes sought to overthrow their exploiters. Marx spent his life trying to understand the nature of economic exploitation and devising measures for ending it (Marx 1867, Marx and Engels 1848).

Max Weber

Marx saw social stratification almost exclusively as an economic matter. Max Weber suggested the major bases were *three:* the economic order, the social order, and the political order. In Marx's view of capilist society, economics and politics were intertwined. Weber separated wealth from power. He also distinguished stratification based on the social order, a form of stratification that involved the distribution of honor, prestige, and deference.

Weber used the term "class" to refer to economic stratification. Like Marx, he considered ownership of property to be the primary index of economic position. Weber used the term "party" to refer to political power, recognizing that some people enjoyed high

---

Karl Marx and the Impoverishment of the Working Class

Karl Marx believed that the capitalist system would cause the increasing impoverishment of the working class. Marx based his theory of social class on extensive study of the life of working people and on the reports of numerous governmental investigations in nineteenth-century England. In his most famous book, *Capital,* he describes the degradation and crushing exploitation of workers during the course of industrialization in Britain. The majority of workers in many industries were women and children, and they were paid very little for long hours of work under appalling conditions. Perhaps the most damaging working conditions were in those industries in which the finishing of machine-made products was done by hand, outside the factory itself. Marx describes the process of lace finishing:

> The lace finishing is done either in what are called "Mistresses' Houses," or by women in their own houses, with or without the help of their children. The women who keep the "Mistresses' Houses" are themselves poor. The workroom is in a private house. The mistresses take orders from manufacturers, or from warehousemen, and employ as many women, girls, and young children as the size of their rooms and the fluctuating demand of the business will

allow. The number of the workwomen employed in these workrooms varies from 20 to 40 in some, and from 10 to 20 in others. The average age at which the children commence work is six years, but in many cases it is below five. The usual working hours are from 8 in the morning till 8 in the evening, with 1½ hours for meals, which are taken at irregular intervals, and often in the foul workrooms. When business is brisk, the labour frequently lasts from 8 or even 6 o'clock in the morning till 10, 11, or 12 o'clock at night. In English barracks the regulation space allotted to each soldier is 500-600 cubic feet, and in the military hospitals 1200 cubic feet. But in those finishing styes there are but 67 to 100 cubic feet to each person.[1]

Marx is describing conditions in England in 1864. It should be easy to understand why Marx, looking at the life of the industrial classes of that time, should decide that poverty and suffering were spreading, that exploitation was far more important than differences in status or honor, and that conflict between the proletariat and the bourgeoisie was inevitable and would continue to be so.

[1]Karl Marx, *Capital* (New York: Modern Library, 1906), pp. 510–11.

Source: Karl Marx, Capital *(New York: Modern Library, 1906).*

standing in society because of their political positions, regardless of whether they owned property. Finally, he used the term "status" to refer to honor, prestige, and deference. He noted that members of a given stratum shared agreements and life-styles, and they interacted with one another to the exclusion of people in other strata (Weber 1925b).

Both Marx and Weber based their theoretical views on observations of the social stratification systems operating around them. They sought to summarize what they observed in the form of ideal types. Neither based his views on the collection of empirical data through which members of a particular community were actually ranked in terms of the community's stratification system. Such studies were being conducted in America, however, beginning around 1925, when Weber's work on class, status, and party was first published.

American Community Studies

During the 1920s and on into the 1940s, a number of American sociologists undertook in-depth studies of social stratification in medium-sized American towns. Their aim was to determine how stratification related to other aspects of middle-American social life.

Robert Lynd and Helen Lynd (1929, 1937), for example, chose to look at Muncie, Indiana, which they subsequently called "Middletown." Examining stratification primarily by way of economic and occupational factors, Lynd and Lynd identified two classes: the "working class" and the "business class." The latter included professionals such as physicians and lawyers. Among other things, Lynd and Lynd were especially interested in the ways in which social status was reflected in the social life of the community. In general, they found that schools, churches, and other institutions and associations were unofficially segregated by status. Identifying the "business-class" churches and the "working-class" churches, for example, was a simple matter.

Perhaps the best-known of the American community studies was W. Lloyd Warner's (1949) examination of Morris, Illinois, which Warner called "Jonesville." For Warner, social class was primarily

a matter of agreement on the part of those living in a society: "By class is meant two or more orders of people who are believed to be, and are accordingly ranked by the members of the community, in socially superior and inferior positions" (1941:82).

Appropriate to this point of view, Warner sought to discover the social-class standing of community members by asking others in the community. Through studies in Jonesville and elsewhere, Warner developed an elaborate typology of American social classes. These are presented in Table 11·1.

Like the Lynds, Warner and others were especially interested in examining the ways social class

Table 11·1 Warner's Typology of American Social Classes

Class	Characteristics
Upper-upper (UU):	Wealthy individuals whose wealth came to them through inheritance over the course of several generations; the "old rich."[a]
Lower-upper (LU):	Newly wealthy individuals; those from modest or poor backgrounds who had made their own fortunes; the nouveau riche.
Upper-middle (UM):	Typically professional people and managers who, although not wealthy, were financially quite comfortable.
Lower-middle (LM):	Lower-level white-collar workers such as clerks and secretaries.
Upper-lower (UL):	Upper-level manual, blue-collar workers, such as skilled craftsmen.
Lower-lower (LL):	Lower-level manual, blue-collar workers, such as unskilled laborers and domestic servants; also includes the unemployed poor.

[a]"Jonesville" was a relatively new community, and Warner found few (and maybe no) residents who could be considered upper-upper there.

was reflected in the life-styles and associations of community members. Indeed, this interest constituted one of the significant aspects of the American community studies conducted during that period.

Notice, however, that the community studies emphasized the separate and distinctive character of the different social classes. The researchers admitted that the lines separating one class from another were not altogether clear. At the same time, they stressed the separateness of classes rather than an unbroken progression from the bottom of the status ladder to the top. That point of view did not come until later.

Talcott Parsons

In 1940, Talcott Parsons, a contemporary American sociologist, published "An Analytical Approach to the Theory of Social Stratification." This article, which appeared in the *American Journal of Sociology,* set forth a theoretical point of view different from those of either Marx or Weber. From Parsons' point of view, stratification was a matter of "moral evaluation." Noting that societies have systems of values, Parsons suggested that a person's relative standing in the society reflected the extent to which his or her characteristics and achievements corresponded to those values.

According to Parsons' view, in a society that shares an agreement on the special value of physical strength, the stronger members will be accorded higher status than the weaker members. In societies sharing an agreement on the special importance of religion, we can expect those occupying religious positions to be accorded the higher status. In a society such as the United States, where economic achievement is a central value, persons with wealth are accorded high status.

Parsons' point of view was important to the development of stratification theories in sociology in two ways. First, it moved the concept of stratification even further from its sole dependence on economic factors by linking it to the central values in a society. Societies that had different agreements as to what was "good" would (and do) have different systems of stratification.

Second, also by linking stratification to other aspects of social structure, Parsons laid the groundwork for a functionalist point of view on stratification.

Kingsley Davis and Wilbert Moore

In 1945, Kingsley Davis and Wilbert Moore published what is now the classic statement of the functionalist point of view on stratification. In "Some Principles of Stratification," they described the functions of stratification for societies. They also concluded that stratification was both universal and inevitable.

The functionalist point of view on stratification is based on three observations about statuses in a society. First, some statuses seem more important than others for the stability and survival of a society. The king, for example, seems more important than any individual commoner. Second, some statuses are more easily filled than others in terms of the skills and training required by the roles associated with those statuses. For example, potentially more people can perform the role of street sweeper than the role of physician. Third, some roles are less "pleasant" than others in terms of the time, physical effort, and working conditions entailed. More is required of corporation presidents than of clerk typists, for example.

For a society to function effectively, however, statuses must be filled—particularly the most "important" statuses—with people qualified and willing to perform the roles associated with them. Social stratification systems, by providing unequal rewards in the form of money, prestige, deference, and privilege, ensure that statuses will be filled and roles performed. Social stratification systems provide *incentives.*

From the functionalist point of view, then, the corporation president receives more money, prestige, deference, and privilege than a secretary because the president: (1) is more important to the corporation and to the larger society; (2) possesses the relatively scarce skills and qualities needed for the position; and (3) devotes more time and effort to the job and suffers more emotional strain from it (or is expected to).

Davis and Moore suggest that every society will necessarily develop some form of stratification system. It will not survive unless it can attract qualified people to important and difficult-to-fill statuses. Stratification systems offer the needed incentives.

Notice that the functionalist point of view is very different from the one we have been discussing so far in this section. For functionalists the issue of distinct social classes with distinct life-styles and patterns of interaction is of secondary or incidental importance. They see the central significance of stratification to be in its functional necessity for societies. From the functionalist point of view, stratification is a matter of gradual progression from the top to the bottom, reflecting the variations in the three aspects of statuses and roles that make stratification necessary.

Conflict Theory and Stratification

Not all sociologists agree with the functionalist point of view. In fact, many disagree strongly and hotly. Conflict theory, which can be traced to Marx, encompasses a very different point of view on stratification. As Gerhard Lenski (1966) points out, conflict theorists are interested in the problem of inequality from the point of view of individuals and subgroups. Where functionalists focus on the needs of society, conflict theorists focus on the needs and desires of individuals. Lenski goes on to say:

> Conflict theorists, as their name suggests, see social inequality as arising out of the struggle for valued goods and services in short supply. Where the functionalists emphasize the common interests shared by the members of a society, conflict theorists emphasize the interests that divide. Where functionalists stress the common advantages which accrue from social relationships, conflict theorists emphasize the element of domination and exploitation. Where functionalists emphasize consensus as the basis of social unity, conflict theorists emphasize coercion. Where functionalists see human societies as social systems, conflict theorists see them as stages on which struggle for power and privilege take place (1966:16–17).

Thus, Ralf Dahrendorf (1959), a contemporary conflict theorist, stresses the importance of "class" over "strata," favoring the analysis of distinct groups rather than positions located on a continuous hierarchy of status. Unlike Marx, who focused almost exclusively on economic factors, Dahrendorf directs his attention to authority. Dahrendorf sees an inevi-

table conflict between the interests of those giving orders and those subjected to them.

The differences between the two points of view —functionalism and conflict theory—are considerable. If you were to look at stratification from a functionalist point of view, you would see statuses arranged hierarchically in such a way as to facilitate the efficient functioning of society. If you were to adopt a conflict point of view, you would see distinct classes of people at odds with one another because of their different economic and political interests. These two basic views are graphically represented in the box on page 274 "Two Views of Stratification."

Each view provides a useful and, in a sense, accurate picture of social stratification in America and other societies. Depending on why you are studying stratification, one of the points of view might be more appropriate than the other.

Before beginning a discussion of some of the dimensions of stratification, I want to make a final comment. Most conflict theorists are quite open in expressing their interest in *changing* the social stratification systems they observe around them. They see most stratification as a matter of exploitation, and they wish to reduce such exploitation or do away with it altogether. The functionalists, in contrast, are often charged with being personally committed to maintaining the **status quo** and being willing to accept the continuation of inequality and exploitation. They themselves hotly deny that charge, however, saying they are interested in understanding the functions of stratification, with its inevitable inequality, and are not necessarily in favor of the particular stratification systems they study.

Dimensions of Stratification

In the preceding discussions of different sociological points of view, I have already touched on a number of the different dimensions of stratification: the qualities according to which people are stratified. I discussed, for example, wealth and power, and, in the discussion of Parsons, I noted that people may be stratified in terms of a society's most important values.

In this section we will take a more comprehensive look at the different agreements that people have

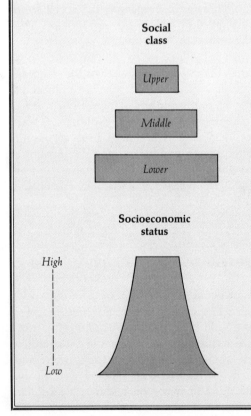

Two Views of Stratification

Sociologists have employed two distinct points of view in examining social stratification. On the one hand, some (for example, Marx and Dahrendorf) have seen discrete social "classes," separate subgroups of society with different interests and life-styles. From the point of view of conflict theory, these social classes are in competition with one another.

On the other hand, some sociologists (Parsons is one) have seen people ranked in a more or less continuous hierarchy from the bottom to the top. The term "socioeconomic status" (SES) has often been used in reference to this view.

Social class

Upper

Middle

Lower

Socioeconomic status

High

Low

created to rank themselves and others. We'll consider the dimensions already mentioned and expand the list considerably.

Family and Kinship

In many societies, your social standing would be based largely on your status within the kinship and family system. Newborn children take on the social status held by their parents. Children of rich parents become "rich children" automatically—even at an age when they think money is just another thing to put in their mouths. Being born into a royal family would give you high social standing that would probably stay with you throughout your life. Less dramatically, being born into a "good family" in a small American community is likely to give you high social status as long as you remain in that community, unless you do something objectionable enough to contradict your high standing.

Age, Sex, Race

In some societies, such as traditional China and Japan, social stratification is related to age. The elders are especially revered and typically exercise more political power than the young. Sometimes this reflects the view that experience provides greater wisdom in the ways of the world. And where authority is based on tradition, the elders of society have more direct knowledge of how things have "always been done."

Modern industrial societies do not typically grant high status to the old. In the United States, for example, the opposite is true. We value youth and generally resist growing old. Toupees, face-lifts, and "mod" clothes are all evidence that high social status does not come with age. I'll have more to say about this in Chapter 12, "Minorities."

Sex and race are also frequent bases for social stratification. In some societies, women have higher status than men; in others, the opposite is true. The relative status of different racial and ethnic groups also varies from society to society. We'll see how race functions as a basis for stratification in the discussion of **caste** later in this chapter, and we'll look at both sex and race in Chapter 12.

"Status symbols" are an aspect of social class. This is sometimes combined with the notion that "bigger is better." (Jill Freedman, Magnum)

Possessions

Money, and lots of it, is perhaps the dimension of stratification that comes to mind most readily for most of us. In American society, and in many others, people are ranked socially on the basis of how much wealth they have. Although money is not everything, all other things being equal, being rich is considered better than being poor.

The valuation of wealth is not a universal agreement. Indeed, wealth is negatively valued within some sets of agreements. Among the Navaho Indians of the American Southwest, for example, the wealthy tribe member is sometimes viewed with suspicion. Often it is suspected and rumored that one's wealth was obtained through witchcraft—a very real possibility within the Navaho point of view.

A somewhat more complicated pattern is found among some Indian tribes in the Canadian Northwest. Wealthy families are expected to give lavish parties —called potlatches—which literally deplete their wealth. Status appears to be gained in proportion to the lavishness of the potlatch. Note that wealth gains status for a family only through its destruction.

Property, such as landholdings, stocks, and bonds, is also a part of one's wealth. Other possessions can symbolize your social standing, too, and a great deal has been written about status symbols. The agreement on what objects symbolize high social status, however, vary from place to place and from

OH PROFESSOR—WHAT A STATUS SYMBOL, FOR YOU TO BE MENTIONED IN A BOOK!!

GREAT PROFESSORIAL FAILURES OF OUR TIME

time to time. Automobiles, shrunken heads, color television sets, seashells, and early-edition comic books are some of the possessions that are important within certain sets of social agreements.

For a college professor, books are an important symbol of high status. Those he or she has written come first, followed by those in which he or she is mentioned. Beyond that, new books symbolize the professor's up-to-date interests, old ones symbolize how long he or she has been a scholar, and a diversity of books indicates a wide-ranging intellect.

We might well consider friends, associates, and memberships in groups as "possessions," as they bear the same relationship to one's social standing as objects do. Belonging to an exclusive country club symbolizes your exclusiveness. Having important and powerful friends suggests that you are important and powerful.

Occupation

Occupation is a critical element in the agreements many societies have on social standing. I've already touched on this in terms of political offices. Kings have higher social standing than commoners, and presidents usually have higher standing than ordinary citizens. From the functionalist point of view, you recall, this follows in part from the differential impor-

tance that different occupations—and other statuses —have in the operation and survival of the society.

In a complex society such as the United States, the multiplicity of occupations would seem to make according a social standing to each one a complicated matter. In fact, however, the general public appears to share rather clear, though informal, agreements in this regard.

In 1947, a group of researchers at the National Opinion Research Center (NORC) in Chicago undertook a study of the social status that Americans granted different occupations (Reiss 1961). This study, named the "North-Hatt study" for Cecil North and Paul Hatt, has become a classic and much-cited resource in American sociology. A national sample of 651 people were presented with a list of ninety occupational titles and asked: "For each job mentioned, please pick out the statement that best gives *your own personal opinion* of the *general standing* that such a job has." The answers were: excellent, good, average, somewhat below average, and poor. The researchers then tallied the answers given for each occupation and ranked them according to their overall ratings.

Sixteen years later, in 1963, another team of NORC researchers repeated the 1947 study to see what changes had taken place in the way Americans rank occupations (Hodge 1964). They found virtually no differences, despite the many changes that have taken place in American society. The results of the two studies are presented in Table 11·2.

Amazed by the consistency of agreements on occupational-prestige ratings between 1947 and 1963, the researchers then turned to a study conducted in 1925. Many fewer occupations were rated in that earlier study, but the overall rankings corresponded very closely to the 1947 and 1963 rankings. Thus, the informal agreements on the prestige of different occupations survived nearly forty years, a catastrophic economic depression, World War II, and great social change in America.

Education

Education is an important aspect of social stratification, especially in developed societies. All other things being equal, a college graduate in America has

Table 11·2 The Prestige of Selected Occupations in America

Occupation	1963 Score	1947 Score	Occupation	1963 Score	1947 Score
U.S. Supreme Court justice	94	96	Newspaper columnist	73	74
Physician	93	93	Policeman	72	67
Scientist	92	89	Radio announcer	70	75
State governor	91	93	Insurance agent	69	68
Cabinet member in the federal government	90	92	Carpenter	68	65
			Manager of a small store in a city	67	69
College professor	90	92	Local official of a labor union	67	62
U.S. representative in Congress	90	89	Mail carrier	66	66
Chemist	89	86	Railroad conductor	66	67
Lawyer	89	86	Traveling salesman for a wholesale concern	66	68
Diplomat in U.S. foreign service	89	92			
Dentist	88	86	Plumber	65	63
Architect	88	86	Automobile repairman	64	63
Psychologist	87	85	Barber	63	59
Minister	87	87	Machine operator in a factory	63	60
Member of the board of directors of a large corporation	87	86	Owner/operator of a lunch stand	63	62
			Corporal in the regular army	62	60
Mayor of a large city	87	90	Truck driver	59	54
Priest	86	86	Clerk in a store	56	58
Civil engineer	86	84	Lumberjack	55	53
Airline pilot	86	83	Restaurant cook	55	54
Banker	85	88	Singer in a nightclub	54	52
Biologist	85	81	Filling-station attendant	51	52
Sociologist	83	82	Dockworker	50	47
Instructor in public schools	82	79	Night watchman	50	47
Captain in the regular army	82	80	Coal miner	50	49
Accountant for a large business	81	81	Restaurant waiter	49	48
Owner of a business that employs about 100 people	80	82	Taxi driver	49	49
			Farmhand	48	50
Musician in a symphony orchestra	78	81	Janitor	48	44
Author of novels	78	80	Bartender	48	44
Economist	78	79	Soda-fountain clerk	44	45
Official of an international labor union	77	75	Sharecropper	42	40
			Garbage collector	39	35
Railroad engineer	76	77	Street sweeper	36	34
Electrician	76	73	Shoe shiner	34	33
Trained machinist	75	73			
Farm owner and operator	74	76			
Undertaker	74.	72			

Source: Selected from data presented in Robert Hodge, Paul Siegel, and Peter Rossi, "Occupational Prestige in the United States, 1925–63," American Journal of Sociology 60(1964):290. Reprinted by permission.

The different dimensions of SES are generally related, but there are exceptions. Street sweepers have low prestige in America, but the 1976 salary for some was $17,000 in San Francisco. (Andy Mercado, Jeroboam, Inc.)

a higher social standing than a person with no education. Part of the high ranking of scientists, college professors, and public school instructors in Table 11·2 reflects the education associated with those occupations. Recall in this connection the Davis-Moore argument that stratification is partly related to the amount of training required to fill a status.

The high social standing associated with education is by no means limited to contemporary American society. Indeed, scholars were accorded very high standing among the ancient Hebrews, and the contemporary Japanese have a higher regard for education than Americans do.

Religion

Persons occupying religious statuses are accorded high social standing in many societies. This is particularly true in societies with agreements that make religion the most important aspect of life. In predominantly Roman Catholic countries, for example, cardinals, bishops, and priests have high social standing. So do "shamans" (religious medicine men) in many primitive societies, the Hindu saints of India, Shinto priests in Japan, and many others.

Even in the United States, with its agreement on the importance of economic values, religious leaders generally have high social standing. In Table 11·2, for example, we note that ministers and priests were ranked higher than others earning much more money.

Power

I've already said a great deal about the place of power in social stratification, both in this chapter and in Chapter 10, in the discussion of political institutions. Bertrand Russell said power was the key concept in social science, analogous to the importance of energy in physics. Dahrendorf sees it as the main dimension of stratification. Weber and others agree that it is important, but feel that there are other dimensions also.

Some power comes as a part of occupying certain statuses, such as political office. We spoke of "authority" in this context as legitimated power. Authority is also granted outside of government, as in the case of business executives or religious leaders. Material goods can be a source of power, aside from considerations of authority. "Money talks" is one way this sociological observation is sometimes expressed.

As I have mentioned, then, people are often ranked in terms of the power they have. Generals rank higher than privates, corporation presidents higher than clerks, and kings higher than commoners. This is undoubtedly a part of the reason why Supreme Court justices and other government officials were ranked high in the list presented in Table 11·2. Agreements granting some people more power than others are always subject to challenge and change, however, as the box on page 280 "Challenges to Power in the Executive Suite" shows.

Many Dimensions of Stratification

As we've seen, sociologists do not all agree on the nature of social stratification. Some take the view that stratification reflects a single dimension, such as property or power. Others argue that stratification either can or does reflect several different variables. This latter view has two implications.

First, if stratification is based on several variables, it means that there are different ways in which you may achieve high social standing. You might gain the respect of the rest of your society by getting a great deal of education, by amassing a vast fortune, by winning high political office, by learning to play the violin excellently, or in countless other ways. The United States has, in a sense, several different stratification systems, and people enjoy high social standing in each of them.

The second implication is summed up in the term **status inconsistency.** This means that your social standing may be quite different according to different sets of agreements. For example, you would have an inconsistent status if you were very wealthy but had little education, or if you were very well educated but poor. Ministers, teachers, and many "self-made" millionaires are examples of people who have inconsistent statuses.

Measuring Socioeconomic Status (SES)

The basis for ranking people in a society varies with the agreements that different societies have about what's important. In part, stratification is a matter of granting some individuals more honor, respect, prestige, and deference than others. In part, it involves the unequal distribution of material objects that make life more or less comfortable.

In studying the relationship between stratification and other aspects of social life, it is essential that sociologists first be able to classify people in terms of where they stand in the stratification system. Researchers taking the conflict point of view, stressing the concept of social class, tend to focus on occupation. Sometimes they divide people into two classes: white-collar and blue-collar. They also make finer distinctions.

Sociologists who view stratification in terms of a continuous hierarchy reflecting several dimensions have a bigger methodological problem. They must combine the several dimensions they consider relevant into a single measure. Typically, they do this by creating an index of **socioeconomic status** (SES), an overall summary of where individuals stand in the social pecking order.

Establishing SES only makes sense as a research technique if the several dimensions considered reflect the same overall stratification hierarchy. We've already seen that when more than one dimension is considered people can have inconsistent statuses. How, then, can sociologists justify the creation of composite SES measures? Data indicate that relationships exist among several dimensions of stratification. We'll see that people ranking high on one dimension tend to rank high on others. Then, I'll show you how sociologists actually create their SES indices.

Relations among Dimensions

In 1974, Americans earned over a trillion dollars in personal income. It will come as no surprise to you that all the members of American society did not share equally in that amount. Some got well over "their" $4,000, and some got much less. In fact, as Figure 11·1 shows, the poorest one-fifth of American

---

Challenges to Power in the Executive Suite

The absolute power of the corporate president and the corporation board is being challenged today from a number of directions. In a recent poll conducted by Peter D. Hart, a public-opinion analyst, "a majority of Americans feel both the Democratic and Republican parties favor big business and that the major corporations 'dominate and determine' the actions of public officials rather than the reverse. Sixty-six percent of those polled were in favor of employee ownership and control of large corporations and 44 percent approved of direct public ownership of natural resources."[1]

Although worker participation in management is only a proposal in the United States, it is becoming a reality in some European countries. For example, for the past twenty-five years, West Germany has had "codetermination" laws, which provide for labor participation on supervisory boards of major corporations. This system has worked so well that the laws will probably be broadened in 1976 to give labor almost equal representation with management on these boards.[2] In other countries, such as Sweden, workers participate in management decisions on the shop floor as well as in the executive suite.

A major question about these innovations is whether they are steps on the road to socialism or new ways of controlling the ordinary working person in the interest of economic stability and higher corporate profits. Newspaper accounts of the West German system suggest that labor participation in top-level management contributes to stability. For example, at the Witten works of the Thyssen corporation, there has not been a real strike for fifteen years although the plant has gone through a reorganization in which a large number of jobs were eliminated.[3]

As long as such changes do not affect the private ownership of industry, socialism is probably not around the corner. On the contrary, such changes may help to perpetuate capitalism by giving workers a higher stake in its preservation. In Sweden, the metalworkers union is pushing for legislation which might take that country further on the road to socialism. "Their aim—denounced by employers as a form of expropriation inconsistent with the spirit of Swedish labor-management cooperation—is a law requiring that all industry's 'excess profits' go into a fund that would eventually be used to buy up control of major companies for the benefit of all unionized workers."[4] It is perfectly possible that "the benefit of all unionized workers" might be something other than maximum profits, or even something other than the survival of any particular corporation. Sweden will be a critical case to watch for an answer to the question of whether increasing labor participation in management means a more stable version of capitalism or a slow transition to socialism.

What do you think will happen?

[1]*New York Times*, January 4, 1976, Section 3, p. 27.
[2]Ibid., January 25, 1976, p. 61.

[3]Ibid.
[4]Ibid., January 4, 1973, Section 3, p. 7.

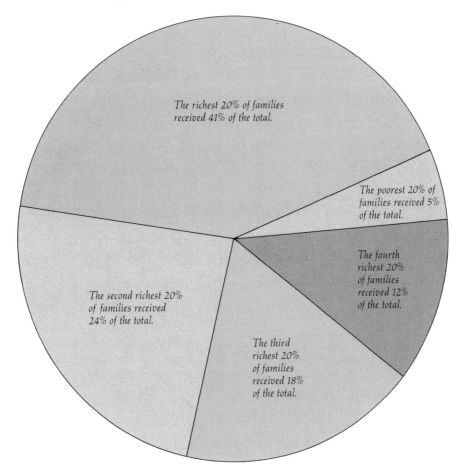

Figure 11•1 The distribution of 1974 income among families in America. Source: U.S. Bureau of the Census, Current Population Reports, *Series P-60, No. 101, 1976, p. 37.*

families received just 5 percent of the total, while the richest one-fifth of families received 41 percent.

The relationship between income and occupation should need no documentation. Persons employed in professional and technical jobs received far higher incomes than those in manual labor, and the impact of unionization has not changed this general pattern. The relationship among stratification variables only begins here, however.

Education and income are also related—in a circular fashion. By and large, persons with the greatest education earn the most money, and children from wealthy families are more likely to get advanced

education than are those from poorer families. Table 11•3 presents the expected lifetime incomes of American males eighteen years of age and older in 1972 according to different levels of education. Notice that men with four or more years of college were expected to earn more than two times as much money as those with less than eight years of schooling.

The relationship between income and education is circular, however, as I mentioned above. In 1972, the Bureau of the Census reported that among families with incomes of under $3,000, 15 percent of the members between eighteen and twenty-four years of age were enrolled in college. This percentage in-

Table 11·3 Estimated Lifetime Earnings of American
Men Eighteen Years Old and Older
as Computed in 1972

Educational level	Estimated lifetime earnings
0–7 years of elementary school	$376,470
8 years of elementary school	421,136
1–3 years of high school	476,703
4 years of high school	563,101
1–3 years of college	659,040
4 or more years of college	872,805

Source: U.S. Bureau of the Census, Current Population Reports,
1974, p. 23.

creased steadily with increasing family income.
Among families with incomes of $15,000 or more,
58 percent were enrolled (U.S. Bureau of the Census
1975a). Education and income are not *always* as directly linked as these data suggest, however, as the
box "Sex Stratification and the Women's Movement"
describes.

To round out our review of the interrelationships
among income, occupation, and education, Table 11·4
presents the percentages of people in several occupational groupings who have completed four or more
years of college. The differences are dramatic, ranging
from 62.9 percent among the professionals and technical workers to less than 5 percent among blue-collar
occupations.

These three dimensions of socioeconomic status,
then, are closely related to one another. Persons who
would be judged as having high status on one are
likely to appear high on the others as well. These
dimensions, moreover, are related to other aspects
of status. For example, income is related to possessions, as you might imagine. The *extent* to which
income determines the material aspect of the good
life, however, is perhaps greater than you imagine.
Table 11·5 presents some data on income and possessions as of 1973.

Indices of Socioeconomic Status

Sociologists often combine several indicators of
socioeconomic status into composite measures to be

Sex Stratification and the Women's Movement

What started the women's movement? One
answer is that women began to realize that
they were not allowed to compete in the same
world of work as men. Many of the women
in on the beginning of today's women's movement had high levels of education. These
women expected their educations to lead to
good jobs with prospects and pay equal to the
prospects and pay of the jobs their brothers
and husbands were getting. Instead, they
found themselves working as secretaries or
permanent "assistants." The jolting recognition of the gap between reality and beliefs
about democracy led to anger, demonstrations,
and demands.

At the same time, researchers found that
the "dimensions of stratification" don't come
together in the same way for women as they do
for men. High income goes along with high
occupational status for men, but women's incomes rise much more slowly as their occupational status goes up. The same thing is true
for education: More education gives men
greater income increases than it gives women.
In spite of laws and court cases upholding
equality of opportunity for women, few
changes seem to have occurred since the
beginning of the women's movement. If anything, the earnings gap between women and
men is increasing. In 1974, on the average,
American women working full-time, year-
round earned only 57 percent of the earnings
of American men; in 1964 they were taking
home 59 percent of the earnings of men. If
these figures are a true indication of the gains
being made, the women's movement is likely
to be around for a long time.

Do you agree?

*Sources: Larry E. Suter and Herman P. Miller, "Income
Differences between Men and Career Women," in* Chang-
ing Women in a Changing Society, *ed. Joan Huber
(Chicago: University of Chicago Press, 1973); Issue on
Women and Work,* Monthly Labor Review *(May 1974).*

Table 11·4 Relationship between Education and Occupation among Americans in March 1974

Occupation group	Percent with four or more years of college
Professional, technical, and kindred workers	62.9
Managers and administrators, except farm	28.0
Sales workers	16.5
Clerical and kindred workers	6.5
Craft and kindred workers	3.1
Operatives, except transport	1.5
Transport-equipment workers	1.3
Laborers, except farm	1.4
Private household workers	2.0
Service workers, except private household	3.0
Farm workers	4.8
All occupational groups	15.5

Source: "Educational Attainment of Workers, March 1974," U.S. Bureau of Labor Statistics Special Labor Force Report 175, 1975.

Income	Score	Education	Score
Under $5,000	0	0–8 years	0
$5,000–7,499	1	9–11 years	1
$7,500–9,999	2	12 years	2
$10,000–19,999	3	13–15 years	3
$20,000 or more	4	16 or more years	4

Composite Socioeconomic Status

Low   → High

0   1   2   3   4   5   6   7   8

Figure 11·2 Hypothetical measurement of SES.

used for classifying people in research projects. The purpose of such measures is to provide an overall ranking of statuses along a continuum (as distinguished from grouping people into discrete social classes). The particular methods used vary from study to study, but a simplified example will illustrate the process involved.

Figure 11·2 describes the construction of an SES index based on two variables: income and education. Suppose for the moment that we have conducted a survey and wish to characterize the survey respondents in terms of their socioeconomic status. Each respondent is given a score (see Figure 11·2) reflecting his or her income and another score reflecting his or her level of education. The higher the income or education, the higher the score. The scores assigned on the two variables are then added, with the result that people are ranked from 0 to 8.

In this example, a person who earns $4,000 a year and has completed six years of school is scored 0 overall. Someone who earns $8,000 a year and has

14 years of school is scored 5 overall. It should be noted that in such a system very different patterns of income and education can produce the same overall score. For example, a person who earns more than $20,000 a year and has a sixth-grade education is scored 4 overall, as is the college graduate who earns less than $5,000 a year. Such cases are the exception, however, and as we have seen in the examination of interrelationships among the different dimensions of stratification, combining scores, as shown in Figure 11·2, generally yields useful social stratification classifications.

Measures of socioeconomic status have two important functions for the sociological study of stratification. First, they permit studies of the factors that seem to produce high or low status. Second, they permit studies of the consequences of different status levels, a topic that we will examine later in this chapter.

Social Classes as Subcultures

We have been looking at social stratification as if it were a continuous hierarchy of strata. In this section, we'll return to the point of view that sees social classes within a society as more or less discrete groups.

The definition of membership in particular social

Table 11·5 Income and Ownership of Family Possessions, 1973

| | Percent of families owning | | | | |
Income	2 or more cars	Color TV	Clothes dryer	Dishwasher	Air conditioner
Under $3,000	8.3	28.6	19.3	5.0	30.0
$3,000–4,999	12.5	36.5	24.9	6.9	38.1
$5,000–7,499	18.4	45.0	33.4	9.2	41.3
$7,500–9,999	28.4	52.3	43.6	13.9	46.3
$10,000–14,999	41.2	65.0	58.9	23.0	53.9
$15,000–24,999	59.4	76.6	72.0	41.7	61.4
$25,000 and over	69.0	82.2	80.8	64.4	68.5

Source: U.S. Bureau of the Census, Statistical Abstract of the United States, *1975, p. 406.*

classes is often unclear and ambiguous, but sociologists do examine the different orientations and lifestyles that generally characterize the different classes. To the extent that social classes have special sets of agreements, they might be examined as subcultures within the same society. Children and adults socialized in terms of the class's shared agreements further consolidate their membership in that class.

As we'll see at the conclusion of this section, the study of social classes as subcultures can also shed light on the power relations within a society. If different classes have different sets of agreements, whose do you suppose are more often established in the main institutions of the society as a whole?

Politics

The classes in America have quite different agreements regarding politics and government. In large part, this reflects their manner of participation in these institutions. The middle and upper classes tend to be the most conservative politically and the most likely to be Republicans. Their political conservatism, of course, supports the maintenance of the status quo, and, almost by definition, they tend to be happy with the way things are. From a middle- and upper-class point of view, the American political system is a good one. Members of these classes are very likely to be involved in politics and government, serving in official positions or working behind the

scenes. Their motives range from feelings of dedication to the well-being of their country as a whole to feelings of dedication to their own well-being.

Members of the working class tend to be more liberal on economic issues and are more likely to be Democrats. They feel that politics should be an instrument of social change since they are not making out as well with the status quo as are the upper and middle classes. Traditionally, many among the working class have been alienated from politics altogether. They have been less likely to believe that government will do anything in their interest, and they are less likely to vote on election day. (It is an axiom of practical American politics that a rainy election day usually costs the Democrats votes.) In recent years, however, the working class has been changing radically in its attitudes toward politics. Labor unions and racial-ethnic movements have increased both the political participation and the political effectiveness of the working class in America.

In many ways, the political point of view of the very poor is an extreme extension of that of the working class. The very poor are the most alienated from politics in general and are the least likely to participate in the political process. They are more likely to regard government as belonging to someone else and as an instrument of their oppression. The situation changed slightly, however, during the late 1960s. The poor became more active in politics and government, partly because of the organization of welfare recipients. When the poor *are* politically active, their point of view tends to be the most radical of all the social classes, calling for the most far-reaching kinds of social and political change.

The preceding comments have dealt mostly with social class and political *economics.* In general, the white-collar portion of America is economically conservative while the blue-collar portion is economically liberal. This is not to suggest, however, that economic orientation extends as neatly to other issues. When racial discrimination, abortion, and other issues of social change are being considered, a very different pattern appears. The white working class and the white poor have tended to be the most conservative with regard to legislation aimed at ending racial discrimination, for example. Similarly, the working and lower-middle classes provided much of the strongest support for the continuation and acceleration of the war in Vietnam.

Religion

As a general rule, white-collar religion in America is relatively reserved and ritualistic, in contrast to blue-collar religion, which has been characterized by more emotional fervor. There is a greater tendency to reify religious beliefs, values, and norms among the lower classes than among the upper classes, and blue-collar religion is generally more fundamentalist and dogmatic. In large part, this difference reflects the educational component of social class. Education, as we saw in Chapter 9, is a natural enemy of dogmatic religious belief, especially as evidenced in the impact of scientific discoveries on traditional religious agreements.

This is only a part of the story, however. The upper classes are more likely to associate themselves with churches than are the lower classes. Moreover, they are more likely to belong to the "right" churches: Unitarian, Episcopal, Congregational, and Presbyterian, most typically. Church membership partly reflects the upper classes' greater participation in all aspects of society. The lower classes are less likely to participate in organized religion just as they are less likely to participate in other aspects of society. When they do join churches, they are more likely to join the Baptists, Missouri Synod Lutherans, or one of the many fundamentalist sects.

Speech

Let's look at something very different from religion and politics. The great majority of Americans speak English as their native language, yet members of different social classes speak it very differently. Moreover, the fact that they *communicate* their class when they speak has been demonstrated in a number of studies. In some, people from different social-class backgrounds were asked to tell familiar children's stories or to count from 1 to 20 into a tape recorder. Groups of judges—typically college students—were then asked to guess the social class of the speakers when the recordings were played. The judges' estimates consistently corresponded very closely to the speakers' actual social-class backgrounds. Even when all the speakers were themselves college students, their speech betrayed their family backgrounds (Ellis 1967).

Class and Societywide Agreements

We have been discussing just a few of the differences in agreements that characterize the American social classes as subcultures. Sociologists have examined many more, though we cannot consider all those here. I want to bring up one additional point, however. The different sets of agreements that classes have are more than merely "different." Sociologists do not hold one set of agreements to be "better" than another, but it is true that the various sets of agreements are not of equal importance.

While you were reading about speech differences, you may have found yourself thinking that the upper class speaks what is considered "good English" while the lower class speaks what is considered "bad English." The upper-class version of English is the dominant one.

Most simply put, there is a tendency for the agreements of the upper classes to be the formal agreements of the society. Functionalists and conflict theorists agree on the existence of this tendency, but they disagree strongly as to its meaning In Parsons' view of stratification as a "moral ranking," people receive high social status to the extent that their conditions and behaviors reflect the general values of the society. The conflict point of view is very different: The upper classes, through their greater power and greater control of the institutions of the society, *impose* their own class agreements on everyone else.

In elaborating on this latter view, Seymour Martin Lipset (1968:160) states, "To a very large degree, lower classes throughout history have acceded to the societal values that define them as being, in various aspects, inferior to those of higher status." We have already seen in the preceding three chapters how this takes place—through socialization into the agreements of the major social institutions. And socialization is all the more effective to the extent that people are brought to reify and internalize the agreements composing those institutions.

Consequences of Social Stratification

As you might imagine, there has been a lively debate in sociology as to whether social stratification, as it operates in a society such as ours, is good, bad, or just a fact of social life. The functionalist point of view tends to see stratification as generally beneficial for the functioning of society—as essential, in fact —and as inevitable anyway. The conflict point of view suggests that our current stratification system has more problems than value. Marxian conflict theorists, moreover, feel that it would be possible to develop a society without stratification, the "classless society" envisioned by Marx.

Sociologists will probably never agree on whether stratification is ultimately good or bad. Even so, it is possible to note some of the consequences of the American stratification system that most sociologists would agree ought to be corrected. It is obvious that people at the bottom of the stratification system often lack the necessities of life: food, shelter, and adequate clothing. Other consequences of stratification are not so obvious.

The poor have poorer physical and mental health than other Americans, or at least this is what a variety of studies suggest. The poor are more likely to be classified as mentally ill and admitted for hospital care. And—when they are released—they are more likely to suffer relapses (Hollingshead and Redlich 1958).

The relationship between mental illness and social class is a particularly complicated one, since there is less agreement on what constitutes mental illness than there is on physical illness. To an extent, members of the lower classes may be considered mentally ill because they fail to behave in the ways upper- and middle-class Americans have agreed are "proper" and "normal." I'll have a good deal more to say about this general issue in Chapter 13 on deviance and social control.

The lower classes have a different experience of war than other Americans, too. Leo Srole and his associates (1962) have shown that the lower classes are more likely to be rejected by the military draft. Other research suggests that those who do enter the military suffer a higher casualty rate (Hoult 1974). One possible reason for this is the fact that the officer corps is drawn primarily from the middle and upper classes.

Ironically, the lower classes—with less money to spend—often pay more for the things they buy than do the upper and middle classes (Caplovitz 1967). Even when they buy a particular item, such as a television set, the poor are likely to pay more for it than those who have more money to start with. This comes about in several ways. When they lack the money to buy something outright, they are forced to buy on installments, and the interest rates are often outrageously high (*and* hidden). Very often, the poor are the targets of out-and-out fraud. Their predators assume that they will not know how to seek official redress or protection.

Although it is possible to focus on the way in which social stratification functions on behalf of society's survival (as the functionalist point of view does), it is equally important to examine the consequences of stratification for the lives of individuals. Americans have liked to think of the United States as relatively classless, at least compared with traditional Europe or other parts of the world, but many sociologists have argued that the matter is quite different. Social classes are very real in America and they matter for the people in them (see, for example, Tumin 1967).

One of the chief problems of social stratification systems is that inequalities tend to be perpetuated across generations. The poor and the powerless of one generation tend to be the children of the poor and powerless of the previous generation and the parents of the poor and powerless of the next. Often, low social status is reified: The poor, for example, are often seen as inferior, weak, and lazy. Their children are assumed to be the same. When the economic facts of life—involving education, nutrition, and health—plus subcultural socialization are added to negative stereotypes, the perpetuation of low social status is likely.

Stratification systems operate like social institutions in that they tend to perpetuate the status quo. They support the survival of society. The advantage to society comes at the cost of individual disadvantage and dissatisfaction, however. There are even disadvantages to the society in the long run, since talented individuals may be effectively prevented from serving the society in positions of responsibility.

In spite of overall, general perpetuation of the status quo, most social stratification systems allow for a degree of movement. In most it is possible for some individuals to rise or fall in social standing, a process called **social mobility**. I want to conclude this chapter with an examination of what sociologists have learned about this process.

Social Mobility

Your social-class standing, to review, is a matter of agreement. To the extent that social class has any "real" meaning, you occupy a particular social status only if other people agree that you do. I'll close this chapter with an examination of the ways in which agreements about social status are changed. "Social mobility" refers to individual and group movement from one social class to another.

We'll begin the section with a brief discussion of the difference between class and caste. Then, we'll look at the nature of group and individual mobility.

Class versus Caste

Sociologists often distinguish between class and caste when they examine social stratification. A "caste" is a stratification category or group whose membership is determined on the basis of **ascribed statuses.** The traditional Indian caste system, which runs from the Brahmins at the top to the "untouchables" at the bottom, is usually mentioned as an example. A person was born into a specific niche in this rigidly stratified system, and there was virtually no hope of moving from that niche. People may have moved up or down within their caste, but there was no possibility of significant social mobility.

In America, various racial groups have suffered the disadvantages of at least a partial caste system. This was certainly the case for black slaves early in our history, and the castelike quality of being black survived the emancipation of the slaves (see Dollard 1937 for a classic discussion of the operation of a caste system in the United States).

Individual Mobility

Most class systems—as opposed to caste systems—allow a degree of upward and downward movement, as we have already suggested in earlier sections of this chapter. Sociologists are interested in both upward mobility and downward mobility, as mea-

sured by a person's change of social status from the status of the family into which he or she was born.

Mobility can be measured in terms of any of the several dimensions of stratification: income, education, occupation, and so forth. The person who gets much more education than his or her parents, for example, would be considered upwardly mobile, while the child of a wealthy physician who becomes an impoverished laborer would be considered downwardly mobile.

Looked at from the point of view of class (as opposed to stratification), social mobility is a matter of learning and accepting a new set of agreements as to what's true, good, and expected. When Professor Higgins tutored Eliza Doolittle, he was attempting to give her this kind of social mobility. Typically, education is critical to the process (as I've suggested earlier). Social mobility can often be a source of strain for the mobile person and for his or her family. Both the child "putting on airs" and the "black sheep" are a source of unhappiness for parents.

Societies differ in the degree to which they permit social mobility, even in the absence of a formal caste system, and sociologists often distinguish between "open" and "closed" class systems. Most would regard the United States as having a relatively open class system, one that permits much social mobility. In fact, the general American agreement on the value of achievement presupposes an open class system.

Still, the American class system is not as open as that general agreement would suggest. The children of poor parents do not stand the same chance of becoming wealthy as the children of rich parents stand of staying rich. The children—the sons at least —of physicians are still more likely than any other group to become physicians themselves.

Group Mobility

Often, an entire group of people within a society can be socially mobile. While, by definition, this means that the individual members of the group are mobile, there is often more at work than individual movement. The emancipation of black slaves in America, for example, marked a degree of upward mobility for all blacks, even though it did not provide

as much mobility as many had hoped. Women, to take another example, have held a second-class status for nearly three-fourths of America's national history. They experienced a degree of upward social mobility when, in 1920, they were given the right to vote.

Legislation is not a prerequisite for group mobility, as the history of America's many immigrant groups has shown. The many German, Irish, Italian, Jewish, Japanese, Chinese, and other immigrant groups began their lives in America at the bottom of the social structure. Most of these groups, moreover, have moved upward, often through national and ethnic self-help associations.

Perhaps the clearest example of this form of group mobility in America can be seen in the case of the Chinese in Hawaii. Originally brought to Hawaii as day laborers for the large sugar and pineapple plantations, the Chinese steadily extricated themselves from the plantations to establish businesses and to invest in land. Today, the Chinese are the wealthiest racial group in Hawaii.

Upward economic mobility—for both groups and individuals—often involves what sociologists have called **deferred gratification.** Rather than spending the money available at a given time, some people save a part of it and invest it in the possibility of upward mobility. Such investments may be made in real property, in education, or in other things that hold the possibility of paying off in the long run. Deferring gratification has been a common practice among the middle class in America, and it has also been the key element in the group mobility experienced by many immigrant groups.

There are many other sources and means of social mobility. Blau and Duncan (1967) have looked at some of the more generally important sources of mobility in America. Historically, they cite the westward expansion—with its vast opportunities for individual advancement—and the growth of technology, which freed people from manual jobs and created a demand for technicians and clerical workers. In more recent times, they find migration (sometimes called "geographical mobility") from farm to city an important source of social mobility.

Overall, Blau, Duncan, and others have stressed the importance of American values. In particular, our general agreements on universalism and on achievement over ascription (see Parsons' pattern variables, Chapter 6) have been identified as important conditions for mobility. Social mobility is more difficult in societies sharing the agreement that who you *are* is more important than what you can *do*. Ultimately, the American social stratification system is a mixture of persistence and change.

Summary

This chapter has dealt with a variety of topics related to social stratification and mobility. Stratification is by definition a matter of inequality, of the unequal distribution of certain desired things. In studying stratification, sociologists make a distinction between social classes—distinct groupings of people—and strata—levels within a continuous hierarchy of status.

There are a number of different sociological points of view regarding stratification. Early observers tended to regard stratification as part of the "natural order of things." The rich were rich and the poor were poor because they were "supposed to be that way." Rousseau and others, however, suggested that most social stratification was a matter of agreement, and this view permitted the possibility that agreements could be changed.

Karl Marx was one of those most interested in changing the agreements regarding stratification. He saw in society a division between two classes of people: the capitalists and the workers. In his view the capitalists exploited the workers, a situation that he spent most of his life trying to correct.

Two different sociological points of view, the functionalist and conflict points of view, are very important in contemporary sociology. The functionalist looks at stratification as a mechanism serving the needs of society; the conflict theorist sees distinct social classes fighting with one another by virtue of their different class interests.

There are many dimensions of stratification. Since stratification is a matter of agreement within

a society as to what's important, different societies have quite different stratification systems. We examined the most important elements of stratification in the United States and saw how sociologists measure social status—typically called socioeconomic status (SES).

Within the view of social classes as distinct groups within a society, social classes can be seen as subcultures in America. There are different class-based agreements with regard to politics, religion, education, and speech. Moreover, the upper classes in a society are more likely than the lower classes to have subcultural agreements similar to those more generally shared in the society as a whole. There is disagreement in sociology as to the reason for this pattern.

Finally, we looked briefly at some of the consequences of the American social stratification system and discussed social mobility, both individual and group. Social mobility consists of changing the agreements about social status.

Suggested Readings

Baltzell, E. Digby
1958 *Philadelphia Gentlemen.* New York: Free Press. Most sociological analyses of particular social classes have focused on those at the bottom of the heap, producing occasional charges of paternalism. Here is a rare examination of the other end of the stratification ladder: the rich and powerful. Baltzell examines the residential, religious, educational, occupational, family, and other aspects of upper-class status.

Bendix, Reinhard and Seymour Martin Lipset, Eds.
1966 *Class, Status, and Power.* New York: Free Press. This massive collection of articles and book excerpts covers virtually all aspects of the sociological inquiry into stratification. Included is Weber's differentiation of three aspects of stratification, the classic Davis-Moore statement of the functionalist view of stratification, and many, many other historical and modern analyses.

Dahrendorf, Ralf
1959 *Class and Class Conflict in Industrial Society.*
Stanford, Calif.: Stanford.
Here's Dahrendorf's modern reformulation of Marx's view of the class struggle. This is an important work in the literature of conflict theory, providing a useful balance to the structural-functional view of stratification exemplified by the Davis-Moore article mentioned in the preceding entry. Dahrendorf's attempt to develop a formal theory of stratification and power is also instructive from the standpoint of sociological theory.

Marx, Karl and Friedrich Engels
[1848] *The Communist Manifesto.* New York:
1955   Appleton-Century-Crofts.
Viewed in historical perspective, this must be rated one of the most influential books of all time. This short, simple, and highly polemical tract outlines Marx's view of history as a matter of class struggle in the face of economic oppression, and, at a more general level, it states Marx's theoretical view of economic determinism.

Episode Eleven

On May 16, 2027, a two-month-old infant was kidnapped from a collapsible stroller at Kennedy Airport in New York City. Two days later a gang of nonmutants converged upon a campsite near Tucson, Arizona. It had been rumored that a young woman and the kidnapped baby were resting there. In the ensuing violence both the woman and baby were fatally shot. Subsequent identification procedures confirmed that the younger victim was indeed the infant who had been seized in New York. An autopsy of the woman accompanying the child revealed "chlorophyll capable of photosynthesis within the epidermis."

May 25, 2027, United States Senator Malcolm Adams, Democrat from Florida, introduced a bill that would officially deny mutants the right to vote in federal elections until their status had been specifically defined as human. The bill would cause bitter and lengthy debate.

On June 5 three unidentified persons drove from Flagstaff, Arizona, to Adamsville where they attacked and murdered one of two chlorophyllic guards. The surviving mutant fired a laser into the escaping auto, killing one of the three and seriously wounding another.

June 10, 2027, the Arizona State Legislature passed two bills. The first, LB 431, demanded that individuals undergo thorough physical examinations

—including biochemical tests—before receiving marriage licenses. The second, LB 432, prohibited marriage between mutants and nonmutants.

On June 15, 2027, FBI Agent K. Jeffers phoned the president of Chicago National Insurance Company. Company employee Gabriel Knapp, he explained, had been visited in his apartment at Lake Shore Towers March 14, 2027, at approximately 6 P.M. by a male in his early twenties. The visitor had been followed from Green Colony, Jeffers related, and was known to have returned there. Jeffers requested that Chicago National forward available information on Gabriel Knapp to the Federal Bureau of Investigation.

June 17 the director of health services for Chicago

National received a memo from the company's president. The memo requested that the file on employee Gabriel Knapp be completed immediately.

That afternoon someone from the health services department contacted the physician who had examined Gabe. Three days later the physician mailed the insurance company the following communication:

"As you know, the doctor-patient relationship demands absolute privacy. Abiding by that professional standard, I have until now offered no one other than Mr. Knapp information concerning his medical examination one year ago.

"It has become less apparent, however, that this individual falls into that category of patients concerning whom a physician is morally and legally bound to secrecy. Therefore, I am enclosing a copy of Mr. Knapp's medical report, compiled last June, 2026."

On June 24, 2027, at approximately 11 A.M. Gabriel's secretary buzzed him on the interoffice communication system. "Mr. Knapp," he said, "the vice president in charge of personnel would like to see you in his office at one o'clock this afternoon."

"Thank you," Gabriel responded mechanically.

Half an hour later Gabe opened his drawer and took out the loaded handgun he had purchased several weeks before. Slipping it into his pocket—as he automatically did now whenever leaving the privacy of either his office or apartment—he rose to exit the office.

At the door he glanced backward into the room that had become a symbol of his success and consequently a source of pride. "Plush place," he remarked to himself, shaking his head. "Damn plush place," he repeated, this time with bitterness, then left the office.

He walked toward the lake as he had done so many times before. The sun felt good against his shoulders; the breeze was warm. His thoughts turned to Monica. He missed her. He had heard through rumor that she had joined Civil Liberty for All. After hearing that, Gabe had begun to hope that she would contact him.

He had reasoned that Monica's enlisting in CLA might mean that she would consider seeing him again. But she hadn't phoned. Gabe had been forced to conclude that the woman's membership in CLA was a result of her conviction that in the United States all

intelligent beings deserved equal representation under the law. Nothing more.

Gabe had avoided making new friends, growing increasingly isolated over the past ten months. Of the three sociologists whom he had seen in the crowd the day of the rescue, it was Constance Batterson with whom he had lately kept closest contact. She had visited his apartment several times. Occasionally Gabe had gone to her office at American University.

"I have so many questions to ask you," Dr. Batterson had grinned. "How many in-depth interviews do you think you can bear?"

"As many as you like," Gabe had replied, figuring the forthcoming discussions might lessen his loneliness.

Dr. Batterson, along with a team of graduate students, had begun to compile results on a questionnaire she had mailed some months before. The research would yield data concerning the extent of and reasons for ungreens' animosity toward greens. Gabriel's understanding of green culture, Constance had explained, would help her interpret this raw data with greater perception.

Batterson and Knapp found themselves talking for hours at a time. "Why do you think ungreens are opposed to greens' gaining status or power in broader society?" Constance asked often. "Is it because those who do have power refuse to share it and consequently deny greens access to that power? Or is it because green religion really does deny some of the basic moral principles upon which our culture is based?"

Once when Constance had asked this, Gabe had thought awhile, then said, "What moral principles does my religion deny?"

"You felt conscience-bound to rescue," Connie offered. "Kidnapping is opposed to our moral code." Batterson meditated a moment. Later she had said, "Maybe it's good for the larger society to deny power to people who would kidnap infants without discretion."

"Maybe," Gabriel had debated, "but it is not good for *green* people to have to sneak around, hiding their mutations, hurrying home to safety once their skin begins to mature. If we knew our children could survive on the outside even after their skin began to change color, there would be no rescue."

"What would green children need in order to survive on the outside?"

Gabe's response was direct. "Respect," he said.

The discussions continued over several months. "What status will you have in Adamsville if and when you return there?" Batterson had asked once.

"Very low," Gabe had replied. "I will be assigned a home in the valley with other dull greens. I won't be allowed to work in any decision-making positions at S.T.I. I won't be able to enter Elderhome. I can join a nurturing contract, but not to raise offspring of pure greens."

"Why?" Connie had questioned.

"Because I lack sufficient allegiance," Gabe had answered straightforwardly. "Therefore I would be considered dangerous in decision-making positions. I would be a scandal in positions of prestige."

"Then your society believes it is functional to deny dull greens equal rights and opportunities?" Dr. Batterson probed.

"Yes."

"But you have a well-educated economic mind and several years' experience with a major insurance company," Batterson pointed out.

"Still," Gabe had replied, "greens with dull skin often do make mistakes. Besides," he added, "many dull greens seem to be really quite lazy. It is as if they were ill."

Often lethargic, dulls moved more slowly than did their counterparts. Prone to dizzy spells, they often found it difficult to complete a regular day's work without either rest or—more often—supplement.

"I see," Connie had responded. "And are they satisfied with their rank?"

"They know that they have been disloyal and so they accept their position."

Gabe recalled parts of these discussions now as he walked near Lake Michigan. He would miss these conversations with Dr. Batterson when he eventually left Chicago for good.

Gabe didn't return to his office until shortly before his one o'clock appointment. Seated at his desk, he drank a cup of coffee and smoked a cigarette. He had forced himself not to think about the forthcoming meeting. When he had smoked a second cigarette, he ground it into an ashtray and proceeded to the executive suite of the vice president in charge of personnel.

"Sit down, Mr. Knapp," the vice president began courteously.

Gabriel sat down.

"I have received information from your examining physician." He looked at Gabe. "You're a green," he said.

Gabe stared into the other man's eyes. "Yes," he said.

"The FBI contacted us several days ago. They wanted your complete file. We cooperated."

The file, Knapp realized, would contain Gabriel's requests to take sick days. A little checking would reveal that Gabriel Knapp had been absent from work June 28, 2026. He was no longer safe on the outside.

"Mr. Knapp," the executive continued, "your work for us has been exemplary. We hate to lose you. But," he paused briefly, "we know that greens make a practice of returning to Green Colony at just about the time they have become most valuable to their employers. Chicago National has already spent a lot of money training you. We have learned to count on you. We don't want to become even more dependent upon your talents and skills only to have you leave us at what might be a critical time."

"We would not leave, sir, if people with green skin could live safely and with respect on the outside."

"Mr. Knapp," the vice president said firmly, "we will have to let you go. I'm sorry."

Gabriel stood and extended his hand. His superior did likewise. "You may finish the week if you like," he said.

Gabriel returned to his own office. He opened his briefcase and emptied into it some personal belongings from his desk drawers. He took a picture of Monica from the top of his desk. Half an hour later, saying nothing to his secretary, he left Chicago National.

He walked to Illinois State Bank where he withdrew the balances from both his savings and his checking accounts.

Later at his apartment he wrote a letter to his landlord explaining that he had been transferred and must vacate the apartment before the termination of his lease.

From his bedroom closet he pulled three suitcases. He would take what he could. He packed cosmetics, clothes, mineral tablets, a thermos, books, a few pictures, his university diploma. When he had finished packing, he stood for a moment, gazing into the fluorescent lights he had ordered installed in his ceiling.

Later he sat at his kitchen table where he composed a short note to Monica. "I'm sorry for the pain I've caused you," he wrote. "I must go home now. I love you." He placed the note into an envelope, then stamped and sealed the letter.

He phoned for a taxi. When it came, he pulled on a topcoat, felt in his pocket for the gun he had learned to carry, and with his luggage and the briefcase departed his apartment.

At O'Hare airport Gabe purchased a ticket.

"Poor time to go to Phoenix," an airline clerk idly remarked as he checked Gabriel's luggage. "Just when summer is getting a good start here."

"Yes," Gabe said.

Questions

1. How is Gabe a victim of a caste system outside of Adamsville? How is he a victim of a caste system within Adamsville?

2. Discuss the place of greens in the ungreen stratification system from a functionalist and from a conflict point of view.

3. What questions does Batterson ask from a functionalist perspective?

4. Give examples of the "self-fulfilling prophecy" in Adamsville and outside it.

12

Minorities

In this chapter, we discuss the minorities who live in a society. A **minority group** is not necessarily small. Indeed, a minority group is sometimes made up of a majority—even an overwhelming majority—of the members of a society. Within the sociological point of view, the term "minority" is used to refer to those people who have a disproportionately small share of the power and "things" that are distributed in the society. They are a group pushed generally to the bottom of a society's stratification system.

Nearly 90 percent of the population of the Union of South Africa, for example, are nonwhite; they are predominantly members of the black native Bantu tribes. The primary political power and wealth of the country, however, are concentrated in the hands of the numerically small white minority. The blacks and other nonwhites are prevented from participation in most sectors of the society and are relegated to third- or fourth-class citizenship. These nonwhites, while constituting a vast majority in terms of numbers, are regarded as a "minority" in the sociological point of view. Later in this chapter, we will discuss women in America as a minority, even though they constitute slightly over half of our population.

The sociological notion of "minorities" in a society, then, is closely related to the stratification process. People constitute a minority by virtue of agreement, nothing more, although you need to remember that one group often imposes social agreements on another. Such agreements, moreover, gov-

ern the behavior of majority and minority groups alike. In this chapter, we will see how members of minorities participate in the agreements that make them a minority, and we'll also see some of the ways in which they work to change such agreements. The agreements that create minority groups are very often reified in societies. People tend to believe that such agreements represent an ultimate reality in the world. One of the first steps in changing those agreements, as will become clear, is to draw attention to the fact that *agreements are only agreements.*

The chapter begins with a general discussion of **prejudice** and **discrimination.** In this, we'll look at the structure of the agreements that create minorities and see how they operate. We'll see the part that **stereotyping** plays in the definition of minorities and in the maintenance of agreements about who belongs in a minority group.

The middle part of the chapter deals with the various kinds of minority groups that have been created in American society. We'll begin with racial minorities, looking at some of the different agreements that exist among the general public and among scientists regarding racial differences. Then, we'll see how those agreements have been made a part of the social structure that shapes social interactions. Next, we'll turn to ethnic or national minorities, looking a bit at the history of some ethnic groups in America that moved from minority to majority status.

A major section of the chapter deals with women

as a minority group. We'll look at the agreements that define women as a minority and some of the results of such agreements. And we'll see how the agreements are changing.

The chapter concludes with an examination of the part that minority group members play in the agreements that define them as minorities. Some, as we will see, simply accept the agreements passively. Others resist the agreements, and some change the agreements. All this will shed light on how social agreements operate in general.

Prejudice and Discrimination

From the sociological point of view, a minority group's place in a society is critical to its general functioning. The agreements relating to minority groups are sociologically important just as are those relating to the family or to stratification generally. We cannot fully understand how a society operates without understanding the agreements defining and governing the majority and minority groups of which it is comprised.

For most American sociologists, the study of minority groups is significant in another way also. Typically, the experience of minority group members in America contradicts official American agreements relating to equality, freedom, and human dignity. Because their identity is usually based on ascribed characteristics, minority groups often function as "castes," as we used and defined that term in Chapter 11.

You should realize that sociologists can approach the study of minority groups from either or both of two distinct points of view. The sociological point of view per se regards the study of minority groups as important to understanding society as a whole. The point of view growing out of traditional American values, in contrast, can lead sociologists to see injustice and inhumanity, quite aside from the functions such inhumanity and injustices serve in the overall operation of the society. Some of the things sociologists say about minority groups reflect one point of view, and other things they say reflect the other. It will be useful for you to keep these two

points of view clear in your own mind, since what sociologists say will sometimes be misleading.

A sociologist might observe, for example, that job discrimination against women in America serves the function of maintaining the traditional structure of the family. Such a statement does not mean, however, that he or she is in favor either of discriminating against women or of maintaining the traditional family. As another example, sociologists often speak out against prejudice against minority group members. This, however, does not mean that they are blind to the fact that such prejudices enhance the self-esteem of the majority group members.

The distinction between the two points of view is especially important as we turn now to a discussion of prejudice and discrimination.

Discrimination

It will be useful to recall the Chapter 4 definitions and discussions of "status" and "role." People occupy various statuses, or positions, in a society; the behaviors expected of people with those statuses are roles. More accurately, roles prescribe the behavior expected of the occupant of one status in interactions with occupants of other specific statuses. Thus, the status "lieutenant" has roles prescribing interactions with privates, other roles prescribing interactions with generals, and so forth.

From this point of view, all social behavior is based on discrimination. We "discriminate"—that is to say, we distinguish—among the different statuses we interact with and form our behavior on that basis. The lieutenant discriminates between privates and generals in choosing an "appropriate" behavior. Ministers discriminate between bishops and parishioners in choosing "appropriate" behavior. The "appropriateness" of behavior is defined by the roles governing the interaction that takes place among occupants of different statuses.

This is *not* the sense in which people typically use the term "discrimination," although the two usages are related. Typically, we talk about discrimination in connection with minority groups. Membership in a minority group (or in a majority group) is a status. The roles associated with minority—and majority—group memberships prescribe the ways in which occupants of those statuses are expected—by agreement—to interact with one another. There are agreements describing the ways in which majority group members act toward minority group members and vice versa.

Usually we talk of discrimination against the members of a minority group, even though discrimination in favor of a group is both a logical possibility and a social reality. As the term is most commonly used, however, discrimination refers to the withholding of scarce commodities—including respect, dignity, and opportunity to achieve—from the members of a minority group. This is the sense in which we will use the term in this chapter.

Discrimination, then, is a matter of *behavior*, as distinct from prejudice (which we'll discuss later in this section), which is a matter of *attitude*, or point of view. Believing all Orientals to be untrustworthy is an example of prejudice; refusing to hire an Oriental on that basis is an example of discrimination.

Discrimination may be based on official, legal agreements, or it may be based on unofficial agreements, such as tradition. Discrimination against American blacks in connection with voting illustrates these two types. Prior to 1870 when the Fifteenth Amendment to the U.S. Constitution was passed, blacks were prohibited by law from voting. Indeed, in the original Constitution, slaves and Indians each counted only three-fifths of a person in computing the populations of states for the purpose of determining the number of representatives to be elected to Congress. During the century following the passage of the Fifteenth Amendment, southern blacks were effectively prevented from voting through a variety of unofficial means. Discrimination against blacks' voting persisted, then, even though the official agreement changed.

Whatever its form, discrimination against minorities usually involves the denial of something that all members of a society consider desirable. Observed patterns of discrimination have most often involved the denial of: life, citizenship, freedom, scarce goods, and the opportunity to earn scarce goods.

In "annihilation," the most severe form of discrimination, the members of a minority group are killed wholesale. The Nazi attempt to exterminate Jews, gypsies, and others is a clear example of this

pattern. Equally clear is the early American attempt to eradicate the native Indian population of the country, based on an agreement that "the only good Indian is a dead Indian."

"Expulsion" is a pattern of discrimination that denies minority group members their citizenship, their very membership in the society. This was the pattern followed when the federal government placed Japanese-Americans in detention camps during World War II. Sometimes, minority group members have been forced to leave their country, as were millions of Germans living in eastern Europe at the end of World War II. Similarly, millions of Moslems were forced to leave India following the 1947 partitioning of Pakistan and India.

"Segregation" is a pattern of discrimination in which minority group members are separated from the rest of society, often geographically. The segregation of blacks in America is probably the most familiar example to you. Sociologists often refer to segregation as an institution in America because it is a relatively integrated and persistent set of beliefs, values, and norms separating blacks from whites in residences, schools, churches, and public services. Although officially outlawed, to some extent Jim Crowism still exists.

Many other groups have been segregated in America, some involuntarily, others by choice. Approximately three-fourths of the nation's Indian population live on or near federal reservations. Many large American cities have a Chinatown. Towns and cities of the American Southwest have Chicano sections. Miami has Cuban sections. Other cities have Irish, German, Polish, Italian, Portuguese, and Puerto Rican sections. Some minority group members willingly accept the agreement on segregation, wanting to live, learn, worship, and relax with others who share their subcultural agreements. Where they do not accept segregation willingly, they often work to change that agreement.

The denial of scarce goods is another common form of discrimination. One example of this pattern is the generally lower pay women receive even when they are doing the same job as men. The denial of membership in exclusive social clubs is another example of the same pattern.

One of the most frustrating patterns of discrimination in America today is the denial of opportunity, and it is related to other forms of discrimination. Members of minority groups are often denied access to the jobs that would allow them to earn scarce goods and to fulfill their individual potentials. They may also be denied access to good education, critical to individual and group mobility.

Discrimination against minorities in America is a complex and often interrelated set of patterns. Because of the neighborhood-school system, segregated housing results in segregated education, which, in turn, results in minority group members' being denied the better-paying jobs that would allow them to move into better neighborhoods and gain better education for their children. The wheel of discrimination goes 'round and 'round.

Prejudice

Like discrimination, the term "prejudice" is commonly used somewhat differently than its definition suggests. Strictly defined, "prejudice" is prejudgment. If you believe that tomorrow will be a rotten day, you have a prejudice. You have prejudged what kind of day tomorrow will be; you have judged it before it happens. In this sense, prejudices are little more than expectations you have about something. They can be positive, negative, or neutral. You can expect tomorrow to be nice, you can expect it to be rotten, or you can simply expect it to come. The last of these is also a prejudgment, or prejudice.

Prejudices are as much a part of our lives as expectations, and they seem very functional in many ways. You can't take a bus without an expectation that it will arrive more or less as scheduled. When you walk across a busy intersection, you do so with the expectation that cars will stop for the red light.

Many of our expectations or prejudices are based on shared agreements, many are based on past experiences, and many more are based on both. Sociologists are interested in all kinds of prejudices, and they are particularly interested in those that relate to social interactions. "Social interactions" refers to our expectations about other people—what they are like and how they will behave. Those expectations affect how *we* behave.

If you expect your instructor to give a very difficult examination, you likely will study harder than if you expect an easy one. In writing this book, I have had countless expectations—prejudices—about you: your abilities, your interests, and what is required to fill the gap between where you were at the beginning of the book and where your instructor wants you to be after reading it. Some of my prejudices were based on experiences with students and sociology instructors, some were based on the agreements as to what sociology is, and many were based on both.

The term "prejudice," however, is normally used with a more limited meaning than the preceding comments suggest. Usually it refers to shared negative beliefs and feelings about all the members of a particular group, especially a minority group. In this sense "prejudice" is an expectation you share about a *group* of people that forms the basis for your expectations about *individual* members of that group. Typically, these expectations are negative.

Sociologists use the term "stereotype" to refer to the pictures people share about a group, pictures that are the basis for expectations. Stereotypes are reified agreements—beliefs—about the characteristics of a group. Stereotypes may or may not be based on actual experiences or observations. They are learned, often during early socialization.

In 1971, a sociological study of stereotyping was conducted among hundreds of second- and third-grade schoolchildren. Each child was asked to describe the "average American" using a five-point scale running between pairs of opposite adjectives. For example, they were asked to describe the "average American" as "very intelligent," "somewhat intelligent," "neither intelligent nor unintelligent," "somewhat unintelligent," or "very unintelligent." Twenty such pairs of adjectives were used (Davis 1971).

Next, children were asked to describe the "average black American," using the same technique and the same sets of adjectives. The purpose of the study was to discover the extent to which young children had come to share negative stereotypes of blacks. On each of the twenty sets of adjectives, blacks were described in less-favorable terms than the "average American." Blacks were portrayed as less intelligent, less hardworking, less honest, and so forth.

What makes this study especially interesting is that it was conducted in Hawaii where blacks constitute less than 1 percent of the population. A large proportion of blacks in Hawaii, moreover, are military personnel, and there were no black children in the classes sampled in the study. It seemed unlikely that the children studied could have had more than the most casual contacts with blacks. Although they might have picked up some stereotypes of blacks from old movies on television, that can't explain children's saying that blacks "smelled bad" compared with the "average American." (See the accompanying box, "The Language of Prejudice.")

Many minority group stereotypes are clearly a product of agreement rather than personal experience. Studies of anti-Semitism (anti-Jewish prejudice) consistently show higher levels of anti-Semitism in areas such as the South and Midwest that have fewer Jews than other areas of the country. Anti-Semitism is also more prevalent in rural areas than in urban areas, although American Jews are heavily concentrated in cities.

Negative minority group prejudices are dysfunctional and unjust in many ways. Two should be noted here. First, it is inappropriate and unjust to apply a stereotype of a group to all individual members of that group. This is the case even when there is a kernel of truth in the stereotype. During the mid-1960s, a Wayne, New Jersey, school board election became the focus of a national controversy when an incumbent member of the board urged the community to vote against two Jewish candidates saying, "They're liberal like all Jews, and they'll spend all our money." Ironically, the man who said this professed to like the two Jewish candidates personally, and sociologists who interviewed him later concluded that he really did. He was puzzled and hurt to find himself labeled a bigot (Stark and Steinberg 1967). He believed—correctly—that American Jews *as a group* had a more liberal voting record than Protestants or Catholics, so he felt justified in applying that characteristic to *all* Jews. Such reasoning can provide a basis for institutional racism, as the box on page 302 "Racism without Racists" discusses.

Second, minority group stereotypes constitute a point of view through which people see the world

—and what they "see" is conditioned by their point of view. If you believe that all women are emotional

The Language of Prejudice

Prejudice in some ways resembles language. Like language, prejudice has a syntax—a system of rules—that designates which adjectives can properly be attached to which social groups. "Primitive," "lazy," and "immoral" are typically applied to blacks, not to Jews. Jews are identified as "rich," "unethical," "clannish"; Italians as "greasy" or "impulsive"; Poles as "dumb"; Mexicans as "shiftless"; Japanese as "sneaky"; Catholics as "priest-ridden" and "superstitious"; women as "passive," "emotional," and "incompetent."

The most important similarity between prejudice and language is the ease with which both are acquired. Prejudice is typically learned as easily, and in much the same way, as language itself. From the time they are very young, children hear the adjective "lazy" attached to blacks, "shady" to Jews, "emotional" to women, just as they learn that men are "strong," the earth is "round," and a particular laundry soap leaves clothes "dazzling."

Once these images are adopted, they operate as filters through which individuals perceive and interpret the world. Should they encounter blacks who appear lazy, they interpret this as confirming the stereotype. At the same time, they filter out all those cases that are inconsistent with the stereotype. Our society has no image of whites as lazy, so the unambitious white, like the industrious black, is either unnoticed or dismissed as an exception. This self-confirming mechanism is part of the reason why people cling to their prejudices so stubbornly. How do you think this process might be changed so as to reduce stereotypes?

Source: Stephen Steinberg, "The Language of Prejudice," Today's Education, February 1971.

and irrational, you are likely to "see" only emotional and irrational women. If you believe that all Germans are rude, you will only meet rude Germans. If a female does something stupid and dangerous on the highway, she is likely to be called a "woman driver"; a male doing the same thing will only be called a "bad" driver.

Reasons for Prejudice

People come to share negative agreements regarding minority groups for many reasons. Scapegoating is one. Troubled by problems, personal, societal, or other, people search for causes. A man who loses his job at a time of high unemployment may seek a "culprit" at work. Blacks, women, or Chicanos may be seen as cutting into the job market by working cheaply; or the "international Jewish banking conspiracy" may be identified as the source of the problem. People unhappy about the general liberalization of sexual attitudes and practices in America may blame the loss of their jobs on Communists, hippies, pornographers, or homosexuals.

Competition is another common reason for prejudice. Competition can center on jobs, houses, education, mates, or any other scarce commodity. Competition from immigrant groups, blacks, and women have fueled prejudices against them.

Projection often lies at the heart of prejudice. We may "see" in others those things we fear in ourselves. Thus, people unsure about their own intelligence willingly agree that the members of some minority groups are less intelligent. People uncertain about their own honesty "see" dishonesty in others.

Racism without Racists

Racism is ordinarily thought of as a trait of individuals who harbor prejudiced beliefs or engage in discriminatory behavior. However, there is another form of racism that is more subtle and more insidious, one that does not involve specific individuals acting in a self-consciously racist manner. This form of racism is called "institutional racism." In their book *Black Power*, Carmichael and Hamilton illustrate the difference between individual racism and institutional racism in the following way:

> When white terrorists bomb a black church and kill five black children, that is an act of individual racism, widely deplored by most segments of the society. But when in that same city —Birmingham, Alabama—five hundred black babies die each year because of the lack of proper food, shelter and medical facilities, and thousands more are destroyed and maimed physically, emotionally, and intellectually because of conditions of poverty and discrimination in the black community, that is a function of institutional racism.

The concept of institutional racism is important because it draws attention to the fact that practices that are not intended to be racist may be racist in their consequences. For example, until recently law schools admitted only students who excelled on their law-school entrance exams. Because racial minorities typically receive inferior schooling and have many other disabilities to overcome, few could compete with white middle-class students on these supposedly "objective" tests. The admissions procedures of law schools, although not overtly racist, had racist consequences. All but a few minority applicants were excluded from the nation's law schools, and minority communities were deprived of badly needed legal representation. This is one of the ways an apparently unbiased practice can unwittingly perpetuate existing inequalities.

Can you think of other examples of institutional racism? What policies are called for to combat institutional racism?

Source: Stokely Carmichael and Charles Hamilton, Black Power *(New York: Random House, 1967).*

More generally, minority groups can represent a threat to the agreements we share because they often share different sets of agreements among themselves. Hindus are a threat to Christians, homosexuals are a threat to heterosexuals, intellectuals are a threat to the uneducated. And when a minority group reifies *its* agreements about what is true, the threat we perceive is all the more pressing. The homosexual who sadly confesses to being "sick" is less a threat to heterosexuals than one who openly declares that homosexuality is right.

In contrast to these factors supporting prejudice is the strongest factor working against it. Research in prejudice has consistently shown that better-educated people are less prejudiced against minority groups than less-educated people. Education generally exposes agreements as only agreements and works against their reification. In large part, this happens because people are exposed to the variety of agreements that others have created in different times and places. They are also exposed to information that contradicts negative stereotypes.

Now that we have considered prejudice and discrimination in general, let's turn to some of the minority groups in America. We'll begin with racial and ethnic minorities, look next at women as a minority, and conclude with a brief examination of some other minorities.

Racial Minorities

Race is a much abused term. In popular usage, it often conjures up the image of "blood" and unchangeable "instincts." Very often it is the basis for ranking groups of people in terms of superiority and inferiority, as the Nazis did in defining the Aryan "super race" as superior to the Jews.

Biologists and physical anthropologists offer no support for these popular notions.

> Anthropologists and geneticists speak of race to refer to a population sharing characteristics known to be inherited genetically. These specialists insist that the major biological types into which mankind is often divided—Caucasoid, Mongoloid, and Negroid—are only convenient statistical categories and that no clear lines of demarcation can be drawn. Ironically, the actual, measurable hereditary differences among human beings are often of little consequence in the affairs of men (Shibutani and Kwan 1965:39).

The agreements people share about "race," of course, are of far greater consequence. If people with quite different genetic makeups agree that they are of the same race or if people of similar genetic makeups agree that they are of different races, then "race" matters greatly. "Race," ironically, is more important in the sociological point of view than in the biological point of view.

Table 12·1 describes the "racial" composition of the population of the United States according to the 1970 census. You should bear in mind that the listing

Table 12·1 The Racial Composition of the United States, 1970

Racial group	Numbers	Percentage
White	177,748,975	87.47
Black	22,580,289	11.11
American Indian	792,730	.39
Japanese	591,290	.29
Chinese	435,062	.22
All other	1,063,580	.35
Total	203,211,926	100.00

Source: U.S. Bureau of the Census, Census of Population: 1970. Characteristics of the Population, *1973, p. 262.*

reflects an agreement as to what a race is and that the data represent the ways in which people classified themselves in completing census forms.

The numbers describing the various groups only tell a part of the story. The remainder of this section is devoted to brief examinations of each of the racial minorities shown in Table 12·1. We'll be primarily interested in assessing the amount of prejudice and discrimination directed against each.

Blacks

Brought to America as slaves from Africa, blacks were legally declared to be human beings by an act of Congress in 1868, following ratification of the Fourteenth Amendment. Their struggle for equality began then and still continues.

In a 1964 national survey, Gertrude Jaeger Selznick and Stephen Steinberg found one white in five saying no when asked: "In general, do you think that Negroes are as intelligent as white people—that is, can they learn things just as well if they are given the same education and training?" (1969:171).

Of southern whites, 37 percent denied that blacks were as intelligent as whites, compared with 12 percent of northern whites. In the same study, 40 percent of all whites agreed that "generally speaking, Negroes are lazy and don't like to work hard" (Selznick and Steinberg 1969:171). Of the southern whites, 55 percent agreed, as did a third of the northerners.

Antiblack sterotypes generally persist, but there have been notable changes. In 1932, a team of Princeton researchers asked undergraduates to select from a list of eight-four adjectives the five that best described each of several groups (Katz and Braly 1933). Eighty-four percent chose "superstitious" as one of the five adjectives best describing blacks, followed by "lazy" (26 percent), "happy-go-lucky" (38 percent), "ignorant" (38 percent), "musical" (26 percent), "ostentatious" (26 percent), "very religious" (24 percent), and "stupid" (22 percent, in addition to the 38 percent for "ignorant").

In 1967, another team of researchers repeated the study among the Princeton undergraduates of that year (Karlins 1969). "Superstitious" had declined to 13 percent, and the combination of "ignorant" and "stupid" accounted for only 15 percent of the choices.

In 1967, the leading choices were: "musical" (47 percent), "happy-go-lucky" (27 percent), "lazy" (26 percent), "pleasure-loving" (26 percent), and "ostentatious" (25 percent).

These data illustrate the persistence of stereotypes in the face of contradictory evidence. In 1966, the Watts district of Los Angeles was rocked by racial riots and violence that captured headlines around the world. In 1967, there were violent riots in Detroit, New York, Rochester, Birmingham, and elsewhere. In that same year, 27 percent of the Princeton undergraduates studied said that "happy-go-lucky" was one of the five adjectives best describing blacks.

Sociological research data also point to the continued willingness of whites to discriminate against blacks in America. Table 12·2 presents some of the data reported in the Selznick-Steinberg study mentioned earlier. Among other things, in 1964 60 percent of the whites interviewed said they thought "there should be a law against marriages between Negroes and whites."

Table 12·2 Whites' Attitudes towards Discrimination against Blacks, 1964

Percent who agreed that	North	South	Total
"An owner of property should not have to sell to Negroes if he doesn't want to."	89	96	91
"A restaurant owner should not have to serve Negroes if he doesn't want to."	47	82	56
"Before Negroes are given equal rights, they have to show that they deserve them."	58	74	62
"To be frank, I would not like my child to go to school with a lot of Negroes."	47	76	54

Source: Gertrude Jaeger Selznick and Stephen Steinberg, The Tenacity of Prejudice. Copyright © 1969 by Anti-Defamation League of B'nai B'rith. By permission of Harper & Row, Publishers, Inc.

Some people are effectively left out of every society. Minority group members are denied an equal share of the good things in life and often pit themselves against the system. (Hiroji Kubota, Magnum)

Table 12·3 Average Incomes for Selected Occupations in 1970: All Men and Black Men

Occupation	Total for men	Black men only
Accountants	$10,627	$ 8,447
Architects	13,447	10,433
Engineers	13,149	10,444
Lawyers and judges	15,000	12,914
Physicians and dentists	15,000	14,380
Social scientists	13,356	11,045
Secondary school teachers	9,002	7,991
Airplane pilots	15,000	8,974
Writers, artists, entertainers	9,444	6,589
School administrators	11,612	7,520
Real estate agents and brokers	10,295	7,869
Retail-sales clerks	5,532	4,511
Bakers	6,422	5,161
Carpenters	7,001	4,545
Assemblers	6,947	6,391
Farm laborers and foremen	2,619	1,866
Policemen and detectives	8,962	8,391

Source: U.S. Bureau of the Census, Statistical Abstract of the United States, 1975, pp. 361–62.

The willingness to discriminate against blacks is mirrored in the actual status of blacks in American society. In 1975, for example, the unemployment rate of blacks (13.9 percent) was almost double that of whites (7.8 percent). Unemployment rates were much higher for persons from sixteen to nineteen years of age in general, but the situation was far worse for blacks (40.6 percent) than for whites (19.2 percent) (U.S. Department of Labor 1976:70, 142).

Even when blacks are employed in "good" jobs, they earn less money, on the average, than whites. The 7 million men employed in professional and technical jobs in 1970 earned an average of $10,735. The blacks among them, however, earned an average of $7,763. Of the men employed as managers and administrators 5 million earned an average of $11,277; the blacks among them earned only an average of $7,439. This discrepancy was not limited to the higher-status jobs. The 50 million men in the labor force in 1970 earned an average of $7,610. Compare

this with $5,194 for black men (U.S. Bureau of the Census 1975a:361). Table 12·3 presents the average incomes of a few selected occupations. Not only are blacks disproportionately employed in lower-paying occupations, then, they are also simply paid less than other workers, even within a particular occupation.

Employment and income are only two among many instances of discrimination against blacks in America. What we have seen in those respects, however, illustrates the pattern that can also be found in relation to education, politics, health care, criminal victimization, and many other areas of life. The box "We Made It, Why Haven't They?" provides an overview of the many special problems facing blacks as a minority group in America.

American Indians

Unlike blacks, the native American Indians were not brought to the United States as slaves. They were here before there *was* a United States, and many, living and dead, have or had good reason to wish there had never been a United States. From the very beginning, the white colonists and settlers of the West robbed the Indians of their lands and carried out atrocities that all races would prefer to forget.

The general status of Indians in America today is worse than that of blacks, as Zanden (1972:188) indicates:

Forty-two percent of Indian school children (almost double the national average) drop out before completing high school; nearly 60 percent have less than an eighth-grade education. Unemployment reaches 40 percent, nearly ten times the national average. Fifty percent of Indian families have incomes below $2,000 a year, 75 percent below $3,000. Overall, poverty is widespread (the oil-rich Osages of Oklahoma are the exception), making the Indians America's most deprived minority. Infant mortality is 36 deaths per 1,000 (at least 10 points above the national average) and average life expectancy is 44 years. Rates of tuberculosis, dysentery, enteritis, trachoma, pneumonia, and alcoholism are high. Even at present, more than 70 percent of reservation Indians haul their drinking water a mile or more, often from unsanitary sources.

"We Made It, Why Haven't They?"

One frequently hears the question: "We made it, why haven't they?" In this case, "we" refers to European immigrants and their children, "they" to blacks and other racial minorities. Typically the question is asked invidiously, that is, to imply that blacks lacked the "guts and determination" or some other quality that is assumed to account for immigrant success. The question received more serious examination by the National Advisory Commission on Civil Disorders, better known as. the Kerner Commission. This commission isolated five factors that explain why blacks have been unable to escape from poverty and the ghetto in the same way that European immigrants have.

1. *The maturing economy.* Immigrants came at a time when the economy was undergoing a tremendous expansion and there was a drastic shortage of workers. Indeed, this is why the nation opened its doors to so many immigrants in the first place. In contrast, blacks have been coming to northern cities at a time of high unemployment. Furthermore, the unskilled and semiskilled jobs that provided an economic foothold for immigrants have been decreasing in number and importance, making it much more difficult to get jobs and escape from poverty.

2. *The disability of race.* Although European immigrants suffered from prejudice and discrimination, it was not as virulent or as pervasive as in. the case of blacks. In the South, blacks were kept down by a ruthless system of exploitation and oppression. And in the North, the industries that provided employment for millions of immigrants typically had a "color line" that excluded blacks altogether. Had blacks instead of immigrants been hired in the growing industries of the North, then we might today be asking why so few immigrants "made it" into the middle classes.

3. *Entry into the political system.* Immigrants had political opportunities that never existed for blacks. Many immigrant groups have had their turn controlling urban political machines, but blacks have rarely controlled even their own communities, much less the enormous resources of urban government.

4. *Cultural factors.* Immigrants were poor at a time when the standard of living was generally low, and they could look forward to a brighter future. As a consequence, they were able to maintain stable families and communities and a sense of optimism. Today, however, ghetto blacks are surrounded by affluence, and their prospects are bleak. It is hardly surprising that severe strains are placed on family and community and that the mood is often one of resignation and despair.

5. *A vital element of time.* Immigrants forget that when they were immersed in poverty, they too lived in slums that produced high rates of alcoholism, desertion, illegitimacy, and other pathologies associated with poverty. Blacks have only recently moved to the cities, and their escape from poverty will also take several generations. The structure of opportunity is less favorable than in the past, however, and the commission's report ended on a pessimistic note: "What the American economy of the late nineteenth century and early twentieth century was able to do to help the European immigrant escape from poverty is now largely impossible. New channels of escape must be found for the majority of today's poor."

What policies or programs do you think are necessary to provide "new channels of escape"?

Source: Report of the National Advisory Commission on Civil Disorders *(New York: Bantam, 1968).*

The original Americans have become a curiosity for the late arrivals. This man does not want to be photographed because he believes that those who have your photograph have power over you. (Henri Cartier-Bresson, Magnum)

An Indian scholar, Chris Cavender (1972), has suggested that the status of Indians in America is related to the negative stereotypes of them that have been maintained by school textbooks. Cavender quotes the following description of a massacre. This description exemplifies the image most Americans have shared regarding the way the "savages" dealt with white settlers.

> They were scalped. Their brains were knocked out; the men used their knives, ripped open women, clubbed little children, knocked them in the head with their guns, beat their brains out, mutilated their bodies in every sense of the word (Dulles 1959:41).

Outrageous? The passage I've just quoted is a description from a white witness of the way *white*

soldiers dealt with the Cheyenne encampment at Sand Creek in 1864. Though Chief Black Kettle had been guaranteed safety for his people, the Colorado militia struck suddenly and killed 500 men, women, and children. A century later, the original Americans have been immortalized as brutal savages.

Asian-Americans

Asian-Americans began migrating to the United States in significant numbers in the later part of the nineteenth century, when they served as imported labor in the development of the West Coast and Hawaii. According to the 1970 census, there were approximately half a million each of Japanese- and Chinese-Americans in the United States.

Early Chinese-American history was woven into the context of western expansion and the California gold rush. Chinese immigrants built railroads, highways, and buildings. They worked the mines. And, as Zanden (1972:207) reports: "By virtue of the shortage of women in the frontier West, Chinese men were also hired to do work usually done by women, such as cooking, washing, and gardening." This historical quirk was to lay the basis for Chinese-American business enterprise later on.

Whenever the economy suffered, as in the business crash of 1876, however, the Chinese-Americans often bore the brunt of peoples' anger and frustration. Cheap Asian labor was often seen as the source of economic ills, and persecution, burning, and bloodshed often were the proposed antidotes.

Japanese-Americans have had a similar history. First brought to this country as plantation workers, they worked hard, saved their money, and slowly left the plantations to establish businesses and enter professions.

Japanese-American progress suffered a severe setback on December 7, 1941. With the bombing of Pearl Harbor, Japanese aliens and citizens of Japanese ancestry alike were cast in the role of potential saboteurs. The informal agreement was formalized on February 19, 1942, with the issuance of Executive Order No. 9066, authorizing the secretary of war to establish detention camps for persons of Japanese ancestry. Approximately 110,000 Japanese—two-thirds of them United States citizens—were taken from their homes and placed in ten "war relocation centers" in the West and Midwest (Masaoka 1972).

Some homes and businesses were confiscated. More fortunate Japanese were able to get friends to occupy their homes and run their businesses during the period of relocation. Others were able to hire "managers" at very high salaries. In 1942, the Federal Reserve Board estimated that the evacuation cost the Japanese residents approximately 400 million dollars (Masaoka 1972).

National and Religious Minorities

Caucasians constitute the dominant majority in American life, but that group is far from homogeneous and contains within it several **ethnic minorities.** Sociologists use the term "ethnic" to refer to religion and/or national origin. Very often, because of the ambiguities inherent in the term "race," the term is also applied to "racial" groups.

In this section, we will look at some of the larger ethnic groups in America, paying special attention to their experiences with prejudice and discrimination.

To set the stage for the discussion, look at Figure 12·1. It describes some ingredients of what is commonly called the American "melting pot." Part of the melting-pot character of the country comes from people's differing religious orientations. Protestants constitute the dominant religious majority in America. Nonetheless, in 1974, approximately one-fourth of the United States population were members of the Roman Catholic church, and approximately 3 percent were members of Jewish congregations, as I reported previously (Table 9·3). We will also discuss these two religious minority groups.

European Immigrants

Most Americans are descendants of immigrants to the New World, most typically from Europe. The earliest immigrants came, of course, from the British

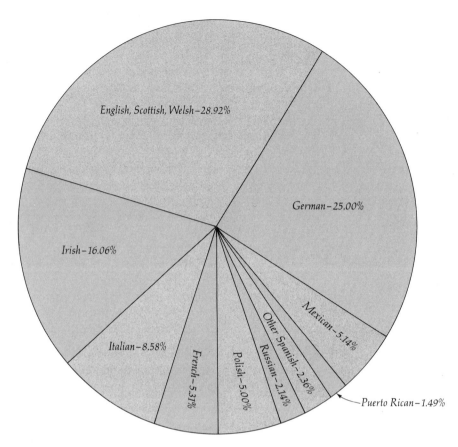

Figure 12·1   National origins of American whites, 1973. Source: U.S. Bureau of the Census, Statistical Abstract of the United States, 1975,*p. 34. (This figure omits the sizeable number of whites that the Bureau of the Census lists as "other," "mixed," and "not reported.")*

Isles, and over a fourth of today's population are English, Scottish, or Welsh by national origin. As a group, they escaped persecution. The culture they brought with them to America, instead, formed the baseline of agreements that permitted the persecution of the native Americans and the subsequent waves of immigration from elsewhere.

From the early days of nationhood, English-Americans feared the influence of other European immigrants. Benjamin Franklin expressed concern over the persistence of German culture and language in the New World (Gordon 1964). Thomas Jefferson was concerned for the survival of major American cultural agreements, suggesting the immigrants would:

bring with them the principles of the governments they leave, imbibed in their early youth; or, if able to throw them off, it will be in exchange for an unbounded licentiousness, passing, as is usual, from one extreme to another. It would be a miracle were they to stop precisely at the point of temperate liberty. These principles, with their language, they will transmit to their children (Quoted in Gordon 1964:91).

The mass immigration that Franklin, Jefferson, and others feared occurred around the middle of the nineteenth century when millions of German, Irish, and other European immigrants came to America seeking opportunity, often in flight from economic depression and political persecution in their native lands.

What many found in the New World was far different from what they had bargained for. They represented an economic threat to many earlier immigrants and their descendants, and their native cultures seemed to differ sharply—as Jefferson had feared—with the mainstream agreements of the new nation. Prejudice, discrimination, even violent riots followed.

The Know-Nothing party of the 1850s was typical of the political-terrorist groups that formed to turn back the waves of foreign immigration. The name of the party was taken from the members' agreement that they would say they knew nothing if questioned by authorities (others felt the label was even more ironically appropriate than intended).

Overall, the European immigrants eventually melted themselves into the American pot, changing American agreements as they did so. But many of the prejudices and stereotypes that marked their arrival in America still persist. In the 1967 study we mentioned earlier in this chapter, Princeton undergraduates said the Irish were best described as "quick-tempered" and "extremely nationalistic." Italians were seen as "passionate" and "pleasure-loving." Germans fared somewhat better, being described as primarily "industrious" and "scientifically minded" (Karlins 1969). These stereotypes are probably a close reflection of the agreements shared by Americans generally, although we should add the Hollywood-perpetuated stereotype of Italians as gangsters.

Jews

It seems likely that Jews have had as much experience with prejudice and discrimination as any group of people in history. Migration to the United States offered little exception to that experience.

In part, the Jews suffered the same prejudice and discrimination as the other European immigrants and for many of the same reasons. Their disagreement with the mainstream Christianity of the nation, however, always set them further apart than the others. The persistence of anti-Semitic stereotypes and prejudice in America is best seen in the findings of the 1964 national survey reported by Selznick and Steinberg. Table 12·4 presents some of the agreements Americans share about Jews.

Table 12·4 Potentially Negative Beliefs about Jews

Belief	True	False	Don't know
Jews still think of themselves as God's chosen people	59	17	24
Jews always like to be at the head of things	54	32	14
Jews stick together too much	52	38	10
Jewish employers go out of their way to hire other Jews	49	32	19
The movie and television industries are pretty much controlled by Jews	47	21	32
Jews are more willing than other people to use shady practices to get what they want	42	46	12
International banking is pretty much controlled by Jews	30	24	46
Jews are more loyal to Israel than to America	30	47	23
Jews don't care what happens to anyone but their own kind	26	62	12
Jews today are trying to push in where they are not wanted	18	68	14
Jews have too much power in the United States	11	77	12
Jews are always stirring up trouble with their ideas	10	70	20

Source: Taken from Gertrude Jaeger Selznick and Stephen Steinberg, The Tenacity of Prejudice. Copyright © 1969 by Anti-Defamation League of B'nai B'rith. By permission of Harper & Row, Publishers, Inc.

The 1964 survey results also point to a continued willingness among Americans to discriminate against Jews or at least to tolerate discrimination. One person in five said they would favor "a law to stop more Jews from immigrating to this country" (Selznick and Steinberg 1969:60–61). Another one person in four didn't care one way or the other. Thus, a bare majority said they would be opposed to such a law.

Apathy toward the discrimination others might wish to practice was a common pattern uncovered by the study. For example, the survey asked: "If a candidate for Congress should declare himself as being against the Jews, would this influence you to vote for him or to vote against him?" A majority (58 percent) said they would vote against such a candidate, compared with only 5 percent who said they would vote for him. The sizable minority remaining, however, said the candidate's anti-Semitism wouldn't influence them one way or the other. Many explained by saying they "vote on the basis of issues," evidently feeling that prejudice and discrimination are not political issues (Selznick and Steinberg 1969:54).

Roman Catholics

A good deal of the hostility and violence greeting the European migrants was directed specifically at Catholics. The Know-Nothing and Anti-Mason parties were formed largely in opposition to the immigration of Catholics. Even the Ku Klux Klan, formally committed to "maintain forever the God-given supremacy of the White Race" (Zanden 1972: 89), has traditionally taken violent exception to Catholics, along with Jews, Communists, and "foreigners."

The accompanying box, "Catholics and Jews in the American University," offers an interesting comparison. The box illustrates the initial differences among ethnic groups arriving in America and the reduction of those differences over time.

Spanish-Speaking Minorities

Recently immigration of people from traditionally Spanish-speaking parts of the world has increased. Few people have come from Spain itself; mostly they have come from Mexico, Puerto Rico, and Cuba. As recent arrivals in the United States, they are currently very visible as a minority group facing much the same out-group treatment that earlier immigrants did. At present, these three major groups are concentrated in different areas of the United States: Chicanos (from Mexico) in Southern California and the South-west, Puerto Ricans in New York City, and Cubans in Miami.

Many Chicanos, the largest of the Spanish-speaking groups, have been visible as agricultural workers, but the great majority of all the Spanish-speaking minorities live in cities. In 1974, when just over two-thirds of all Americans lived in metropolitan areas, for example, the figure for Spanish-speaking people was 82.5 percent overall and even higher among the Puerto Ricans (94.2 percent) and Cubans (91.4 percent) (U.S. Bureau of the Census 1975b:27).

Economically, Spanish-speaking Americans fall between other whites and black Americans. Table 12·5 presents Department of Labor statistics for 1974, showing the median family incomes for the several Spanish-speaking groups, in comparison with other whites and blacks. The table also shows the percentages in each group earning less than $5,000 and more than $15,000 as indications of poverty versus moderate wealth.

As Table 12·5 shows, the Cubans stand out among the Spanish-speaking minorities in America. Most of them came to the United States shortly after Fidel Castro came to power in Cuba; many were educated professionals and business people (Rose and Rose 1972). At first, they settled in Miami with the expectation of returning to Cuba when Castro

Table 12·5 Annual Family Incomes in America, 1974

Type of family	Median	Percent below $5,000	Percent $15,000 or above
All American families	$12,044	14.1	39.8
Whites	13,356	11.1	42.0
Blacks	7,808	29.5	22.3
Spanish total	8,715	23.0	18.4
Mexican	8,435	23.3	15.8
Puerto Rican	6,779	33.5	12.5
Cuban	11,191	15.5	27.7
Other	7,203	20.4	19.6

Source: *U.S. Bureau of the Census*, Current Population Reports, *Series P-20, No. 280, 1975, p. 32; Ibid., Series P-60, No. 101, 1976, pp. 11, 19, 27.*

Catholics and Jews in the American University

Historically, Jews in America have produced a disproportionate number of the nation's scholars and scientists. Catholics have, in contrast, been underrepresented in American colleges and universities relative to their number in the general population. A common explanation for this difference is that Jewish religion and culture place a high value on intellectual achievement, whereas Catholics regard education with suspicion, fearing that it will undermine faith and morals. A recent study casts doubt on this popular cultural theory.

Data indicate that Catholics have been increasing their representation among faculty in American colleges and universities. This is shown in the table below, which reports the religious background among faculty of different ages.

Among the oldest group of faculty—those over 55—Catholics were only 14.8 percent of the total. But among younger groups, this figure rises steadily—from 14.8 to 16.9 to 19.2 to 20.5 percent. Among graduate students planning a career in college teaching, Catholics are 22.2 percent, which is almost as high as the Catholic proportion in the nation as a whole (25 percent). Thus, within the foreseeable future Catholics will be producing their numerical share of the nation's scholars. The figures indicate, in contrast, that Jewish representation has been tapering off.

Why, then, did Jews get a head start in American higher education, and how is it that Catholics have been able to close the gap? The answers to these questions seem to have little to do with culture as such, and more to do with differences between Catholics and Jews in their countries of origin. In Eastern Europe most Jews lived in urban areas. When they immigrated to America they brought industrial skills that were in great demand at that time. Unlike Jews, most Catholic immigrants came from peasant backgrounds. They had a much higher rate of illiteracy and lacked occupational skills relevant to urban and industrial conditions. The two groups had "unequal" beginnings, and it has taken Catholics longer than Jews to work their way into the middle class. However, as Catholics have gradually improved their economic and social position, their children are increasingly going to college, and as in every group, a certain number of them pursue careers as scholars and scientists. Social class, then, appears to be at the root of whatever cultural differences once existed between Catholic and Jewish immigrants.

How does this discussion apply to groups other than Catholics and Jews? Can you think of other examples where "achievement" is better explained in terms of social class rather than in terms of culture?

Religious background	Age of faculty				Graduate students planning a career in college teaching
	55+	45–54	35–44	34–	
Protestant	75.7%	69.0%	63.2%	62.6%	57.8%
Catholic	14.8	16.9	19.2	20.5	22.2
Jewish	5.5	8.2	9.5	9.6	9.6
Other	2.1	2.9	4.4	3.9	4.5
None	1.9	3.0	3.7	3.4	5.9
Total	100.0%	100.0%	100.0%	100.0%	100.0%

Source: Adapted from Stephen Steinberg, The Academic Melting Pot: Catholics and Jews in American Higher Education. © 1974 by McGraw-Hill Publishing Co., Inc. Reprinted by permission.

was ousted. As it became clear that Castro would remain in power, the Cuban refugees began to migrate to other large cities and to attempt to integrate themselves in American life, although there are almost half a million Cubans still in Miami. Many were educated urban people and adjusted rapidly; many opened small stores and made the same kind of adjustment as Europeans had earlier. They have met discrimination, but they have not had the same difficulties as Puerto Ricans or Mexican-Americans.

Like many European and Asian immigrant groups before them, the Spanish-speaking minorities have faced a language problem, though Department of Labor studies (1973:94) show that this problem is decreasing. Illiteracy in English still exists among older people, but almost all the young are literate. Related to literacy in English, educational levels are being upgraded among Spanish-speaking Americans. As of March 1974, members of the American labor force 55 years of age and older had a median education of 12.1 years. The Spanish-speaking members of that age group had only 8.2 years of education. Among workers aged from 16 to 19, however, the figures were 11.5 for all workers as compared to 11.1 for the Spanish-speaking (U.S. Bureau of the Census 1975b:66). On balance, then, conditions are improving for the Spanish-speaking minorities in America. As a group, however, their status is still well below the status of Americans as a whole.

America has countless other ethnic minorities, and it would be impossible to discuss them all here. I would like you to know that I regret not doing so, since the agreements that keep minority groups in their disadvantaged status have always persisted most when ignored. Each of the racial and ethnic minority groups discussed so far has at one time or another been described as the "invisible Americans" or the "forgotten Americans." The first step in changing the agreements upon which minority group status is based is awareness that the agreements are agreements only, nothing more.

Women as a Minority Group

We turn our attention now to a "minority" group that in numbers composes a slight majority of the American population: women. Women are clearly a minority group as the term is used within the sociological point of view. Throughout our national history, women have been denied equal participation in countless sectors of society. Black Americans were denied the right to vote until 1870, but it took women another half century to get that right.

The status of women in America has, in large part, grown out of our agreements regarding the family, discussed in Chapter 8. A persistent American agreement has been summarized in the cliché: "A woman's place is in the home." More specifically, the woman's "place" has been in the kitchen—with periodic trips to the children's rooms, the laundry room, and the master's bed.

A variety of stereotypes have effectively kept the American woman in her "place." She has been depicted as emotional, flighty, weak, irrational, and impractical. While these are not the characteristics you might prefer in those chosen to socialize society's new generations, women have frequently been told they were best equipped for raising children. When they objected to that, they have been assured that child rearing is a vital function.

You should not think that American men are a clique of evildoers who have simply bedazzled or subjugated women with such ideas. What I've been describing represents generally shared agreements, and many women—past and present—have accepted those agreements, often willingly. Men and women alike have been socialized into a general acceptance of the roles appropriate to their own sex and the roles appropriate to the other one.

In spite of these factors, both men and women in recent years have begun to recognize such agreements for what they are: agreements. Progress seems slow and painful, but both men and women are working to change those agreements. In this section, we'll look primarily at the status of women in relation to occupational roles in American society. One of the main goals of the American woman's movement has been equal opportunity in the economy.

Participation in the Labor Force

Women in America have never been kept totally at home. There have always been some who found

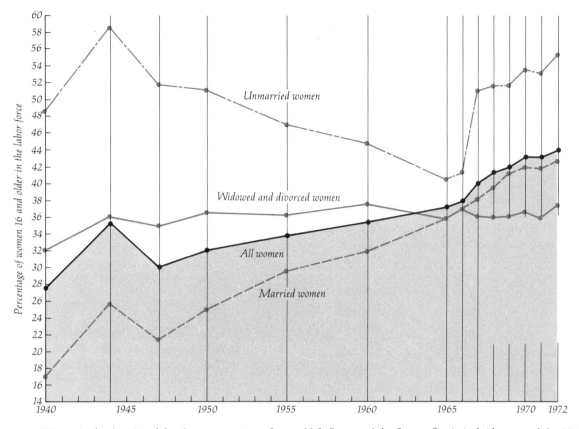

Figure 12•2   Women in the American labor force, 1940–1972. Source: U.S. Bureau of the Census, Statistical Abstract of the United States, 1975, *p. 345.*

employment in the labor force. During wars, in fact, women have been encouraged to take over vital production jobs and fill other positions outside the home.

In recent years, even in peacetime, more women than ever before have sought and found employment. Figure 12•2 shows the percentages of all women sixteen years of age and older who were in the civilian labor force during selected years between 1940 and 1972. In addition to showing the participation of women in general, I have presented married women, unmarried women, and those widowed and divorced.

Figure 12•2 suggests several patterns worth noting. First, we see a general increase in women in the labor force overall: from 27.4 percent in 1940 to 43.6 percent in 1972. Notice that the participation rates of unmarried, widowed, and divorced women—while fluctuating over the three decades—are about

the same in 1972 as they were in 1940. The participation of married women, however, has increased dramatically: from 16.7 to 42.1 percent. This pattern suggests a growing agreement in America that a woman can hold a job and fill family roles at the same time. (It has always been agreed that men could do that.)

Occupation Types

Participation in the labor force is only part of the story, however. *How* women participate is another matter. The American occupational structure has always been quite closely related to sex. There have been a number of agreements defining those jobs more "appropriate" for men and those more "appropriate" for women.

As a general pattern, women have been nurses, not physicians; secretaries, not executives; teachers, not principals; stewardesses, not pilots; clerks, not managers; cooks, not chefs. As these examples illustrate, women have typically filled positions closely associated with, but of lower status than, those of men. Even when men and women served in exactly the same roles, we have often found it necessary to apply different labels to those roles: A woman can be a poetess but not a poet, an actress but not an actor. Other occupational labels have seemed to exclude women altogether: fire*man*, police*man*, mail*man*, chair*man*.

The reification of the agreements linking sex to occupations has become especially evident as more and more people have started to violate them by "crossing over." Male nurses, female jockeys, male typists, and female police officers have seemed "unnatural" to many. When Burt Reynolds posed nude for a centerfold in *Cosmopolitan* magazine, many of those who for years had enjoyed *Playboy* and *Penthouse,* magazines that feature nude women, were horrified.

It is important to realize that many of the agreements Americans share with regard to sex-linked occupations are *not* shared elsewhere. Only 3 percent of lawyers in America are women, but 38 percent of those in the U.S.S.R. are women. Women constitute less than 1 percent of American engineers, but 37 percent are women in the U.S.S.R. Women make up 6 percent of the medical profession in America, but they are an astounding 76 percent of the U.S.S.R. medical profession (Sullerot 1974). The shared American belief that women are intellectually and emotionally ill-equipped to be doctors, lawyers, and engineers (thereby excluding them from such professions) was and is only an agreement.

Income

When women do work, they are often paid less than men, as Figure 12•3 shows. Between 1950 and 1971, women in the American labor force earned roughly half as much as men. And while the average incomes of both men and women have increased (as has the cost of living) during the past two decades, women's *relative* income status has gotten worse. In 1950, the average woman in the labor force earned

Double Jeopardy

Every minority status involves a social stigma and carries with it numerous disadvantages. To occupy more than one minority status, however, amounts to double jeopardy. A prime example of double jeopardy is the case of black women. They are confronted with one set of disabilities because they are black and another set because they are women.

The combined effect of racism and sexism manifests itself most clearly in the job marketplace. Black women are heavily concentrated in the most exploitative sectors of the economy. Large numbers work as domestics and hospital workers; many others work in the garment trades and as low-level clerical workers. These jobs involve menial, dirty, and often backbreaking work at pitifully low wages. The net effect of double jeopardy in terms of wages is demonstrated in the following figures, which show the incomes of white and black men and women in 1967:

White Males	$6,704
Nonwhite Males	4,277
White Females	3,991
Nonwhite Females	2,861

As the figures show, white women earn substantially less than white men and nonwhite men alike. The wage scale for nonwhite women is the lowest of all.

This is only one of the more conspicuous ways in which black women suffer from a double jeopardy. Can you think of others?

Source: Frances M. Beal: "Double Jeopardy: To Be Black and Female," in Liberation NOW! *(New York: Dell, 1974).*

55 percent as much as the average man. In 1971, she earned 48 percent as much. As the accompanying box ("Double Jeopardy") shows, black women carry a double burden.

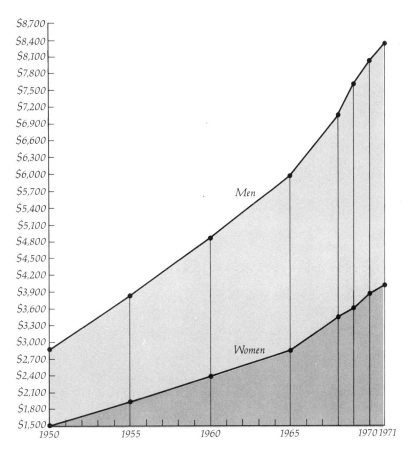

Figure 12•3   Average incomes of employed civilian men and women, 1950–1971. Source: U.S. Bureau of the Census, Statistical Abstract of the United States, 1974, *p. 361.*

Part of the explanation for women's generally lower incomes lies in their general concentration in lower-paying occupations, as I have mentioned earlier. Nurses earn less than physicians; secretaries earn less than executives.

Even this is not a sufficient explanation, however, since women earn less money on the average, even when they are employed in the same occupations as men. Table 12•6 presents a more general comparison of the incomes earned by men and women in several occupational categories. Notice that women earn less on the average than men in *each* occupational category.

While women's incomes vary from 28 percent (sales workers) to 65 percent (nonfarm laborers) of men's incomes, this variation does not seem to be

related to either the general level of income for the category or the predominance or absence of women in it. "Private household service worker" is the most poorly paid category for both men and women, and it is the most nearly all-woman category. Women earn 52 percent as much as men on the average. While the greater participation of men in college might account for some of the income differences in higher-status occupations, it would have no bearing on those occupations where college experience is neither required nor common. Women earn less than men in all occupational categories.

Researchers at the University of Michigan (Levitin, Quinn, and Staines 1970) undertook a national survey on occupation and employment to examine in detail the charge that women are discrim-

Table 12·6   Average Incomes of Men and Women in Occupational Categories, 1970

Occupational category	Average income		Average women's income as percentage of average men's	Women as percentage of category
	Men	Women		
Professional and technical	$10,735	$6,034	56	47
Managers and administrators	$11,277	$5,495	49	17
Sales workers	$ 8,451	$2,338	28	40
Clerical workers	$ 7,265	$4,232	58	74
Artisans	$ 8,172	a	a	a
Operatives				
Transportation	$6,903	$2,574	37	4
Other	$6,730	$3,635	54	39
Service workers				
Private household	$1,891	$ 986	52	97
Other	$5,100	$2,320	45	56
Laborers				
Farm	$2,570	$1,087	42	17
Other	$4,617	$2,988	65	83

ªData not reported for women.

Source: Calculated from data presented in U.S. Bureau of the Census, Statistical Abstract of the United States, *1975, pp. 361–64.*

inated against in income. They began their analysis of the data by selecting half the men surveyed and by studying carefully the relative importance of different factors in determining their incomes. They considered the type of occupation, years of experience in it, education and special training completed, and many other relevant factors. They were able to construct out of those factors a complex equation that they felt would predict the income a given person might expect to receive.

When the researchers applied the equation to the qualifications of the men not used in the construction of the equation, their income estimates were off by about $30 a year (thus reassuring them that they had discovered the determinants of different income levels). When the same equation was applied to the qualifications of the women surveyed, however, the researchers found that those women actually earned over *$3,000 a year less* than their qualifications predicted.

Liberating Both Men and Women

I'd like to conclude this discussion of women as a minority group by observing that the same sets of agreements that have kept women in their "place" have also kept men in their "place." While the man's "place" has generally seemed better than the woman's, neither has been wholly satisfying.

The same agreement that has labeled women "overemotional" has prevented men from learning to express *their* emotions. We have a comic expression that we "hate to see a grown man cry." In practice, "hating to see a grown man cry" is a serious agreement among Americans, even when men have good reasons to cry. The same agreement that labels women "weak" and "soft" requires that men of all ages maintain a strong and tough exterior, even when they don't feel strong and tough.

In reifying our agreements about the differences separating men and women, we have hindered our realization of ourselves as *people*. The liberation of women will inevitably liberate men in the bargain.

There are many other minority groups in America. Among those sociologists have studied are old people, young people, homosexuals, the mentally retarded, to name a few. The preceding discussions, however, should give you a comprehensive view of the experience of minority groups in society. Now let's consider some of the ways minority group members respond to those experiences.

Minority Group Responses

Earlier in the chapter, I indicated that members of minority groups participate in the agreements defining their status as a minority. By this, I mean that minority group members frame their behavior in terms of the agreements just as majority group members do. Thus, the agreement that women are incapable of analytical thought may lead one woman to behave emotionally and another to prove her analytical abilities by devoting her life to the mastery of theoretical physics. Both participate in the agreement to the extent that it determines their actions, even though one participates by denying its truth.

Submission to the Agreements

Some minority group members simply accept that the agreements regarding their status represent "reality." Examples include the black who believes that blacks are "really" less intelligent and lazier than whites and the woman who believes that women are "really" more emotional and irrational than men.

This response should not come as a surprise when you realize that minority group members are—to some degree at least—socialized into the same set of agreements as members of the majority. Young blacks attend schools that offer an educational experience designed primarily by whites. Young girls sit through television commercials that impress on them that their major accomplishment in life will be to get clothes "whiter than white."

When minority group members submit to such agreements, they perpetuate them. If blacks believe

themselves to be less intelligent than whites, they lend support to the reification of the agreement for whites as well.

Modes of Disagreement

Minority groups sometimes respond to the agreements making them a minority with resistance, even with violent aggression against the majority group. Race riots, economic boycotts, and symbolic protests are examples of such resistance.

Flagrant violations of the prevailing agreements can have two quite different consequences. First, such actions can draw attention to the existence of unjust agreements. By making members of the minority group more aware that the agreements are merely agreements, the potential for group solidarity and the creation of power is enhanced. Sometimes, the majority group can be frightened into modifying its agreements.

Resistance can also have a negative effect. It can solidify the prevailing agreements even further by bringing the majority group to their defense. It can make an established point of view more "real." Thus, race riots have often strengthened agreements that the minorities involved represented a threat to a "way of life." Disagreement does not always produce this response, however.

Civil disobedience is a term closely associated with three men—Henry David Thoreau, Mahatma Gandhi, and Martin Luther King, Jr.—and it will be useful to distinguish it from the idea of resistance. "Civil disobedience" has come to mean the acknowledgment of an agreement's existence and the refusal to be governed by it. Thoreau, Gandhi, and King all shared the point of view that aggression against a distasteful agreement meant that the person resisting that agreement was being controlled by it as much as the one who accepted it eagerly. Without violence and without withdrawing into their subcultures, each simply refused to be controlled by those agreements that he did not share. Each continued to live in the society in which the agreements prevailed.

On December 1, 1955, Rosa Parks, a Montgomery seamstress, was riding the city bus home after a hard day's work. In Alabama at that time, there was an agreement that blacks sat in a special section in the back of the bus, and that's what Parks was doing. As the bus became more crowded and the "white" section was filled, the bus driver ordered Parks and three other blacks to give up their seats to whites just getting on the bus.

Rosa Parks chose not to be controlled by the agreements that December day, and in so doing she sparked a revolution in black-white relations in America: a revolution that is still continuing. Parks's refusal and her immediate arrest drew national attention to the situation prevailing in Alabama, showing other blacks that agreements were only agreements and that it was possible not to be run by them.

Montgomery blacks chose to dramatize their disagreement with a nonviolent boycott of the city bus system, forming car pools and walking to work. Black community leaders met to organize the boycott and elected to lead it the Baptist minister Martin Luther King, Jr.

To everyone's surprise, the black boycott of the bus system was virtually total. Blacks had created their own agreement in the midst of the larger society. Very soon, the white power structure began *resisting* the black agreement, which made it more "real." Car-pool drivers were harassed and ticketed by police, and King and other boycott leaders were put in jail. Yet the nonviolent boycott continued. The white resistance drew international attention to the boycott, and support for the blacks came from around the world.

The black leaders in Montgomery had at first envisioned a one-day, symbolic boycott. White resistance changed all that, and the black agreement took on the force of law in November 1956 when the U.S. Supreme Court ruled the segregation of buses unconstitutional. The strength of the agreement within the black community by that time is illustrated in the following account by Ira Peck (1974:41):

> Later that night the Ku Klux Klan rode. Forty cars full of hooded Klansmen drove through the Negro section of town. In the past, the Negroes would probably have gone inside their homes, locked the doors, and turned off the lights. Not this time. They sat on their porches with the lights on. Some even waved at the Klansmen. The KKK couldn't believe it. They quit in disgust after riding a few blocks.

People like Thoreau, Gandhi, and King often seem a people apart, as though they were living in a different reality than the rest of us. In a sense they are, in that they create their own agreements and refuse to have their lives run by agreements they find unjust. Mocked, jailed, beaten, and finally assassinated, King chose to govern his own behavior by a set of agreements he felt were more proper for human relations. A minister, he spoke of the society those agreements represented as a "promised land."

On April 3, 1968, Martin Luther King, Jr., gave his final public speech in Memphis. He had been warned that he would be killed in Memphis. He chose to go anyway, and part of his speech concerned death.

> It doesn't really matter with me now, because I have been to the mountaintop. And I've looked over, and I've seen the promised land. I may not get there with you. But I want you to know that we as a people will get to the promised land. So I'm happy tonight. I'm not worried about anything. I'm not fearing any man (Quoted in Peck 1974:92).

Assimilation

Minority groups often become assimilated into the larger society. The notion of an American "melting pot" is based on the idea of assimilation. Over time, the members of a minority group may come to share many of the predominant agreements of the larger society, becoming for the most part an indistinguishable part of it. Germans, Italians, and Irish people, for example, have largely been assimilated into American society.

The process of **assimilation,** however, affects the larger society's agreements as well. The subcultural values of the groups being assimilated often become a part of the more general culture. Milton Gordon (1964:71), in a pioneering work, has suggested the following steps in the process of assimilation:

1. Change of cultural patterns to those of host society.
2. Large-scale entrance into cliques, clubs, and institutions of host society, on primary group level.
3. Large-scale intermarriage.

4. Development of sense of peoplehood based exclusively on host society.
5. Absence of prejudice.
6. Absence of discrimination.
7. Absence of value and power conflict.

Developing Subcultural Agreements

Very often minority groups respond to the prevailing agreements by withdrawing into their own subculture and developing more consciously their own subcultural agreements. The recent black emphasis on African culture and the growing attention American Indians have given their own cultural heritage are good examples of this response.

Minority groups, then, may acknowledge that their group agreements are different from those of the dominant majority while denying that they are inferior. Sometimes they simply acknowledge that different sets of cultural agreements are *only* different; sometimes they assert that their minority agreements are superior to those of the majority. The latter course, much as aggressive resistance, may spark a counterresponse from the majority.

The general response may also take an extreme form, that of self-segregation, physical separation of the minority from the majority. Frequently in American history, for example, black militants have advocated the establishment of a separate black nation in America or the return of black Americans to Africa. American Indians have sometimes responded in a similar manner.

The accompanying box (titled "What Ethnic Revival?") examines data relevant to the issues of

What Ethnic Revival?

During the 1960s it was widely assumed that the nation was undergoing an "ethnic revival." The revival began with the "soul movement" among blacks, then spread to other Third World groups—Chicanos, Asians, Indians, and Puerto Ricans. Eventually white ethnics got on the ethnic bandwagon, as Jews, Irish, Italians, Poles, and other immigrant groups sought to reaffirm and strengthen their ethnic identities.

Recent studies raise questions concerning the depth and significance of the ethnic revival. For example, a study by Richard Alba[1] of Catholic national-origin groups found that the proportion of people marrying outside their own ethnic group is very high. The figures in the table are based on a 1963 national sample of Catholic people between the ages of twenty-three and fifty-seven.

A study of Jews[2] also found that intermarriage is on the upswing. Among Jews marrying between 1956

[1]Richard D. Alba, "Social Assimilation Among American Catholic National-Origin Groups," *American Sociological Review* (October 1976).

[2]"Intermarriage," National Jewish Population Study, Council of Jewish Federations, New York City.

Ethnic group	Rate of intermarriage
Irish	69%
German	68
Polish	59
French	43
Italian	41

and 1960, only 6 percent married non-Jews. For the period between 1961 and 1965, the figure rose to 17 percent. And by the period 1966–72, the rate of intermarriage again rose sharply—to 32 percent. In other words, among Jews marrying between 1966 and 1972, one out of every three had a non-Jewish spouse.

Instead of asking whether the nation is experiencing an ethnic revival, it might be more appropriate to ask whether ethnic groups are on their way to vanishing altogether.

What do you think? Will they vanish? What sociological factors might keep ethnic groups alive and distinct?

assimilation versus subcultures as responses to minority group status in America. Let's conclude this discussion with an alternative that somewhat bridges the gap between the two.

The Pluralist Society

Pluralism refers to the coexistence of differing points of view in a society. In a pluralistic society members of minority groups are able to maintain their subcultural sets of agreements without withdrawing from the larger society. This differs from the assimilation characteristic of the "melting pot" in which subcultural differences essentially vanish.

The state of Hawaii offers the clearest example of pluralism in the United States. In 1970, whites constituted 39 percent of the state's population, Japanese were 28 percent, Filipinos were 12 percent, Chinese were 7 percent, Hawaiians and part-Hawaiians were 9 percent, and the remaining 5 percent were native Hawaiians, Samoans, Puerto Ricans, blacks, and many other groups (Gardner and Nordyke 1974).

In 1974, Hawaii's voters elected two men of Japanese ancestry as governor and lieutenant governor, and the state was represented in the U.S. Congress by two men and a woman of Japanese ancestry and a man of Chinese ancestry. The state legislature and the agencies of state government were peopled by a variety of races and nationality groups. The mayors of the state's four counties included men of Filipino, Portuguese, and Japanese ancestry, plus an Italian-American from Hartford, Connecticut.

Despite instances of prejudice and discrimination, the many subcultures of Hawaii's people generally flourish. Individuals participate in a variety of subcultures other than their own in clothing styles, food, entertainment, and friends. Intermarriage between racial and ethnic groups is high.

Life in a pluralistic society is not necessarily one of complete harmony and comfort. Many whites migrating to Hawaii are uncomfortable being in a "minority" group, and they are often quick to sense prejudice and discrimination directed against them as whites.

The maintenance of subcultural agreements —necessary in a pluralistic society—appears to require a certain degree of reification. To continue sharing in your own subculture's agreements, you must to some degree feel they have a *special* value, that they are in some ways "better" than the agreements of other subcultures. The Hawaiian experience, however, has shown that it is possible to maintain divergent sets of agreements side by side without violence or the subjugation of one group by another.

Summary

In this chapter, we have examined a variety of topics related to the status of minority groups in a society, especially minorities in America. We began by noting that "minorities," as the term is used in the sociological point of view, are not necessarily numerical minorities. They are groups who have a disproportionately small share of the power and "things" that are distributed in a society.

The first major section of the chapter dealt with the concepts of prejudice and discrimination. Although some discrimination is inherent in all status relations, we saw that the term is typically used in the sense of discrimination *against* the members of a minority group.

Discrimination is a matter of action, but prejudice is a point of view that typically involves negative stereotypes or pictures of a minority group and the negative feelings associated with those pictures. We concluded the discussion with a look at some reasons for prejudice.

The bulk of the chapter was taken up with a few of the various racial and ethnic minorities in American society: blacks, Indians, Japanese, Chinese, Puerto Ricans, and Cubans. Women were also considered as a minority group.

Stereotypes are the pictures that people have about a particular group, and prejudice is the assumption that all members of the group in question have the characteristics making up the stereotype. Discrimination is action taken on the basis of prejudice and stereotypes. Americans have many agreed-on stereotypes about ethnic and racial minorities, and prejudice and discrimination have often flowed from those stereotypes.

Minority groups react in many ways to the agreements that define them as minorities. Sometimes they join in those agreements, either actively or passively. Sometimes they resist the agreements, and that resistance often makes the majority's commitment to the agreements even stronger. Sometimes minority group members engage in civil disobedience, choosing to live in accordance with agreements they feel are more appropriate, without resisting the majority agreements.

Societies are structured around minority groups in different ways. Minority groups may withdraw into subcultures, isolating themselves from the dominant culture. Pluralism is a situation in which different subgroups' points of view are represented in the larger society and coexist with one another. Assimilation refers to the integration of minority groups into the dominant culture—typified by the idea of a "melting pot."

Suggested Readings

Glock, Charles and Ellen Siegelman, Eds.
1969 *Prejudice U.S.A.* New York: Praeger.
During the early 1960s, the Survey Research Center at Berkeley undertook a number of comprehensive studies of contemporary American prejudice. In 1968, the center sponsored a national conference in which leaders from the nation's major institutions were asked to respond to the research findings. This book, drawn from the conference proceedings, offers both sociological and institutional views of prejudice in government, religion, education, the economy, and the mass media.

Gordon, Milton
1964 *Assimilation in American Life.* New York: Oxford University Press.
In this modern classic (sociology has a lot of "classics"), Gordon carefully examines the various ways in which different racial, religious, and national subcultures accommodate one another. Gordon discusses the assimilation of minority groups into the dominant Anglo culture, the proverbial "melting pot," and the issue of cultural pluralism. Throughout, he draws out the implications of such patterns for intergroup relations.

Rose, Arnold and Caroline Rose, Eds.
1972 *Minority Problems.* New York: Harper & Row.
This collection of sociological and nonsociological pieces provides an omnibus view of America's many minority groups. It provides a wealth of historical and statistical data, analytical interpretations, and a human sense of the situations within which minority group members find themselves.

Sullerot, Evelyne
1974 *Woman, Society and Change.* New York: McGraw-Hill.
The nation's oldest and youngest minority group makes up more than half our population. In this examination of women in America, Sullerot examines the history of discrimination and sets the American situation in world context through the reporting of comparative national statistics on employment and other institutional matters.

Episode Twelve

Gabriel Knapp arrived at Phoenix airport at 5 P.M. June 25. Immediately upon entering the terminal he telephoned Jacob Lockwood.

"This is Gabe," he said when he heard his friend's voice. "I'm here in Phoenix. I just got in."

There was a pause.

"What the hell did you say to Dan?" Jacob responded finally. "He's got half of Adamsville convinced you're a heretic."

Gabriel shook his head, shifted his weight. "We just got talking," he explained into the mouthpiece. "I thought maybe I could make him understand." Abruptly Gabriel changed his manner. "Listen," he said, "I've got to get home. They're on to me. I was fired yesterday."

"We can't send anyone for you, Gabe. It's too rough out there. All our posers are home now. No one goes out."

"How's the border? Can I get in?"

"We had some shots fired again yesterday. They're coming from all over now. A group came down from San Francisco last week, threatening to burn S.T.I. They left a pipe bomb near the guard shelter at the south gate." Jacob paused. "You'll have to be very careful," he advised.

"Which is the safest gate?" Gabe asked.

"The north one, I think."

"I have to get in tonight," Gabe said anxiously. "Can I make it through?"

"The FBI is at the south gate," Jacob said. "They're supposed to keep order and protect us. The state patrol is up at the north gate. They should help you get in safely. You haven't broken any laws, have you?"

Gabe laughed aloud at the naiveté of the question.

"I mean *besides* the rescue. You know they can't trace that to you. You didn't leave any evidence."

"Yeah," Gabe responded weakly. By now, he thought to himself, they knew that he had called in sick Wednesday, June 28, 2026.

"Listen, Gabe," Jacob's voice suddenly quickened. "Larry's insisting we don't let you in. He says you've relinquished your right to membership in the community."

"That's impossible! I'm green!"

"Larry says heretics cannot be members of the colony."

"What do the Elders say?" Gabriel asked.

"They want to let you in. They know you don't have anywhere else to go."

"Well, who's in control there, for God's sake?" Gabriel demanded nervously.

"Elderhome officially," Jacob answered, then changed his tone. "Listen, I'll do all I can. I'll phone Elderhome now and have them okay your entry with the guards at the north gate."

Gabriel hung up. He collected his baggage and walked to a coffee shop where he purchased a carton of milk from a vending machine. He walked to a booth where he rented an automobile, later tossed his cases into the trunk, and—checking his rearview mirror often—left the airport.

As Gabe drove toward Adamsville, he smiled at the strength of the Arizona sunshine. In many respects it would be good to get home, he thought. No longer would he pretend he was something that he was not in order to gain employment or friends.

Knapp proceeded along Highway 60 through Fort Apache Indian Reservation, eventually entering St. Johns, Arizona. He was reminded of the two brutal murders his people had suffered there many years before. David and his sister Mary had not been murdered because they had done anything wrong, he knew from history. They had been beaten to death because David's skin was green.

As Gabe progressed still closer to Adamsville, he noted the increasing number of vehicles and pedestrians along the road. Here and there crowds gathered. People were yelling to one another. Some carried clubs. A few displayed rifles. Gabe drove ahead, keeping his eyes on the highway in front of him. His hands had begun to sweat. "You waited too long," he admonished himself aloud.

But when he finally approached the north gate to Adamsville, he found himself greeted by a single state patrolman. Gabe parked the car he had driven several yards from the entrance and removed his suitcases from the trunk. He intended to leave the car there. Once safely inside he would telephone the rental agency, informing them of the vehicle's whereabouts.

The patrolman whom Gabe had seen as he neared the gate approached. "Going somewhere?" the officer asked abruptly.

"Sir," Gabe stammered, "I live here."

"The hell you do!" the other guffawed. "Only greenfaces live in there." He took hold of Gabriel's arm. "Come on," he urged, "why don't you just go on home. They aren't hurtin' you any right now. They're monsters, I have to admit, but so far, at least, I have to protect them. That's my job."

Gabriel Knapp's mind had stopped at the term "greenfaces." He had never heard the expression before. Insulted to a degree he had not previously experienced, he felt himself resist the strength of the trooper's grip.

"Listen, buddy," the officer went on, "I've got to insist you don't go any closer to that gate. I hate them too, you know what I mean? I've got little kids too. You think I want them out kidnapping and killing little kids? But so far the law says I've got to keep peace around here, so let's go."

"Sir," Gabe said meekly, "I *am* one of them. If you would just take my name and relay it to the

guards at the gate, they would verify it." He spoke with deferent politeness, having regained his composure.

"You?" the patrolman sneered. "You're one of those greenfaces? ... What's your name then?"

"Gabriel Knapp."

"That your car?"

"It's a rented car, sir."

The officer checked the vehicle's registration. "If you're one of them, I'm not going to let you take this automobile inside," the trooper said, reluctantly approaching the guards' shelter.

Gabriel waited, pacing. When the officer returned he said, "Okay. They say to let you through."

Carrying his briefcase and one suitcase, Gabe walked toward the gate as it opened electronically before him. Once he had set these inside the gate, he went back outside for the rest of his belongings and rushed into what he hoped was safety within Adamsville.

Inside he was met by Jacob Lockwood. The two old friends embraced one another.

"It's been a long time," Jacob said. "Come on, I'll take you into town."

Gabe threw his luggage into the back of Jacob's solar vehicle and got in. As they drove, Jacob said, "After you called from the airport I contacted Elderhome to tell them you were coming. You can stay with me for a while. Later they'll give you a place in the valley."

The valley had become populated during the previous fifteen years. Located on the outskirts of town, it housed only mutants with dull skin. Generally those in the valley worked at S.T.I.'s routine factory jobs or served as janitors, maintenance workers, and waste collectors. Valley residents raised goats, drinking their milk for supplement. Jacob drove awhile, not saying anything. Finally Gabriel broke the silence.

"It's almost time for light-break," he said, making conversation.

"Do you still practice light-break?" Jacob asked.

"It's difficult," Gabe explained, "when you're on the outside. I had trouble finding somewhere to go in downtown Chicago during my lunch hour."

Jacob said nothing.

"In the summertime I walked along the lake or

in the parks," Gabe continued. "Cloudy days I just stayed in and maybe went to a lunch counter somewhere to get a glass of milk."

"Dan was right then. You're still taking supplement."

Gabriel didn't answer. He sensed the regret in his companion's voice.

"They have a word for that now—for greens who don't stop taking supplement." Jacob swallowed. "They call them 'milk-whites'."

Gabriel turned the phrase in his mind. He was a "milk-white" here, he thought, and out there a "greenface." He grimaced bitterly at the irony of it.

Suddenly Jacob slammed his foot against the brake pedal. The car came to a screeching halt. Gabe looked up to see several men and women in the road ahead. They all wore face masks.

Before he realized what was happening, three greens pulled him from the auto and threw him to the ground. He felt a blow to the middle of his back. He was pummeled about the face and head. Someone kicked him in the side.

Jacob had attempted to protect his passenger, but could not. He was being held by two of the attackers. The blows to Gabe's body continued until Gabe lost consciousness.

When he awoke he was in Adamsville Hospital. A physician stood over him.

"Hello, Gabriel," he said sympathetically.

Gabe blinked. His chest hurt; his head throbbed. His body felt crushed, broken.

"You have some fractured ribs," the doctor was saying, "along with many lacerations and bruises. We stitched up a long gash on your head. We'll tape those ribs in place and soon you'll be able to get around."

Gabe nodded and fell asleep.

During the days that he remained in the hospital, he was visited once by Ruth Jones-the-Elder. "You came home," she said simply, entering his room.

"Yes, Elder," Gabe responded, his jaw aching.

"We are sorry about what happened here," Ruth said.

Gabe did not respond.

"Jacob says they all wore masks," Ruth continued. "He knows it was Larry Jones and some others, but he didn't actually see that it was Larry." She paused. "Did you see any of their faces?"

"No," Gabe murmured.

"I'm sorry," Ruth repeated. Then, changing the subject, she said, "According to the law, you must make a public confession."

"I know."

"We have scheduled it for July 2. Your physician says you will be well enough by then." Ruth smiled firmly. "And of course you will mature at the autumnal equinox," she added.

Gabe nodded.

"There's a vacant apartment in the valley," the Elder said then. "You may move into it when you like." She rose to leave. "Now," she said, "I'll let you get some sleep."

When Bradley Duncan left the conference on human mutations he had addressed May 10, he returned to his office at American University. There he began to prepare a paper that he would mail to Elderhome.

The Elders had allowed him to stay in Adamsville partially because they hoped that his observations would help them solve their internal problems. Consequently, he would offer the Elders what insights he could.

Duncan's eventual correspondence suggested that Adamsville posers who had shown themselves disloyal by putting off participation in the maturation ceremony had done so because going home often offered the prospect of downward mobility.

Duncan suggested that the belief that mutants did not physically mature because they had harbored thoughts of disloyalty proved a "self-fulfilling prophecy." A poser who waited in disappointment while his skin did not change color would eventually question the wisdom of his return home. To return meant to accept a position of low rank and general humiliation.

As a solution Duncan suggested that posers who did not become luminous be considered equal to their fellows. They would return more readily, he wrote, if they could participate in the maturing ceremony without feelings of inferiority—and if after the ceremony they could hold positions of honor, trust, and prestige.

Finally, Duncan pointed out that for Adamsvillers to define dull skin as evidence of inward disloyalty could actually be dysfunctional to the community. Dull greens were men and women of experience and expertise in many diverse fields. They might act as public relations persons or sales representatives for S.T.I., or as ambassadors to foreign nations, or lobbyists in Washington, D.C., or state capitals. Because they could travel more inconspicuously than their green fellows, they could do many things that were now left to young posers with little business or political experience.

The Elders received Duncan's paper on July 1, 2027.

Gabriel left Adamsville Hospital on June 30, five days after his attack. He went to stay with Jacob until he had fully recovered and could move into the valley apartment.

On July 2, the day scheduled for his public confession, Gabriel bathed, dressed, and walked with Jacob to the park.

The Elders had declared a religious holiday. Already a crowd of several hundred had formed. Gabe recognized Larry Jones; Daniel Adamson; Jacob's cousin, Rebecca Lockwood; and other bright greens standing together in one section of the sacred space.

The Elders had ascended to the ceremonial platform. Pain shot through Gabe's torso as he approached the same platform. At the microphone he spoke to the crowd.

"I am standing before you now," he began, his stomach growing sick with both humiliation and pain, "because I have sinned by disloyalty. I have refused to mature spiritually and therefore my skin has not matured physically." He swallowed, clenching his fists as they hung at his sides. "I come before you now," he forced the words, "to beg forgiveness."

Then suddenly the audience witnessed an unprecedented and surprising sequence of events. Michael and Ruth Jones-the-Elder moved closer to Gabriel and kissed him on each cheek.

"Gabriel Knapp should not have been required to request public forgiveness," Michael said. "He came to us last year a rescuer and a hero."

The crowd murmured.

"He will not live in the valley," Ruth proclaimed.

Many in the crowd shouted angrily. Gabriel had chosen a life of collaboration with ungreens, they raved. For that there was only lasting humiliation.

The Elders motioned for quiet. Still the angry voices in the throng rumbled. "He is a milk-white," they jeered. "Milk-whites will destroy Adamsville!"

Questions

1. How are Adamsville residents members of a subculture?

2. As a "milk-white," Gabe is a member of a minority within a minority. Explain.

3. How does the episode illustrate prejudice? Are there incidents of discrimination within this or previous episodes?

4. Greens might respond to ungreen hostility in a number of ways. What are they, and what do you think would be the consequences of each?

5. Discuss all the ways greens might be regarded as a minority group within American society.

Part Four
Changing Social Agreements

Part Three consisted largely of an examination of institutional structures. In those chapters, we looked at some ways our institutional agreements—our agreement reality—shape our thoughts, feelings, and actions. We saw how institutions are essential to the survival of society, governing individual experiences so as to serve group needs. We also saw how the quality of individuals' experiences of institutional structures is often, for one reason or another, unsatisfying.

Agreements are necessary. The problem lies in how we perpetuate them. We reify and internalize them, and in the process we often forget that our agreements are only agreements and mistake them for ultimate truth or reality. They become that much more difficult to change.

In spite of the persistence of social agreements, they do change. In Part Four, we're going to focus on changing social agreements, or the more disorderly side of social affairs. We're going to look at some ways people break established agreements, how people disagree, how they act spontaneously in groups, outside of established agreements, and how agreements change.

Chapter 13 takes up the topic of deviance. I know you've heard someone referred to as a "deviant," and maybe you've been called one. Early in the chapter, you'll discover that *you* are a deviant—we all

are. Deviance is basically a matter of breaking the established agreements of society, and all of us do that in various ways. Only certain kinds of deviants are deemed sufficiently threatening to society to warrant serious attention. We'll look at how the decision is made, and at the social control mechanisms that are brought to bear on people in the enforcement of agreements.

Chapter 14 takes up a variety of topics that sociologists call "collective behavior": fads, crazes, riots, and other spontaneous group actions. In part, we'll see how people join together in creating agreements in the heat of the moment. And we'll also look at the way fashion trends spread. Chapter 14 also includes a discussion of social movements. Social movements, in contrast to the spontaneity of collective behavior, aim deliberately at having a long-term effect on established agreements. Not all social movements aim at changing agreements, however; some have the opposite intent.

Chapter 15 is addressed to disagreements, or social conflict. We are going to discover that a frequent consequence of social conflict is the modification in a variety of ways of established agreements.

Part Four covers the dynamic aspects of social life, as distinguished from the more static quality of social structure. After you finish Part Four, you should have a balanced view of how societies operate.

13

Deviance
and Social Control

The first half of this book has focused largely on the agreements that members of a society share. For the most part, societies function smoothly and harmoniously when their members keep agreements. "Conformity" is a term used to describe behavior that keeps society's agreements. When sociologists talk about conformity, they don't make moral judgments about whether it's "right" or "wrong" to keep the agreements. Keeping the agreement not to murder other people is no different, in this sense, from being a woman, a black, or a poor person and "staying in your place" without causing trouble. All illustrate conformity to the existing agreements, and the society operates smoothly and harmoniously—and the institutions survive—when people conform.

This chapter has a rather different focus. In large part, we'll be looking at **deviance:** the breaking of existing social agreements. We'll also examine, though more briefly, **social control:** the process of enforcing agreements by preventing deviance and punishing deviants.

Most people have a relatively simple notion of deviance as something that involves perversity and immorality. The term "deviant" is likely to bring forth pictures of criminals, prostitutes, dope addicts, and the like. If you saw the movie *Dr. Strangelove,* you may recall when Keenan Wynn as Colonel Bat Guano leveled his submachine gun at Peter Sellers, playing the British naval officer Mandrake, and said,

"I think you're a deviated prevert." That's the view of deviance that many people have.

This chapter begins with an examination of the sociological point of view on deviance and deviants. We'll see that the matter is far more complex than you might imagine. All of us are deviants in a sense; and, at the same time, the most hardened, incorrigible criminal keeps most of society's agreements. Many sociologists are coming to conclude that, ultimately, deviance is mostly a matter of what and who gets "labeled" as deviant.

None of this makes deviance unimportant in the study of society, however. Breaking the agreements—along with our reactions to other people's breaking the agreements—has critical implications for the functioning and survival of society. Sociologists have, accordingly, studied many different forms of deviance, and we'll look at some of those. We'll see how each fits—and conflicts—with the body of social agreements.

We'll turn next to some of the explanations sociologists and others have given for deviance. Some of us break agreements that others keep, and we'll look at some of the reasons for that. Is it a matter of biology, psychology, social conditions, or what? We'll look at all those possibilities.

The chapter concludes with an examination of social control: its purposes and mechanisms. Beginning with the socialization process as an example of social control, we'll zero in on those persons and groups that have a special responsibility for enforcing the law: police, courts, and prisons. We'll also see some of the ways in which social control creates problems.

On Deviance and Deviants

In this section, I want to show how two seemingly straightforward concepts become more complex when we look at them carefully. We're going to find out that it matters greatly *who* breaks *what* agreements, to what *degree,* whether he or she gets *caught,* and how *other people* feel about it.

You Are a Deviant

In the preceding discussions of this book, it should have become apparent that most societies have literally millions of agreements relating to symbols, beliefs, values, and norms. Many of these agreements contradict one another, so it is simply impossible for a person to avoid breaking some of the agreements every day. We saw several examples of this agreement breaking in the discussion of role conflict in Chapter 4. Further, if you have ever driven too fast, lied, worn your hair "too long" or "too short," been late, or done something "surprising," you are a deviant.

Like prejudice, deviance is normally viewed in a negative light. Strictly speaking, the negativity need not be. Albert Einstein was as much a deviant

as Jack the Ripper. Mahatma Gandhi was as much a deviant as Adolph Hitler. Their ways were simply different.

Sociologists, however, have tended to follow common usage in directing their attention to those forms of deviance that are regarded as "bad," or defined as "bad" by general agreement within the society.

We Are All Deviants

You are not the only deviant in your sociology class, even when deviance is defined conventionally as breaking norms in a "bad" way. Look around you the next time you are in class, and realize that you are surrounded by deviants. We're all deviants.

J. L. Simmons (1969:44) has discussed degree of deviance as follows:

> *The rules are to be bent but not broken.* The prevailing practices in a society are the divergencies most common and most acceptable. Deviance is simply divergence that is much greater than the divergence of the majority, or at least the majority of the groups and classes in power.

Deviants, then, seem to be people who deviate *more* than the rest of us—people who go "too far." The expectation that we'll all deviate from prescribed norms at least somewhat is illustrated by our general reactions to people who "overconform," who follow all the agreements as closely as humanly possible. By driving strictly within posted speed limits, for example, "overconformers" aggravate other drivers who express their disapproval with blasting horns and shaking fists. When such people insist that others strictly adhere to the agreements, they are ridiculed, ostracized, and sometimes assaulted. Unquestionably, the person who managed to keep all his or her society's agreements would be regarded as the supreme deviant.

How far is "too far" in deviating from the norms is not clear. People have different views on it. Even if we draw the line at "breaking the law"—even serious laws—the prevalence of deviance in America is astounding. Robert Merton, a prominent American sociologist, has summarized the results of a survey conducted during the more "law-abiding" 1940s:

A study of some 1,700 prevalently middle-class individuals found that "off the record crimes" were common among wholly "respectable" members of society. Ninety-nine percent of those questioned confessed to having committed one or more of 49 offenses under the penal law of the State of New York, each of these offenses being sufficiently serious to draw a maximum sentence of not less than one year. The mean number of offenses in adult years—this excludes all offenses committed before the age of sixteen—was 18 for men and 11 for women. Fully 64 [percent] of the men and 29 [percent] of the women acknowledged their guilt on one or more counts of felony which, under the laws of New York, is ground for depriving them of all rights of citizenship (1957a:144).

I don't want to encourage you to take up a career in crime. I just want to indicate the extent to which deviance—what virtually everyone would agree is deviance—pervades our society. Deviants, however defined, are scarcely a "people apart" from you and me.

Mostly We Conform

Although all of us are "deviants," there's another side to the coin. Simmons (1969:40) has stated it nicely:

> All deviants are conventional in the vast majority of their beliefs, attitudes, and activities. Even the most unconventional denizens of our society, for instance, prefer ground beef to rotted camel meat, speak a language which is unmistakably a mid-century American dialect of English, drive on the right-hand side of the road, and take aspirin for a headache. The vast bulk of a deviant's characteristics will be statistically common and morally accepted. Our upbringing in the same historical place and time gives us all —deviant and straight—a thousand common bonds.

Saint and sinner alike share countless agreements, and in most of our behavior we conform to those agreements. Otherwise, prostitutes would walk naked in the streets to advertise and murderers would murder everyone in sight. Thieves wouldn't steal, by the same token, if they didn't share in a variety of agreements regarding the purpose and value of

All of us are deviants, some, such as this man, more than others. Notice, however, the number of ways he agrees with the norms of American society. (Ronald Goor, Black Star)

money. All in all, we deviants are a pretty conformist lot.

What Is Deviance?

My purpose so far in this section has been to loosen up and expand your views on deviance and deviants. Now let's look at several different *sociological* points of view on deviance, gaining, in the process, a better understanding of how societies operate. I'll touch on these points of view briefly here and elaborate on them later in the chapter.

The **labeling** point of view on deviance suggests that people are deviants only or primarily because they are "labeled" as deviant. You are "mentally ill" if a psychologist or physician says you are. You are a "criminal" if a court says you are. In short, you become a deviant as a result of an *agreement* that you've broken the agreements. Two people might both break the same agreement, but only one of them might be labeled a deviant. The soldier and the (privately) hired killer both kill people, but only the latter is labeled a deviant.

The conflict point of view in sociology suggests that deviance and social control are elements in the struggle between social classes or other groups in society. This is most clearly exemplified in "collective" deviance, such as riots, protest marches, and anti-war-tax movements. Moreover, conflict theorists see social control through laws, police, courts, and jails as an overt act of those in power to suppress those who lack power.

The functionalist point of view regards deviance as a threat to the stability and persistence of a society and its agreements. Different functionalists might differ, however, on whether that's "good" or "bad."

The functionalist and conflict points of view both grant that a lot of agreements are being broken in any society at any time. They differ on the kinds of agreement breaking they label and treat as deviant. The conflict point of view is interested in the breaking of agreements that protect the existing distribution of power in the society; the functionalist point of view looks to the breaking of agreements that support major institutions. The threat to institutions may often be indirect. Prostitution and homosexuality, for example, may be seen to represent an indirect threat to the institution of the family—because they challenge its monopoly on sexuality.

Quite aside from these different points of view, most sociologists recognize that deviance per se has a function for society. The identification and punishment of deviants draw the attention of others to the existence and "importance" of the agreements the deviants broke. Making "an example" of deviants

can keep others on the straight and narrow. The identification of deviants can strengthen the solidarity of the rest of society. You may recall from Chapter 6 that in-group solidarity is strengthened by the presence of out-groups. The identification and labeling of deviants in a society have the effect of creating an out-group that everyone else can feel superior to and united against.

Who, then, are the deviants in American society? When Simmons (1969) asked a sample of 180 people to "list those things or types of persons whom you regard as deviant," the variety of answers given was staggering.

The sheer range of responses included such expected items as homosexuals, prostitutes, drug addicts, beatniks, and murderers; it also included liars, democrats, reckless drivers, atheists, self-pitiers, the retired, career women, divorcees, movie stars, perpetual bridge-players, prudes, pacifists, psychiatrists, priests, liberals, conservatives, junior executives, girls who wear makeup, and know-it-all professors (p. 224).

Table 13·1 presents a summary of Simmons's findings. Since he asked his respondents to identify

Table 13·1 Who Are America's Deviants?

Response	Most frequent responses to the question "What is deviant?" (% of 180 respondents)
Homosexuals	49
Drug addicts	47
Alcoholics	46
Prostitutes	27
Murderers	22
Criminals	18
Lesbians	13
Juvenile delinquents	13
Beatniks	12
Mentally ill	12
Perverts	12
Communists	10
Atheists	10
Political extremists	10

Source: J. L. Simmons, "Public Stereotypes of Deviants," Deviants (Berkeley: Glendessary, 1969).

America's deviants in their own words, there are some overlapping categories in the table. For example, it contains both homosexuals and lesbians, and it lists murderers and juvenile delinquents in addition to criminals in general.

Though Simmons's study was done in the mid-1960s, the results are probably not too different from what would be found today. In any event, it contains most of the groups that sociologists examine most in the study of deviance, so let's see what sociologists have learned.

Forms of American Deviance

In this section, we're going to look at some of the major forms of deviance in American society. We'll consider crime, juvenile delinquencey, sexual deviance, alcoholism, drug use, and mental illness. While this list does not exhaust the popular or sociological views of deviance in America, it provides enough variety for you to broaden your understanding of deviance in general as well as your understanding of the relationship between deviance and society.

Crime

Crime is a clear case of deviance since it represents the breaking of formal, legal agreements in a society. Wearing your hair too long or too short violates unstated, informal agreements, and its status as deviant behavior is, therefore, somewhat ambiguous. Breaking the law—stealing and killing—is not ambiguous in that regard.

We have already gotten a sense, earlier in this chapter, of the extent of lawbreaking in America—even by middle-class, seemingly law-abiding citizens. Yet there is a vast difference between breaking the law and getting caught. There is also a difference between crimes committed and crimes reported to the police. Table 13·2 reports the numbers of crimes "known to police" in recent years.

You might notice a number of points in Table 13·2. First, crimes against property greatly outnumber crimes against persons. The ratio is currently about six to one. The number of crimes against property would be even greater if robbery were added to the category.

Second, the number of major crimes *known to police* is simply staggering. In 1974, almost 5 major crimes were known to police for every 100 people in the United States population.

Third, both the number of crimes and the crime rate have been increasing dramatically over the period shown. The crime rate, a figure that is arrived at by dividing the number of crimes by the population size, more than tripled during the fourteen-year period. The number of crimes more than quadrupled.

Table 13·2 Major American Crimes Known to Police, 1960–1973

Crime	1960	1965	1970	1973	1974
Violent crimes	286,000	384,000	733,000	869,000	970,000
Murder and nonnegligent manslaughter	9,000	10,000	16,000	19,500	20,600
Forcible rape	17,000	23,000	38,000	51,000	55,200
Robbery	107,000	138,000	348,000	383,000	441,000
Aggravated assault	153,000	213,000	331,000	416,000	453,000
Property crimes	1,734,000	2,553,000	4,848,000	7,769,000	9,222,000
Burglary	900,000	1,266,000	2,177,000	2,541,000	3,021,000
Larceny, $50 and over	507,000	794,000	1,750,000	4,304,000	5,228,000
Auto theft	326,000	493,000	922,000	924,000	974,000
Grand total	2,020,000	2,937,000	5,581,000	8,638,000	10,192,000

Source: Federal Bureau of Investigation, Uniform Crime Reports for the United States, *1975, p. 59.*

There are some things you should be aware of in reading tables such as Table 13·2 that report data on crime rates. First, crime rates, like other society-wide phenomena, are strongly influenced by the age distribution of the population. In this instance, the rapidly increasing crime rate partly reflects the "baby boom" following World War II. As we'll see later in this section, crime rates are higher among young people in America than among older people, so the disproportionately large number of young Americans at present results in higher nationwide crime rates.

Second, data on "crimes known to police" reflect enforcement policies. Whenever the police decide to "crack down" on drug use, for example, crime statistics will give the appearance of an increased crime rate in that area. DeFleur's (1975) analysis of drug arrests in Chicago between 1942 and 1970 graphically demonstrates the influence of enforcement policies on apparent crime rates.

Finally, more crimes are known to victims than are known to police. Countless informal agreements contribute to this discrepancy. Crimes committed by family members or friends against one another often go unreported for obvious reasons. Similarly, in areas that support organized crime (ranging in type from neighborhood gangs to syndicates), victims and witnesses alike may keep quiet for fear of retribution. And many people share an agreement that calling in the police won't bring anything but trouble. Rape victims, for example, often conceal the fact in order to avoid ugly publicity, painful questioning, and, some victims report, police suspicions that they encouraged the assault.

It's impossible to know exactly how many crimes go unreported each year, but we can make some estimates. During 1965–66, the National Opinion Research Center (NORC) of the University of Chicago undertook an interview survey with 10,000 households in America. Respondents interviewed by NORC were asked whether they or anyone else in their household had been the victim of a crime during the preceding year. The answers given in the survey made it possible to estimate the nation's crime rate from the point of view of its victims and to compare that estimate with official police figures. Table 13·3 reports that comparison.

Table 13·3 Estimated Crime Rates as Reported by Victims and by Police

Type of crime	Rates reported by households, 1965–1966[a]	Rates reported by police, 1965[a]
Violent crimes	357.8	184.7
Willful homicide	3.0	5.1
Forcible rape	42.5	11.6
Robbery	94.0	61.4
Aggravated assault	218.3	106.6
Property crimes	1,761.8	793.0
Burglary	949.1	299.6
Larceny, $50 and over	606.5	267.4
Motor vehicle theft	206.2	226.0

[a]All rates represent the number of crimes per 100,000 population. The "police" reports, moreover, are limited to crimes against individuals (as opposed to organizations), which permits an appropriate comparison with the National Opinion Research Center data.

Source: Adapted from The President's Commission on Law Enforcement and Administration of Justice, The Challenge of Crime in a Free Society, 1967, p. 21.

The data shown in Table 13·3 suggest that the number of major crimes committed in America is more than double that indicated by official police statistics. Forcible rapes are about four times as prevalent, and the ratio is probably even greater than that. A great deal has been written recently about rape victims' reluctance to expose themselves to public view by reporting the attack to police, and the data substantiate that. It stands to reason, moreover, that many victims might even be reluctant to report such attacks to survey interviewers.

You may find the data on property crimes unsettling, but you are probably more concerned about crimes directed against your person. Getting killed is more upsetting than getting robbed. Sociologists have discovered an interesting, though unsettling, pattern in crimes of violence. As summarized by the President's Commission on Law Enforcement (1967:18), "nearly two-thirds of all aggravated assaults and a high percentage of forcible rapes are committed by family members, friends, or other

persons previously known to their victims." The box on page 338 "Who Is Most Likely to Harm You?" elaborates the point.

I'm not sure you should take comfort in the discovery, but if you are going to be killed, raped, or assaulted, it'll probably be done by a friend or relation. And given that, you may not report it to the police.

A great deal of sociological attention has been paid to the characteristics of those arrested for committing crimes. As reported by the President's Commission on Law Enforcement and Administration of Justice (1967:44), the largest number of crimes overall are committed by white males over 24 years of age. In particular, this group acccounts for a large majority of the arrests for fraud, embezzlement, gambling, drunkenness, vagrancy, and crimes within the family. Other crimes, however, are more typical among other social categories.

> The 15-to-17-year-old group is the highest for burglaries, larcenies and auto theft. For these three offenses, 15-year-olds are arrested more often than persons of any other age with 16-year-olds a close second. For the three common property offenses the rate of arrest per 100,000 persons 15 to 17 in 1965 was 2,467 as compared to a rate of 55 for every 100,000 persons 50 years old and older. For crimes of violence the peak years are those from 18 to 20, followed closely by the 21 to 24 group. Rates for these groups are 300 and 297 as compared with 24 for the 50-year-

old and over group (President's Commission on Law Enforcement 1967:44).

The commission's report goes on to indicate that men are far more likely than women to be arrested for committing crimes. This, in fact, is the most salient characteristic distinguishing those arrested from the population at large. The sex difference has been decreasing in recent years, however, especially in larceny offenses.

Race is almost as important as sex in distinguishing persons arrested from the general public. Blacks commit fewer crimes than whites, but crime *rates* are considerably higher among blacks. Racial differences appear largely to reflect differences in socioeconomic status and other social variables (President's Commission on Law Enforcement 1967:44).

Juvenile Delinquency

Sociologists, like others in the society, tend to treat crime by minors separately from that by adults. Partly this reflects the different patterns of crime for people of different ages, as indicated in the "portrait" presented above. In addition, many acts are considered criminal *only* when committed by young people. Adults committing the same act would not be considered deviant.

Consider the following California statute stating the conditions under which a minor may be declared a ward of the state:

> Any person under the age of 21 years who persistently or habitually refuses to obey the reasonable and proper orders or directions of his parents, guardian, custodian or school authorities, or who is beyond the control of such person, or any person who is a habitual truant from school within the meaning of any law of this State, or who from any cause *is in danger* of leading an idle, dissolute, lewd, or immoral life, is within the jurisdiction of the juvenile court which may adjudge such person to be a ward of the court (Quoted in Kassebaum 1974:12; emphasis added).

These "status crimes" add to the "criminal" *potential* of young people compared with adults by giving them more agreements to keep and, hence,

Who Is Most Likely to Harm You?

Where does one turn for an accurate picture of violent crime in America? Certainly not to current television shows. They consistently portray rapists as psychopaths and murderers as evil men usually affiliated with organized crime. Most often, in TV shows, the violent criminal is a stranger to his victim.

Some classic sociological studies suggest a different profile of violent crime and the criminal-victim relationship. One such study is Marvin Wolfgang's[1] analysis of homicides committed in Philadelphia in the years 1948–1952. Wolfgang reports that many homicides are crimes of passion or the outgrowth of quarrels between spouses, lovers, relatives, friends, or acquaintances. One in every four homicides is "victim-precipitated"; the victim strikes the first blow or first produces a deadly weapon. (Other studies have found as many as one-third of criminal homicides to be "victim-precipitated.") Wolfgang's data indicate that 65 percent of homicide victims know their killer. Relatives are involved in 25 percent of homicides.

A second important study involves rape. Menachem Amir reviewed all rape cases reported to the Philadelphia police in 1958 and 1960 (remember,

most rapes are never reported).[2] His analysis suggests that rapes by total strangers occur less often than current stereotypes suggest. In 48 percent of the cases, the attacker was an acquaintance of the victim. In general, the closer the relationship between victim and offender, the greater the use of physical force against the victim. Clearly, the "Jack-the-Ripper" model does not appear often in Amir's data.

Reporting these studies is not meant to give you a cynical view of the victim as someone "who asks for it." The point is to demonstrate the complexity of violent crime and the difficulty in preventing such crimes. Who is most likely to harm you? Probably not the stranger. The chance of the average American's being the victim of a violent attack by a stranger is 1 in 550. His or her chances of being harmed by a family member or acquaintance are twice as great. Perhaps we should fear ourselves the most. Statistics tell us that suicides occur at least as often if not more often than homicides.

What are the implications of these research findings for the prevention or reduction of crime? What laws or law enforcement practices do you think would be most effective?

[1]Marvin E. Wolfgang, "Victim-Precipitated Criminal Homicide," *Journal of Criminal Law, Criminology, and Police Science* 48(1957):1–11.

[2]Menachem Amir, *Patterns in Forcible Rape* (Chicago: University of Chicago Press, 1971).

more to break. Few status crimes apply only to adults (statutory rape is one).

In terms of arrests, juveniles account for more than their share within the general population. This is particularly so for burglary, larceny, and car theft. On the whole, however, most juvenile crimes are less serious.

Juveniles are most frequently arrested or referred to court for petty larceny, fighting, disorderly conduct, liquor-related offenses, and conduct not in violation of the criminal laws such as curfew violation, truancy, incorrigibility, or running away from home (President's Commission on Law Enforcement 1967:56).

The president's commission went on to note that in 1965, over half the girls referred to juvenile court had only violated status crimes, those that would not have been regarded as criminal if committed by adults. This was true for only one-fifth of the boys.

Juvenile status crimes highlight the fact that deviance is purely a matter of agreement within society. A given act by a given person is "criminal" only if we agree that it is. Thus, it has been agreed at times that drinking alcohol is a deviant act for a person 17 years and 364 days old, but not a deviant act for a person 1 day older. As we've seen, society's agreements are largely arbitrary. We've also seen that societies can't survive without agreements. These two characteristics of agreements are a source of continuing strain within society, and the strains are aggravated according to the degree that agreements are reified and internalized. Nowhere is this clearer than in the case of agreements pertaining to the structuring of sexual experiences.

Homosexuality

Homosexuality falls within a general category of deviance that sociologists often refer to as "crimes without victims." Murder has its murder victim and robbery has a robbed party, but homosexuality is an unconventional activity entered into voluntarily.

The "unconventional" nature of homosexuality comes from its violation of the agreement that sexual relations should be limited to persons of opposite sexes. This agreement extends well beyond sexual intercourse, however, and generally includes other intimate acts and even feelings of love.

The American agreements pertaining to homosexuality are rather complex and largely unstated. For example, most young children engage in sexual experimentation with members of the same sex. Although this experimentation is typically discouraged by adults, the label of homosexuality is seldom attached to it. Moreover, Americans are more permissive with women in this regard than with men. Adult women may acceptably hug, kiss, and hold hands in public, but men may not do so as acceptably. It is worth noting that many other contemporary societies—in Latin America and Europe, for example—do not make the same distinctions North Americans do about proper behavior for men and women.

The term "homosexual" is typically used to refer to men only; "lesbian" is the term used to refer to female homosexuals. (Recall the distinction made earlier in Table 13·1.) Clearly, male homosexuality has been regarded as a more serious deviation in America than has lesbianism.

The agreements relating to homosexuality are further complicated by the existence of bisexuals, or ambisexuals: people who engage in both heterosexual and homosexual relations. Such people often have conventional marriages and are parents. Their homo-sexuality is merely an addition to conventional sex and marriage patterns.

Estimates of the extent of homosexuality in America are approximate at best. Fearing loss of jobs and legal and other sanctions, many homosexuals conceal their disagreement with prevailing sexual norms. Moreover, a great many Americans have had homosexual encounters, at least as children, but have accepted heterosexual patterns afterward. The best available estimates suggest that perhaps 4 percent of the male population is exclusively homosexual (Weinberg 1974).

The American agreements regarding homosexuality are clearly changing. Although homosexuality is still against the law in most states, several, including California and Illinois, have recently decriminalized it among consenting adults. Other states will undoubtedly follow suit. At the same time, many homosexuals have "come out of the closet," publicly acknowledging their homosexuality. "Gay lib" has joined the list of minority groups openly demanding equal treatment in American society.

Prostitution

Prostitution, another sexual crime without victims, represents an agreement between a prostitute and her client. It provides an excellent contrast to homosexuality. Although both men and women are involved in prostitution, women are the most likely to be identified with it and punished for it. In 1975 55,800 people were arrested for "prostitution and commercialized vice." Three-fourths of these were women; and many of the men arrested were procurers rather than clients (Federal Bureau of Investigation 1975:121). Only recently have police begun arresting clients as well as prostitutes, spurred largely by charges that previous arrest patterns have constituted sex discrimination against women.

Prostitution, sometimes called the "oldest profession," is usually heterosexual in America. Although it supports the agreement on heterosexuality—too much, some would feel—it violates other agreements. First, it violates the agreement limiting sexual relations to the family, between married partners. In addition, it violates more informal agreements that

European men can kiss each other on the mouth without fear of sanction. Contemporary American norms, however, would cast this as a deviant act. (Dorka Raynor, Photo Researchers, Inc.)

sexual relations should be associated with feelings of love and lasting commitment.

The combination of prostitution's illegal status and its persistent popularity has created a secondary problem that seems clearly more serious than its simple existence. Prostitution in America has become an important industry within organized crime, although no one knows to what extent. Many independent entrepreneurs exist, but a large number of prostitutes are forced to ply their trade as employees of pimps, mobs, and syndicates. In those areas where prostitution is generally organized, the would-be self-employed prostitute risks severe punishment. And, because prostitution is itself illegal, she has no recourse to the police.

Alcoholism

For the most part, drinking alcoholic beverages is legal in America, and it is hardly considered deviant. If anything, total abstention from alcohol is the deviant pattern in terms of our informal agreements.

Deviance is largely a matter of labeling. Drinking by itself is not sufficient for you to be labeled a deviant. (Gary Renaud, Magnum)

Exceptions include the period of national Prohibition from 1919 to 1933, the prohibition of alcohol in individual "dry" states, and laws denying alcohol to minors. In addition, state and municipal laws specify who may make and sell alcoholic beverages and the conditions under which it may be sold and consumed. In spite of all these restrictions, people take a drink now and then.

In 1974, the per capita consumption of alcoholic beverages in America was 31.0 gallons of beer, 2.90 gallons of whiskey, and 2.40 gallons of wine. Compared with 1950, this represented a 96 percent increase for whiskey and an 80 percent increase for wine (U.S. Bureau of the Census 1975a:750).

Drinking may be normative in America, but getting drunk, ironically, is another matter. Drunkenness per se is not illegal, but state and municipal laws prohibit you from being drunk in a public place, being "drunk and disorderly," and "driving while intoxicated." The president's commission (1967:223) reported about 2 million arrests for drunkenness annually.

Our informal agreements on drunkenness appear to discriminate by sex in a manner exactly opposite to our agreements relating to same-sex hugging and kissing. We are more permissive with men than with women. Americans are relatively tolerant of a "bunch of the boys whooping it up" as a sign of healthy camaraderie, and the man who refused to participate in such festivities would probably be regarded as deviant. Women gathering together to "tie one on," however, would be met with severe disapproval; they would probably be suspected of all manners of other deviant behaviors, too.

Sociologists have given special attention to one class of drinkers. This class is composed of "alcoholics," people who, by medical definition, are dependent on the consumption of alcohol. Cahalan (1970) has estimated that between 6 and 10 percent of the adult population of the United States are alcoholics, although the ambiguities of definition and the stigma attached to alcoholism make precise estimates impossible.

Alcoholism illustrates an irony that is present in many forms of social deviance. As we've seen, Americans share a general agreement that the consumption of alcohol is expected. Drinking is the norm, and those who refuse to drink at all are regarded as deviant. Yet there's also an agreement that you shouldn't drink "too much." Abiding by the first norm sets up the risk of violating the second, and the "proper" middle ground—drinking the "right" amount —is not precisely defined. The same irony appears in connection with drug taking.

Drug Use

In 1973, Americans spent over 9 billion dollars on drugs, a statistic that suggests the existence of an agreement in support of drug taking. That same year, the nation's drug companies spent 245 million dollars on television advertising alone. This is more than was spent to perpetuate the agreement that we transport ourselves in automobiles (217 million dollars) or the agreement to get clothes whiter than white and to keep sinks spotless and shiny (192 million dollars). Only food (332 million dollars) and toiletries (371 million dollars) had higher television advertising expenditures. American drug companies produced 16,076 tons of aspirins in 1973 (U.S. Bureau of the Census 1975a:70, 88, 793).

We are clearly a drug-taking society. Some people suggest that we have a "drug problem." In saying that, however, they usually do not refer to taking aspirins. Instead, they refer to deviant drug use, drug use (and abuse) that involves illegal sub-

stances such as heroin, cocaine, LSD, and marijuana. Sociologists have been interested in studying the use of illegal drugs.

Figures are highly unreliable, but it has been estimated that perhaps 2 million Americans have used heroin, a morphine-derived depressant, at least once, and there may be as many as 400,000 heroin addicts, people who are physiologically dependent on continued use (Weinberg 1974).

Cocaine is a stimulant, not a depressant like heroin. It is derived from the leaves of South American coca plants. Cocaine, which is typically ingested by sniffing, was a popular drug in America a few decades ago. It went out of fashion, but it has recently regained popularity, especially among the middle and upper classes. In contrast to heroin, it is not known to be physically addictive. Weinberg (1974) estimates that perhaps 4 million Americans have tried cocaine at least once, though it is likely that the new wave of popularity and publicity has increased previous figures.

During the 1960s, considerable national attention was focused on the use of LSD, a powerful manufactured hallucinogenic, or psychedelic, drug. First popularized primarily by college students, its use spread to high school and even elementary school students. Hailed as a "consciousness-expanding" drug, LSD largely replaced and outstripped use of peyote and mescaline, "organic" drugs that produce similar effects.

While LSD and the other hallucinogens are not known to produce physical addiction, mass-media reports of extremely heavy and continued use by a few users produced fears of psychological dependence. Moreover, an unresolved controversy has raged in medical circles as to possible genetic damage resulting from heavy and continued use. After reaching a peak in the mid-to-late 1960s, LSD use appears to have declined in America.

Easily the most talked-about and most popular illegal substance in recent years has been marijuana, derived from the female hemp plant. Used for years in black ghettos, it came to national attention in the 1960s when it was discovered by large numbers of middle- and upper-class college students. By the early 1970s, as estimated from Gallup polls during 1971 and 1972, over 40 percent of American college students and one adult in nine had tried marijuana at least once.

Marijuana is the least powerful—in its mind-altering effects—of the drugs we have been discussing. Its effects seem to depend largely on the user's state at the time of ingestion, though it is typically relaxing, and it produces a degree of euphoria and heightens the user's awareness of body sensations. Marijuana is nonaddictive and has no known, long-term, negative side effects.

All the substances we have mentioned have one special potential side effect, however. In 1974, 3,938 Americans were tried in U.S. district courts for violations of antimarijuana laws, and 77 percent were convicted, with 8 percent of those convicted being sentenced to five or more years in prison (U.S. Bureau of the Census 1975a:165). The British approach to the "drug problem," described in the box on page 344 "Dealing with the Drug Problem: Legalistic versus Medical Model," provides an interesting contrast.

With millions of Americans—many of them in the middle and upper classes—having used marijuana, there has been increased public support for its legalization or at least for a reduction in the penalties for its use. The growing agreement that it is no more harmful than alcohol has very recently begun to find expression in the revision of antimarijuana laws. In some states and municipalities, the possession of marijuana has been given the status of a "petty misdemeanor," and violations are handled much like parking and traffic violations.

Mental Illness

For many years, sociologists have been interested in the phenomenon of mental illness as a persistent and often tragic form of deviance. It is still a topic of concern and research for sociologists, and the sociological point of view on mental illness has been shifting in recent years.

The term "mental illness" suggests a medical model of disease, a suggestion echoed in the slang expression "sick in the head." Much medical research, moreover, is devoted to the search for organic causes of mental illness such as malfunctions within the nervous system. Psychologists and psychiatrists have added another dimension to the picture of mental illness through the examination of emotional strains and stresses in interpersonal relations—in the family, for example.

Traditionally, sociologists have examined the epidemiology of mental illness, its distribution throughout the population, noting the social characteristics most commonly associated with it. Hollingshead and Redlich (1958), in a classic study, examined different rates of mental illness within different social-class groups.

Notice that I haven't defined mental illness or even given examples to illustrate it. This reflects in part recently emerging scientific points of view on mental illness: what it is and what causes it. To many scientists today, "mental illness" is largely a meaningless term. Thomas Szasz (1961) has written persuasively about the "myth of mental illness." Szasz does not deny that people have the symptoms associated with the term "mental illness," nor that those symptoms can be dysfunctional for the individual, particularly in his or her interactions with others. Szasz objects, however, to the use of a medical model in approaching those symptoms, a model that suggests there is something wrong with the person that needs curing. The medical model overlooks, for example, the possibility that a person's interpersonal difficulties might be related to situations. Suppose the FBI and CIA were "really" tapping your telephone and fol-

Dealing with the Drug Problem: Legalistic versus Medical Model

Narcotic addiction is a source of great concern to most members of our society. If we have not personally seen the devastating effects of heroin addiction on individuals and entire segments of our population, we have certainly viewed documentary evidence. Increasingly, we put pressure on the legislature and law enforcement agencies to combat the "hard-drug" problem. Few of us ever consider the possibility that our legal approach to the narcotic problem is the wrong approach.

Perhaps this society is too quick to turn to legal models to solve social problems. Legal remedies are often useless; in some instances, they seem to make the problem worse. The point is well illustrated by Edwin Schur, who has compared the American and British approaches to the drug problem.

The American response to the heroin problem has been to make it illegal for anyone to possess or sell narcotics and illegal for doctors to prescribe narcotics to addicts. As a result, argues Schur, the drug addict is isolated from the medical profession. What is basically a medical problem is dealt with by legal authorities, not by physicians. This produces a large black market and high prices for narcotics, which, in turn, lead to "secondary crime," robberies and thefts by addicts to support their habits. There is little evidence that our legal approach has succeeded in reducing narcotic addiction in this society.

Great Britain, on the other hand, has chosen to handle its drug problem by treating addiction as a medical instead of a legal problem. Doctors may supply addicts with narcotics at low cost. An attempt is made to cure the addict, but it is also recognized that, in some cases, refusal to supply the drug may cause serious problems for the addict and the society. The British approach seems to have resulted in better societal control over the addiction problem and has reduced it considerably. Black-market drug traffic has decreased, and so has "secondary crime." The British system has not eliminated the drug problem by any means, yet drug abuse seems definitely less a social problem in England than in America.

Attempts have been made in this country to implement a medical model through use of methadone clinics. Some say these attempts have been a failure. Others charge that we have not given the medical, nonlegal approach a fair trial. Whatever the answer, it is clear that we should examine our present legal policies, determine their effectiveness, and, if necessary, consider other approaches to the drug problem.

Do you feel we rely too much on the law to solve our problems? Consider other social problems we face, prostitution, for example. What nonlegal approaches could be used in dealing with prostitution?

Source: Edwin Schur, Narcotic Addiction in Britain and America: The Impact of Public Policy (Bloomington: University of Indiana Press, 1962).

lowing you around town. In the medical model you'd still be tabbed a "paranoid" and sent off for treatment.

In another criticism of the conventional view of mental illness, Thomas Scheff (1966) has suggested that it's primarily a matter of labeling: We are mentally ill if others agree that we are mentally ill and especially if we ourselves join in that agreement. There is not total agreement among scientists on the Szasz and Scheff points of view, but no scientist

suggests that the definition of mental illness is an easy one.

Like other forms of deviance, what we call mental illness is a matter of breaking agreements. People who are "too" excitedly outspoken in a group or who are "too" quiet and withdrawn may be suspected of harboring some mental "problem" or "disorder." The person who is easily angered or upset, the person who "flies off the handle" with little provocation, and the person who sobs uncontrollably over what seem like minor upsets are also likely to be regarded as abnormal or "just not right."

The more severe forms of what we call mental illness involve a person's "losing touch with reality." The paranoid who sees a secret conspiracy to "get" him or her is one familiar example. Or what about someone who is convinced that the world is flat and is trying to convince *you* of that belief?

Anyone who believes that the world is flat is clearly "mentally ill." Right? Seven or so centuries ago in Europe, however, anyone who believed the world was round was just as clearly "mentally ill." Both of these people break the prevailing agreements as to what's true. "Reality," after all, is a matter of agreement, and "losing touch with reality" is nothing more than breaking agreements about reality. People who broke agreements about reality were once regarded as being possessed by devils and demons and therefore evil. We now regard them as sick and pitiable. Always, however, the notions of mental illness or insanity depend on the reification of agreements within the larger society. It is the process of reification that transforms "different" into "crazy."

The purpose of these comments is not to persuade you that mental illness is merely a fiction that ought to be ignored. Rather, I'd like you to see how complicated and often arbitrary it is.

The ambiguities surrounding the notion of mental illness make it impossible to determine its extent. One study (Srole 1962) of nearly 1,700 residents of New York City reported that 80 percent of those studied had, at the time of the study, at least one psychiatric symptom. Nearly one-fourth of the sample was found to be "impaired because of psychiatric illness."

Earlier in this chapter, I stated that all of us are deviants. It seems likely that a case could be made for each of us in some way being "mentally ill." As a practical matter, however, only a small fraction of us are formally labeled in that fashion. At the end of 1974, there were 215,573 resident patients in the nation's state and county mental hospitals. Many more were being treated by outpatient clinics (U.S. Bureau of the Census 1975a:84).

It should be apparent by now that a great many people are, one way or another, defined as deviant in American society. I have emphasized the extent to which deviance is a matter of labeling, and I'll return to that topic shortly. Whether a matter of labeling or not, however, it still is true that some people commit murder while others do not, some become addicted to heroin while others do not, and some people do things that result in their being called mentally ill while others do not. It makes sense, then, to ask what the causes of deviance are. Why do some people break social agreements that other people keep? The answer to this question will further clarify the web of agreements and disagreements that underlie human societies.

The Causes of Deviance

Throughout much of human history, people have believed deviance to have a biological cause: Some people were simply "born to be bad." This view gained academic support during the nineteenth century, especially in the writings of the Italian physician Cesare Lombroso (1911). Lombroso believed that it was possible, in fact, to recognize "criminality" in people's faces, and he arranged to have the pictures of notorious criminals displayed in the corridor outside his office. They are said to have been a "criminal-looking" lot.

No reputable scholar now agrees with the **Lombrosian view,** and the ugly and the handsome alike are arrested for crimes every day. Indeed, biological explanations are in general disrepute, though recent discoveries regarding the XYY chromosome pattern spurred a reconsideration of the matter.

Sociologists have given more credence to psychological explanations of deviance. The Freudian point of view, for example, suggests that all people have antisocial impulses that would result in deviant acts were it not for socialization. The development of the individual's superego, the internalization of social agreements, thus prevents deviance. Those who do break the agreements, in this point of view, were improperly socialized.

Unstable or broken families are often seen as the source of improper or inadequate socialization. Those deprived of normal family relations, it is suggested, are more likely to become deviant than those who are not. Illustrating this point of view, a gang member in *West Side Story* sings, "I'm depraved because I'm deprived."

Sociologists have paid considerable attention to psychological factors in the study of deviance, but there are also more strictly social causes. We are going to look at some of those in this section, beginning with Robert Merton's classic examination of **social disorganization.** Then we'll look at some of the other explanations sociologists have offered, concluding with a look at the ways in which labeling can *cause* deviance as well as define it.

Social Disorganization

Robert Merton and other sociologists have suggested that deviance results from social disorganization and the feelings of anomie (sense of "normlessness") that it produces. In particular, Merton has focused attention on the disparity between social agreements relating to goals and means.

As we have seen throughout this book, every society has shared agreements pertaining to what is valued and desired. Wealth, for example, is an agreed-on goal for individuals in many societies. Societies also have agreements regarding the acceptable means for achieving goals. The problem comes when individuals who internalize the agreements regarding goals lack the agreed-on means for achieving them. The person who accepts the desirability of a college diploma but lacks the scholarly abilities to achieve it has such a problem. This person might adopt other means—such as cheating on examinations—to achieve the desired goal. The potential discrepancy between goals and means led Merton to construct a typology of possible responses to both goals and means. His typology is shown in Table 13·4.

Merton (1957a) describes four major types of deviance that result when goals are not integrated with means. "Innovation" is his term for the acceptance of agreed-on goals coupled with the rejection of agreed-on means (the means are often rejected because they are not available). Thus, the child of a poor ghetto family may find himself or herself unable to pursue the goal of wealth through conventional means and substitutes other means such as stealing or cheating. "Ritualism" is Merton's term for the situation in which a person conforms to the agreed-on patterns of behavior but lacks a real commitment to the goals associated with that behavior. A clerk may continue going to work at an office, doing his or her job as prescribed, but may do so without any commitment to getting rich. "Retreatism" is a pattern of withdrawal from society. Heroin addiction is an extreme case of the rejection of both agreed-on goals and means.

Finally, "rebellion" is characterized by the rejection of both agreed-on goals and agreed-on means

Table 13·4 Merton's Typology of Deviance and Conformity

Term	Acceptance of agreed-on Goals	Means	Examples
Conformity	+[a]	+	The nondeviant
Innovation	+	−[b]	The thief, the "crooked" businessman
Ritualism	−	+	The lower middle-class office worker with little ambition
Retreatism	−	−	The tramp, the drug addict, the skid-row dropout
Rebellion	±[c]	±	The political revolutionary

[a] + Accepts the agreement.
[b] − Rejects the agreement.
[c] ± Replaces the agreement with another one.

Source: Robert Merton, Social Theory and Social Structure (Glencoe, Ill.: Free Press, 1957); see especially pp. 139–57.

and their replacement with new goals and means. The person who rejects the economic goals of individualistic capitalism as well as the accepted patterns of participation in it and who works for the establishment of a socialist economy is an example of a person in rebellion.

You may have noticed how closely Merton's examination of social disorganization and deviance relates to the discussions of institutionalization in Part Three. Recall how institutionalized agreements are frequently the source of individual dissatisfaction. Now we've seen more specifically how those dissatisfactions are manifested in the form of deviance.

Many people although motivated to engage in deviant behavior fail to do so. A variety of social control mechanisms prevent them. When the social control mechanisms are weak, however, deviance may result.

Lack of Social Control

Whereas psychologists have explained deviance largely in terms of the failure of internal controls, some sociologists have looked to the failure or lack of external controls. Travis Hirschi and Hanan Selvin (1967), for example, found this point of view useful in examining the frequently noted relationship between broken homes and delinquency.

According to Hirschi and Selvin, broken homes do not per se foster delinquency. It is the lack of adult supervision, more typical in broken homes, that has this effect. Children living in families with both a father and a mother are more likely to have after-school supervision than those living with only their mother, since she is likely to be out of the home working. In families where children *do* have adult supervision, broken homes produce no more delinquency than unbroken ones.

The importance of informal social control mechanisms for deviant behavior is also illustrated in a recent study of marijuana use among students at the University of Hawaii (Takeuchi 1974). The study began with the observation that even though many people have tried to explain drug use among students, no one has ever thought to ask why students drink beer. Indeed, the student who steadfastly refused to drink beer would probably be regarded as deviant.

The study took the point of view, then, that marijuana was like beer and that all college students would be motivated to try it because of its popularity and publicity. The study asked why some students did *not* try it. Three different social constraints were suggested to explain nonuse. It was found that women were less likely than men to smoke marijuana because American society is generally less permissive with women in terms of illegal behavior. Second, it was found that students living at home with their parents and those living in dormitories were less likely to smoke marijuana than those living in apartments. The first two groups experienced greater social control from adult authorities. Finally, it was found that Oriental students were less likely to smoke marijuana than non-Orientals, and it was suggested that Oriental subcultures in America have traditionally been more insistent about law-abiding behavior.

When these three forms of social constraints were combined, they provided a greater prediction of marijuana use or nonuse than any of the study's measures of students' attitudes or orientations. Among Oriental women living at home, for example, only 10 percent had ever tried marijuana. At the other extreme—non-Oriental men living in apartments—77 percent had tried marijuana.

Realize that the lack of social constraints did not cause students to smoke marijuana any more than the lack of adult supervision in the home caused the Hirschi-Selvin delinquents to be delinquent. Many people are motivated to be deviant, but only some of them are prevented from it by external social controls.

Deviant Subcultures

The "deviance" of many "deviants" is actually a matter of conformity, as I have suggested earlier in this book. While deviance is regarded as breaking the agreements of the larger society, many subcultures have their own agreements that vary from those of the larger society. Thus, a person may be regarded as deviant from the point of view of the larger society at the same time that he or she is seen as conformist from the subculture's point of view. Many sociologists, in fact, have regarded "deviance" as a matter of being socialized within subcultures.

The classic statement of this point of view may

be found in Sutherland's (1924) notion of **differential association.** Sutherland argued that the socialization process was essentially the same, regardless of whether the agreements being transmitted were conformist or deviant. The explanation for "deviance," in this view, was to be found in the social groups with whom one associated. The member of a juvenile gang learns and accepts the agreements of the gang, just as the Boy Scout learns and accepts the agreements of scouting and—by extension—the agreements of the larger society.

Interestingly, this point of view provides a basis for criticism of prisons and other penal institutions. Prisons are sometimes referred to as "schools for crime." Associating with no one but criminals can have the effect of further socializing people in criminal agreements. There is a wealth of anecdotal material describing people who were imprisoned for relatively minor offenses but who became dedicated and well-trained criminals during their stay in prison.

The Labeling of Deviants

While all of us are deviants in one way or another, only a few of us get labeled as such. Some sociologists have pointed out that the process of labeling can itself be a cause of deviance. The accompanying box, "Resistance to Labeling," suggests how the process might work.

Edwin Lemert (1951) has distinguished between **primary deviance** and **secondary deviance.** The first of these—primary deviance—refers to deviant behavior that is generally tolerated by those around you (perhaps because it seems trivial) or deviant acts that you successfully conceal from others. In either event, nobody considers you a deviant nor do you consider yourself one. While you might be able to continue your particular deviancy forever with impunity, it can also provide a basis for your being labeled a deviant.

Suppose, for example, that you are a young girl growing up in a small town with very strict, traditional standards regarding sexual behavior. Premarital intercourse is prohibited in this town and almost nobody does it, especially young girls from respected families like yours. Suppose you did it anyway. That would be an example of primary deviance, and it

might not amount to anything as long as nobody else knew about it. If word got around, however, you might find yourself branded as "loose," "easy," or worse. The boys might treat you as though you wanted to have sex with everyone, and the girls might avoid you—perhaps at their parents' urging—as immoral and a bad influence. Eventually, you might give in to the group's agreement and start behaving the way they all seemed to expect you to. Your sexual behavior at this point becomes an example of secondary deviance, illustrating the powerful effect of labeling in perpetuating standards and in structuring the experiences of individuals in society.

Howard Becker in *Outsiders* (1963) devoted special attention to the manner in which people develop self-identities as "deviants," based on their being so identified by others. Another sociologist, Erving Goffman, has addressed the same issue with regard to patients in mental institutions (1961) and persons with physical deformities (1963).

Individual and Society

Our discussion of deviance has come quite a distance from Bat Guano's "deviated prevert." One issue runs throughout. The issue is the relative responsibility to be assigned individuals or the society for the existence of deviance. People disagree.

On the one hand, it is argued that deviants themselves are responsible for their behavior and for the punishment they may suffer because of it. On the other hand, it is argued that the very structure of society and the actions of those in power create deviance, and that deviants are themselves the victims.

This disagreement has persisted throughout history, with occasional swings of the pendulum from one side to the other. It is a critical issue in the area of social control, especially with regard to the punishment or other treatment of deviants.

Social Control

If deviance is the breaking of agreements, "social control" is the enforcement of agreements. Every society has mechanisms for the enforcement of agreements. We have already discussed two important social control mechanisms in earlier chapters: socialization and peer-group pressure. In addition, certain agencies in society have social control as their specific function. Some of these we're going to examine now.

Police

The most visible agents of social control in modern societies are the police officers. Their job is to see that other members of society keep the agreements and that those who break the agreements are

Resistance to Labeling

The label "criminal" and its effects involve more than the seriousness of the crime committed. The results of a few studies illustrate this point clearly.

In a well-planned field experiment by Steffensmeier and Terry,[1] an actor deliberately shoplifted a store item under direct observation of an unsuspecting customer. After the "thief" moved away, two other actors appeared on the scene as "store employees." The first "store employee" simply rearranged items on shelves, giving the customer the opportunity to report the crime. If no report was made, the second "employee" replaced the first and told the customer he suspected that a shoplifting had occurred. The customer was asked if he or she had seen anything suspicious. The experiment was repeated with 212 customers.

Characteristics of the "thief" were varied with each episode. The shoplifter appeared either as a female or a male and as a "hippie" in appearance or a "straight"—four possible types of offenders. The sex of the offender made little difference to the customer, but the offender's appearance greatly influenced the customer's willingness to report the crime. "Hippies" were reported far more often than "straights" for exactly the same crime. Whether or not one receives the label "criminal" obviously involves more than violating the law.

The effects of labeling also involve more than the seriousness of the crime committed. In another field experiment, Schwartz and Skolnick[2] distrib-

uted employment folders to potential employers of unskilled workers. The folders were alike in every aspect but one: criminal record. Some folders noted that the employment applicant had been convicted of assault in court. Other folders indicated that the applicant had been tried for assault but acquitted. Still other folders indicated a trial for assault and subsequent acquittal and included a letter from a judge affirming the individual's innocence. Finally, some folders simply made no mention of a criminal record. Employers were consistently willing to hire the individual with no record and less willing to hire even those acquitted individuals with a letter from a judge. Even the suspicion of a label was detrimental for the unskilled worker.

Schwartz and Skolnick also studied the results of malpractice suits brought against doctors.[3] In contrast to the experience of the unskilled workers described above, the suggestion of a deviant label had no ill effects for the physicians. In fact, in most instances, their practices improved! Practices improved even when the court ruled in favor of the suing patient and against the doctor. The authors suggest that many things determine the effects of a label. As we see here, social class, professional status, demand for services, and publicity are but a few of the factors that must be considered.

Recently some citizens have expressed concern about the mild sentences many of the Watergate-related offenders have received for their crimes. With the above examples in mind, what does this complaint suggest about differences in individuals' ability to resist the effects of labeling?

[1]Darrell J. Steffensmeier and Robert M. Terry, "Deviance and Respectability: An Observational Study of Reaction to Shoplifting," *Social Forces* 51(1973):417–26.
[2]Richard D. Schwartz and Jerome H. Skolnick, "Two Studies of Legal Stigma," *Social Problems* 10(1962):133–38.

[3]Ibid.

brought to the attention of the group for possible punishment.

In recent years, the American police have been increasingly scrutinized by sociologists and the general public. Predominantly white and of the lower middle class, police are generally conservative politically and share the biases of their racial and socioeconomic classes. The abuse of power by police officers during the civil rights and peace movements has been widely reported, and many communities have instituted civilian review boards to oversee police activities.

In *Police Riots,* Rodney Stark (1972) undertook a careful examination of the events taking place in several campus outbreaks during the 1960s. In many of those, he found that relatively peaceful demonstrations had turned to violence when the police intervened. Sometimes the presence of large numbers of police sparked a reaction from campus demonstrators. Many times, unprovoked attacks by police led to counterattacks by demonstrators.

Much of the criticism of police is directed at their discretionary powers. The extent of lawbreaking in a society such as ours is too great to permit total enforcement. Police must choose which laws they will enforce and in what ways. To take a limited example, the police simply could not apprehend every person exceeding speed limits by 1 mile per hour, so their efforts are limited to those speeding "too much." Notice that the officer on the beat gets to decide what constitutes "too much," and there is evidence that other factors are involved in such decisions besides the number of miles per hour a person is speeding.

To test the possibility, a sociology class at the University of California conducted a simple experiment. Twelve students with previously clean driving records put "Black Panther Party" bumper stickers on their cars. In 2½ weeks, they had received thirty police citations at a cost of $1,000 (Mitford 1973).

The most damning criticism lodged against police is that of corruption. By giving police special authority to employ force and violence, we expect them to keep the agreements of society even more faithfully than the rest of us. A number of studies suggest they are not always successful.

Albert Reiss, Jr. (1971), and a team of researchers accompanied urban patrolmen on their rounds. They were astounded by the extent of crime practiced by the officers in their presence. Police rolled drunks, took objects from burglary scenes, accepted bribes, and assaulted numerous individuals without provocation. Overall, one officer in five was observed to commit a crime during the course of the study, and the researchers could only guess at the extent of such crime when the police were not accompanied by researchers.

The President's Commission on Law Enforcement and Administration of Justice (1967:99) asked the National Opinion Research Center to conduct a nationwide survey on public attitudes toward the police. Less than two-thirds of the whites questioned and only 30 percent of the nonwhites said they felt the police in their neighborhoods were "almost all honest." Indeed, 10 percent of the nonwhites said they were "almost all corrupt." Not surprisingly, the commission found attitudes toward the police worse in high-crime areas of the nation's urban slums and ghettos than in other areas.

Courts

The aspect of formal social control that begins with the police often—though not always—involves another social control agent: the courts. In theory, the police *allege* that individuals have broken society's agreements; the courts make the final decision and determine the sanctions warranted.

The police-courts system of social control is illustrated graphically in Figure 13•1, which also shows the number of persons "processed" in 1965 and the public costs involved.

In 1965 for every 16.5 crimes known to police, 1 person was fined or imprisoned. Only a fraction of those arrested by police were eventually found guilty of an offense. There are a variety of different explanations for such statistics. Some are quick to suggest that overly lenient judges "mollycoddle criminals," while others suggest that the system would work better if the police only arrested guilty people. Whatever point of view is adopted, however, it is clear that the American criminal-justice system is not

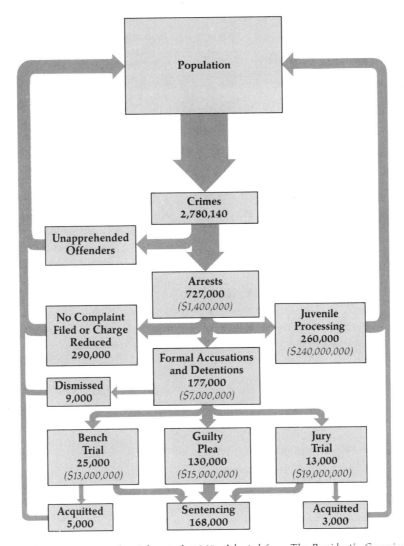

Figure 13•1   The police/court system of social control, 1965. Adapted from The President's Commission on Law Enforcement and Administration of Justice, The Challenge of Crime in a Free Society, *1967, pp. 262–63.*

a particularly efficient or effective component of American society.

Another thing is clear. People who commit crimes and are sentenced are not a cross section of America's criminals. They are disproportionately poor and nonwhite. Whites and the wealthy stand a better chance than poor nonwhites of avoiding conviction and punishment if they are arrested.

Prisons

Near the end of the criminal-justice system lie the nation's several thousand prisons and jails. Exclusion from the normal activities of society is one possible punishment for the breaking of agreements.

Ever since prisons first gained popularity 150 years ago, there has been a continuing disagreement as to their purpose. Four primary purposes have enjoyed the greatest agreement:

1. *Protection of society.* Locking offenders away prevents them from committing crimes against the rest of society.

2. *Punishment.* Suffering is a morally just payment for causing suffering to others.

3. *Deterrence.* The threat of imprisonment and the example made of offenders will deter others from committing crimes.

4. *Rehabilitation.* Offenders should be resocialized to permit their return to normal, productive social lives.

The prison system would seem to serve partially the purpose of protecting society from criminal assault. Those in prison do not, in fact, commit many crimes against those on the outside *during their time in prison.* They *do* commit crimes against each other, however: homosexual assault, extortion, assault, and murder.

The punishment purpose of prisons depends so directly on one's point of view on morality that its success or failure is difficult to test except by definition. Evidence suggests that the general public emphasizes the punishment purpose less than it once did.

The deterrent purpose of prisons surely has some effect on crime rates. The threat of imprisonment is a part of the external controls that discourage some people from committing deviant acts. The continual growth in crime rates nationally, however, indicates that it is scarcely a *sufficient* deterrent to crime. The box "Does the Death Penalty Deter Murder?" raises further questions.

Finally, many sociologists and others have been particularly attentive to the rehabilitative purpose of prisons. Countless innovative programs have been instituted with a rehabilitative aim. This emphasis is reflected in the language we attach to prisons, calling them "correctional" institutions and (those for youth) "reform" schools.

How successful have prisons been in this regard? Gene Kassebaum (1974:80–81) sets the stage for an evaluation:

The highest priority concerns of 20th-century evaluation of correctional programs revolve around whether the offender shows signs of change and whether the recidivism rate goes down or up. Modern correctional philosophy implicit in the origins of the juvenile court and explicit in the new ideology of adult corrections is necessarily dependent on proof that its programs produce effects. It has nothing else to argue; without this evidence, or in the face of evidence to the contrary, modern juvenile and adult corrections is a pretense that falls short of justice and cure alike.

Recidivism refers to the return to prison by those previously imprisoned and released: the "repeat offenders." The success of prisons' rehabilitative function is measured by the extent to which ex-convicts stay out of prison after their release.

By the recidivism standard, the American corrections system is not very successful. The president's commission (1967:259) reported that between one-third and two-thirds of those released from prison return and that an innovative program producing "a return rate of between one-seventh and one-eighth is remarkable." The general failure of the corrections system to "correct" has led some critics to conclude that the only thing prisons are known to cure is heterosexuality.

Does the Death Penalty Deter Murder?

The U.S. Supreme Court has recently been considering the constitutionality of capital punishment. One of the key issues in the debate over the death penalty is whether or not it deters people from committing serious violent crimes like murder and rape. This issue reflects a central sociological interest in punishment and social control: Can we deter deviance through strict penalties?

In one important study, William C. Bailey collected data on homicides in forty-one states for the years 1967 and 1968. He divided his data into two categories: first-degree murders (killing with premeditation) and second-degree murders (killing without premeditation). Next, he computed homicide rates for each state, that is, the number of first- and second-degree murders for every 100,000 people in a state. For example, Illinois had 1.17 first-degree murders per 100,000 of its citizens in 1968. (Bailey's data are not totally reliable because they cannot account for plea bargaining, which resulted in murder charges being reduced to lesser charges. Even so, they are probably the best data we have.)

Bailey divided the forty-one states into two groups: those states with capital-punishment laws and those without capital-punishment laws. If capital punishment deters murder, states with the death penalty should have lower murder rates than states without the death penalty.

Does capital punishment deter murder? Bailey's study suggests that it does not. In fact, as the table below shows, capital-punishment states have higher homicide rates than non-capital-punishment states.

Bailey also compared murder rates for states that are geographical neighbors but differ in death-penalty policies. Again, he found higher murder rates among states with capital-punishment laws.

Some people note that states with the death penalty have not recently used it. Hence, they argue, it cannot be expected to deter murder. Murderers are sure that they will never be put to death for their crimes. To check this, Bailey looked at death-penalty states and compared the murder rates of states with more executions and states with fewer executions. He found that more frequent use of the death penalty by a state has little to do with its murder rates.

The evidence compiled by Bailey and others suggests that, at least in regard to the death penalty and murder, punishment does not deter deviance. The Supreme Court justices must decide the capital-punishment issue by sorting out the validity of many different arguments, both pro and con.

Do you feel that Bailey's evidence might convince the justices that the deterrence argument is invalid?

Average Rate Per 100,000 Population of First- and Second-Degree Murders for Capital-Punishment and Non-Capital-Punishment States, 1967 and 1968

	Non-capital-punishment states		Capital-punishment states	
	1967	1968	1967	1968
First-degree murder	.18	.21	.47	.58
Second-degree murder	.30	.43	.92	1.03
Total murders	.48	.64	1.38	1.59

Source: Text and table adapted from William C. Bailey, "Murder and Capital Punishment," in Criminal Law in Action, ed. William J. Chambliss. Copyright © 1975 by John Wiley & Sons, Inc. Reprinted by permission of John Wiley & Sons, Inc.

Do prisons accomplish their purpose? The question still cannot be answered. We do not have satisfactory alternatives for dealing with serious deviance. (Paul S. Conklin)

source of change in a society. A society's agreements only change when individuals break agreements and substitute others in their place. Albert Einstein was a deviant who broke our agreements regarding the nature of reality. Martin Luther King, Jr., was a deviant who broke our agreements regarding black-white relations.

Social control, by definition, militates against social change—including changes that we might later agree are for the better. Social control systems have the effect of reifying agreements, and social control agents often behave as though all agreements are sacred.

This phenomenon is clearly illustrated by the following comment from Harry Anslinger of the Federal Bureau of Narcotics in response to a medical report suggesting that marijuana is harmless:

> Of course, the primary interest of the Bureau of Narcotics is the enforcement aspect. From this point of view it is very unfortunate that Doctors Allentruck and Bowman should have stated so unqualifiably that the use of marijuana does not lead to physical, mental or moral deterioration (Quoted in Arnold 1967:127).

Enforcement of antimarijuana laws makes no sense if marijuana is harmless. From an enforcement point of view, it is reasoned, the harmlessness of marijuana would be "unfortunate." Social control represents a point of view that conflicts with others in society. The box "What Lies behind the Attempt to Outlaw Certain Behaviors?" elaborates on this matter.

Dysfunctions of Social Control

Throughout this section, I have pointed to various dysfunctions in systems of social control. Among other topics, we have looked at abuses of power by police and at the problems of prisons. In these final comments, I'd like to examine a dysfunction inherent in social control more generally.

Although deviance is generally regarded in a negative light, we have also noted that it is the only

Summary

In simplest terms, deviance is the breaking of society's agreements. The matter is more complicated than that, however. First, all of us are deviants in that we break many of our society's agreements every day. At the same time, all of us—including the most hardened criminals—conform most of the time.

Deviance, then, is a matter of (1) breaking an agreement and (2) being socially identified or labeled as a deviant. Labeling theory in sociology addresses

What Lies behind the Attempt to Outlaw Certain Behaviors?

Emile Durkheim once noted that crime is an integral part of any healthy society. He was referring to the fact that members of society are made more aware of the values they hold in common when they react to a crime. Social solidarity is then increased. Various forms of "deviance" may also stimulate needed change in a society. The civil rights sit-ins of the 1950s and the race riots of the 1960s forced society to confront problems it was ignoring. In his book *Wayward Puritans,* Kai Erikson[1] suggests that deviance may force a society to define more clearly its boundaries of acceptable behavior and the type of society it wishes to be.

The larger and more complex a society, the more likely that the outlawing of a particular form of behavior is functional for certain interest groups in their struggles with other interest groups. Often, as Joseph Gusfield[2] points out in *Symbolic Crusade,* the behavior that is contested is symbolic of deeper issues. Thus, the temperance movement's struggle for passage of the Prohibition Act in 1919 repre-

sented more than a fight against alcoholic-beverage consumption. It symbolized the struggle for supremacy between the forces of traditional, Protestant, rural, middle-class America and America's newcomers—the urban, predominantly Catholic immigrant class. The repeal of the Volstead Act in 1933 signaled the beginning of major changes in American life and a symbolic defeat for the traditional classes and their values.

We should look beyond contested behaviors for the issues they mask. The legislation and enforcement of drug laws in the 1960s may have represented more than an antidrug movement. The war on drugs may have symbolized a condemnation of "new-left," "unpatriotic," antiwar, anticapitalist youth by the forces of "middle America" trying to preserve traditional values.

We are currently debating the legality of pornography. Is it only pornography that is at issue? Or is the pornography debate symbolic of a deeper controversy about general sexual and moral values in this society? Think about liberalized homosexual laws, abortion, gun control, and mercy killing. What greater issues lie behind the attempts to outlaw or legalize these behaviors?

[1]Kai Erikson, *Wayward Puritans* (New York: Wiley, 1966).

[2]Joseph Gusfield, *Symbolic Crusade* (Urbana: University of Illinois Press, 1963).

this two-dimensional concept of deviance. Some labeling theorists speak of primary deviance (breaking an agreement, even though it may go unnoticed) as distinct from secondary deviance (deviant behavior that follows from a person being labeled deviant and taking on the expectations of that status).

The functionalist and conflict points of view picture deviance differently. From the functionalist point of view, deviance is seen as a threat to social stability. From the conflict point of view, deviance is sometimes seen as a challenge to established authority and a source of social change.

There have been countless theories of the causes of deviance: some biological, some psychological, and some strictly sociological. Some sociologists have examined deviance in terms of social disorganization

(the disparity between agreed-on goals and agreed-on means of achieving them). Others have focused on the lack of effective social control, while still others have seen it as a matter of socialization into "deviant" subcultures.

Social control refers to the enforcement of society's agreements. Socialization and peer-group pressures are examples of social control, and every society has certain persons and agencies with special responsibilities for this function. Police, courts, and prisons are prime examples in our society.

Social control mechanisms—charged with enforcing and maintaining the established agreements—can also be dysfunctional for society. They are an impediment to social change, preventing and slowing even those changes that we might all agree later were important and just. Social control is an important factor in the reification of society's agreements.

Suggested Readings

Becker, Howard
1963   *The Outsiders.* New York: Free Press.
Here's an early statement of the labeling view of deviance by one of its main proponents. Writing prior to the general, informal acceptance of marijuana use, Becker devotes much of his attention to the subcultural aspects of that grass-roots movement and the nature of social control, zeroing in on what he calls the "moral entrepreneurs."

Goffman, Erving
1961   *Asylums: Essays on the Social Situation of Mental Patients and Other Inmates.* Chicago: Aldine.
No one has portrayed the life of inmates more vividly and perceptibly than Goffman. Focusing primarily on mental hospitals—with references to prisons, naval ships, monasteries, and other "total institutions"—Goffman examines both structural and interactionist aspects of life "on the inside." He brings his sociological insights together in a discussion of the ways in which inmates "make out" by learning and playing the system.

Kassebaum, Gene
1974   *Delinquency and Social Policy.* Englewood Cliffs, N.J.: Prentice-Hall.
Kassebaum presents the many sides of juvenile delinquency as he summarizes the theories and research concerning the nature and causes of a persistent social problem. In part, however, the "problem" lies in the social-structural agreements that define deviance. A variety of "status crimes," for example, define certain behaviors as criminal for young people but legal for adults. Kassebaum examines the role of public policy in resolving delinquency as broadly understood.

Scheff, Thomas
1966   *Being Mentally Ill: A Sociological Theory.* Chicago: Aldine.
The ambiguities of defining and treating "mental illness" are examined in detail in this application of labeling theory. In a direct challenge to the "medical model," Scheff places this form of deviance within the context of social agreements, laying the basis for a more humane understanding and handling of emotional differences among people.

Episode Thirteen

Thunderstorms drenched Chicago July 4, 2027. The American University faculty sailboat regatta which was to take place in Lake Michigan had to be canceled. Instead, faculty members and friends milled about the university campus. Louise, Brad, and Connie and their spouses gathered near the bowling lanes in the university student center. With them were Monica and several friends she had met through her membership in Civil Liberty for All.

Brad lowered his right knee and let go of the bowling ball. "Strike!" he roared, jumping up. "This beats flies and mosquitoes any day." He penciled his score onto the scoresheet. "Actually I'm glad it rained. I hate picnics."

"It's un-American to hate picnics, Bradley," Constance joked, scooping up a handful of salted, roasted soybeans. "It's deviant behavior."

Monica's thoughts had meanwhile turned to Gabriel. She had received the note he had written her his last day in Chicago. He would have been nervous and fidgety, Monica noted now, on a day like today. Rain always irritated him.

Louise Roanoke understood the shadow that had spread across her niece's face. "He'll be safer in Adamsville," Dr. Roanoke said, reading the younger woman's thoughts.

During the months that Monica had refused to see Gabe, she had been active with both former and new friends. While immediately after the termination of their relationship, Gabriel had occupied virtually all Monica's thoughts, she found that as the months progressed her mind turned to him less frequently.

When she did think of him, it was often his involvement in the Lake Hospital kidnapping that was foremost in her thoughts. She wondered about the victimized mother of the stolen infant; she wondered how the baby himself was getting along in Adamsville.

Now she said—more to herself than to anyone in the group—"I don't think I will ever respect him again after the kidnapping."

"But he doesn't see the rescue as a crime, Monica," Bradley Duncan offered. "In Gabriel's culture what he did was not wrong but something to be admired."

"Kidnapping ought to be wrong in any culture," Monica replied. She placed her thumb and fingers into a bowling ball.

Connie Batterson joined the conversation. "Monica," she said, "you're a member of CLA now. Would you defend Gabe if he were arrested for the kidnapping?"

"He would deserve the best possible defense he

could get," Monica said. "But that doesn't lessen the fact that stealing babies from their parents is wrong."

"Only because some people have decided it is," Brad said flatly, then hurled a heavy ball onto the alley before him.

"And because to permit kidnapping would be harmful to society," Louise added. She raised the ball until it was level with her chin, looking past it intently to the three pins she would drop for a spare.

"Kidnapping is wrong because those who are in power see it as wrong and have the strength to impose their morality upon others," Connie suggested.

Monica slammed her bowling ball onto the rack beside her. "Sometimes I get sick of this sociological game playing," she exploded suddenly. "Kidnapping is wrong because it's wrong, that's all. It's a lousy, rotten, criminal thing to do!"

Louise rushed to her niece, wrapping her arm around Monica's shoulder.

Batterson spoke. "I'm sorry, Monica. Really. I guess we sociologists forget how much our professional objectivity can irritate people."

Duncan scurried to a portable bar on the other side of the room and returned with two beers. He handed one to Monica. "Here," he said, "let's drink to the Fourth of July. I'm sorry."

The strong odor of gunpowder assaulted Gabriel's nostrils as he made his way from Adamsville cemetery toward the community's southern entrance. It was the Fourth of July, and Gabe expected the air near the entrance to be heavy with gunpowder. Yet the smell frightened him. He wondered how he would know as he stood guard during the night whether the explosive claps he heard were innocent fireworks or shots aimed toward his colony.

Two days earlier, on the afternoon of Gabriel's public confession, Larry Jones had successfully insisted that Knapp be assigned night guard duty at the south gate.

Jones had followed Ruth and Michael to Elderhome after watching in horror their performance at Gabriel's public confession. He had found his great aunt and uncle seated in the front parlor.

"Why did you do such a thing?" he had demanded. "What you said from that platform was against everything Adam stood for. It was wrong!"

Ruth handed Larry Duncan's sociological report. Slowly Larry had read it. Finally he asked, his voice loud with anger, "Why did you let them come here? Adam never allowed outsiders in! Why did you do it?" Larry grew furious, shaking his fist. "Now you're following their advice! Your foolish collaboration with these—these protein-consuming social scientists

—goes against all Adam taught!" The Elders remained calm, showing almost no reaction.

His anger increasing, Larry waved the report at them. "So this is why you made a mockery of the public confession? This is what led you to announce that Knapp won't have to live in the valley?"

"We studied the paper for several hours before doing what we did," Michael had said.

"We decided not to cancel Gabriel's confession, but to use it as an opportunity to demonstrate that Adamsville would begin to rethink its policy concerning dull greens."

Larry's voice grew sullen. "So you've begun to let ungreens tell you what's good for greens," he sneered. "If you plan to let Knapp live outside the valley," he said, "then I'm going to insist he take duty at one of the gates."

"He has considerable managerial experience," Ruth had ventured. "We thought we could use him at S.T.I. Perhaps after the furor over his rescue mission recedes, he could even travel for us."

Larry Jones glared. "I've got a lot of people on my side," he said coldly. "If you refuse to assign Knapp guard duty, I promise you your authority will be seriously challenged."

The next day Gabriel received an official communiqué from Elderhome. Gabe was invited to move into a glass fourplex located near the center of Adamsville. It was a habitat until now reserved for bright greens.

Also, the message read, Gabe was to replace a not-yet-matured young green named Peter Adamson as night guard at the south entrance beginning the next day, July 4.

Now Gabriel walked nervously toward his first night's watch. It was 4:30 P.M. He was scheduled to begin duty at 5.

Gabe had spent the earlier part of the afternoon at Adamsville cemetery, sitting beside Jonathan's simple headstone. Still aching from the blows he had suffered the previous week, he had gone to the graveyard to keep a belated vigil for the soft parent whom he had loved very much.

He sat quietly for a long time near the grave, soaking in the reality of Jonathan's death. He would have liked to ask Jonathan's forgiveness for his negligence as a son. Tears had filled Gabriel's eyes.

Sometime during the vigil Loretta Larson, Gabe's stern parent, approached. She had come to bring some desert flowers to place near Jonathan's grave.

"What are you doing here?" she had asked, startled. It was the first time since Gabe's return that she had spoken to him face to face.

"Just thinking, I guess," Gabriel said. "I miss him."

"You're too late for the vigil, you know. You didn't come home when you should have."

Gabriel had said nothing.

"Jonathan talked about you often, especially after the rescue last year. He was very fond of you, you know."

"I didn't know he was dead until Dan came," Gabe said. "Why didn't you call me when he died? I would have come for the vigil."

"Gabriel," Loretta said, "Adamsville has not ignored you. You have ignored Adamsville."

Gabe looked into the woman's face. "Remember how well we used to get along, you and me?"

Loretta studied Gabriel. "I'm told you still drink supplement," she said.

"Why does that have to matter?" Gabriel had demanded, suddenly desperate in his fear that the isolation he had known on the outside might continue in Adamsville.

"Drinking supplement at your age is a sign of disloyalty, Gabriel," Loretta reminded. She turned to leave. "It's wrong," she had added, walking away.

The conversation between Gabe and Loretta Larson had taken place hours before. Now Gabe entered the glass-roofed guard shelter. "How's it been?" he asked Ann Sullivan, the mutant he was to relieve.

Ann Sullivan was a chlorophyllic of fifty-three whose skin had never become more than faintly green. She lived in the valley, sharing an apartment with two other dull greens. Always tired and considered lazy, Ann was one of Adamsville's least valued citizens. While she had matured ceremonially when she was twenty-seven, the fact that the color of her skin remained dull was taken as a sign that she persisted in some sort of disloyalty.

Ann looked up at Gabriel. She said, "Some people came around yelling 'Kill the greenfaces'. And a lot of fireworks have been going off. But otherwise it's been pretty quiet." She rose to leave. "Well," she said slowly, "I guess I'll be going on home."

Gabriel sat down in the chair which Ann had vacated. He set a sack which he had carried onto the table in front of him. From it he pulled his thermos and poured himself a cup of milk.

"Can I have a swig of that?" Ann asked. "It's a long walk home, and I'm feeling a little weak."

"Are you sick?" Gabe noted that she looked faint.

"I don't think so," Ann responded. Gabriel offered her the milk he had poured. "From one milk-white to another," he said, pleased to be talking with a fellow dull green. "Now go home and get some rest."

"Thanks," she smiled. She swallowed the milk and was gone.

Gabe Knapp placed the palms of his hands against the sides of his body, applying gentle pressure to his aching ribs. Several hours passed. Loneliness crept into the shelter with the lengthening shadows. The pain in his jaw and ribs only accentuated his feelings of desolation.

He dug into his pockets for cigarettes. There was no place to buy them in Adamsville; greens did not smoke. He planned to quit what he knew was a bad habit when those he had brought with him from the outside were gone. Finding a rumpled package, he lit one of his few remaining smokes.

A car neared the gate. From the passenger window someone hurled an empty bottle. Seconds later Gabriel heard the squeal of tires and the evening was quiet.

For reasons which Gabriel didn't understand, his thoughts turned to the chromosomal mother of the infant he had rescued. It had been reported in the papers that she had suffered a nervous breakdown. Perhaps the rescues were wrong. Sometimes anyway. Perhaps Monica was right after all.

Knapp poured himself a cup of milk from the thermos. He was convinced now that what he had suggested to Daniel when the two had talked in his Chicago apartment was true. Religious loyalty had nothing at all to do with the color of his skin. He resolved to talk with Ann Sullivan about it soon.

It had grown dark. Three cars approached the gate from the outside. Their headlights went out. Gabe heard car doors open and shut, followed by approaching voices and footsteps. He stood, grabbing a solar laser projector from its position on the wall beside him.

The outsiders came closer.

"This is a lynch mob!" one of them yelled. Gabe heard them laugh.

He stepped from the shelter. "This is private property," he said. "If you come any closer, you'll be trespassing."

"Greenfaces don't own nothing but what they can steal," the response pierced the darkness.

"The state patrol is out there," Gabriel called. "They'll arrest you."

"We passed them down the road," someone answered. "They didn't pay us no attention."

"Stop!" Knapp shouted into the darkness. "I have a solar weapon. I'll shoot."

Suddenly one of them grabbed him from behind. Pain screeched through Gabe's body as he felt new blows to his already hurting ribs. The laser projector was knocked from his hand and lost in the darkness.

Someone grabbed Gabriel's ankles. Another held his arms, while still a third hit him about the head and chest.

"Hey, greenface," he heard one of them taunt, "how many babies have you stolen?"

"Hey, greeeeeeeeenie," another called, "it's the Fourth of July. Want to help us celebrate the Fourth of July?"

Half conscious, Gabriel vaguely perceived the arrival of a fourth vehicle. Two state police officers stepped out. A spotlight glared, flooding the area. As Gabriel lay limp on the sandy ground, he felt his attackers pulled away from him.

Later he was handcuffed along with the others. He felt himself being helped into the back seat of an automobile.

"We're taking you all in to St. Johns," one of the agents was saying. "We'll contact headquarters in Phoenix and decide what to do with all of you then."

At the tiny St. Johns police station, Gabe was escorted to a long, wooden bench. He sat across the room from his attackers. Bruised and bleeding, he felt himself growing sick to his stomach. He wished they would turn on more lights.

An officer approached. "What's your name?" he asked.

"Gabriel Knapp."

"You a resident of Adamsville?"

Gabe nodded. The officer left. When he returned a few minutes later, he said, "We're booking the others for disturbing the peace."

Gabe looked up. "Can I go home?" he asked. "They can take care of me in the hospital at home."

"Not if you're Gabriel Knapp," came the reply. "You're wanted for kidnapping."

Questions

1. How does the dialogue in this episode illustrate the labeling point of view on deviance? The conflict point of view? The functionalist point of view?

2. How do Monica's remarks illustrate the reified agreements of her own culture?

3. Using social disorganization theory, can you explain what "caused" Gabe to kidnap?

4. Gabe is a deviant in everybody's eyes. How might this result in secondary deviance inside and outside Adamsville?

5. Have the Elders been deviant in their treatment of Gabe? Has Larry Jones been deviant in challenging the authority of the Elders? How do you suppose others in Adamsville regard these actions?

Types of Collective Behavior

Fads, Fashions, and Crazes
Rallies
Mass Hysteria and Panic
Terrorist Mobs
Riots

Theoretical Points of View

Le Bon
Freud
Blumer
Smelser
A Note

Types of Social Movements

Expressive
Reactionary
Conservative
Reformist
Revolutionary

Elements in the Study of Social Movements

Conditions
The Role of Success
Leaders
Ideology
Membership and Participation
Organization

Summary

Suggested Readings

14

Collective Behavior
and Social Movements

Throughout Part Three of this book, we discussed some of the ways in which human behavior is organized and governed by integrated systems of agreements. In Chapter 13, we examined some of the ways in which individuals break those agreements. In the present chapter, we'll consider the ways in which groups of people operate outside the established agreements of society, often breaking them, and always creating new agreements in the process.

Collective behavior is a term that sociologists apply to spontaneous and disorganized group action such as panics and riots. Collective behavior is distinguished from **institutionalized behavior.** If all the workers at a factory show up for work on time, that is an example of institutionalized behavior. If, on the other hand, they stay away from work on a wildcat strike or burn the factory to the ground, that is an example of collective behavior.

This is not to say that collective behavior does not have organized aspects. Either the strike or the factory burning could have been planned in advance by some of the workers. To the extent, however, that the group behavior lies outside institutionally established agreements and is somewhat spontaneous, sociologists are likely to regard it as collective behavior.

As we will see, collective behavior is a process in which some established agreements get broken and new ones are created. Agreements are created, moreover, through action rather than deliberation and

negotiation. Think for a moment about some of the agreements we have regarding behavior in a theater. People are expected to sit quietly in their seats during the performance, and when they move up and down the aisles, they are expected to do so in an orderly fashion. Individuals are expected to respect the rights of others, and pushing and shoving are a clear violation of those agreements. When a fire breaks out in a theater, though, all those agreements disintegrate, and a new set of agreements is struck in the mad rush for exits.

Theater panics are only one type of collective behavior. Many different types have interested sociologists, and we'll begin the chapter with an examination of them. Then we'll look at some of the theoretical points of view that have been offered to explain collective behavior.

Social movements are similar to collective behavior in that they are group actions that diverge from established agreements. Social movements often grow out of collective behavior. They are distinguished from collective behavior by being more persistent and more organized. Over time, social movements may result in significant alterations to a society's agreements. The civil rights movement is an example.

Following the discussion of collective behavior, we'll look at some different kinds of social movements. After describing social movements, we'll take a look at the elements that make them up. The chapter concludes with a case study.

Types of Collective Behavior

We'll examine two forms of collective behavior in this section. The first involves the actions of a group, a lynch mob, for example, gathered together and *acting as a group.* This type of collective behavior occurs in **crowds,** audiences, and mobs.

The second form of collective behavior, the one that we'll begin with, doesn't involve an assembled group. It is a *mass* phenomenon, exemplified by fads, fashions, and crazes. Later, we'll look at two additional examples of this in Chapter 18 on communication: rumors and public opinion.

Fads, Fashions, and Crazes

Sociologists use the terms **fad,** "fashion," and "craze" to refer to widely shared points of view or practices that last a limited time and are about matters generally agreed to be unimportant. Certain voguish phrases and manners of speech are examples: "right on," "far out," "where it's at," "stonewall 'em," "expletive deleted," and "that explanation is now inoperative."

Dance crazes are another example of this form of collective behavior, ranging through the lindy, the

IT'S THE LATEST CRAZE TO SWEEP AMERICA.....

Charleston, the jitterbug, marathon dancing, the tango, the mambo, the twist, the frug, the monkey, Kung Fu dancing, and other things that people do with their bodies to music.

Even a partial listing of the various crazes that have swept America during this century alone may cause you to wonder how we survive as a society: goldfish swallowing, telephone-booth crowding, miniature golf, canasta, flagpole sitting, Monopoly, karate, barbeques, chain letters, grass, acid, pocket calculators, astrology, Mah-Jongg, massage, Hula-Hoops, drive-ins, and topless dancers.

The popularity of entertainers and other public figures is another example of fads and crazes. Different generations of Americans have become ecstatic and fainted over Rudy Vallee, Bing Crosby, Eddie Fisher, Frank Sinatra, Elvis Presley, the Beatles, and John Denver. Harry Truman, who was often unpopular as president, is becoming a folk hero as this is being written.

Clothing fashions and hairstyles go in and out of vogue. Women's hemlines and the length of men's hair have gone up and down for generations. Cardigans go in and out of fashion. So do cosmetics. Women curl their hair, then straighten it. Men grow beards, then shave them off. Hair has been a source of changing agreements for a long time, as the box "The Fad" details.

Fads, crazes, and fashions are fun, and for many people, they break the monotony of drab existence. They provide a sense of excitement and identification with others, a sense of belonging.

Rallies

People often engage in expressive group behavior, working themselves into a frenzy of oneness. College football rallies, religious revival meetings, political nominating conventions, rock concerts, peace marches, holiday celebrations, and the like are all examples. Individuals invest a part of their emotional beings in the whole of the group and feel themselves to be almost inseparable parts of it. Swept up in the spirit of the moment, they behave in ways they would otherwise avoid totally and do things that would be seen as inappropriate anywhere else.

The Fad

Long hair and beards have always been a matter of controversy. Dispute was on the meanings they represented, and the meanings changed with changes in people's opinions and moods.

In the eleventh century the Pope decreed against long hair. Men with long hair, he said, should be excommunicated and not prayed for after death. A knight in England was so guilt-stricken by his locks that he had a nightmare: The devil sprang upon him and tried to choke him with his own hair.

During the rise of Puritanism in England, the country was divided into Roundheads and Cavaliers. Puritans cut their hair short and saw vice in the curly tresses of the monarchist Cavaliers. A man's locks were the symbol of his political and religious creed. The more abundant the hair, the weaker the faith; and the balder the head, the more sincere the piety.

The severest attack on the beard came during the reign of Peter the Great, during the late seventeenth and early eighteenth centuries, in Russia. Russians loved to grow beards, especially as a mark of distinction from beardless foreigners. Peter ordered the beards to be shaved and imposed a "beard tax" of 100 rubles. For many years, large revenues were collected from this source, proof that many preferred to defy the decree and pay the tax.

After that, rulers of Europe refrained from dictating on hair and beard style. But moustaches were another matter. The king of Bavaria signed an ordinance in 1838 forbidding citizens to sport moustaches and ordering police to arrest and shave the offending growth. "Strange to say," a journal reported, "moustaches disappeared immediately, like leaves from the trees in autumn."

Source: Adapted from C. Mackay, "The Influence of Politics and Religion on Hair and Beards," in Extraordinary Delusions and the Madness of Crowds *(New York: Farrar, Straus & Cudahy, 1962).*

Mass Hysteria and Panic

Neil Smelser (1962) defines a hysterical belief as:

a belief empowering an ambiguous element in the environment with a generalized power to threaten or destroy. Examples of hysterical beliefs are premonitions of disaster and bogey rumors, both of which frequently build up as a prelude to panic (p. 84).

On October 30, 1938, Orson Welles broadcast a radio dramatization of H. G. Wells's science-fiction classic, *The War of the Worlds.* The program used the format of "news reports" of a flying saucer invasion of Earth from Mars. Reporters "on the scene" told of mass destruction by martian death rays. Before the program was over—the "invaders" were done in by bacteria—thousands of Americans had fled their homes, and highways were jammed with frantic motorists attempting to flee the invaders. This is a perfect example of mass hysteria and panic.

When we want to describe some act as maliciously irresponsible, we often say "it was like yelling 'fire' in a crowded theater." Crowded theaters have often been the scenes of panic. Eddy Foy, an entertainer, described the pandemonium he witnessed at the Iroquois Theater fire.

Somebody had of course yelled "Fire!"—there is almost always a fool of that species in an audience; and there are always hundreds of people who go crazy the moment they hear the word. . . .

The horror in the auditorium was beyond all description. There were thirty exits, but few of them were marked by lights; some had heavy portieres over the doors, and some of the doors were locked or fastened with levers which no one knew how to work. . . . The fire-escape ladders could not accommodate the crowd, and many fell or jumped to death on the pavement below. Some were not killed only because they landed on the cushion of bodies of those who had gone before. . . . In places on the stairways, particularly where a turn caused a jam, bodies were piled seven or eight feet deep. . . . The heel prints on the dead faces mutely testified to the cruel fact that human animals stricken by terror are as mad and ruthless as stampeding cattle (Foy and Harlow 1928:96–97).

The Iroquois Theater fire lasted from eight to ten minutes. During that time over 500 people died, and the final death toll from the panic was over 600.

The stock market is a frequent scene of panic as rumors of impending economic collapse send stockholders into a frantic flurry of selling. In the two months following the stock-market crash of October 29, 1929, a widely shared agreement held that prices would continue to go down. To avoid economic disaster, individuals unloaded their stock holdings—at low prices if necessary—which, of course, drove prices down. Some 15 billion (in 1929 dollars) was lost in the panic selling as tens of millions of stocks traded hands. To make matters more tragic, many of those who suffered financial ruin ended up taking their own lives as well.

Terrorist Mobs

Panics represent a retreat from a real or imagined danger; terrorist mobs, in contrast, represent an attack. The lynch mob is the most frequently cited type of terrorist mob. Typically, the mob grows out of an agreement that institutional agents of social control are not "doing their duty." The angry mob then takes the matter into its own hands.

Terrorist-mob actions almost always reflect more than the specific situation triggering them. The specific "evil" is usually the focus of a more general hostility and frustration among those joining the mob. Once the mob begins to act, the target of its attack often widens broadly, and increasing numbers of victims are added to its fury. The 1930 lynching in Leeville, Texas, is an example.

> When the mob discovered that their would-be victim was confined in the vault of the courthouse and was not readily accessible, they turned their fury on the courthouse itself, burning it recklessly and gleefully. Then, having killed their now accessible victim, they took his body to the Negro section of town, mutilated and burned it, and wreaked havoc on the property of many innocent Negroes (Turner and Killian 1957:133).

Though nearly 2,000 people—mostly black—have been lynched in America during this century, it is today a relatively rare event. Other forms of terrorist-mob behavior persist, however.

Riots

Riots are similar to terrorist mobs in hostility and violence, but they are generally more haphazard in their targets. In race riots, all members of the hated race become equal targets for violence, and once riots begin, violence for its own sake often becomes the norm. Race, religion, social class, ethnicity, and nationality have all provided the basis for riots. Often, several such bases are involved.

Midway through the Civil War, in 1863, the federal government enacted the nation's first draft law. It called for the conscription of young men into the Union army and allowed men to buy exemption from the draft for $300. The $300 exemption immediately outraged poor workers and labor organizations. The Civil War was already unpopular in the North, and the draft law was viewed as an attempt to force poor people to fight it.

Ironically, blacks—the poorest of all—became the chief *target* of the riot. Most simply put, poor white workers felt they were being forced to fight for the liberation of blacks who would then flood an already-tight job market. This sentiment was strongest among the newly arrived Irish workers of New York City. The "New York draft riots" of July 1863 were probably the most severe riots in American history. An estimated 2,000 people were killed, and property worth millions of dollars was damaged. One newspaper at the time called it "a perfect reign of terror" and expressed the belief that "not a single negro will remain within the metropolitan limits" (Quoted in Lofton 1957:136).

Riots did not begin nor did they end in 1863, and you are probably already familiar with some of the more recent riots in America such as the "big-city" riots in New York, Detroit, Newark, and elsewhere during the late 1960s and the many campus disturbances of that same period.

Riots present a challenge to social control agents such as police that cannot be ignored. Local police have often, in the past, looked the other way when lynchings were taking place, but full-blown riots must be faced by institutionally constituted authorities. And, as noted in Chapter 13, the police themselves often become swept up in the hysteria of the moment, needlessly destroying, hurting, and killing.

As we've seen, the term "collective behavior" covers a wide variety of actions. Some, like fads, fashions, and crazes, are basically harmless (if you're not a goldfish) and simply fun. Others, like panics, riots, and lynch mobs, are another matter. What are some of the explanations sociologists offer for this wide variety of behavior?

Theoretical Points of View

In this section, we are going to review the history of theoretical views on collective behavior. We'll begin with some early points of view and move to those that currently enjoy widely shared agreement among sociologists.

Le Bon

Gustave Le Bon's classic study *The Crowd* was first published in 1895 and was very popular at that time. It is today generally regarded as the first major work on collective behavior.

Le Bon was personally bothered by the excesses of the French Revolution and by the increasing militancy of workers during the Industrial Revolution. He also held a scientific point of view regarding crowds and collective behavior. He said that "the crowd is always intellectually inferior to the isolated individual" (Le Bon 1895:33) and went on to state what he saw as the special characteristics of crowds:

> impulsiveness, irritability, incapacity to reason, the absence of judgment and of the critical spirit, the exaggeration of the sentiments, and others besides— which are almost always observed in beings belonging to inferior forms of evolution—in women, savages, and children, for instance (pp. 35–36).

Much of Le Bon's attention was directed at what he called the "law of mental unity of crowds." Individuals gave up their mental individualities to the "group mind," forming a new entity akin to a biological organism. Le Bon stressed the degree of emotional contagion and suggestibility that prevailed under such conditions. If one person became angry, that

anger could sweep across the others in the crowd. If one became violent, so did the others.

It seems fair to say that Le Bon reified the crowd, saw it as a real entity. He often spoke of how the *crowd* thought, felt, and acted. The crowd was, for Le Bon, a hideous beast, threatening civilized society. More to the point, he had seen what crowds had done to the old, aristocratic order of France, a set of agreements that he clearly shared.

Freud

The year in which *The Crowd* first appeared also saw the publication of *Studies in Hysteria* by Breuer and Freud, a work dealing primarily with individual hysteria. Freud's later work on group psychology moved into the area of collective behavior, and Freud himself acknowledged his respect for Le Bon's work (Freud 1921).

Despite his general praise of Le Bon, Freud suggested that Le Bon's theory of crowds was wrong. Freud saw collective behavior (as he saw everything else) as largely a matter of the repression of basic drives and traumatic experiences in the individual's unconscious. Participation in crowds could be seen as a return to infancy. Individuals could experience dependence on a parentlike leader, identify with the leader, and take on the leader's characteristics, thoughts, and emotions as their own. As members

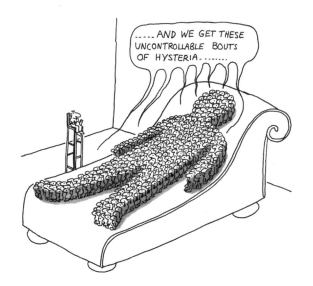

..... AND WE GET THESE UNCONTROLLABLE BOUTS OF HYSTERIA........

Herbert Blumer 1900– (The American Sociological Association)

of a crowd, moreover, individuals could also experience the sense of omnipotence that infants appear to experience before they differentiate themselves and their bodies from their environment.

Blumer

In 1939, Herbert Blumer, whose ideas on symbolic interactionism we discussed in Chapter 2 sought to describe the specific mechanisms through which contagion operated in crowds. Blumer defined his concept of "circular reaction" as "a type of inter-stimulation wherein the response of one individual reproduces the stimulation that has come from another individual and in being reflected back to this individual reinforces the stimulation" (Blumer 1946:170).

Blumer's examination of collective behavior reflected a more general interactionist point of view. Blumer thought the circular reaction of crowds was unlike the thoughtful reasoning that characterized other social interactions, and he likened it to the collective mindlessness of cattle.

> One sees the process clearly amidst cattle in a state of alarm. The expression of fear through bellowing, breathing, and movements of the body, induces the same feeling in the case of other cattle who, as they in turn express their alarm, intensify this emotional state in one another. It is through such a process of circular reaction that there arises among cattle a general condition of intense fear and excitement, as in the case of a stampede (1946:170).

Pursuing this bovine metaphor, Blumer saw "milling" as a basic form of behavior in crowds: "individuals move around amongst one another in an aimless and random fashion, such as in the interweaving of cattle and sheep who are in a state of excitement" (1946:174). The circular reaction fostered by milling set the stage for the development of rapport among crowd members, collective excitement, social contagion, and, finally, spontaneous behavior (1946).

For Blumer, collective behavior, with its circular reaction and contagion, was a source of more general social unrest, resulting in social movements and revolutions. Collective behavior forged individual "restlessness" into social unrest. Blumer saw social unrest, at the same time, as an "incipient preparation for new forms of collective behavior" (1946:173).

Smelser

The view that general social unrest *produces* collective behavior is more structuralist than interactionist. The structuralist point of view on collective behavior has been most thoroughly stated by Neil Smelser, a student of Talcott Parsons, in the classic *Theory of Collective Behavior* (1963).

Smelser's examination of collective behavior is patterned after the economic **value-added** model. In this model new "value" is added at each stage in the processing of a resource as it becomes a usable commodity. As iron ore becomes steel, for example, then the parts of a machine, and finally the assembled machine itself, it becomes gradually more valuable. In a similar fashion, Smelser (1963) traces the "production" of collective behavior from start to finish. Let's look at each of the stages in Smelser's model.

1. *Structural conduciveness.* To begin, in Smelser's view, collective behavior cannot occur unless certain structural conditions permit it. Using an economic example, he notes that a financial panic cannot occur under conditions in which property can only be passed from father to eldest son at the father's death. By the same token, a race riot cannot develop without races, nor a confrontation with police without both police and confronters.

2. *Structural strain.* Next, collective behavior requires some degree of "disagreement," as we have used that term in this book. It requires conflicting points of view. They may occur in disagreeing groups, such as racial, ethnic, or religious groups. There may also be a disagreement between ideas—between the general value placed on economic success and beliefs about the future of the economy, for example.

3. *Growth and spread of a generalized belief.* Members of a group must create and share their own agreements, such as the belief that Martians are invading earth or that blacks are invading Cicero, Illinois. Such agreements can take the form of hysterical beliefs about present or future events, hostile beliefs about out-groups, and the like.

4. *Precipitating factors.* Against the backdrop of general unrest, something must occur that brings matters to a head. In a situation of general concern over the possibility of residential integration, a black family's moving into a white neighborhood may be sufficient. At a time of general economic concern and uncertainty, the meeting of high-level economic officials may be the precipitating factor for a financial panic.

5. *Mobilization of participants for action.* Collective behavior needs a triggering event. Sometimes it takes the form of a fistfight in an assembled crowd. A financial panic may be triggered by

the sale of a large block of stocks. Stark (1972) has suggested that the arrival of police at a demonstration can trigger a riot. At the Iroquois Theater it was someone screaming "Fire!"

6. *The operation of social control.* Finally, Smelser discusses the effects of social control agents on collective behavior. "Stated in the simplest way, the study of social control is the study of those counter-determinants which prevent, interrupt, deflect, or inhibit the accumulation of the determinants just reviewed" (1963:17).

In applying his value-added model to the control of hostile outbursts such as a riot, Smelser (1963:267) summarizes the following principles for maintaining order and preventing violent collective behavior:

1. Prevent communication in general so that beliefs cannot be disseminated.

2. Prevent interaction between leaders and followers so that mobilization is difficult.

3. Refrain from taking a conditional attitude toward violence by bluffing or vacillating in the use of the ultimate weapons of force.

4. Refrain from entering the issues and controversies that move the crowd; remain impartial, unyielding, and fixed on the principle of maintaining law and order.

A Note

Collective behavior per se is neither good nor bad. It is only collective behavior. If I have stressed lynch mobs and riots, it is only because these have most captured the attention of sociologists as usually representing compelling social problems.

The Boston Tea Party and the colonial stand at Lexington and Concord are both examples of collective behavior. Many people at the time regarded them as disquieting and terrorist events. King George III surely regarded them with the same horror that later-day Americans have found in mob violence directed against blacks and civil rights workers in the 1960s or in the My Lai massacre a decade later. The "goodness" or "badness" of a particular instance of collective behavior depends on your point of view.

Many forms of collective behavior have functions even from the point of view of the general society as a continuing set of agreements. Collective behavior often serves as a safety valve for structural strains, permitting things to be depressurized and to return to normal. Religious revivals, for example, may allow the economically depressed to vent their frustrations nonviolently, without threatening the established economic order. The study of lynchings suggests that they have the effect of reducing frustrations and tensions among the lynchers, causing a considerable delay until the next lynching. These functions may not strike you as "happy," nor are they intended to seem that way. These are simply some of the issues that sociologists must examine in order to understand how societies operate.

The dysfunctions of collective behavior are evident. Such behavior often challenges institutions and the authority and strength of social control agents. If it is successful, important changes in the structure of society and its agreements can result. In short, it can result in social movements, and we'll turn to that topic now.

Types of Social Movements

Blumer defines a social movement as "collective enterprises to establish a new order of life" (1946: 199). He goes on to say that social movements "have their inception in a condition of unrest, and derive their motive power on one hand from dissatisfaction with the current form of life, and on the other hand, from wishes and hopes for a new scheme or system of living" (1946:199).

Along the same lines, William Cameron says, "A social movement occurs when a fairly large number of people band together in order to alter or supplant some portion of the existing culture or social order" (1966:7). A social movement, then, is an attempt to alter a society's agreements. Collective behavior such as riots may have the consequence of changing agreements, but changing agreements is the overt purpose of social movements.

All sociologists agree that there are different types of social movements, but they disagree on what the types are. Blumer (1946), for example, refers to "general" social movements, such as the peace movement and the labor movement, as distinct from "specific" ones for reform and revolution. He also distinguishes "expressive" movements (for example, religious, fashion) from "revivalist" and "nationalistic" movements.

Cameron (1966) speaks of four major types: "reactionary," "conservative," "revisionary," and "revolutionary." Smelser (1963) distinguishes "norm-oriented" from "value-oriented" movements. Louis Wirth (1957) has suggested four types among minority groups: "pluralistic," "assimilationist," "secessionist," and "militant." Other sociologists, as you might imagine, have suggested other classification schemes. In this section, we'll examine some of the major types of social movements that we have mentioned.

Expressive

As the name suggests, expressive social movements have the primary purpose of allowing the expression of feelings. Religious revivals such as those led by Dwight Moody, Billy Sunday, and—more recently—by Billy Graham are good examples of expressive social movements. They draw on individuals' inner feelings and provide a vehicle for their expression. The encounter-group movement is a secular example.

Such movements focus directly on individuals, but they typically have social goals as well. To those participating in them, they offer a set of beliefs, values, and norms different from the agreements prevailing in the general society. Understandably, participants in such movements wonder what society would be like if all its members could experience and accept the new set of agreements. In some cases—as in Billy Sunday's support of Prohibition—expressive movements seek a more direct influence on society.

Reactionary

Some social movements represent a reaction to real or perceived shifts in society's agreements that is characterized by seeking to replace the new agreements with old ones. Religious revivals—as the term "revival" suggests—sometimes have this flavor. So do a variety of cultural and political "nativistic" movements. These movements are characterized by efforts of the original residents of an area to restore patterns threatened or destroyed by newcomers.

During the early 1870s in California and during the 1890s elsewhere, native Americans gave birth to a movement popularly called the "Ghost Dance," which foretold a time when all American Indians would be reunited and their past glory restored. The whites who stole away their lands would be no more, and they would live happily without death, disease, or misery (Mooney 1939). The more recent militancy of native Americans and the rebirth of aboriginal Indian culture is a nonmystical nativistic movement, at least in part.

As indicated in Chapter 12, every major wave of immigration to America has been met with nativistic resistance from earlier immigrants. Longing for "the good old days" and urging the restoration of old values, groups such as the American Protective Association, the Ku Klux Klan, and the John Birch Society are examples of reactionary, nativistic social movements.

Conservative

Conservative social movements are similar to reactionary ones, except that they seek to maintain the agreements that they regard as being *in danger* of change. The distinction between the two types, then, depends on whether you think the old agreements have already changed or not.

During the late 1960s and early 1970s, the loosely organized movement in support of American involvement in Vietnam could be considered an example of a conservative social movement. The antiwar movement was correctly seen as a challenge to the influence of the military and the role of military solutions in American foreign policy.

Reformist

Crossing the line between stability and change, we find a wide variety of social movements dedicated overtly to the change of society's agreements. Such movements typically have specific and limited goals, as distinct from revolutionary movements, which we'll discuss shortly. Opponents of reformist movements may damn them as revolutionary whether they are or not.

The tremendous variety in reformist movements is perhaps illustrated by the following goals: prohibition of alcoholic beverages, legalization of marijuana, declaring war on Cuba, withdrawing from the war in Vietnam, promoting birth control, giving women the vote, and ending the death penalty.

Revolutionary

Whereas reformist movements seek to improve on existing social structures by changing some specific agreements, revolutionary movements have a broader goal: to supplant all or most of the structure with something new. The fight for American independence, then, was revolutionary in the sociological point of view as well as in our everyday language.

The extent of change sought by revolutionary social movements varies, although it usually includes a change in the form of government institutions. The border line between reformist and revolutionary movements is as fuzzy as the one separating reactionary and conservative movements. More generally, you should realize that all social movements have such a variety of characteristics and their participants such a variety of motivations that easy classification is precluded.

Elements in the Study of Social Movements

Merely cataloging social movements according to "type" doesn't tell us very much about the ways societies operate, although an examination of their similarities and differences is a first step toward understanding. Sociologists have devoted most of their attention to an analytical dissection of the several aspects of social movements. In this section, we'll review some of the things sociologists have looked at and what they've seen.

Conditions

The expression "an idea whose time has come" probably describes *all* social movements to an extent. No social force can become a movement unless it appears among people who are somewhat receptive to it. The agreements it proposes to protect or change must seem in need of being protected or changed.

Marx and Engels began the *Communist Manifesto* with the cry: "Workers of the world, unite! You have nothing to lose but your chains." They touched a well of preexisting frustration and misery throughout the European Industrial Revolution. The same pronouncement today at a labor union's national convention would probably produce little more than yawns or embarrassment.

There have been supporters of sexual equality throughout our nation's history. The centennial celebration of 1876 was "marred" by the opposition of feminist activists who loudly protested a century of sexual discrimination. Yet the women's movement in America continued to ebb and flow, requiring a century and a half of nationhood before women were allowed to vote. It has taken another fifty years to reach the eve of full equality.

The Role of Success

It seems logical to predict that social movements will flourish and grow when they are successful and wither away when they fail. This prediction is not necessarily accurate, however. Movements may lose support as they begin to achieve their objectives, thereby reducing the discontent that was their source and falling short of full success.

More interesting are those movements that suffer clear and undeniable setbacks, such as happens with religious movements that are given to prophecy. What happens when the prophecies fail to come true?

During the first half of the nineteenth century, an American preacher, William Miller, announced that he had calculated from Biblical sources the time of Christ's Second Coming and the attendant ending of the world. The result of his preaching was the Millerite movement of people who began giving up their worldly goods to prepare for the millennium. When the world failed to end on the day prophesied, Miller recomputed doomsday, and his followers began preparing anew, urging their friends and relations to join them. Although the world still refused to end, the movement became organized in 1863 as the Seventh Day Adventist church.

Leon Festinger and his colleagues (1956) discovered a similar phenomenon when they set out to study a small group in the Midwest who had been warned of doomsday by visitors on flying saucers. Only a chosen few were to be rescued from the doomed planet, and members of the group feverishly attempted to get friends and relations to join with them. When the rescue saucer failed to appear on schedule, a new time of departure was set, and the members worked all the harder to get others to join them.

Festinger, a psychologist, saw the renewed proselytization as a way of resolving "cognitive dissonance," the conflict between beliefs and experiences. "If more and more people can be persuaded that the system of belief is correct, then clearly it must, after all, be correct" (1956:28). Lofland (1966) reached the same conclusion in his study of a Korean-based doomsday cult.

Sometimes when people fail, they try harder, become desperate, and seek to gain broader agreement that what they are doing is right. Sometimes when they succeed, they become complacent and lose their dedication to the cause. The role of success is not as straightforward as might be imagined.

For the most part, social movements feed on feelings of discontent: fear, frustration, anger. Few grow purely from feelings of love, joy, or hope. Even expressive religious movements or utopian movements such as recent communalism represent a disillusionment with the way things are in the general society. The current environmental movement, for example, comes less from a love of nature than from a fear of its destruction. Social movements provide

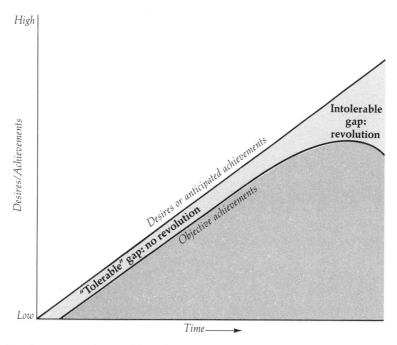

Figure 14•1 A model of revolutionary conditions. Adapted from James Davies, "A Theory of Revolution," American Sociological Review 27 (February 1962):6. Reprinted by permission.

an outlet for such feelings and a vehicle for changing the conditions that cause them. Unless the conditions are present, however, the social movements will not develop.

Sociologists have found "discontent" to be a complex phenomenon. Relative deprivation, for example, appears to be a more powerful source of social movements than objective deprivation, as students of revolutions have discovered.

James Davies (1962) has suggested a model of the conditions under which revolutions are the most likely to occur. His model is based on the gap between what people have and what they want. "Revolutions are most likely to occur when a prolonged period of objective economic and social development is followed by a short period of sharp reversal" (1962:6). Davies's model is represented graphically in Figure 14•1.

Economic deprivation per se, then, does not produce revolutions; rather it is the discrepancy, or disagreement, between what is wanted and what is gotten. Even there, it appears that people will tolerate some "gap," be willing to live with somewhat less than they want. As conditions improve, however, their desires expand accordingly, and they continue expanding even when objective circumstances become less favorable. Ironically, people who have lived quietly in abject poverty may revolt after a period of substantial improvement, a situation often referred to as "the revolution of rising expectations."

What we have just said about economic conditions holds for freedom as well. Revolutions do not occur because people have little or no freedom; they occur only when freedoms are reduced. The Berkeley free-speech movement of 1964, for example, occurred when students were told they could *no longer* sell political materials on campus. This was after years of a gradual liberalization of such activities. It would not have occurred to earlier generations of students to protest such a lack of freedom.

It was in this context, the context of reducing freedoms already held, that Smelser warned against vacillation by social control agents in preventing or quelling hostile outbursts such as riots. Remaining firm and unswerving throughout a confrontation was less likely to produce violence than was a tightening up of controls after allowing more freedom.

Leaders

Regardless of the degree of discontent among people, social movements do not occur without leaders, people who are willing and able to direct the energies of others. They focus discontent and point to actions to remedy it. Some leaders volunteer, others (like Martin Luther King, Jr.) are drafted, and others have to compete for the position.

The leaders of social movements differ so greatly in background and temperament that they can't be generally characterized. Adolph Hitler was an uneducated paperhanger when he began the Nazi movement in Germany. Paul Ehrlich was a Stanford biologist when he began the organization called Zero Population Growth as a way of focusing concern over the problem of overpopulation. Gandhi was a contemplative lawyer prior to becoming a revered religious and political leader.

Smelser (1963) notes that social movements require two types of leaders at different points in their histories. The agitator is important in getting the movement going, but as the movement develops and expands, more bureaucratic skills are needed. Offices must be opened, clerks hired and supervised, mail answered, membership lists maintained, and so forth.

Leadership of a social movement requires the establishment of authority through noninstitutionalized means. Who gets to be president of the United States is not very problematic because we have established means for selecting the president. There are no agreed-on means for selecting the leader of a movement to abolish the income tax or stop a war, however. As a result, **charisma** plays an important part in the selection of leaders.

Ideology

In a sense, social movements grow out of inarticulate agreements: the dissatisfactions, fears, and frustrations that many individuals have in common.

Hitler's drive to establish national socialism, using torchlight parades, mass rallies, and terrorist-mob action, illustrated many aspects of collective behavior and social movements. (The National Archives)

Individuals feel the pressure of population growth, and Zero Population Growth emerges. Individuals feel that a war is unjust, and an antiwar movement emerges. Social movements, then, are vehicles for articulating and integrating the feelings that individuals have in common.

An ideology is a relatively coherent and integrated set of agreements describing a movement's point of view, and ideologies have several functions for social movements. First, they reinforce the feelings of initial participants and place those feelings within a more coherent point of view. Individuals frustrated by unemployment and inflation, for example, get validation for their feelings—learning that others share them—and they discover who is "to blame" for the unsatisfactory situation.

Holding no political office and refusing all forms of violence, Mahatma Gandhi led a massive social movement that ultimately freed India from British colonial rule. (Henri Cartier-Bresson, Magnum)

Second, ideologies point toward actions that might remedy the dissatisfactions. They specify the changes that must be made and suggest the means for making them.

Another important function of ideology is education. Ideologies can be written down, published, and circulated, thereby bringing attention to problems. The women's liberation movement, for example, has frequently focused around "consciousness-raising" groups. Women who have reified the agreements making them inferior are brought together and exposed to the movement's point of view, its ideology.

Membership and Participation

Who participates in social movements? All kinds of people. For one thing, different social movements appeal to the feelings and interests of different groups. The women's movement obviously has a special appeal for women, the black power movement a special appeal for blacks, and the poverty rights movement a special appeal for poor people.

Cameron (1966) has listed some of the kinds of statuses that different social movements appeal to: age, sex, occupation, economic class, education, racial or ethnic background, religion, political faith, geographical location, and language. In addition to making direct appeals to the specific interests of particular groups, different social movements attract different groups to varying degrees. For example, those supporting the war in Vietnam were generally older than those opposing it. Sociologists frequently examine the characteristics of participants in social movements as a means to understanding the nature of the movements.

People join social movements for a variety of reasons aside from their particular self-interests. Politicians may join in search of voters. Business people may join in search of business. People may feel they will gain prestige by becoming identified with certain movements. And most find the fellowship of primary-group relations in working with others on a cause.

Some students of social movements have suggested that certain types of people are *generally* more likely to join movements. Eric Hoffer (1958) called

these people "true believers," and he noted, for example, that Hitler drew many of his Nazi recruits from Communist groups, even though the two movements were ideologically opposed.

Most social movements have their beginnings among friends and relations, and they grow initially through communication with such networks. This is not surprising since people tend to associate with others who share the same points of view (see Lofland and Stark 1965).

The growth and spread of a social movement beyond kinship and friendship networks is a function of its appeal, of course, but also is governed by the movement's attitude toward membership. Some secret societies, for example, are exclusive and restrict membership. Others are merely receptive to new members, and still others actively seek members through proselytization. The last of these is no doubt the most common.

Finally, something should be said about the difference between support, participation, and membership. Some people may be in sympathy with the goals and purposes of a social movement without actually *doing* anything on behalf of the movement. Others may participate in movement activities, such as attending public meetings and marches or writing letters to public officials. Still others may become formal members in organizations associated with the movement. In studying social movements, sociol-

YOU CAN ONLY JOIN OUR SOCIETY IF YOU CAN SPELL PROSELYTIZATION

ogists often measure the degree of individuals' involvement by the kinds of activities they engage in.

Organization

If social movements are to succeed in changing the agreements of a society, they must be organized. They must form organizations, whether formally constituted or not. Movement activities must be organized and coordinated. Money must be raised and spent. Letters must be written and typed. Members must be kept informed. The endless list of bureaucratic, organizational tasks is often disillusioning to the idealistic supporter. Margaret Sanger, the founder of the birth control movement in America, said of her earliest supporters: "When they remained they found work, work, work, and little recognition, reward, or gratitude. Those who desired honor or recompense, or who measured their interest by this yardstick are no longer here" (1938:354–55).

The business of social movements requires a variety of tasks and talents, and organizations create the division of labor needed. In the most otherworldly religious revival, for example, someone must collect contributions and someone must count the money and decide how it should be invested. The fact that such organizational necessities can create serious role strains for those involved bears repeating. Organizational necessities can threaten the goals of the movement, as in the case of the idealistic, populist political candidate who feels obliged to make somewhat shady deals in order to win the still-higher office that will put him or her in a position to "really" change things. Such a person may become so socialized into the wheeling and dealing as to lose sight of the lofty ideals that started the movement in the first place (see Selznick 1952).

You may have noticed a parallel between this latest discussion of the problems created in the organization and bureaucratization of social movements, on the one hand, and the general problems associated with institutionalization as discussed in Chapters 7 through 10 earlier. The parallel is a direct one, since we have been discussing the institutionalization of a social movement. All these discussions point to a persistent social dilemma.

We have seen that individuals' desires and aspirations can often best be achieved through some form of organized group life. Yet, organized group life has "system needs" of its own, and those latter needs often conflict directly with the initial desires and aspirations of the individuals involved. This dilemma was caricatured years ago in a satirical advertisement placed in a college newspaper: "There will be an organizational meeting of the American Anarchist Association next Tuesday night."

We've now examined those aspects of social movements that are of special interest to sociologists, and you've seen what social movements look like from the sociological point of view. I'd like to conclude this chapter with a short case study of a social movement that emerged recently in Honolulu (see the box "Saving Wawamalu: A Case Study" on pages 378–379).

I have a couple of reasons for presenting the case study. It illustrates a number of the points I have made in the chapter. But, more important, it also illustrates the application of sociological training to bringing about a change in social agreements. Since sociologists usually study the way things are, there is a danger, as I've mentioned earlier in the book, that you might assume sociologists are in favor of the way things are. That's not so, as the case study illustrates.

This account is personal. My wife, Sheila, and I organized the group discussed in the report, and I served as president of it. Throughout the organization of the group and the direction of its activities, I knew that my sociological background was invaluable even though I did not set out to use specific sociological principles. I think you'll see that as the story unfolds.

This report of the struggle to save Wawamalu tells only a few of the highlights. A great many people did a great deal of work of all kinds. We received assistance from many public officials, some volunteering their support, others yielding reluctantly. None of us had ever organized a social movement before, so we learned as we went along. People who had never been involved in politics at all found themselves testifying before the legislature on technical matters quite new to them. Ultimately, though, it was possible to change a set of agreements that had seemed immutable.

Summary

I began this chapter by distinguishing collective behavior from institutionalized behavior: The former is more spontaneous and disorganized, less governed by preestablished agreements. Agreements are created in collective behavior as participants share in beliefs, feelings, and actions.

Social movements represent a more persistent and ultimately more organized form of noninstitutionalized behavior. They aim at changing social agreements. Social movements often develop out of collective behavior.

Sociologists have distinguished many forms of collective behavior. Some require the presence of a crowd; others occur across a society. Fashions, fads,

Saving Wawamalu: A Case Study

In June 1971, a major Honolulu land developer, in collaboration with the city planning department, held a public information meeting to announce plans for the development of a major resort and residential complex near the popular surfing area of Sandy Beach. The purpose of the meeting was to inform nearby residents of the development plans and to indicate that the planning department was considering whether to recommend approval of the plans.

The meeting ended in an uproar with a loud protest against the proposed development. Foremost among the protesters were members of a group made up of surfers and environmentalists, but they were joined by older residents, including a state representative.

Residents left the meeting feeling that they had clearly demonstrated their opposition to the proper authorities and that the project would be scrapped. In December 1971, a rumor began circulating that the planning department was on the verge of recommending approval of the project. My wife, Sheila, and I met with a small group of residents to discuss the possibility of stopping the project.

A decision was reached to call another public meeting, this one sponsored and run by the residents themselves. Arrangements were made to rent a school cafeteria, and announcements of the meeting were hastily printed and circulated. The city planning director was invited to attend, but declined the invitation, saying he would prefer to receive written questions from residents and promising to answer any that were received.

The public meeting was held within a week of the decision to act. Approximately 150 residents turned out to learn about the proposed development and to voice their opinions. The main purpose of the meeting was to find out what residents wanted to know. Ninety-seven questions were recorded and sent to the planning department. The questions ranged from such matters as planned public facilities (schools, parks, health care, and so forth) to issues of traffic congestion, mass transportation, sewage disposal, and tidal-wave protection.

People attending the public meeting were urged to write directly to the planning director and other public officials asking that the project not be approved until the many questions raised had been answered. Many did so, and the planning department delayed action on the project for a month while it prepared a thirty-page response to the questions.

During that time, the organization—by then named the Save Wawamalu Association (Wawamalu was the traditional Hawaiian name of the beach)— was busy conducting research of its own. A public health graduate student began conducting water-quality tests near the outfall of the existing sewage-treatment plant and analyzing department of health statistics. Sheila and I designed, organized, and supervised a public-opinion poll of residents to learn their sentiments toward the proposed development. Two women drove the whole length of the highway connecting the community to downtown, counting the number of driveways feeding into it. This information was combined with official traffic studies to produce estimates of the added traffic congestion that would be produced by the development.

By the time the planning department had completed its response to the original ninety-seven

and crazes are examples of collective behavior that do not require the assembly of a group of people. They typically last for a short time and deal with some trivial aspect of life. Mass hysteria and panic are other forms of collective behavior. Panics may occur in an assembled crowd—as in a crowded theater—or can occur across a society—as in the mass selling of stocks. Terrorist mobs represent an attack against a perceived threat, whereas panic is a retreat. Riots are generally more haphazard in their selection of targets for aggression, though terrorist-mob actions can result in riots.

Once we examined different forms of collective behavior, we turned to some of the scientific points of view that have been used to understand it. Le Bon was chiefly concerned with the irrationality and im-

---

questions, we had many additional questions, supported this time by empirical studies. The planning department went back to work, and we began preparing a fact sheet describing the probable impact of the development.

As of February 1972, the planning department still had not made a recommendation, much to the consternation of the developer. As the state legislature opened its annual session, we arranged with our local legislators to have a resolution introduced that would declare the area in question a state park. At the legislative hearings on the resolution, the Save Wawamalu Association and some fifteen other organizations (representing a broad political spectrum) presented a carefully coordinated testimony in opposition to the development and in support of the park. Only the developer and the landowner testified against the resolution.

As an intergovernmental courtesy, the city planning department deferred its recommendation until the state legislature handled the park resolution. The decision was, thereby, effectively delayed until around May, when the legislature would recess.

During this same time, another important event occurred. The city councilman representing the area in question resigned to accept a judicial appointment, and a special, no-primary election was called for June. A variety of candidates began announcing for the post.

By this time socialized into the norms of American politics, the original small group of residents gathered in a dimly lit, smoke-filled bar to discuss whether to run a candidate for the council on a platform of opposition to the development.

The decision was yes, and a candidate was picked. I was chosen campaign manager.

As the campaign became more intense, it became clear that the proposed development at Wawamalu was to be the key issue, but in a peculiar fashion: All seven candidates were against it and debating who opposed it the most! Finally, the planning department announced plans for the official, public hearing—scheduled to occur one week before the city council election.

The Save Wawamalu Association immediately set about organizing testimony for the public hearing, as we had done for the legislative session; 7,000 leaflets were printed to inform residents of the meeting. With the prospect of seven city council candidates all testifying against the development, however, the developer withdrew its request and asked that the meeting be canceled. The reason given for this surprise move was that the developer wished to make slight modifications to its request. A revised request was to be submitted within a few weeks.

Then, however, the campaigns for the regular 1972 elections were beginning with United States representatives, a mayor, and state legislators to be elected. We immediately prepared and mailed a questionnaire to all political candidates asking for their positions on the proposed development. All were against it.

The next three years were a standoff, and the developer never did submit the "revised proposal." In 1975, with little or no fanfare, the state began the incremental purchase of Wawamalu for a park.

What elements of a social movement are illustrated by this example?

pulsiveness of crowds, and he saw them as a threat to "civilized" social life. Collective behavior fit neatly into Freud's general psychoanalytical theory. Freud regarded it as an attempt to return to infancy, and he felt crowd members regarded their leaders as parent-figures.

Blumer, an interactionist, has been particularly interested in the contagious nature of emotions in crowds, suggesting "circular reaction" as the way in which the emotions expressed by one person were reflected back by another, thereby reinforcing that emotion in the first person. Blumer likened collective behavior to the herd behavior of cattle.

Smelser presented a more structuralist point of view, outlining the stages in the development of collective behavior through the use of a "value-added" model. The several stages are: structural conduciveness, structural strain, the growth and spread of a generalized belief, precipitating factors, the mobilization of participants for action, and the operation of social control.

Next, we turned to social movements, looking first at some of the different types sociologists have studied. Expressive movements, such as religious revivals, have the primary purpose of letting individuals vent their feelings, though such movements typically have social goals as well.

Reactionary social movements, such as nativistic movements, represent a concern for perceived changes in society's agreements and a longing for a return to the "good old days." Conservative social movements are based on the belief that social agreements *may* change, and they seek to maintain the status quo.

Reformist social movements seek relatively specific and limited changes to social agreements without overturning basic structures. Revolutionary movements are more radical and ambitious in their objectives—seeking a major restructuring of society.

When sociologists study social movements, a number of things interest them. First, they often examine the conditions that give rise to movements. In the case of revolutions, we noted that they most frequently occur as a result of relative deprivation and rising expectations, quite aside from the objective conditions.

Sociologists have been particularly interested in

the characteristics of leaders of social movements, though they differ so greatly as to preclude general characterization. Different types of leaders are needed at different times in the history of a movement. The fiery and emotional agitator may be needed to get it started, with more bureaucratic leadership required later on.

Ideology serves several functions for social movements. It makes the feelings of individuals more coherent and validates the feelings. It also makes education of the general public possible.

Different social movements appeal primarily to different types of people, sometimes, but not always, because of their relevance to special group interests. People participate in social movements for a variety of reasons, and the organizational needs of movements may require them to do things they feel are unrelated to the movement's goals. Movements must become organized (with a corresponding division of labor) if they are to be successful.

Suggested Readings

Cameron, William
1966   *Modern Social Movements.* New York: Random House.
In this excellent little book, Cameron has reviewed the major sociological points of view on social movements, providing a useful introduction to the topic. He discusses typologies of social movements, examines leadership, followership, and the development of movements over time. All this is fleshed out with numerous illustrations.

Lofland, John and Rodney Stark
1965   "On Becoming a World-Saver: A Theory of Conversion to a Deviant Perspective." *American Sociological Review* 30:862–75.
This article is interesting from two perspectives. First, it offers an inside view of a religious movement, based in Korea and active in America, that the authors have disguised as the "divine precepts" movement of "Mr. Chang." Second, their participant-observation of the movement's growth in California provides the basis for the development of a theory of religious conversion.

Smelser, Neil
1963 *Theory of Collective Behavior.* New York: Free
      Press.
Utilizing the "value-added" model developed in
economics, Smelser traces the development of the
many forms of collective behavior and social movements. Since Smelser takes a structural-functional
view, this book provides about the best analysis of
structural strain available.

Stark, Rodney
1972 *Police Riots.* Belmont, Calif.: Wadsworth.
While the police are a formally established agency of
social control, Stark's chronicling of student-police
clashes during the 1960s shows that social control
agents are themselves subject to collective behavior.
In addition, the book contains valuable insights for
social policy regarding protest. A wealth of examples
point to the likely possibility that riots are generated
by the application of excessive force.

Episode Fourteen

Gabriel Knapp's trial opened in Chicago October 1, 2027. Monica Roanoke represented him. When Gabriel phoned her from Phoenix July 5, she had first suggested she find him another attorney, explaining that she knew several qualified lawyers who would take his case. But Gabe had insisted she defend him herself. With mixed emotions she had agreed.

Knapp had been held without bond. On July 29, still in custody, he was sent to Illinois where subsequently he spent nearly two months in Cook County jail awaiting trial.

Because a large majority of prospective jurors admitted upon questioning that they had already reached a conclusion regarding Knapp's guilt, attorneys took nine days to choose a jury.

Gabriel's arrest in Phoenix July 4 had sparked an increase in national violence. On July 10 a truck loaded with S.T.'s heading for an automobile factory in Detroit was hijacked and set ablaze near Battle Creek.

Meanwhile rumors had sprung up in and around Denver that members of a commune west of that city were descendants of a second kind of mutants. Commune members, many believed, were mentally deficient monsters whose pastimes included torture and mutilation of animals and children.

On July 29, 2027, several persons from Denver joined activists from Steamboat Springs, Aspen, Colorado Springs, and Vail. The mob converged upon the suspected commune, set fire to the main house, and fatally stabbed and shot the twenty-five women, men, and children who resided there.

The following day, in a separate incident, three homemade bombs exploded simultaneously in the Phoenix airport, killing fifteen and injuring thirty. Concerned Citizens for National Defense claimed responsibility for that act of terrorism.

On August 2 a Union Pacific railroad train carrying S.T.'s to East Coast factories was purposely derailed near Des Moines. The engineer was shot four times in the head.

By the end of August most major cities had summoned state national guards. Federal infantry divisions were stationed in New York, Los Angeles, San Francisco, Chicago, St. Louis, and Phoenix.

Meanwhile the periodic border disturbances that had plagued Adamsville for nearly ten years had intensified. FBI personnel, although their numbers had been substantially increased, found it increasingly difficult to maintain order near the colony's gates.

Inside Adamsville Larry Jones insisted that S.T.I. impose a boycott immediately, refusing to market its solar transistors within the United States. The national economy, he reasoned, having grown increasingly dependent upon S.T.'s, could not survive without them for longer than a few days. Once Adamsville held outsiders in this economic vise, greens would be in a position to voice their demands: the establishment of a separate and independent green nation, consisting of what now were the states of Arizona and New Mexico.

The Elders, on the other hand, procrastinated, fearing that to impose the boycott might further limit Gabriel's already tenuous chance for a fair trial. Furthermore, they refused to see the future of Adamsville in terms of a separate nation.

On August 10 the epidemic upheaval that troubled the nation outside infected Adamsville itself. A tiny solar explosive device, manufactured at S.T.I., was discovered upon the steps to Elderhome. The device had been placed there by some of the community's radical militarists.

Hundreds of miles to the east the faculty at American University in Lake Michigan had been placed under heavy security. Sociologists and other faculty members had received telephoned threats to their homes. Duncan, Roanoke, Batterson, and several others had been assigned personal bodyguards.

The night of October 5, four days after Gabriel's trial opened, 200 vigilantes battled with FBI agents outside Adamsville's gates. While many hurled grenades, fashioned from pop bottles and tin cans, others struggled with green guards. Amid the chaos two ungreens managed to sneak into Adamsville. Before they escaped the two had murdered three greens. The murders would not be discovered by residents until the following morning. Dead were Rebecca Lockwood, Leonard Decker, chromosomal father of the infant Gabe had taken from Lake Hospital, and their sixteen-month-old rescued son.

Members of the press, now permanently camped near Adamsville, reported the killings the following morning. Gabriel learned of the murders from a United States marshal who escorted him from his cell to the courtroom.

Gabe sat pale and unresponsive through that morning. Shortly before noon he asked Monica to request a short recess so that he could go to the rest room. Once inside the lavatory, he lay his head into a washbasin and heaved, first liquid and then nothing, until finally he was taken, limp and perspiring, to his cell. The court remained adjourned—a jury still not selected—until October 8.

On October 6 Solar Transistors, Inc., shut down. Ruth and Michael Jones-the-Elder had consented to

impose the boycott. Three of their people had been murdered in cold blood. Some action had to be taken —in spite of the possible repercussions the decision might have upon Gabriel's trial. Wall Street brokers predicted a crash within thirty days should the boycott continue. Power companies along the Eastern Seaboard, having grown dependent upon solar transistors, cut down production, causing brownouts from Florida to Maine.

Threats of violence enveloped Chicago and the federal courts building October 11 as Monica began her opening statement.

"Ladies and gentlemen," she began, assuming a position close to the jury box, "the prosecution has promised to prove that the defendant, Gabriel Knapp, sneaked into Lake Hospital June 28, 2026, kidnapped an infant from the second-floor nursery, then boarded a plane and flew with the child to Phoenix, ultimately delivering the victim to an Arizona community known as Green Colony or Adamsville.

"The prosecution must have facts to support this argument! . . . I beg you to remember your obligations as members of this jury. You are commissioned with two equally important responsibilities: One is to see that justice is done in this specific case; the other is to assure that this nation's legal system is neither sacrificed nor weakened. . . . We must not forget that if we deny the full benefits of the law to Mr. Knapp today, then another jury can more readily deny *you* those same benefits tomorrow. . . . We cannot convict Mr. Knapp simply because we believe he is green."

Monica was seated next to Gabe. "This is a political trial," she whispered to her client.

The prosecution called as its first witness the vice president in charge of personnel from Chicago National. He testified that he knew Knapp to be a green. He had discovered such, he said, on June 22, 2027, when he received a letter from a physician who had examined Gabriel one year before.

Monica objected on the grounds that what transpires during a physician-patient relationship is privileged information, and therefore the doctor's letter was inadmissible. The court sustained her objection and advised the jurors to ignore the testimony.

Next the prosecution called Garcia, the agent who had followed Daniel Adamson to Gabriel's apartment.

She testified that she had tailed a young man from Adamsville to Chicago where on the evening of March 14, 2027, he spent two hours with the defendant in his apartment. Garcia testified further that upon leaving Knapp's apartment, the young visitor had returned directly to Adamsville.

On cross-examination Monica asked, "Do you *know*, Ms. Garcia, whether Mr. Knapp is a green?"

"I know that he was visited by one."

"But you do not know that he himself is a green, isn't that correct?"

"Yes," Ms. Garcia said.

During the next several days the prosecution called twenty-three witnesses, all of them minor acquaintances of Gabriel Knapp. They testified that he often refused or skipped meals, that many times they had heard him complain about the dim lighting in a room, that he seemed always to want the lights turned up as far as they would go, and that he generally "acted a little different."

Gabriel's secretary, Mr. Jacobs, testified that often he saw his boss drink milk, but couldn't recall ever seeing him eat anything solid. Jacobs testified also that he had watched Knapp grow increasingly nervous over the past year and a half, "especially since the day he received the report of his physical."

Monica had already determined that her client would not take the stand. She would simply rebut the facts presented, ultimately arguing that the prosecution had presented insufficient evidence for conviction.

On the seventh day of testimony the prosecution called the FBI agent who had read Knapp's file compiled at Chicago National Insurance Company. He testified that, according to information from that file, Gabriel had called in sick the morning of June 28, 2026, complaining of a "summer cold."

Monica rose for cross-examination. "Do you know for sure," she demanded, "that Mr. Knapp was *not* home suffering from a cold June 28, 2026?

"No," the witness responded, "not absolutely for sure."

"It is entirely possible, then, as far as you know, that Mr. Knapp stayed home from work June 28 because he was ill with a cold, is it not?"

"Yes," the agent muttered, "it's possible."

Later the prosecution called the Lake Hospital nurse who had directed Gabriel to the nursery. Producing a tan jacket and wig recovered by police from the rest room of a filling station across the street from Lake Hospital, the district attorney asked whether the witness had seen either of the items before.

The nurse said she couldn't be sure, but perhaps the jacket looked familiar. Gabriel was ordered to put on the jacket and wig.

"Is that the man who asked directions to the nursery?" the prosecution asked.

"I just can't be sure," the nurse replied.

While Monica fought for Gabe's freedom in court, the attention of those outside the courtroom had been diverted to the nation's economic crisis. The stock market had plummeted. Newspapers, politicians, labor leaders, and industry alike predicted returning depression. By the time Gabriel's trial had reached the seventh day of testimony, Adamsville's Elders had made their demands nationally understood. The Associated Press, in a story datelined "Adamsville," reported on October 19 that unless colony representatives were invited to attend and vote at the upcoming conference on human mutations, S.T.I. would not resume manufacture of solar transistors.

On October 20, the eighth day of testimony in Gabriel's trial, the prosecution called Bradley Duncan.

"State your full name," the prosecuting attorney said when Brad had seated himself in the witness chair.

"Bradley Clarence Duncan."

"Your occupation?"

"Sociologist."

"You spent several months in Green Colony, did you not?"

"In Adamsville. Yes."

"Did you spend the afternoon of June 28, 2026, in Green Colony?"

"In Adamsville; yes, I did."

"Will you tell this court, Mr. Duncan, what took place"—the attorney hesitated—"in Adamsville the afternoon of June 28, 2026?"

Duncan cleared his throat. "I cannot answer that question," he said. "It is privileged information." The judge ordered Duncan to answer the question. The sociologist persisted in his refusal. Fifteen minutes later he was sentenced to ten days in Cook County jail for contempt of court.

The prosecution then called Dr. Constance Batterson and, later, Dr. Louise Roanoke, who likewise refused to testify and were similarly sentenced.

Later that afternoon the prosecution called a representative from the U.S. Department of the Interior. She testified that her special area of expertise included knowledge of green culture patterns and that she knew for certain that under some circumstances greens believed in kidnapping infants.

The next day the prosecution summoned to the stand the steward who had hosted Gabriel on his June 28 flight from Chicago to Phoenix. The steward testified that he had seen a man resembling Gabe with a newborn infant aboard US-Russian Airlines Flight No. 742.

Monica cross-examined the witness. "What was the passenger who carried the baby wearing that day?"

The steward said he could not be sure.

"How was the baby wrapped?" Monica asked.

"In a blanket, I think."

"What color was the blanket?"

"I don't remember for sure."

"You are quite certain that this is the gentleman whom you hosted, but you don't know what he had on or how the baby he supposedly carried was dressed?"

"I know that the man with the baby looked like that man," the steward pointed toward Gabriel.

"But you can't be absolutely certain that this *is* the man, can you?"

"Not absolutely certain."

On October 23, the day before Monica would deliver her closing argument, the U.S. secretary of the interior consented to the mutants' demands. Furthermore, at Adamsville's subsequent insistence, the conference was scheduled six months earlier than had been previously planned. Delegates to the conference would meet in Omaha November 15, 2027.

Monica Roanoke began her closing argument October 24, 2027. "Ladies and gentlemen of the jury," she announced, "this is a political trial. My client is not on trial here as a human being who has transgressed the law, but as a representative of a group hated and feared within our society.

"The prosecution has attempted to prove that Mr. Knapp is a chlorophyllic. Because of that—and only because of that—he is charged here with a serious federal crime. . . . This morning the prosecution has based its closing argument on two things primarily: that Mr. Knapp is a chlorophyllic and that chlorophyllics believe in something they call rescuing. I am not here to argue these two assertions, nor am I here to argue that I believe kidnapping is ever honorable. I am simply here to remind you that these two assertions alone are not sufficient evidence to convict Mr. Knapp of the Lake Hospital crime. There are no facts sufficient to convince us beyond a reasonable doubt that Gabriel Knapp kidnapped an infant."

The jury deliberated two days before agreeing that the prosecution had failed to prove defendant Gabriel Knapp guilty.

Questions

1. How many different kinds of collective behavior can you identify in the past two episodes?

2. How do events in this and previous episodes illustrate the concepts of "precipitating events" and "contagion"?

3. How is the radical militarist social movement an example of a "conservative social movement"?

4. How would Smelser analyze the formation and development of the radical militarists' movement?

15

Social Conflict
and Social Change

Societies exist by agreement. To the extent that people within a society continue to agree, the society persists. Societies change through disagreement, and when the prevailing agreements of a society are changed, we might even say that a *new* society has been created, even though it will resemble its predecessor in many ways.

Social conflict is a matter of disagreement. When people have different points of view, they often engage in activities aimed at gaining agreement for *their* point of view over others. Thus, for example, two children (of any age) may have different points of view regarding who is the stronger and will start a fistfight in an effort to gain agreement on one or the other point of view. Nations (of all ages) engage in the same sort of activity.

Put more formally, "social conflict" is an activity engaged in by two or more parties with differing points of view, each of which is attempting to gain agreement for its point of view. The forms of social conflict vary greatly, ranging from debates, economic competition, and political campaigns to revolutions and thermonuclear wars. Sometimes, one party to the conflict clearly wins over the other. Sometimes, as I mentioned in the discussion of the Hegelian dialectic in Chapter 2, the result of the conflict is a synthesis of the opposing points of view. In this chapter, we'll look at some of the different forms of social conflict and the points of view sociologists take in

studying them. We'll also consider some of the functions of conflict for the parties involved and for society as a whole.

This chapter also discusses **social change,** the changing of social agreements. It seems reasonable to assume that if people agree totally in their points of view, if there is no social conflict, the agreements people share will never change. We can only "assume" that would be the case because there has never been a society in which everyone agreed on everything. There is always some degree of disagreement and conflict, and there is always social change. In the second part of this chapter, we'll look at some of the forms social change takes—giving special attention to national **modernization**—and the different points of view that may be taken in the examination of change. We'll see, incidentally, that the question of how to study social change can itself be a source of disagreement and conflict—for sociologists. Is change inevitable? Does it proceed in a straight line or is it cyclical? These are some of the questions that sociologists disagree about. Let's begin with a look at the basic nature of social conflict.

The Nature of Social Conflict

The potential for social conflict is always present, for people never agree totally. No two people agree with one another on everything. Social conflict always exists everywhere around us in the form of conflicting points of view. The term "social conflict," as I've indicated, however, is used in reference to the *actions* people take in the attempt to get greater agreement for their particular points of view.

A fundamental issue is involved in the notion of social conflict. The issue has to do with "human nature" and what parts such qualities as cooperation and competition, harmony and hostility, and love and aggression might play in it. Thomas Hobbes in *Leviathan*, you'll recall, suggested that people were "naturally" inclined to engage in social conflict, and he spoke of the prehistoric "war of all against all." Recall also that Freud saw civilization as a device for harnessing and repressing our antisocial drives. The debate continues.

Some scholars have focused their attention on animal behavior (a study called ethology), hoping to learn about people from an understanding of our more distant relatives. Konrad Lorenz (1966), for example, finds aggression to be an innate drive in animals, usually aimed at establishing territorial rights, dominance within a group, or mating rights. Lorenz also suggests that species which have the greatest physical ability to kill other members of their own species also have behavioral patterns to keep the killing in check. Winning and losing among these species is accomplished without killing. When wolves fight among themselves, for example, the losing wolf rolls over and exposes an unprotected neck. The victor simply terminates the fight at that point, refusing to make the kill. If aggression is innate in animals, it seems that other behavioral patterns keep it in check.

Pierre van den Berghe, a sociologist, agrees with Lorenz, and he suggests that human beings are more vicious than other animals—because of the patterns Lorenz noted. Van den Berghe (1975) points out that humans are not well endowed biologically for killing one another: Neither our teeth nor our claws are especially lethal. Our species could survive without instinctual behavior patterns such as those that keep wolves from killing one another. We have made up for our biological weakness through technology, however, and have become uniquely violent and aggressive.

Man's aggressiveness is uniquely frightful for two reasons. First, man, especially the male of the species, seems to get a greater kick out of killing than almost any other animal. Many other animals kill for food, but only man, it seems, kills for the sheer fun of it. . . .

Second, man is the most lethal animal to his own species. . . . Man is not only bloodthirsty, but his equipment to deal instant death to members of his own species is far more developed than that of any other mammal or bird (Van den Berghe 1975:260).

Van den Berghe is clear in his belief that human aggressiveness is innate rather than socially caused. If anything, he suggests that (1975:45) "social order . . . imposes some restraints on our homicidal propensities."

The theory that man is by nature gentle and is made nasty through a vicious social system is wrong. If anything, the reverse is true: through life in society we sometimes learn to suppress the most damaging aspects of our aggressiveness.

Without suggesting that humans are warm and wonderful by nature, Ralf Dahrendorf (1968: 127) places a greater stress on the *social* sources of conflict. As you'll recall from Chapter 2, Dahrendorf suggests that social order is a result of power and constraint. Some members of society are able to exercise their will over others. This constraint is, for Dahrendorf, itself a source of conflict, which explains the fact that conflict is always with us:

We assume that conflict is ubiquitous, since constraint is ubiquitous wherever human beings set up social organizations. In a highly formal sense, it is always the basis of constraint that is at issue in social conflict.

Whether human aggressiveness and conflict are innate in our species or are generated by social structure is a question that has been debated for a long time. That social conflict exists in various forms is not debatable. Let's look at it.

Microconflict

Sociologists sometimes use the term "microconflict" to refer to disagreements between individuals—

Social conflict reflects the different points of view people have. Individuals disagree, and so do groups. (Jean-Claude Lejeune, Black Star)

situations in which each attempts to gain agreement for his or her point of view. Property is a common focus of social conflict because of disagreements over who should own or use it. Beliefs, values, and norms provide other bases for microconflict. Suppose you have just informed your parents that you have moved in with your true love as a trial run for marriage, and they announce they've just been elected to head the local Stamp Out Sin committee. That's the stuff microconflict is made of.

Although the goal of all social conflict is the same —making your point of view dominant—a variety of methods are available for achieving it. Arguments, debates, and attempts at persuasion are physically nonviolent means. The control of social interaction is another means that might consist of, for example, your

encouraging others to ostracize the person you disagree with. The threat of violence is also a means for settling disagreements, as is, of course, violence itself.

Within-Group Conflict

Social conflict often occurs within groups, as the members disagree on matters relating to the group itself. Factions may form around different points of view relating to policies, actions, leadership, or the like. Family disputes and civil wars are equally examples of within-group conflict.

Conflict is likely to be the most hostile within groups normally characterized by close, intense ties among members. As Lewis Coser (1956:68) has observed:

Individuals who participate intensely in the life of such groups are concerned with the group's continuance. If they witness the breaking away of one with whom they have shared cares and responsibilities of group life, they are likely to react in a more violent way against such "dysloyalty" than less involved members.

As Coser (and Georg Simmel before him) observed, conflict within a group threatens the definition of the group and its boundaries. It can threaten the very survival of the group, whether it is a small clique or a nation. Consider, for example, the reaction to domestic communism within the United States. For many Americans, the "enemy within" is far more to be feared than Russian or Chinese military divisions. Emotion-charged terms such as "turncoat" and "traitor" are used in reference to those group members who once agreed with "us" and now disagree. Thus, Benedict Arnold is regarded as more despicable than King George III in American history. In contemporary Communist nations, "revisionists" are similarly despised.

Between-Group Conflict

In contrast to conflict within a group, which threatens its solidarity and survival, conflict between groups can strengthen each. Recall the discussion in Chapter 6 of in-groups and out-groups. A Democratic primary may weaken the Democratic party *as a group* but strengthen both the conservative and liberal factions within it *as factions.*

Groups, like individuals, often have conflicting points of view. Factions of a political party disagree on what policies and programs the party as a whole should pursue and on who its candidates for office should be. Colleges have conflicting points of view on athletic superiority. Nations have conflicting points of view about who should control certain areas of the world. Social conflict between groups occurs in convention halls, on football fields, and on battlefields.

The hostility of intergroup conflict is greater when the conflicting points of view have been reified, when the individuals involved believe they are fighting on behalf of "truth." As Coser notes:

It appears . . . that conflict pursued with a "good conscience" . . . is generally more radical and merciless than where such inner support is lacking. For example, one reason for the apparently decreased combativeness of American management in labor struggles today, as compared with fifty years ago, can perhaps be found in a decreased belief in the absolute righteousness of maximizing profits both in the society at large and in the business community itself (1956:113).

The perceived "righteousness," the "rightness," of your point of view increases the viciousness with which you seek to gain agreement for it, and it has been observed that religious wars are the bloodiest wars.

Class Conflict

One type of between-group conflict that sociologists have studied extensively is the conflict that takes place between social classes. I've mentioned this from time to time throughout the book, and I'd like to give it special attention here.

The sociological study of social conflict began with the study of the class struggle in the writings of Karl Marx (in the 1860s). As you'll recall from Chapter 2, Marx thought all social organization was a consequence of economic organization. During his own lifetime, he saw unfettered capitalism create two major classes of people: the "bourgeoisie" (the owners of the means of production) and the "proletariat" (the workers). The oppression of workers was seen as a condition that would drive the oppressed to realize their true class interests, to organize politically, and eventually to revolt in an overthrow of capitalism itself.

With the benefit of clear-eyed hindsight, we may now regard Marx's view of history (and of the future) as somewhat simplistic. Nowhere did he anticipate the development of corporations, which spread economic ownership more broadly across populations. He did not anticipate the union movement that would result in better pay for skilled workers than for, say, teachers, either. Despite Marx's lack of "foresight," many sociologists still find value in his basic concept of a struggle between different social classes.

Nikolai Lenin (1870–1924) transformed Marxist thought into violent social conflict. The institutionalization of the Marxist-Leninist point of view in Russia brought about enormous social change, touching all aspects of life. (American Russian Institute)

Ralf Dahrendorf, a contemporary sociologist, has attempted to update and systematize Marx's concept of **class conflict.** Dahrendorf has often had to reject a Marxian generalization and substitute specifics. Where, for example, Marx saw violence and civil war as inevitable, Dahrendorf (1959:136) concludes that

the empirical hypothesis is false that insists that this class conflict must always assume the form of violent

civil war and "class struggle." Indeed, it seems plausible that under certain conditions (which it is possible to determine) class antagonism becomes latent or is reactivated from a state of latency.

Dahrendorf goes on (1959) to construct a formal theory describing the conditions under which the intensity and violence of class conflict will be heated or cooled. He suggests that when different aspects of the class conflict are separated from one another, the intensity will be less than when they coincide. A closed class system will produce a more intense class conflict than an open class system. In Dahrendorf's theory, separating authority and economic rewards will also lessen the intensity of the conflict.

Although Dahrendorf and other contemporary sociologists have rejected aspects of Marx's view on class conflict, the overall notion of the struggle between social classes as a central factor in the structure and operation of society lives on. Like other persistent points of view in sociology, it pulls together and explains a set of observations about how social life is conducted, even in modern industrial society. It seems likely that some sociologists will continue to study class conflict for as long as social stratification persists—which promises to be a long time. Let's turn now to another persistent form of conflict.

War

War is the most dramatic example of social conflict, visiting death and destruction on hundreds, thousands, or millions of individuals. The German military strategist Clausewitz defined war as "the pursuit of politics by other means." As offensive as this definition may seem to you, it illustrates the fact that war is, ultimately, only another way of trying to gain agreement for your particular point of view. The "noble" end is permitted to justify any means.

The agreement that "war is terrible, *but* . . ." appears to be broadly shared. Few Americans would quarrel with the "justice" of the American Revolution of 1776 or our fight against fascism in World War II, even though many Americans opposed both of those wars at the time. Yet many who regard the American Revolution as unquestionably "just" find no justice in the "wars of national liberation" now occurring in Asia and other parts of the globe.

Woodrow Wilson probably summarized what was a general human agreement when he characterized World War I as "the war to end all wars." We tend to see each war as *the* one that is fought to gain agreement for our point of view, the one that will establish "truth" and "justice." Each war is the last because further wars could only threaten the "right" point of view. Arabs and Israelis, for example, alter-

nate in their support of war or peace depending on whose territorial point of view was victorious in the last war.

Wars do not necessarily grow out of disagreements between total populations of nations, however. Throughout world history, bloody wars have been fought to settle the disagreements of kings, dictators, and ruling elites. In *The Causes of World War Three* (1958), C. Wright Mills suggested that this pattern is still with us. Mills was especially concerned over the rise of an American ruling elite—the "military-industrial complex":

> The top of modern America is increasingly unified and often seems willfully co-ordinated. . . .
> The power of decision is now seated in military, political, and economic institutions. Other institutions are increasingly shaped and used by these three. By them the push and pull of a fabulous technology is now guided, even as it paces and shapes their own development (1958:21).

Mills stresses the fact that the "fabulous technology" paced and shaped the power elite: The growth of a war-oriented economy developed imperatives of its own. In the interest of military preparedness, great amounts of capital had to be invested in industries that could develop and produce the weapons of war, and that very investment made it necessary that more and more weapons be developed and produced continually. Halting war production in times of peace would, presumably, have serious economic consequences.

As political, business, and military leaders cooperate with one another in the interest of military preparedness, Mills argues, they develop a militaristic point of view, one that they have the power to act on at a national level.

> The power elite are not merely men of good will who are doing their best. They are also men of power. No doubt they are all honorable men, but what is honor? Honor can only mean living up to a code that one believes to be honorable. There is no code upon which all men are agreed. The question is not: Are these honorable men? The question is: What are their codes of honor? The answer is: They are the codes of their own circles . . . (1958:40–41).

DESPERATE MESSAGE FROM H.Q. FRED — — WE'RE NOT USING ENOUGH BOMBS TO KEEP UP WITH PRODUCTION IN MUNITION FACTORIES!!

Mills's fear, then, was that the power elite would act "in good faith" from their point of view of military preparedness. He wrote (1958:47), "The immediate cause of World War III is the military preparation of it."

While polemical in flavor, Mills's analysis points out that wars need not be caused by leaders who want war. They can happen accidentally. As a footnote to Mills's study, it might be noted that the controversial "Pentagon Papers," made familiar by virtue of the competing attempts to publish or suppress them, were originally commissioned by Robert McNamara, then secretary of defense, for the purpose of finding out how an intellectual, peace-loving administration could have blundered inadvertently into a war in Vietnam, all the while trying to avoid just that.

The idea that conflicts need not be intentional should be familiar to you. Several of the sociologists considered in this chapter have suggested that conflict is generated by social structure itself. As long as society exists, there will be conflict between different groups within it. Even the structural-functionalists recognize the persistence of conflict in real-life societies, though their interpretation of it is, of course, quite different from that of the conflict theorists we've been examining.

The Functionalist View of Conflict

You'll recall from the discussion of social systems theory in Chapter 2 that the notion of "equilibrium" was central. The "balancing" of elements in a system leads to the persistence of the system as a whole. Early functionalists often likened society to the human body, which—biologically—maintains a state of equilibrium through self-regulating mechanisms. In the body, such mechanisms keep body temperature from rising too high or dropping too low, for example; in society, a set of functionally interrelated beliefs, values, and norms maintains social harmony. From this point of view, social conflict—as well as deviance—is seen as "pathological" in the same sense that an irreversible fever in the body is pathological. Conflict threatens the survival of society just as a fever threatens the survival of the human body.

This view of conflict and deviance has bothered other sociologists because it seems to suggest that only conformity is proper. It takes no account of *what* people are asked to conform to. This is the sense in which some sociologists regard functionalism as basically conservative.

Contemporary functionalists, such as Talcott Parsons, do not speak of conflict as pathological or "evil," although they do regard it as a threat to the equilibrium of the system. The American Revolution was an example of social conflict that, while not evil in the eyes of contemporary Americans, clearly disrupted the political equilibrium of the British Empire.

Functionalists have come increasingly to speak of a "moving" equilibrium as distinguished from a "static" equilibrium. In this view, it is possible for a social system to undergo change continually all the while it is maintaining its equilibrium. A factory could grow in size and in the specification of functions and still maintain integration and cooperation among the multiplying specialists. The factory doing this is an illustration of "moving equilibrium."

Where social conflict fits into the functionalist point of view is still not clear. At the very least, social conflict appears to serve as a propulsion mechanism to keep a system in "moving equilibrium" *moving.* Without conflict, social relations would undoubtedly stagnate into a state of monotony. Conflict is an important source of social change.

Views on Social Change

Social change, as I've indicated, means a change in a society's agreements. Such changes may occur with regard to beliefs, values, or norms. Thus, for example, secularization, which Max Weber regarded as one of the most significant changes taking place in modern societies, represents a shift from religious to nonreligious beliefs.

Consider a situation in which the value on economic success takes priority over values on kinship relations. This shift has occurred in numerous societies recently, and it, too, is an example of social change.

The emancipation of blacks and of women in America represents social change relating to norms. Other American examples are the increasing number of supermarkets, which supplant family-run stores, and the great increase in the educational levels people achieve.

Social change, of course, has been taking place since human societies began. Many of these changes were related to technological developments, such as the invention of the wheel, the forging of metals, and the establishment of agriculture. Of special interest to contemporary sociologists, however, is the increased *rate* of social change. Things are changing faster than ever, and the pace is likely to accelerate.

Alvin Toffler (1970:13–14) quotes the economist Kenneth Boulding as saying "I was born in the middle of human history, to date, roughly. Almost as much has happened since I was born as happened before." Toffler continues:

> This startling statement can be illustrated in a number of ways. It has been observed, for example, that if the last 50,000 years of man's existence were divided into lifetimes of approximately sixty-two years each, there have been about 800 such lifetimes. Of these 800, fully 650 were spent in caves.
>
> Only during the last seventy lifetimes has it been possible to communicate effectively from one lifetime to another—as writing made it possible to do. Only during the last six lifetimes did masses of men ever see a printed word. Only during the last four has it been possible to measure time with any precision. Only in the last two has anyone anywhere used an electric motor. And the overwhelming majority of all

the material goods we use in daily life today have been developed within the present, the 800th, lifetime.

The increasing rapidity of technological and social change has led Toffler to a concept he calls "future shock." In much the same way that persons first confronting the agreements of a strange culture experience what is called "culture shock," Toffler suggests that our own society will, in the years to come, seem equally strange and "shocking."

In the remainder of this section, we are going to look at some points of view that sociologists and others have taken in the examination of social change. In the following section, we'll take a special look at the phenomenon of modernization.

Discoveries and Inventions

As I've already suggested, discoveries and inventions are an important source of social change. From a sociological point of view, for example, Columbus discovered America, regardless of whether he was the first European to arrive in the New World. It was his "discovery" that spurred the vast social change that followed the subsequent waves of European migration. Similarly, the invention of television early in the century radically changed most aspects of social life: family activities, entertainment, information transmission, politics, economics, and so forth.

From the standpoint of social change, then, discoveries and inventions are less important than their adoption and use. Accordingly, sociologists have been especially interested in the manner in which such innovations gain widespread agreement.

Diffusion

Ideas, discoveries, and inventions do not stay at the point of their origin. They spread. Thus, two Americans flew the first motorized airplane, a German developed the first jet plane, the Russians orbited the first satellite, and the Americans first put people on the moon.

Diffusion refers to the spread of agreements from one place to others. Donald Schon (1971) has described two models of diffusion. These are pre-

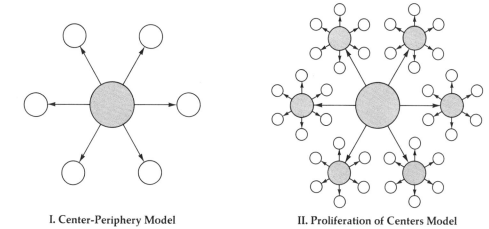

I. Center-Periphery Model   II. Proliferation of Centers Model

Figure 15•1   Two models of diffusion. Figure from Donald Schon, Beyond the Stable State *(New York: Random House, 1971).*

sented in Figure 15•1. The "center-periphery model" is characterized by one source of innovations and several receivers of innovations; the "proliferation of centers model" describes the case in which the receivers of innovations become innovators in their own right.

Sociologists often use the term **cultural lag** to refer to the gap between the appearance of an innovation and its subsequent adoption through widespread agreement. Although the term is often used in connection with the adoption of technological innovations, it is by no means limited to that use. The periods separating the legal from the actual first-class citizenship of blacks and women in America are periods of cultural lag.

Sociologists examine the appearance and spread of specific innovations. They and others also take a much broader view of social change, one that involves long-term, global patterns. Let's turn now to some of the points of view relevant to this.

Linear Theories of Change

A number of social thinkers have suggested that some types of social change represent a linear development in a particular direction. Further, it is thought that such developments represent general tendencies among human beings. The trend from small, primi-

tive societies to large and complex civilizations is commonly put forth as an example.

Table 15•1 illustrates the extent to which sociologists have seen linear developments in their examinations of human social life. Many of the names and terms in the table will be familiar to you from earlier discussions. You may recall in addition that Durkheim saw an ever greater division of labor as an inherent feature of social development, and Weber wrote of the secularization process through which religious bases for society were steadily replaced by rational, secular ones.

In contrast to the social change that may result from inventions, discoveries, and other specific events, the views represented in Table 15•1 relate to a more general process of long-term change. Implicit in them is the idea that social forms evolve over the course of history. Indeed, the idea of "social evolution," akin to Darwin's notion of biological evolution, has been popular in sociology from time to time. Herbert Spencer (1820–1903), for example, argued that societies evolve over time through "natural selection" and "survival of the fittest," terms originally used by Darwin.

During much of the twentieth century, the notion of social evolution has not been very popular in sociology. Its critics generally consider it to be naive, a judgment partly in reaction to the zealous optimism

Table 15·1 Some Concepts of Linear Social Change

Year[a]	Writer	Concepts
1855	Auguste Comte	Theology $\longrightarrow$ Metaphysics $\longrightarrow$ Science
1867	Karl Marx	Capitalism $\longrightarrow$ Socialism $\longrightarrow$ Communism
1876	Herbert Spencer	Simple forms $\longrightarrow$ Complex forms
1887	Lewis Morgan	Savagery $\longrightarrow$ Barbarism $\longrightarrow$ Civilization
1887	Ferdinand Toennies	Gemeinschaft $\longrightarrow$ Gesellschaft
1893	Emile Durkheim	Mechanical solidarity $\longrightarrow$ Organic solidarity
1909	Charles H. Cooley	Primary groups $\longrightarrow$ Secondary groups
1922	Max Weber	Charisma $\longrightarrow$ Tradition $\longrightarrow$ Rational bureaucracy
1941	Robert Redfield	Folk society $\longrightarrow$ Urban society
1950	David Riesman	Tradition-directed $\longrightarrow$ Inner-directed $\longrightarrow$ Other-directed
1951	Talcott Parsons	Particularism $\longrightarrow$ Universalism
		Ascription $\longrightarrow$ Achievement
		Affectivity $\longrightarrow$ Affective neutrality
		Functional diffuseness $\longrightarrow$ Specificity
		Collectivity orientation $\longrightarrow$ Individual orientation

[a]Year of major publication discussing the concepts.

of the early evolutionists, who felt that things were getting better and better as societies evolved. Faced with growing social problems, overpopulation, environmental pollution, the alienation of mass society, and the threat of thermonuclear war, twentieth-century sociologists have been less willing to regard "progress" as automatically good.

Recently, social theorists have separated the idea of social evolution from the starry-eyed view that such evolution is necessarily moving in a desirable direction. *Macrosociological* studies (studies of total societies) over time by Parsons (1964) and Lenski (1974), for example, present reconsiderations of the evolutionary view.

Sociologists also have recognized that social change does not occur in a smooth unfolding of ultimate forms. Progress, even in a given direction, often occurs in leaps and bounds. Sometimes there is forward development, and sometimes there is none. Sometimes things even seem to be going backward. And some movement is linear; some is geometric.

Wilbert Moore (1963) has diagrammed various models of social change that sociologists work with. Figure 15·2 presents four of Moore's diagrams.

Model 1 represents the most simplistic view of linear, evolutionary social change. It suggests that societies steadily and smoothly get more and more "civilized." No sociologist today could defend such a model.

Model 2, though also simplistic, is a more accurate picture of long-term social change. We might, for example, see hunting and gathering as the first stage of development, followed by a step up occasioned by the development of agriculture. Later steps might be based on subsequent technological and economic developments. Clearly, however, such steps are not as regular and evenly spaced as the diagram suggests.

Model 3 represents social change as a succession of spurts in which societies move forward, stay the same for a time, then move forward again. Model 4 is a modification of model 3, allowing for periodic retrogressions. The history of black equality in America might be described by model 4 because it is characterized by gains, setbacks, more gains, and more setbacks, all taking place within an overall framework of movement toward equality with whites.

None of these models is intended to be a precise

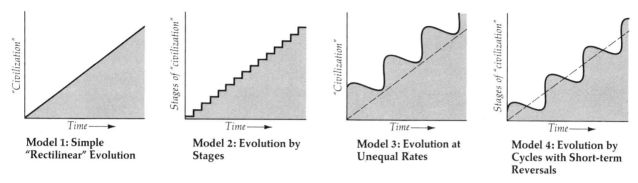

Figure 15·2 *Some models of social change. Figure adapted from Wilbert Moore,* Social Change *(Englewood Cliffs, N.J.: Prentice-Hall, 1963), Figure 1, page 38.*

and accurate picture of social change. To begin, the dimension of "civilization" is too ambiguous to permit the mathematical graphing of social change. And if measurable social changes were to be graphed, it is unlikely that any would be as smooth and regular as shown. These models are nonetheless useful in suggesting the variety of patterns in which social change occurs.

Notice that each model suggests a movement toward some final condition. Some writers have been optimistic about the final states. Comte and Marx, for example, foresaw science and communism, respectively. Others, such as Riesman, with his view of other-directedness in American society, have been less optimistic. All the thinkers shown in Table 15·1, however, have generally seen social change as being in a given, and possibly irreversible, direction. The implication is that technology will become increasingly complex rather than simpler and that roles will continue becoming more specialized and interdependent rather than more general and independent, and so forth.

Cyclical Theories of Change

Several students of social change have suggested that it is not linear at all. The German historian Oswald Spengler (1880–1936), for one, suggested that societies were like people: They were born, grew rapidly, reached full maturity—which he called the "golden age"—declined, and died. Spengler's (1932)

suggestions that Western civilization was in the process of declining and that nothing could be done to halt the inevitable process were unpopular.

The British historian Arnold Toynbee (1889–) has suggested that societies pass through cycles of "challenge" and "response": As each challenge is met by society's response, a new challenge arises. More optimistic than Spengler, Toynbee sees societies progressing toward perfection, or at least sees that as possible (in contrast to a prediction of sure decline) (Toynbee 1962–64).

The sociologist most associated with the cyclical view of social change is Pitirim Sorokin (1889–1968), an immigrant to America following the Russian Revolution. Sorokin thought that three points of view characterized societies from time to time. The "sensate" point of view defines reality in terms of sense experiences. Science is important in such a point of view. The "ideational" point of view, by contrast, places a greater emphasis on spiritual and religious factors. Unlike Comte and others, who saw a linear evolution from religion to science, Sorokin suggested that these two points of view alternated cyclically in societies. Finally, Sorokin's third point of view, the "idealistic," combined elements of the sensate and ideational in an integrated, rational view of things (Sorokin 1937–40).

Figure 15·3 presents Moore's diagram of Sorokin's cyclical model of social change. Notice that this model does not imply a long-term direction of social change: There is no implied final condition,

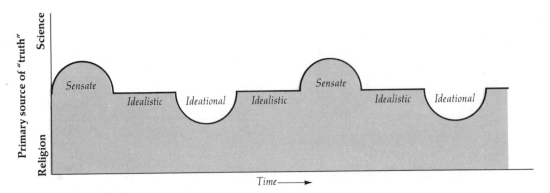

Figure 15•3 Sorokin's cyclical model of social change. Figure adapted from Wilbert Moore, Social Change *(Englewood Cliffs, N.J.: Prentice-Hall, 1963), Figure 13, page 43.*

Pitirim Sorokin 1889–1968 (The American Sociological Association)

such as civilization, science, rationality, or utopia.

To review, then, there are two major points of view on long-term social change. One of these sees a linear progression from one type of society or charac-

teristic of social life to another. Some of the theories representing this point of view have been evolutionary in that they suggest that "higher" social forms (such as civilization) evolve from "lower" ones (such as barbarism). These theories have typically been optimistic about the future. The other major point of view suggests that social change is more cyclical, representing alternations among types of societies, for example, rather than proceeding in a given direction.

Some phenomena make more sense when viewed linearly. Other phenomena make more sense when viewed cyclically. It is worth noting that modern physicists sometimes view light as made up of particles (photons) and sometimes as a wave phenomenon (like ripples in water). Each of these conflicting points of view makes sense in understanding certain phenomena. With social change, matters are somewhat simpler: Some types of social change are linear, while others operate in cycles.

Moore (1963:34–35) cites "*average* increase in productivity (output per man-hour of work) over an entire economy such as the United States" as an example of social change that appears to approximate closely the linear model (model 1 in Figure 15•2). As an empirically observable example of cyclical change (Figure 15•3), he cites (1963:43) "the short-term course of marriage rates and birth rates in contemporary western societies." Observations of social change indicate clearly that no single model encompasses all, and sociologists seek to discover the particular models that best represent specific aspects of social change.

Modernization

The final section of the chapter addresses a particular form of social change that is very common in the contemporary world. In a general way, the term "modernization" is used to refer to the process of social change that characterizes the development of simple, agrarian societies into complex, industrial ones. Economic changes are typically the most visible aspect of modernization, and they may also be the first changes to occur. Realize, though, that modernization eventually touches all aspects of social life—all the society's agreements.

While it makes sense to talk of the modernization of the United States (Lipset 1963) or of Britain, the term is more specifically used in reference to the current process through which the poorer countries of Asia, Africa, and Latin America are attempting to "catch up" with the wealthy, "developed" nations of the world. India's development of nuclear power plants and the development of oil-rich Arab states are examples of modernization, as sociologists customarily use the term.

Economic Change

For the most part today, modernization comes about as a result of economic diffusion. The economic

and technological developments of wealthy, industrial countries are exported to poorer, less developed ones. All this occurs as part of a global drama in which poor—typically Third World—nations of the world attempt to catch up with the rich ones.

Despite the worldwide trend toward modernization, there are still enormous differences in the economic statuses of different nations. Table 15·2 shows the current level of economic development in five nations of the world: United States, Japan, Greece, Ecuador, and India.

The data shown in Table 15·2 reveal the gap separating the developed from the undeveloped nations of the world. Comparing the United States and India, for example, on a per capita basis, we find that the United States consumes 62 times as much energy and 41 times as much steel, has over 300 times as many telephones, almost 80 times as many radios, and nearly 5,000 times as many television sets. This is the gap that the undeveloped nations of the world are seeking to close; this is modernization as such countries see it. In a later discussion of environmental matters, we'll return to this issue.

Modernization per se relates less to the gap than to its *closing*. Consider the performance of Japan. Almost destroyed by World War II, Japan has "risen from the ashes" to become one of the world's leading industrial nations. India, on the other hand, has had a much harder time modernizing. Figure 15·4 illustrates the relative economic growth experienced by Japan and India in recent years, in comparison with the United States.

The graphs in Figure 15·4 tell a number of stories. First, the United States is more industrially developed in each of the indicators shown than either India or Japan. In each case, Japan is more developed than India.

Japan's *rate* of economic growth was also uniformly greater than India's. Thus, if the trends shown were to continue, the gap between Japan and India would increase rather than decrease.

In cement, steel, and motor-vehicle production, Japan has clearly been closing the gap with the United States. It had a greater rate of growth than the United States in each of those industries during the period shown, and by 1972 its absolute levels of production were relatively close to those of the United States.

Table 15·2 Selected Economic Indicators for Five Nations

Indicator	United States	Japan	Greece	Ecuador	India
a. 1974 Gross National Product in millions of U.S. dollars per capita	5,979	3,697	1,691	309	98
b. 1973 energy consumption in the equivalent of kilograms of coal per capita	11,960	3,601	1,828	321	188
c. 1971 production of electric energy in kilowatt-hours per capita	8,295	3,684	952	167	110
d. 1973 steel consumption in kilograms per capita	711	805	172	20	14
e. 1971 steel production in pounds per capita	1,163	1,865			25
f. Motor vehicles per 1,000 population in 1971	537	188	43	10	3
g. Telephones per 1,000 population in 1973	657	357	187	19	3
h. Pieces of domestic mail sent per capita in 1971	420	115	24		11
i. Radio receivers per 1,000 population in 1971	1,622	573	111	270	21
j. Television sets per 1,000 population in 1971	449	222	10	24	.09

Sources: a. U.S. Bureau of the Census, Statistical Abstract of the United States, 1975, p. 845; b. United Nations, Statistical Yearbook 1974, 1975, pp. 359–62; c. U.S. Bureau of the Census, Statistical Abstract of the United States, 1973, p. 815; d. United Nations, Statistical Yearbook 1974, 1975, pp. 546–47; e. U.S. Bureau of the Census, Statistical Abstract of the United States, 1973, p. 815; f. Ibid., p. 825; g. United Nations, Statistical Yearbook 1974, 1975, pp. 534–35; h. U.S. Bureau of the Census, Statistical Abstract of the United States, 1973, p. 827; i. Ibid.; j. Ibid.

If the trends shown were to continue, Japan would overtake and surpass the United States in each of those three industries.

Social Change

Economic change is only a part of modernization. Many of a society's agreements change in the process. Some of these change as a result of economic devel-opment; others must change to permit it. Table 15·3 summarizes some of the changes typically occurring in noneconomic institutions during the modernization process. The box on page 402 "Consequences of Modernization: The Family" elaborates on one of the changes.

Modernization produces frequent conflict between economic development and cultural patterns. Consider what happens to agreements on sex roles,

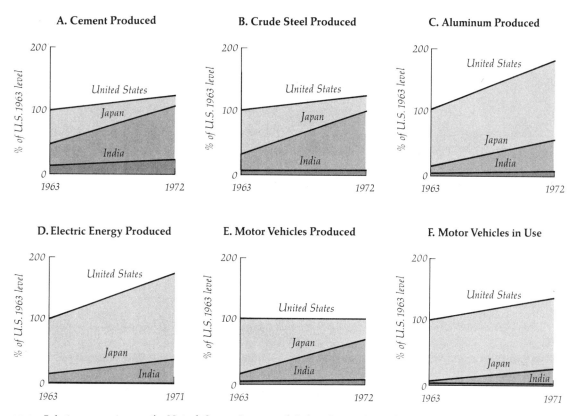

Figure 15•4   Relative economic growth: United States, Japan, and India. Source: United Nations Statistical Yearbook 25(1973): *294–95, 297–98, 309–10, 363–64, 367, 417–19.*

Table 15•3   Summary of Noneconomic Institutional Changes Associated with Modernization

Family

1. Family changes from economic production unit to economic consumption unit.
2. Women freed from family functions for participation in the economy.
3. Birth rate declines.
4. More families reside in urban centers.
5. Family consumption patterns reflect mass production of goods.

Religion

1. Greater secularization in society.
2. Religious status becomes less significant than economic status in general social stratification.
3. Religious values and norms modified to support economic development.
4. Religions become more bureaucratically organized.

Education

1. Education becomes more open to women and dispossessed minorities.
2. Scientific, technical education strengthened.
3. Education becomes more formalized.
4. Volume of book publishing increases.
5. General literacy rate increases.

Government

1. Greater government support and regulation of industry.
2. Government becomes larger.
3. Government becomes increasingly bureaucratized.
4. Greater national unity.
5. Relations with other nations become more significant.

Consequences of Modernization:
The Family

One of the earliest changes experienced by newly modernizing countries is the reduction of infectious disease through the diffusion of public health technology. Public health technology lowers the death rate, especially among infants and children, causing rapid population growth. Since most of the people of less-developed nations live in rural areas that cannot absorb the increased population, unemployment presses people off the land. They tend to migrate into urban areas where newly developing industry and commerce and modern consumer goods and services offer hope for employment and a better life. Unfortunately, the opportunities are more apparent than real; and often the transition is more painful than pleasant.

In the course of the transition from agrarian life to modern urban living, the family undergoes major changes in function, structure, relations, and style. Functionally, the family changes from a production unit to a consumption unit. No longer is there need for a large multiworker household to operate the family's farm interests, and the extended-family household changes to the one containing only a core nuclear family. In the city children become economic liabilities rather than economic assets, and eventually families have fewer of them. Wives lose their functions as producers and maintainers of the labor force and become free to pursue extra-household activities.

The modern economy forces work outside the home away from kinfolk. Not only the father but also the mother is forced into the marketplace or factory to obtain enough money for the family to survive in a pecuniary economy. Without the extended-family household, no one remains at home to supervise children so they are left on their own. They may be sent into the streets to earn money. Daily life be-

comes filled with more secondary than primary relations. There is an erosion of family control over individual members. Still, extended families survive as mutual-aid societies in a city of strangers. One of their most important tasks is to provide shelter, food, and employment assistance to newly migrated relatives until they can stand on their own feet.

Scarce urban housing forces overcrowding in both dwelling and neighborhood. Dense structures with common halls, stairways, and utilities cause more intensive contact with neighbors than in rural villages. Loss of rural courtyards, oven rooms, and large family areas drives group activities such as cooking, eating, and sitting into small rooms or city streets. More positively, household furnishings change as families are able to acquire the high-status accoutrements of modern living such as kerosene burners for cooking (replacing dung cakes) and beds (instead of mats).

These innovations in family functions, structure, relations, and style take time to diffuse throughout the society. For instance, a family that engaged in a handicraft industry prior to urban migration may reestablish itself as a producing unit in the city and maintain an extended household with large numbers of economically active children. Cultural lag is also seen among the nuclear consumer families that continue to reproduce nonproductive children. Indeed, even in the United States, cultural lag is evident in a relatively small number of large nuclear families, reflecting agreements of a traditional agrarian society.

Is there evidence of other cultural lags in modern industrialized societies? Can you imagine the kinds of within-group conflict which might result from these changes in the family?

an excellent illustration of this conflict. Japan traditionally has been a male-oriented society, one in which women have been restricted largely to family roles. With economic development, this situation

has changed drastically. Japanese women have become actively engaged in various occupations, in offices, factories, and stores. The Japanese experience is not unique.

Japan is a striking example of the modernization process. The mother and child, representative of traditional patterns, contrast sharply with the background of modern industrialization. (Henri Cartier-Bresson, Magnum)

The transition from being a traditional society to being a modern one is often painful for those involved in it, as Daniel Lerner (1964) has amply documented in the case of Turkey. For the Turks that Lerner called the "traditionals," national modernization has meant the need to think about societywide problems and to consider other areas of the world and strange people; in short, it has meant the need to give up much of what was comfortable and familiar. When Lerner sought to tap such broader viewpoints, many of his Turk respondents refused to engage in "modern" thinking. When they were asked where they would like to live other than Turkey, half the "traditionals" could not imagine doing that, many of

them saying that they would rather die.

For many people around the world, modernization—and the economic benefits it brings—means giving up a variety of accustomed beliefs, values, and norms. It may mean moving from the farm to the city, breaking up families, weakening religious ties, assuming unaccustomed occupational roles. Some may seem to gain, and others may seem to lose. All will probably feel uncomfortable to some extent.

The foregoing are some aspects of modernization facing many countries around the world. We will examine other aspects of modernization and social change in Chapters 16 and 17, dealing with **population, technology, urbanism,** and the environment.

Summary

Social conflict arises from disagreements and is characterized by the attempt of one party to gain agreement for its point of view at the expense of a conflicting one. College debates are one form of social conflict. Thermonuclear war is another.

The study of social conflict has covered a variety of topics: philosophical discussions of ultimate "human nature" and examinations of animal and primitive behavior. All these inquiries suggest that conflict is probably as "natural" as cooperation.

Some social conflict occurs in a "micro" setting, such as a disagreement between two individuals. Sometimes it is useful to examine social conflict as occurring within a group; other times it is more useful to examine it as occurring between two groups. Very often, both points of view can be used in the study of a given instance of social conflict, and each might yield special insights.

War is the most dramatic form of social conflict, and many sociologists have studied wars and worried about preventing them. C. Wright Mills thought that the roots of modern war grew out of the "military-industrial complex"—the increased interdependence among government, industry, and the military. He said that the immediate cause of World War III would be the preparation for it.

The functionalist point of view sees social conflict largely as a threat to the equilibrium of a social system. The survival of a society depends on its balancing and integrating its many components, and conflict is a source of imbalance. Not all functionalists see all conflict as "bad," however. Indeed, conflict is a form of propulsion for what they call "moving equilibrium"—the continued rebalancing in societies undergoing continual change. Without conflict, societies would likely stagnate.

Much of this chapter has been devoted to the examination of social change: alterations to a society's body of shared agreements. Examples of broad social change include secularization, industrialization, growing equality of the sexes and of ethnic groups, and the general shift from simple, primitive societies to complex, industrial civilizations.

Inventions and discoveries are important sources of social change. Of special interest to sociologists is the process of diffusion whereby innovations are transmitted from one social group to another.

In studying social change generally, sociologists have employed two distinct points of view. Many have seen social change as a linear process, moving in a particular direction. The overall trend from simple to complex societies is an example of linear change.

The second point of view that sociologists have brought to bear on social change sees it as more cyclical: Change fluctuates through recurring conditions rather than progressing continuously in the same direction. Both points of view are useful to sociology, as some social change appears to be primarily linear while other social change seems to be more cyclical.

"Modernization" is a special kind of social change that is important to an understanding of the contemporary world scene. Typically, the term refers to the process of urbanization and industrialization among the "developing" countries of the world. Japan is a good example of a society that has modernized; India exemplifies those that are still struggling with the painful process.

Modernization, like all social change, involves the changing of social agreements. Largely spurred by economic change, modernization touches all aspects of social life: family, religion, politics, education, and others. Often, it brings dysfunctions and unhappiness for the individuals involved.

Suggested Readings

Coser, Lewis
1956 *The Functions of Social Conflict.* New York: Free Press.
Building on the earlier work of Georg Simmel, Coser elaborates the many ways in which social conflict strengthens group life rather than weakens it. Coser's attempt to develop formal, theoretical propositions regarding conflict are instructive from the standpoint of sociological theory and ought to be compared with the propositions developed by Dahrendorf (suggested reading in Chapter 11).

Lenski, Gerhard
1974 *Human Societies.* 2nd ed. New York: McGraw-
      Hill.
Here's the big picture, as Lenski traces the evolution
of societies from the simplest to the most complex.
An excellent resource for the study of social change,
Lenski focuses his attention on the development of
social institutions and their interrelations with one
another. The examination is filled with cross-cultural
data drawn from important anthropological sources.

Moore, Wilbert
1963 *Social Change.* Englewood Cliffs, N. J.: Prentice-
      Hall.
In this small, readable book, Moore has summarized
all the major theoretical points of view regarding
social change, both linear and cyclical. He carefully
examines small-scale and global change, and the

final chapter on modernization is likely to be a useful
introduction to the topic for many years to come.

Van den Berghe, Pierre
1975 *Man in Society.* New York: Elsevier.
Subtitled "a biosocial view," this provocative book
examines human beings as animals—in both the
biological and pejorative senses of the term. In large
part, van den Berghe finds that technological developments have canceled out the natural, biological checks
against human aggressiveness, leading to the creation
of inhumane social institutions. This is not the jol-
liest of views, and van den Berghe summarizes the
tone when he concludes (p. 278): "If I leave my readers
with a gnawing and lingering dissatisfaction with
their society, their place in it, and my own irreverent
and impertinent remarks about it, I shall consider
that I have accomplished my purpose."

Episode Fifteen

Gabriel evidenced almost no emotion when the jury foreman pronounced the verdict, "Not guilty." He was exhausted. The child for whom he had risked his life had been brutally murdered. The baby's chromosomal mother remained under treatment in a Chicago mental hospital. While Monica had defended Gabe illustriously, she had simultaneously dashed any hopes he had nursed for resuming their previous relationship. His ribs and skull sometimes still ached from the injuries he had suffered several months before.

The courtroom emptied. Gabriel sat quietly in the place he had occupied throughout the trial, staring at his clasped hands. Monica stood next to him.

"You're free now," she forced, breaking the long silence between them.

"Yes," Gabe nodded. "Thank you." Suddenly he added, "I'm sorry for all the deception before."

Monica leaned toward Gabe and kissed him. "Take care," she whispered, then turned to leave the courtroom.

It was 1 P.M. when the wire services reported Knapp's acquittal. Demonstrations both for and against the verdict erupted across the country. Later that afternoon, however, Gabriel would return to Adamsville without incident.

Using a pseudonym and accompanied by four secret service agents, he flew to Tucson. From there he was driven in a government limousine to the colony.

Gabe remained silent during most of the journey. Occasionally he poured milk from his thermos, gulping it, hoping to replenish temporarily his waning strength. "A greenface on the outside," the words nagged him as he rode, "and a milk-white at home."

Two miles outside Adamsville's southern entrance, Arizona state authorities stopped the car. Only after Knapp's escorts had convinced the local officers of their identities was the party allowed to proceed.

This heightened security was new to Gabriel. "No one within 2 miles of the borders now," one of the escorting officers explained. "New orders issued yesterday from Washington." The speaker grunted. "They don't want another boycott."

Minutes later the car stopped. Just ahead stretched the colony's south gate. "I'll get out here," Gabe said, reaching to open the door. The residents were expecting him: He had phoned Elderhome from Tucson.

Ann Sullivan advanced from within the guard shelter. "Gabe?" she called. "That you?"

"Yes." He moved quickly toward the electronic gate which had already begun to open. When he reached Ann, he took her hands. Although he didn't know the woman well, he had found himself thinking of her during his trial.

While the two stood facing one another, Gabriel attempted to assess his feelings about being home—wondering at the same time whether he could ever be really "home." Meanwhile the limousine in which he had arrived disappeared to the south, returning to Tucson.

"The Elders and Jacob Lockwood are here to greet you," Ann said. "Alexander brought them down. They're waiting a little way up the road. They'll take you into town."

Knapp and Sullivan walked northward a few hundred feet. When Ruth, Michael, and Jacob caught sight of Gabriel's advancing silhouette, the three rushed toward him.

Michael put his brilliant green arms around Knapp's neck. "Gabriel, Gabriel," he breathed, "you have suffered so much."

Ruth kissed Gabe on the cheek. "We're glad to welcome you back," she said. "We were very afraid that they would find you guilty—even without the evidence."

Gabriel said nothing. Unnoticed Ann Sullivan had returned to the guard shelter.

Michael said, "You won't take guard duty again. It was a mistake. You would not have been arrested if you had not taken guard duty."

"That's over now," Gabe murmured.

"Welcome home," Jacob said then, extending his lime green hand toward his friend. "We missed you."

"You had a fine attorney," Michael said. "You made a good choice."

"Yes." Gabriel looked down at his feet.

"You missed the autumnal equinox," Ruth smiled. "Three greens matured."

"I will mature at the spring ceremony," Gabriel assured them, again aware of his fatigue.

"We've moved your things into the house you were assigned before your arrest," Jacob said. Gabriel

remembered: It was the large, glass house near central Adamsville. He stood quiet for several seconds.

"I would like to live in the valley," he announced softly. "I would be more comfortable there."

"That's ridiculous," Michael exclaimed.

Duncan's paper, which Elderhome had received July 1, had eroded their confidence in the belief that dull greens must be disloyal sinners. Now the Elders had come to view valleyites as victims of genetic misfortune. Knapp had suggested to Dan Adamson that failure to mature might be the result of a green's possessing fewer mutant chromosomes. It now seemed clear to the Elders—and to all the cooperationists—that valleyites were genetically inferior, and that explained their well-known tendency to disease.

"The valley people are often sick, Gabriel," Ruth reminded. "You would not enjoy living there."

"I am one of them," Gabriel responded.

"You have never appeared very ill to me," Jacob retorted. "You must have been fairly healthy to accomplish what you did at Chicago National."

"I am one of them," Gabriel insisted.

Michael broke in. "Let's not discuss it now. Gabriel is exhausted: He's had a grueling experience. We're all emotionally drained. We'll consider this again in the morning."

"Gabriel," Jacob offered, "why don't you stay with me tonight? You can decide on this tomorrow."

The four entered the waiting limousine.

The following morning Gabriel came to realize to what extent dissent had come to pervade Adamsville. According to the agreement made between Elderhome and Washington, the colony would send three voting delegates to the third conference on human mutations. Who these representatives would be had grown into a major controversy.

All Adamsvillers agreed that to send the community's greenest members would not only be unnecessarily dangerous but also politically foolish. Ungreen delegates, shocked and startled at the sight of the mutants, would ignore any rational arguments these greens might pose.

The answer was to send either young, not-yet-matured mutants or dull greens from the valley. Gabriel found his people angrily divided upon which was the better solution.

Larry Jones and the radical militarists, still strongly convinced that failure to physically mature was evidence of spiritual transgression, argued that the only trustworthy delegates would come from the ranks of the young.

Elderhome, on the other hand, influenced by Duncan, held that older, more experienced mutants might perform better as delegates. Many dull greens had spent several years on the outside before their final return to the colony.

While it was true, Elderhome and the cooperationists argued, that valleyites tended to be physically weak and often ill, that fact did not necessarily lessen their potential as influential delegates. "We will choose the most experienced and best qualified of our valleyites," Ruth had summed up Elderhome's position, "and they will do a good job."

As residents took sides on this issue, the purpose for attending the conference became still another source of contention. Elderhome wanted a scientific resolution that photosynthetic creatures should be considered "just as human" as ungreens.

Larry Jones, however, argued that the delegation's role should be to dramatize S.T.I.'s political and economic threat. Adamsville, he often yelled from the platform in the community's public park, must demand establishment of a separate green nation, consisting of the present states of Arizona and New Mexico.

Simmering dissent threatened to erupt into a full boil when, on Sunday, November 2, 2027, Larry Jones again climbed the steps to the community's sacred platform. Gradually a crowd gathered, many of the onlookers armed with the guns Bradley Duncan had noted more than a year before.

"Tomorrow the Elders will choose our representatives," Larry called, his fists clenched and raised, his voice dramatically passionate. "Fellow greens, true followers of Adam, we cannot send our sinners! What people sends its lowest—those of whom it is ashamed —to represent them? Tell me! What government has ever purposefully commissioned people it could not trust to speak for it?"

The approximately 50 Adamsvillers to whom Larry spoke cheered. Others joined the crowd until, thirty minutes later, Jones bellowed his message to 300 greens.

"Now I wonder," Larry thumped, "just why Michael and Ruth govern Adamsville? Who is it that gave them such authority? Was it Adam Jones III, their father, my great-grandfather? Maybe—but we have no written documents to that effect. Adam left no specific rules for choosing who would govern after him. When he died he left a family, the beginnings of a nation—but not a nation.

"Who then decided that Michael and Ruth should govern us? *They* did!" Larry paused, allowing his audience to absorb his message. When he began again his voice was softer.

"And that was fine with all of us so long as the Elders followed the traditions and philosophy established by our prophet, Adam."

Gabriel and Jacob joined the crowd; Gabriel recognized his sister, Elizabeth, near the platform.

"But Ruth and Michael have not continued to follow Adam's wishes," Jones went on. "Not only have they allowed outsiders into Adamsville, but they have taken ungreens' advice! By their actions they have implied that outsiders apparently know better than we do what is good for us.

"In saying this they have sinned against our prophet and father, Adam. They have admitted that they do not really—genuinely—believe that our people are the future people of earth; for if they really believed this, they would trust their own judgments above those of outsiders!"

Gabe whispered to Jacob, "Will the Elders respond to this?"

"They may come to the park to make an official statement later," Jacob answered.

"Adam, our founder and prophet," Larry called, "established Adamsville as a separate colony. He discouraged his children from leaving the colony, and, later, he erected fences to ensure Adamsville's separatism. Why is it then that now Ruth and Michael refuse to follow this tradition of separatism? Are they afraid?"

Ann Sullivan and several others from the valley had wandered into the park. They collected near the rear of the cheering throng.

"This is no time to be afraid," Jones bellowed, "for we have already proven that we can bring American industry to its knees! Why then are the Elders afraid? Or is it that they are really not afraid: that really they are ashamed of their color and of their calling?"

The crowd had grown unruly. Larry flung his arms about him as he yelled his message, his face growing darker with increased emotion. It was as if a dam within him had broken; all the power welled up in him came rushing, washing through the crowd, carrying it along in deep, turbulent waves.

Spontaneously refueled by the crowd's collective response, Jones raised his voice. It was as if he gained strength from his followers' shouts of approval.

"Maybe," he screamed now, "maybe Michael and Ruth aim to surrender Adamsville! Perhaps they are traitors! I think—don't you—that they are ashamed of their sacred mutations. And that shame has caused them to plan to surrender all of us!"

Larry Jones had never gone this far before. The crowd grew suddenly quiet. The orator swallowed, then went on.

"This is why they want to send our least acceptable residents as delegates. This is why they plan to send disloyal sinners! Only the scum of our community could be persuaded to deliver us into the hands of our enemies. Only our most deceitful members, those milk-whites who harbor secret sins and who sometimes openly promote heresy, only these most despicable—"

The crowd rumbled.

"—only these would be capable of Elderhome's treasonous plan."

Larry paused momentarily, then shouted as with sudden vision. "Valleyites," he screeched," are parasites!"

Suddenly the sound of a gunshot cracked the air. Amid the screaming and pushing that followed, Larry Jones fell to his knees. His right hand clutched his chest. Seconds later he was dead.

Unknown to anyone present, Ann Sullivan had in a moment of uncontrolled anger issued the fatal bullet.

Questions

1. Individuals can sometimes effect widespread social change. How is this true of Gabe? Monica? Ann Sullivan? Larry Jones?

2. How is social conflict evidenced in this episode?

3. How does the situation within Adamsville demonstrate class conflict?

4. Can you describe the events of this episode from the functionalist, the conflict, and the symbolic interactionist points of view?

Part Five
Mass Society

In Parts One through Four of this book, we've been looking at the major aspects of how social agreements are created, perpetuated, and changed. I want to conclude this introduction to sociology and the sociologist's view of society with a special focus on mass society. "Mass society" is a term sociologists and others use to refer to large, industrialized societies in which a large proportion of the population live in large urban centers. It is what most of the evolutionary models of Chapter 15 showed as the societal form toward which evolution moves.

In Chapter 16, we'll address the "mass" aspect of mass society, focusing on the topic of population. I'll introduce the sociological subfield of "demography": the scientific study of population. We'll see how populations increase in size and what difference the increase makes. We will also consider the now widely discussed notions of overpopulation and population explosion.

Medicine has played a major part in the growth of populations all over the world. As modern medical science has found preventions and cures for a variety of diseases, more of us escape death in infancy and have longer life expectancies. In view of this, the concluding portion of Chapter 16 is devoted to a look at medicine as sociologists have studied it.

Technology and urbanism are also integral aspects of mass societies, and Chapter 17 addresses them. We see that both phenomena are intimately entwined with social agreements. Chapter 17 concludes with an examination of the effects of population growth, technology, and urbanism on the physical environment in which they occur, and I describe the part that sociology must play in the ultimate solution to environmental problems. Although such problems as pollution and the depletion of natural resources have typically been regarded as requiring technological solutions, I want you to see the extent to which they will require social solutions as well.

Chapter 18 focuses on a more specific topic relating to mass society: communication. We will see how central communication is to social affairs in general, and that social interaction is, in an important sense, merely a process of communication. We then look at how communications are structured in mass society and what these structures mean.

I've concluded this book with a chapter about sociologists themselves. I know that most introductory textbooks appear to present their subject matters as lifeless bodies of knowledge and ideas, and I'd like to show you there's some life in sociology. Like society in general, sociology has people living in it, and I'd like you to get more familiar with them.

In case I haven't already communicated it, I'd like you to know that I find sociology about the most exciting thing there is to do. Sociology is a way of viewing society and a way of participating in it. I've found sociology a nice place to visit *and* a nice place to live, and I want to invite you to move in.

16

Population and Health

Early in this book, I described a society as a social system with people living in it. More recently I've said that one characteristic of mass society is *lots* of people. This characteristic of mass society highlights a fundamental aspect of society in general. Societies are made up of individual human beings, each following his or her individual course, and all that individual behavior adds up to what's going on in the society at large. Throughout the book, we've seen the countless ways in which social structures influence the actions of individuals, but I know you've probably also had a sense that society is the uncontrollable sum of what individuals do. One person throws a candy wrapper on the ground, others do too, and eventually an enormous amount of litter has accumulated. The unplanned, incidental, aggregated result of individual actions often appears as a frightening surprise.

The creation of human populations is something like the creation of litter (this is not intended to be a pun). Becoming a parent seems like a very personal thing. Nonetheless, when individuals—moved by all sorts of personal, individual reasons—have babies, all those babies form what is probably the most significant group product in social affairs. Sociologists study this aspect of group life.

Demography is the scientific study of population. Demography is often regarded as a subfield of sociology and taught within sociology departments. At the same time, demography has become sufficiently specialized and developed to be seen as a separate discipline. Some colleges and universities have departments of demography outside the departments of sociology.

Demography is addressed (1) to measuring the size and composition of human societies, (2) to understanding the factors involved in determining population size and composition, and (3) to understanding their consequences. In this chapter, we are going to examine some of the concepts and theories that have been developed in demography, and we'll also look at what demographers have discovered in their empirical studies of population.

You may have already recognized that the scientific study of population has a pressing, "real-life" significance. A great deal has been written in recent years about the population explosion and the problems of overpopulation. We're going to look at these topics in the chapter, seeing how demography fits into the picture.

When we look at the causes of population growth, we're going to see that medicine has played a critical role. By defeating many of the diseases that prevented population growth during most of human history, modern medicine has sparked a geometric increase in the numbers of people on the planet. In the later part of the chapter, we'll look at the place of medicine in societies. Sociologists have looked at medicine from a variety of perspectives—quite aside from its influence on population growth.

In many ways, the sociological study of medicine offers a microcosm of the study of society in general. The creation, structuring, learning, and changing of agreements that characterize social life generally are all to be found in matters of illness and health. We'll see that even death is a matter of social agreements: its definition, its meaning, and how people behave in relation to it.

By the time this chapter is completed, you should have a clearer picture of how human beings—as biological entities—fit into the social side of things. Let's begin, then, with an overview of population size, composition, and growth in the world and, more specifically, in the United States.

A "Head-Counting" Overview

One of the oldest methods of empirical social research is the **census:** the enumeration (counting) of populations. Records show that this practice existed at least as long ago as the ancient Egyptian civilizations. In part, the ancient Egyptian rulers counted the members of their societies so as to tax them. Later, the Romans conducted censuses throughout their far-flung empire for the same purpose, and the Bible tells us that Jesus was born in Bethlehem because Joseph and Mary were required to journey there—Joseph's ancestral home—to be counted.

In more recent times, methods of census taking have been developed to considerably greater scientific precision. Not all contemporary societies have developed scientific enumeration procedures, however, so it is difficult to determine the actual population of the world at any given time. Indeed, all we can do is *estimate* it. Such estimates, moreover, must be even rougher when we are estimating the population of the world centuries ago. Still, they can be very valuable in understanding the contemporary population situation, especially when we turn to the consideration of overpopulation.

World Population

The United Nations (1974:81) has estimated that the 1973 population of the entire world was about 3,860,000,000, nearly 4 billion people. Since it is difficult to conceive of so many people, I will give you some "visual" guides. In the world today there are roughly 1,500 people for every letter in this book. Placed head to toe, they would reach from the earth to the moon nine abreast. If, on your birthday, you decide to have a party for everyone else with the same birthday, you'll need over 10 million party hats and you'll have to rent Tokyo, Paris, or New York City for the party. (If your birthday is February 29, however, you can get by with Boston or Pittsburgh.)

Table 16·1 presents the populations estimated by the United Nations for different areas of the world

Table 16·1   World Population Estimates, 1950–1973

Area	1950	1960	1970	1973	Growth 1950–1973
World	2,486,000,000	2,982,000,000	3,632,000,000	3,860,000,000	55%
Africa	217,000,000	270,000,000	344,000,000	374,000,000	72
North America	166,000,000	199,000,000	228,000,000	236,000,000	42
Latin America	162,000,000	213,000,000	283,000,000	309,000,000	91
Asia	1,355,000,000	1,645,000,000	2,056,000,000	2,204,000,000	63
Europe	392,000,000	425,000,000	462,000,000	472,000,000	20
Oceania	12,600,000	15,800,000	19,400,000	20,600,000	63
U.S.S.R.	180,000,000	214,000,000	243,000,000	250,000,000	39

Source: United Nations, Demographic Yearbook, 1973 *(New York: United Nations, 1974), p. 81.*

from 1950 to 1973. Several things are apparent in the data. First, over half the world's population lives in Asia, with the percentage increasing slightly between 1950 and 1973. Overall, the population growth rates for different parts of the world vary a great deal, ranging from 91 percent in Latin America for the twenty-three-year period to 20 percent for Europe. This difference is also illustrated by a comparison between Latin America and North America. In 1950, the population of Latin America was 98 percent as large as the population of its northern neighbors; in 1973, its population was 31 percent larger than that of North America. As a general observation, the underdeveloped areas of the world have experienced a much greater growth of population than the more developed areas, and we'll see why shortly.

To round out the picture of current population size in the world, Table 16·2 presents the populations of the world's largest nations, showing all those with 50 million or more people. Taken together, these fifteen largest nations account for over two-thirds of the world's population. Indeed, more than one-fifth of the world's population lives in China alone.

Table 16·2 Population Estimates for the World's Largest Nations, 1973

Nation	Population
China	814,280,000
India	574,220,000
U.S.S.R.	249,750,000
United States	210,400,000
Indonesia	124,600,000
Japan	108,350,000
Brazil	101,710,000
Bangladesh	71,610,000
Pakistan	66,750,000
West Germany	61,970,000
Nigeria	59,610,000
United Kingdom	55,930,000
Italy	54,890,000
Mexico	54,300,000
France	52,300,000

Source: Demographic Yearbook, 1973 *(New York: United Nations, 1974), pp. 82–87.*

If current population estimates lack total accuracy, estimates of earlier years and centuries are even more approximate. Nevertheless, scholars have found it useful to make such estimates. One of the most frequently cited estimates was developed by A. M. Carr-Saunders in 1936: He estimated world and area populations for the period from 1650 to 1900. Carr-Saunders suggested that the total world population increased from 545 million to 1.608 billion during that period.

Other estimates (Durand 1968) suggest there were 5 million people on earth in 8000 B.C. and perhaps 300 million at the time of Christ. Figure 16·1 provides a graphic illustration of world population growth from 8000 B.C. through estimates for the year A.D. 2000. The precise population figures for any given year are irrelevant in comparison with the general story that the graph tells.

Throughout most of human history, world population hardly increased at all. The number of people was governed by the same natural checks and balances that keep other species from overflowing the earth. Only during the past 300 or 400 years has the rate of population growth increased dramatically, and demographers have been especially interested in this.

One of the ways demographers measure population growth is by the length of time it takes a population to double in size, called the "doubling time." Thus, it took several hundreds of thousands of years for a human population of one-quarter billion to develop in the world, a figure achieved by about the time of Christ. It took 1,650 years for the figure to double again. The next doubling took about 200 years: a population of 1 billion around 1850. The second billion was achieved about 80 years later, in 1930; and the fourth billion was achieved 45 years later, in 1975. It has been estimated by the United Nations that our current doubling time is 35 years. This means that we'll achieve a world population of *8 billion* around the year 2010. Nobody cares to estimate what the doubling time will be then.

United States Population

As of its 1790 census, the new United States had a population of just under 4 million. The 1975 popu-

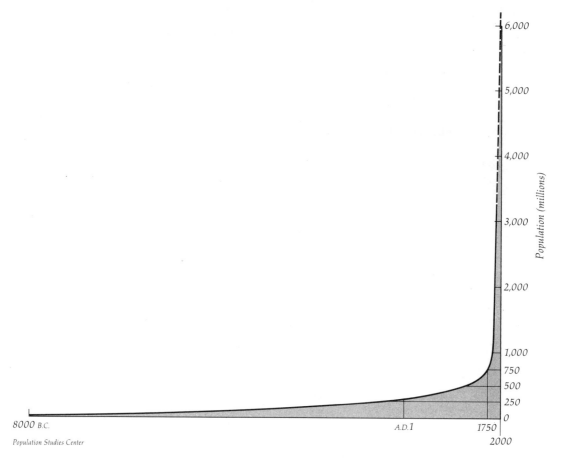

Figure 16•1   Long-term world population growth. Redrawn from John Durand, "The Modern Expansion of World Population," Pro-ceedings of the American Philosophical Society, June 1967, as reprinted in Charles Nam, ed., Population and Society *(New York: Houghton Mifflin, 1968), p. 111.*

lation was estimated at around 213 million, or about fifty-five times what it had been 185 years earlier (U.S. Bureau of the Census 1975a). Figure 16•2 shows the American census counts from 1790 to 1970 and Census Bureau population projections through the year 2000.

Early in our national history, the United States had a shorter doubling time than the world as a whole. It has become longer than the world average during this century as the figures to the right indicate.

Year	Population	Doubling time (years)
1790	4 million	
		24
1814	8 million	
		24
1838	16 million	
		23
1861	32 million	
		30
1891	64 million	
		45
1936	128 million	
		56
1992	256 million	

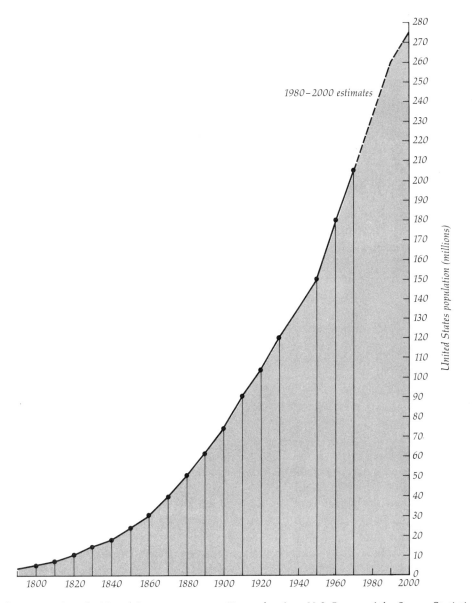

Figure 16•2   Population growth in the United States, 1790–2000. Data taken from U.S. Bureau of the Census, Statistical Abstract of the United States, *1975, pp. 6–7.*

This is not an indication that population growth has become insignificant in the United States. During the five years from 1970 to 1975, we *added* double the 1790 population. And as the following chapter will show, American population growth has an environmental significance far beyond sheer numbers of people.

We'll look at some of the causes and components of population growth in the next section of this chapter. Before that, however, let's look at the methods by which population data are compiled. How does anybody know how many people there are?

United States Census

Because congressional representation was to be based on each state's population size, regular censuses were provided for in Article I of the Constitution: "The actual enumeration shall be made within three years after the first meeting of the Congress of the United States, and within every subsequent term of ten years, in such manner as they shall by law direct" (U.S. Constitution, Art. I, sec. 2).

The first census, in 1790, was conducted by several hundred United States marshal's assistants; in it was recorded the number of persons in each household, classified by sex, age, race, and status (whether free or slave). Since 1790 the census has grown in many ways: the number of people enumerated, the number of questions asked, and the analyses undertaken once the data are collected. It is one of the most important research undertakings in America today.

To enumerate some 200 million Americans requires hundreds of thousands of census workers. The actual enumeration proceeds through an intricate geographical division and subdivision of the nation. Cities and towns are divided into census tracts, which are further divided into enumeration districts. The people hired to undertake the actual enumeration of households within enumeration districts are called census enumerators.

From the beginning until 1970, all enumerations were conducted through personal interviews. An enumerator walked systematically through a district, stopping at each household and conducting an interview with either the head of the household or another adult member of it. One interview is collected per household, but information is collected about *each person* living in the household, as well as about the dwelling itself.

In the 1970 census, the enumeration of many urban households was conducted by mail. Personal interviews were conducted when the questionnaires were not returned, however, and the enumeration of rural areas proceeded in the traditional manner.

As I mentioned, the census was initially intended primarily as a method of determining the proportional representation of the several states in the U.S. House of Representatives. Now it has become a major research project, providing a variety of data relevant to national planning. To accommodate the mushrooming variety of information desired, the Census Bureau now employs sampling techniques. Longer questionnaires are administered to 20, 15, or 5 percent samples of the households. The sampling procedures are so designed that from these questionnaires estimates can be made about the entire population for all questions.

While most people think of the Bureau of the Census in terms of the decennial censuses, its most important work is conducted on a continuing basis. One of its publications, *Current Population Survey,* provides a regular flow of information from a carefully selected, rotating sample of about 47,000 households across the nation. These sample surveys are generally more accurate than the decennial censuses of the entire population, because they are more manageable and can be conducted by the bureau's regular, professional staff. In fact, each decennial census is followed by a sample survey designed to determine the extent of error in the total enumeration.

In addition to the decennial censuses and continuing sample surveys, a great volume of data is

Demography is the scientific study of births, migrations, and deaths, the human substance of organized social life. (Burk Uzzle, Magnum)

collected regularly by government agencies at all levels. Birth, marriage, and death records, for example, provide valuable information for demographers. What are some of the things demographers *do* with the great volumes of data available to them?

The Components of Population Growth

The size of a society's population changes as a function of three factors: births **(fertility)**, deaths **(mortality)**, and migration. The term **natural increase** refers to the excess of births over deaths, and the difference between in-migration and out-migration is referred to as the "net" gain or loss due to migration. To take account of different population sizes in understanding and projecting population change, however, demographers work with *rates* rather than numbers.

Birth Rates

The simplest measure of births in a society is called the **crude birth rate:** the number of births divided by the size of the population. Typically, the number of births during a given year is divided by the total population as of the beginning or the midpoint of that year. This rate is most often expressed as the number of births per 1,000 population. In 1973, for example, the United States crude birth rate was 15 per 1,000. The highest national crude birth rate in 1973 was 52.3 in Swaziland; West Germany, by contrast, had 10.2 births per 1,000 population (United Nations 1974:94–98).

While the crude birth rate figures directly in the year-to-year change in population, a fuller understanding of population change involves the concepts of **fecundity** and **fertility.** "Fecundity" refers to the biological ability of women within a particular age range to bear children. Societies with more women in the childbearing years have a greater potential for births than those with fewer such women, regardless of the total population sizes.

The "fertility rate" used by demographers is the number of births divided by the number of women in their childbearing years. Although women vary in the number of their childbearing years, a specific period of years, such as from ages fifteen to forty-nine, is typically used for the calculation. A society's fertility rate for a given year is thus the number of babies born per 1,000 women between the ages, say, of fifteen and forty-nine.

Death Rates

Asked "What's the death rate in these parts?" a Vermont farmer is reported to have replied, "One apiece." Undaunted by this native wit, demographers pay as much attention to death rates as to birth rates. The **crude death rate,** as you might imagine, is the number of deaths in a year per 1,000 population. The United States crude death rate in 1973 was 9.4 per 1,000. In Africa, by contrast, the average annual death rate between 1965 and 1973 was 21 (United Nations 1974:81, 94–98).

Since everyone is biologically capable of dying in any given year, it makes no sense to limit the calculations to a particular sex or age range as is done with fertility rates. Even so, demographers often compute "infant mortality rates": the number of deaths

among children under one year old, divided by the number of live births during a given year. The infant mortality rate is important for many reasons. For example, those who die in infancy cannot have children of their own and thus will not add to population growth.

Infant mortality rates are also closely related to birth rates. Throughout much of human history, most children have not survived infancy, and societies have only survived because they had very high birth rates. By way of illustration, Ralph Thomlinson (1967) dedicated his book *Demographic Problems* (Encino: Dickenson, 1975) to Wolfgang Amadeus Mozart, saying:

> One of seven children, five of whom died within six months of birth;
> Father of six children, only one of whom lived six months;
> Himself a survivor of scarlet fever, smallpox, and lesser diseases,
> Only to die at the age of thirty-five years and ten months
> From a cause not diagnosable by the medical knowledge of his time;
> Thus making his life demographically typical of most of man's history.

This historically typical pattern is still maintained in many underdeveloped countries. Table 16·3 presents some illustrative birth and infant mortality rates.

Table 16·3 Selected Birth and Infant Mortality Rates, 1973

Area	Crude birth rates	Infant mortality rates
High rates		
Niger	52.2	200.0
Rwanda	51.8	132.8
Dahomey	50.9	109.6
Low rates		
Luxembourg		
United States	15.0	17.6
Japan	19.4	11.7

Source: Demographic Yearbook, 1973 *(New York: United Nations, 1974), pp. 94–98.*

Natural Increase

While birth and death rates among the nations of the world generally correspond, the disparity between them is what causes the overall increase in world population. Most simply put, there are more births than deaths each year. From 1965 to 1973, the average annual crude birth rate for the world was 34; the corresponding death rate was 14. As a result, the world's population increased an average of 20 per 1,000, or 2 percent per year (United Nations 1974:81).

The excess of births over deaths—natural increase—is a worldwide pattern although an uneven one. Societies have survived by matching high birth rates with high death rates, but many have experienced a lag between the decrease in the death rate and the subsequent decrease in the birth rate. Latin America offers a clear illustration of this situation.

Until recent decades, most of Latin America had been characterized by the high birth and death rates that still characterize much of Africa. The vast improvement in public health and other medical conditions, however, has drastically reduced the death rate in Latin America, bringing it to about the same as that in North America in 1973. Birth rates, however, have stayed at the same high levels that were needed to offset the earlier death rates. With an annual death rate of 10 between 1965 and 1973, Latin America had a birth rate of 39. This is in contrast to 18, the number for North America (United Nations 1974:81).

Figure 16·3 presents the birth and death rates of several societies over a forty-year period. Notice the lag between decreasing death and birth rates; notice, too, how birth rates are almost always higher than death rates.

The United States and Japan illustrate the pattern in which birth and death rates generally decrease together, although the American "baby boom" of the 1950s and the war-related fluctuations in Japan vary from the general pattern. Puerto Rico illustrates the lag between decreasing death and birth rates: About ten years' time separates the start of a steady decline in the death rate and the steady decline in the birth rate. Mexico, on the other hand, illustrates the case in which the death rate declines significantly while the birth rate remains essentially unchanged. Finally, notice that even when both rates decrease, the birth rate remains higher than the death rate. That persistent disparity is why populations continue to grow even though birth rates decrease.

Demographic Transition Theory

Patterns of birth and death rates such as those we've just seen have led many demographers to distinguish them in the form of typologies. The United Nations' (1956:26–33) population division, for example, has suggested a fivefold classification as follows:

Type	Birth rate	Death rate	Examples
I	High	High	Central Africa
II	High	Declining	Northern Africa, much of Asia
III	High	Low	Latin America, Southern Africa
IV	Declining	Low	Chile, Argentina, Brazil
V	Low	Low	United States, Western Europe

Societies around the world have frequently been seen to move through these several steps in order, as they have become industrialized and urbanized. As a result, demographers have formulated the **theory of demographic transition** to refer to the process. Figure 16·4 provides a simple graphic picture of the theory. The actual processes are far more complex.

Declining death rates have a rather complicated effect on birth rates, relating to changes in life expectancies. In 1973, for example, the nation of Guinea in Africa had a life expectancy of 26 years for men and 28 years for women, as compared with 67.4 years for men and 75.2 years for women in the United States. In part these figures reflect grossly different rates of infant mortality: 201.3 per 1,000 in Guinea and 17.6

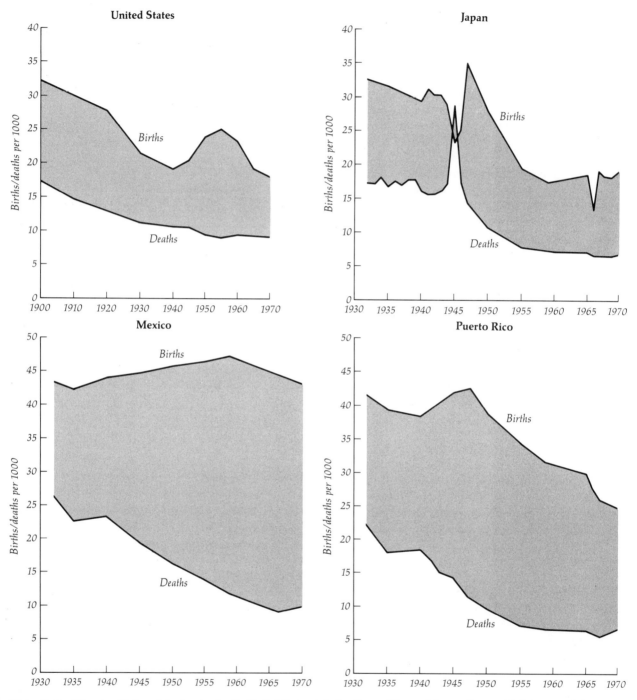

Figure 16·3   Changing birth and death rates for the United States, Mexico, Puerto Rico, and Japan. Sources: U.S. Bureau of the Census, Historical Statistics of the United States: Colonial Times to 1957, 1960, pp. 23, 27; U.S. Bureau of the Census, Statistical Abstract of the United States, 1973, p. 52; others: United Nations, Demographic Yearbook, 1948, pp. 260–65, 312–17; ibid., 1960, pp. 476–83, 498–505; ibid., 1969, pp. 256–65, 582–87; ibid., 1973, pp. 225–30, 279–85.

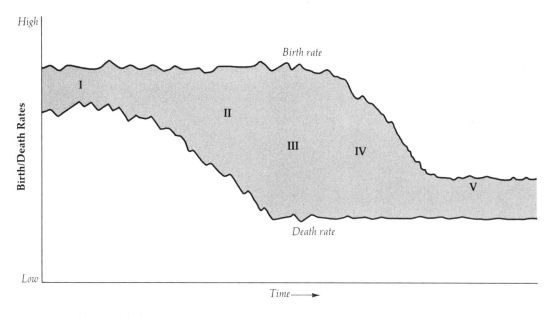

I: High birth and death rates
II: High birth rate, declining death rate
III: High birth rate, low death rate
IV: Low death rate, declining birth rate
V: Low birth and death rates

Figure 16·4   The theory of demographic transition.

in the United States. But they also reflect a difference in the average longevity of those who survive infancy (United Nations 1974:94–98).

Since women's ability to bear children extends, on the average, to their mid- to late forties, low life expectancies have a limiting effect on birth rates. As death rates go down and people—especially women—live longer, more babies will be born unless people change their patterns of reproduction.

As death rates are further reduced and life expectancies further extended, however, the effect on birth *rates* is reversed. More and more people living beyond their childbearing years does not increase the number of babies born, but it does increase the total population, thereby decreasing at least the crude birth rate. For example, if 400,000 babies are born in a society with a population of 10 million, that society will have a crude birth rate (40 per 1,000) twice as high as the society of 20 million that produces the same number of babies.

The decrease in death rates, then, eventually creates at least the appearance of declining birth rates. Because the appearance may not reflect the reality, demographers pay more attention to fertility rates. These rates give a clearer picture of future population growth in societies. Where even more sophisticated models are needed, demographers compute "age-specific fertility rates." These are fertility rates for women in different age categories.

Later in this chapter, we'll return to an examination of some other reasons why birth rates decline as societies become more urban and industrial. Before doing that, let's look at the manner in which demographers view the composition of populations.

Age-Sex Profiles

The potential for population growth can be assessed from the **age-sex composition** of a group. The potential for growth is greater if a large proportion

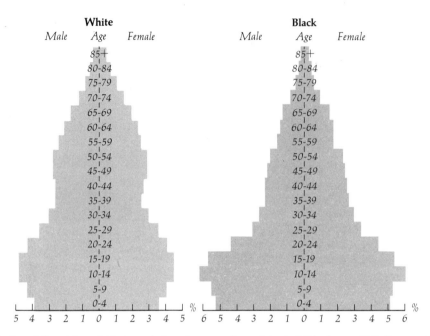

Figure 16·5   *Distribution of the white and black populations by age and sex, July 1, 1973. Source: U.S. Bureau of the Census,* Current Population Reports, *Series P-25, No. 519, April 1974, p. 4.*

of the women are in their childbearing years. Depending on the agreements governing mating, the sex ratio of the group is also important. In a monogamous society like the United States, for example, an equal balance of men and women creates an optimum condition for growth: There is a potential father for every potential mother.

The importance of age and sex distributions for population growth has led demographers to develop methods for analyzing them. Chief among these methods is the age-sex pyramid, a graphic description of the proportional composition of the population by age and sex. Two age-sex pyramids are shown in Figure 16·5.

One of the pyramids describes the white population of the United States as of July 1, 1973, the other, the black. From the standpoint of population-growth potential, the two age-sex pyramids indicate that more blacks than whites are entering the childbearing years. This means that if both black and white couples starting families in the next few years have the same number of children per couple, the crude birth rate

for blacks will be higher than for whites. "Couples having children" will make up a larger proportion of the black population than of the white population. (Whites greatly outnumber blacks overall, however, so the number of white babies born will be greater than the number of black babies.)

Age-sex pyramids, then, are important for understanding the future potential for population growth in a society or subgroups of it. Age-sex pyramids can also reflect the history of societies as we'll see shortly as we turn to the final aspect of population growth: **migration.**

Migration

We've seen that population size increases because of births, that it decreases because of deaths, and that the excess of births over deaths is called the "natural increase." The natural increase is the chief source of population growth in virtually all nations of the world, but it is not the only one. Populations in a society also grow and decline because of migration: people moving in and out.

The reasons for migration are many. Demographers often speak of "push" and "pull" factors. People can be "pushed" out of an area because of unsatisfactory conditions there. Wars, unemployment, persecution, famine, blight, and pollution are but a few of the many reasons why people may choose to pack up and leave the place where they are living. Correspondingly, people may be "pulled" to areas because of good economic opportunities, good climate, congenial political and social conditions, and a countless variety of other reasons. Very often, migration reflects both push and pull factors, as in the migration of many people from Ireland to the United States in the 1840s. Ireland was suffering a devastating potato famine, while the United States was regarded as the land of golden opportunity.

Aside from the direct and immediate consequences of migration on population growth, there may also be indirect and long-term consequences depending on the *kind* of people migrating. As a general rule, young immigrants, because of their potential for childbearing, will have greater consequences than old ones. Thus, for example, the large migration of retired people to Florida creates less long-term population growth there than the migration of young people to California.

Sex is also an important consideration in determining the impact of migration on population growth. Unless there is a reasonably even sex ratio, having a large proportion of a population in the childbearing years has little consequence for population growth. But men and women do not always migrate in equal numbers. Look at the example of Hawaii.

Late in the nineteenth century, large numbers of young Japanese and Chinese men were brought to Hawaii to work on the large agricultural plantations. This event is reflected in the first age-sex pyramid (*a*) of Figure 16•6. In 1900, nearly one-third of the total population was composed of young men between twenty and thirty-five years of age. Many of them eventually decided to remain in Hawaii beyond the period of their labor contracts, brides were imported from Asia, and by 1920, as we see, the sex ratio had nearly evened out (*b*). During the military build-

up prior to World War II, however, the number of young men in Hawaii was again out of proportion (*c*), and the continued military presence in 1970 (*d*) provides for the same peculiarity.

Population growth, in summary, is the result of an often intricate and complex interaction among births, deaths, and migration. Perhaps the only simple thing about population growth is that it's a simple fact of life around the world today, and it has been for the past 200 years. For many years nations regarded growth as good and encouraged their citizens to be fruitful and multiply. Why is population growth now regarded as bad?

The Problem of Overpopulation

People have for a long time thought that "bigger is better," and public officials have pointed to population growth with pride. Yet now many people regard population growth as the world's most pressing problem. Why? Even the threat of thermonuclear war is not always with us. Population growth, however, continues without abatement.

To set the stage for this discussion, you might want to review Figure 16•1, which shows the long-term pattern of world population growth. The rapid increase in numbers of people on this planet is a rather recent thing, really getting under way only around the time of the Industrial Revolution. That the world population will double every 35 years at its present rate of growth is a staggering thought: Today's 4 billion becomes 8 billion, which becomes 16 billion, which becomes 32 billion—an eightfold increase in just over a century.

People have been on this earth for about a million years. Yet Ansley Coale (cited in Nam 1968:63) has calculated that if we continue increasing at our present rate for another 6,500 years, people will be piling on top of each other around the entire globe, and the mass of bodies will be moving into outer space at a rate faster than the speed of light.

It seems relatively safe to assume that this forecast won't come true. The reasons why it won't, however, point to the reasons why even lower rates

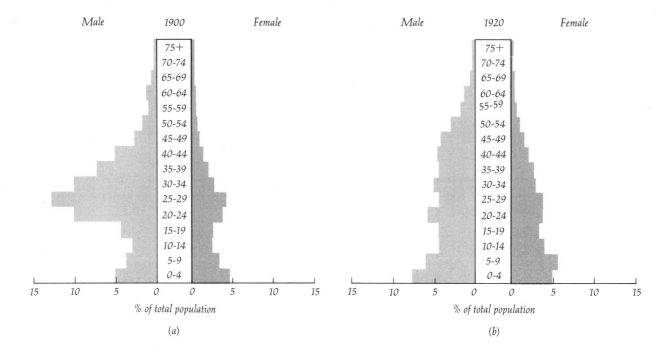

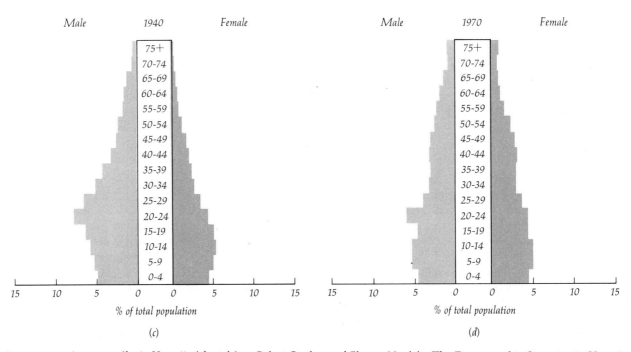

Figure 16•6   *Age-sex profiles in Hawaii. Adapted from Robert Gardner and Eleanor Nordyke,* The Demographic Situation in Hawaii *(Honolulu: East-West Population Institute, 1974), pp. 14–19.*

of population growth are a problem. Let's look at some of them.

Food

Long before people begin literally piling on top of one another across the face of the earth, many will starve to death. The relationship between population growth and food shortages is a compound one. With a fixed amount of food, of course, more mouths to feed mean less food for each. Perhaps two can live as cheaply as one (I doubt that), but one person's food cannot indefinitely sustain 2, 4, 8, 16, or 32.

Of course, the amount of food is not fixed. During your lifetime, agricultural advances have greatly increased the yield per acre of many crops, and the world's food supplies have been steadily increasing. They haven't been increasing fast enough, however.

In 1798, Thomas Robert Malthus, a British economist, published his work entitled *An Essay on the Principle of Population*. Malthus's primary thesis was that while food production increases *arithmetically*, population growth is *geometrical*. These two types of mathematical progressions are illustrated below:

Thomas Malthus 1766–1834 (Bulloz)

Arithmetic (Food)	Geometric (People)
1	1
2	2
3	4
4	8
5	16
6	32
.	.
.	.
.	.

Malthus recognized that the discrepancy between population and food could not continue growing indefinitely: Starvation would prevent unlimited population growth if nothing else did. Since Malthus believed that people were so sexually driven that they could not control their fertility, however, he concluded that there would always be great masses of people on the brink of starvation. Mass poverty would always exist.

Many of Malthus's specific points have been rejected, but population growth has continued to outstrip food production in the world as a whole. To make matters worse, population growth increasingly places limits on the amount of food that can be produced. The need for housing, for example, has resulted in the conversion of vast amounts of farmland into subdivisions in the United States. The amount of food produced has not been decreased yet, but the potential future growth in food production is continually being limited.

Present and potential food shortages are sometimes difficult for Americans to conceive of, since many of us worry more about being overweight than about getting enough food to survive. It has been estimated, however, that only half of the world's population currently gets enough of the right kinds of food to be adequately nourished. Prospects for the future are sufficiently grim to lead some analysts to urge that the United States begin giving food aid only to those nations certain to survive with such aid—cold-bloodedly denying any assistance to pop-

One of the many consequences of overpopulation is hunger. (Thomas Hopker, Woodfin Camp)

ulations that might not survive even with the aid (Paddock and Paddock 1967).

Even when mass starvation is averted, unchecked population growth will often result, as Malthus suggested, in mass poverty. You'll recall from the discussion of social stratification earlier in this book that status is largely a matter of sharing in the scarce commodities in a society. As numbers of people increase, such commodities become relatively scarcer.

Crowding

Studies of the ways animals behave in crowded conditions provide a useful backdrop for the exami-

nation of human crowding. Studies of rats, elephants, deer, monkeys, and other animals show that crowding produces a variety of problems, among them aggression, infertility, high mortality rates, and erratic behavior. Many of the animal responses to crowding, as you may have noted, have the effect of reducing population size.

Studies of the effects of human crowding are more complicated. The behavior of small groups crowded together under experimental conditions may not reflect the effects of crowding in natural social settings, such as crowded apartment buildings. On the other hand, studies of natural crowding— numbers of people per acre or people per room—are com-

plicated by difference in social class and cultural patterns. Thus, when studies show that crime rates are higher in densely populated areas of a city than in more sparsely populated areas, part of the answer may lie in the generally lower social status of the more crowded areas. (Research problems such as this are one of the reasons that sociology is so fascinating and challenging.)

Recognizing the shortcomings of research in this area, it is nonetheless worth noting that crowding has been found to be related to higher crime rates, higher incidences of mental illness, greater competition, less cooperation, and similar social problems. (For an excellent review of studies on crowding, see Fischer et al. 1974.)

War

Overpopulation has often been cited as a factor in creating international hostilities. German aggression in World War II, for example, was often justified by the need for "lebensraum"—living space. As a nation begins to outgrow its space, it may look elsewhere, across its borders.

This problem is complicated by another factor. National policies of population growth are often justified as a means to developing military potential—

for defense, of course. Small nations sometimes fear that their size makes them weak in relation to larger neighbors. So they grow, eventually running out of space, and they need to look around for "lebensraum." Notice how this parallels the nuclear arms race, as nations compete with one another for the security of military superiority, increasing the danger of war in the same process. So it is with the "population bomb" as well.

Environment

Much of Chapter 17 will deal with the impact of human beings on the natural environment. In the present context, however, I should note that population growth has two major effects on the environment: the depletion of nonreplaceable, natural resources and the creation of pollution.

From an environmental point of view, then, overpopulation is not merely a matter of numbers. It is also a matter of per capita impact on the environment. The United States, because of our high standard of living, has been called the most overpopulated country in the world, despite our *relatively* small and slowly growing population. Composing only from 5 to 6 percent of the world's population, it has been estimated that we account for about half the world's consumption each year.

These are but a few of the problems created by overpopulation. Other problems are recognized today, and more will undoubtedly become apparent. The box "Population Problems" on page 430 summarizes several distinct points of view that people have taken with regard to population growth. Let's turn now from the problems of population growth to partial solutions.

Stemming Population Growth

If the world's population is to cease growing, the global birth rate must equal the global death rate. Beginning where we are today, then, either the birth rate will have to be reduced or the death rate increased. No one seriously suggests raising the death rate to halt population growth, so we will devote this section to a discussion of lowering birth rates.

Population Problems

During the 1960s and early 1970s increased interest in population, particularly concerns with overpopulation, moved the subject from scholarly and professional discussion into the political arena. Currently, there exist at least four distinct positions on population as a problem. There is population as crisis, so grave that catastrophe is near unless steps are immediately taken to limit fertility and stop population growth. There is population as a multiplier and intensifier of other social problems, such as crime, food and energy shortages, and environmental pollution. There is population as a nonproblem (or even a false problem with imperialist overtones), the real problem being development or how to bring about socialist organization of society or how to redistribute income or how to improve the status of women or how to rectify social injustice or how to promote technological change. In this third view, any population "problem" will be taken care of automatically as a by-product of other fundamental social changes. Then there is the view that underpopulation, not overpopulation, is the problem. To gain more workers for modernization, some governments such as Saudi Arabia and Rumania are offering financial stipends to encourage marriage and child production. In short, although the nature of the population problem varies, the consequences of population growth for human life and for social structures are under close scrutiny by research workers, politicians, and the public.

Which of the four views described above comes closest to *your* view? Why?

Source: Adapted from Ronald Freedman and Bernard Berelson, "The Human Population," Scientific American, September 1974, pp. 31–51.

Zero Population Growth

The term **zero population growth** (ZPG) has become a popular one in recent years, largely be-

cause of the efforts of the American organization of that name. The ZPG concept is simple in theory, but it is more complicated in actual application to human populations.

Basically, "ZPG" refers to the condition in which a population merely reproduces its number generation after generation. This can happen if each person in the world produces one and only one person to replace himself or herself. Given the dyadic way we reproduce, this equation is often stated in terms of each couple's producing two and only two children. To put this notion in perspective, Figure 16·7 shows the population sizes resulting from patterns in which couples produce 2, 3, and 4 children each.

As indicated in Figure 16·7, the pattern in which each couple produces only two children leads to population stabilization over the course of the generations. Each person in one generation is replaced by one person in the next. The patterns in which each couple produces more than enough children for simple replacement, of course, result in population growth over the generations. Most dramatic is the case of four children per couple, since this results in a doubling of the population each generation.

The enormous implications of geometrical progressions such as these are sometimes difficult to understand. Consider the pattern of four children per couple for a moment. In this pattern each person in a given generation is replaced by two in the next. Beginning with a single couple, this pattern could produce a population equal to half the current world total in only thirty generations. Now, how many more generations would it take to equal our current population of 4 billion people? Only one more. It would happen in the very next generation—the thirty-first.

The patterns illustrated in Figure 16·7 are somewhat simplified. In practice, it doesn't really matter how many children a couple produce, but how many of their children go on to produce children, who then produce children, and so forth. Many primitive societies in the past have been able to produce a dozen or so children per couple without increasing their population size significantly from one generation to another. This is because few of their children lived to produce more children. High rates of infant mortality kept population growth at a low level. Reducing infant mortality rates and increasing life expectancies be-

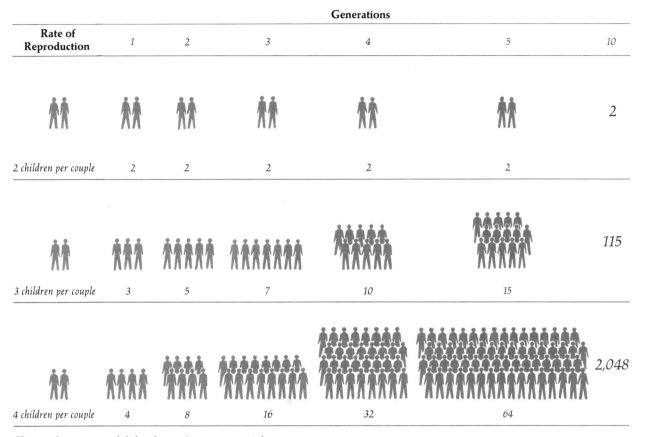

	Generations					
Rate of Reproduction	*1*	*2*	*3*	*4*	*5*	*10*
2 children per couple	2	2	2	2	2	*2*
3 children per couple	3	5	7	10	15	*115*
4 children per couple	4	8	16	32	64	*2,048*

*Figures shown are rounded, though exact figures were carried
forward in computing subsequent generations.

*Figure 16•7   Populations resulting from different reproductive patterns. (The figures shown are rounded, although exact figures were carried
forward in computing subsequent generations.)*

yond average childbearing ages, however, have freed
these societies from that check-and-balance system.

Some children still die in infancy in every society
and some adults never bear or father children. Because of these facts, it is estimated that a society like
the United States could stabilize its population over
the generations if each couple produced an average
of approximately 2.11 children. Interestingly, the
United States has actually reduced its reproduction
below this level. Given the proportion of the United
States population in or approaching their childbearing
years, however, it will take us about fifty years at
current birth rates to reach a point where our total
population stops growing. Moreover, the United

States is hardly typical. Recall that *worldwide* birth and
death rates at the present time are such that global
population will double every thirty-five or so years.
This is not very different from the most extreme
pattern shown in Figure 16•7. And since the less-
developed countries of the world have larger proportions of their populations in the childbearing years,
it would take them even longer than the United States
to reach a point of population stability.

Childbearing Agreements

Sociologists are particularly interested in the
levels and changes in birth rates because these re-

flect social agreements. Whereas death rates are largely—though not exclusively—a function of medical knowledge and practices, birth rates depend more directly on social norms.

People have three general kinds of agreements regarding childbearing:

1. An agreement to bear whatever number of children result from sexual behavior

2. An agreement that *more* children is better

3. An agreement that *fewer* children is better

The first of these agreements undoubtedly characterized most of human history. People engaged in sexual relations without even realizing that it was related to reproduction, and they took what they got. The race survived because the numbers of children produced in that fashion more or less matched the relatively high death rates.

The second kind of agreement—that having lots of children is good—has appeared many times in human history. Early American settlers needed many children to assist them in settling the wilderness. Small, weak nations as well as small minority groups within a given nation have sometimes seen population growth as a means to political power. And numerous religious groups have taught that bearing many children glorified their god, adding ever larger

Demographic Variables and Household Structure

Typically a family comes into being when a couple is married. From its formation to its dissolution, a family passes through a series of distinct stages called the family life cycle. At first the family gains in size with the birth of each child. From the time when the last child is born until the last child leaves home, the family size remains relatively stable. Then, as children leave home for marriage or employment, the size of the family shrinks back to the original two persons. Finally one and then the other of the parents dies, and the family life cycle ends.

Demographic variables, such as birth and death rates, have implications for this family life cycle, family size, and for the structure of kinship and household groups. In the table, representative ages of the husband and wife in the life cycle of the family in rural India are compared with corresponding information from the United States.

In the United States, low death rates, a long life expectancy, effective medical and health care, and widespread use of birth control methods assure a married couple of long life together. These conditions enable couples to take on long-term responsibilities for starting a nuclear family in a household apart from their parents, rearing children, and setting aside provisions for old age. In Banaras, India, the age at marriage is extremely low and birth and death rates are high. Under these conditions the existence of the nuclear family is precarious. Only the extended family has a good prospect for continuity. When two or more couples pool their resources and their labor they are able to supply minimum needs better than they could living as separate nuclear groups. When one adult dies, others remain to care for orphaned children.

Another purpose of childbearing in a society where kinship is a primary basis of social organization is to assure sons to carry on the family line. Thus, it is easy to discover a justification for high fertility in rural India. Despite the high reproductive rates, twenty-two percent of Banaras parents are often deprived of sons, a dreadful liability according to Hindu doctrine. Aging parents deprived of sons may still be assisted by grandchildren and nephews living with them in the extended group. The degree of independence enjoyed by the nuclear family in America would be out of the question in rural India.

Source: Adapted from Andrew Collver, "The Family Cycle in India and the United States," American Sociological Review 28(1963): 86–96.

generations of believers. The box "Demographic Variables and Household Structure" places this second kind of agreement in a statistical context.

The third agreement—fewer children is better—has been increasing in popularity in the United States and in other developed countries. The source of popularity is at two levels. First, increasing numbers of people are recognizing the dangers of overpopulation both in societies and around the globe. Second, people have come to recognize that small families have economic and other advantages at the individual family level. It has been estimated, for example, that raising a child from birth through independence now costs the average American about $40,000. And

increasingly, young couples are coming to recognize and reject the loss of freedom that children impose upon parents.

Average family sizes in America have been getting smaller for some time (U.S. Bureau of the Census 1975a:39). Attitudinal surveys have shown a fairly steady decrease in the number of children *desired* by American couples as well. A 1971 survey conducted in connection with the U.S. Commission on Population Growth and the American Future, for example, indicated that the average "ideal family size" included 2.33 children (Ehrlich and Ehrlich 1972).

People's *desires* regarding family size are important, of course, because, unlike the situation for most

Median Ages of Husbands and Wives at Each Stage of the Family Cycle, in the U.S.A. (Based on Census Data) and a Sample of Hindu Villagers, Banaras, India

Stage of family cycle	Median age of husband				Median age of wife			
	Banaras 1956	U.S.A. 1890	1950	1970	Banaras 1956	U.S.A. 1890	1950	1970
Marriage								
Shadi (Indian marriage ceremony: After Shadi a couple continues to live with their own parents)	13.6	......	......	......	10.9	......	......	......
Guana (start of conjugal cohabitation)	17.3	26.1	22.8	23.6	14.6	22.0	20.1	21.7
Birth of first child	20.9	27.1	24.5		18.2	23.0	21.8	
Birth of last child	39.7	36.0	28.8		37.0	31.9	26.1	
Marriage of first child	36.9	51.1	46.0		34.2	47.0	43.3	
Marriage of last child	55.7	59.4	50.3		53.0	55.3	47.6	
Age at own death	54.5	66.4	71.6		54.5	67.7	77.2	
		Industrializing				Industrializing		

Source: From O. A. Collver, "The Family Cycle in India and the United States," American Sociological Review 28 (1963):86–96. The 1970 figures are from Vital Statistics Reports.

of the time our species has been around, we now have a choice in the matter. Even after our ancestors became conscious of the link between reproduction and intercourse, there wasn't much they could do to separate the two, and of course there wasn't much pressure in that direction until recently. Having a choice, however, doesn't necessarily mean that people exercise it.

Birth Control

Contemporary methods of birth control are many and varied: birth control pills, condoms, diaphragms, intrauterine devices, foams, jellies, and sterilization. Some people attempt to control conception through practices including celibacy, withdrawal prior to ejaculation, the "rhythm method" (limiting intercourse to infertile periods of a woman's menstrual cycle), astrology, breast feeding, and a variety of douches.

The study of birth control often involves "knowledge, attitudes, and practices" studies. Demographers and others have been interested in learning what people know about birth control methods, how they feel about those methods, and what methods if any they actually practice.

Knowledge of birth control methods is largely a function of educational level—both within societies and across them. David Heer (1966) has concluded that the general relationship between economic development and reduced birth rates probably reflects "an increased flow of communications concerning birth control." Many nations of the world have not experienced the economic development Heer spoke of.

Paul Ehrlich and Anne Ehrlich (1972:311) describe the general situation in the world's underdeveloped countries:*

In most UDCs [underdeveloped countries], few people know anything about birth control (often, only about 10–20 percent of the adult population), and

*From *Population, Resources, Environment: Issues in Human Ecology*, 2nd ed., by Paul R. Ehrlich and Anne H. Ehrlich, copyright 1972 by W. H. Freeman and Company. Reprinted by permission.

knowledge is mainly restricted to withdrawal. Only a fraction of those who know about birth control practice it. But among people interviewed in surveys, including those previously ignorant of birth control, interest is high, especially in couples with three or more children.

The birth control movement in the United States and around the world has throughout its history often been involved in controversy. Special resistance has come from Roman Catholics (although not limited to Catholics), reflecting the anticontraception teachings of the church. Not surprisingly, different people have quite different feelings about birth control, both for themselves and for others. Overall, however, support for birth control has been growing steadily in the United States.

The *practice* of birth control has also increased greatly in the United States in recent years. In 1970, over half the couples in America were using some form of effective birth control (Westoff 1972). Increasing numbers of American Catholics, moreover, are breaking with church doctrine in this regard.

The increased acceptance and practice of birth control in America has many sources. The women's movement, for example, has gotten agreement for the position that women have functions other than the bearing of and caring for children. Increased availability of occupational careers for women has had a similar, related effect. This latter factor has become increasingly important as young couples have sought to achieve and maintain reasonably high standards of living during times of economic inflation. The birth of a new child both adds family costs and takes away the wife/mother's income.

Contraception is only one form of birth control. Norms that delay marriage and cohabitation until later in life also have the effect of reducing birth rates. Abortion is another alternative to contraception and a hotly controversial one.

The traditional American image of the "abortionist" plying an evil trade in the back rooms of sleazy hotels and boardinghouses is giving way to the reality of legal, clinical abortions in hospitals and doctors' offices. Table 16·4 presents data on the numbers of legal abortions performed in various countries in recent years.

Table 16·4 Legal Abortions in Selected Countries

Country	Year	Legal abortions
Japan	1971	739,674
United States	1971	480,259
Yugoslavia	1968	245,783
Poland	1972	204,562
Hungary	1972	179,035
United Kingdom	1972	167,493
Bulgaria	1972	154,415
Czechoslovakia	1972	93,697
Canada	1972	38,905
Sweden	1972	24,170
Tunisia	1971	12,974
Norway	1972	12,203
Denmark	1971	11,522

Source: Demographic Yearbook 1973 *(New York: United Nations, 1974), p. 248.*

People are attempting in some localities and in several different ways to take control of their own reproductive capacity. I would not want to create the impression that individual practice of birth control around the world reflects a general concern for overpopulation, however. After all, *one* baby more or less does not make or break a population explosion, and while some people report that overpopulation figured in their decision to limit their families, most birth control activities reflect individual, personal objectives. Leon and Steinhoff (1975), for example, report that the most common reason for seeking an abortion under Hawaii's liberalized abortion law was that the prospective mother was unmarried. Following that, the most common reasons given were (1) financial, (2) interference with woman's education, (3) inability to "cope with a child at this time," (4) having enough children already, and (5) the prospective mother's feeling that she was too young.

Let's move on now to a topic that is intimately connected with population. We've already seen that population growth primarily reflects dramatic reductions in death rates around the world and other advances in human health. The concepts of health, illness, and death, however, are complex. Let's see how sociological points of view can reveal and clarify that complexity.

Health, Illness, and Death

Any comprehensive examination of population dynamics should consider the topics of health, illness, and death. As suggested earlier, the radical acceleration of population growth in recent centuries is largely a product of reduced death rates. Vaccinations, sanitation, and improved medical treatments have all had a part in reducing infant mortality and in extending the life expectancies of those who survive infancy.

Beyond demographic considerations, sociologists are also interested in health, illness, and death because they—like all aspects of social life—are a matter of agreement, and people have created a wide variety of agreements concerning them. In this section, we'll take a special look at different definitions of health and illness, the different social organizations created in relation to them, and also the matter of death.

Defining Health and Illness

You might imagine that health and illness are fairly clear and unambiguous concepts, more in the realm of medicine than sociology. Not so. We have already talked about the social definition of mental illness earlier in the book. Physical illness is also a matter of social agreement.

John Clausen (1963:139–40) has stated the case clearly:

> Health and disease are often conceived exclusively as states of the organism, but they represent social definitions as well. What one does in the presence of a given symptom or discomfort depends on whether one regards the symptom as an inevitable consequence of being alive or as a condition remediable by a professional healer or by a regime of care. This is true both at the societal level and at the family or individual level.

The social definition of illness that Clausen spoke of is susceptible to subcultural variations within a given society. The accompanying box, "Differential Pain Experience," describes Mark Zborowski's research on that topic.

Sick Role

From a sociological point of view, being ill is the basis for a special social status. Talcott Parsons (1951), among other sociologists, has looked at some of the roles associated with being sick both in America and other modern societies. To begin, being labeled as sick exempts you from other responsibilities that you would normally be expected to carry. You're not expected to take exams when you have a 103° F. fever, for example. At the same time, sickness is

regarded as a form of deviance that disrupts social relations. (Don't tell your instructor you're glad you got the flu.) It is *not* typically blamed on the deviant, however; sick people are usually not blamed for being sick. (Remind your instructor that there's a lot of flu going around.) Finally, the sick person *is* expected to seek recovery, especially through cooperating with medical professionals. (Take two aspirins every four hours, drink lots of liquids, and rest.) Failure to seek recovery (or to *appear* to seek recovery) cancels out the agreement about not blaming sick people for being sick.

The theoretical concept of "sick role" has been the source of considerable research in medical sociology. Some sociologists (for example, Mechanic and

Differential Pain Experience

The physiology of pain does not explain the *pain experience*. It does not explain, for example, the acceptance of intense pain during torture nor does it explain the strong emotional reactions of certain individuals to the sting of a hypodermic needle.

Mark Zborowski deals in his research with the cultural components of pain. He attempts to understand the significance and role of social and cultural patterns in the pain experience. Zborowski selected three ethnocultural groups for intensive study. These groups included patients of Jewish, Italian, and "old American" stock at the Kingsbridge Veterans Hospital, Bronx, New York. Jews and Italians were selected for study because medical people described these groups as tending to "exaggerate" their pain. "Old Americans" were chosen because the values and attitudes of this group dominate in this country, are the same values and attitudes that currently dominate in the medical profession, and are the attitudes immigrants to America tend to adopt. Members of the "old-American" group were defined as white, native-born individuals, usually Protestant, whose grandparents, at least, were born in the United States and who did not identify themselves with any foreign group, either nationally, socially, or culturally.

The study was qualitative in character. The main techniques used in data collection were open-ended interviews with patients of the selected groups, observations of their behavior when in pain, and discussion of the individual cases with doctors, nurses, and other people directly and indirectly involved in the pain experience. In addition, "healthy" members of each group were interviewed on their attitudes toward pain. The researchers, in certain cases, interviewed a member of the patient's immediate family in order to check the report of the patient on his pain experience and in order to find out family attitudes toward the patient's experience. The interviews, which lasted approximately two hours, were recorded and transcribed verbatim for analysis.

What Zborowski found were patterned differences by cultural group in attitude and response to pain. For example, although Jews and Italians reacted similarly to pain, their attitudes toward pain were clearly different. Italian patients concerned themselves with the immediacy of the pain experience and the actual pain sensation they experienced. The Italian patient expressed in his behavior and complaints the discomforts caused by the pain and the effects of pain on his immediate situation in terms

Volkart 1961, Suchman 1965) have sought to explain why some people assume the sick role more readily and more frequently than others. Others (Brown and Rawlinson 1975) have focused their attention on the factors related to giving up the sick role after surgery. Still others (for example, Reynolds et al. 1974) have sought to formalize the concept as a "social indicator," a measure of the relative health and illness of societies.

Social Organization of Health Care

Every society has special statuses for healers, though they may be combined with other statuses. In many primitive societies, for example, religious and healing functions are linked. This makes a great deal of sense, of course, in a point of view in which illness has a supernatural component. Among the Navaho Indians, steeped in witchcraft, the same people are believed both to cure and to cause disease. (This belief has the latent function of facilitating "one-stop shopping.")

Contemporary, developed countries have done more than differentiate the healing function from others. Indeed, specialization *within* the healing function is one of its more striking characteristics. The country doctor of America's romantically recalled past is virtually gone. This development has brought with it both good and bad.

On one side, medical specialization has meant

of occupation, economic situation, and so forth. The Jewish patients primarily focused on the symptomatic meaning of pain and on the significance of pain to general health, welfare, and eventually the health and welfare of their families.

Attitudes of Italian and Jewish patients toward pain-relieving drugs mirrored these different attitudes toward pain. When in pain Italians called for pain relief and concerned themselves mainly with the analgesic effects of the administered drugs. Once pain was relieved Italian patients forgot their suffering and manifested a happy, even joyful, disposition. The Jewish patient, however, often only reluctantly accepted drugs. Jewish patients felt drugs only temporarily relieved pain and did not cure the underlying cause of pain. Nurses and doctors reported Jewish patients hiding pills, preferring to suffer rather than relieve the pain. These reports were confirmed in patient interviews.

"Old Americans" displayed another attitude toward pain and pain-relieving drugs. These patients rarely complained or reported their pain and were stoic and unemotional in their response to pain. "Old Americans" like Jewish patients were concerned with the origin of pain but the "old Americans" were more optimistic about treatment processes than were Jewish patients. An important element in their optimistic outlook was a faith in the progress of science. The security and confidence of "old Americans" increased in direct proportion to the number of tests, X rays, injections, and the like that they received. In short, the "old American" was disturbed by the symptomatic and incapacitating aspects of pain but expressed confidence and optimism rather than skepticism with the treatment processes.

This research and its findings contribute to an understanding of differential pain experiences. These differences may play an important part in the evaluation of organizational settings which deal with pain, in administration of analgesics, and in related attitudes toward health, disease, medication, hospitalization, and medicine in general. Moreover, there may be differences in pain experiences by age, sex, and social position of individuals within particular cultural groups. These differences are yet to be explored in sociological research.

Source: Adapted from Mark Zborowski, "Cultural Components in Responses to Pain," Journal of Social Issues 8(1953):16–31.

greater effectiveness in treatment. By devoting an entire career to the understanding of a particular disease, part of the body, or medical technique, a specialist can know more about what lies within his specialty than someone attempting to deal with many diseases and techniques and with the whole body.

On the other side, medical specialization has been a source of concern and unhappiness. The traditional family physician is remembered for his breadth of concern for the whole patient. In contrast specialists sometimes are charged with narrowly probing into their special area while forgetting other aspects of the whole person.

The narrowness of specialized points of view has been seen to have two different kinds of dysfunctions: one technical and one more generally human. It has been feared that specialists will seek specialized success only: taking pride in repairing the ruptured aorta even though the patient dies. There is also considerable concern that as medicine has become scientifically specialized, physicians have become more impersonal and detached in caring for patients. Both physicians and patients have complained about "assembly-line" medicine in which sick people are processed like television sets or automobiles in need of repair.

Medical care may or may not be getting more impersonal and dehumanized. And the question does not seem to be directly linked to scientific orientations of physicians. In a national survey of medical school faculty members in departments of medicine and pediatrics (Babbie 1970), I found—as expected—that physicians varied in styles of patient care. Some seemed to exhibit more compassion toward patients than others. Some maintained a direct responsibility for patients assigned to them, while others were more inclined to turn over responsibility to their assistants. Yet none of these differences appeared to reflect different degrees of "scientific" orientations. The "scientists" were no more or less compassionate or responsible than the "nonscientists."

Even the image of the "mad scientist" in medicine appears unfounded. When I asked respondents whether they felt that medical experimenters themselves should participate in experiments that might be dangerous to subjects, the scientists were as likely

as the nonscientists to feel morally obliged to take the same risks they would ask of others.

Scientifically inclined specialists may be no less compassionate than general practitioners, but the danger that specialists will overlook matters that lie outside their specialties remains. One solution to this problem has been sought in "comprehensive-care" programs aimed at training medical students to see the whole patient (see Merton et al. 1957). Another solution is medical "teamwork." Typically, the team is headed by a general "attending physician" who requests and coordinates the work of specialists. While retaining responsibility for the overall well-being of the patient as a whole person, the attending physician takes advantage of the greater depth of knowledge and insight that specialists have within their particular specialties. The main dysfunction of this approach appears to be its astronomical cost.

Sociologists have also looked to medical education and medical school students' experiences for insights into the more philosophical issue of "idealism." Lying behind the matters of compassion and responsibility is the traditional view of the physician as an altruistic healer. Becker et al. (1961), in intensive participant-observations among medical school students, suggested that medical education dampened altruism. In the students' view, they came to medical school motivated to help others and left, four years later, more intent on being personally and professionally successful. In the course of their training, for example, they tended to give up plans to become general practitioners who would care for the multifaceted needs of whole patients and to move in the direction of lucrative and less demanding specialties.

The view of physicians as altruistic, while traditional in America and elsewhere, is a complex matter. The codes of ethics of the American Medical Association, for example, devote considerably more attention to the obligations of physicians to one another than to their obligations to patients (Babbie 1970). Nowhere has the issue of altruism been more hotly debated, however, than in the question of who deserves to receive medical care and under what conditions.

Health as Right or Privilege

Modern medicine has faced the persistent philosophical question of whether physical health is a right deserved by all people or a privilege to be bought and sold in the economic marketplace like other scarce goods and services. Agreements in this area have varied from place to place and time to time.

Throughout much of American history, medicine has operated on a "fee-for-service" basis. Physicians have offered the benefits of their training and experience in return for payments from those receiving the benefits. There have always been exceptions, however, and American physicians have traditionally offered free care to other physicians and their families and to the clergy. On a more discretionary basis, they have given free care to the poor, although American codes of medical ethics have warned doctors against taking potential fees out of the marketplace in this fashion.

Early American medicine, as elsewhere, sometimes was funded on a "capitation" basis. Members of a community would agree to contribute a certain amount apiece to pay for having a physician serve their community. Modern health insurance programs, both private and governmental, are an extension of this kind of system.

Government health programs have clearly reflected the point of view that good health is a *right* rather than a privilege. Socialized medicine—in England and in socialist countries around the world—is

the fullest implementation of this agreement. Health care is based on medical need rather than on the ability to pay for it.

By and large, American physicians have opposed any program approaching socialized medicine. Their opposition has been most clearly seen, perhaps, in the American Medical Association's opposition to Medicare. Many physicians have also opposed private, prepayment health programs such as those established by the late Henry Kaiser.

Agreements on health care as a right or as a privilege reflect more general points of view concerning individual responsibility. Those who emphasize the concept of "free will" and regard each person as the master of his or her destiny tend to consider medical care a privilege to be earned. This point of view also produces opposition to welfare programs and regards deviance as something to be punished. The more "deterministic" point of view suggests that individuals are largely a product of their environments: that poor people are the victims of the economic system, that juveniles become delinquent because of social conditions, and that people should not be held personally responsible for either getting sick or being unable to pay for medical care. These conflicting points of view underlie countless disagreements in society, especially concerning matters of "social legislation" (see Babbie 1970).

Aging and Death

Advances in medicine, coupled with declining birth rates, have the effect of increasing the average age of the members of a population. Improvements in medical technology give people longer life expectancies. The declining birth rate, resulting in fewer young children, has the effect of making older people a larger *proportion* of the population. Both these processes have been at work in the United States in recent years. The implications of these processes are many and have interested sociologists, other scholars, and policymakers alike.

The aging of a population has a number of societal consequences. Demographers speak of a "dependency ratio," for example, a ratio representing the proportion of the population too young or too old to contribute to the economy. As a somewhat arbitrary rule of thumb, demographers in the United States often calculate the dependency ratio as the percentage of the population who are either under age fifteen or over age sixty-five. To the extent that persons over sixty-five are unable to contribute to the economy, a growth in the percentage in that age category places an increasing burden on those who are in the labor force.

In large part, however, sociologists have given more attention in recent years to the problems faced by the older people themselves. These problems are of two broad types. One has to do with the biological consequences of having aged a certain number of years. Most notably, this state is characterized by failing health and all the implications that holds for mobility, activities, and general satisfaction in life.

The problem of the biological state of old age, however, often seems pale in the face of the other type of problem: that created by social agreements regarding old people. People differ greatly in degree of physical deterioration and diminished mental capacity during old age, but our general agreements about old people don't acknowledge those differences. By and large, people are expected—required in many cases—to stop working at age sixty-five, regardless of their abilities to continue making meaningful contributions through their work.

For most people, forced retirement brings a severe financial hardship. Families headed by someone over sixty-five in 1969 had average incomes of less than half those of families headed by someone between age sixteen and age sixty-four (Atchley et al. 1972). The great majority of retired people live just this side of abject poverty, and many are not that lucky. Most live on government and private pensions that typically do not keep pace with rising costs of living.

The financial side of retirement is only a part of the picture. Forced retirement from a lifetime occupation represents a social agreement that the retiring person has outlived his or her usefulness, that he or she is "over the hill." For many, the psychological blow is devastating. If financial problems make them dependent on their children or others, the sense of worthlessness is likely to be increased.

In societies with extended family systems, old

Many societies revere their elderly people, but the United States is more youth-oriented. Many older Americans feel they have no purpose, no human worth. (Elizabeth Crews)

people live out their later years with the children they raised. Old age is usually revered in such societies, and the old are treated with respect and deference. In the United States, with its nuclear-family pattern and its emphasis on youthfulness, older people present a problem for young and old alike. One solution has been the nursing home for the elderly. While some such facilities provide medical care and supervision for those who need it and meaningful activities for those who desire them, others appear little better than prisons (Townsend 1971). Even under the best conditions, nursing homes can be seen as a way of getting old people out of the way, convenient places for them to await their deaths.

Social agreements surround, modify, and define growing old and dying in all societies. The box "Cause of Death" illustrates the complexities of determining the cause of death and suggests the part agreements might play in the process.

Although there are different points of view on what happens after death, in the West we have typically seen death as an abrupt and irreversible event. Many Eastern religions see death quite differently. For Buddhists and Hindus, life is a continuing, inextinguishable unity that repeatedly manifests itself in the form of finite life forms on earth. Within the Shinto point of view, dying merely represents a joining together with ancestors in a different form of participation in earthly existence.

Death has been so wrapped in grief, tragedy, and embarrassment in the West that it has long been a taboo topic for sociologists, and that taboo is only beginning to be removed. In a moving report on her interviews with dying hospital patients, Elisabeth Ross (1970) discusses the typical norms for dealing with the dying and the cruelty those norms impose.

> Unfortunately, we feel a need to cheer our patients up. We more often than not enter such a room and say, "Come on, now, it's not so bad." We discourage them from grieving and do not appreciate that it takes courage and strength to acknowledge that life comes to an end. Patients who are discouraged from expressing their anger and their sadness feel much more alone in their grief (p. 167).

> If we are uncomfortable in the face of a young dying patient we may block out these communications and the patient may never be able to communicate what he wants to share with another human being. We deprive him and ourselves of an important experience (p. 169).

We tend to shield ourselves from the fact of death. Dying people are often placed in institutions, away from family and friends. Dead bodies are covered by sheets.

Sociologists have increasingly studied death, however. Some, like Ross, have interviewed the dying and talked about death. Others have studied attitudes toward death in the general population. Both sociologists and anthropologists have studied the rituals that different societies surround death with.

Cause of Death

Gathering and interpreting statistics on mortality is not easy. Physicians are responsible for assigning "cause of death," or "the disease or condition directly leading to death." It is listed on the death certificate. Heart failure can be a cause of death, for example.

Death, however, is typically the effect of a number of factors, some of them nonbiological. As an illustration, suppose that a number of persons are in an accident and sustain identical injuries. After treatment, two-thirds of the persons recover. This fact alone would lead to some hesitation in assigning the "accident" as cause of death. Of those that die in the accident, one was an elderly man whose lesions healed too slowly; one was a woman who had a chronically weak heart; one, a black, was denied admission to the nearest hospital; and one, a member of the Christian Science church, refused medical treatment on religious grounds. Yet the death certificates of all these persons would list the accident as "the" cause of death. Other biological and nonbiological circumstances might be included as contributory factors, but many would not be mentioned. Even if the physician were to list religion or race as the cause of death, the coroner could refuse to accept the certificate by declaring that "race is not a disease," just as air pollution and religion are not diseases and are not listed on the death certificate.

Summary

Demography is the scientific study of population and is often considered a subfield of sociology. Demographers examine population size, composition, change, and the factors involved in each of those.

The current population of the world is approximately 4 billion people and growing more than 2 percent a year. At the current growth rate, the world's population will double about every thirty-five years.

If you live another seventy years and population growth continues at the same rate as now, there will be four times as many people around you as now.

Rapid population growth is relatively recent. It got its first significant boost with the invention of agriculture and exploded following the Industrial Revolution and the important advances made in the fight against disease.

The first United States census, conducted in 1790, offers a good illustration of the current methods employed in learning how many people live in a society as well as the characteristics of those people.

Essentially, three factors determine changes in the size of a society's population: births, deaths, and migration.

Birth and death rates differ greatly among the various societies in the world today, and these patterns change over time in a given society. The demographic transition theory suggests that many societies move through stages as they industrialize.

Overpopulation in the world is a problem that must be solved or it will solve itself. Most simply put, world population would stop increasing if every person alive today were replaced by only one person in the next generation: if birth and death rates were equal. As a rough rule of thumb, this would occur if every couple were to limit themselves to no more than two children. Given the current age structure of the world's population, even this practice would produce population growth for the next half century or so, but the population would then stabilize. The situation in which population does not grow from one year to the next is called zero population growth.

High birth rates and resistance to birth control are largely functions of implicit or explicit agreements regarding childbearing. Those societies that have an implicit agreement to take what they get will experience rapid population growth when death rates decline. Those sharing agreements in favor of large families will show the same pattern.

Health and illness, like everything else in society, are importantly a function of agreements. Illness occurs in all societies, and it makes sense to speak of the "sick role": the behaviors expected of sick people.

Many sociologists have studied the organization of health care. They have looked at the history of agreements defining the conditions under which

medical expertise is made available to those requiring it. We noted that there are still disagreements regarding the provision of health care: people disagree about whether health is a right or a privilege.

Finally, we have looked at aging and death as sociological topics. There are biological problems to be faced in old age, but social agreements regarding old people intensify those problems and create others in the process. Death has long been a taboo topic for sociologists, but a number of researchers have begun addressing it in recent years.

Suggested Readings

Becker, Howard et al.

1961 *Boys in White.* Chicago: University of Chicago Press.

What's it like to become a physician? That's the question asked by Becker and his colleagues at the outset of this classic study in medical sociology. To find the answer, a team of participant-observers moved in with a group of entering medical students and observed them over the course of their medical training. A key finding was that medical training tends to decrease the sense of idealism that students bring to medical school.

Ehrlich, Paul

1971 *The Population Bomb.* New York: Ballantine. Nearly two centuries after Malthus, overpopulation was an idea whose time had come when biologist Paul Ehrlich published this controversial little book. Ehrlich's purpose was to draw people's attention to the dismal implications of demographic research: That radically increasing population in the United States and around the world was pushing humanity to the brink of global disaster.

Hardin, Garrett, Ed.

1969 *Population, Evolution, and Birth Control.* San Francisco: Freeman.

As the subtitle suggests, this is a "collage of controversial ideas," as the noted biologist, Garrett Hardin, brings together the wide range of points of view regarding population and overpopulation. The 123 short selections include scientific, religious, and other views, both historical and contemporary. Of special note is Hardin's famous "tragedy of the commons."

Suchman, Edward
1965 "Stages of Illness and Medical Behavior." *Journal of Health and Social Behavior* 15:271–88.

When you're sick, you're sick. Right? Nope. As mentioned in the chapter, "being sick" is a very complex matter involving several sociological variables. Suchman examines the critical factors involved in recognizing illness, assuming the sick role, and seeking medical care.

Episode Sixteen

Amid the thunder of national dissent, the third conference on human mutations opened November 15, 2027. Gabriel Knapp, Ann Sullivan, and Daniel Adamson made up the Adamsville delegation.

Gabe Knapp, milk-white heretic, had emerged as a leader among his people.

Seconds after Larry Jones was murdered, Gabriel had sped toward Elderhome. "Get the Elders," he had demanded, pushing past Mr. Alexander and into the front parlor. "Larry Jones has been shot!"

Within seconds Ruth and Michael appeared.

"You'll have to come to the park," Gabriel had urged when he realized their shock and confusion. "You must quiet the radicals; we could have civil war by this afternoon!"

But both Ruth and Michael proved unequal to the challenge, and it was Gabe who succeeded in delivering his people from the crisis.

"This felled leader," Gabe had called from beside Jones's assassinated body, "will have a hero's burial . . ."

Steadily the crowd had grown quiet. While Jones's followers were both stunned and angered, no leader appeared from within their ranks. The radical cause, it seemed, would be severely weakened with Larry Jones's death.

On Tuesday, November 4, Gabriel requested a conference with Ruth and Michael.

"I think it would best serve Adamsville now," Gabriel proposed, "if you were to send to the conference two dull greens from the valley and one we consider a pure green, not yet physically matured."

The Elders hesitated. Then Ruth said, "Gabriel,

would it be too dangerous for you to go?"

"Washington has pledged our delegates protection equal to what they give their president when he's away from the White House," Michael reminded her.

"I am planning to go," Gabriel said firmly. "I will take Ann Sullivan and Daniel."

"Ann Sullivan is sick and not up to this," Ruth said. "She is genetically impoverished."

"Ann is weak from malnutrition," Gabe replied, his jaw set. "Some of Adamsville's ways have not been good for her. She will go with me."

Ironically Larry Jones's untimely death had accomplished his own driving purpose: The Elders had, during the crisis that followed, relinquished— although inadvertently—their authority.

Now, eleven days later, Louise Roanoke, Constance Batterson, and Bradley Duncan took their places among fellow conference members in the hotel auditorium. Tension, like summer humidity, hung in the room. Outside, secret service personnel guarded entrances. Beyond them milled groups of demonstrators. Occasionally the strained order erupted into violence as protesters confronted one another.

The conference would open in just a few minutes. "Monica didn't come then?" Constance asked Louise in an attempt to lighten the atmosphere. Louise shook her head, obviously relieved that her niece had chosen to remain in the relative safety of Chicago.

While Monica had entertained the notion of joining other CLA members in demonstrations at the conference, she had ultimately decided against it. Her presence, she reasoned, might serve to remind attending scientists of Gabriel's trial—and consequently of greens' political-religious conviction that kidnapping is sometimes honorable.

For the third time attending scientists watched and listened as the conference opened. "We have the unprecedented presence of three green delegates with us," the United States secretary of the interior was saying.

Upon introduction the delegation from Adamsville stood, turned to face the apprehensive audience. Daniel stared, stone-faced. Gabriel searched eyes, looking for faint glimmers of empathy. Ann smiled, aware that not even Gabriel knew to what extent his being in Omaha was a result of her own impulsive and angry action.

"*Are* they human, Brad?" Louise whispered to Duncan, seated next to her. "In your objective, detached, scientific judgment?"

"There is no such thing," Duncan chuckled under his breath.

Constance Batterson had overheard the exchange.

"Go to hell," she sneered good-naturedly to Brad.

"Mr. Knapp," the secretary of the interior was explaining, will address this conference first . . ."

Soon Gabe approached the podium. He stood for a time in silence. When he opened his mouth, the words fluttered. "I'm nervous," he said, managing a smile. "It's a human quality."

The audience murmured.

"Some of my people," Gabe said in clear tones now, "believed that we should come here with threats."

The attending scientists shuffled.

"But that's not why I'm here," Gabriel continued. "I'm here rather to suggest that from a scientific, genetic, and evolutionary point of view, we green photosynthesizers are the answer—or can be the answer—to world food shortages . . .

"Adamsvillers who possess so much chlorophyll within their skin that their flesh is green virtually never need to ingest protein. In sufficiently lighted environments, they can live by drinking only water.

"Greens like myself whose skin does not contain that much chlorophyll exist with varying levels of required food intake. Throughout my lifetime I have ingested milk and little else . . .

"It seems to us, esteemed scientists, that whatever your distaste for us, we are the most promising hope for surviving the next century on this planet. We mutants are in the evolutionary sense a messianic breed who must be allowed to multiply throughout earth in order that humankind will not starve to death. But in order to save this species we must be considered human beings."

To many Gabe's was an illustrious presentation. Some few stood in applause.

Would greens be defined as human beings? Discussion and debate ravaged the group for days. Biochemists were split on the issue. Economists warned of the danger posed by the ever-present possibility of further S.T. boycotts. A historian asked whether officially to define greens as human beings wouldn't serve to legitimate their "violent attacks upon infants and young children."

Louise Roanoke answered that once the mutants were permitted to live openly—no longer posing and free to communicate their mutation to future mates—rescuing would no longer serve a manifest function for greens. What latent functions the practice filled could be performed by various, less threatening, functional alternatives.

A psychologist suggested that a definition of greens as human beings wait "until we are absolutely certain about relative aggression levels."

Bradley Duncan responded that after living among greens for ten months he felt very comfortable in concluding that greens were neither more nor less aggressive than were other Americans.

Daniel Adamson, throughout the long discussions, threatened. Ann Sullivan pleaded for understanding. And Gabriel reiterated his formal argument.

At 7:12 P.M., November 20, 2027, by a ten-vote margin, the conference passed a resolution. "The term 'human beings'," the final document stated, "shall be understood to include both those Homo sapiens who do and those who do not possess chlorophyll within their epidermal tissue."

Duncan and Batterson supported the resolution. Louise had abstained. "We have no more evidence than we did six months ago," she explained to Connie. "This is not a vote by scientists but by people invested with ideological values."

"Aren't we all?" Brad retorted.

Questions

1. Gabe argued that allowing greens to interbreed freely would solve the problem of food shortage associated with overpopulation. What other problems of overpopulation would it solve? Which would not be solved?

2. Ann Sullivan is considered "sick" by a majority of Adamsvillers. What sociocultural factors influence this agreement? In what type of society would she not be considered ill? *Is* Ann Sullivan sick? Why? (Why not?)

3. This conference has come to an agreement concerning greens. What sociological factors influenced that agreement?

4. Louise believes that the delegates voted according to their political ideologies instead of science. Duncan says it's always that way. What do you think?

5. If there really were greens, would they be human beings or not?

Three Views of Nature

    Subjugation by Nature
    Harmony with Nature
    Mastery over Nature
    The Ecosystem Point of View

Technology

    Food Production
    Medicine
    Industry
    Transportation

Urbanism

    The Chicago School
    Mass Society

Environmental Consequences

    Resource Depletion
    Air Pollution
    Water Pollution
    Sociology and the Environment

Summary

Suggested Readings

17

Technology, Urbanism, and Environment

This chapter deals with the different points of view people have regarding the physical environment. Florence Kluckhohn and Fred Strodtbeck (1961:13) have described three views that are especially relevant to our discussions. They are:

1. Human subjugation by nature
2. Human harmony with nature
3. Human mastery over nature

We're going to look at each of these points of view and the agreements different societies have created around them. We'll see that technology has gone hand in hand with the view of mastery over nature and that urbanism has gone hand in hand with technology. Much of this chapter is devoted to an examination of the technological and urban aspects of social life. It concludes with a look at the implications for the future of modern social life on what has aptly been called Spaceship Earth.

Three Views of Nature

In this section we'll examine each of the attitudes identified by Kluckhohn and Strodtbeck. We'll also explore the modern ecological point of view, noting the relationship between that and the three different points of view that different societies have agreed on.

Subjugation by Nature

As nearly as we can tell, our earliest ancestors regarded themselves as being at the mercy of the environment. Their existence on earth seemed dependent on the whims of climate, weather, vegetation, and hungry animals. Lightning burned the forests around them, droughts drove them from place to place, predators drove them into hiding, and ice ages forced them to relocate permanently.

The earliest men and women probably differed little from other animals in being run by the forces around them. By virtue of their greater brain capacity, however, people were able to reflect on their condition, as the other animals could not. Human beings *knew* they were subject to the forces of nature; they knew how bad things were and thought about it.

Much of our speculation about the point of view shared by the earliest humans comes from what anthropologists and others have learned about contemporary preliterate societies. Much of their religions, for example, is devoted to the "propitiation" of nature, to gaining the good graces of all-powerful natural and supernatural forces. The Tsembaga of New Guinea, for example, thank their ancestors for assistance in war and seek continued support.

Rappaport (1969) describes the ritual in which they plant the *rumbin* plant and say, in essence:

> We thank you for helping us in the fight and permitting us to remain on our territory. We place our souls in this *rumbin* as we plant it in our ground. We ask you to care for this *rumbin*. We will kill pigs for you now, but they are few. In the future, when we have many pigs, we shall again give you pork and uproot the *rumbin* and stage *a kaiko* (pig festival). But until there are sufficient pigs to repay you the *rumbin* will remain in the ground (p. 191).

From this point of view, human survival occurs at the pleasure of forces in the environment that people cannot control, although a variety of religious practices are aimed at seeking the favor of these forces. Realize that there is considerable empirical evidence to support this point of view in the experiences of people who share it. Fear and discomfort, starvation, and violent death provide ample evidence for people to conclude that men and women are mere pawns in a cosmic chess game.

Harmony with Nature

Another point of view shared by many people around the world and through history suggests that human beings are equal partners with other animate and inanimate forms in nature. Rather than controlling or being controlled by the environment, people are merely a part of it. They exist in harmony with it.

Many Eastern religions, such as Buddhism and Hinduism, share a point of view regarding the sanctity of all elements in the environment. Members of the Jain sect of Asia, for example, are especially careful not to tread on insects and worms; and they cover their mouths with cloth to avoid inadvertently swallowing and killing tiny flying insects.

This point of view has been presented to a Western audience recently in the form of several popular books. Among them are the "Don Juan" books of Carlos Castaneda (1969, 1971, 1972, 1974) and Robert Pirsig's *Zen and the Art of Motorcycle Maintenance* (1975).

It is important to distinguish stated agreements from practices in this regard, however, as Paul Ehrlich and Anne Ehrlich (1972:352) have cautioned.

While Chinese religions, for example, stressed the view that man was a part of nature (rather than lord of it) and should live in harmony with it, the Chinese did not always live by this belief. . . . By the twentieth century, China's once plentiful forests had been nearly destroyed to build cities and clear the land for agriculture. . . . Ironically, the present government, which explicitly rejects the traditional religions, has attempted to restore the forests on a large scale.*

Mastery over Nature

You are no doubt most familiar with the last of the three points of view described by Kluckhohn and Strodtbeck: human mastery over nature. This is the point of view that best characterizes the developed nations of the world. It has produced great industrial engines, brought manifold increases in the productivity of the soil, cured disease, tamed wild animals and raging rivers, and placed men on the moon.

In acting on this point of view, we have had two important advantages over the other animals: our large brains; and the thumbs that can be pressed against our fingers, giving us great manual dexterity. We have added to these advantages a willingness to manipulate our environment. Whereas other animals, along with our earliest ancestors, adapted themselves to the whims of an all-powerful nature, we have more recently put our energies into adapting nature to suit *our* whims and desires.

This point of view finds considerable support in the Judeo-Christian tradition. Beginning with the Book of Genesis, human beings are given dominion over the other creatures of the earth. Ehrlich and Ehrlich argue (1972) that Christianity—in comparison with other religions—has created a mood of indifference to other elements in the environment, permitting them to be manipulated in the service of human beings.

We'll turn our attention shortly to the manner in which people have acted out the mastery-over-nature point of view: through technology and urbanism, in

*From *Population, Resources, Environment: Issues in Human Ecology,* 2nd ed., by Paul R. Ehrlich and Anne H. Ehrlich, copyright 1972 by W. H. Freeman and Company. Reprinted by permission.

particular. Before doing that, however, it will be useful to examine another point of view regarding the place of human beings in their environment: that of the modern, ecological sciences.

The Ecosystem Point of View

Ironically perhaps, modern ecologists take an environmental point of view strikingly similar to that of the Eastern mystics: Humans exist in harmony with the rest of the environment. It's not so much that we *should* but that we have no choice in the matter.

To understand the ecological point of view, it is necessary to recall the notion of **homeostasis** from the discussion of social-systems theory in Chapter 2. The Greek term *stasis* means literally "a standing," as in a stoppage in the flow of blood from a body. "Homeostasis," then, essentially means "staying the same," and what the term suggests is very similar to the notion of social stability discussed earlier in this book.

Our physical environment, including us, is a system: an ecosystem. Like a social system, the ecosystem is made up of interrelated components. Each component affects and is affected by all the other components in the system. The rain accelerates the growth of grass, which cows eat, thereby providing milk, and so forth. If people transform the fields of grass into subdivisions and parking lots, there is less

grass for the cows to eat, so there may be less milk, and the rain runs off the concrete, causing floods. Everything is related to everything else, and someone has said that the first law of ecology is that you can't do just one thing. Anything you do has many, many subsequent effects.

In a system where everything is related to everything else, two kinds of things can happen. The components of the system can balance and counterbalance each other, creating homeostasis over time, or a series of events can create continuing and often accelerated change in the state of the system. Some examples will illustrate these two different possibilities.

Imagine water leaking through a tiny hole in a dam. The water trickling out erodes the edges of the hole, making it larger. As the hole enlarges, more water pours out faster, causing more erosion. This chain of events is creating a continuing and accelerating change in a system. By contrast, consider this example of homeostasis in a system. Some forms of automobile antifreeze contain tiny magnetic pellets. Whenever the antifreeze begins leaking through a hole in the radiator, the magnetic pellets stick to the edges of the hole, eventually clogging it up and stopping the leak.

To take another example, imagine a case of social conflict: labor talks with management, for example. Two things can happen during the negotiations. The two sides may move toward agreement, reaching a compromise settlement acceptable to both, or their disagreements may grow more extreme. Their points of view may polarize, with each side making ever more extreme demands, widening the gap between them, until the talks break down altogether.

The much-discussed "wage-price spiral" illustrates a lack of homeostasis in an economic system. Wage increases among workers in manufacturing industries result in higher prices, thereby raising the cost of living and necessitating further pay raises. Population growth, as discussed in Chapter 16, is another example. An excess of births over deaths results in more people to have more children who can have more children who can have more children and so forth.

In the case of social conflict versus stability, homeostasis means the survival of some sets of agreements. Whether that survival is "good" or "bad" depends on your point of view regarding the agreements. If increased conflict means the downfall of capitalism and the cooling of the conflict means capitalism's persistence, how you feel about capitalism determines which is preferable.

In the case of our physical environment, homeostasis means the survival of the ecosystem, the continuing possibility of life on earth, including us. Ecosystem survival is not intrinsically "good," but virtually everybody on earth *agrees* that it's good. Let's turn now to a consideration of some of the tinkering we've done with that ecosystem and how our tinkering has affected the chances for homeostasis.

Technology

Gerhard Lenski (1974:38) has defined "technology" as "the information, techniques, and tools by means of which men utilize the material resources of their environment to satisfy their varied needs and desires." In its conventional usage, the term suggests "artificial" manipulations of the environment, "unnatural acts." Picking wild nuts and berries would be different from planned, active cultivation.

Typically, technology is represented by a contrived tool or practice that is more efficient in meeting our needs and desires than what we imagine would be the case if we lived like our earliest ancestors. Thus, the automobile seems more efficient for meeting our needs and desires to travel than walking barefoot through the forest. But what is the cost?

It is important to realize that human beings have an impact on the ecosystem simply by being here, and we have an impact with everything we do. We breathe in oxygen and breathe out carbon dioxide, thereby modifying the atmosphere surrounding the planet. Plants take in carbon dioxide and give off oxygen, so that there is a balance more or less, given the right numbers of plants and people. We have an impact on the environment when we eat the wild nuts and berries, but we also fertilize the soil so as to produce more nuts and berries later.

Technology is "special" in this context, however, in that it has tended to increase the magnitude of our impact on the ecosystem. Moreover, the speed of

recent technological developments has made it increasingly difficult for other components of the ecosystem to adjust to those impacts. If there were only one lumberjack on earth, working with only a hand ax, he or she could chop down trees all day, every day, forever with no significant effect on the homeostasis of the ecosystem. The natural rates of germination and death of trees would take up the slack. Technology, however, makes possible the mass "harvesting" of whole forests, and the homeostasis is disrupted. If there were only a single internal-combustion engine on earth, it could be run day and night forever with no significant impact. Fossil fuels would be created fast enough (even though it would take millions of years) to replenish the gasoline used, and the pollutants put into the atmosphere would be accommodated. The hundreds of millions of such engines that are running at this very moment are a different matter.

This is not to say that all technology is all bad from the standpoint of ecosystem homeostasis. Indeed, some forms of technology actually minimize our impact on earth. Simple tools like the lever and the wedge allow us to expend less energy, which means that we require less food to replace the energy expended. Certain forms of social organization (the bucket brigade, for example) probably have the same effect. It would be possible, therefore, to develop social and physical technologies that would have as their purpose the lessening of our impact on the ecosystem and the maintenance of homeostasis. But these are not the types of technology we have developed.

How can some of the technology we *have* created be described? In seeking a partial answer to this question, we'll pay special attention to the ways in which technological developments have affected social life. In the concluding section of the chapter, we'll look at the environmental consequences.

Food Production

As nearly as we can tell from the archaeological record, our kind began as foragers, hunting and gathering what we could find to eat. Early technological developments that supported those activities included spears, arrows, clubs, axes, and tools for digging. These rudimentary innovations probably were what enabled the species to survive.

Around ten thousand years ago, we began cultivating the soil in the Mesopotamian basin. People's discovery that they could cultivate the soil was surely one of the most significant technological developments in human history. The necessity for migration was reduced, and people stuck around to harvest the crops they planted. Cultivation, moreover, increased the amount of food produced in a given area over what could be found growing wild. Thus, people were able to live together in somewhat larger groups.

We know little about the history of agricultural specialization, but by the time of the first written records, many members of society were freed from the need to engage in food production. (Somebody wrote those records, for example.)

Later agricultural development has been largely in the direction of greater intensity. A smaller and smaller proportion of a population has become able to produce food enough for the remaining members. Nowhere has this tendency been illustrated more dramatically than in the United States, where the absolute *number* of farm workers decreased by 60 percent between 1950 and 1974. During that same period, farm output in America *increased* by 214 percent (U.S. Bureau of the Census 1975a:358, 607).

The increased productivity of American farmers, of course, is based on countless technological developments. A variety of planting, harvesting, and processing machines have played a major role. Chemical fertilizers have increased the productivity of the soil, just as chemical pesticides have decreased crop losses resulting from insects and worms.

Several social impacts have been felt as a result of technological developments in food production. Most evident has been the freeing of many men and women for nonagricultural functions. Indeed, fewer than 4 percent of the American work force are currently engaged in agriculture. A variety of social organizations and interactions have grown up around the distribution of food, however, including, for example, grocery stores, supermarkets, and restaurants.

The relative abundance of food—most evident in the United States, but true everywhere when a very long historical perspective is taken—has also had the effect of lowering death rates and increasing population. This effect may also be seen whenever grain shipments are sent from the developed nations of the world to starving populations elsewhere.

Not so obvious, perhaps, as the fact that food production has become an activity that few of us engage in, is the fact that food has become *power* in human social relations. Those who produce or control food have political leverage over those who do not. The exercise of such power may be seen in international grain shipments (as just mentioned) or—at the domestic level—in food stamp programs.

These are but a few of the ways in which technological developments relating to food have reshaped social structure and interaction. Future developments, involving the production of totally artificial foods, for example, or the development of new food sources in the ocean, will have further effects on the way we run our day-to-day lives.

Medicine

Technological developments in medicine have combined with increases in food production to decrease death rates and extend our life expectancies. The earliest medicine probably consisted mostly of the use of herbs and religious remedies, although the surgical procedure of "trepanation" (punching holes in the skull) is evident in many of the earliest fossil remains of human beings.

The most significant medical developments over the course of human history might be classified as follows:

1. Drugs for curing illness, such as penicillin

2. Inoculations for preventing illness, such as smallpox vaccinations

3. Surgical remedies for illness, such as appendectomies

4. Public health measures, such as sanitation

5. Other preventive medical developments for avoiding onset or seriousness of illness, such as knowledge of nutrition

The impact of such medical developments on population growth is only one of the ways in which social life has been affected. The development of medicine as an institution is another, involving medical roles and relations, hospitals, clinics, health insurance, and so forth.

Interestingly, the technological advance of medicine has not resulted in a uniform decline in all forms of disease. Reflecting other facts of social life, some causes of death have become more prevalent while others have remained unchanged. Table 17·1 compares some selected causes of death in America in 1900 and 1973. It was not possible for people to die in auto accidents in 1900, but notice that cancer and heart disease have also increased over the half century reported.

The extension of life expectancies brought by medical developments has brought about many changes in social life. The potentially productive life spans of individuals have been lengthened, permitting greater contributions to society. At the same time, an overabundance of workers has been created at times, which complicates economic systems. And as we saw in Chapter 16, it has also produced a class of people who live in society without being capable

Table 17·1   Selected Causes of Death in America, 1900 and 1973

Cause of death	Deaths per 100,000 1900	1973
Decreased		
Tuberculosis	194.4	1.8
Typhoid and paratyphoid fever	31.3	0.0
Influenza and pneumonia	202.2	29.8
Stable		
Suicide	10.2	12.0
Increased		
Malignant neoplasms (cancer)	64.0	167.3
Major cardiovascular-renal diseases	354.2	494.4
Motor vehicle accidents	0.4[a]	26.5

[a]Rate for 1906.

Sources: U.S. Bureau of the Census, Historical Statistics of the United States: Colonial Times to 1957, 1960, p. 26; U.S. Bureau of the Census, Statistical Abstract of the United States, 1975, p. 64.

of contributing in proportion to their needs: The very elderly have become like the very young in this respect.

Medical developments have both permitted and, to an extent, encouraged people to live in ever denser populations in cities. Large cities were nearly wiped out in the plagues of the Middle Ages, but modern sanitation methods in concert with modern medicines make such plagues unlikely in developed nations. Moreover, city populations are more easily served by medicine than scattered, rural populations, particularly when medical care requires complicated and expensive equipment.

Industry

A good deal has already been said earlier in this book about the history of industrial development, and there is no need to repeat it here. It will be useful, however, to look briefly at some of the social consequences of industrial development.

Technological developments in industry, as discussed in Chapter 10, moved the locus of work out of the family and into the factory. Except for during the early years of the Industrial Revolution, this relocation of work removed children from the labor force and removed men from the family for much of the day. In more recent years, it has increasingly removed women from the home as well, with the result that family life is being restructured.

The development of interchangeable parts paved the way for industrial mass production based on assembly lines. It would be impossible to overstate the importance of these developments in regard to, among other things, the differentiation of function, the relation of the worker to the product, and social stratification. All aspects of mass industry, in fact, have influenced stratification and political power.

Automation is a recent technological development in industry that is further restructuring social relations. In many industries—such as petroleum processing, for example—unskilled laborers have been replaced by computer-directed equipment. The human jobs that remain require special technical training and skills, and there is no room for unskilled workers. Automation is certain to prove one of the most significant developments in industry in the years to come, and one of the changes it will necessitate is a reassessment of agreements concerning the righteousness of work.

Transportation

On or about April 1, 4837 B.C., Mary Gar was coming over the crest of a hill in the forest on her way home. Because she stepped on a fallen log, she inadvertently began a revolution in transportation. Her weight on the log dislodged it, and it began rolling down the hill. Mary, arms flailing in the air, managed to stay atop the rolling log, like a prehistoric lumberjack, as it rumbled down the hill, crushing saplings and bushes in its path. Lying dazed in a heap at the bottom of the hill, Mary realized that she had cut twenty-three seconds from her normal commute time and decided to capitalize on it. She borrowed a chain-saw from a neighbor, lopped four cross sections off the log, and invented the little red wagon. (Well, it probably happened *something* like that.)

Technological developments in transportation have revolutionized social relations in countless ways. Some of these can best be seen by an enumeration of those aspects of modern life that would be impossible if walking were still the only means of human transportation. You might get a sense of the magnitude of the revolution by merely reviewing the things you've done today. Don't limit yourself to your own move-

ments. Think about the food you've eaten, the clothes you're wearing, the buildings you've been in, and so forth. How many of those things could be the way they are if human foot power were the only means of transportation?

The automobile has, of course, had many obvious impacts on social life in developed nations. Many regard the automobile as a necessity rather than a luxury, especially given the extent to which interactions are organized around it. As serious efforts are being made to create more reliance on public, mass transit, we are learning of more and more functions cars have for us. Cars give us status. We eat meals and watch movies in them. They give us freedom, opportunities to escape parents and crowded cities. Cars made suburbs possible. People get engaged in cars, and some start families there. Imagine robbing a bank and then jumping aboard a bus for your getaway.

In 1974, there were 130,751,000 registered motor vehicles in the United States, or one for every 1.8 men, women, and children in the nation. There were approximately the same number of registered motor vehicles as there were licensed drivers. Moreover Americans owned nearly half the motor vehicles in the entire world (U.S. Bureau of the Census 1975a: 570, 573).

Technological developments relating to travel through the air have been even more impressive. A mere sixty-six years—around the length of the average American life span—separated the twelve-second Wright Brothers flight at Kill Devil Hill in Kitty Hawk, North Carolina, from the *Apollo 11* landing in the Sea of Tranquillity on the moon. Forty-four years separated Kitty Hawk from the first supersonic flight, in 1947; and twenty years later, the fixed-wing aircraft speed record rested at just under seven times the speed of sound.

Larger, faster passenger transports have reshaped many aspects of social life. Consider, for example, the effect of greater migration and travel on ethnocentric attitudes, as people from different cultures come into increased contact with each other.

Transportation is often discussed as a subcategory of the category "communication." Chapter 18 will deal with developments in other aspects of communication.

Robert Park 1864–1944 (The American Sociological Association)

Urbanism

Technology has also had an enormous impact on patterns of human residence. Most simply put, technological development has gone hand in hand with the rise of urban population centers. Whereas our ancestors may have started out in bands of a dozen or so, many people today live in cities and metropolitan areas with populations running over 10 million. The relationship between technology and urbanism has been one of mutual support.

Technology has supported urbanism by making population concentrations possible. As we noted earlier, the development of agriculture several thousand years ago made it possible for large populations to subsist in relatively small areas, a situation impossible in hunting-and-gathering economies. Public-sanitation innovations made even larger concentrations possible. So did a variety of other technological developments.

Urbanism has also supported technology. The early growth of agriculture depended on the availability of large markets for food. Factories have depended on the concentration of labor forces. Mass-transit systems could not develop without masses to be transported.

The city has been a focus of sociological attention for years. Particularly interested was a group of scholars at the University of Chicago earlier in this century.

The Chicago School

The "Chicago school" has many referents in sociology: a place, an era, a group, and certain points of view. The place was the University of Chicago; the era was primarily the 1920s and 1930s. For present purposes, the group of sociologists included Robert Park, Ernest Burgess, W. I. Thomas, Ellsworth Faris, Emory Bogardus, Stuart Queen, and Louis Wirth. The point of view that interests us here is to be found in their fascination with the city. As Robert Park said in his 1926 presidential address before the American Sociological Society:

> Ecology, in so far as it seeks to describe the actual distribution of plants and animals over the earth's surface, is in some very real senses a geographical science. Human ecology, as the sociologists would like to use the term, is, however, not identical with geography, nor even with human geography. It is not man, but the community; not man's relation to the earth which he inhabits, but his relations to other men, that concern us most.

Sociologists needed, Park continued, to examine the structure, the growth, and the changes in modern, American urban centers. He saw the modern city as being organized around the marketplace. This characteristic largely determined the distribution of businesses, residences, and interactions. Related to the economic issues were the waves of European and Asian immigrants arriving in Chicago, creating subcultural concentrations within the city. These needed to be studied.

The urban sociology most characterizing the Chicago school consisted of on-location examinations of the different faces of the city: ghettos, boarding

Urban renewal has become an integral part of urban life. Although it may solve some urban problems, it frequently creates others. (Bruce Davidson, Magnum)

houses, red-light districts, and so forth. These special-topic studies were woven into the mosaic that was Chicago in the 1920s and 1930s as sociologists recorded "social distances" and behavior patterns on geographical maps. Typical of this method perhaps is the following report on "whorehouses":

> In order to get an accurate picture of the exact regions in which commercialized vice exists, a spot map was made from the location of "vice resorts." . . . Transferred to E. W. Burgess' chart describing the natural organization of the city, the commercialized vice areas as revealed by this spot map are found to be implanted upon the central business zone (Zone I), the zone of transition (Zone II) with its slums, immigrant and racial colonies . . . (Reckless 1926:194).

The "chart describing the natural organization of the city," created by Burgess and augmented by the research of others, was to become one of the best-known products of the Chicago school of urban sociology. Figure 17·1 shows Burgess's concentric zone theory of urban expansion as it applied to Chicago.

As you can see, for Burgess, Chicago's commercial Loop serves as the hub for several concentrically arranged social bands. Nearest the central business district (zone I) was the deteriorating residential area (zone II) containing the city's slums. Social class increased the farther one moved from the hub: The working class lived in zone III, the middle class in zone IV, and the urban fringe of the commuters in

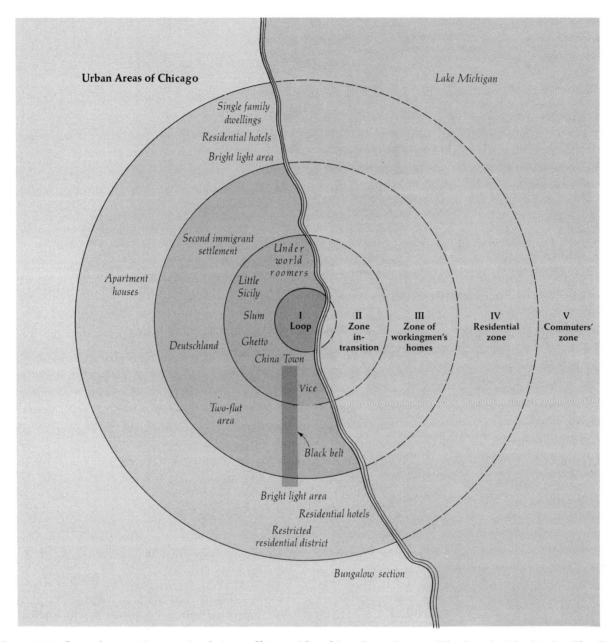

Figure 17•1 Burgess's concentric zone point of view on Chicago. Adapted from Ernest Burgess, "The Growth of the City," in The City, *ed. Robert Park, Ernest Burgess, and R. D. McKenzie. Copyright 1925 by the University of Chicago Press. Reprinted by permission.*

zone V, where the suburbs were located. Burgess cautioned that the city's social structure was not as neatly layered as the concentric circles might suggest, but the model was reasonably accurate. The growth of Chicago, moreover, had proceeded from the center outward. Over the years, the residential area nearest the center, zone II, had become the home of the city's poorest residents, with the wealthier people moving

**Three Generalizations of the
Internal Structure of Cities
District**

1. Central business district
2. Wholesale light manufacturing
3. Low-class residential
4. Medium-class residential
5. High-class residential
6. Heavy manufacturing
7. Outlying business district
8. Residential suburb
9. Industrial suburb
10. Commuters' zone

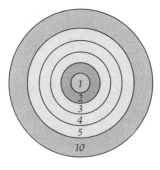

Concentric Zone Theory

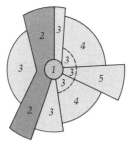

Sector Theory

Multiple Nuclei

Figure 17•2   Three city models. Reprinted from "The Nature of Cities" by Chauncy D. Harris and Edward L. Ullman in volume 242 of the Annals of the American Academy of Political and Social Science. *Copyright © 1945 by the American Academy of Political and Social Science. Reprinted by permission.*

away from the center, resulting in the picture presented in Figure 17•1.

Burgess further cautioned that the concentric zone model might not fit all cities, and a number of sociologists developed other models. Harris and Ullman (1945) summarized three models, including the concentric zone model. Those three models are presented in Figure 17•2.

Some cities are structured pretty much the same way Burgess suggested in his studies of Chicago. Others, as indicated in the sector theory disgram, are organized more as spokes radiating from a central hub than as concentric bands around it. Still others, as illustrated in the multiple nuclei diagram, are organized around several more-complex structures.

As these diagrams indicate, no single pattern describes the organization of urban areas. You'll recall from the discussion of institutions that a variety of forms serve the functions required for group survival. Similarly, a variety of layouts work for cities.

For the most part, sociologists have studied the largely unplanned ways in which cities have evolved in response to technological developments, population growth, and a host of other stimuli. In more recent years, however, sociologists have been more involved in planning the process. Working with architects and city planners, sociologists have participated in planning "new towns" and "planned communities" with the purpose of creating physical and spatial designs that will take account of patterns

of social interaction. Communities such as Reston, Virginia, represent an attempt to accommodate social as well as engineering factors in community design.

With the development of urban technology—such as high rises, freeways, and similar engineering feats—conflicts between technology and social patterns have appeared. Consider what sometimes happens with urban renewal programs. The construction of a new freeway, for example, can cut neighborhoods in half, disrupting and redirecting patterns of interaction. Families who were once close friends may find they must travel miles to the nearest freeway interchange and an equal distance back to be with former friends. The friendships may not survive the trip. Urban renewal projects can involve the "improvement" of living conditions, as slum areas are torn down and replaced by modern apartment buildings. Frequently, however, the new residences are inappropriate to the needs, desires, and financial abilities of the former residents. Where people once interacted regularly on doorsteps and in the street, these patterns are often no longer possible. The failure of urban renewal efforts to take account of social-interaction patterns has been a source of concern for many sociologists (among them, Greer 1966).

Mass Society

A city is a large aggregation of people in a densely populated area, but "how many people" and "how

Table 17·2 The Relative Pros and Cons of City Life

Advantages of city	*Disadvantages of city*
1. Sense of being where the "action" is.	1. Higher crime rates.
2. Greater variety of people to interact with.	2. Higher rates of mental illness.
3. Freedom to rise above family origins.	3. More pollution.
4. Variety of occupational choices.	4. More crowding.
5. More extensive cultural and entertainment options.	5. More impersonal, anonymous interactions.
6. Better medical facilities.	6. Less access to top leaders.
7. Closer to government agencies.	7. Social problems more difficult to remedy.
8. Easier mobilization of people for social action and social change.	8. Harder to reach agreement among populace.
9. Quicker access to technological advances.	9. More competition for jobs.
10. More innovation; tradition less restricting.	10. Less that you can depend on (because of more social change).

densely populated" are matters of arbitrary definition. For its bookkeeping, the United States census defines a city as an incorporated area with 2,500 or more residents. As sociologists use the term, however, no population size can define a city. A "city" is a form of social organization, the existence of which is related to population size and density but is not synonymous with them. Sociologists contrast the term "urbanization," the demographic and structural characteristics of a city, with "urbanism," people's experience of that way of life. The two are described in the box "Urbanization versus Urbanism: More Than a Matter of Definition."

What a city *is* can best be seen in comparison with what noncities—towns and villages—are. Most simply put, a city is organized as a gesellschaft; it does not have the gemeinschaft character of towns and villages (as discussed in Chapter 6). Most urban interactions are secondary rather than primary. City dwellers depend on countless people whom they don't know by name and may never see face to face, whereas small-town residents are all likely to know one another.

In all large societies, some people prefer country life while others prefer the city. Until the last decade or so, there was a general agreement in America that city life was "superior" to country life: Country folks were depicted as naive bumpkins, and every decennial census documented a continuing migration from rural to urban areas. The last few years have seen

a modification in this agreement, however. Migration is beginning to be away from the central cities.

Table 17·2 summarizes some of the pros and cons of city life and country life. It describes the relative "quality of life" that each has to offer and illustrates the trade-offs people must make in deciding which best matches their own preferences. Realize, as you look over the list, that the notion of "choosing" where to live is a relatively new one in human history. For thousands of years, most people have simply lived where they were born without even being aware that there *were* other places they might live.

Also notice in the lists of advantages and disadvantages of city life that some of the "good" and "bad" aspects of the city are inseparably paired. The much-discussed anonymity of urban society, for example, has advantages. Small, rural societies in which everybody knows everybody else make social mobility and personal growth difficult. If you were a big-city fire fighter, on the other hand, it would be easier for you to organize your fellow workers to strike for better wages. But you would also be more likely to suffer through a police or garbage workers' strike. City life can also free you from the stagnation of small-town traditions, but continuing social change can produce a sense of anomie. In fact, urban dwellers often have negative images of the cities they live in. The box "Urban Imagery: Its Negative Connotations" on page 462 discusses this aspect of the rural-urban trade-off.

Urbanization versus Urbanism: More Than a Matter of Definition

The distinction between "urbanization" and "urbanism" is an important one. "Urbanization" has two essential characteristics: (1) Demographically, the term refers to a level of population concentration whereby people live under high densities; (2) in terms of social structure, the term refers to the change in economic and social organization that a society undergoes as a greater proportion of its population lives in cities. Urbanization, in this latter sense, is usually viewed as a companion of industrialization even though it is difficult to tell which determines the other.

"Urbanism," however, refers to the way of life experienced by city dwellers. People must adapt psychologically to the demands of the city. One facet of this adaptation is making their behavior conform to the social values of fellow urbanites.

According to these definitions, it is fairly easy to see how a country can have a large proportion of its inhabitants living in cities (high level of urbanization) while its citizens are still basically rural regarding their values and social identification (low degree of urbanism). Many large cities in Africa, for example, appear to have populations that still cling to rural values and attitudes. A country like the United States, in contrast, with its advanced technology and communication systems, is felt to have high levels of both urbanization and urbanism.

What social and personal problems do you think are common among societies with high urbanization and low urbanism?

Frustrated and disillusioned with city life, many young people have sought refuge in the rural, agrarian social patterns of an earlier era. Being socialized into the modern world, however, may make returning to the past difficult. (Bob Fitch, Black Star)

The fact that city life has both advantages and disadvantages has produced worldwide an ecological hybrid: the suburb. By living in small towns and villages on the fringes of large, metropolitan centers, people have discovered a way of enjoying the best of both worlds. Thus, the resident of, say, Tenafly, New Jersey, can live in a relatively large house with a large lawn and friendly neighbors all the while he or she is in driving distance of the commercial and cultural life of New York City. This development has serious costs, however.

The flight of wealthier residents to the suburbs has undercut the tax base of the cities. Suburban residents do not pay property taxes within the city, but they "use" the city's facilities: its parks, streets, libraries and museums, and so forth. There is no less need for police, sanitation workers, and the others that keep a large city functioning. There are simply fewer people to pay for those facilities and services.

Urban Imagery: Its Negative Connotations

Thomas Jefferson took a very dismal view of the city. He felt that the virtue of his new nation's government lay in its willingness to remain agricultural. In 1800, Jefferson wrote: "I view great cities as pestilential to the morals, the health and the liberties of man." Although most Americans today would not take so dismal and pathological a view of the city, there can be no doubt that the image many Americans have of the city is not a positive one. When one mentions Cleveland, we often think of the Cuyahoga River's catching fire in the late sixties. The names of Detroit, Newark, Gary, and New York City usually conjure images of crime, pollution, congestion, and, in general, nearly intolerable conditions. Rural America is equated with the simple and clean life while urban America is seen as a modern Sodom and Gomorrah (with an overdose of air pollution thrown in for good measure).

Urban residents have a kind of negative "self-image" regarding the city they live in and how it reflects upon themselves. All too often, positive images of the city have related only to the general character of the city as a whole. The negative images are at the level of the individual. Chicago was "hog butcher to the world," while Jacksonville, Florida, is the "bold, new city of the South!" It is difficult for the typical urbanite to see himself as a "hog butcher to the world" or as a "bold new person." But when Atlanta is called "crime capital of America," it has meaning at the individual level. One can see it reflected in the everyday life of people staying off the streets at night, having double locks on their doors, and doing everything possible to keep the crime imagery from being a personal reality.

When you think of a large American city, what images come to your mind? How do you think these images affect the lives of urban dwellers and how they relate to the city they live in?

Thus, in 1975, the city of New York requested federal assistance in the amount of 1 *billion* dollars to help it survive as a municipality.

The rise of suburbs in the United States and other developed nations, combined with population growth in general, has given rise to another social phenomenon: the "megalopolis." A few decades ago, most developed nations consisted of a few large cities surrounded by rural areas. More recently, the cities have become ringed by suburbs, with the rural expanse beyond them. Now, increasingly, one "metropolitan area" (an urban center plus its suburbs) merges into another. Although cities and suburban communities may still exist as independent political units, they are *sociologically* components in the same, larger whole. It is now possible to drive from Boston to Washington, D.C., and beyond with little sense of ever leaving "the city." People cross state as well as town and city borders in the unbroken flow of daily life. The sense of discrete towns, cities, and states is largely gone.

Figure 17·3 shows the megalopolises we may anticipate in the future in America. Based on the assumption of two children per family, this map indicates the location of America's "supercities" in the year 2000.

The urbanization of America that we've been discussing is only a slight exaggeration of a worldwide trend. Table 17·3 shows the extent of urbanization in several countries around the world during the period from 1965 to 1973, as reported by the United Nations. Though the definitions of "urban" are not strictly comparable across all the countries, the general pattern of urban growth is clear with very few exceptions. The box on page 465 "Are Some Developing Nations 'Overurbanized'?" examines a particular dilemma faced by a majority of the world's nations as they experience the trend toward urbanization.

Urbanization, coupled with population growth, is clearly one of the most significant trends in the world today. In the final section of the chapter, we'll look at some of the ways in which it *is* significant.

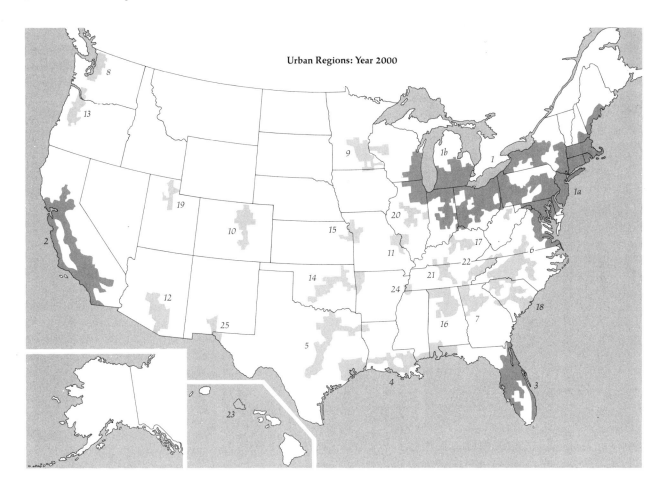

Figure 17·3   *Anticipated American megalopolises in the year 2000 (based on two-child family projection). Source: Presidential Commission on Population Growth and the American Future, 1972.*

Environmental Consequences

Like all living things, human beings modify the physical environment by taking things away from it and adding things to it. These two human activities are referred to by the terms "resource depletion" and "pollution." Human beings are not alone in depleting the world's resources and in polluting. Other animals do it, too—but we are special.

When wild goats deplete their food resources through overgrazing, for example, the situation is remedied by natural checks and balances. Many of the goats starve to death, and their population is reduced to the point at which grass, trees, and shrubs

Table 17·3 Worldwide Urbanization, 1965–1973

Nation[a]	Percent of population in urban areas	
	1965	1973
Afghanistan	20.0	15.0
Algeria	39.0 ('66)	50.4
Belgium	86.6	87.1
Botswana	4.5	13.2
Brazil	50.6	58.3
Bulgaria	46.5	56.2
Colombia	54.3	63.4
Cuba	53.1	60.5 ('71)
Cyprus	37.7	43.1
East Germany	73.2	74.3
Egypt	40.0	43.2
Ethiopia	6.8	11.0
Finland	43.9	57.1
Hungary	44.7	49.3
Iceland	82.5	85.6 ('72)
India	18.8	20.2 ('72)
Indonesia	11.6	17.5
Iran	37.5	42.6
Iraq	51.1	61.4
Japan	68.1	72.1 ('70)
Libya	25.4	29.3
Luxembourg	63.2 ('66)	68.3
Mexico	54.7	61.2
Mongolia	39.6	46.4
Morocco	29.9	36.8
Netherlands	78.4	77.4
New Hebrides	11.8	19.3
New Zealand	61.4	81.4 ('71)
Norway	40.9	44.9 ('72)
Panama	44.5	49.0
Sikkim	4.6	5.3
Sudan	10.3	12.8
Turkey	34.4	38.6
U.K. (England/Wales)	79.1	77.9 ('72)
U.S.S.R.	52.9	59.2
Venezuela	71.6	75.7 ('70)
Zaire	21.8	25.1

[a]Nations for which 1965–1973 (or close) data were available.

Source: Demographic Yearbook, 1973 *(New York: United Nations, 1974), pp. 108–22.*

can recover. Our technological ingenuity, however, has allowed us to devise stopgap measures of our own to put off nature's reckoning. In the process, we have created forms and levels of pollution well beyond the abilities of other animals.

Resource depletion and pollution have serious implications for the ecosystem. Of what relevance is sociology? What can the understanding of social agreements contribute to the solution of environmental problems? Let's see.

Resource Depletion

"In April 1968, a group of thirty individuals from ten countries—scientists, educators, economists, humanists, industrialists, and national and international civil servants—gathered in the Accademia dei Lincei in Rome . . . to discuss a subject of staggering scope—the present and future predicament of man" (Meadows et al. 1972:9). Eventually calling itself "The Club of Rome," this group commissioned a series of research projects aimed at determining the long-term effects of human consumption of global resources and the production of pollution.

In 1972, a major report on the research was published, and *The Limits to Growth* by Donella Meadows and her colleagues at M.I.T. became one of the most important and most controversial books of the generation. Using advanced computer-simulation techniques, the researchers constructed computer programs and models that explored the implications of factors and relationships governing past and present human behavior. Population growth, resource utilization, and pollution were among the factors considered. The programs resulted in forecasts, some of which were extremely dismal. They indicated that past patterns simply could not continue without totally exhausting certain resources.

The research findings were perhaps more shocking in regard to "nonrenewable natural resources": the fuels and minerals that require millions of years for natural production. Table 17·4 shows some of the researchers' forecasts (Meadows et al. 1973). Estimates of how long various resources will last depend on two important variables. First, do we currently know the volume of resources available to us, or can we expect to discover more in the future? Second, will

Are Some Developing Nations "Overurbanized"?

Over 65 percent of the world's population live in countries termed "developing countries." These nations lag technologically behind the Western World in varying degrees. A fundamental question is whether or not they will be able to cope with their own urbanization. Each year millions of rural peasants crowd into the cities of Third World nations. They settle in squalid living areas where employment is low or nonexistent and the prospects for a better future are bleak.

When the proportion of people engaged in agricultural activity falls below the proportions established by developed, urbanized nations, a country is said to be "overurbanized." Egypt, for example, is more urbanized than France in relation to its level of economic development, even though Egypt, according to its per capita income, is a developing nation. Egypt's economy cannot support its urban population. Overurbanization is usually attributed to "push" factors of severe economic conditions. These drive rural peasants to the city in

hopes of bettering their lives. The consequences of overurbanization are typically viewed as negative. A country must allocate too much of its economic resources to support parasitic urbanites, which means that its overall economic growth is impeded.

Some scholars, however, criticize the notion of "overurbanization." They say it is a value-laden concept too strongly based on a definition of development that is culturally bound to Western nations. They also believe that new peasant migrants to a city usually become more productive (even though minimally at first) for a nation's economy than they would be if they remained in rural areas. The viewpoint taken has implications for the economic and growth plans of developing nations as well as for our understanding of the urbanization process in these nations.

If you were a leader of a developing nation labeled overurbanized, what "danger signs" would you pay attention to?

levels of production (consuming the raw materials) continue at current levels, or will production rates continue to grow in the future as they have been growing in the past? Table 17·4 considers each of these possibilities.

Resources like coal, petroleum, and iron are called "nonrenewable" because of the millions of years it takes nature to produce them. Other resources, such as lumber, food crops, and water are regarded as "renewable" because of the *relative* speed with which they are produced. Even with renewable resources, consumption often matches and temporarily exceeds production. The global food shortage has been discussed elsewhere in this book. In many places in the world, water consumption is reaching its local limits, and timber "harvesting" has often completely denuded forest areas for decades or longer.

Earth's ecosystem is for all practical purposes a "closed system." This means that nothing is permanently taken away from it. When iron ore is taken

out of the ground and processed into steel, it remains in the ecosystem, but in a transformed state. The transformations we work, however, have an impact on other aspects of the environment. Let's look at some of those.

Air Pollution

The massive atmosphere surrounding the planet has been visibly and invisibly changed in many significant ways by our activities. The clouds of smog hovering over most modern cities, often extending out to sea or merging with the smog of other cities, is the most visible evidence of our impact. This painful fact of modern life has drawn our attention to the problem of air pollution, but it has also deceived us. What you see is not all you get, and it may not even be the most dangerous part.

Paul Ehrlich and Anne Ehrlich (1972:147) state the case clearly:

Air pollution is now recognized not only as an agent that rots nylon stockings and windshield wiper blades, that corrodes paint and steel, blackens skies and the wash on the clothesline, and damages $500 million worth of crops annually; it is recognized as a killer of people.*

Smog comes from such sources as pulp and paper mills, power plants, refineries, steel mills, and other industrial activities. In the United States, automobile exhausts are a key source. Citing U.S. Public Health Service data, Ehrlich and Ehrlich (1972:147) report that:

> In the late 1960s our 90 million motor vehicles annually spewed into the atmosphere 66 million tons of carbon monoxide, 1 million tons of sulfur dioxides, 6 million tons of nitrogen oxides, 12 million tons of hydrocarbons, 1 million tons of particulate matter, and assorted other dangerous substances, such as tetraethyl lead.*

Air pollution of this magnitude affects hearts, lungs, and eyes. It kills crops that might have been consumed and poisons those that are. All this seems trivial in comparison with what air pollution may be doing to the atmosphere itself and the gaseous layers beyond it: reducing the radiant energy reaching earth from the sun while allowing more-deadly radiation to pass through, changing the earth's climate.

Water Pollution

Water is as essential to sustained life on earth as air, and various of our activities are converting this source of life into a deadly poison. Sewage disposal in waterways adds disease-causing and death-dealing bacteria and viruses. Industrial wastes contaminate water with no-less-deadly inorganic materials such as lead, mercury, and sulfuric acid. Agricultural pesticides and herbicides also end up in the rivers, streams, and springs that supply us with drinking water.

*From *Population, Resources, Environment: Issues in Human Ecology*, 2nd ed., by Paul R. Ehrlich and Anne H. Ehrlich, copyright 1972 by W. H. Freeman and Company. Reprinted by permission.

Table 17·4 Estimates of the Future of the World's Natural Resources

| Resource | Years to deplete resource assuming | | | |
| | Current consumption | | Increased consumption[a] | |
	Low estimate[b]	High estimate[c]	Low estimate[b]	High estimate[c]
Aluminum	110	340	33	49
Chromium	730	1,300	115	137
Coal	3,100	5,100	118	132
Cobalt	190	420	90	132
Copper	52	160	27	46
Gold	7	25	6	17
Iron	840		154	
Lead	38	490	28	119
Manganese	710	1,200	106	123
Mercury	25	84	19	44
Molybdenum	390	1,400	65	92
Natural gas	30	300	19	58
Nickel	130	350	50	75
Petroleum	38	110	23	43
Platinum	100	140	41	49
Silver	18	32	15	23
Tin	88	160	62	92
Tungsten	39		27	
Zinc	280	930	76	115

[a]Based on estimates by the U.S. Bureau of Mines.
[b]Assumes currently known resources; i.e., no new discoveries.
[c]Includes new resource discoveries as estimated by the U.S. Geological Survey and others.

Source: *Adapted from Dennis Meadows et al.,* Dynamics of Growth in a Finite World *(Cambridge, Mass.: Wright-Allen Press, Inc., 1973), pp. 372–73.*

Only a portion of these poisons reach people directly through their drinking water. Others are introduced into the complex food chain that eventually reaches dinner tables. Poisons in the water are ingested in algae, for example, which are in turn eaten by small fish which are then eaten by bigger fish, the last of these being caught and eaten by people. Not only are the poisons transmitted from step to step in the food chain, but many of them become more concentrated at each step.

The complexity of relationships in the ecosystem often causes a delay between pollution and the appearance of its consequences. Researchers have only recently discovered mercury concentrations in some Antarctic animals. These are believed to have resulted from the gold-mining practices of the California gold rush of 1849! Recent discoveries on the lasting effects of DDT in the ecosystem are probably only the tip of a noxious iceberg that will surface in the years to come. By the time we begin noticing the effects of the deterioration of the ozone layer surrounding the earth's atmosphere, there will probably be no way to remedy it.

These are but a tiny fraction of the number of examples that might be discussed in relation to pollution around the world today. Many excellent, recent books explore these matters in more detail (Helfrich 1970, Reinow 1967, Ehrlich 1971, Hardin 1969, Anderson 1970, Carson 1962, Landau and Rheingold 1971).

Sociology and the Environment

What has all this to do with sociology? Don't the problems discussed above all fall within the realm of other scientists? Aren't they problems to be worked out by physicists, chemists, and biologists? No.

The point of view that saw human beings as masters over nature has produced a myth that the technology that has created environmental problems will be sufficient to save us from those problems. Most physicists, chemists, and biologists do not agree with the myth. For example, Garrett Hardin (1968:1243), an eminent biologist, has defined the technical solution as: "one that requires change only in the techniques of the natural sciences, demanding little or nothing in the way of change in human values or ideas of morality." Hardin is clear that such technical solutions have limits, that they are not enough, no matter how tempting it is to think so. The concentration of people in cities even now taxes our technology, as is suggested in the box on page 468 "The Space Race in Urban America."

As we have seen throughout this chapter, our behavior as human beings, including our use of technology in our relationship to the ecosystem, is part of our values and ideas of morality. Those values and ideas, in turn, are a function of social agreements. We have already discussed the critical agreement regarding our mastery over nature. An equally critical issue may be seen in what Hardin calls the "tragedy of the commons."

Many years ago, the British "commons"—and, later, the American ones as well—were grassy areas owned by the public. The Boston Common is today a park, for example. In earlier times, however, the British and American commons were used primarily for the grazing of cattle privately owned by individual farmers.

Individual farmers eventually found it was in their *individual* interests to increase the sizes of their herds if possible. Since the grass was free, only a little more work resulted in considerably more milk and meat. As all the farmers increased their herds, though, the commons became overgrazed, and there wasn't enough food for any of the cattle. Each individual, pursuing his or her self-interest, ultimately destroyed the commons for *all* individuals and for the society as a whole.

The conflict between individual and societal advantage is one of the most persistent dilemmas of social life. It should be made clear that the individual pursuit of individual self-interest does, in fact, work to the individual's advantage for at least a time, as was the case with the commons. Ultimately, however, it can be *self*-defeating as well as work a hardship on all other members of the society.

Social agreements are what prevent most people from killing each other in the streets. The desires of individuals are fettered in the interests of the common good. Social agreements are what keep most people from stealing what they want from others. While technological advances—such as the Meadows' computer-simulation techniques—will assist in solving the problems of pollution and re-source depletion, they clearly will not be enough (any more than the development of effective birth control techniques has been enough to halt population growth). The ultimate solution to environmental problems—like the problems of war, prejudice, and crime—rests with human behavior and the agreements that shape it. If sociologists are not able to understand the operation of those agreements, nobody will.

Sociologists will have to take the lead in the restructuring of human beliefs, values, and norms

---

The Space Race in Urban America

In 1970, there were about 10 acres of land in the United States per American, but what does that mean? Is 10 acres a little or a lot? Should we say "only" 10 acres or "fully" 10 acres? The issue is a complex one.

To begin, it is unrealistic to imagine the American population spread evenly across the nation, each of us with his or her own private 10 acres. This would necessitate some living in the middle of the desert, some atop mountains, and others on glaciers in Alaska. Not all our land area is readily inhabitable by people.

An indication of the even habitability of the American landscape may be found by looking at where people *do* live. Most of us live together in dense, urban areas. Seventy-three percent of us, in fact, live on less than two percent of the nation's land area—about the size of Florida.

This does not mean, of course, that only our current urban areas are inhabitable by large numbers of people. Even granting that many areas are virtually uninhabitable, there is still plenty of space left for far greater numbers of people—especially if they were to reside in new urban areas. But is that really the case? Is there really room for many more?

The problem involved in the relationship between space and people is not one of living space alone. It involves the heavy taxing of natural re-sources and other environmental matters. Land is needed for growing food, for lumber, and for mining. Transportation and other public facilities use up land area. Many argue that recreational land is a necessity rather than a luxury. Added population places an increased burden on these other support functions of land, all the while using up part of that land for housing.

In some ways, cities represent an efficient use of land, in that the dense urban concentrations house large numbers of people on relatively little land. Public transportation facilities use less land per capita than interstate highway systems connecting small, scattered settlements. Yet, urban concentration is not a sufficient answer in the long run.

Water supplies in southern Florida and elsewhere are seen as dangerously low. Pollution levels in southern California are viewed as detrimental to health. By 1980, it is estimated that solid-waste disposal will average between 25 and 30 tons per American a year, and experts still do not know how to deal with this volume of waste. These problems, and countless more like them, will tax our ecosystem regardless of whether people are concentrated in cities or spread across rural areas.

How would you suggest that we begin solving the kinds of problems just discussed? How do you feel about "your" 10 acres: Is it a little or a lot?

and in the creation of institutions that support the ecosystem rather than undermine it. As Ehrlich and Ehrlich (1972:347–48) indicate*:

> Our problems cannot be solved by destroying our existing institutions, however; we do not have the time or the wisdom to dismantle them and put them back together again in better ways. But these institutions must be successfully altered—and soon—or they and we will not survive. Whether significant changes in attitudes and institutions can occur fast enough to affect mankind's destiny is an open question.

In the concluding chapter of this book, I'll discuss the role of sociologists in mass society. It is worth noting here that individual sociologists have often been in the forefront of social movements. They have been among the most active participants in movements relating to labor organization, civil rights, peace and war, and the liberation of women. Many are actively at work on the problems of the environment today. Many more will be active in the future.

Summary

This chapter began with a discussion of three different points of view that people have had regarding the relationship between human beings and the physical environment: (1) subjugation by nature, (2) harmony with nature, and (3) mastery over nature. Following that discussion, we examined the modern, ecosystemic view suggested by ecological scientists, a view strikingly similar to that of many ancient, Eastern religions. We are a part of nature and must exist in harmony with it and its other components.

Technology, we saw, represents the most extensive application of the view that we can master nature. We reviewed a few of the significant technological advances that have been made in the areas of food production, medicine, industry, and transportation. At

*From *Population, Resources, Environment: Issues in Human Ecology*, 2nd ed., by Paul R. Ehrlich and Anne H. Ehrlich, copyright 1972 by W. H. Freeman and Company. Reprinted by permission.

the same time, we noted how social relations have been modified in many, many ways by those technological developments.

Urbanization is one of the clearest and most far-reaching consequences of technology and the population growth that has accompanied it. The "Chicago school" was a group of sociologists who, during the 1920s and 1930s, developed the notion of "human ecology" and applied it to an understanding of the ways in which cities are formed and grow.

Some of the consequences of technology in the ecosytem are clear today; others are only becoming clear. Many of the earth's life-support elements—air, water, soil—have been severely damaged by the fruits of technological "progress" and urbanization. Radical changes are needed in social agreements if basic biological processes are to continue.

This has been a rather negativistic chapter. If the term "dismal science" had not already been assigned, with justification perhaps, to economics, it would surely be attached to the science of ecology. An empirical examination of current ecosystemic trends and our role in those trends cannot produce any but dismal results.

It is by now evident that technology will not provide sufficient solutions to the various problems that make ecology such a dismal field of study. It has been evident throughout the chapter that many ecosystemic problems arise directly out of agreed-on patterns of social behavior. Other agreements prevent us from taking advantage of technological solutions. There is every reason to conclude that sociology will play an increasingly important part in the solution to environmental problems.

Suggested Readings

DeBell, Garrett, Ed.
1970 *The Environmental Handbook.* New York: Ballantine.
As environmental consciousness has increased in America and elsewhere, many people have expressed frustration over the complexity of the problems involved. Ecosystems are complicated and not fully

understood by anyone. This book, prepared in connection with the April 22, 1970, national teach-in on the environment, provides some practical guides. The several articles describe various aspects of our environmental problems and suggest how *you* can work on solving those problems—both in your day-to-day behavior and in an attempt to bring about social change.

Greer, Scott
1966   *Urban Renewal and American Cities.* Indianapolis, Ind.: Bobbs-Merrill.
The renewal of the nation's decaying cities has seemed like a good idea in general, but it has often produced disasters in practice. Established social networks are destroyed as freeways cut through neighborhoods. Poor people are evicted from substandard homes and are unable to afford the modern housing built in their place. Greer offers data and a sociological point of view on understanding the problem.

Meadows, Donnella et al.
1972   *The Limits to Growth.* New York: Universe.
Like Ehrlich's *Population Bomb,* this is one of the most powerful influences in the growing environmental concern of the present day. Utilizing computer-simulation techniques, the researchers have traced out the likely implications of recent patterns of population growth, resource utilization, and pollution. Their main conclusion is contained in the title. We can't continue into the future without radically modifying some past patterns of behavior.

Vayda, Andrew, Ed.
1969   *Environment and Cultural Behavior.* Garden City, N.Y.: Natural History Press.
This collection of ethnographic reports gives an excellent picture of cross-cultural variations in human responses to the natural environment. You'll see many of the ways preliterate societies have created social patterns that permit them to live in harmony with the rest of the ecosystem.

Episode Seventeen

Gabe nudged Ann Sullivan toward a sundries counter in the main terminal of the Phoenix airport. "Let's take a look at how the *Phoenix Herald* is reporting the conference vote yesterday," Gabriel said, plunking down a ten-dollar bill on the counter.

"I'm so tired," Ann smiled apologetically, "I don't even think I care."

Gabe gazed at his companion, then returned his attention to the counter clerk. "And give me a jar of those protein capsules," he said.

Gabriel pocketed his change, then handed the vial of tiny pills to Ann.

"What's this for?" she asked.

"Protein," Gabe said, matter-of-factly. "Take one. I found I needed them once in a while in Chicago. I took them all through the trial. You won't feel so tired."

"Thank you," Ann said simply. "Thank you." She put the vial of pills into her shoulder bag.

Daniel approached. "Where have you two been?" he demanded. "I've got the luggage. Alexander's here to take us home. Secret Service will escort us to the gates."

Daniel led Sullivan and Knapp to the waiting limousine.

"You three are heroes at home," Alexander announced, turning his vehicle to exit the airport. "We've got a big welcome planned. The band's been practicing all night long."

Gabriel sat quietly, remembering the time he had returned only to be attacked by Larry Jones's thugs. "Things change," he said finally.

"They're already talking about hiring outsiders at S.T.I. someday. The only thing that holds back expansion is our small labor force."

"Who's talking about that?" snapped Daniel.

"Mostly Jacob. He thinks it would be a good idea. Now that some of the greatest scientists in the world have defined us as human, he says, maybe outsiders will begin to stop threatening us."

The limousine wound its way up an entrance ramp to a divided highway. Inconspicuously Ann Sullivan placed a protein capsule upon her tongue and, working her cheeks to salivate, swallowed the energy source without water.

"The Elders won't be at the gates to meet us," Alexander informed his passengers later. "Ruth is in the hospital. The physicians say it could be serious."

"How serious?" asked Ann, surprised.

"Pretty serious," Alexander responded in his typical cursory manner.

"How is Michael taking it?" Gabriel inquired.

"Not well. He's doing almost nothing. Just sits in the parlor. Doesn't seem to care about much of anything now." Alexander paused. "But he does want to see you all today."

"When did Ruth become ill?" questioned Daniel.

"The morning after you left. I took her to the hospital that afternoon. She ordered that no one try to get a message to you. She wanted you to be able to concentrate on your work."

When the limousine passed the guard shelter and entered Adamsville, the group was met with band music and wild cheering. Greens of various shades spilled into the road both ahead and behind the advancing automobile. "Welcome, welcome," the throng chanted even above the blare of the band. "We're human!" many called.

Once in front of Elderhome Gabe, Ann, and Daniel were escorted up the front steps. But as the three moved to enter Elderhome, the spectacular celebration suddenly became a debacle. "Is Sullivan to come in too?" Gabriel overheard Daniel challenge Alexander.

Momentarily confused by Dan's question, Alexander hesitated. Before he opened his lips to respond, Gabriel had acted.

"Of course Ann's coming in with us," Knapp shouted while Adamsville watched in apprehension.

"She's a milk-white," Dan breathed from between clenched teeth.

At that moment Jacob appeared. "Welcome back, Gabe," he said calmly, extending his hand in an attempt to appease his long-time friend. "It's really very good to have you all home safely."

"What's going on here?" Gabriel demanded, still angry.

"Nothing. It's nothing. Ann can go in. After all," Jacob looked toward Daniel, "she's a hero."

Gabriel stared defiantly at Jacob. "That's not good enough," he shouted for all to hear. The crowd was silent with anticipation. "That's just not good enough anymore! Ann Sullivan goes in because she's green, because she lives here in Adamsville, because she's a good citizen of this community—or neither of us go in. She doesn't enter Elderhome as an exception to any rule about dull greens and their spiritual or genetic deficiences. She enters as a valleyite—healthy and proud."

His words still resounding in the ears of his listeners, Gabriel stormed from Elderhome's front steps. Ann Sullivan, along with other dull greens, followed. That afternoon Gabe moved his belongings to an apartment in the valley.

Once the dissenters had departed, the crowd stood dumbfounded. The band director motioned quickly and again music played. Jacob led the throng across the street to the park where he urged they rest and take a quiet light-break "in thankful meditation for our victory."

Meanwhile Michael-the-Elder remained inside his home, wondering what was to become of Adamsville—and of his sister, Ruth. Daniel slumped into Sunlight Liquidhouse and ordered a glass of water. He would sit there brooding throughout the afternoon.

Three days later Ruth-the-Elder died. The morning of her burial Michael sent for Jacob. He directed that Larry Jones's shares of S.T.I. stock—since he had died intestate—be divided among Gabriel, Daniel, and Ann Sullivan in recognition for their accomplishments at the third conference. Then he signed his own and his sister's stock to Jacob. And he informed the younger man that, beginning the next day, it was to be Jacob who would govern Adamsville.

On November 29, 2027, in an elaborate ceremony Jacob was officially named "Successor Elder." During his speech which followed, he announced that S.T.I. would begin to plan for expansion. There would be diversification, including funding for genetic research on human mutations. Results from this kind of research would someday allow descendants of mutants to establish by computer the amounts of protein intake they individually required. "Technological knowledge such as this," Jacob promised, "can one day work to decrease both greens' and ungreens' fear of assimilation."

Gabriel Knapp was not to remain in Adamsville, however, to watch these planned technological changes become reality. "I think we should move down to Phoenix," he said one day in December to Ann Sullivan.

"Move?" she repeated.

"Yes. The whole lot of us. There are no services here for us. We have to go several miles to buy protein. We still stand huddled in frightened little groups near the edges of the crowd when anyone speaks from the platform. Jacob, in his fear of disturbing the remaining radical militarists, has not officially changed any of the rules that discriminate against us."

"Move?" Ann said again.

"Here you work as a guard," Gabriel pursued, "and I put in routine hours at S.T.I. In Phoenix we could at least try to find work we like."

He paused, trying to read the woman's thoughts.

"You wouldn't have to sneak your protein capsules for fear of ridicule in Phoenix," he said. "The whole group of us from the valley could go. We could find ourselves an area of the city we like and live there together."

"I have to think about it," Ann said.

The thinking and planning lasted several weeks. To fellow valleyites Gabriel argued that in Phoenix dull greens would spend most of their time in their own neighborhood, just as was true in Adamsville. But in the city valleyites would be virtually unrecognizable outside their own neighborhood. It was true that when ungreens recognized them as mutants, his people could expect to suffer from discrimination. But for the most part, valleyites would go unnoticed. "How many of you will go?" Jacob inquired of Gabriel during an official conference at Elderhome.

"Twenty-five. Maybe thirty," Gabe said.

"We need those people at S.T.I.," insisted Jacob.

"We need a larger place," Gabriel answered.

Questions

1. How did changes in the formal definition of greens give rise to new technology that promises to influence greens' lives still further?

2. If ungreens were hired to work in the S.T.I. factory, what consequences would that have for the institutionalized agreements of Adamsville? How might it affect religion, for example?

3. What established agreements among the greens are dysfunctional for economic expansion? What will happen to those agreements?

4. Why does living in Phoenix seem better to Gabe than remaining in Adamsville? What sociological concepts does this decision of Gabe's point out?

5. Where will the decision that greens are human have its greatest impact: in Adamsville or in the rest of American society?

18

Communication in Mass Society

Wilbur Schramm, a pioneer in the sociology of **communication,** describes his subject as follows:

> *Communication* comes from the Latin *communis,* common. When we communicate we are trying to establish a "commonness" with someone. That is, we are trying to share information, an idea, or an attitude (1955:3).

At the microlevel of individuals, communication is a process through which one person's experience or point of view is transmitted to another person for the purpose of gaining agreement. Suppose, for example, that you find yourself feeling friendly toward a person you approach on the street. You may attempt to communicate that feeling to the other person by smiling and saying "hello" in a cheerful voice. The communication of your experience of friendliness is completed when the other person acknowledges the communication: agreeing that *you* feel friendly toward him or her. Typically, this will happen by means of the other person's smiling and saying "hello" back to you. Whenever this acknowledgment occurs, your experience of friendliness gains "reality" through agreement.

In Chapter 1 and throughout the book, I've stressed the extent to which our views of what's real in the world around us depend on the agreements we share with others. As the above example suggests, reality of our inner feelings also depends in large part on agreements. Imagine for a moment that the person you met on the street simply stared at you as though you were a stranger. What would happen to your feeling of friendliness then? It would probably disappear.

This chapter begins with a discussion of communication as a means for transmitting points of view and for creating agreements about reality. We'll look at the ways this occurs in the process of social interaction. For the most part, however, this chapter doesn't deal with the microlevel of face-to-face interaction.

The subject of this part of the book, Part Five, is mass society, and this chapter is mostly concerned with the nature of communication on a large scale. An important part of communication in a mass society occurs outside the face-to-face sharing of points of view. Many of our agreements about reality arise from a communication process in which some participants have considerably more influence than others. In large part, we'll be examining the role of the **mass media**—television, radio, and newspapers—in the creation of social reality.

It is often said that "knowledge is power," meaning that learning what's true in the world around you gives you a special power. But think of the power you'd have if you were the *source* of other people's knowledge about the world. Think how many people have this power. As we've seen throughout this book, most of what you've learned about the world originated in other people's experiences and their subsequent communications to you. You've learned about the moon, the American Revolution, and countless other subjects without personally experiencing any of them. Other people created what you learned.

We're going to examine a number of the processes through which people create and communicate views of reality: rumors, propaganda, advertising, and mass-media news reporting. Yes, we'll see that even the 6 P.M. news and your daily newspaper are *creating* what's happening, not just reporting it. We'll see that this issue has both a cynical and a fatalistic side to it. It's possible to view the mass-media creation of news as a conscious activity, reflecting individual and organizational biases, akin to propaganda. At the same time, however, it will become clear that the mass media have no choice but to create the news. The sheer volume of information that might be reported simply must be edited.

Since this book has focused so much on the forces acting on people in society—determining what they think, feel, and do—I think it's appropriate to end this chapter with an examination of **public opinion.** In many ways, public opinion is the outcome of all the communications being transmitted throughout mass society—all the rumors, propaganda, face-to-face interactions, and news reports—as filtered through the individual members of the society. We'll look at some of the things sociologists have learned about public opinion and how it forms. We'll also look at the ways sociologists and others measure public opinion.

To begin, then, let's take a closer look at communication as an interpersonal process. This will give us a basis for seeing how communication occurs on a large scale in mass society.

The Nature of Communication

From a physiological point of view, action is impossible without communication. You can't pick up a coffee cup and take a sip without the transmission of signals from your brain to your hand and arm, followed by "feedback" signals, augmented by communications from your eyes, lips, and tongue. Your body is continually filled with electrical communications—far more sophisticated than the most extreme advances of our electronic technology.

Similarly, "inter"action is impossible without communications. Indeed, you could usefully adopt the point of view that interaction is merely a form of communication. Even in a fistfight, throwing a punch at your opponent is a way of communicating your intention to dominate that person. The purpose of that communication, moreover, is to gain agreement on your dominance.

Gently nibbling someone's earlobe is a way of communicating your feeling of love or affection and an attempt to gain agreement on that feeling. (More vigorous nibbling might communicate feelings of cannibalism, so be gentle.)

Communication, then, begins with inner feelings and is an attempt to create an external reality for those feelings through agreement. Communication itself, moreover, depends on agreement. Gestures, words, and acts must have agreed-on meanings if they are to serve the purpose of communicating feelings and points of view. If there were no agreement linking friendliness with turning up the corners of your mouth and twinkling your eyes, smiling would be useless in promoting it. People would just think you had something wrong with your face, and your inner feeling of friendliness would gain no external reality.

Not all communication occurs face-to-face, of course. Increasingly with technological advances, interpersonal communication has taken place over great distances. First postal services, then telegraph and telephone have made it possible for individuals to communicate with each other across thousands of miles. While these methods have facilitated communication, they have also complicated it by removing the nonverbal cues to meaning, such as facial expressions.

Communication over great distances did not begin with the pony express. Drums and smoke signals have served this function since early in human history. And scientists are now taking increased interest in the claims of telepathic communication among some primitive people. In 1946 Jean Cocteau, the French writer, told of an African woman in an "uncivilized" tribe who was observed to go under

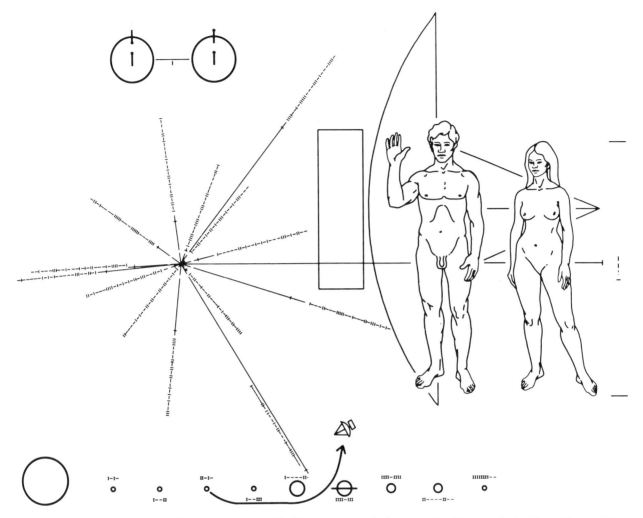

Figure 18•1   An attempt at interstellar communication. The Pioneer *spacecraft plaque carries pictures and scientific notations, which are intended to transcend culture-based communication systems.*

a "magic" tree and speak a message intended for her husband, several hundred miles away. Asked by the Western observer why she had done that, the woman replied, "Because I am poor. If I were rich I should have the telephone" (Cited in Pauwels and Bergier 1968:167).

Communicating across cultures is an especially difficult task since the sender and the receiver may use different agreed-on systems of meaning. A Tibetan sticks out his or her tongue as a form of greeting; the same gesture communicates contempt in the West. Try to imagine how you would communicate with intelligent life forms on other planets in the universe. Figure 18•1 shows the plaque attached to America's *Pioneer* spacecraft in an attempt to inform the scientifically inclined of other worlds where the spacecraft came from.

Communication, to review, is a process in which a sender attempts to gain agreement on his or her feelings and points of view by recreating them in a receiver. You communicate your anger, for example, by recreating the sense of anger in another person.

You needn't make the other person angry. Recreating the sense of anger lends reality to your feeling.

Thus far, I've been talking solely about communication between individuals. One person sends a communication and another receives it. A great deal of communication—especially in mass societies—is of a different sort. A message may be sent with the intention that it will be received by many people. The term "mass media" is commonly associated with this form of communication. Let's turn to that now.

The Mass Media

Charles Wright has defined "mass communication" in terms of its audience, the communication experience, and the communicator, thereby distinguishing mass communication from, say, face-to-face conversations among individuals.

1. *Audience.* Mass communication is directed toward a relatively large, heterogeneous, and anonymous audience.

2. *Experience.* Mass communication may be characterized as public, rapid, and transient.

3. *Communicator.* Mass communication is organized communication. Unlike the lone artist or writer, the "communicator" in mass media works through a complex organization embodying an extensive division of labor and an accompanying degree of expense (1975:5,6,7).

Mass communication is relatively recent in human history. It is customarily traced to Gutenberg's invention of movable type some 500 years ago, which made possible the mass production of lengthy written works such as books.

Gutenberg's printing press could produce around 600 pages a day, a marked improvement over the slow and laborious process of hand lettering. No substantial improvements were made for another 350 years, until the Industrial Revolution mechanized printing as it had manufacturing. Steam power and subsequent innovations made it possible in the 1870s to print 18,000 newspapers in an hour (Emery et al. 1973).

The development of mass communications depended only in part on the ability to print communications. It also depended on the ability to read. When Gutenberg published the Bible, only a tiny fraction of the world's population could read. The worldwide literacy rate has increased continuously since then, and it is currently estimated that around half the world's population is literate. There are extreme variations from society to society, however, and in some—such as the United States and Japan—literacy is nearly universal.

Unlike direct, face-to-face communication, mass communication is typically a one-way process. The receivers of mass-media communications are, for the most part, unable either to acknowledge receipt of a message or to respond with messages of their own. Interactive communications are largely impossible, which produces frustrations on both ends of the mass-communication process.

A good deal has been said about the frustrations of consumers of mass media. When you hear a point of view you disagree with, you are nearly precluded from responding to it. The communicators are also frustrated because they aren't immediately acknowledged. There is the feeling of emptiness experienced by the radio announcer, for example, whose rip-roaring joke is met with the unamused silence of the broadcast booth. Indeed, the media try to reduce the artificiality and strangeness of unacknowledged communications by using television "laugh tracks" and by filming shows before live audiences.

The speaker at a large political rally has the advantage of a microphone. The football-team cheerleader has the advantage of a megaphone. Still their audiences can—because of their physical presence—acknowledge and respond to communications. They can be supportive or opposing. Even their silence communicates. The television news announcer, in contrast, addresses tens of millions of receivers with no immediate feedback. Let's look a little more closely at the no-feedback form of communication in mass society. We'll begin with the printed media and move to the electronic media.

Printed Matter

In newspapers, magazines, and books, writers—through editors, perhaps—seek to create verbal images. Schramm (1955:4) describes the process as one that involves the encoding of messages by the sender. "That is, he takes the information or feeling he wants to share and puts it into a form that can be transmitted. The 'pictures in our heads' can't be transmitted until they are coded."

I have already commented on the beginnings of mass printing as a means of encoding and transmitting messages. Books continue to be the most durable printed verbal communications, and the volume of book production has grown immensely since the time of Gutenberg. In the United States alone, each year sees the publication of some 38,000 books (about one-third of these being new editions of previously published books) and book sales of around 2.5 billion copies. Educational textbooks at all levels of instruction account for about a third of the dollar sales (Emery et al. 1973). Books are not the most voluminous print medium, however.

The first European newspapers appeared shortly after the invention of movable type, and many of the familiar features of modern newspapers appeared in Germany during the 1600s (DeFleur 1966). In America, newspapers began during the colonial period, but it was not until the 1830s and 1840s that the so-called penny press created mass consumption of daily newspapers.

The growth in newspaper circulation in America presents an interesting pattern. As you'd expect, circulation has grown steadily over the years: from a daily circulation of 758,000 in 1850 (U.S. Bureau of the Census 1960:500) to 61,877,000 in 1974 (U.S. Bureau of the Census 1975a:523). In terms of circulation per household, however, the trend has been curvilinear. Newspaper circulation in 1850 amounted to .21 copies per household, a figure that rose to 1.38 per household in 1919, a peak not subsequently matched (DeFleur 1966). In 1973, newspaper circulation in America was .89 copies per household (U.S. Bureau of the Census 1975a:40, 523). This relative decline in newspaper circulation coincided with the arrival first of radio and then television.

Magazines and other periodicals such as academic and scientific journals are another form of printed mass media that have appeared in the relatively recent past. Magazines lie between books and newspapers in permanence and frequency of publication, and they cover a variety of topics: news, instruction, entertainment, opinion. I'll have more to say about the role of magazines and other printed media in society later in this chapter.

Radio

Unlike the telephone and telegraph, which are characterized by person-to-person communication, radio may be regarded as the first electronic *mass* medium—it beams its messages to anyone who cares to receive them.

The basic radio technology was developed during the later part of the nineteenth century. Guglielmo Marconi's transmission of "wireless" telegraph messages set the stage for the transmission of voice and music. This new technology might never have formed a new mass medium except for the brainstorm of a young engineer, David Sarnoff. In 1916, Sarnoff wrote to his superiors at the American Marconi Company:

> I have in mind a plan of development which would make radio a "household utility" in the same sense as the piano or phonograph. The idea is to bring music into the house by wireless. . . .
>
> The same principle can be extended to numerous other fields as, for example, receiving lectures at home which can be made perfectly audible; also events of national importance can be simultaneously announced and received. Baseball scores can be transmitted in the air by the use of [a transmitter] installed at the Polo Grounds (Quoted in DeFleur 1966:56).

Sarnoff's plan for financing radio assumed that broadcasters would be the ones selling radio receivers. In 1920, Frank Conrad of Westinghouse began broadcasting from a transmitter in his garage, his family assisting him in playing records on the family Victrola. Conrad's signal was picked up mostly by people who had built amateur receivers of their own. He was an immediate success. Conrad's audience increased rapidly, and he was soon swamped with requests for favorite songs. The box "Popular Music and Popular Money" on page 480 offers an interesting contrast to Frank Conrad's undertaking.

Popular Music and Popular Money

Richard Peterson and David Berger took a look at the issue of variety and diversity in the popular music industry from 1948 to 1973 and found that "popular tastes" are in large part controlled by record companies.

In the beginning there was moon and June, Doris Day, Vaughn Monroe, Tony Bennett, and four companies that dominated the record field—RCA Victor, Columbia, Decca, and Capitol. They produced around 80 percent of the hit tunes that made the weekly list of the Top 10 best-selling records. How? By controlling or being linked to the movie industry and Broadway shows where musicals defined the hit tunes, the network variety shows, and recorded music programs. With these outlets in their hands, companies could also control the writers, composers, and performers. If an independent company produced a hit song, the four big companies produced "cover" records. They rushed out their own (often sanitized) version of the tune and blanketed the independent. Long-playing records were cheap to produce (as little as from $200 to $300), and to manufacture and market them required only a few thousand dollars more. But to get air time, or exposure in musicals, or to prevent "covering" was very difficult. Homogeneity was the result. Competition among the big four was intense, but there was little incentive for innovation or diversity.

Starting about 1955 the number of radio sets increased by a third, largely due to cheap portable transistors. This increase provided small independent record producers with an outlet ignored by the giants, the local, non-network radio station, and an outlet that could be directed to groups with special musical tastes. The unsated demand for variety already was showing itself in the increase in live performances of jazz, rhythm and blues, country and western, gospel, folk, and rock'n' roll music. Record sales shot up; cover renditions disappeared; and a single Bing Crosby record did not stay in the Top 10 for months. New recording companies, talent scouts, and distributors appeared. The shock to established lyric formulas "where sexual references are allegorical and social problems are unknown" was profound, as was the shock to the profits of the major companies and the major stars.

The corporate giants were down, but hardly out. RCA got Presley from the independents, and in the early 1960s, the majors began picking distinctive new talent, such as the Beach Boys and Dylan. From about 1964 to 1969 a second generation of non-giant rock innovators reached the market, with more diversity in lyrics and styles. But the giants were ready. By buying up labels and artists and diversifying within themselves, the four leading majors (in 1973, Columbia, Warner Brothers, Capitol, and the new entry, Motown) achieved a concentration of power approaching that of 1948. They were ready to capitalize on "the vagaries of public tastes" as the president of Columbia put it, by having the resources to cover each fad. We are not back to the bland sameness of the 1930s and 1940s, but the top hits now stay there for weeks rather than days, there are fewer companies that make the Top 10; there are fewer performers who make the Top 10, and they tend to be established ones working for the majors.

What did it? Organization and control of the "factors of production" as the economists call them—gaining control over artistic creation, merchandising, and distribution. With these, the issue of content, or tastes, becomes secondary, and the diversity of styles, reflecting diverse publics, becomes a victim.

Do you agree with this assessment, or do you feel that listeners and record-buyers have more to say in the market?

Later in 1920, the Westinghouse Company, using a large transmitter in East Pittsburgh, established station KDKA to support their manufacture and sale of receivers. Radio as a mass medium then became very popular, as DeFleur (1966:59) reports:

By 1922, the manufacture of home receivers was lagging hopelessly behind the receipt of orders. New

Modern communications techniques are a force for social change around the world. This African woman is in touch with a class of events that her parents would never have learned about in their lifetimes. (Guy Le Querrec, VIVA)

stations were being built at a staggering pace. In the last half of 1921 licenses were issued for thirty-two new stations, but in the first half of 1922, this number had risen to 254!

Radio had become a central medium for the transmission of information and entertainment. Family social life became centered around the "music box." Americans from Maine to California could listen to the same national events as they occurred. Radio enhanced the stature of political and cultural heroes and created many of its own.

Today, radio is a nearly universal fact of American life. In 1974, Americans purchased over 30 million radios, almost two-thirds of them portables,

and it has been estimated that 99.9 percent of American homes have at least one radio (U.S. Bureau of the Census 1975a:723, 766).

Although Americans own nearly half the world's three-quarters of a billion radios, it is an important mass medium in many societies (Emery et al. 1973).

Film

Of the four media discussed in this section, film has the least immediacy. Films can require several years to produce, and then they must be distributed for viewing. Immediacy is often irrelevant, however, and film is a dramatic and very powerful mass medium in America and elsewhere.

Practical film technology has a longer "pre-history" than radio, but it, like radio, was developed in the late nineteenth century. Moving through silent films, talkies, technicolor, drive-ins, 3-D, and the wide screen, the film as a mass medium reached a peak in America during the 1940s. It has declined in popularity somewhat since then, though the 1970s have seen a slight upsurge. Still, 1949 remains the "top" year for American film in at least two respects. Tickets sold each week numbered 90 million, and over 400 new films were released.

Newspapers and radio have offered both information and entertainment, but film has been predominantly, though not exclusively, addressed to entertainment. As we will see shortly, entertainment offers a picture of reality that shapes people's points of view about life.

Television

Combining the visual appeal of film with the immediacy of radio, television is, in many respects, the most important mass medium in America today. It started as a vehicle for mass communication on the eve of World War II. It grew little during the war, but its use skyrocketed subsequently. The number of television sets in America rose from some 8,000 in 1946 to 110 million in 1973 (U.S. Bureau of the Census 1960:491, 1975a:859). In 1974, 99.9 percent of American households with electrical power had television sets; 71.5 percent had color televisions (U.S. Bureau of the Census 1975a:723).

As with radio, the United States has more than its share of the world's television sets: about one-third of the quarter billion in use around the globe (U.S. Bureau of the Census 1975a:859). The establishment of television broadcasting stations and the proliferation of private receivers is a mark of development throughout the world today.

Mass-Media Content

Harold Lasswell (1948), a political scientist long involved in the study of communication, has suggested that the mass media serve three primary functions for society: (1) a "surveillance," or news, function by providing information about events, (2) a "correlation," or editorial, function by interpreting the significance or implications of that information, and (3) the function of "transmitting" a cultural heritage from one generation to another.

To Lasswell's list, sociologist Charles Wright (1975) adds a fourth: entertainment. Commentators on this last function are divided in their assessments, regarding the entertainment provided as ranging from culturally enriching to escapist and worse.

Each medium discussed fulfills each of the four functions. Newspapers have from the start provided more than the news. DeFleur (1966:10) reports that the early seventeenth-century German newspapers had "many of the features of the modern newspaper, such as the editorials, sports articles, illustrations, political columns, and even comics." During the course of newspaper history, different periods and papers have emphasized one or another of these types of content, but the overall tendency has been to cover them all.

Radio began as an entertainment medium, but its potential was far different, as anticipated in Sarnoff's historic memo (quoted earlier). Its subsequent development in America and elsewhere has more than realized that anticipated potential. Today, some stations broadcast only news and editorial opinion, but all stations broadcast some.

Films, throughout their history, have strongly emphasized entertainment but not exclusively. A few decades ago, newsreels like *The March of Time* provided American moviegoers with an important source of news, a delayed but visual forerunner to the evening news on TV. Thousands of documentary films have informed people of current and recent events, and both government and commercial propaganda films offer editorial interpretation. D. W. Griffith's *Birth of a Nation*, an early classic in American filmmaking, depicted the birth and spread of the Ku Klux Klan in a favorable light, spurring a controversy that even now periodically renews itself.

Television, the newest mass medium, has been especially broad in its content. Information is offered on news programs, in documentary films, and on hundreds of "educational" stations. Editorial opinions are sometimes expressed by station personnel in connection with news broadcasts and special programs. Formats—such as panel discussions—seek to encompass divergent points of view. Many have suggested that the manner in which "news" is selected and presented has an inevitable editorial aspect in television as in other media, and we'll return to this issue shortly. The entertainment aspect of television requires no documentation.

Finally, all the media serve the function of cultural transmission. Each provides a record of the events of human social epochs. Today's archaeologists dig and scratch for clues to the social life of ancient civilizations; the archaeologists and historians of the thirtieth century, say, will find themselves awash in a sea of data describing the life and times of the twentieth century.

Finance and Control

The financing of films and books is relatively direct and logical. Individuals wishing to view or read them pay amounts sufficient to cover the costs of producing them, at least within a private-enterprise economy. Filmmakers and publishers cannot know in advance, however, how well specific films and books will be received, so they lose money on some and make money on others.

David Sarnoff envisioned an equally rational system of finance for radio. The money paid to manufacturers would be used to provide programming. As the costs of broadcasting increased during the mid-1920s, however, a variety of financing plans were considered. Listeners were asked to contribute funds voluntarily. They didn't. Sarnoff suggested that philanthropists might endow radio stations as they had endowed libraries. They didn't. Some felt those owning radio receivers ought to be taxed. They weren't.

The solution to this financial dilemma had begun evolving in 1922, when station WEAF permitted a Long Island realtor to talk about available property *for a fee.* Companies next began sponsoring entertainment shows. The snowball had begun to roll, despite the protests of Secretary of Commerce Herbert Hoover that "it is inconceivable that we should allow so great a possibility for service, for news, for entertainment, and for vital commercial purposes to be drowned in advertising chatter" (Quoted in Goldsmith and Lescarboura 1930:279). Radio had discovered the source of support that newspapers had known about for a long time. Television made the same discovery.

The extent of advertising on radio and television in America today is simply staggering. In 1974, over 4 billion dollars was spent on television advertising; another billion and a half was spent on radio. Newspaper advertising, nonetheless, was greater than television and radio combined: almost 8 billion dollars. Another billion and a half was spent on magazine advertising. Nearly two-thirds of the 26 billion dollars spent on advertising in 1973 was channeled through these four media (U.S. Bureau of the Census 1975a:791).

Advertising is not the only source of broadcasting's financial support in the United States. Educational radio and television stations are supported by government and foundation grants and in some cases by "subscriptions." A growing number of cable TV stations (in addition to providing better reception of commercial broadcasts) offer programming of their own.

Elsewhere, such as in the U.S.S.R. and China, radio and television are government activities. England's BBC and Japan's NHK are examples of government-sanctioned, noncommercial networks financed as public corporations through license fees.

The airwaves over which broadcast signals are relayed are an environmental resource, though a strange one: They are undiminished by use. Today's broadcast in no way diminishes the possibility of broadcasting something different tomorrow. Despite this unique characteristic, however, the airwaves are limited, at least in our current technology. Only a limited number of messages can be broadcast at any one time.

This finiteness of the airwaves—coupled with the undeniable power inherent in mass communication—has produced an agreement shared across most societies, the agreement that the airwaves are public property. It is generally agreed that they ought to be used in the "public interest." In some societies, such as the U.S.S.R. and China, use of the airwaves is limited to government. In others, like the United States, private use of the airwaves is regulated by government. The Federal Communications Commission in this country, for example, establishes guidelines for broadcasters' activities, suggesting

Figure 18•2 Some of the people who brought you Society by Agreement. *Courtesy of Dan Whiteman.*

what should and should not be broadcast. It also specifies—through licensing—who may broadcast at all. In practice, it should be noted, the FCC has seldom made use of its power against broadcasters.

The Structure of Mass Media

Mass-media communication is a function of organizations. Even when the apparent initiator of a communication is a single person, the actual transmission involves a team of specialists most of whom are unknown to the recipient of the message.

Television news broadcasts involve producers, editors, reporters, photographers, secretaries, office managers, salespersons, camera operators, electronic technicians, carpenters, custodians, and many others —including the person you see on your television screen. Newspaper teams are equally complex, as are those who facilitate radio, films, and other mass media.

Book publishing is no different. While one or a few authors write the manuscript that ultimately reaches you as a book, that's only the tip of the iceberg. Figure 18•2 describes *some* of the other people who were involved in producing *Society by Agreement*.

Exposure to Mass Media

Considerable research has been done on the extent to which people expose themselves to the mass media—particularly in America. In part, such research has had a direct, commercial purpose. Those wishing to advertise through the mass media wish to know about how many people their advertisements will actually reach. At the same time, sociologists and others have studied this matter in the interest of understanding the flow of communication in a mass society such as ours.

Throughout this section, I've presented data on exposure to the mass media in terms of the numbers of radios, television sets, and newspapers that people buy. As regards the use of these, the best data available relate to television. Schramm and Alexander (1975:29) have summarized some of the recent television data: "According to the Nielsen Television Index, during the measurement period ending in March of 1972 the average American home used its

television receiver forty-two hours and fourteen minutes a week, or just over six hours a day."

An analysis of *who* is watching shows produces various results over the course of the day. The daytime audience is made up predominantly of women and children; the whole family watches during "prime time" (3 P.M. to 10 P.M.). As a national profile, Schramm and Alexander (1975:30) indicate, "In ten representative homes, we should expect in prime evening time to find about six sets in use, about thirteen people viewing, of whom four would be men, five women, one or two teen-agers, and perhaps two or three children."

Data are harder to come by for radio exposure, though it is usually estimated to be about half as many hours as television. More *people* are likely to listen to the radio in a given day or week, even though more *time* is spent with television (Schramm and Alexander 1975).

Why do sociologists care about exposure to the mass media? The answer to this question involves far more than the desire to know how people spend their time. The mass media, because they communicate messages to so many people, are an important source of agreements in mass society. To the extent that people reify the messages received from television, radio, newspapers, and so forth, the media become a source of reality. You might say that the mass media are in the business of creating reality.

The Creation of Agreement Reality

Recall from Chapter 1 that what we regard as "reality" is actually a function of agreements that we have with one another, agreements that take the form of beliefs, values, and norms. Such agreements take on the appearance of "reality" through reification. Reification, moreover, is a function of our awareness of the extent of agreement. If you learn that just about everyone around you agrees that the Oakland Raiders are a better football team than the San Francisco Forty-Niners, you are likely to believe that it's "really true." Finally, the awareness of agreement is a function of communication. We discover that our points of view agree by communicating them.

The mass media have a special power for creating the appearance of agreement because they communicate the same point of view to millions of people at the same time. They have the capacity to plant the same point of view in millions of individuals who may then discover agreements among themselves. This potential has not escaped the attention of those people who have an interest in consciously creating reality.

Propaganda

Social scientific interest in propaganda has probably never been higher than it was during World War II. Both sides were interested in using and combating it. Hitler likened it to the use of artillery in preparation for an attack, saying "Our strategy is to destroy the enemy from within, to conquer him through himself" (Quoted in Bruner 1954:492).

Hitler and his minister of propaganda, Joseph Goebbels, operated on the principle of the "big lie": People would believe anything that was repeated often enough. They used this principle to create unity and solidarity within Germany and to create divisions among people elsewhere. In large part, the Jews were the focus of the Nazi "big lie." The German people were told repeatedly that Jews were traitors to the fatherland, that they had been responsible for Germany's defeat in World War I, and that their greed had produced the economic troubles that followed the war. All "good and true" Germans were urged to unite in support of the fatherland and in opposition to the Jews.

Beaming the same message abroad, they sought to turn gentiles against Jews in America, Britain, and elsewhere. They sought to pit workers against "Wall Street" and to create national divisions and hatred among the Allies. Americans were told they were being dragged into the war by British trickery and treachery.

Propaganda is not limited, of course, to wartime politics. Quite possibly, it is inherent in all politics, domestic or international, in peace or war. Those who seek to gain and hold power do so, at least in part, by creating a view of reality that is favorable to their holding of power and unfavorable to their opponents' gaining power. This is clearly the case in those nations whose governments totally control the mass media.

In America, political campaigns provide a clear example of the political use of propaganda, typically called "public relations." Steven Chaffee and Michael Petrick (1975) report that the total cost of the 1972 political campaigns was around 400 million dollars, with a fourth of that being spent on the presidential campaigns.

Political candidates are now "packaged" and "sold" in the same fashion as drugs, detergents, and dog food. Most campaigners consider a candidate's "image" to be far more important than political philosophy or points of view on specific issues (see, for example, Schwartz 1974).

Commercial advertising is another form of propaganda, one that is deeply embedded in the mass media. It offers additional views on reality. Commercials tell us that we will live richer, fuller, more satisfying lives if we have clean shirt collars, don't sweat, and avoid bad breath. They tell us that it is somehow possible for clothing to be whiter than white. They assure us that brand X is better, faster, more effective, longer lasting, softer, stronger, and better smelling than brand Y.

The points of view that commercials put forward often disagree with those suggested by logic and scientific examination. In recent years, government agencies such as the Federal Trade Commission and the Food and Drug Administration have begun crack-

ing down on the more outrageous claims made by advertisers, and it seems likely that further control will be exercised in the future. In part, the growing concern over advertising excesses stems from the tendency of children to reify what they see on television.

Commercial advertising creates "reality" in many subtler ways than simple product propaganda. It implies values, for example. Mouth-wash commercials suggest that people with bad breath are somehow beyond the pale, out of it. Detergent commercials suggest that clean laundry has high moral value. Commercials also create pictures of social life and stereotype social statuses. Women are often portrayed as having no social function outside the kitchen, nursery, and laundry. Men, on the other hand, are portrayed as totally inept in those areas, being superior in the things that "matter." Increased public objection has changed things somewhat in recent years, but as this is being written, an evening of television programming and commercials leaves little doubt that women are basically inferior to men.

Sex and Violence

The mass media create pictures not only of current events but of current social life as well. In their entertainment function, for example, the media portray various aspects of life: family, work, adventure. Their power in this regard is tremendous. As actor David Carradine has said: "We, as the movie makers, have the power to do anything. We can make our characters live or die, triumph or fail" (Quoted in Kilday 1975:127).

Recognizing this form of moviemaker omnipotence, many people have protested the entertainment industry's portrayal of sex and violence in everyday American life. Serious resistance to the portrayal of violence is recent, but resistance to the portrayal of explicit sexual activities and the use of sexual language has been evident for some time. Sociologists and other social scientists have been involved in both controversies.

The findings of social scientific research on the consequences of pornography and television violence have clashed with agreements on those topics. When the National Commission on Obscenity and Pornog-

raphy reported there was no evidence linking sex crimes to exposure to sexual materials, President Nixon condemned the report as "morally bankrupt" (Chaffee and Petrick 1975).

When, on the other hand, the United States surgeon general's million-dollar, three-year study of violence on television concluded that it had an adverse effect on American society—encouraging violence and dulling sensitivities to the violence of others—NBC-TV President Robert Howard was moved to suggest that "research does not replace common sense" (TV Guide, June 14, 1975, p. 6). Edith Efron (1975:22) argued against the report by saying that "the social sciences are not true sciences."

Perhaps one of the most telling arguments against violence on television has come from science-fiction writer and scientist Isaac Asimov. While noting that violence was a requirement for survival in early human history, Asimov (1975:31) suggests all that is past.

> We've got to get rid of violence for the simple reason that it serves no purpose any more, but points us all in a useless direction. . . .
> The new enemies we have today—overpopulation, famine, pollution, scarcity—cannot be fought by violence. There is no way to crush those enemies, or slash them, or blast them, or vaporize them.

Regardless of how people feel about the merits of sex and violence on television and in the other media, all are more or less agreed on the power of the media to *create* implicit pictures of reality. But what about their reporting of the "real" reality? Don't the media also communicate the plain facts of the events happening around us each day?

Reporting the "News"

One of the chief functions of the mass media—and of communication more generally—is the transmission of information. The editorial function of the mass media is recognized as involving a point of view; the "news" function, however, has generally been regarded as different. As Richard Salant, president of CBS News, has indicated: "Our reporters do not cover stories from *their* point of view. They are presenting them from *nobody's* point of view" (Quoted

in Epstein 1974: opening page). The assumption, then, is that "facts are facts," "reality is reality," and that "news" is merely a statement of reality as it *is*.

This point of view does not have complete agreement. Many people have come to a view more akin to the title of a 1975 newspaper-subscription advertisement: "The World You See Depends on the News You Get" (*Christian Science Monitor,* June 24, 1975). Even if you could assume that a purely objective reality of situations and events existed in the world, the simple *volume* of messages that would be required to report it in its entirety would make the reporting impossible. Inevitably, the course of day-to-day events must be sifted and filtered in what Edward Epstein (1975) has aptly called "the selection of reality." The box "Creating Reality" on pages 490–91 presents a case study of this process.

Reporters devote time and energy to the "search" for news, but you should not assume that the mass media have any trouble finding enough news to fill their papers, magazines, and news broadcasts.

> Most media operations face a situation of having more material available to them than they have time or space to use. A large daily newspaper, for example, might be able to use only one-tenth of all the materials which flow into the newsroom on any given day. In radio and television newscasts, the fraction is quite likely smaller than that (Chaffee and Petrick 1975:28).

The filtering process through which the "news" is created is multistaged. Many individuals are involved in the determination of what is worth printing or broadcasting. Figure 18·3 illustrates that process, tracing the flow of news through the Associated Press, a national wire service, to newspaper readers in Wisconsin.

Salant's disclaimer notwithstanding, the news media do report through points of view. The *New York Times*'s promise "All the News That's Fit to Print" implies a point of view on "fitness." When news people discuss this issue, moreover, they often speak of "newsworthiness," "significance," "interest," and "balance"—none of which can be defined or measured scientifically. Each requires the exercise of a point of view. In the interest of "balance," for example, a television newscast may devote ten seconds to an excerpt from a sixty-minute political speech and another ten seconds to a one-minute protest that interrupted the speech. The suggestion is that the speech was continually heckled. But should the heckling have been ignored altogether, creating the impression that everyone loved the speech?

Given the limitations of time, space, and cost, the mass media have no choice but to *create* "reality" in their reporting of the "news." Whatever they do represents a point of view—implicit, explicit, or accidental—and forms the basis for agreement as to what's "really so." While some media people may consciously seek to "slant" the news to reflect their personal biases, not even the most honest and honorable can avoid having an impact on what the remainder of mass society will come to regard as "facts."

The Effects of Mass Media

The concern over sex and violence in the mass media as well as the concern over how and what news is reported all reflect the point of view that the mass media have an effect on people's thinking and behavior. This is more a point of view than a firm research finding, however. Even the surgeon general's report on TV violence cautioned that its conclusions were tentative.

Even where research findings are not tentative regarding the effects of the mass media, it is not necessarily possible to state general conclusions.

The News Flow   **News flows into the AP and goes**

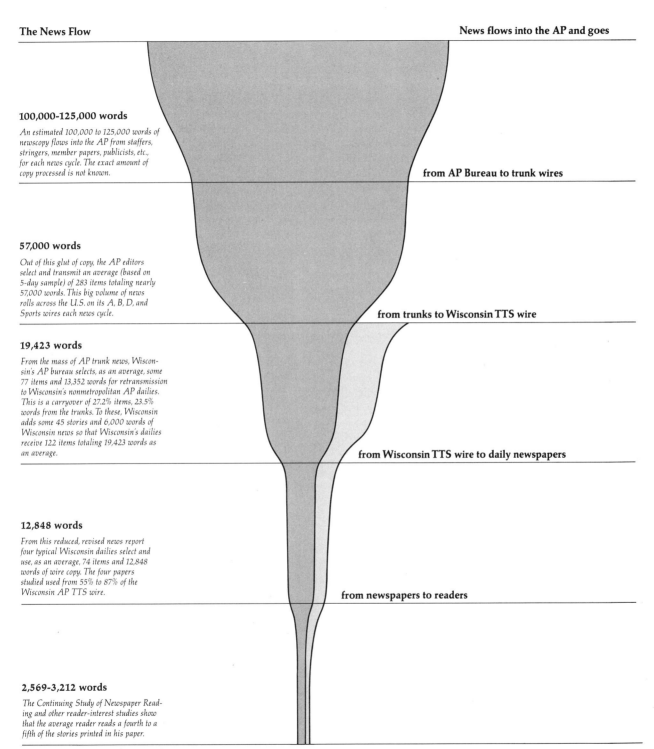

100,000-125,000 words

*An estimated 100,000 to 125,000 words of
newscopy flows into the AP from staffers,
stringers, member papers, publicists, etc.,
for each news cycle. The exact amount of
copy processed is not known.*

from AP Bureau to trunk wires

57,000 words

*Out of this glut of copy, the AP editors
select and transmit an average (based on
5-day sample) of 283 items totaling nearly
57,000 words. This big volume of news
rolls across the U.S. on its A, B, D, and
Sports wires each news cycle.*

from trunks to Wisconsin TTS wire

19,423 words

*From the mass of AP trunk news, Wiscon-
sin's AP bureau selects, as an average, some
77 items and 13,352 words for retransmission
to Wisconsin's nonmetropolitan AP dailies.
This is a carryover of 27.2% items, 23.5%
words from the trunks. To these, Wisconsin
adds some 45 stories and 6,000 words of
Wisconsin news so that Wisconsin's dailies
receive 122 items totaling 19,423 words as
an average.*

from Wisconsin TTS wire to daily newspapers

12,848 words

*From this reduced, revised news report
four typical Wisconsin dailies select and
use, as an average, 74 items and 12,848
words of wire copy. The four papers
studied used from 55% to 87% of the
Wisconsin AP TTS wire.*

from newspapers to readers

2,569-3,212 words

*The Continuing Study of Newspaper Read-
ing and other reader-interest studies show
that the average reader reads a fourth to a
fifth of the stories printed in his paper.*

Figure 18•3   The multistage filtering of news. Source: Scott M. Cutlip, "Content and Flow of AP News—From Trunk to TTS to Reader,"
Journalism Quarterly, *Fall 1960, p. 386. Reprinted by permission.*

Creating Reality

Most of what we know about what is going on in our community and beyond does not come from firsthand experience. It comes one way or another from the mass media. To paraphrase Walter Lippmann, "the pictures [of reality] in our heads are the pictures we have seen on television." Thus, an important question: Since television seems to provide our best possible and, certainly today, our most ubiquitous substitute for firsthand experience, is it possible that what we see on television can communicate an impression significantly different from what we would get if we were physically present at an event? Two sociologists, Kurt Lang and Gladys Lang, then graduate students at the University of Chicago, provided what has come to be considered a classic demonstration of the way in which television can portray an event as differing substantially from the impressions of firsthand observers.

In the fall of 1951 President Harry Truman had relieved General Douglas MacArthur of his command in Korea. The already legendary general returned to the United States for the first time since before World War II, and a series of triumphal appearances, parades, receptions, and celebrations were staged in his honor in various cities across the country. From reports on radio and television and in newspapers, a wave of national indignation about MacArthur's seemingly abrupt dismissal seemed to be sweeping the country. Wildly enthusiastic crowds, enthusiasm bordering on "mass hysteria," greeted him wherever he appeared. Chicago announced a planned visit and a MacArthur Day celebration. In anticipation of an opportunity to study such crowd activity firsthand, the Langs formed a group of thirty-one participant-observers who stationed themselves at important points along MacArthur's route. Each observer was instructed to report what he or she saw and particularly to note the talk and other behavior of spectators. Another set of observers monitored the event on television, reporting the picture and verbal commentary, as well as their general impression of what was happening.

The contrast between the two reports was striking. Here is a typical example. MacArthur had just passed State and Jackson in the heart of the Loop. No observers in the area mentioned the event in an extraordinary context. One observer reported as follows:

> Everybody strained but few could get a really good glimpse of him. A few seconds after he had passed most people merely turned around to shrug and to address their neighbors with such phrases: "That's all," "That was it," "Gee, he looks just as he does in the movies," "What'll we do now?" Mostly teenagers and others with no specific plans flocked into the street after MacArthur, but very soon got tired of following as there was no place to go and nothing to do. Some cars were caught in the crowd, a matter which, to the crowd, seemed amusing.

The same event was reported as a high point in the television presentation, "the moment when the crowds broke into the parade by surging out into State Street." One video monitor reported:

> The scene at 2:50 p.m. at State and Jackson was described by the announcer as the "most enthusiastic crowd *ever* in our city. . . . You can feel the tenseness in the air . . . . You can hear that crowd roar." The crowd was described as pushing out into the curb with the police trying to keep it in order, while the camera was still focusing on MacArthur and his party. The final picture was of a bobbing mass of heads as the camera took in the entire view of State Street northward. . . . this mass of people appeared to be pushing and going nowhere. And then, with the remark, "The whole city appears to be marching down State Street behind General MacArthur," holding the picture just long enough for the impression to sink in, the picture was suddenly blanked out. . . . the last buildup on TV concerning the "crowd" (cut off as it was, abruptly at 3:00 p.m.) gave me the impression that the crowd was pressing and straining so hard that it was going to be hard to control. My first thought, "I'm glad I'm not in that" and "I hope nobody gets crushed."

Clearly the perspective presented by television was different from that of the spectator in the crowd. The camera zeroed in frequently to show what appeared to be a unified mass of cheering spectators, but observers in the crowd reported little cheering and a good deal of confusion and disappointment expressed because people could not see and did not know what was going on at the moment. In fact, it was reported that "the cheering, waving, and shouting was often largely a response to the aiming of the camera." In particular, the commentary on television implied that the crowd's reaction was similar to that possible for each TV viewer by emphasizing close-ups of MacArthur. An announcer shouted, for example, "Look at that chin! Look at those eyes!" But most people in the crowd caught only a glimpse of that chin and those eyes and had no opportunity whatsoever to see themselves in a face-to-face relationship with the man. As Lang and Lang conclude, "The selectivity of the camera and the commentary gave the event a personal dimension, nonexistent for the participants in the crowds, thereby presenting a very specific perspective which contrasted with that of direct observation."

What accounts for this discrepancy between the television presentation and firsthand observations of the same events? One does not have to assume that television personnel deliberately intended to create an event different from the reality of firsthand observers. On the basis of the cumulative media reports of similar events, it was reasonable to expect that MacArthur Day in Chicago would be an "exciting and dramatic event," one that justified television's rearranging everyday scheduling and allocating considerable resources to attract an anticipated, unusually large, interested audience. The event was simply presented in conformity with the announced program, presumably fulfilling the preexisting expectations of the television industry and their audience. It was the job of the TV news personnel to use the TV camera and to construct commentary to fit the specified program: dramatic public event. They did their jobs in conventional fashion. In this case, the program created a reality for the television audience demonstrably different from that of direct observers. The media impression of overwhelming and enthusiastic support for General MacArthur (and by implication, for his position on the Korean war) was not an impression that could reasonably be gotten from participation in the crowd watching the parade and ceremonies. Perhaps the "camera does not lie," but it obviously can be used selectively, wittingly or unwittingly, to create specified impressions.

More specifically, Lang and Lang point to three aspects of television presentation that can be used to structure an event to fit TV-program expectations:

1. Technological bias, that is, the necessarily arbitrary sequence of telecasting events and their structure in terms of foreground and background, which at the same time contains the choices on the part of the television personnel as to what is important

2. Structuring of an event by an announcer, whose commentary is needed to tie together the shifts from camera to camera, from vista to close-up, helping the spectator to gain the stable orientation from one particular perspective

3. Reciprocal effects, which modify the event itself by staging it in a way to make it more suitable for telecasting and creating among the actors the consciousness of acting for a larger audience

A good deal of what we know beyond firsthand experience is the world shown to us on TV, and we should fully understand the way in which TV creates reality and what that perspective is. Impressions obtained from TV are no more "our own" than any other impressions based on mediated communication.

Source: Kurt Lang and Gladys E. Lang, "The Unique Perspective of Television and Its Effect," American Sociological Review 18 (February 1953):1. Reprinted by permission.

What is communicated to whom under what conditions all seem to determine whether people are influenced by what they see, hear, and read in the media.

During World War II, for example, the popular singer Kate Smith broadcast an eighteen-hour radio marathon urging people to buy war bonds. She received pledges for 39 million dollars' worth of bonds. Repeating the marathon a year later, she raised over 100 million dollars. A few years later, just after the war, a number of organizations launched an intensive mass-media campaign spanning a six-month period to educate the public about the newly formed United Nations. The campaign involved radio, newspapers, pamphlets, signs, posters, meetings, and speeches. Surveys conducted before and after the campaign indicated that it had had little or no effect (Wright 1975).

Hiebert et al. (1974) suggest three possible media effects: (1) People may learn and understand things; (2) their attitudes and values may change; and (3) their behavior may change. The first of these effects, dealing with cognition and comprehension, occurs frequently, as is probably obvious. You know about the American Revolution without having participated in it or talking to people who did. You know about it because of the mass media: textbooks, novels, magazines, and so forth.

Attitude and value changes appear less likely as consequences of the mass media than learning and understanding. Joseph Klapper (1960), Wilbur Schramm (1964), and others suggest that the mass media are more effective in creating *new* agreements than in changing old ones. If a war were to break out tomorrow between Honduras and Nicaragua, it is unlikely that many people in the United States would have an immediate preference for one side or the other. The mass media would be able to shape people's attitudes. Consider, on the other hand, a firmly established agreement such as the one prohibiting incest. It is unlikely that a mass-media campaign would be very successful in changing that agreement.

Paul Lazarsfeld and Robert Merton (1960) go a step further to suggest that a major effect of the mass media is the enforcement of the established standards of society. In this regard, the media are a force for conformity in mass society.

All this is not to suggest that the media are incapable of effecting radical changes in attitudes and values. To take a historical example, there is no denying the influence of abolitionist newspapers such as William Lloyd Garrison's *Liberator* and books such as Harriet Beecher Stowe's *Uncle Tom's Cabin* in changing attitudes regarding slavery in America. More recently, mass-media coverage of the Vietnam war clearly had an effect on American attitudes.

In the examples just cited, not only attitudes and values but behavior as well were changed. The mass media *do* have an impact on people's behavior, but, in general, producing "new" behavior seems more likely than changing "old" behavior. Thus, Hiebert et al. (1974) suggest that the media may influence the use of leisure time and may stimulate particular interests: an interest in French cooking, for example. Attempts to change old behavior patterns are less successful, as the campaign against tobacco smoking has illustrated.

A variety of factors influence the effect of the mass media on people's cognition, attitudes, values, and behavior. Hiebert et al. (1974) point out that the fewer the skills required for access to a medium, the greater its potential impact. It becomes available to more people. Television is more accessible than an advanced textbook. Styles of presentation matter also. Witness the effectiveness of "Sesame Street" (discussed in Chapter 9) as compared with more conventional educational-television formats. Exposure to the message influences its impact. This research conclusion is anticipated by politicians and advertisers who repeat the same message over and over. Finally, the environment in which the message is received has an influence. Some environments, such as the home, contain numerous distractions; others, such as movie theaters, do not.

The variety of factors operating in the question of the possible influence of the mass media no doubt contributes to the inconsistency of research findings and personal convictions regarding media effectiveness. The demonstrable fact that a calculated use of the mass media *can* have an impact—in the political propaganda campaigns of totalitarian regimes, for example—has been a source of worry for many observers. Periodically, legislation has been addressed to the prevention of media monopolies, to ensuring the balanced reporting of different points of view, and so forth.

All such concerns basically revolve around the notion of "public opinion": what Hennessey (1975:5) defines as *the complex of preferences expressed by a significant number of persons on an issue of general importance.* Put another way, "public opinion" refers to the attitudes and values generally shared by the members of a population. In an important sense, public opinion is, no matter how arrived at, the end of the road for mass-media communications. Let's turn to that topic now.

Public Opinion

From the beginning, this book has focused on the many agreements that members of a society share, among them, beliefs, values, and norms. In the discussions of social structure, we have concerned ourselves with that more or less persistent body of agreements that is passed from one generation to another. In this section, we are going to be looking at a form of social agreement that is more transitory and changing in societies: public opinion. Public opinion continually forms and reforms in regard to a variety of issues that gain and lose importance for members of a society over time.

In 1886, George Thompson addressed the implicit role of public opinion in the form of government envisioned by the U.S. Constitution, and he also noted the confusion that surrounds the concept.

> People may disagree about the facts; or agreeing about the facts, they may differ in their calculations; or agreeing in the calculation that a certain course will attain one object at the sacrifice of another, they may differ in their estimation of the relative worth of these objects . . . (1886:7).

Thompson went on to caution that "public opinion" and "the will of the nation," along with other

such commonly used phrases, "are really nothing but metaphors, for thought and will are attributes of a single mind, and 'the public' or 'the nation' are aggregates of many minds."

The Jeffersonian view of American democracy anticipated that citizens would have different points of view in regard to the issues facing them as a society but that the give-and-take of public debate (as occurred in the New England town meeting) would create a group course of action. This is the sense in which Blumer (1966:48) characterized public opinion as a "collective product," noting that "it is not a unanimous opinion with which everyone in the public agrees, nor is it necessarily the opinion of a majority." As Blumer indicated it is often possible for a minority group to exercise an influence in the discussion of ideas that is greater than the group's weight in numbers.

The Jeffersonian view of public opinion as the product of rational debate has been increasingly criticized in the context of mass society. Their sheer mass prevents people from coming together to discuss, debate, and decide. Add to this the speed with which many societal decisions must be made and the complexity of many modern issues, and you have something quite different from what Jefferson had in mind when the Constitution was written two centuries ago.

The implications of mass society for public opinion and democracy have raised two major concerns for many observers. First, public policymaking has been increasingly given over to public officials who are susceptible to relatively small pressure groups. The collective wisdom of the members of the society in general has grown less important.

Second, the inability of citizens to gather together for discussion has led to a view of public opinion as only an aggregation of individual opinions rather than a collective product. Even this type of public opinion, many fear, is largely a function of what people learn through the mass media.

Before turning to the role of the media in shaping public opinion, however, we are going to look at a different, less-structured way in which public opinion is often formed. Rumors create reality through covert agreement, in contrast to the mass media, which do

Television has revolutionized most aspects of American life, including the news, entertainment, commerce, and politics. The power of modern, electronic communications represents both a promise and a threat to participatory democracy. (Cornell Capa, Magnum)

it more overtly. The study of rumors provides a useful background for the study of mass media and public opinion.

Rumors

Rumors are a form of communication, a fascinating form. This fascination partly reflects the excitement of those issues that become the subject of rumors, but it also reflects the spontaneous, informal, and unpredictable nature of rumor as a social process.

Tamotsu Shibutani has called rumors "improvised news," suggesting that they reflect a desire to understand ambiguous situations. Where "firm" information is both desired and unavailable, people create their own and pass it around. Shibutani (1965:17) thus defines rumor as

> a recurrent form of *communication through which men caught together in an ambiguous situation attempt to construct a meaningful interpretation of it by pooling their intellectual resources. . . .* To act intelligently such persons seek news, and rumor is essentially a type of news.

In taking this view, Shibutani notes that the common view of rumors assumes them to be inaccurate. Indeed, much of the laboratory research on rumor transmission has focused on the manner in which stories get changed as they are passed from person to person. Arthur Ponsonby (1930) has provided an excellent illustration of this process in analyzing

Table 18·1 Public Attitudes toward the Mass Media, 1970

Which of the media	Television	Newspapers	Radio	Magazines
Gives the most complete news coverage?	41%	39%	14%	4%
Presents the fairest, most unbiased news?	33	23	19	9
Present things most intelligently?	38	28	9	18
Gives you the clearest understanding of the candidates and issues in national elections?	59[a]	21	3	8

[a]The percentages do not total 100 because some respondents expressed no opinion.

Source: Reprinted, with permission, from the June 11, 1973 issue of Broadcasting.

the successive newspaper reports on the fall of Antwerp, Belgium, to the Germans in World War I. Notice how the initial report that German churches in Germany heralded the victory by ringing their bells got continuously reinterpreted and revised—even in *Le Matin*, which reported the story twice.

When the fall of Antwerp got known, the church bells were rung (*Kolnische Zeitung* [Germany]).

According to the Kolnische Zeitung, the clergy of Antwerp were compelled to ring the church bells when the fortress was taken (*Le Matin* [France]).

According to what Le Matin has heard from Cologne, the Belgian priests who refused to ring the church bells when Antwerp was taken have been driven away from their places (*Times* [England]).

According to what the Times has heard from Cologne via Paris, the unfortunate Belgian priests who refused to ring the church bells when Antwerp was taken have been sentenced to hard labor (*Corriera della Sera* [Italy]).

According to information to the Corriera della Sera from Cologne via London, it is confirmed that the barbaric conquerors of Antwerp punished the unfortunate Belgian priests for their heroic refusal to ring the church bells by hanging them as living clappers to the bells with their heads down (*Le Matin* [France]).

This transformation of presumably happy German priests into martyred Belgians illustrates the "distortion in serial transmission" that has been the focus of most scholarly studies of rumor. Shibutani, however, points out that rumors needn't be inaccurate. Barbara Suczek (1972), in her examination of the rumor of Beatle Paul McCartney's death, concludes that some rumors don't even change through communication: "Among its believers, the story was taught and learned, deviations from the theme were definitely discouraged, and the fundamental details were memorized like a litany" (p. 71).

Rumors are a form of collective behavior—like panics and fads—and a form of communication through which people create a reality by agreement. Sometimes the mass media participate in rumors—reporting them or fueling them—and sometimes they do not.

Mass Media and Public Opinion

Undeniably, much of the information that goes into the formation of public opinion in a mass society comes through the mass media. People have become increasingly dependent on television for such information. Table 18·1 reports some of the results of a recent survey of public attitudes toward the different media.

Sociological research spanning several decades, however, suggests that the impact of the mass media on public opinion is more complex than might appear. In particular, the research of Elihu Katz and Paul Lazarsfeld suggests that the mass media influence general public opinion in a "two-step flow of communication."

In Lazarsfeld's *The People's Choice,* the researchers developed a hypothesis that the mass media had their primary impact on the opinion leaders or the "influentials" of a community—respected business, governmental, and professional people—and that they, in turn, influenced the general public opinion. In this view, information and ideas flowed directly from the mass media to the community's influentials and then to the general public through networks of social interaction involving those influentials.

This hypothesis was tested by Katz and Lazarsfeld (1955) in a study of Decatur, Illinois, in the early 1950s. The results of the Decatur study, plus subsequent studies by Irving Allen (1975) and others, confirm the "two-step flow" hypothesis. These findings bear an interesting relationship to the eighteenth-century idea of participatory, democratic public opinion. On the one hand, public opinion does indeed appear to grow out of interaction and discussion, as studies show the extent to which people report learning things about current events in discussions with friends. On the other hand, the special opinion-forming role played by the influentials contradicts the democratic aspect of the process. As Blumer pointed out, "public opinion" is not necessarily the opinion of the majority.

Measuring Public Opinion

In a mass society, public opinion and governmental policies do not always coincide. Indeed, the theory of representative democracy assumes that representatives will sometimes go against the wishes of the people, exercising "a greater wisdom" by virtue of their special expertise and knowledge. Nonetheless, public opinion is relevant to government.

Public officials who must seek reelection to office—plus those who serve at the will of those who must be reelected—have an interest in following (or appearing to follow) the public will. Many public officials, moreover, genuinely feel that they *should* reflect the feelings of those who elected them. By extension, people with a special point of view they wish to see enacted have a special, persuasive weapon if they can show that their point of view is supported by the general public.

During the Vietnam war, for example, many public officials began by supporting the war effort and later changed their minds. Public opinion on the wisdom of the war also changed over time, as Table 18·2 indicates. Some public officials were instrumental in changing public opinion, others changed their opinions on the war at the same time and for the same reasons as the general public, and other public officials undoubtedly changed their opinions in order to remain on the side of the majority.

Knowing what public opinion is on a given issue, then, is of more than passing interest. Not surprisingly, many people are eager at any given time to tell us. Journalists have done this for years, based on their "sense" of what the "common person" is thinking, as assessed from interviews and observations.

The empirical measurement of public opinion has been practiced with varying degrees of success for years. Earlier in this century, political elections in the country have been predicted in a number of ways. Movie theaters have offered patrons a choice of popcorn bags printed with elephants (Republican) or donkeys (Democrats) in an effort to determine behavior at the polls. The same symbols have been printed on grain bags in agricultural areas as a means for predicting the farm vote.

For the most part, however, public-opinion measurement at the present time is undertaken through the use of the survey-research methods discussed in Chapter 3. Political and public-opinion polls conducted by commercial organizations such as Gallup (Table 18·2), Harris, and Roper, plus those done by university researchers, give us our primary insight into public opinion.

To review the earlier discussion, effective public-opinion polling depends on selecting proper samples of respondents, asking proper questions, and interpreting the responses properly. (See Chapter 3 to learn what's "proper.") Of these three aspects, the

Table 18·2   Public Opinion on the Vietnam War

"Some people think we should not have become involved with our military forces in Southeast Asia, while others think we should have. What is your opinion?"

Date of answer	Should have	Should not have	No opinion
January 31, 1965	50%	28%	22%
May 16, 1965	52	26	22
November 21, 1965	64	21	15

"In view of the developments since we entered the fighting in Vietnam, do you think the United States made a mistake sending troops to fight in Vietnam?"

Date of answer	No mistake	Made mistake	No opinion
June 3, 1966	49%	36%	15%
September 30, 1966	49	35	16
February 26, 1967	52	32	16
May 14, 1967	50	37	13
July 30, 1967	48	41	11
October 25, 1967	44	46	10
January 3, 1968	46	45	9
March 10, 1968	41	49	10
May 1, 1968	40	48	12
March 23, 1969	39	52	9
June 28, 1970	36	56	8
June 6, 1971	28	61	11

Source: George Gallup, The Gallup Poll, vol. 3 (New York: Random House, 1972), pp. 1921, 1940, 1971, 2010, 2031, 2052, 2063, 2074, 2087, 2099, 2109, 2125, 2189, 2254, 2309.

formulation and asking of "proper" questions is perhaps the trickiest. Variations in the wording of questions or variations in the ways they are asked by interviewers—if interviewers are used—can significantly affect the answers obtained from respondents.

It is clear that questions can be biased. For example, the question "Don't you agree with everyone else that . . ." is clearly likely to produce more agreement than an unbiased, neutral question on the same topic will. Or consider this question, asked by Karl Marx in his little-known 1880 survey of French workers: ". . . does your employer or his representative resort to trickery in order to defraud you of a part of your earnings?" (see Bottomore and Rubel 1843:208).

Bias can operate more subtly than these examples suggest, however. During the early years of World War II in Europe, Hadley Cantril conducted two national surveys to determine how Americans felt about the likelihood of the United States getting involved in the conflict. The surveys were designed and conducted in such a manner that each should have given the same, accurate picture of public opinion at that time. In one survey, respondents were asked "Do you think that the United States will succeed in staying out of the war?" Most (55 percent of those with an opinion) said yes. In the other survey, a slightly different question was asked: "Do you think the United States will go into the war before it is over?" Most (59 percent of those with an opinion) said yes. What was public opinion, then? Did people think we'd stay out of the war or get into it? There isn't an answer to these questions.

In an important sense, public-opinion polling *creates* public opinion. In this sense, it doesn't exist until people are asked for their individual opinions, and the manner in which they are asked often shapes the manner in which they answer (see Babbie 1975).

Over the years, pollsters have grown increasingly aware of the fact that many people do not have an opinion on many issues. They have also discovered that such people are reluctant to admit it, saving face instead by reporting some opinion. This is seen most clearly in studies that have asked for opinions on fictitious issues. In a political poll in Honolulu recently, respondents were given a list of public figures and asked several questions about each, beginning with whether they had ever heard of the person. Nine percent of the sample said they were familiar with a fictitious person (made up by the researchers). Of those, half reported seeing the person on television, and the same proportion had seen him in person.

This troublesome tendency has led George Gallup to use what he calls a "quintamensional" approach to the study of issues. Respondents are asked, in order, whether they have heard anything about a particular issue, then (if yes) what they have heard, how they feel about it, which of several specific positions (provided by the interviewer) comes closest to how they feel, and how strongly they feel about their position.

Despite the difficulties involved in measuring public opinion, and several historical embarrassments notwithstanding, current activities by qualified and established pollsters provide a useful insight into the public's thinking. This is validated periodically in relation to political polls conducted before elections. The 1968 presidential election in the United States provided an extremely difficult test of the accuracy of current polling methods. All indications suggested that the contest between Nixon and Humphrey would be very close, although the third-party candidacy of George Wallace confused the matter somewhat. George Gallup's last preelection poll missed the Nixon vote by only 0.5 percentage point and the Humphrey vote by 0.9 percentage point.

In recent years, the commercial pollsters have grown more sophisticated in the analysis of public opinion. They have become more effective in handling the implications of "don't know" responses. In the case of preelection polls, for example, the experience of previous elections and polls has made it possible for them to estimate the voting patterns of those who report no opinion at the time of polling. The commercial pollsters have also increasingly analyzed and reported their findings in terms of the various subgroups making up the general population: by sex, age, race, religion, education, and so forth. It becomes clear that different public "opinions" exist in different subgroups, and knowledge of those differences makes it easier to discover the meanings that lie behind opinions.

Summary

Communication is the creation of "commonness" with someone: the sharing of information, ideas, and attitudes. Between individuals, communication of an experience and acknowledgment of the experience make the experience more "real" for the person who had it.

In modern, mass societies a great deal of communication occurs outside the context of face-to-face interactions. Technology has made it possible for individuals to communicate with one another across long distances. Equally important, mass media such as books, newspapers, magazines, films, radio, and television represent a communication system in which one communicator addresses a large number of receivers who are unable to respond directly to the communication.

By their nature, the mass media have a special potential for creating agreements about reality. This potential is clear in the case of propaganda, where the communicator explicitly attempts to create particular attitudes and beliefs. Political and commercial advertising are seen as special examples of this.

Considerable controversy exists over the portrayal of sex and violence in the mass media, based in part on the awareness of its potential for the creation of agreement reality. Children, in particular, it is argued, will be led to accept violence and sexual deviance as facts of life in our society and encouraged to engage in them. The research on these topics suggests that the media do not have the expected effect with regard to sex, while the research findings are not consistent with regard to violence.

Even the reporting of "news" is an act of creating reality for viewers. So many events occur every day that the media must be selective in their reporting. Such selectivity inevitably shapes the picture of reality that viewers form.

The transmission and reception of information is only one of the possible consequences of mass communications. Researchers have also looked at the potential for changing attitudes, values, and behavior. Overall, it appears that the media are more effective in creating new attitudes, values, and behaviors than they are in changing old ones.

"Public opinion" refers to the generally shared set of attitudes and preferences in a society, and it can be seen, in part, in the final outcome of mass communication. How do people feel about events and issues once they have been exposed to the mass media and have participated in interpersonal communications about them? The Jeffersonian model of democracy placed considerable importance on public opinion, assuming that citizens would rationally discuss and debate issues and arrive at consensus.

The nature of modern, mass society, including the role of the mass media, has led many people to doubt the accuracy of that view.

The measurement of public opinion is currently a well-developed, scientific activity. Using the methods of survey research discussed in Chapter 3, a number of private polling companies—such as Gallup, Harris, and Roper—and university researchers frequently sample public opinion on a wide variety of topics.

Public opinion is perhaps an appropriate topic to end our extended study of society with. Throughout this book, we've been looking at the established structures that shape people's social lives and how they experience living within those structural constraints. The value to be gained from such an examination is enormous, but there is a corresponding danger that we might lose sight of the fact that people create the agreements that subsequently shape their lives. Public opinion is an example of the agreements that people create.

Suggested Readings

Hennessey, Bernard
1975   *Public Opinion*. North Scituate, Mass.: Duxbury Press.

Here's an excellent and readable introduction to the topic of public opinion. Hennessey examines the political history of the concept in America (its implications for democracy), some of the research findings that reveal how public opinion is formed, and the techniques by which researchers study it.

Lazarsfeld, Paul et al.
1944   *The People's Choice*. New York: Columbia.

I suppose it's possible that you're not really interested in why some voters in Erie County, Ohio, favored Franklin Roosevelt for president while others preferred Wendell Wilkie. (You don't know who Wilkie was!) Never mind. Lazarsfeld's analysis of voting preferences in Erie County was a milestone in the study of electoral decision making. I've described many of those findings in the chapter, but you'll get a lot of value from reading the "real" thing.

Shibutani, Tamotsu
1966   *Improvised News: A Sociological Study of Rumor*. Indianapolis, Ind.: Bobbs-Merrill.

Psssst. Did you hear that . . . Everybody enjoys a juicy rumor, and Shibutani's sociological examination of what he calls "improvised news" is both enjoyable and informative reading. He looks at the reasons why rumors start and how they are passed around. Incidentally, he notes that rumors aren't necessarily wrong, so you might reconsider that rumor you dismissed out of hand yesterday.

Wright, Charles
1975   *Mass Communication: A Sociological Perspective*. New York: Random House.

Here's a very readable introduction to the sociology of mass communications. Wright provides data on the mass media, theoretical points of view to use in understanding mass communications, and generally demonstrates how sociologists examine this aspect of mass society.

Episode Eighteen

"Dry-roasted soybeans!" Ann Sullivan giggled, lifting a jar from the shipping crate she was unpacking and placing it on a shelf above her head.

"Chocolate-covered raisins?" Gabriel laughed, setting the vacuum-packed container on another shelf opposite Ann. "You've got to be kidding!"

It was evening, March 19, 2028. Four months earlier the two had returned victorious from the third conference on human mutations.

"You know what I miss?" Gabe said, suddenly melancholy. "I miss spring in Chicago."

"You're not happy here in Phoenix?" Ann questioned.

During the previous January Gabriel and twenty-seven other valleyites had moved into a modest neighborhood on the northeast edge of Phoenix. With dividends drawn from Gabriel's and Ann Sullivan's S.T.I. stock, the group had purchased three small homes, a rooming house, and a vacant storefront in which Ann planned to open a delicatessen. Gabriel lived in the rooming house while Sullivan shared one of the homes with several other valleyites, among them her former roommates.

"It's Lake Michigan, I guess," Gabe said now, more to himself than to his companion. "I miss the way the wind comes in over the lake."

"Maybe you can go back someday," Ann cheered. Then she paused; when she spoke again her voice was lower. "Are you glad you came to Phoenix, Gabriel?"

Gabe smiled. "I think we will make ourselves a comfortable neighborhood here," he said. "I just wish the desert had one of the great lakes, that's all."

"And I just wish this place were ready to open," Ann played. "I'd invite everyone down after the ma-

turing ceremony for a refreshment-filled weekend."

Gabe laughed. "Can't you just see Dan Adamson in here? 'How about some salted peanuts, Dan? Care for an apple?' 'Oh, thank you, no,' he'd say. 'Actually I'm too perfect to need to eat'."

It was the eve of Gabriel's maturation ceremony. "I have to go back for it," he had explained earlier to some other former valleyites. "Jonathan, my soft parent, would want it."

Ann Sullivan set the last jar of roasted soybeans in place and bent to take the empty shipping container outside. Near the doorway she stopped, turning back toward Gabriel. "Did you see the paper today?" she asked.

"No. Why?"

"The *Phoenix Herald* did a front-page feature on the maturing ceremony tomorrow. I haven't had a chance to read it closely. Take a look."

Gabe recovered a newspaper that lay on the floor amid an assortment of partially unpacked boxes. The *Phoenix Herald* had, since its first spectacular story on the mutants, remained interested in Adamsville, and now the prospect of an article on the maturation ceremony intrigued Gabe.

He read for several seconds, noting the general accuracy of presentation. It was evident that the journalist responsible for the story had done some homework.

When he had completed what was carried of the story on the front page, he moved to open the paper to page 4 where the piece continued.

Suddenly his attention was grabbed by a headline positioned in the lower right-hand corner of the front page. Ann must have missed this, he thought, his heart beginning to pound.

"Mother of Kidnapped Chicago Infant Commits Suicide," the headline clamored. Gabriel read the story:

"Chicago—Sarah Welsh, mother of the infant boy kidnapped from Lake Hospital June 28, 2026, has hanged herself at a local mental hospital here. She was found in her room shortly before 5 A.M., authorities said . . .

"It was widely circulated at the time of the kidnapping that the infant was stolen by green mutants whose religion makes virtue of such practice . . .

"Gabriel Knapp, once an executive with Chicago National Insurance and, according to reputable sources, a green mutant, was tried and acquitted of the kidnapping. According to reports he now resides in Phoenix."

Ann returned to the room. "Is it *that* biased?" she asked, noting the expression on Gabriel's face.

"I've got to go," he said, rising to leave and handing the newspaper to Ann. "I'll see you in the morning."

Three cars filled with former valleyites arrived at Adamsville the next forenoon. "It doesn't look like they've had any recent border trouble," Ann remarked, noting the relaxed posture of the young green in the guard shelter.

"And no more state police," Gabe said, recalling the first time he had heard the derogatory term "greenface."

That day at noon Gabriel donned a velvet ceremonial cloak and, with five others from the community, ascended the sacred platform. He looked out into a sea of green faces. Behind him on the platform sat Michael, weak with age.

When he had removed his green cape, Jacob began the politico-spiritual litany. "We are the future people of the earth," he chanted. "We are the culmination of God's evolutionary plan."

That afternoon inside the Great Hall Gabriel grew pensive. Incidents from recent years, in no apparent order, crowded into his brain. He recalled lying upon the earth, sand grinding its way into his face and eyes.

He recalled Monica and the July Fourth picnic he once shared with her. He remembered the day he received the medical report; he pictured his office at Chicago National. He recalled the rescue. The trial. He remembered peering curiously into a tiny baby's eyes while he sat holding him on an airplane. He recalled vomiting into a dirty lavatory sink the day he heard that the child was dead.

He thought of the physical beauty of Rebecca Lockwood—and of Larry Jones. He recalled Jonathan Knapp, his soft parent. He thought of his long, academic discussions with Connie Batterson. And of his tormenting confession to Monica. And he thought of a woman whom he had never met: Sarah Welsh.

Jacob approached. "Congratulations, Gabe," he said, embracing his friend. "How long can you stay? I have plenty of room, you know."

"I think we'll be getting on back tonight," Gabe said. "Several of us have to work tomorrow."

Jacob stood a minute, not sure of what to say. "Well," he forced a grin, disappointed to see his friend leave so soon, "maybe someday I'll get down to Phoenix. Think it's safe for bright greens like me yet?"

"Not yet. Someday maybe," Gabe said.

Jacob drew in a breath, changing the subject. "Michael would like to visit with you before you go."

When Gabriel entered Elderhome an hour later, he was ushered by Alexander to Michael's private bedroom. The old man lay quietly upon his bed, bathed in a sea of fluorescent light.

"Elder?" Gabriel spoke softly.

"Gabriel," Michael murmured. "I am about to die."

Gabe sat down on a chair beside Michael's bed, saying nothing.

"I'm glad you matured," Michael said.

"Yes," Gabriel whispered.

"Do you enjoy living in Phoenix?"

"It is not paradise," Gabriel smiled. "But it is a place for us."

Michael struggled with his words. "Tell me, are you glad that you were raised here in Adamsville?"

Gabe stared. "I had never thought about it that way," he said. "I am a green; it was necessary that I be raised here."

"You are thankful then that you were rescued?"

"Of course, Elder."

"I'm glad," Michael said. "I'm very glad."

The two sat for a long time. "Can I get you anything?" Gabe offered.

"Our people are beginning to question now," Michael said, peering into the light above him. "Some outsiders work at S.T.I. now. They raise questions. Adamsvillers have begun to wonder."

"Wonder about rescuing?" Gabriel asked.

Michael nodded.

Gabriel took Michael's thin, green hand. "I am glad that I was rescued," he reaffirmed. "It was necessary."

It was to be the last conversation Gabriel would have with Michael-the-Elder.

A few minutes before midnight the party arrived back in Phoenix. As Gabe walked alone to his rooming house, Ann Sullivan came up behind him, taking his sleeve. "Can we talk a minute?" she asked.

"Sure," he said, turning in the darkness, "what is it?"

"No one mentioned Larry Jones today. Did you notice?"

Gabe shuffled. "To keep talking about him would only stir up old animosities," Gabe suggested. "It's better this way."

"Gabriel," Ann said, "why did you never attempt to find out who shot him?"

"There would have been no point to it," he said. "After the assassination Jacob and I discussed it and he felt the same way. To go through a long investigation would only have ripped apart a community that was already dangerously divided."

"I killed him," Ann confessed suddenly.

Gabriel stepped back. "Why are you telling me this now?"

"I don't know," she said. "It haunts me."

"I understand that," Gabe responded, his mind turning again to Sarah Welsh. "I have been responsible for death also."

Questions

1. "Agreement reality" is created through communication. As Gabe and Ann stock shelves for her delicatessen, what agreement realities are the two creating?

2. Ann and Gabe agree that the *Phoenix Herald* article describing the maturing ceremony was accurate. Does that mean it was "really" accurate? Can accurate communications be distinguished from inaccurate ones except through agreement?

3. Somebody at the *Phoenix Herald* decided to place the story of the suicide on the same page as the story about the green maturing ceremony. Discuss the several different reasons which might have led to that decision.

4. Reified agreements are challenged through communication. How has the hiring of outsiders at S.T.I. challenged certain Adamsville agreements?

5. Why does Michael-the-Elder feel the need to talk with Gabe before he (Michael) dies?

19

Sociologists in Mass Society

Throughout this book, I've been telling you how sociologists look at society, and I've mentioned the names of more than a few sociologists in the process. Still, it seems likely to me that you may not have a very clear picture of who or what sociologists *are*. How would you recognize one on the street or on campus? What do sociologists do, really? What good are they?

I want to deal with questions like these in this final chapter. We'll begin with a brief look at sociology as a profession: how sociologists are organized and what they do. The remainder of the chapter is addressed to the ways in which sociologists can, do, and will have an impact on the rest of society. In both these topics, I'll focus primarily on sociology in America.

The Profession of Sociology

It is no more possible to point to the beginning of sociology as a profession in America than it was possible in Chapter 2 to point to the beginning of sociology as a point of view. For the better part of this century, however, the professional life of sociologists has been linked to and reflected in their professional association. The American Sociological Society was organized in 1905, with Lester Ward its first president. In 1959, the group was renamed

the American Sociological Association. You'll be able to understand why this was done since you've read Chapter 4: Professional groups are voluntary associations, not societies. It seemed especially important for sociologists to be clear about such terms. The initials of the earlier organization had nothing to do with it.

The annual meetings of the ASA and of the many regional sociological associations provide an opportunity for communication. Sociological journals are another means for communication. The *American Journal of Sociology* was established in 1895 at the University of Chicago, where it is still published and is still a major sociological journal. For about forty years, it served as the unofficial journal of American sociology. Then, in 1936, the American Sociological Society began publication of the *American Sociological Review.* In the years that have followed, the association has added a number of official periodicals reflecting the various needs and interests of the profession.

Book reviews are now published in a separate journal: *Contemporary Sociology.* Research and commentary regarding the profession as well as association business are communicated through *The American Sociologist* and a tabloid called *Footnotes.* Three other ASA journals address special sociological interests: *Journal of Health and Social Behavior, Sociology of Education,* and *Sociometry.*

In addition to these official ASA journals, a great many others of interest to sociologists are published by allied professional associations with substantial sociological memberships. A few of these are *Social Problems, Social Forces, Journal for the Scientific Study of Religion, Journal of Marriage and the Family,* and *Population Studies.* Added to these sources of sociological research and commentary are non-American sociological journals, journals published by regional associations, and those of related disciplines such as anthropology, psychology, and political science.

When they are not reading journals or attending professional meetings, sociologists engage in a variety of activities reflecting their special expertise. The great majority of sociologists are employed as faculty members in colleges and universities. You already know part of what they do there. They train new generations of sociologists and add a sociological component to the general education of other students. Teaching is not the only college function of sociologists, however. Many also do research and participate in the college administration.

Some sociologists are employed outside colleges and universities. Some work for government agencies such as the Bureau of the Census, the Department of Labor, and the Department of Health, Education, and Welfare. Others conduct research for private organizations.

The remainder of this chapter is devoted to an examination of the impact of sociology on society. We'll begin with a discussion of the different ways in which sociology makes a difference in society. We'll conclude by considering the place of personal values in sociological pursuits and looking at the future prospects of sociology.

The Impact of Sociology on Society

Sociologists, using their sociological skills, influence social life in countless ways. Some of these have been touched on already. Sociologists conduct political polls and advise political candidates, for example. Some assist minority groups living in poverty areas to organize and work together to gain better living conditions. Industrial sociologists study ways

for improving working conditions, morale, and productivity.

In this section, I'm going to present a few examples to illustrate the diversity of ways in which sociological research has affected society. These are not necessarily the most important influences of sociology in American society, and they surely do not exhaust the impact of the profession. Still, they should give you a sense of the broad potential for sociological participation in day-to-day social life. The first example comes from World War II.

Bringing the Boys Home

During much of the Vietnam war, "Bring the boys home" was a rallying cry at many antiwar demonstrations. At the end of World War II, bringing the boys home was a different kind of problem. With the German and Japanese surrenders, millions of American military personnel were psychologically ready to go home from the war. There were too many people in uniform, however, to simply let everyone go at once, and the American military high command was faced with deciding who should be released first.

After the German surrender, troops in the European theater were released in accordance with a "point system" that took account of such things as combat duty, length of service, family status, and so forth. With the Japanese surrender, however, the War Department received considerable pressure from important generals to release the least experienced soldiers first, retaining those with more combat experience. General George Marshall was concerned that such a decision would have disastrous effects on morale, so he instructed Samuel Stouffer and his research branch to conduct a survey of soldiers' attitudes on the matter.

The results of the survey confirmed Marshall's fear. Of those surveyed, 60 percent said the points given for combat duty should not be changed, while another 20 percent felt the points should be increased. Only 4 percent favored lowering the number of points given for combat duty. (The remainder had no opinion.) To the suggestion of early release for those who "have been in the Army too short a time to complete their training," four out of five were totally opposed.

As a result of Stouffer's survey, the Army decided to continue the point system unchanged, releasing soldiers in a fashion that reflected what the soldiers themselves felt was fair (Stouffer 1962).

William Graham Sumner 1840–1910 (Yale University Library)

Educating Blacks and Whites

Sociologists have been involved in American race relations in countless ways. Their impact in this issue has been as visible in terms of public education as in any other aspect, and it illustrates the different implications that can be drawn from sociological research.

In 1896, the U.S. Supreme Court established the principle of "separate but equal" as a means of reconciling the equality guaranteed blacks by the Fourteenth Amendment with the norm of segregation that prevailed throughout the South. While the case (*Plessy* v. *Ferguson*) had to do specifically with public transportation, the ruling was to influence public education for years to come.

Sociologists were not asked to research the subject and none were cited directly, but it is generally agreed (Rose 1959) that the Court was influenced by the writings of William Graham Sumner (1840–1910),

who was later to become the second president of the American Sociological Society. By the time of the Plessy case, Sumner (1894) was well known for his view that the mores and folkways of a society possessed a power that could not be significantly altered by legislation and social planning. Thus, the Court ruled that it could not accept the assumption that "social prejudices may be overcome by legislation," and it denied the wisdom of "laws which conflict with the general sentiment of the community" (Reprinted in Blaustein and Zangrando 1970:308).

The doctrine of "separate but equal" was not overturned until 1954. In *Brown* v. *Board of Education of Topeka*, the Supreme Court ruled the doctrine unconstitutional. In part, the decision was based on the conclusion that segregation had a detrimental effect on black children. In a footnote accompanying this decision, the Court cited several sociological and psychological research reports (Reprinted in Blaustein and Zangrando 1970).

The more recent controversy that has surrounded the "Coleman report" (1966) (discussed in Chapter 9) is evidence of continued sociological involvement in the issue. Coleman and his colleagues, in a massive national survey sponsored by the U.S. Office of Education, found that students' home environments had a far greater influence on academic achievement than either integration or school facilities and expenditures. The controversy sparked by the report will likely continue for some time.

Recasting the Passion Play

For nearly two thousand years, Christians and Jews have debated the role played by the ancient Jews in the Crucifixion of Christ. The epithet "Christ killers" has served as justification for countless anti-Semitic atrocities.

From 1962 to 1965, the hierarchy of the Roman Catholic church met at Vatican City in Rome in what came to be known as Vatican Council II for the purpose of updating church practice and doctrine. Among the measures proposed before the council was formal passage of a statement denying the doctrine of Jewish guilt for the Crucifixion. Conservative members of the council objected, saying the church had never taught the doctrine of Jewish guilt and therefore had nothing to deny.

As the council proceedings were under way, sociologists Charles Glock and Rodney Stark were just beginning their analyses of a large-scale survey of Christian church members, seeking to discover any existing religious sources of anti-Semitism. The results of the study were published in 1966 in the book *Christian Beliefs and Anti-Semitism.* Early reports of the study's findings, however, were forwarded to the Vatican. Regardless of whether the church had formally taught the doctrine of Jewish guilt, the findings showed, 61 percent of the Roman Catholic church members surveyed believed that the Jews were the group "most responsible for crucifying Christ" (Glock and Stark 1966:54).

The Glock-Stark research findings reinforced the view that the church had a moral obligation to speak out against the doctrine. Ultimately, a statement denying Jewish guilt was passed (Stark et al. 1971).

Free without Bail

It has been a tradition in American criminal law to set bail for persons accused of crimes, a practice provided for in the Constitution. The amount of bail in any given case is established by the judge, who seeks to ensure that the defendant will later appear in court for a trial. Often the bail is actually posted by professional bail bondsmen, who collect 10 percent of the bail amount from the accused as compensation for taking the risk that the accused will leave town. In rare cases, persons deemed especially trustworthy by the court have been released without bail.

In 1961, a team of researchers in New York City conducted an experiment in which they made predictions on the likelihood of defendants' appearing in court for trial on the basis of interviews. With the cooperation of the New York judiciary, a number of those deemed good risks by interviewers were released without bail. Only 1 percent failed to appear in court.

The consequences of the experiment have been widespread. First the city of New York established the interviewing system as a permanent feature of its court system. Subsequently, most large cities and many rural areas adopted the same system (Zeisel 1967).

This handful of examples should give you an idea of the many ways in which sociological research can have a direct impact on the functioning of mass society. The potential influence of sociologists on their societies, however, must be viewed within a larger, more philosophical context. We are going to see that sociologists disagree among themselves as to the "proper" uses of their discipline.

Values, Scholarship, and Social Policy

It is clear that sociologists can and do use their professional skills to change the nature of the society they live in. Sociology is a potential instrument for social action, for social reform. As you can imagine, this potential has not escaped the attention of sociologists themselves, nor has it been only recently recognized. Consider, for example, the three lead articles in the first (February 1936) issue of the *American Sociological Review:*

F. Stuart Chapin, "Social Theory and Social Action"

Pitirim A. Sorokin, "Is Accurate Social Planning Possible?"

E. A. Ross, "Some Contributions of Sociology to the Guidance of Society"

Chapin's article, a reprint of his 1935 presidential address, expressed the aspirations of many American sociologists at a time when their discipline seemed to be coming of age. As the nation was recovering from an unprecedented economic depression, experimenting with active federal governance under the Roosevelt administration, Chapin called for the establishment of social scientific advisory boards.

> Such persons should be actually advisory in the sense of being consulted *before* and *not after* administrative decision is made. They should render an expert opinion by stating the alternatives of social action and/or the probable consequences, and submit this statement to the proper public official or leader. Finally, this expert opinion should be considered and studied by administrators before the decision is announced publicly (1936:11).

What Chapin had in mind was probably something like the contemporary President's Council of Economic Advisors. Nothing like that has quite come about, however. The reasons why Chapin's vision was never realized have more to do with the subject matter of sociology than with the abilities of sociologists to make expert contributions to social administration.

Sociology is typically addressed to subjects that have day-to-day reality to members of society. Moreover, most people have personal points of view on such things, points of view that often reflect ideologies and are often reified.

When sociologists study and draw conclusions about such things as prejudice, religiosity, politics,

education, and the family, they venture into areas in which everyone is an "expert." Were the world's most renowned sociologist to conduct the world's greatest research project and conclude that the nuclear family was dysfunctional for both society and individuals and urge legislation to ban it in the United States, it is unlikely that such legislation would even be considered seriously, let alone passed and enforced. As we saw in Chapter 8, our personal notions about the family have been reified and firmly linked with other institutions.

Sociologists, then, study things that most people already have strong personal feelings about. Sociological research often threatens people's personal values and ideologies. To make matters worse, sociologists are people, with their own values. Can we be sure that sociologists can prevent their own personal values from interfering with the scientific quality of their research and conclusions? This is something that has concerned sociologists themselves for a long time.

In 1918, the great German sociologist, Max Weber, addressed students at Munich University on the topic of "Science as a Vocation." In that talk, he put forth a point of view that has figured importantly in sociology ever since. Weber was concerned over the great popularity of professors who took political positions in the lecture hall that pleased students, and he suggested that these professors were behaving improperly. Science, including sociology, needed to be "value-free" if it was to make its special contribution to society, Weber argued (Weber 1925a). In scientific research and teaching, the scientist needed to set personal values aside.

Few scientists would disagree with Weber's position that scientists should not allow their personal values to distort their research findings. Yet there is and has been considerable disagreement on whether scientific activities can be totally devoid of personal-value influences. And American sociology has a long history of disagreement on whether sociologists should use their professional expertise to seek the realization of social and political ideals.

Lester Ward (1841–1913), the first president of the American Sociological Society, was a social-action sociologist. He didn't hesitate to address policy issues in his research nor to draw policy conclusions from

Lester Ward 1841–1913 (Brown University Archives)

his research—providing scientific, sociological bases for sexual equality, democracy, and racial unity (Odum 1951). A similar orientation is to be found in Albion Small (1854–1926), the fourth president of the association. Small's determination to *do something* with the results of scholarship led him, in 1904, to lash out at historians:

> The quarrel of the sociologists with the historians is that the latter have learned so much about how to do it that they have forgotten what to do. They have become so skilled at finding facts that they have no use for the truths that would make the facts worth finding. They have exhausted their magnificent technique in discovering things that are not worth knowing when they get through with them (Quoted in Barnes 1948:768).

The activist zeal of some of the earlier American sociologists often was a product of their religious and

vocational experiences. Small, for example, was a minister and the son of a minister, and much of his sociology can be read as an attempt at the secular salvation of society. Also, many of the early sociology departments were combined with departments of social work, providing an additional social-action component.

The openly activist example set by the association's first president (Ward) was contradicted by the second president, William Graham Sumner. Sumner felt that attempts at social change were useless. And like Chapin who was to follow, he felt sociologists could best serve society by observing scientifically and reporting what they observed. Their own personal values had no place in such an endeavor.

While Sumner's conclusion regarding the impossibility of planned social change has been proved wrong, the debate over the "propriety" of sociologists' using their science to further particular values has continued. Overall, the Weberian view of "value neutrality" seems to have predominated in American sociology in recent decades. Even the staunchest supporters of this view, however, would undoubtedly make some exceptions.

No sociologist would be criticized for saying his or her research was aimed at achieving world peace. No one would condemn eradicating poverty as the motivation behind a research project. Sociologists also more or less agree that prejudice and bigotry are "bad." Glock and Stark (1966:xxi) candidly opened their study of anti-Semitism saying, "obviously our decision to undertake such a study was not dispassionate. If the churches, no matter how inadvertently, lead men to hate Jews, we mean to raise the alarm." Some sociologists and church people were displeased with the study's empirical findings and interpretations, but no one seriously questioned the propriety of using sociology to fight bigotry. Nobody criticizes the cancer researcher for being "against" cancer.

The question of personal values and professional scholarship is a complex one. In his 1961 presidential address to the Society for the Study of Social Problems, Alvin Gouldner (1962) criticized the Weberian view, referring to "the myth of value-free sociology." Gouldner suggested that it was simply impossible for a scholar's personal values to be totally divorced from his or her scholarship.

I have gone into the complications of this issue at length because the dilemmas it poses are not unique to sociology. Many physicists were rudely awakened by the atomic bombing of Hiroshima in 1945. Biologists have seen their discoveries used to lay the foundation for biological warfare. Statisticians see their findings used to promote and defend unwise and inhumane policies. Scientists from all disciplines have begun asking whether it is possible to be *just* a scientist.

Issues such as these make another point. The debate over unresolved issues shows sociology to be a living, vibrant undertaking. Sociology is no dusty storehouse of established facts and techniques. It is continually growing and developing. Sociologists are very much alive in the world today, and they will be tomorrow too. Let's look at what sociologists are likely to be doing in the years to come.

Prospects for the Future

It is sometimes useful to divide sociology—and other sciences—into two branches: pure and applied. This is one of those times.

By "pure" sociology, I mean sociological inquiry that has no direct or immediate use. At the least,

such inquiry is not motivated by plans for the application of what is learned. The political sociologist who is interested in understanding the dynamics of voting behavior but who has no plans to use that understanding in actual political situations is engaged in pure sociology.

Sociologists are certain to continue working in the area of pure sociology. We can anticipate the development of new theoretical points of view in the future, just as we've seen a continuing evolution of theory in the past. We can also anticipate a continuing development of new, more sophisticated statistical and methodological techniques. There's little risk in making predictions like that, but what is likely to be the nature of such theoretical and methodological developments?

I suspect we will see more basic inquiry directed at the dynamic aspect of society, more attempts made to understand and measure social process. While we have made considerable progress in formally conceptualizing the structure of agreements in society, we do not have the formal theoretical and methodological tools appropriate to understanding how those agreements operate or how they change. We can observe and measure social change by comparing structures at different points in time, but we cannot measure and understand what goes on in between the points. Sociology of the future, then, is likely to be more involved in matters of process than structure.

It is far easier to predict—with greater specificity—what applied sociology will address in the years to come, since the application of sociology has typically linked the discipline to social problems and planning. During the last third of this book, we have looked at a number of the social problems that have attracted sociologists' attention: crime, poverty, discrimination, and prejudice, among others. It is unlikely that sociologists will either lose interest in or totally solve such problems very soon.

Our examination of mass society has pointed to certain problems that are becoming more important than they have seemed before. The field of demography, for example, has become far more vital as we've begun recognizing the dangers of overpopulation. Increasingly, demographers have directed their attention to the issue of family planning, seeking

Any two people on earth have things in common and things that make them different. Social life is a continuing process of discovery. As we discover the similarities and differences that link us with others, we discover ourselves. (Earl Dotter, BBM)

to discover factors that will facilitate the use of contraceptives and reduce family size.

Environmental concern has redirected interests and activities in the physical sciences, and we can expect something similar in sociology. As we saw in Chapter 17 and elsewhere in this book, merely recognizing that many human practices threaten the physical ecosystem does not lead to a change in those practices. We must understand more fully the social agreements shaping the ways people view and treat their planet. Such knowledge is as important as chemical or biological knowledge.

Applied sociological activities in the future will very likely take place in the context of increased attempts at social planning. Many of those planning activities will occur within a government framework, adding intensity to the debate over values and sociological inquiry. The social-planning context has implications for the techniques sociologists will use as well. First, we can expect a mushrooming of activity in connection with **social indicators**. (The accompanying box, "'Social Indicators' and the Quality of Life," discusses this aspect of social research.) Second, evaluation research, mentioned frequently in earlier portions of the book, is likely to become an important specialty in sociology. No longer will administrators experiment with new programs—in prisons, hospitals, schools, and elsewhere—without including a formal

"Social Indicators" and the Quality of Life

How would you rate the "quality of life" in:

Massachusetts?	Florida?
New York?	Louisiana?
Illinois?	California?
South Dakota?	Texas?
Ohio?	Alabama?
Pennsylvania?	North Carolina?
Minnesota?	

If you're like most Americans, you would probably put these states in roughly the order shown. California might be higher, South Dakota might be lower, there might be differences of detail, and we'd have to allow for your home-state patriotism, but generally shouldn't the "quality of life" be higher where the people are healthier, wealthier, and, if not wiser, at least better educated? In fact (ever since the journalist H. L. Mencken tried to identify "the worst American state" fifty years ago—it was Mississippi), statistical measures of quality of life have given just about this result.

It seems reasonable that if we ask people whether they like their state as a place to live, we will get about the same order again. Shouldn't people be happier with states where the quality of life is higher? Apparently not. When residents of these thirteen states were asked in 1968, "Would you say that [your state] is the best state in which to live?" only about 50 percent of those in the top three states said yes, compared with around 60 percent in the next six states, around 70 percent in California and Texas, and around 80 percent in Alabama and North Carolina![1]

In recent years, sociologists and other social scientists have attempted to develop "social indi-cators," measures of social well-being analogous to the economic indicators familiar to all of us. The foregoing example may suggest why the search for such social indicators has been so difficult.

If you had to select social indicators to go into an annual "social report" (like the President's annual *Economic Report*), what statistics would you choose? Crime rates? Disease rates? Measures of inequality in the distribution of income? Here are some questions to think about:

1. What is the rationale for including each item? Is there a national consensus that it is a "good thing"? Does it promote individual happiness? Social justice? What if it promotes one but not the other?

2. Are there items that ought to be included for which we don't have any measures? Two recent studies have shown that relations with family and friends are probably the most important predictors of individual happiness.[2] How could these be measured?

3. What is the cost (in dollars and otherwise)? Do we have a measure of it? We might agree that low crime rates are good. What if reducing them requires greatly extended police surveillance and interference?

4. If we are including items because they produce greater happiness, why not just measure happiness directly and be done with it? Are people reliable reporters of their own happiness?

What would you suggest as social indicators for measuring our quality of life?

---

[1]Merle Black, "North Carolina: The 'Best' American State?", in *Politics and Policy in North Carolina*, ed. Thad L. Beyle and Merle Black (New York: MSS Information Corp., 1975), pp. 13–36.

[2]"Measuring the Quality of Life in America: A New Frontier for Social Science," Newsletter of the Institute for Social Research, University of Michigan, II (Ann Arbor, Summer 1974), pp. 3–8.

Modern societies bring together a variety of points of view. The survival of human group life requires the continual making and remaking of social agreements that permit social interaction. (Andy Mercado)

research component to measure the effectiveness of the experiment.

The earlier discussion of modernization suggests a whole host of pure and applied activities for sociologists of the future, but it also suggests something more. I suspect that sociology of the future will follow the lead of the large corporations in becoming transnational. Sociologists must eventually take on a global point of view. Through population growth and improved communications, we are fast becoming a global society, and the study of single, national societies becomes increasingly artificial.

As the many diverse peoples of the world come into closer and more frequent contact with one an-

other, the variety of agreements that I've discussed throughout the book will come into confrontation as never before. If we are to survive that confrontation, it is essential that we understand what agreements are, how they are formed, and how they operate. Only then will *people* be able to construct institutions that will both promote group survival and enhance individual satisfaction.

A few hundred pages ago, I suggested to you that sociologists see a rich and fascinating world. It has been a special honor and a delight for me to be able to share that world with you, and I hope you will find it as fascinating as I have.

Suggested Readings

assessment of modern sociology is stimulating reading.

Barnes, Harry Elmer

1948   *An Introduction to the History of Sociology.* Chicago: University of Chicago Press.

Although dated, this large volume provides an excellent and engaging history of American sociology and its European origins. Barnes intertwines history, biography, and sociological concepts in such a way as to give you a comprehensive view of how sociology operates in practice. This kind of presentation puts life into what might otherwise seem a dreary collection of facts and theories. Sociology lives!

Gouldner, Alvin

1971   *The Coming Crisis in Western Sociology.* London: Heinemann.

Not only does sociology live (see above), but sociologists sometimes disagree with one another, as I've tried to indicate throughout the preceding discussions. Alvin Gouldner has been known to disagree with various sociologists from time to time, and this examination of contemporary and recent sociology describes his reservations about structural-functional points of view. Both scholarly and polemical, this

Lazarsfeld, Paul et al., Eds.

1967   *The Uses of Sociology.* New York: Basic Books.

Is sociology really worth the effort? I trust that I've answered that question for you (the answer was yes) in this chapter, but the Lazarsfeld collection provides a much broader view of the many ways sociology is involved in your daily life. Organizing the presentation around major institutions, the editors have brought together a mass of examples regarding the impact of sociology in medicine, education, and so forth, pointing also the the potential uses of sociology in those areas.

Odum, Howard

1951   *American Sociology.* New York: Longmans.

This is an excellent reference book for studying the history of American sociology. Odum largely organizes his presentation around the several presidents of the American Sociological (Society) Association through 1950. The book is of special interest in showing the shifts in substantive interests of sociologists over the years. He also discusses, more briefly, related professional associations and a number of professional journals.

❧

Episode Nineteen

It was in late June of the year 2032 that Monica appeared at Gabriel's door. She arrived with Louise Roanoke.

Gabriel had just returned from his office at Southwest Insurance and changed his clothes when he heard the bell. Flicking off the exposed fluorescent tubing in his bedroom he walked, curious, through a large, glass-roofed garden room to open his front door.

"Gabe?"

He recognized the voice even before he looked into her face.

"It's been over four years!" he heard himself exclaiming seconds later.

"Louise and I are on our way back to Chicago from Mexico City," Monica was explaining. "We're between planes. We thought we'd stop."

"Come in," he managed.

When his guests were seated he asked whether they would like something.

"Maybe some wine," Monica said.

"Yes, thank you, Gabriel," Louise added, "wine would be good."

Gabriel went to a wet bar, removed the cork from a bottle of burgundy, and carried it and three glasses into the garden room. Returning to the bar, he fixed a plate of soybean chips and assorted cheeses.

"Snacks?" Monica asked upon seeing the food. "Gabriel Knapp, you've changed!"

"Not as much as you might think," he responded. "But I keep a few things around now. I like a little cheese every so often. Remember Ann Sullivan? Or perhaps you didn't meet her. *You* met her though, Dr. Roanoke"—he turned to face the older woman, already aware that he had begun to ramble nervously—"well, Ann Sullivan opened a little deli a few blocks from here about four years ago now. I helped her

stock the shelves. Handling all that silly stuff made me curious, I guess." Gabriel stopped abruptly. "What are you doing now, Monica?"

"I'm still with the firm," she said. "Although I'm thinking about leaving soon. I'd like to take off on my own. Open a little office somewhere in a low-rent neighborhood and answer my own phone. That sort of thing."

"Are you still with Civil Liberty for All?"

"Oh, yes," she said, "I've tried several cases for them. Nothing as spectacular as yours though."

Gabriel took a swallow of wine. "Will you stay in Chicago?" he asked.

"Probably," she said. "We like Chicago."

"We?"

She gazed at him. "I married two years ago," she said.

He didn't reply.

"We have a little girl."

"Oh," he answered, "wonderful." His voice trailed off. He remembered that he and Monica used to talk about that sometimes.

"Tell me, Gabriel," Louise said, "how is Daniel Adamson, the other delegate who came with you to the conference?"

"Fine," Gabe said. "Just fine. He's still up in Adamsville, of course. He matured last year. His skin is brilliant. He publishes a newspaper in the colony now. Quite a radical, very separatist paper, from what I've seen. But generally the community is more liberal now. Daniel speaks to a minority."

"And Ann Sullivan owns a delicatessen here, you say?" Louise pursued, academically curious.

"Yes. She's running for the Arizona State Legislature. She worked very hard to get the state's ban on intermarriage declared unconstitutional last year."

"Whatever happened to the federal bill that would have denied greens the right to vote in federal elections?" Louise asked Monica.

"It was permanently tabled shortly after the third conference," Monica replied. She turned toward Gabe. "I read a few years ago in the papers that you matured," she said.

"Yes," Gabe answered.

"Do you go back to Adamsville often?" Monica asked, placing a slice of cheese on a soybean chip.

"Every few months." He paused. "There are unpleasant memories there, but then there are many good ones too." "Well, tell me," he shifted, "how is Bradley Duncan?"

"He's down in Brazil now," Louise said, "doing a study on possible ways to improve the health of native tribes."

"And drinking Brazilian beer," Monica added with a laugh.

"I went to the university library here and looked up his journal article on word meanings in Adamsville," Gabriel said. "I enjoyed it."

"What he's doing now may prove even more useful to a greater number of people," Louise smiled.

"And where is Dr. Batterson?" Gabe asked.

"She and her husband are in Africa," Louise answered, "helping to organize the labor movement there. The study she was doing on discrimination toward greens was published in *Transaction* last year."

"Some sociologists from the University of Arizona," Gabriel offered, sipping his wine, "are doing research on problems our children may face when they begin to attend school here in Phoenix."

"Your community here is growing then," Monica concluded.

"Yes," Gabe nodded. "We have done well here. We have encountered some discrimination, of course, but we expected that. We have been very lucky that even in spite of prejudice many of us have found satisfying jobs—often in the areas for which we were educated and trained while posing." He shifted, conscious that he had gone on too long. "And, Louise, what are you doing now?"

"I'll be teaching at the University of Mexico City this fall. That's why I spent the last two weeks there. I wanted to check into living space, things like that. Monica came along for a vacation." Dr. Roanoke drank from her glass of burgundy.

"Tell me more about Adamsville," Monica requested. "It must be quite different now in some ways."

"Well," Gabe began, "pure greens continue to live within the boundaries. The fence is still up, and guards are still posted. But for the most part there is no trouble near the borders, and the guards are more a tradition than a necessity. A friend of mine from childhood, Jacob, is Elder. He moved into Elderhome after Michael's death.

"Many outsiders work at S.T.I. now. Their presence has influenced some changes. Some residents are beginning to talk about electing a mayor by secret ballot, as outsiders do, rather than accepting Jacob as Michael's chosen successor."

"Has Adamsville's religion changed?" Louise asked.

"Some, yes," Gabe said. "Light-break, for example, is now considered more a necessity to a mutant's good health than a religious exercise. Few would consider it prayer. But there remain those orthodox greens—many who once supported Larry Jones—who insist that the truths set down by Adam must never change. This is one reason I persuaded many from the valley to come to Phoenix. In Adamsville many continued to think of us as spiritually degenerate. And even the liberals considered us sick, genetically deficient."

"And are you happy here now?" asked Monica.

"Yes," Gabriel affirmed. "I'm comfortable here."

"Do you live here alone?"

"No," Gabe answered. "Three others whom neither of you know and I entered a five-year friendship contract last summer. We designed and built this home last fall shortly after one of us was admitted to practice medicine on the staff at Central Hospital —and after I was promoted at Southwest Insurance."

"You're back in the insurance business then," Monica smiled.

"Yes," Gabe nodded. "We're developing standards of coverage for both pure and partial mutants.

There's no doubt in my mind that we'll be offering health coverage to greens within five years."

Louise glanced at her watch. "I'm sorry this visit was so brief," she apologized, standing up. "But I'm afraid it's time we were getting back to the airport."

"I'll take you," Gabriel offered.

"No," Monica said. "It's already been arranged. A taxi is coming for us." She paused, aware of Gabe's —and her own—disappointment. "We couldn't be sure whether we'd find you—or whether you'd be free—"

"I understand," Gabe interrupted her explanation.

The cab had returned and was parked near the curb. Louise shook Gabriel's hand. "I very much enjoyed seeing you again," she said. "Thank you for the wine and food." Then she left the home and walked toward the waiting taxi.

"Listen," Gabe said to Monica, "keep in touch."
"You too," she said, turning to leave.

Questions

1. In what ways did Roanoke, Duncan, and Batterson—as sociologists—affect the lives of greens generally and Gabe Knapp in particular?

2. To what extent did the sociologists' behavior in the story reflect their training as sociologists and to what extent was their sociology irrelevant? Be specific.

3. Do you think that sociologists should keep their personal values separate from their science? Do you think they can?

Glossary

Achieved status. Social position gained through your actions, such as college graduation or ax murder. Contrasted with **Ascribed status.**

Age-Sex composition. (1) The numbers (or proportions) of males and females in various age groups that make up a population; often presented by demographers in the form of an age-sex pyramid. (2) The way you size up a party as soon as you arrive.

Aggregation. As distinguished from group, this refers to a gathering of people in the same location, such as the people who gathered to watch you let the air out of your instructor's tires. (Money will probably weaken their memories.)

Agreement. Condition of being the same, often in terms of sharing the same point of view or expectation. Some social agreements are recognized by people as agreements; some are mistaken for reality. Some are entered into voluntarily; some are a matter of coercion or custom.

Agreement reality. Your picture of the way things are based on your acceptance of the agreements you share with those around you.

Ascribed status. Social position established at birth, such as sex or race. Contrasted with **Achieved status.**

Assimilation. Process through which the subcultures of a society are merged into the dominant culture, losing their groups' differences and becoming a part of the whole. The American "melting pot" is an example of the assimilation process,

to the extent that the concept "melting pot" is characteristic of the United States at all.

Association. A type of secondary group, organized around a shared interest or view.

Attribute. Characteristic of a person or thing. A set of logically related attributes make up a **Variable.**

Authority. Person's agreed-on right to exercise power in a group. See also **Legitimation.**

Belief. Reified view of what's true, usually shared as an agreement among a group.

Bilineal descent. (1) Kinship agreement in which people trace their ancestry through both their male and female forebears. Contrasted with **Matrilineal descent** and **Patrilineal descent.** (2) Walking down a moving escalator.

Bureaucracy. (1) Form of social organization characterized by specific procedures and status relationships. (2) Government in the hands of a clique of cabinetmakers.

Capitalism. (1) Economic system in which the means to production are owned by private individuals. Contrasted with **Socialism.** (2) A big-letter fetish.

Caste. (1) Category of people in a stratification system, similar to a social class, but preventing movement to another place in the system. Caste is an **Ascribed status.** (2) The actors in a British play.

Category. As distinct from group, this refers to people who merely share a particular characteristic in common, such as left-handed people.

Census. (1) Enumeration, or counting, of the members of a society's population. This is what the U.S. Bureau of the Census does every ten years. (2) Sight, hearing, taste, smell, touch.

Charisma. (1) Special, personal quality that sets those who have it apart from other people; may be based on unusual strength, grace, beauty, or the ability to inspire others to follow. (2) A psychopathological delusion that your automobile is your mother.

Charismatic authority. Ability to exercise power on the basis of **Charisma.**

Church. Form of religious organization characterized by relatively restrained and formal behavior. Compared with **Sects** and **Cults.**

Civil disobedience. Conscious, nonviolent act of breaking group agreements for the purpose of dramatizing disagreement and drawing attention to the inappropriateness of the agreements being broken. This method of collective behavior is most closely associated with Gandhi, Thoreau, and Martin Luther King, Jr.

Class conflict. (1) Societywide struggle for dominance between broad social classes; a process stressed by Marx, who saw the workers struggling to escape the oppression of the ruling capitalists. (2) Enrolling in two courses that meet at the same time.

Collective behavior. Spontaneous group behavior that, while forming patterns, occurs outside institutional prescriptions for behavior. Examples are fads, riots, and panics. (2) What the Mob engages in when you fail to pay off your gambling debts.

Communication. Process of transferring points of view from one party to another. Wilbur Schramm described it as an attempt to establish a "commonness" with someone else.

Communism. Economic system in which all property is owned in common by the group; denies the possibility of private property.

Community elites. **Power elites** of specific, local communities.

Conceptualization. Mental process whereby fuzzy and imprecise notions (concepts) are made more specific and precise. See also **Operationalization,** which chums around with conceptualization.

Conflict theory. Theoretical point of view that focuses on social disagreements and the struggle among individuals and groups to impose their points of view on others. Stresses the role of power in social affairs. Associated with Marx, Coser, Dahrendorf, and others.

Content analysis. (1) Research method involving the examination of human communications. (2) Studying the examination your instructor gave last term.

Control group. (1) Group of subjects in an experiment who are not exposed to the experimental stimulus; used to isolate the effects of the stimulus per se. (2) Riot squad sent to your sociology class in connection with the unannounced mid-term exam.

Crowd. (1) Gathering of people sharing a common interest or purpose, such as a crowd gathered to hear a street-corner orator. Crowds hold the potential for **Collective behavior.** (2) What the British rooster did evuray mawning.

Crude birth rate. (1) Number of births in a population during a given year, divided by the size of the population. (2) An increase in the birth rate following a barbarian invasion.

Crude death rate. The number of deaths during a year divided by the total population size.

Cult. (1) Form of religious organization characterized by emotional, religious expression and often using ritual practices—such as snake-handling—that lie outside the established social agreements. (2) A British aristocrat's baby horse.

Cultural lag. Failure to adapt established agreements to changing conditions. The electoral college—created in connection with a loose federation of sovereign states—is an example.

Cultural relativity. Recognition that the agreements different groups share are only different, with none being better or worse than another. Contrasted with **Ethnocentrism.**

Culture. (1) Shared symbols, beliefs, values, norms, and other agreements of a group such as a society. (2) What you were sent to couth school to get. (3) What you wash your ears to avoid.

Deductive. (1) Logical model in which specific expectations are derived from general principles. (2) From a duck.

De facto. Actual state of affairs, regardless of how things are supposed to be. De facto segregation refers to the existence of racial segregation even in the face of laws prohibiting it.

Deferred gratification. (1) Foregoing something pleasurable now as a means of getting even more later. Usually involves investing time and money. Instead of eating out, you use the money to buy a textbook that will teach you things that will make you rich and powerful so that you can eat out any time you please. (2) The joy of being rejected by the army.

Democratic. Form of government in which political authority is derived from the consent of the governed.

Demography. (1) Scientific study of populations, their compositions and changes. (2) Taking pictures of prominent Democrats.

Dependent variable. In a causal relationship, it is the "effect" variable and must occur after the **Independent variable.** If the number of hours spent studying affects examination grades (who knows, it may), grades are the dependent variable.

Descriptive analysis. (1) Manipulation of data for the purpose of describing the characteristics of the group under study, without looking for the reasons for those characteristics. (2) Psychotherapy that only tells you how bad off you are without telling you how to get better.

Determinism. Point of view implicitly assumed in science, holding that every event has a set of prior causes that determine it. In the context of *social* science, this view conflicts with the notion of individual freedom and choice (see also **Free will**). All your thoughts and actions are seen as the effects of something else.

Deviance. Breaking the agreements of a group, though it matters greatly whether people are **Labeling** you as deviant.

Dialectical materialism. Marx's reformulation of the Hegelian view of history as a succession of thesis, antithesis, synthesis. Hegel was concerned with ideas; Marx substituted economic factors.

Differential association. Explanation for deviance that emphasizes the part played by socialization into a deviant subculture.

Diffusion. Spread of cultural elements from one group to another; the reason you can enjoy TV dinners in Paris.

Disagreement. Condition of being different, often in terms of different points of view or expectations. Disagreements are a source of **Social conflict** and **Social change.**

Discrimination. Actions taken on the basis of **Prejudice** and **Stereotypes.**

Dyad. (1) Two-person group. (2) Hair-color commercial.

Ecclesia. Officially established religion having special rights and powers in a society.

Economic determinism. Karl Marx's theoretical point of view, suggesting that all aspects of social life are a result of economic forces.

Economy. (1) Social institution dealing with the production, distribution, and consumption of scarce goods and services. (2) Being cheap.

Education. Social institution dealing with the transmission and transformation of knowledge.

Empirical verification. The testing of expectations through the observation of real-life events. You may be certain that you did well on your final exam, but your grade is a means of empirical verification.

Ethnic minority. Social category—based on racial, religious, or national-origin similarities—whose members are denied proportionate shares of power, wealth, and opportunities within a society.

Ethnocentrism. Feeling that the agreements of your group are real, true, and better than the agreements of some other group.

Ethnomethodology. Theoretical point of view that focuses on the ways in which people pretend to agree when they actually don't. Probes the most implicit agreements shared by a group.

Exchange theory. (1) Theoretical point of view that adapts an economic model to social affairs generally. Interactions are seen as events in which individuals enact cost-benefit arrangements with one another. (2) Your belief that if you help your friend on this exam, your friend will help you on the next one.

Experiential reality. Your picture of the ways things are based on your own personal experiences. Contrasted with **Agreement reality.**

Experiment. (1) Research method involving the controlled manipulation of variables, often in a laboratory situation. Evaluation research involves "natural experiments." (2) Mess around.

Experimental group. Group of subjects exposed to a stimulus in an experiment. To see if paying students to learn sociology will have any effect, you pay the experimental group and don't pay the **Control group** and find out which learns better.

Explanatory analysis. (1) Manipulation and interpretation of data for the purpose of discovering associations among variables and explaining how people come to be the way they are. (2) Tells you *why* you're that bad off and that you can't get better. See **Descriptive analysis** (2).

Expressive functions. Term used by Talcott Parsons and Robert Bales regarding a family's needs with reference to internal operations; creating a climate of cooperation and emotional support is an example of this function. Contrasted with **Instrumental functions.**

Extended family. Family structure composed of more than two generations. An example is a family composed of children, their parents, and their grandparents. Contrasted with **Nuclear family.**

Fad. Form of collective behavior, very popular for a short period of time and involving something generally regarded as trivial, for example, goldfish swallowing, Hula-Hooping, flagpole sitting. Sociology is definitely not a fad.

Family. Social institution dealing with the group need for the replacement of members through reproduction and nurturance. The term is also used to refer to specific social organizations operating within the institutions such as "your family" and "my family."

Fecundity. Women's *potential* capacity for childbearing, whether or not realized. Contrasted with **Fertility.**

Fertility. Women's *actual* rates of childbearing, contrasted with **Fecundity.**

Field research. (1) Research method that involves the direct observation of social events in progress. (2) Fooling around a lot prior to selecting a spouse.

Free will. (1) Point of view that holds individual actions to be the product of free, personal choice. This view conflicts with the deterministic view that is assumed by science. (2) One of the many benefits of having a friend who is an attorney.

Functionalism. (1) Theoretical point of view aimed at understanding the elements in a system in terms of their contributions to the whole. (2) Going to a party every night.

Gemeinschaft. The term used by Ferdinand Toennies meaning "community" and implying a preponderance of primary relations. Contrasted with **Gesellschaft.**

Generalized other. (1) Term used by George Herbert Mead in illustrating how we learn about overall community agreements. Having looked at things through the points of view of many different people, we develop a sense of how people in general—the generalized other—see things. (2) A friend who gets promoted to general while you're still a private.

Gesellschaft. Term used by Ferdinand Toennies meaning "society" and implying a preponderance of secondary relations. Contrasted with **Gemeinschaft.**

Homeostasis. (1) Relative stability of a social system, brought about by the balancing and counterbalancing of the different elements in the system. (2) Latin for people who never leave their houses.

Hypothesis. (1) Expectation about the way things are, derived from a theory. (2) Student paper explaining why hypopotamuses are the way they are.

Hypothesis testing. (1) Mode of research in which empirical observations are used to verify or disconfirm the expectations derived from a theory. (2) Oral examination centering around a student paper explaining why hypopotamuses are the way they are. See **Hypothesis** (2).

Ideal type. (1) Simplified model highlighting the essential features of some class or phenomenon. Weber's description of bureaucracy is an example. (2) Without typographical errors.

Imperatively coordinated associations. Term introduced by Weber and used by Dahrendorf to reflect the coercive side of social relations. An

ICA is a group held together and coordinated by the exercise of power.

Independent variable. (1) In a causal relationship, it is the "cause" variable and must occur prior to the **Dependent variable.** Education generally seems to make people less prejudiced; it is the independent variable in that case. (2) Variable that refused to roll over or lick your hand.

Inductive. (1) Logical model in which general principles are created from specific observations. (2) The feeding of ducks.

In-group. Group you feel you belong to, but exclude other people from. See also **Out-group.**

Institution. Set of established and persistent agreements governing a broad aspect of social life. Sociologists use this term to refer to such things as the family, religion, education, politics, and economics. The primary function of an institution is to shape individual experiences in such a way as to support the survival of the group.

Institutionalization. Process whereby agreements are established and perpetuated. **Institutions** are sets of interrelated, institutionalized agreements.

Institutionalized behavior. (1) Actions that follow patterns established as appropriate by institutionalized agreements. Listening attentively to your sociology instructor's lecture is an example. Throwing rotten eggs and apples is not an example; see **Collective behavior.** (2) Banging your tin cup on the bars of your jail cell.

Instrumental functions. (1) Term used by Talcott Parsons and Robert Bales regarding a family's needs in relating to its *external* environment; thus, earning a wage in the economy in order to support the family is an example of the instrumental function. Contrast with **Expressive functions.** (2) Jam sessions.

Internalization. Process through which you make the agreements of your group a part of your own personal feelings about things.

Labeling. Theoretical point of view on deviance that stresses the impact of people's being labeled as deviant. Indeed, being labeled deviant can have greater social consequences than actually breaking the agreements.

Latent function. Hidden, indirect, or unanticipated consequence of something. A latent function of education, for example, is the removal of young people from the job market.

Legitimation. Process through which certain actions or relationships are made legitimate by agreement. Sociologists most frequently talk of this in terms of power relationships in a group. When the exercise of power by certain people become legitimated, they are said to have **Authority.**

Lombrosian view. Outdated theoretical point of view on deviance put forward by Cesare Lombroso holding that (a) deviance is biologically determined and (b) it is possible to identify criminals by the way they look.

Looking-glass self. (1) Term coined by Charles Horton Cooley to refer to the way you see yourself as a reflection of the way other people seem to see you. (2) That friend you talk to in the bathroom when you think no one is watching.

Manifest function. (1) Avowed purpose of something; its justification for being. The manifest function of education is the transmission of agreements. Contrast with **Latent function.** (2) Party at which a revolutionary document will be read.

Mass media. Communication agencies such as radio, television, and newspapers. They are very powerful in a mass society in that they address vast audiences, permitting little or no response from the members of that audience.

Matriarchal. Agreement pertaining to power relations within the family, in which the woman is dominant. Contrasted with **Patriarchal.**

Matrilineal descent. (1) Kinship agreement in which people trace their ancestry through their female forebears only. Contrasted with **Bilineal descent** and **Patrilineal descent.** (2) Riding the rapids on an air mattress.

Matrilocal. Family residency agreement in which the new couple moves in with the woman's parents. Contrasted with **Neolocal** and **Patrilocal** residency.

Migration. (1) Movement from one place to another; demographers study the movement of people from one society to another and from place to place within a given society because of its applications for population size and composition. (2) The headache that kept you from attending your eight-year-old brother's tuba recital.

Minority group. A racial, religious, or ethnic group which occupies a disadvantaged position within a society.

Modernization. Form of social change common today, as the less-developed countries of the world seek to urbanize and industrialize. Such changes, typically focusing on economic matters, affect virtually all aspects of social life.

Monogamy. (1) Agreement limiting people to one spouse at a time. Contrasted with **Polygamy.** (2) Situation in which there's only one game in town.

Mortality. Death; used by demographers in reference to death rates.

Natural increase. (1) Growth of a population caused by an excess of births over deaths. (2) Raising the bet in poker when you were dealt a straight flush.

Neolocal. Family residency agreement in which the new couple establishes a residence separate from either of their parents. Contrasted with **Patrilocal** residence and **Matrilocal** residence.

Norm. (1) Agreement on the behavior expected of people; shaking hands when meeting someone is a norm. (2) Residential building for college students with colds.

Nuclear family. Family structure composed of parents and their children only. Contrasted with **Extended family.**

Operational definition. Concrete and specific definition of the operations by which observations are to be categorized in relation to a concept. The operational definition of "earning an A in this course" might be getting 90 percent of the final exam items right.

Operationalization. (1) One step beyond conceptualization. This is the process of developing **Operational definitions.** (2) Fancy term for surgery, used to justify high medical costs.

Out-group. (1) Those people who are excluded from a particular **In-group** or from the rest of society. (2) Unsuccessful batters in a baseball game.

Participant-Observation. Data-collection method used by sociologists, involving the direct personal observation of real social events as they occur.

Patriarchal. Agreement pertaining to power relations within the family in which the man is dominant. Contrasted with **Matriarchal.**

Patrilineal descent. Kinship agreement in which people trace their ancestry through their male forebears only. Contrasted with **Bilineal descent** and **Matrilineal descent.**

Patrilocal. Family residency agreement in which the new couple moves in with the man's parents. Contrasted with **Neolocal** and **Matrilocal** residency.

Peers. (1) Your peers are the people like you that you identify yourself with. They play an important part in your **Socialization.** (2) Stares through a keyhole.

Pluralism. Sociocultural situation in which subcultural differences are perpetuated side by side in the same society, each subculture being allowed to retain its distinctive agreements; also assumes that each subculture has a reasonably fair share of power in the society.

Pluralistic power. Exercise of power by a variety of groups within a society, such as by business, labor unions, the professions, the military, and consumer groups.

Point of view. Way of seeing things; literally, a place from which to view. People occupying different social statuses typically have different points of view.

Political ideology. Set of interrelated political beliefs that provide the basis for authority in a political institution.

Polygamy. Agreement permitting people more than one spouse at a time. Contrasted with **Monogamy.**

Population. Members or residents of a geographical area, such as a community, a nation, or the world.

Positivism. (1) Philosophical point of view introduced to sociology by Auguste Comte, stressing scientific inquiry based on the assumption of a knowable, objective reality. (2) Smugness.

Posttesting. (1) Measurement made among experimental and control groups following administration of the experimental stimulus; compared with the results of **Pretesting.** (2) Washing your arm after an exam; see **Pretesting** (2).

Power. Ability to make other people do what you want them to do even if they don't want to.

Power elite. (1) Term used by C. Wright Mills to describe the small group of politicians, business people, and military leaders who exercise tremendous power in the national affairs of the United States. The term, of course, is not limited to the United States. (2) Presidents of gas and electric companies.

Prejudice. (1) Prejudging individual members of a group or category on the basis of **Stereotypes** or pictures you have about the group in general. Also refers to negative feelings associated with stereotypes. (2) Your instructor's irrational and unjust feelings about people who read newspapers in class.

Pretesting. (1) Measurement made among experimental and control groups prior to exposure to the experimental stimulus; subsequently compared with results of **Posttesting.** (2) Copying this entire glossary onto your arm before an exam.

Primary deviance. (1) The simple act of breaking agreements aside from the consideration of labeling and sanctions; this is often rationalized as nondeviant by the person involved and tolerated by others in the group. Contrasted with **Secondary deviance.** (2) Tampering with the votes in a primary election.

Primary group. Group characterized by **Primary relations.** Now guess what a secondary group is.

Primary relations. (1) Close, intimate relationships, such as those among friends; characterized by a "we feeling." (2) Political hanky-panky.

Public opinion. (1) General pattern of attitudes that the members of a society have regarding a particular issue, such as public opinion on equal employment opportunitites for women; sometimes used more specifically to refer to the dominant attitude in the society. (2) How you feel about crowds.

Race. Human category based on biological and genetic similarities. While there is little scientific agreement on the value of such categories, the caucasoid, negroid, and mongoloid are sometimes cited as the three main racial types. The social **Labeling** of races seems to have more significant consequences than biological factors.

Random selection. Probability sampling technique that gives members of a population equal chances of being chosen for a sample; it ensures that samples are representative.

Rational-Bureaucratic authority. Ability to legitimately exercise power on the basis of bureaucratic organizational rules.

Recidivism. Return to prison by those who have previously served time and have been released. (2) If you fail this course, they make you take it over again.

Reference group. Those people you compare yourself with or model yourself after.

Relative deprivation. (1) Feeling that you have gotten a bad deal in comparison with other people, especially in comparison with your **Reference group.** (2) Having your in-laws move out.

Religion. Social institution dealing with people's ultimate concerns, often—but not always—involving agreements about supernatural beings and forces. The term is also used to refer to specific social organizations operating within the institution, such as Roman Catholicism.

Religiosity. Religiousness.

Replication. Duplication of a research project to see if the same findings are produced. An essential aspect of scientific inquiry that guards against drawing conclusions from faulty or peculiar observations.

Representative sample. (1) Group of people (typically) selected from a population such that the characteristics of the sample are closely similar to the characteristics of the whole population. This permits a sociologist to study the sample and draw conclusions about the population. (2) The bite your dog takes out of a campaigning Congress member's leg.

Research methods. Modes of empirical observation and interpretation used in scientific inquiry. See also **Survey research, Experiment, Content analysis, Participant-Observation.**

Resocialization. Learning a new set of agreements to replace those previously learned in connection with an earlier status. Soldiers must be resocialized: learning military agreements that may conflict with civilian ones.

Riot. (1) Form of collective behavior, involving mass violence and mob action. (2) Opposite of leoft.

Role. (1) The behavior expectations associated with a social **Status.** The things you are expected to do because of the status you occupy; for example, students are expected to study. (2) Snake-eyes, boxcars.

Role conflict. (1) Condition of occupying two statuses that carry incompatible role expectations; for example, as a student you should study, but as a lover you should do whatever lovers are expected to do. (2) A biscuit war.

Role strain. (1) Condition in which the role expectations associated with a particular status are too demanding on the person occupying it; what you experience when it seems impossible to do everything a college student is expected to do. (2) Popping a button because you ate too many biscuits.

Role theory. (1) Theoretical point of view that places the sociological concept of "role" within a theatrical analogy. (2) A biscuit recipe.

Routinization. Process through which interactions and relationships become traditional, or "routine." Weber used this term to describe the transition between charismatic and traditional authority.

Rumor. (1) Form of collective behavior involving an unconfirmed story that spreads through a group; it need not be accurate. Shibutani calls rumors "improvised news." (2) Somebody who pays to live at your house.

Sampling. Process of selecting a subset from a population in order to study the subset (sample) and draw conclusions about the whole population from which it was drawn. The Gallup poll selects about 1,500 voters for interviewing and predicts how all voters will vote.

Science. Form of inquiry that is based on careful, empirical observation and the logical interpretation of what is observed with the purpose of creating a general understanding of something.

Secondary deviance. Deviant behavior that grows out of being labeled and treated as a deviant. A case in which people label you and treat you as a troublemaker and you begin behaving that way as a result is an example of secondary deviance. Contrasted with **Primary deviance.**

Secondary group. Group characterized by **Secondary relations,** such as an association.

Secondary relations. Casual, impersonal relationships as contrasted with **Primary relations;** usually aimed at accomplishing a specific purpose.

Sect. (1) Form of religious organization characterized by deep religious feelings, active participation, and conversion rather than inheritance as an avenue to membership. Sects often evolve into **Churches.** (2) The back two-thirds of a bug.

Social change. (1) Modification in the elements of a culture; a process of changing agreements. See also **Modernization.** (2) Relocating the senior prom from Chi-Chi's Bottomless Bar and Grill to the high school gym. (3) Mad money.

Social class. (1) Category of people occupying a particular location in a **Social stratification** system and often sharing the same subcultural agreements. (2) Finishing school. See **Culture** (2).

Social conflict. (1) Process of noncooperative interaction between individuals or groups based on disagreements; a struggle to gain dominance for competing points of view. It can occur between individuals (microconflict), within groups, between groups, between large social classes, and between societies in the form of war. (2) Getting two party invitations for the same night.

Social control. Enforcement of a group's agreements, accomplished by a variety of mechanisms and agencies.

Social disorganization. Lack of integration among a group's agreements or a conflict between agreements and conditions; a source of deviance.

Social evolution. Theoretical point of view that regards the development of society over time as moving in a particular direction, typically involving a shift from simple to complex structures.

Reflecting the Darwinian view in biology, in sociology it was popularized by Herbert Spencer.

Social indicators. Statistical measures that reflect general social conditions in a society, such as crime rates, quality of schools, and physicians per capita. Similar to economic indicators that reflect the health of the economy.

Social interaction. The process in which one person directs a communication and evokes a response from the other that is conditioned by the initial communication. Realize in this that "communication" includes physical actions as well as words. Typically, it goes back and forth, back and forth, like a windshield wiper. Also, any number can play.

Socialism. (1) Economic system in which the means to production are owned by government. Contrasted with **Capitalism.** (2) Going to a lot of parties.

Socialization. Process through which people learn the agreements of their group.

Social mobility. Movement of an individual or a group within a stratification system.

Social movement. Organized group action aimed at influencing the society's agreements. Reactionary movements seek to restore prior agreements; conservative movements seek to maintain current ones; reform movements seek modification of current agreements; revolutionary movements seek to replace current agreements with a new set.

Social relationships. The structure of links between social statuses, as specified by the roles associated with each. For example, a social relationship exists between the statuses "mother" and "son" in that we have agreements about the behavior of each toward the other.

Social stratification. (1) Process of arranging people and groups hierarchically within society on the basis of wealth, prestige, power, or other variables. See also **Social class.** (2) Bunk beds in a dormitory.

Social structure. (1) Established network of relationships connecting different statuses in a group, including the norms for interactions among different statuses. (2) Cocktail lounge.

Social systems theory. Theoretical point of view that approaches society as a system comprised of interrelated parts, analogous to a biological system such as the human body. Chiefly associated with Talcott Parsons.

Society. Group of people sharing a common culture; typically a political unit such as a nation, living within defined geographical boundaries. A social system with people living in it.

Socioeconomic status (SES). Measurement of someone's location within a system of **Social stratification.** Typically, such measures reflect several aspects of social status, such as income, education, and occupation.

Sociology. The study of human group life. See Babbie, *Society by Agreement* (Belmont, Calif.: Wadsworth, 1977), for more on this.

Status. A location within a social network. "Student" is an example of status.

Status inconsistency. (1) Occupying statuses that have different implications for your location in a system of **Social stratification;** a millionaire shoe shiner is an example. (2) Telling your friends you make more money than you told the Internal Revenue Service.

Status quo. (1) Current state of affairs. Those benefiting most from a particular set of social agreements tend to want to maintain the status quo. (2) Latin for "you're standing on my foot."

Stereotype. Picture of a group or category of people that serves as the basis for assumptions about all such people. If you believe all sociologists are swell and wonderful, that is a stereotype. (It's true, of course, but still a stereotype.)

Strata. Particular level or ranking within a system of **Social stratification.**

Subculture. (1) **Culture** of an identified group within a society, such as a minority group. (2) The set of agreements shared on submarines, such as not sleeping with the window open.

Survey research. Research method utilizing questionnaires, either self-administered or administered by interviewers.

Symbol. (1) Representation of something else; a flag is a symbol of a nation. (2) Symphonic alarm clock for those who didn't attend couth school. See **Culture** (2).

Symbolic interactionism. (1) Theoretical point of view introduced by George Herbert Mead, focusing on the ways in which people interact and create shared meanings. (2) Shadowboxing.

System imperatives. Term used by Talcott Parsons to refer to those functions that must be served in order for a social system to survive; adaptation, goal attainment, integration, and latency.

Technology. (1) Means we've created for transforming our environment, particularly our physical environment; typically reflects the application of scientific knowledge. (2) Driving across town in forty-five minutes instead of walking in thirty.

Theory of demographic transition. Theoretical model in demography describing a common pattern of population changes during the course of modernization: beginning with high birth and death rates; death rates are decreased while birth rates remain high, causing population growth; then birth rates decrease, reducing the rate of population growth.

Totalitarian. Form of government in which all aspects of life are controlled by a central, political institution.

Totemism. Preliterate form of religion in which the socioreligious group identifies itself with some animal or object (the totem).

Traditional authority. Agreement that the exercise of power by certain people is legitimate by virtue of its "always having been that way."

Traditional autocratic. Form of government in which a single ruler, supported by a small elite, runs things on the basis of **Traditional authority;** more common among small, underdeveloped countries.

Transformation function. Primary function of economic institutions; to transform the physical environment so it provides for human needs and desires; people are also transformed into roles within the economy.

Triad. (1) Group comprised of three or more people. (2) Commercial introducing a new product.

Urbanism. Concentration of populations into cities, as opposed to rural patterns of social organization.

Value. View about what's preferred over something else, usually shared as an agreement among a group. (2) Technical term in advertising for something worth $.10 that you can buy (this week only) for $1.50 instead of the customery $1.98.

Value-added. Analytical model for the study of social processes; "something" is transformed by stages as a series of new elements are added. Marx introduced this model in studying economic production (workers added the value of their labor to raw materials), and Smelser adapted the model to the study of developing collective behavior.

Variable. Logical grouping of **Attributes.** "Sex" is a variable made up of the attributes "female" and "male."

Voluntary association. Specific-purpose, secondary group that like-minded people form in order to share an interest or achieve a purpose.

Zero population growth. Situation in which a given population retains the same size from one generation to the next; requires a balancing of births and in-migration with deaths and out-migration.

Bibliography*

Allen, Irving
1975   "Social Relations and the Two-Step Flow: A Defense of the Tradition." In *Mass Media and Society*, ed. Alan Wells. Palo Alto, Calif.: Mayfield.

Anderson, Walt, Ed.
1970   *Politics and Environment.* Pacific Palisades, Calif.: Goodyear.

Andrain, Charles
1974   *Political Life and Social Change.* Belmont, Calif.: Wadsworth.

Arnold, David
1967   "The Meaning of the Laguardia Report: The Effects of Marijuana." In *Marijuana: Myths and Realities*, ed. J. L. Simmons. North Hollywood, Calif.: Brandon.

Aronoff, Joel and William Crano
1975   "A Re-Examination of the Cross-Cultural Principles of Task Segregation and Sex Role Differentiation in the Family." *American Sociological Review* 40:12–20.

Asimov, Isaac
1975   "Violence—As Human as Thumbs." *TV Guide,* June 14.

Atchley, Robert et al.
1972   *Ohio's Older People.* Oxford, Ohio: Scripps Foundation for Research in Population Problems.

Babbie, Earl
1966   "The Third Civilization." *Review of Religious Research* 7:101–21.

1970   *Science and Morality in Medicine.* Berkeley: University of California Press.

1975   *The Practice of Social Research.* Belmont, Calif.: Wadsworth.

Bales, Robert
1950   *Interaction Process Analysis: A Method for the Study of Small Groups.* Reading, Mass.: Addison-Wesley.

Ball, Samuel and Gerry Bogatz
1970   *A Summary of the Major Findings in "The First Year of Sesame Street: An Evaluation."* Princeton, N.J.: Educational Testing Service.

1971   *The Second Year of Sesame Street.* Princeton, N.J.: Educational Testing Service.

Bandura, A.
1969   "Social-Learning Theory of Identificatory Processes." In *Handbook of Socialization Theory and Research*, ed. D. A. Goslin, chap. 3. Chicago: Rand McNally.

*Brackets indicate original publication date.

Banfield, Edward
1961   *Political Influence.* New York: Free Press.

Barnes, Harry Elmer
1948   *An Introduction to the History of Sociology.* Chicago: University of Chicago Press.

Barry III, Herbert, Margaret K. Bacon, and Irvin L. Child
1955   "A Cross-Cultural Survey of Some Sex Differences in Socialization." *Journal of Abnormal and Social Psychology* 55:327–32.

Becker, Howard
1963   *The Outsiders.* New York: Free Press.

Becker, Howard et al.
1961   *Boys in White.* Chicago: University of Chicago Press.

Bellah, Robert
1959   *Tokugawa Religion.* Glencoe, Ill.: Free Press.
1967   "Civil Religion in America." *Daedalus* 96:1–2.

Bem, Sandra and Daryl Bem
1971   "Training the Woman to Know Her Place: The Power of a Nonconscious Ideology." In *Understanding American Society,* ed. Robert Atchley. Belmont, Calif.: Wadsworth.

Bennis, Warren
1971   "Beyond Bureaucracy." In *Sociological Realities,* ed. Irving Louis Horowitz, Mary Symons Strong, pp. 143–47. New York: Harper & Row.

Berelson, Bernard, Paul Lazarsfeld, and William McPhee
1954   *Voting: A Study of Opinion Formation in a Presidential Campaign.* Chicago: University of Chicago Press.

Berle, A. A.
1958   *Economic Power and the Free Society.* New York: Fund for the Republic.

Bernard, Jessie
1972   *The Future of Marriage.* New York: Bantam.

Biddle, Bruce and Thomas Edwin
1966   *Role Theory: Concepts and Research.* New York: Wiley.

Blau, Peter and Otis Dudley Duncan
1967   *The American Occupational Structure.* New York: Wiley.

Blaustein, Albert and Robert Zangrando, Eds.
1970   *Civil Rights and the Black American.* New York: Washington Square Press.

Blood, Robert and Donald Wolfe
1960   *Husband and Wives: The Dynamics of Married Living.* New York: Free Press.

Blumer, Herbert
[1939] "Collective Behavior." In *Principles of Sociology,* ed. Alfred McClung Lee. New York: Barnes & Noble.
1946

1966   "The Mass, the Public, and Public Opinion." In *Reader in Public Opinion and Mass Communication,* ed. Bernard Berelson, Morris Janowitz. New York: Free Press.

1969   *Symbolic Interactionism: Perspective and Method.* Englewood Cliffs, N.J.: Prentice-Hall.

Bottomore, T. B. and Maximilien Rubel, Eds.
[1843] *Selected Writings in Sociology and Social Philosophy.*
1956   Trans. T. B. Bottomore. New York: McGraw-Hill.

Brown, Julia and May Rawlinson
1975   "Relinquishing the Sick Role Following Open-Heart Surgery." *Journal of Health and Social Behavior* 16:12–27.

Bruner, Jerome
1954   "The Dimensions of Propaganda: German Short-Wave Broadcasts to America." In *Public Opinion and Propaganda,* ed. Daniel Katz et al. New York: Dryden.

Burgess, Ernest
1925   "The Growth of the City." In *The City,* ed. Robert Park, Ernest Burgess, R. D. McKenzie. Chicago: University of Chicago Press.

Cahalan, Don
1970   *Problem Drinkers.* San Francisco: Jossey-Bass.

Cameron, William
1966   *Modern Social Movements.* New York: Random House.

Campbell, Angus, Gerald Gurin, and W. E. Miller
1954   *The Voter Decides.* Evanston, Ill.: Row, Peterson.

Caplovitz, David
1967   *The Poor Pay More: Consumer Practices of Low Income Families.* New York: Free Press.

Caplow, Theodore
1959   "Further Development of a Theory of Coalitions in Triads." *American Journal of Sociology* 64:488–93.

1969   *Two Against One: Coalitions in Triads.* Englewood Cliffs, N.J.: Prentice-Hall.

Carr-Saunders, A. M.
1936   *World Population.* Oxford: Clarendon Press.

Carson, Rachel
1962   *Silent Spring.* Boston: Houghton Mifflin.

Castaneda, Carlos
1969   *The Teachings of Don Juan.* New York: Ballantine.

1971   *A Separate Reality.* New York: Simon & Schuster.

1972   *Journey to Ixtlan.* New York: Simon & Schuster.

1974   *Tales of Power.* New York: Simon & Schuster.

Cavender, Chris
1972   "A Critical Examination of Textbooks on Indians." In *Minority Problems,* ed. Arnold Rose, Caroline Rose. New York: Harper & Row.

Chaffee, Steven and Michael Petrick
1975   *Using the Media: Communication Problems in American Society.* New York: McGraw-Hill.

Chapin, F. Stuart
1936   "Social Theory and Social Action." *American Sociological Review* 1:1–11.

Christian Science Monitor
1975   April 30, p. 21.

Clausen, John
1963   "Social Factors in Disease." *The Annals of the American Academy of Political and Social Science* 346:138–48.

Coleman, James
1966   *U.S. National Center for Educational Statistics: Equality of Educational Opportunity.* Washington, D.C.: U.S. Government Printing Office.

Cooley, Charles Horton
[1902] *Human Nature and the Social Order.* New York:
1964   Schocken Books.

1909   *Social Organization.* New York: Scribners.

Cooper, David
1974   "The Death of the Family." In *Social Problems: The Contemporary Debates,* ed. John Williamson, Jerry Boren, Linda Evans. Boston: Little, Brown.

Coser, Lewis
1956   *The Functions of Social Conflict.* New York: Free Press.

Dahl, Robert
1961   *Who Governs.* New Haven, Conn.: Yale.

Dahrendorf, Ralf
1959   *Class and Class Conflict in Industrial Society.* Stanford, Calif.: Stanford.

1968   *Essays in the Theory of Society.* Stanford, Calif.: Stanford.

Davies, James
1962   "A Theory of Revolution." *American Sociological Review* 27:5–19.

Davis, Kingsley and Wilbert Moore
1945   "Some Principles of Stratification." *American Sociological Review* 10:242–49.

Davis, Thomas
1971   "A Technique for the Identification of Negative Black Stereotype Biases in Elementary School Children." M.A. thesis, University of Hawaii.

DeFleur, Lois
1975   "Biasing Influences on Drug Arrest Records: Implications for Deviance Research." *American Sociological Review* 40:88–103.

DeFleur, Melvin
1966   *Theories of Mass Communication.* New York: McKay.

De Tocqueville, Alexis
[1835,   *Democracy in America.* New York: Vintage
1840]   Books. Originally published in 2 vols.
1945

Dollard, John
1937   *Caste and Class in a Southern Town.* New Haven,
        Conn.: Yale.

Dulles, Foster
1959   *"The Indian Menace," The United States Since
        1865.* Ann Arbor, Mich.: University of Michi-
        gan Press.

Durand, John
1968   "The Modern Expansion of World Popula-
        tion." In *Population and Society,* ed. Charles
        Nam, pp. 108–20. New York: Houghton
        Mifflin.

Durkheim, Emile
[1893]   *The Division of Labor in Society.* New York:
1964   Free Press.

[1895]   *The Rules of Sociological Method.* Glencoe, Ill.:
1950   Free Press.

[1897]   *Suicide.* Glencoe, Ill.: Free Press.
1951

[1915]   *The Elementary Forms of Religious Life.* Trans.
1954   Joseph Swain. Glencoe, Ill.: Free Press.

Dye, Thomas and L. Harmon Zeigler
1975   *The Irony of Democracy.* North Scituate, Mass.:
        Duxbury.

Edmiston, Susan
1973   "How to Write Your Own Marriage Con-
        tract." In *This Is a Sociology Reader,* ed. Angela
        Lask, Richard Roe, students. San Francisco:
        Rinehart Press.

Education Yearbook 1973–74
1973   New York: Macmillan Educational Corpora-
        tion.

Efron, Edith
1975   "Does TV Violence Affect Our Society? *NO.*"
        TV Guide, June 14.

Ehrlich, Paul
1971   *The Population Bomb.* New York: Ballantine.

Ehrlich, Paul and Anne Ehrlich
1972   *Population, Resources, Environment: Issues in Hu-
        man Ecology.* San Francisco: Freeman.

Ellis, Dean
1967   "Speech and Social Status in America." *Social
        Problems* 45:431–37.

Emery, Edwin et al.
1973   *Introduction to Mass Communications.* New York:
        Dodd, Mead.

Encyclopaedia Britannica
1975   *Britannica Book of the Year.* Chicago: William
        Benton.

Epstein, Edward
1974   *News from Nowhere.* New York: Vintage Books.

1975   "The Selection of Reality." In *Issues in Broad-
        casting,* ed. Ted Smythe, George Mastroianni.
        Palo Alto, Calif.: Mayfield.

Erikson, Erik
1963   *Childhood and Society.* New York: Norton.

Erlenmeyer-Kimling, L., and L. F. Jarvik
1963   "Genetics and Intelligence." *Science* 142:1477–
        78.

Ervin-Tripp, S.
1964   "An Analysis of the Interaction of Language,
        Topic and Listener." *American Anthropologist*
        66:94–100.

Etzioni, Amitai
1964   *Modern Organizations.* Englewood Cliffs, N.J.:
        Prentice-Hall.

Executive Office of the President, Office of Management and the Budget
1974   "Social Indicators, 1973." Washington, D.C.:
        U.S. Government Printing Office.

Faris, Ellsworth
1937   *The Nature of Human Nature.* New York:
        McGraw-Hill.

Federal Bureau of Investigation
1975   *Uniform Crime Report of the United States.* Wash-
        ington, D.C.: U.S. Government Printing
        Office.

Festinger, Leon, Henry Riecken, and Stanley Schacter
1956   *When Prophecy Fails.* Minneapolis: University of Minnesota Press.

Fischer, Claude et al.
1974   "Crowding Studies and Urban Life: A Critical Review." Berkeley: Institute of Urban and Regional Development, University of California, working paper no. 242.

Foss, B. M.
1973   "Ability." In *The Seven Stages of Man,* ed. Robert Sears, S. Shirley Feldman, p. 19. Los Altos, Calif.: Kaufman.

Foy, Eddie and Alvin Harlow
[1928] *Clowning Through Life.* Reprinted in part in
1957   *Collective Behavior,* ed. Ralph Turner, Lewis Killian. Englewood Cliffs, N.J.: Prentice-Hall.

Frazier, E. Franklin
1939   *The Negro Family in the United States.* Chicago: University of Chicago Press.

French, David
1974   "After the Fall: What This Country Needs Is a Good Counter Counterculture Culture." In *Social Realities,* ed. George Ritzer. Boston: Allyn and Bacon.

Freud, Sigmund
[1909] "The Origin and Development of Psycho-
1957   analysis." In *A General Selection from the Works of Sigmund Freud,* ed. John Rickman. Garden City, N.Y.: Doubleday.

[1920] *A General Introduction to Psychoanalysis.* Trans.
1949   Joan Riviere. Garden City, N.Y.: Doubleday.

[1921] "Group Psychology and the Analysis of the
1957   Ego." In *A General Selection from the Works of Sigmund Freud,* ed. John Rickman. Garden City, N.Y.: Doubleday.

[1927] *The Future of an Illusion.* Trans. W. D. Robson-
1957   Scott. Garden City, N.Y.: Doubleday.

1930   *Civilization and Its Discontents.* Trans. Joan Riviere. Garden City, N.Y.: Doubleday.

Funkhouser, G. Ray
1973   "The Issues of the Sixties: An Exploratory Study of the Dynamics of Public Opinion." *Public Opinion Quarterly* 37:62–75.

Galbraith, John
1969   *How to Control the Military.* New York: Signet Books, New American Library.

Gallup, George
1972   *The Gallup Poll.* 3 vols. New York: Random House.

Gardner, Robert and Eleanor Nordyke
1974   *The Demographic Situation in Hawaii.* Honolulu: East-West Population Institute.

Garfinkel, Harold
1967   *Studies in Ethnomethodology.* Englewood Cliffs, N.J.: Prentice-Hall.

General Services Administration
1974   *Inventory Report on Real Property Owned by the United States throughout the World.* Washington, D.C.: U.S. Government Printing Office.

Gerth, Hans and C. Wright Mills, Trans., Eds.
1946   *From Max Weber: Essays in Sociology.* New York: Oxford University Press.

Glock, Charles
1964   "The Role of Deprivation in the Origin and Evolution of Religious Groups." In *Religion and Social Conflict,* ed. Robert Lee. New York: Oxford University Press.

Glock, Charles and Rodney Stark
1965   *Religion and Society in Tension.* Chicago: Rand McNally.

1966   *Christian Beliefs and Anti-Semitism.* New York: Harper & Row.

Goffman, Erving
1961   *Asylums: Essays on the Social Situation of Mental Patients and Other Inmates.* Chicago: Aldine.

1963   *Stigma: Notes on the Management of a Spoiled Identity.* Englewood Cliffs, N.J.: Prentice-Hall.

1964   *Presentation of Self in Everyday Life.* New York: Free Press.

Gold, Raymond
1969   "Roles in Sociological Field Observation." In *Issues in Participant Observation,* ed. George J. McCall, J. L. Simmons. Reading, Mass.: Addison-Wesley.

Goldsmith, Alfred and Austin Lescarboura
1930   *This Thing Called Broadcasting.* New York: Henry Holt.

Golenpaul, Ann, Ed.
1975   *Information Please Almanac.* New York: Goldenpaul.

Goode, William
1961   "Family Disorganization." In *Contemporary Social Problems,* ed. Robert Merton, Robert Nisbet. New York: Harcourt, Brace.

Gordon, Milton
1964   *Assimilation in American Life.* New York: Oxford University Press.

Gouldner, Alvin
1962   "Anti-Minotaur: The Myth of Value-Free Sociology." *Social Problems* 9:199–213.

Graubard, Allen
1973   "The Free School Movement." In *Education Yearbook.* New York: Macmillan Educational Corporation.

Greenstein, Fred
1963   *The American Party System and the American People.* Englewood Cliffs, N.J.: Prentice-Hall.

Greer, Scott
1966   *Urban Renewal and American Cities.* Indianapolis, Ind.: Bobbs-Merrill.

Hall, Edward
1959   *The Silent Language.* Greenwich, Conn.: Fawcett.

Hammond, Phillip and Robert Mitchell
1965   "Segmentation of Radicalism: The Case of the Protestant Campus Minister." *American Journal of Sociology* 71:133–43.

Hardin, Garrett
1968   "The Tragedy of the Commons." *Science* 162: 1243–48.

Hardin, Garrett, Ed.
1969   *Population, Evolution, and Birth Control.* San Francisco: Freeman.

Harris, Chauncy D. and Edward L. Ullman
1945   "The Nature of Cities." *Annals of the American Academy of Political and Social Science* 242:12.

Havighurst, Robert and Bernice Neugarten
1968   *Society and Education.* Boston: Allyn and Bacon.

Heer, David
1966   "Economic Development and Fertility." *Demography* 3:423–44.

Helfrich, Harold, Ed.
1970   *The Environmental Crisis.* New Haven, Conn.: Yale.

Henderson, L. J.
1935   *Pareto's General Sociology: A Physiologist's View.* Cambridge, Mass.: Harvard.

Hennessey, Bernard
1975   *Public Opinion.* North Scituate, Mass.: Duxbury.

Hiebert, Ray et al.
1974   *Mass Media: An Introduction to Modern Communication.* New York: McKay.

Hirshi, Travis
1969   *Causes of Delinquency.* Berkeley: University of California Press.

Hirshi, Travis and Hanan Selvin
1967   *Delinquency Research.* Glencoe, Ill.: Free Press.

Hobbes, Thomas
[1651] *Leviathan.* New York: Collier Books, Macmillan.
1962

Hodge, Robert, Paul Siegel, and Peter Rossi
1964   "Occupational Prestige in the United States, 1925–63." *American Journal of Sociology* 60: 286–302.

Hoffer, Eric
1958   *The True Believer.* New York: New American Library.

Hollingshead, August
1949   *Elmstown's Youth.* New York: Wiley.

Hollingshead, A. B. and F. C. Redlich
1958   *Social Class and Mental Illness.* New York: Wiley.

Holsti, Ole
1969   *Content Analysis for the Social Sciences and Humanities.* Reading, Mass.: Addison-Wesley.

Homans, George
1961   *Social Behavior: Its Elementary Forms.* New York: Harcourt, Brace & World.

Horowitz, David and Reese Erlich
1972   "Litton Industries: Big Brother as a Holding Company." In *The Social Scene,* ed. Robert Browne et al. Cambridge, Mass.: Winthrop.

Hoult, Thomas
1974   *Sociology for A New Day.* New York: Random House.

Humphreys, Laud
1970   *Tearoom Trade: Impersonal Sex in Public Places.* Chicago: Aldine.

Hyman, Herbert
1972   *Secondary Analysis of Sample Surveys: Principles, Procedures, and Potentialities.* New York: Wiley.

Hyman, Herbert and John Reed
1969   "Black Matriarchy Reconsidered: Evidence from Secondary Analysis of Sample Surveys." *Public Opinion Quarterly* 33:346–54.

James, William
1890   *Principles of Psychology,* vol. 1. New York: Holt.

Jencks, Christopher et al.
1973   *Inequality: A Reassessment of the Effect of Family and Schooling in America.* New York: Harper & Row, Colophon Books.

Jennings, J. Kent and Richard Niemi
1975   "Continuity and Change in Political Orientations: A Longitudinal Study of Two Generations." In *The Irony of Democracy,* ed. Thomas Dye, L. Harmon Zeigler. North Scituate, Mass.: Duxbury.

Jones, H. E.
1946   "Environmental Influences on Mental Development." In *Manual of Child Psychology,* ed. L. Carmichael, p. 622. New York: Wiley.

Karlins, Marvin, Thomas Coffman, and Gary Walters
1969   "On the Fading of Social Stereotypes: Studies in Three Generations of College Students." *Journal of Personality and Social Psychology* 19:1–16.

Kassebaum, Gene
1974   *Delinquency and Social Policy.* Englewood Cliffs, N.J.: Prentice-Hall.

Katz, D. and K. W. Braly
1933   "Racial Stereotypes of 100 College Students." *Journal of Abnormal and Social Psychology* 28: 280–90.

Katz, Elihu and Paul Lazarsfeld
1955   *Personal Influences.* New York: Free Press.

Kilday, Gregg
1975   "Happy Endings—Have They All Vanished into the Sunset?" In *Mass Media and Society,* ed. Alan Wells. Palo alto, Calif.: Mayfield.

Klapper, Joseph
1960   *The Effects of Mass Communication.* Glencoe, Ill.: Free Press.

Kluckhohn, Florence and Fred Strodtbeck
1961   Variations in Value Orientations. Evanston, Ill.: Row, Peterson.

Kohlberg, Lawrence and Card Gilligan
1971   "The Adolescent as a Philosopher: The Discovery of the Self in a Postconventional World." *Daedalus* 100:1051–86.

Komarovsky, Mirra
1962   *Blue-Collar Marriage.* New York: Random House.

Kornhauser, William
1959   *The Politics of Mass Society.* Glencoe, Ill.: Free Press.

1966   "'Power Elite' or 'Veto Groups.'" In *Class, Status, and Power,* ed. Reinhard Bendix, Seymour Martin Lipset. New York: Free Press.

Kuhn, M. H. and T. S. McPartland
1954   "An Empirical Investigation of Self-Attitudes." *American Sociological Review* 19:68–76.

Landau, N. J. and P. G. Rheingold
1971   *The Environmental Law Handbook.* New York: Ballantine.

Lasswell, Harold
1948 "The Structure and Function of Communication in Society." In *The Communication of Ideas*, ed. L. Bryson. New York: Harper.

Lazarsfeld, Paul, Bernard Berelson, and Hazel Gaudet
1944 *The People's Choice*. New York: Columbia.

Lazarsfeld, Paul and Robert Merton
1960 "Mass Communication, Popular Taste and Organized Action." In *Mass Communication*, ed. Wilbur Schramm. Urbana: University of Illinois Press.

Le Bon, Gustave
[1895] *The Crowd*. New York: Viking.
1960

Lemert, Edwin
1951 *Social Pathology*. New York: McGraw-Hill.

Lenski, Gerhard
1966 *Power and Privilege*. New York: McGraw-Hill.
1974 *Human Societies*. 2nd ed. New York: McGraw-Hill.

Lenzer, Gertrud, Ed.
1975 *Auguste Comte and Positivism: The Essential Writings*. New York: Torchbooks, Harper & Row.

Leon, Joseph and Patricia Steinhoff
1975 "Catholics' Use of Abortion." *Sociological Analysis* 36:125–36.

Lerner, Daniel
1964 *The Passing of Traditional Society: Modernizing the Middle East*. New York: Free Press.

Levitin, Teresa, Robert Quinn, and Graham Staines
1970 "Sex Discrimination Against the American Working Woman." Report of the Institute for Social Research, University of Michigan.

Lieberman, Seymour
1963 "The Effects of Change in Roles on the Attitudes of Role Occupants." In *Personality and Social System*, ed. Neil Smelser, William Smelser, pp. 264–79. New York: Wiley.

Linton, Ralph
1936 *The Study of Culture*. New York: Appleton-Century.

Lipset, Seymour M.
1963 *The First New Nation: The United States in Historical and Comparative Perspective*. New York: Basic Books.
1968 *Revolution and Counterrevolution: Change and Persistence in Social Structures*. New York: Basic Books.

Lofland, John
1966 *Doomsday Cult*. Englewood Cliffs, N.J.: Prentice-Hall.

Lofland, John and Rodney Stark
1965 "On Becoming a World-Saver: A Theory of Conversion to a Deviant Perspective." *American Sociological Review* 30:862–75.

Lofton, Willis
1957 "Northern Labor and the Negro During the Civil War." In *Collective Behavior*, ed. Ralph Turner, Lewis Killian. Englewood Cliffs, N.J.: Prentice-Hall.

Lombroso, Cesare
1911 *Criminal Man*, ed. Gina Lombroso Ferrero. New York: Putnam.

Lorenz, Konrad
1966 *On Aggression*. New York: Harcourt, Brace & World.

Lynd, Robert and Helen Lynd
1929 *Middletown*. New York: Harcourt, Brace.
1937 *Middletown in Transition*. New York: Harcourt, Brace.

Marx, Karl
[1867] *Capital: A Critique of Political Economy*. New York: Modern Library.
1906

Marx, Karl and Friedrich Engels
[1848] *The Communist Manifesto*. New York: Appleton-Century-Crofts.
1955

Masaoka, Mike
1972 "The Evacuation of the Japanese Americans and Its Aftermath." In *Minority Problems*, ed. Arnold Rose, Caroline Rose. New York: Harper & Row.

McCandless, Boyd R.
1969   "Childhood Socialization." In *Handbook of Socialization Theory and Research*, ed. D. A. Goslin, chap. 19. Chicago: Rand McNally.

McClosky, Herbert, Paul Hoffman, and Rosemary O'Hara
1960   "Issue Conflict and Consensus among Party Leaders and Followers." *American Political Science Review* 406–27.

Mead, Margaret
1935   *Sex and Temperament in Three Primitive Societies.* New York: Morrow.

Meadows, Dennis et al.
1973   *The Dynamics of Growth in a Finite World.* Cambridge, Mass.: Wright-Allen.

Meadows, Donella et al.
1972   *The Limits to Growth.* New York: Universe Books.

Mechanic, David and Edmund Volkart
1961   "Stress, Illness Behavior, and the Sick Role." *American Sociological Review* 26:51–58.

Merton, Robert
1957a   *Social Theory and Social Structure.* New York: Free Press.

1957b   "The Role Set: Problem in Sociological Theory." *British Journal of Sociology* 8:113f.

Merton, Robert et al.
1957   *The Student-Physician.* Cambridge, Mass.: Harvard.

Mills, C. Wright
1958   *The Causes of World War Three.* New York: Simon & Schuster.

1959   *The Power Elite.* New York: Oxford University Press.

Miner, Horace
1956   "Body Ritual Among the Nacirema." *American Anthropologist* 58:503–7.

Mitford, Jessica
1973   *Kind and Usual Punishment.* New York: Knopf.

Miyamoto, S. Frank and Sanford Dornbusch
1956   "A Test of Interactionist Hypotheses of Self-Conception." *American Journal of Sociology* 61 (5):399–403.

Mooney, J.
1939   *The 1870 Ghost Dance.* Berkeley: University of California Press.

Moore, Wilbert
1963   *Social Change.* Englewood Cliffs, N.J.: Prentice-Hall.

Morris, Charles, Ed.
1934   *Mind, Self, and Society.* Chicago: University of Chicago Press.

Morse, Nancy and Robert Weiss
1955   "The Function and Meaning of Work and the Job." *American Sociological Review* 20:191–98.

Moursund, Janet
1973   *Evaluation: An Introduction to Research Design.* Monterey, Calif.: Brooks/Cole.

Mussen, Paul H., John J. Conger, and Jerome Kagan
1974   *Child Development and Personality.* New York: Harper & Row.

Nam, Charles, Ed.
1968   *Population and Society.* New York: Houghton Mifflin.

Nasatir, David
1967   "Social Science Data Libraries." *The American Sociologist* 2:207–12.

Niebuhr, H. Richard
1960   *The Social Sources of Denominationalism.* New York: Meridian Books.

Odum, Howard
1951   *American Sociology.* New York: Longmans.

Otto, Herbert
1974   "Communes: The Alternative Life-Style." In *Social Realities*, ed. George Ritzer. Boston: Allyn and Bacon.

Paddock, William and Paul Paddock
1967   *Famine 1975! America's Decision: Who Will Survive.* Boston: Little, Brown.

Park, Robert
1926   "The Urban Community as a Spacial Pattern and a Moral Order." In *The Urban Community*,

ed. Ernest Burgess. Chicago: University of Chicago Press.

Parkinson, C. Northcote
1957   *Parkinson's Law.* Boston: Houghton Mifflin.

Parsons, Talcott
[1940] "An Analytical Approach to the Theory of
1954   Social Stratification." *American Journal of Sociology* 45:841–62. Reprinted in Talcott Parsons, *Essays in Sociological Theory,* chap. 4. Glencoe, Ill.: Free Press.

1951   *The Social System.* New York: Free Press.

1957   "The Distribution of Power in American Society." *World Politics* 10:123–43.

1964   *Societies: Evolutionary and Comparative Perspectives.* Englewood Cliffs, N.J.: Prentice-Hall.

Parsons, Talcott and Robert Bales
1955   *Family, Socialization and Interaction Process.* Glencoe, Ill.: Free Press.

Pauwels, Louis and Jacques Bergier
1968   *The Morning of the Magicians.* New York: Avon.

Peck, Ira
1974   *The Life and Words of Martin Luther King, Jr.* New York: Scholastic Book Service.

Peter, Laurence and Raymond Hull
1969   *The Peter Principle.* New York: Morrow.

Piaget, Jean
1954   *The Construction of Reality in the Child.* Trans. Margaret Cook. New York: Basic Books.

1965   *The Moral Judgment of the Child.* Trans. Marjorie Gabain. New York: Free Press.

Pirsig, Robert
1975   *Zen and the Art of Motorcycle Maintenance.* New York: Ballantine.

Poloma, Margaret and T. Neal Garland
1972   "The Married Professional Woman: A Study in the Tolerance of Domestication." In *Sociology, Students and Society,* ed. Jerome Rabow. Pacific Palisades, Calif.: Goodyear.

Ponsonby, Arthur
1930   *Falsehood in Wartime.* London: G. Allen.

President's Commission on Law Enforcement and Administration of Justice
1967   *The Challenge of Crime in a Free Society.* Washington, D.C.: U.S. Government Printing Office.

Queen, Stuart, Robert Habenstein, and John Adams
1961   *The Family in Various Cultures.* Chicago: Lippincott.

Rappaport, Roy
1969   "Ritual Regulation of Environmental Relations Among a New Guinea People." In *Environment and Cultural Behavior,* ed. Andrew Vayda. Garden City, N.Y.: Natural History Press.

Reckless, Walter
1926   "The Distribution of Commercialized Vice in the City: A Sociological Analysis." In *The Urban Community,* ed. Ernest Burgess. Chicago: University of Chicago Press.

Reinow, R. and L. T. Reinow
1967   *Moment in the Sun.* New York: Dial.

Reiss, Albert, Jr.
1971   *The Police and the Public.* New Haven, Conn.: Yale.

Reiss, Albert, Jr., Otis Dudley Duncan, Paul Hatt, and Cecil North
1961   *Occupations and Social Status.* New York: Free Press.

Reynolds, W. Jeff et al.
1974   "The Validation of a Function Status Index." *Journal of Health and Social Behavior* 15:271–88.

Riesman, David, Nathan Glazer, and Reuel Denney
1953   *The Lonely Crowd: A Study of the Changing American Character.* New York: Anchor Books, Doubleday.

Ritzer, George, Ed.
1974   *Social Realities.* Boston: Allyn and Bacon.

Roethlisberger, F. J. and W. J. Dickson
1939   *Management and the Worker.* Cambridge, Mass.: Harvard.

Rogoff, Natalie
1961   "Local Social Structure and Educational Selec-
        tion." In *Education, Economy, and Society*, ed.
        A. H. Halsey et al. New York: Free Press.

Rose, Arnold
1959   "Sociological Factors in the Effectiveness of
        Projected Legislative Remedies." *Journal of
        Legal Education* 11:470.

Rose, Arnold and Caroline Rose, Eds.
1972   *Minority Problems.* New York: Harper & Row.

Rosenberg, Morris
1965   *Society and the Adolescent Self-Image.* Princeton,
        N.J.: Princeton.

Rosenthal, Robert and Leonore Jacobson
1969   *Pygmalion in the Classroom.* New York: Harper
        & Row.

Ross, Elisabeth
1970   "The Dying Patient's Point of View." In *The
        Dying Patient*, ed. Orville Brim. New York:
        Russell Sage.

Rousseau, Jean Jacques
[1750] "Discourse on the Origin and Foundation of
 1964   Inequality of Mankind." In *The First and
        Second Discourses*, trans. Rodger Masters,
        Judith Masters. New York: St. Martin's.

[1762] *The Social Contract.* Trans. Willmoore Kendall.
 1954   Chicago: Regnery.

Russell, Bertrand
1938   *Power: A New Social Analysis.* New York:
        Norton.

Sanger, Margaret
1938   *An Autobiography.* New York: Norton.

Sapir, Edward
1960   *Culture, Language and Personality: Selected Essays.*
        Berkeley: University of California Press.

Scanzoni, Letha and John Scanzoni
1976   *Men, Women, and Change.* New York: McGraw-
        Hill.

Scheff, Thomas
1966   *Being Mentally Ill: A Sociological Theory.* Chicago:
        Aldine.

Schon, Donald
1971   *Beyond the Stable State.* New York: Random
        House.

Schramm, Wilbur
1955   *The Process and Effects of Mass Communications.*
        Urbana: University of Illinois Press.
1964   *Mass Media and National Development.* Stanford,
        Calif.: Stanford.

Schramm, Wilbur and Janet Alexander
1975   "Survey of Broadcasting: Structure, Control,
        Audience." In *Issues in Broadcasting*, ed. Ted
        Smythe, George Mastroianni. Palo Alto,
        Calif.: Mayfield.

Schutz, Alfred
1962   *Collected ·Papers I: The Problem of Social Reality.*
        The Hague: Martinus Nijhoff.

Schwartz, Tony
1974   *The Response Chord.* Garden City, N.Y.: Anchor
        Books, Doubleday.

Selznick, Gertrude Jaeger and Stephen Steinberg
1969   *The Tenacity of Prejudice.* New York: Harper &
        Row.

Selznick, Philip
1952   *The Organizational Weapon.* New York:
        McGraw-Hill.

Shibutani, Tamotsu
1961   *Society and Personality: An Interactionist Approach
        to Social Psychology.* Englewood Cliffs, N.J.:
        Prentice-Hall.

1966   *Improvised News: A Sociological Study of Rumor.*
        Indianapolis, Ind.: Bobbs-Merrill.

Shibutani, Tamotsu and Kian Kwan
1965   *Ethnic Stratification: A Comparative View.* New
        York: Macmillan.

Shils, Edward and Morris Janowitz
1948   "Cohesion and Disintegration in the Wehr-
        macht." *Public Opinion Quarterly* 12:280–94.

Simmel, Georg
[1908a] *Conflict and the Web of Group Affiliation.* Trans.
 1955   Kurt Wolff. Glencoe, Ill.: Free Press.

[1908b] *Sociology.* Trans., ed. Kurt Wolff. *The Sociology
 1964   of George Simmel.* New York: Free Press.

Simmons, J. L.
1965   "Public Stereotypes of Deviants." *Social Problems* 13:223–32.

1969   *Deviants.* Berkeley, Calif.: Glendessary.

Skinner, B. F.
1953   *Science and Human Behavior.* New York: Macmillan.

Smelser, Neil
1963   *Theory of Collective Behavior.* New York: Free Press.

Smith, Huston
1958   *The Religions of Man.* New York: Harper & Row.

Sorokin, Pitirim
1937–   *Social and Cultural Dynamics.* 4 vols. New York:
40   American Book.

Spencer, Herbert
1898   *The Principles of Sociology,* vol. 2, bk. 2. New York: Appleton.

Spengler, Oswald
1932   *The Decline of the West.* New York: Knopf.

Srole, Leo et al.
1962   *Mental Health in the Metropolis.* New York: McGraw-Hill.

Stark, Rodney
1972   *Police Riots.* Belmont, Calif.: Wadsworth.

Stark, Rodney and Charles Glock
1968   *American Piety: The Nature of Religious Commitment.* Berkeley: University of California Press.

Stark, Rodney and Stephen Steinberg
1967   "It *Did* Happen Here: An Investigation of Political Anti-Semitism: Wayne, New Jersey, 1967." Berkeley: Survey Research Center, University of California.

Stark, Rodney et al.
1971   *Wayward Shepherds: Prejudice and the Protestant Clergy.* New York: Harper & Row.

Stouffer, Samuel
1962   *Social Research to Test Ideas.* New York: Free Press.

Stouffer, Samuel et al.
1949   *The American Soldier,* vol. 1, Princeton, N.J.: Princeton.

Suchman, Edward
1965   "Stages of Illness and Medical Care." *Journal of Health and Social Behavior* 6:114–28.

Suczek, Barbara
1972   "The Curious Case of the 'Death' of Paul McCartney." *Urban Life and Culture* 1:1.

Sullerot, Evelyne
1974   *Woman, Society and Change.* New York: McGraw-Hill.

Sumner, William Graham
1894   "The Absurd Effort to Make the World Over." *Forum* 17(March):92–102.

Sutherland, Edwin
1924   *Principles of Criminology.* Philadelphia: Lippincott.

Szasz, Thomas
1961   *The Myth of Mental Illness.* New York: Hoeber-Harper.

Takeuchi, David
1974   "Grass in Hawaii: A Structural Constraints Approach." M.A. thesis, University of Hawaii.

Thomas, W. I.
1932   *The Child in America.* New York: Knopf.

Thomlinson, Ralph
1967   *Demographic Problems.* Belmont, Calif.: Dickenson.

Thompson, George
[1886] "The Evaluation of Public Opinion." In
1966   *Reader in Public Opinion and Communication,* ed. Bernard Berelson, Morris Janowitz. New York: Free Press.

Tillich, Paul
1952   *The Courage To Be.* New Haven, Conn.: Yale.

Tobin, Bob
1975   *Space-Time and Beyond.* New York: E. P. Dutton.

Toennies, Ferdinand
[1887] *Community and Society.* Trans. Charles Loomis.
1957   East Lansing: Michigan State University Press.

Toffler, Alvin
1970   *Future Shock.* New York: Random House.

Townsend, Claire
1971   *Old Age: The Last Segregation.* New York: Bantam.

Toynbee, Arnold
1962–   *A Study of History.* 12 vols. New York: Oxford
64   University Press.

Tumin, Melvin
1967   *Social Stratification: The Forms and Functions of Inequality.* Englewood Cliffs, N.J.: Prentice-Hall.

Turner, Jon
1974   *The Structure of Sociological Theory.* Homewood, Ill.: Dorsey.

Turner, Ralph and Lewis Killian, Eds.
1957   *Collective Behavior.* Englewood Cliffs, N.J.: Prentice-Hall.

Tzu, Lao
1965   "The Way and Its Power." In *The Religions of Man,* ed. Huston Smith. New York: Harper & Row.

United Nations
1956   "The Past and Future Population of the World and Its Continents." In *Demographic Analysis: Selected Readings,* ed. Joseph Spengler, Otis Dudley Duncan. Glencoe, Ill.: Free Press.

1974   *Demographic Yearbook, 1973.* New York: United Nations.

1975   *Statistical Yearbook: 1974.* New York: United Nations.

U.S. Bureau of the Census
1960   *Historical Statistics of the United States: Colonial Times to 1957.* Washington, D.C.: U.S. Government Printing Office.

1973   "Census of Population: 1970." Vol. 1. *Characteristics of the Population.* Pt. 1, United States Summary, Sect. 1. Washington, D.C.: U.S. Government Printing Office.

1974   "Educational Attainment in the United States: March 1973 and 1974." In *Current Population Reports,* Series P-20, No. 274. Washington, D.C.: U.S. Government Printing Office.

1975a   *Statistical Abstract of the United States.* Washington, D.C.: U.S. Government Printing Office.

1975b   "Persons of Spanish Origin in the United States: March 1974." In *Current Population Reports,* Series P-20, No. 280. Washington, D.C.: U.S. Government Printing Office.

1975c   *Current Population Reports.* Series P-25, No. 541. Washington, D.C.: U.S. Government Printing Office.

1976   "Money Income in 1974 of Families and Persons in the United States." In *Current Population Reports,* Series P-60, No. 101. Washington, D.C.: U.S. Government Printing Office.

U.S. Bureau of Labor Statistics
1973   *Manpower Report of the President.* Washington, D.C.: U.S. Government Printing Office.

1975a   "Employment and Unemployment in 1974." *Monthly Labor Review,* February, pp. 3–14.

1975b   "Educational Attainment of Workers, March 1974." *Monthly Labor Review,* February, pp. 64–69.

1975c   *Directory of National Unions and Employee Associations.* Washington, D.C.: U.S. Government Printing Office.

1976   *Employment and Earnings,* January, vol. 22, no. 7.

Van den Berghe, Pierre
1975   *Man in Society.* New York: Elsevier.

Wallace, Walter
1971   *The Logic of Science in Sociology.* Chicago: Aldine-Atherton.

Warner, W. Lloyd and Paul Lunt
1941   *The Social Life of a Modern Community.* New Haven, Conn.: Yale.

Warner, W. Lloyd et al.
1949   *Democracy in Jonesville.* New York: Harper.

Weber, Max
[1905] *The Protestant Ethic and the Spirit of Capitalism.*
1958   Trans. Talcott Parsons. New York: Scribners.

[1917– *Ancient Judaism.* Glencoe, Ill.: Free Press.
1919]
1952

[1920– *The Religion of China.* Glencoe, Ill.: Free Press.
1921]
1951

[1922] *The Sociology of Religion.* Boston: Beacon Press.
1963

[1925a] *From Max Weber: Essays in Sociology.* Trans.,
1946 ed. Hans Gerth, C. Wright Mills. New York: Oxford University Press.

[1925b] *The Theory of Social and Economic Organization.*
1964 Ed. Talcott Parsons. New York: Free Press.

Weinberg, S. Kirson
1974 *Deviant Behavior and Social Control.* Dubuque, Iowa: Wm. C. Brown.

Westoff, Charles
1972 "The Modernization of U.S. Contraceptive Practice." *Family Planning in Perspective* 4:9–12.

Whyte, William
1956 *The Organization Man.* Garden City, N.Y.: Doubleday.

Wildavsky, Aaron
1964 *Leadership in a Small Town.* Totowa, N.J.: Bedminster.

Williams, Robin
1959 *American Society: A Sociological Interpretation.* New York: Knopf.

Wilson, Bryan
1959 "An Analysis of Sect Development." *American Sociological Review* 24:3–15.

Winch, Robert
1971 *The Modern Family.* New York: Holt.

Wirth, Louis
1957 "Types of Minority Movements." In *Collective Behavior,* ed. Lewis Killian. Englewood Cliffs, N.J.: Prentice-Hall.

Wright, Charles
1975 *Mass Communication: A Sociological Perspective.* New York: Random House.

X, Malcolm and Alex Haley
1965 *The Autobiography of Malcolm X.* New York: Grove Press.

Yinger, J. Milton
1963 *Religion, Society and the Individual.* New York: Macmillan.

Zanden, James Vander
1972 *American Minority Problems.* New York: Ronald.

Zeisel, Hans
1967 "The Law." In *The Uses of Sociology,* ed. Paul Lazarsfeld et al. New York: Basic Books.

Name Index

Subject Index

To the owner of this book:

I hope that you have enjoyed *Society by Agreement* as much as I enjoyed writing it. I'd like to know as much about your experiences with the book as you care to offer. Only through your comments and the comments of others can I learn how to make *Society by Agreement* a better book for future readers.

School _____ Your Instructor's Name _____

1. What did you like *most* about *Society by Agreement*? _____

    _____

2. What did you like *least* about the book? _____

    _____

3. Were all of the chapters of the book assigned for you to read? _____

    (If not, which ones weren't?) _____

    _____

4. How interesting and informative was "The Discovery of Adamsville" for you? _____

    _____

    _____

5. Would you like to see the book continue to include "The Discovery of Adamsville," or a fictional story like it, in future

    editions? Why or why not? _____

    _____

    _____

6. If you used the Glossary, how helpful was it as an aid in understanding sociological concepts and terms? _____

    _____

    _____

7. How useful were the book's graphics (figures, tables, cartoons, and photographs) in helping you learn more about

    sociology and its findings? _____

    _____

    How would you compare the graphics in *Society by Agreement* to those in other college textbooks you have read? _____

    _____

8. In the space below or in a separate letter, please let me know what other comments about the book you'd like to make. (For example, were any chapters *or* concepts particularly difficult?) I'd be delighted to hear from you!

    _____

Optional:

Your Name _____   Date _____

May Wadsworth quote you, either in promotion for *Society by Agreement* or in future publishing ventures?

Yes _____   No _____

Aloha nui loa,

_____

_____
FOLD HERE

_____
FOLD HERE

FIRST CLASS
PERMIT NO. 34
BELMONT, CA

BUSINESS REPLY MAIL
No Postage Necessary if Mailed in United States

Dr. Earl R. Babbie

Wadsworth Publishing Co., Inc.
10 Davis Drive
Belmont, CA 94002

The Discovery of Adamsville

Cast of Characters

Louise Roanoke Sociologist primarily of the functionalist perspective; at American University, Chicago.

Constance Batterson Sociologist primarily of the conflict perspective; American University.

Bradley Duncan Sociologist primarily of the symbolic interactionist perspective; American University.

Gabriel Knapp Posing green; employed by Chicago National Insurance Company, Chicago.

Monica Roanoke Attorney in the Chicago area.

Larry Jones Charismatic leader of the radical militarists in Adamsville.

Ruth and **Michael Jones** Ruling Elders in Adamsville; the only remaining living children of Adam Jones III.

Jonathan Knapp Gabe's soft parent.

Loretta Larson Gabe's stern parent.

Daniel Adamson Young, not-yet-matured green; sent to visit Gabe at Shore Towers.

Jacob Lockwood Gabe's friend from childhood.

Rebecca Lockwood Jacob's distant cousin; niece of Ruth and Michael Jones.

Ann Sullivan A "dull" or "less" green; Adamsville valley resident.

Adamsville's Original Settlers

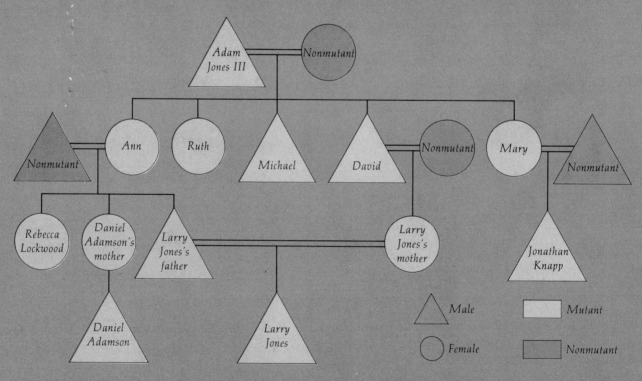